DICKENS STUDIES ANNUAL

Essays on Victorian Fiction

DICKENS STUDIES ANNUAL

Essays on Victorian Fiction

DICKENS STUDIES ANNUAL

Essays on Victorian Fiction

VOLUME
42

Edited by
Stanley Friedman, Edward Guiliano,
Anne Humpherys, Natalie McKnight, and Michael Timko

AMS PRESS, INC.
New York

Dickens Studies Annual
ISSN 0084-9812

Dickens Studies Annual: Essays on Victorian Fiction welcomes essay- and monograph-length contributions on Dickens and other Victorian novelists and on the history of aesthetics of Victorian fiction. All manuscripts should be double-spaced and should follow the documentation format described in the most recent *MLA Style Manual*. The author's name should appear only on a cover-page, not elsewhere in the essay. An editorial decision can usually be reached more quickly if two copies of the article are submitted, since outside readers are asked to evaluate each submission. If a manuscript is accepted for publication, the author will be asked to provide a 100- to 200-word abstract and also a CD-ROM containing the final version of the essay. The preferred editions for citations from Dickens's works are the Clarendon and the Norton Critical when available, otherwise the Oxford Illustrated or the Penguin.

Please send submissions to The Editors, *Dickens Studies Annual*, Ph.D. Program in English, The Graduate Center, CUNY, 365 Fifth Avenue, New York, NY 10016-4309. Please send inquiries concerning subscriptions and/or availability of earlier volumes to AMS Press, Inc., Brooklyn Navy Yard—Unit #221, 63 Flushing Ave., Brooklyn, NY 11205-1073.

Dickens Studies Annual: Essays on Victorian Fiction is published in cooperation with Queens College and the Graduate Center, CUNY.

International Standard Book Number
Series ISBN-10: 0-404-18520-7
Series ISBN-13: 978-0-404-18520-6

Vol. 42 ISBN-10: 0-404-18942-3
Vol. 42 ISBN-13: 978-0-404-18942-6

All AMS books are printed on acid-free paper that meets the guidelines for performance and durability of the Committee on Production Guidelines for Book Longevity of the Council on Library Resources.

AMS PRESS, INC.
Brooklyn Navy Yard, 63 Flushing Avenue—Unit #221
Brooklyn, NY 11205-1073, USA
www.amspressinc.com

Manufactured in the United States of America

Contents

Preface

The varied essays in this volume indicate that Dickens, nearly two centuries after his birth, still speaks to us. By chance, of the fifteen contributors to this volume, six are just beginning their scholarly careers, two have reached relatively early stages, five are well-established, and two now enjoy retirement (as professors emeriti) after long academic service. These contributors reside in diverse regions of the United States and also in Canada and the United Kingdom. Moreover, five of the articles in this issue, as well as the survey, happen to consider Dickens's close relationship to some aspects of popular culture, either in our time or in earlier periods. The articles in this issue—once more, by chance—devote attention to a number of Dickens's narratives, ranging from very well-known to less familiar texts, and including examples from every stage of the author's long career.

We thank Shari Hodges Holt for her comprehensive, insightful review of Dickens-related work published in 2009, a survey that includes discussion of graphic versions of Dickens's narratives and also of recent fiction that draws on his creations and on his life.

For practical assistance, we again express appreciation to various academic administrators: President William P. Kelly, Provost Chase Robinson, Ph.D. Program in English Executive Officer Mario DiGangi, and Nancy Silverman, Assistant Program Officer, Ph.D. Program in English, all of The Graduate Center, CUNY; and President James L. Muyskens, Dean of Arts and Humanities Tamara S. Evans, and Department of English Chair Nancy R. Comley, all of Queens College, CUNY.

We are grateful to John O. Jordan, Director of The Dickens Project at the University of California, Santa Cruz; JoAnna Rottke, Project Coordinator for The Dickens Project; and Jon Michael Varese, the Project's Research Assistant and Web Administrator, for placing on the Project's website the tables of contents for volumes 1–27 of *DSA*, as well as abstracts for subsequent volumes. (These items are included in a link to *Dickens Studies Annual* on the Project's website, which can be reached at <http://dickens.ucsc.edu>.)

We thank Gabriel Hornstein, President of AMS Press, for his continued confidence and generous support; Jack Hopper, retired Editor-in-Chief at AMS Press, for his expertise in many areas; and David Ramm, Editor-in-Chief at AMS Press, for prompt, effective help with various problems. Finally, we are very grateful to our editorial assistants, Brett Kawalerski and Julia Fuller, doctoral students at The Graduate Center, CUNY, for their skill and care in fulfilling many essential tasks.

—The Editors

Notes on Contributors

JIM BARLOON is Associate Professor of English at the University of St. Thomas in Houston. He has published essays on Dickens, Hemingway, Conan Doyle, Faulkner, and Cather.

ROSEMARIE BODENHEIMER, Professor of English at Boston College, is currently thinking about how nineteenth- and twentieth-century British novelists put London on the page. In her two most recent books, *Knowing Dickens* and *The Real Life of Mary Ann Evans: George Eliot, Her Letters and Fiction*, she explored ways of doing biographical criticism by intertwining a writer's letters with his or her published works.

SUSAN COOK is Assistant Professor of English at Southern New Hampshire University. She received her Ph.D. from the University of California, Santa Barbara, and was a Provost's Postdoctoral Scholar at the University of South Florida. She is currently completing a project on incorporation in the Victorian novel and beginning a study of nineteenth-century visual culture and literature. She has published in *Discourse* and *English Literature in Transition, 1880–1920*.

DEHN GILMORE is Assistant Professor of English at the California Institute of Technology. She is currently completing a book project entitled ''Forms of Regard: The Victorian Novel and the Place of Art.''

MARK M. HENNELLY, JR. is Professor Emeritus and former English Department Chair at California State University, Sacramento. He is also a trustee of the International Dickens Society and has published widely in Victorian fiction. His most recent work appears in *Victorian Literature and Culture*, the online journal *Le Fanu Studies*, and *The [Alfred] Hitchcock Annual Anthology*, ed. Sidney Gottlieb and Richard Allen (Wallflower, 2009).

SHARI HODGES HOLT is Instructional Assistant Professor of English at the University of Mississippi. She is the co-author, with Natalie Schroeder, of *Ouida the Phenomenon* (U of Delaware P, 2008) and has written articles on

Charles Dickens and film that have appeared in *Dickens Studies Annual* and *Literature/Film Quarterly*. She is currently completing a monograph that examines cinematic and television adaptations of Dickens's novels as examples of how Dickens is "read" in other media and under varying cultural and historical circumstances.

JESSICA KILGORE recently received her Ph.D. in English from the University of Texas at Austin. Her research interests include Victorian perceptions of political economy and the relationship between economics and literature. Her dissertation, entitled "Benevolent Failures: The Economics of Philanthropy in Victorian Literature," examines the influence of the tension between political economy and literature on literary representations of charity.

KAREN E. LAIRD received her Ph.D. in English from the University of Missouri, where she currently teaches in the Honors College. Her dissertation, "Melodrama's Afterlife: *Jane Eyre, David Copperfield,* and *The Woman in White* from the Victorian Stage to the Silent Screen," was awarded the 2010 Walter L. Arnstein Prize for Dissertation Research in Victorian Studies by the Midwest Victorian Studies Association. Her article on *Masterpiece Theatre*'s new approach to Victorian adaptation (co-authored with Nancy West) is forthcoming in *Literature/Film Quarterly*.

MAIA MCALEAVEY is Assistant Professor of English at Boston College. She received her Ph.D. from Harvard University in May 2010. Her essay "Soulmates: *David Copperfield*'s Angelic Bigamy" appeared in *Victorian Studies* in Winter 2010 (52.2). She is completing a book entitled "The Shadowy Third: Bigamy and the Victorian Novel," which argues that the surprisingly prevalent plot of bigamy provides an important narrative and cultural frame for Victorian fiction.

GOLDIE MORGENTALER is Professor of English at the University of Lethbridge. She is the author of *Dickens and Heredity* (2000) and of numerous essays on Dickens. Her essay on Dickens and dance will be appearing in the journal *Partial Answers* in 2011. Her translations from Yiddish to English, especially of the work of Chava Rosenfarb, have won several awards, including an MLA book award in 2006.

MARC NAPOLITANO is Assistant Professor of English at the United States Military Academy in West Point. He received his Ph.D. in English from the University of North Carolina at Chapel Hill in 2009. His primary areas of interest include Dickensian literature, the nineteenth-century novel, and stage and screen adaptations of Victorian texts. He has previously explored the use of music in adaptations of *A Christmas Carol, Oliver Twist, Nicholas Nickleby*, and *The Mystery of Edwin Drood*. Along with his interest in musical performance, he also enjoys giving dramatic readings of Dickens's works for his students, colleagues, and family.

DAVID PAROISSIEN, Emeritus Professor of English, University of Massachusetts, Amherst, and Professorial Research Fellow, University of Buckingham, edits *Dickens Quarterly* and co-edits The Dickens Companion Series with Susan Shatto. He has contributed two volumes to the series (*Oliver Twist* and *Great Expectations*) and recently edited *A Companion to Charles Dickens* (2008), a series of essays contributed by Dickensian scholars from around the world and designed to place Dickens's writing in its literary and historical context. He is currently working on a project related to Dickens's political views and his writing about history.

LESLIE SIMON has recently completed her doctoral studies in the Department of English at Boston University, and will begin work as an assistant professor in the Philosophy and Humanities Department at Utah Valley University this fall. Her dissertation, ''Novel Relations: Dickens, Narrative Realism, and Nineteenth-Century Mathematics,'' reflects the interdisciplinary nature of her research, which locates aesthetic and epistemological connections between the literature and mathematics of the nineteenth century.

SHARON ARONOFSKY WELTMAN is Professor of English and Director of Graduate Studies in English at Louisiana State University. The author of two books, *Performing the Victorian: John Ruskin and Identity in Theater, Science, and Education* (Ohio State UP, 2007) and *Ruskin's Mythic Queen: Gender Subversion in Victorian Culture* (Ohio UP, 1999), Weltman has published on a wide array of Victorian authors besides Ruskin, including Charles Dickens, Christina Rossetti, Oscar Wilde, Charlotte Brontë, and Anna Leonowens. Known also for her work on Victorian theater, she has most recently published an essay on Victorian pantomime and is preparing a scholarly edition of George Dibdin Pitt's 1847 melodrama *The String of Pearls, or the Fiend of Fleet Street* for a special issue of *Nineteenth-Century Theatre and Film*, which she is guest-editing. Her current book project, ''Victorians on Broadway: The Afterlife of Victorian Literature on the American Musical Stage, 1951–2000,'' demonstrates the surprising extent to which our current understanding of Victorian literature and culture has been formed by the music, lyrics, dance, and spectacle of American musicals. It includes chapters on *The King and I, Oliver!, Sweeney Todd, Goblin Market, Jekyll and Hyde*, and *Jane Eyre: The Musical*.

DAVID WILKES is currently the Chair of English and Modern Language at Mount Vernon Nazarene University, where he teaches nineteenth-century British Literature. He has published articles on several of Dickens's novels in *Dickens Studies Annual* and *Dickens Quarterly*.

Terms of Art: Reading the Dickensian Gallery

Dehn Gilmore

In this article, I re-contextualize Dickens's reception as a commercial writer by setting it against the development of a heated commercial art market in the middle of the nineteenth century. In the worlds of both literary and visual arts, an ongoing democratization of patronage was accompanied by the evolution of new styles to meet new consumer appetites. I show how concern over the nature of Dickens's innovative fictional technique was framed in the terms of art-world anxieties about a new prominence for contemporary art; how exhaustion at how much the novel now crammed in (and how many novelistic pieces the cramming necessitated) was diagnosed through allusions to galleries so full of wares that they could hardly be processed by the eye. The new art critics tried to create a language and metric to describe and direct the shifts of their world; Dickens's first readers picked up this language as they tried to make sense of (and perhaps to make the career of) their own novel quarry.

I

When Victorian literary critics talked about literature, they drew very often on the language of visual art. In a negative review of *Armadale* by Wilkie Collins, a painter's son, a writer for the *Westminster Review* admonished the novelist: ''to admire the plot and to forget the characters is like admiring the frame instead of enjoying the picture'' (''Armadale'' 159). In a criticism of

---

one-time architect Thomas Hardy, a critic for the *Athenaeum* condemned *The Return of the Native*: "There is just that fault which would appear in the pictures of a person who has a keen eye for the picturesque without having learned to draw" ("The Return of the Native," Cox 57). In an assessment of work by sometime art critic and sometime *künstlerroman*-ticist Thackeray, reviewer John Foster criticized *Henry Esmond* for "wasting the genius and resources of an admirable colourist on pictures false in drawing and perspective" ("Henry Esmond," Tillotson and Hawes 145–46). Not all such references to art worked to a negative end—I've chosen the examples just given for their "lively" qualities. But in all of these reviews and many more like them, we can witness a vocabulary of "pictures" and "painting," of "daubs" and "drawing," of old masters and new photographic effects, and we can see how this vocabulary is observably present both in the writing of more sophisticated, art-informed reviewers, and in the writing of reviewers whose allusions seem more amateurish, or haphazardly selected.

Charles Dickens, the author whose Victorian reception will be my subject in what follows, is the one writer who, based on any informed current critical intuition, we might most expect to present an exception to the rule described above. Because of the way that our own present-day scholarship has become concerned to highlight the art-world connections of novelists like Thackeray and Collins, the Victorian critical move to "frame" these authors through recourse to a visual vocabulary makes ready sense. But Dickens is someone who tends to get posed as a figure apart. If they take up the subject of Dickens and the visual arts at all, older historicist projects typically start in a vein of apology, and then stay in a nervous crouch; their investigations invariably stick close within narrow confines—totting up lists of Dickens's more informal and personal connections to the art world, without any suggestion of their impact on his practice.[1]

Meanwhile, newer historicist evaluations of Victorian text and image evince an even more surprising degree of avoidance, and it is quite remarkable to trace, or more appropriately, to mark, what seems a lately inaugurated tradition of aporia, given how, in a series of recent and excellent works tying various Victorian writers to the visual arts, Dickens never really makes it into the "picture." Necessarily, he has a place in considerations of the "sketch" (how could an author who started by writing *Sketches by Boz* fail to?); but he is not allowed to transcend this connection into a more diversified relation to art; he never gets his chapter fronting due like Eliot, Scott, or the day's other great realist bards.[2] Those who would marry Dickens with the visual field admittedly brush up against stark truths—that, unlike Collins or Thackeray, Dickens lacked both formal artistic training, and a consistent art critical voice. And his manifest, well-known connections to more performative artistic modes (e.g., the theater, the circus, the diorama, and the fair) can make a central focus on visual art seem willfully eccentric.[3] But, as I will argue, the tendency to absent the artistic represents a missed chance when it comes to how we understand Dickens's historical situation and sphere of influence—and this is especially the case when it comes to how we understand how he was read and perceived by his peers.

For Dickens's work, perhaps even *more* than that of his fellow novelists, elicited a series of projected artistic allusions by nineteenth-century readers, and I believe that we must heed this to make sense not only of his place in the Victorian scene, but also of the nature of his nineteenth-century reception. Leafing through the views of his first readers, we encounter Dickens as a writer who might be gifted with the ''eye of a Dutch and also an Italian artist for all external effects,'' yet a writer, too, who could manifest a degree of ''Pre-Raphaelite toil'' (Horne, Collins 150–51; Stothert, Collins 296). We see him as a portrait painter, but also as a worker of ''photographic landscape'' (Cleghorn 78). And we see him as quite like Hogarth, but not to be removed too far from Teniers: ''He is the literary Teniers of the Metropolis'' (''Sketches by Boz'' 196). His virtues can be described with terms of art— R. H. Horne, for example, felt that the novelist's ''Dutch'' and ''Italian'' ''eye'' meant that ''A street, a dwelling, a rural scene, and the human beings therein are so *painted* to the life [in Dickens] that no one who has ever seen them can doubt the resemblance'' (Horne, Collins 150–51). So, too, were Dickens's flaws defined; seethed E. B. Hamley: ''One tells him whatever he does to be sure to be graphic; and accordingly the obedient author *paints* every scene and every character, no matter what degree of importance, with a minuteness far surpassing that of the most laborious limner of *the Dutch school*, till *still life* has no atom left in natural indistinctness'' (495). But if it can perhaps be hard to find critical metaphors consistent with one another in the shapes they take, or the evaluations they support, *that* Dickens is to be logically tied to the figures and trends of his era's art historical moment was once a truth universally acknowledged, and in this essay, my goal will be to study the shape and import of why it was.

In what follows, my project is to reconnect Dickens and his art historical milieu in multiple ways, and in so doing, both to come to a new understanding of how his role and production as a writer were perceived by the Victorians, and to reexamine the motivation and shape of an important Victorian critical impulse—the use of ''terms of art'' for literary analysis. In a notable sense, the work I do will join the trend of new attention to the use of artistic language by the eighteenth- and nineteenth-centuries' literary worlds, and it will join in a much more longstanding tradition of considering *pictura* and *poesis* together. In very interesting recent studies by scholars such as Richard Sha, Alison Byerly, and Ruth Bernard Yeazell, there has been an illumination of the vocabulary of the ''sketch'' and of certain crucial phrases like ''Dutch

Painting'' as these terms were employed to articulate something about the practice and development of literary realism. In the wake of important work on the evaluative and potentially moralizing vocabulary of art reviewing by such scholars as Kate Flint and Elizabeth Prettejohn, ever more panels at interdisciplinary conferences concern themselves with narrative art, broadly construed.

At the same time, however, in looking to Dickens, and in considering how his first readers experienced and described his novels, I also want to push beyond the limits of these considerations, and, ultimately, to make what I see as two more large-scale observations about how scholars think about the literary turn to art. First, I will suggest that the scholarly move to place someone like Dickens beyond some perceived bounds of what might make a writer's visual artistic connections significant should be seen as a signal that our present intuition about the limits of the nineteenth-century's artistic intersections is not sufficiently developed or broad; I will emphasize how often, and in how many ways the literary world could intersect with the art world even when an authorial expertise wasn't the driving force of the connection. Concurrently, I will propose that our understanding of how an author like Dickens was read (or might be read in the future) gains greatly from re-imagining the possibilities and significations that the Victorians saw in visual artistic invocation. Today scholars and critics have come to assume that when reviewers use ''terms of art,'' they do so (or did so) to describe something about forms of *writing*; whether we talk about the ''broad canvas novel''—and mean that a given book is full of characters and details—or whether we consider the applications of a term like ''Dutch painting''—something Yeazell has done brilliantly, to find it ''a kind of shorthand for many of the characteristics we now associate with the bourgeois novel''—we center our own language and discussion on matters of subject and style (Yeazell xv). Reviewers are seen always to be saying something about aesthetic production.

Yet such writerly bearing was not always seen as the sole import of artistic language, and I will emphasize that, for readers in the Victorian period, the use of artistic terms was actually quite variously conceived. Victorian reviewers turned to art to comment on production, but they used it just as frequently, to describe something about *consumption*. And, specifically, in looking at the reception of Dickens, I will show that artistic language comes in almost more often to describe something about his reviewers' *readerly* experience than it does to say something about his writerly practice. Dickens's initial evaluators bring Dickens and the art world together, as I will, in broad structural terms, with an eye to a new, sphere-spanning set of developments around art and commerce, and in their emphasis not only on what they saw, but also in how they saw, they seek to diagnose a new kind of phenomenological experience.

The variety of visual metaphors that they used in their critical descriptions can be taken to refer directly to two strands of new developments that affected aesthetic consumption in the nineteenth century, and their metaphorical usage underscores a vital, and yet understudied link that existed between these strands. On the one hand, the visual artistic recourse of Dickens's critics almost invariably seems to have highlighted what, for them, appeared most strikingly new about Dickens—his new brand of detail-oriented realism, the tendency of his books to seem as though they were made up of disparate parts (or, thanks to serialization, actually to *be* so made up), and perhaps above all, his new and amazing dimension of mass appeal, and his related status as a commercial figure. On the other hand, as we will see in the first part of my discussion, the art world that the critical discourse pointed to was itself a space undergoing a series of revolutions that affected reception. It was the nature of these changes—changes in many cases that had exact parallels in the Dickens-fronted ones described above—that I will argue as having made logical the literary writers' allusive choices.

In the world of the visual arts, as around the work of Dickens, an ongoing diffusion downward of patronage meant that a common audience found itself newly able to spend a few guineas and to get either a whole painting, or a couple of newly published books (Altick, *Paintings* 77). This democratization of the buying public was accompanied by the rise of a new style, and, just as important, of new volume to meet new imperatives of appetite. Questions about aesthetics—but also about phenomenological response—were the result of those developments in the relationship between art and commerce. Genre paintings got hot; new tastes emerged; and market incentives produced crowded walls. To match concerns over the nature of Dickens's new fictional technique, there were tandem art-world anxieties about what might manifest itself concurrent with a new prominence and legitimacy for contemporary art. Juxtaposed with an exhaustion over how much the novel now crammed in, there were complaints about galleries so full of wares that they could hardly be processed by the eye. Those who wrote about the art world sought to describe and to diagnose a new set of pressures on visual attention—if also a new sense of possibility that lay behind what J. B. Atkinson (disdainfully) called an "amazing increase in production" ("Decline" 2). A body of literary reviewers borrowed often from the resultant vocabulary, as they too sifted and sorted, and as they themselves tried to proffer instructions for consumption—their own view on the union of aesthetics, information, and market forces. Seemingly casual descriptions that cast Dickens's writing as resembling the work of a painter still produce strong local images in the mind; how vivid indeed to state like George Brimley, that *Bleak House* suffers artistically, "so crowded is the canvas which Mr. Dickens has stretched" (284). But I think that, in its moment of circulation, such language had a more pointed, yet also a more global significance. If Dickens's *writing* was painterly, the experience of *reading* Dickens (and reading him in a world where tastes competed and attention was divided) could very often seem to be the experience of entering a space—that space seemed very much like the space of a commercial gallery of art.

In one of the more famous descriptions of Dickens that has ever been written, Walter Bagehot saw Dickens as "a special correspondent for posterity"—his beat was London life: "London is like a newspaper. Everything is there and everything is disconnected" (468). Yet just a few pages before Bagehot got to this metaphor, he offered something else: "An artist once said of the best work of another artist, 'Yes it is a pretty patch.' " Bagehot then commented, "If we might venture on the phrase, we should say that Mr. Dickens's pictures were graphic scraps; his best books are compilations of them" (464). Before Dickens was a correspondent, he was a collector; before his works were broadsheets they were pictorial collections. "Dickens" the institution, and the commercial art institutions of his day, come together here; in the course of what follows, I will show just how often and in how many ways they did.

II

The rise of a thriving commercial art market, and of two important commensurate phenomena—the new class of patrons to fuel it, and the commentators who would mediate it—was part of a large art historical trend in nineteenth-century Britain: a constant enlargement in both number and nature of the pool of people who came into contact with art, and these people's increasing appetite for further and more meaningfully personal encounters. Janet Minihan has written that the "expansion of the audience for art" was "the most significant cultural development of the nineteenth century," and though the force of her assertion may be debatable, the fact of the growth she cites clearly is not (4). In the museum world, the National Gallery and the British Museum swelled their visitor rolls tenfold in mere ten-year periods—with the Gallery's numbers climbing from 60,321 visitors in 1830 to 503,011 in 1840 (Minihan 52), and the British Museum's attendance figures shooting from around 80,000 in the late 1820s to over a million in 1851 (Altick, *Shows* 454; Crook 196). In the sphere of the exhibition, the era's grand shows like the Crystal Palace and the Manchester Art Treasures Exhibition were newly welcoming to what the *Illustrated London News* described as everyone between "the wealthier classes and their dependents" ("A New Result" 608). In the commercial art world, also, there were moves towards increased and diversified involvement.

In the nineteenth century's early decades a boom of print production and print shops or so-called "poor-man's picture galleries" (Altick, *Shows* 109) led to a situation where everyone might be familiar with the same works. Dickens wrote confidently to Forster from Italy in 1845: "The most famous oil paintings in the Vatican you know through the medium of the finest line-engravings in the world" (*Letters* 4: 276). In the 1830s, the founding and then surging popularity of the art union movement brought "art into the homes of a wider public than ever before" by offering cheap reproductions of art to subscribers (Minihan 61). And through the middle of the century, even the Royal Academy made a slow transition from being a "resort of men and women of title and wealth" (Altick, *Shows* 406) to being a space that Dickens could identify, writing to Forster in 1841, as being of a much wider cultural significance: "that hallowed spot on which the eyes of Europe and the beating hearts of the civilized world are unalterably fixed" (*Letters* 2: 277–78).[4] Whether the Academy was familiar to the majority of Britons because they had entered its doors, or because they had seen engravings of its works, or because they had read press reports on its exhibitions, it was becoming a space so familiar to Dickens's readers that they could reasonably be asked to make sense of a reference to it.[5] And, in *Little Dorrit*, Arthur Clennam, considering Christopher Casby, muses how "whereas in the Royal Academy some evil old ruffian . . . will annually be found embodying all the cardinal virtues, on account of his eyelashes . . . so in the great social exhibition, accessories are often accepted in lieu of internal character" (*Little Dorrit* 152–53; bk. 1, ch. 13). Art was increasingly a part of (more) people's lived experiences, and the rise of a popular art market was becoming part of a broad, multi-institution transformation.

At the same time as the evolving art market was part of an "expansive" trend, it was also characterized by a set of particular features all its own. It was defined, first, by changes in the nature of the patronage that the enlargement of the audience encompassed, and, second, by a spike not only in the number of art-interested viewers and potential buyers, but also in the volume of art on view and for sale. Looking back on the 1839 founding of the *Art-Union*, S. C. Hall revealed a certain gift for hyperbole when he claimed that before his periodical began, "There was literally no 'patronage' for British Art." Even Hall went on to clarify his terms: "Collectors—wealthy merchants and manufacturers did indeed buy pictures as befitting household adornments, but they were 'old masters' with familiar names" (197). But hyperbolic or not, his comments point us towards two important art-market tropes. The first (less overt) is that those who were doing the bulk of the "collecting" by midcentury were no longer the aristocrats or churches and were, instead, the rising commercial classes. And the second, which will be evident from the thrust of his remarks, is that what was being collected was shifting also, as old masters and contemporary works came into competition for buyer attention, with the result that ever more art seemed fit for show and demanding of evaluation.

That, by midcentury, the middle classes did indeed newly hold "the purse strings," as *Fraser's* contributor William George Clark called their new buying power, was a fact universally apparent (708). It was, as Richard Altick notes, wholly clear that "a new, demotic market for art had materialized," and, in 1862, J. B. Atkinson summarized accordingly in *Blackwood's*: "Patronage is now not solely in the sovereignty of the state or in the power of the church, but in the hands of the people . . . the people, both for evil and for good, have, throughout Europe, grown into a power and pictures, accordingly, are made to pander to the wants of a dominant democracy" (Altick, *Paintings* 77; Atkinson, "Pictures" 360). The day's more famous and renowned works were bought by industrial barons rather than by aristocrats. Affluent men of the middle class commissioned the lion's share of new, contemporary works. And while some, like Clarke, celebrated the middle's new power: "The actor, author, artist, must act, write, and paint up to our level or down to our level, if he means to live by his profession" (Clarke 708), others, like Dickens, worried about too much market-born calculation by artists producing "a horrible respectability" in English art (*Letters* 7: 742–43).

Down the scale, too, there was novelty in the character of potential consumers. As a business in the fraudulent production of "Old Masters" boomed and flooded the market to bring down the cost of legitimate works, it became possible that you might get a "Titian" for just a few pounds (Hall 204). Mr. Meagles in *Little Dorrit* is proof enough of this, and, referring to one of his many souvenirs, he remarks to Clennam and Doyce, "Titian, that [picture] might or might not be—perhaps he had only touched it" (199; bk. 1, ch. 16). But, more legitimately, there were also diversifying developments. On the one hand, as Altick suggests (in a union of his interests in book history and popular arts), "Hundreds of pictures exhibited at the British Institution and the Society of British Artists were priced at only a few guineas, no more than would have bought two or three recently published books," and he adds, pictures at this price—"ordinary small cabinet pictures"—appealed to middle-class buyers and "swell[ed] the [purchase] records of nineteenth-century British Painting. This was the bargain basement precinct of contemporary art, where the prevailing taste was reflected *en masse*" (Altick, *Paintings* 77).[6] On the other hand (albeit on what Atkinson might have seen as the dreg level of the "dominant democracy"), there were also the "patrons" in the membership of the country's nascent Art Unions—men and women who paid cash subscriptions for a lottery stake towards the acquisition of original works, and a guaranteed ownership of engravings based on works bought in their original form by much richer people. Such men and women (members like Dickens, an initial subscriber, excepted) were generally even poorer than those who shopped the Institute's "bargain basement"; so, as Janet Minihan writes: "The significant achievement of the art unions was to bring art, even if not a very exalted kind, into the lives of people socially below the prosperous middle and upper-middle classes" (77–78; 61).

Dickens was first in line to satirize one outcome of the ascent of the new kind of patron, and he found much to mock in a group of people whose security about taste and judgment could be slower to emerge than was their financial power. In a *Household Words* piece called "The Toady Tree," he told readers to: "take Dobbs . . . a well-read man" and a man "perfectly clear in his generation that men are to be deferred to for their capacity for what they undertake, for their talents and worth, and for nothing else." We then find that this poor, would-be aristocrat of talents is keenly obsequious to a marquis, whose ease and comfort in the space of the Royal Academy's exhibition clearly accentuates his elevated birth. As Dickens observes, wryly: "I have seen Dobbs dive and double about that Royal Academy Exhibition, in pursuit of a nobleman . . . when the Marquis has entered . . . I have known of the Marquis's entrance without . . . turning my head, solely by the increased gentility in the audible tones of Dobbs's critical observations" ("Toady Tree" 3: 301). In an anecdotal commentary such as this, we can see how there would be many who would rue the power of the "dominant democracy" and how it would be true, as Kate Flint suggests, that a "resentment of the linkage between art and commerce was something of a commonplace throughout the period" (*Victorians* 176).

But Dickens was also prescient when he recognized that there were more tangible—and potentially positive—sides to the expansion of who held the "purse-strings" of the age, and in his novels there are plenty of subtle signs that indicate as much. In the great number of pictures (portraits and genre scenes especially) that deck the illustrations for his novels, we witness the newly diffuse ownership literally framed as fact—for example, all but one of the *Bleak House* illustrations that show interiors have pictures in them (the plate "Sunset in the long Drawing-room of Chesney Wold" shows a gallery).[7] Meanwhile, the texts of his novels casually cast the new demographic range of patron as quotidian reality, and in *David Copperfield*, even humble Mr. Peggotty has "some common coloured pictures, framed and glazed, of scripture subjects," while the much more high-toned Steerforths deck their bedrooms with "pictures in crayons of ladies with powdered hair and bodices," and a "likeness of Miss Dartle" (30; bk. 1, ch. 3; 272; bk. 1, ch. 20; 277; bk. 1, ch. 20). In *Little Dorrit*, a "few prints" "poorly decorat[e]" the room of Mr. Dorrit in the Marshalsea, while rather more impressive portraits feature in the rather more impressive rooms of a character like Flora (87; bk. 1, ch. 8; 291; bk. 1, ch. 24). And in *Our Mutual Friend*, "a coloured picture beautiful to see" hangs over the bed of poor dying orphan Johnny, as, in a very different corner of society, the Veneerings, "bran-new people in a bran-new

house'' are also ''bran-new'' patrons, with pictures of ''bran-new pilgrims
on the wall, going to Canterbury in more gold frame than procession'' (320;
bk. 2, ch. 9; 6; bk. 1, ch. 1; 17; bk. 1, ch. 3).

Throughout these descriptions we see Dickens registering the diversifica-
tion of artistic patronage, and about all of this there is the sense, as George
Orwell once wrote of Dickens, that ''Everything is seen from the consumer
angle,'' though now we might use that comment as a lens on a very specific
kind of consumption (48). The same heterogeneous public that helped the
novel to become a major market force and cash cow (especially with the
advent of Dickens) was becoming newly able also to help the works of visual
artists earn financial rewards.[8] And when Dickens wrote to S. C. Hall in 1839
to congratulate him on the founding of the *Art-Union*, and to wish him ''All
good fortune to the *Art-Union*'' his acknowledgment of Hall's ''good idea''
and savvy in capturing ''the only unoccupied [periodical] field'' was significant (*Letters* 1: 509). Just as the swelling roster of readers was hungry for
guides to direct its inclinations and to mediate its new relations to literacy,
so too those for whom artistic encounter had newly personal stakes also
looked for guidance.

III

Indeed, whatever their education, and whatever their role, patrons and critics
confronted a changing art and an experience of it that was also changing.
And here we encounter the second broad thematic shift that characterized the
dynamics of the artistic marketplace as the nineteenth-century developed.
Namely, that the rise of middle-class buyers was accompanied by a phenomenon to which it bore something of a ''chicken and egg'' relationship—a rise
in the volume of art on show, and one enabled in significant part by a new
admixture of circumstances and tastes. There was a ''surge of patriotism''
that came in the wake of the Napoleonic Wars, and that cut two ways—first
fueling a desire to beat out the Continent for acquisition of newly available
Old Masters, but also undergirding an impulse more xenophobic; for after
the wars, as Richard Altick suggests, ''the productions of native artists . . . aroused keener interest and commanded higher prices'' than they ever had
before (*Shows* 404). There was also, a new, much more positive valuation
for genre painting and for contemporary work. While many of the new buyers
wanted to emulate the artistic preferences of the aristocrats who had preceded
them as buyers, many, too, wanted to acquire pictures that seemed to be
about *their lives* and *their* world. And so, as Helene Roberts writes, by mid-
century ''[t]he former strict hierarchy of subject categories which placed
historical subjects at the top and genre and still-life painting near the bottom

had largely broken down'' (17). And on the highest level of exhibition and acquisition, these developments, and particularly the ''breakdown'' cited by Roberts, meant that modern works and Old Masters squared off. They competed for pride of place on gallery walls, and for the attention of high-rolling purchasers like *Bleak House*'s own Lord Dedlock—a man who surveys ''with approbation'' his ''pictures ancient and modern'' before the omniscient narrative voice describes them as ''they would best be catalogued like the miscellaneous articles in a sale'' (395). Meanwhile, at the lower end of the market, new so-called ''furniture pictures''—a species of canvas meant to be purely decorative and reflective of the owner's life and tastes, or works that seemed, in the horrified identification of *The Saturday Review*, ''but a portion of domestic furniture''—vied with imitations and reproductions of old classics for middle-brow affection and a place in middle-class homes (''The Royal Academy Exhibition'' 475).

The result of such contests would ultimately determine everything from the future of the National Gallery's purchasing decisions to what decked out the spaces that a boom in middle-class housing produced, the new ''wall areas offering so many more millions of square feet to hang pictures on, even if the individual paintings had to be small'' (Altick, *Pictures* 79–80). The result of the *contretemps* was also, significantly, an ongoing theoretical debate about the place of the past in relation to the present. Did Old Masters, as Dickens suggested while in Italy in 1844, perhaps instantiate ''rules of art'' that could be ''much too slavishly followed, making it a pain to you, when you go into galleries day after day, to be so very precisely sure where this figure will be turning round . . . a perfect nightmare'' (*Letters* 4: 221).[9] Or were they still vital sources to be learned from and esteemed?—as he himself claimed at another point, this time taking the Pre-Raphaelites to task: ''There is something so fascinating . . . in the notion of ignoring all that has been done for the happiness and elevation of mankind during three or four centuries of slow and dearly bought amelioration'' (''Old Lamps'' 521). These were important abstract questions. But, perhaps most perceptibly, what the continuing interest in the old *and* a newfound appreciation of the contemporary became associated with was a different kind of evaluative need, and a previously unknown kind of phenomenological competition. Crowds of people were linked to newly crowded gallery walls, and the new experience that *both* multiplying pictures *and* multiplying viewers produced, centered in a highly distinctive new aesthetic.

Just as they are famous for writing very long books, the Victorians are also known for having crowded their walls with pictures. A constant of the Victorian art-viewing experience was often a sense of confusion and excess—and this was something to be undergone in private estate house and public museum alike. Consistently, works in all of the Victorians' spaces of display baffled with their lack of organizing rubric. Not until the Manchester Art Treasures show of 1857 was a practice of chronological hanging employed in Britain, while in institutions like the National Gallery the hanging policy was, as Kate Flint comments, one full of "chance juxtapositions" that were "driven by the demands of fitting together a geometric puzzle of rectilinear forms" (*Victorians* 191–92).[10] Works fought with each other for attention, amidst what Dickens called the usual "glare and bustle" ("Meeting" 215).[11] Viewers complained *ad nauseum* about the resulting pressures all public art encounters put on the senses, and as a despairing Henry Morley rued, viewing art wherever the Victorians hung it could lead to a "mind confused by quick jolting along a line of ideas between which there are no links or association, with attention much distracted by a babble at each ear" (695). In crowding their walls (and their rooms), the museum, the grand-scale show, and the commercial exhibition were alike in promoting such confusion. Surely this was stressful.

At the same time, however, for all that an intensity of cramming and surfeit was a regular feature of artistic encounter in the nineteenth century, there were also ways in which the changing art marketplace and the exhibitions that were its most public manifestation fostered a kind of evaluative need and competition that the private collection did not, and that the museum alone had not. Indeed, the market's aesthetic was one that a series of distinctive properties helped make into one of distinct confusion. First, as a simple arithmetic fact, the conferral of approval on, and market interest in, new genres and new artists as fit for acquisition and display, inherently meant that the amount of art to be considered increased, and so one exhibition-associated change to the period's volumetric experience or dynamic of art was purely *quantitative*. The new acceptance of previously unappreciated or undervalued works by schools like the early Germans meant that suddenly there was a flood of old canvases due new consideration ("Manchester Exhibition" 758). But, more overwhelmingly, the legitimization of contemporary painting meant that there would *always* be more to look at and to evaluate, and with each passing year, the pressure mounted. In 1865, J. B. Atkinson wrote that: "The London Art-Season, which in some degree is an epitome of the world's art, has now swelled into such magnitude of dimension . . . that to survey its vast extent, or to grasp it in its grand entirety, were more than we can hope to compass within the limits of a single article" (234). Such expansion led to a new experience of infinity that tested the limited of what *could* be counted. And, as year flowed into year, there further arose an accounting problem that was distinctly diachronic. In 1872 Henry Morley calculated that it would take a viewer twenty-five hours to view a Royal Academy show at the rate of a minute spent per picture—but once you'd run that gauntlet, your task was still incomplete: "Did anybody ever go to a private view at the Academy without being asked, whether he thought this exhibition better or worse than the last? And did anybody . . . ever feel that he was really able to compare the recollection of 1,500 works . . . with the impression made by another 1,500 now before his eyes?'' (694). The act of viewing had come not only to involve comparing the works of separate countries, separate artists, separate schools, or even separate epochs, but also of separate *years*, and it was standard to start a review as William George Clark did in 1855 with a version of this note: ''The general impression which the exhibition of the present year leaves upon one's mind is, that it is neither better nor worse than those of other years'' (709). It was common to frame any perceived teleology in discrete annual increments, as did Thackeray (as Titmarsh) in 1843: ''I think every succeeding year shows a progress in the English school of painters'' (214). These comments indicate a kind of comparison viewers did not make in looking at a museum collection that retained a stable core, or in looking at the works in a grand exhibition that happened once in a lifetime. Surely, if perhaps confusingly, one new element of consciousness involved being driven to restless summarizing, and in both analeptic and proleptic ways. The effort to grapple with immensity and to shuffle among myriads was dizzying.

But the specific presence of newly accepted genre works and newly pro-duced contemporary pictures also effected a more local or micro-level set of pressures on one's eye. And in confronting a single gallery room, or even a lone gallery wall, visitors had to consider the traits that defined these kinds of work—their tendency to be figurative or anecdotal in nature, often natural-ist in style, and small in size. These traits augmented elements of the already jostling pictorial relations detailed above, now in ways that seemed more *qualitative*. To take the case of the exhibitions' portraits, for instance, is to find that they had a novel relationship to the sensory experience of crowding, and this was that they worked to literalize it. Portraits were ever-bigger busi-ness in the Victorian era—for obvious reasons of vanity, but also because they helped people in new class positions mark and consolidate their ascent—and accordingly all commercial galleries overflowed with them. Dickens was prompted by this surfeit to describe the gallery viewing experience as one in which the viewer could feel drawn into a confused fellowship: ''all the people in the pictures pointedly referred to me in every cock of their highly feathered hats'' (''An Idea of Mine'' 20: 161). For him the solution was sardonically clear. Although he sarcastically proposed that there be a moratorium on model-sittings, he comments: ''Whether the withdrawal of the Models would reduce our men of genius, who paint pictures, to the shameful necessity of wrestling their great art to the telling of stories and conveying of ideas, is a question upon which I do not feel called to enter'' (20: 165). *Punch* likewise noted drily that an 1847 show would be ''an object of interest to those who are fond of self-contemplation'' (''Ensuing'').

But for other writers, the problem was not funny, and, particularly at the Royal Academy, debates about the prevalence of portraits were fierce. An Academician had the prerogative to submit up to eight paintings for a given show, thereby bypassing a tough juried system that, in representative year 1848, left two-thirds of submitted works out in the cold ("The Royal Academy: The Eightieth Exhibition" 165). And since the R. A. members who most often took up this chance were the portrait painters (Roberts, 11), the walls of the show could come to seem a sea of faces, often with dizzying effect. As a scornful *Art-Union* reviewer wrote, there could easily be "human forms and faces of all conceivable expressions, literally covering the walls of 'the great room.' North, South, East, and West . . . carry your eye round the huge apartment, and you see a crowded assemblage of inanities for whom the world knows, and for whom it cares, nothing" ("The Royal Academy" 179). For a landscape to compete for attention with "moving heads," as it might do in the National Gallery was one thing. For "human forms and faces of all conceivable expressions" to go "head to head" with their real life counterparts was a different kind of confusion altogether and might need a new set of dictates for proper viewing.

Certainly, then, a new eye, or a new focus was needed if one sought to move beyond the portraits to a consideration of the newly prominent genre pictures, or to a more general consideration of a particular wall or room. Given the smaller size of the newly valued works, a visitor might well wish for some kind of ocular assistance. One reason, indeed, that the Royal Academy could include ever more works on its walls—something it certainly did, as it moved from showing 1,278 to 2,000 pieces in its annual shows between 1830 and 1899 (Altick, *Paintings* 72)—was that the kinds of works that it was hanging were literally changing shape. The shows' (and market's) tendency to value highly "genre" paintings, portraits, and even miniatures—which Clark believed to be a special site of English "excellenc[ce]" (715)—alongside (or in place of) history and landscape, meant that even more paintings could be placed on the average wall than would be done in the museum, for the simple reason that these pictures were often comparatively small.[12] Or, as a despairing reviewer for *Blackwood's* wrote in 1858: "What are things coming to? Certain artists and critics seem tacitly to have conspired in order to defraud our national art of her grandeur and dignity. Just in proportion as our empire widens in extent, do our pictures lessen in size; in proportion as great thoughts struggle for utterance do our artists play trivially with small ones" ("London Exhibitions" 181). Clearly important in his assessment is the appeal to the national self-image. But just as notable is an implication about how its dimunition practically plays out: where previously visitors might have had to shuffle among a few works on a wall, now here was a need to look up and down as well as back and forth and all over. Some disorientation and certainly some

distraction are potential outcomes, and we can perhaps consider their condensation, in Dickens if we look at the advertising board Miss La Creevy hangs
in her lodging in *Nicholas Nickleby*. There, in a single "large gilt-frame"
(still small enough in size to fit "upon the street door") there are hung what
seem to be dozens of miniatures, with not just "two portraits of naval dress
coats . . . one of a young gentleman in a very vermilion dress coat . . . one of
a literary character . . . a touching representation of a young lady . . . and a
charming whole length of a large-headed little boy." In addition, "[b]esides
these works of art, there were a great many heads of old ladies and gentlemen
smirking at each other . . . and an elegantly written card of terms with an
embossed border" (25–26; ch. 3). To have room for the card and yet such a
"great many heads" was impressive; to try to take in all these images within
a short time was formidable.

Elements of the new style levied their own (un)sightly requirements, and,
in addition to having a tendency to be focused on real life, the contemporary
pictures shown in the exhibition often featured a new version of a realist
effect, with the result that they could seem *internally* crowded in a novel or
unfamiliar way. Those who followed the dictates of Ruskin or the example
of the Pre-Raphaelites not only had canvases crammed into shows, but, as
far as many traditional viewers were concerned, the artist also crammed any
given canvas. A *Blackwood's* critic lamented that "Instead of the grandeur
of the storm, the gloom of the mountain, the infinity of space, the spectator
must botanize among foreground flowers, watch the bee . . . or shudder at the
spotted serpent gliding in the dewy grass" ("London Exhibitions" 186–87).
He rued, in other words, that the spectator must risk getting lost in a swamp
of minutiae. Meanwhile, Dickens again commenting on the Pre-Raphaelites,
mocked the group's devotion to detail. One expected to find at the next Royal
Academy show, he wrote in 1850, "some pictures by this pious Brotherhood,
realizing Hogarth's idea of a man on a mountain several miles off, lighting
his pipe in the upper window of a house in the foreground. But we are
informed that every brick in the house will be a portrait . . . and that the
texture of his hands (including four chilblains, a whitlow, and ten dirty nails)
will be a triumph of the painter's art" ("Old Lamps" 524).

The pictures that Dickens and his compatriot referred to reflect what Kate
Flint calls "a significant feature of the period: its dependence, across a variety
of fields, on the accumulation and precise recording of detail" (*Victorians*
19). But the effect of these works' timeliness, at least in some cases, was
clearly not what the Pre-Raphaelites and their ilk hoped for—a felt testament
to God, and (again as per Flint) "spiritual significance made manifest"
(20)—and was instead a concern that a writer for the *Saturday Review* phrased
when he wrote English painters were vesting too much in the insignificant:
"such gifts as they possess are so largely thrown away on meanness of

subject . . . [on, for example,] the most trivial incidents of family life.'' The effect was also a worry that the distinction between ''grandeur'' and grass, between background and foreground, might be lost amidst a new opportunity for visual fatigue and a sense of competing draws on the eye (''The Royal Academy Exhibition'' 475).

New patrons, new pictures, new crowds, a new sense of visual crowding—this was the dynamic and sometimes disorienting artistic moment in which Dickens worked, and in which, as we have seen, he was much more thoroughly and typically situated than we often give him credit for being. This was the art world that he knew, one with many contradictions—between the positive side of democratized artistic encounter and the more shadowy or laughable dimensions of open access, between the relative value of Pre-Raphaelite avant-gardism and that of warmed-over Old Master imitations. This was a world that he drew on as he offered a pronouncement like this, to supporters of the Artists' Benevolent Fund about his ''strong belief that the neighborhoods of Trafalgar Square, or Suffolk Street [homes of the Royal Academy and the British Artists' Society], rightly understood, are quite as important to the welfare of the empire as those of Downing Street or Westminster Hall'' (''Artists' '' 268–69). This was the shape of the commercial side of his sister art, or what Dickens himself called his ''near relation'' in a ''family party,'' as he sought to make his own navigations between ''significance'' and ''meanness'' (''Royal Academy Banquet'' 264–65). And, in seeing all of this, what we will now see is how Dickens's own act of self-alliance to the visual arts was one refracted, mirrored, reimagined, and above all, *repeated* time and again by his critics—and in ways, as I suggested at the outset, that have vital implications for our understanding of not only their quarry, but also, of themselves and their practice.

IV

Dickens's critics began using an art-inflected language to describe his fiction almost as soon as it was put in front of them. As was perhaps only appropriate in considering a writer whose first preface—that to *Sketches by Boz*—had promised ''little pictures of life and manners as they really are,'' a pictorial vocabulary was in wide and diverse circulation from the time of his first work.[13] Already, in the first crop of notices, his critics likened Dickens to Teniers, a Dutch painter of genre scenes, because of how the former ''paints the lower orders of London with . . . exactness and . . . comic effect'' (Buller 52–53). They criticized Dickens for being, as Abraham Hayward said, a mere ''copyist'' rather than a good ''portrait painter'' (something ironically resonant, here, of course, with Dickens's suggestion that models should be prohibited, the better to incite actual *ideas*) (497). And they instituted the first instances of what would come to constitute a career-spanning practice of linking Dickens to Hogarth—with both men as artists of London life, as portrayers of people in and of the streets, artists to be regarded as quintessentially *English* institutions, or, more abstractly, as practitioners who somehow worked along the same general lines.[14] As a summary (and representative) piece in an 1838 *Edinburgh Review* proposed,

> We would compare [Dickens] rather with the painter Hogarth. What Hogarth was in painting such very nearly is Mr. Dickens in prose fiction. . . . Like Hogarth he has a keen and practical view of life—is an able satirist— . . . peculiarly skillful in the management of details, throwing in circumstances which serve not only to complete the picture before us, but to suggest indirectly antecedent events which cannot be brought before our eyes.
>
> (Lister, Collins 72)[15]

These first reviews offer much that resounds with strains of the art world debates that the first part of this essay detailed, and already they nod to the popularity of the genre scenes that defined the art world in Dickens's day (and that made painters like Teniers a hot seller). In them there is a transformal concern that with the production of art to meet taste, what was artistic might be lost—or that the public market would feature a "copy" rather than a "portrait." In them, too, there is a sense that Dickens's popularity has something to do with a new delight in "details," and the new sense that no work of art—whether visual or verbal—is complete without them.

But it is also the case that these early reviews were only setting the stage, and in surveying the developing field of Dickensian criticism, we can see how intricately and with what nuance the connections established around *Sketches by Boz* and *Pickwick* developed. More generally, in looking over Dickens's career span, we can see that his critics consistently used a borrowed vocabulary to try to understand the source and shape of his unprecedented degree of commercial success, and to articulate Dickens's particular fashion of combining information and aesthetics. In a closer survey, we see that as they did this, they did it along two lines. Playfully, it might be said that one body of allusions—the body that developed first, but persisted—cast Dickens as artist, and his works as things that might hang *on a wall*, while another body of allusions posed Dickens as a collector or curator, and his works as presenting the experience of looking at *an entire wall itself*. Practically, it will be seen that his critics' metaphorical language moved to emphasize that the novelty of Dickens lay as much on the side of the experience of reading him and considering his *ouevre* as it did on the side of anything about his subject, his style, or a particular book. The reviews of *Pickwick* tend to show us an image of Dickens as painter, to use an artistic vocabulary to describe his writerly practice, and to assume a stable art viewing experience. By the time we get to career summations of Dickens at the end of his life, he is not only a painter, but also an arranger, ever putting on shows. His critics now use an artistic vocabulary to describe a range of phenomenological experiences (some a bit unwieldy); they use it to describe and diagnose what a reader might expect from a Dickensian brush. And in a look at *Our Mutual Friend*, we are told by no less a figure than E. S. Dallas, to prepare to be overwhelmed, to "see what a mass of matter he lays before his readers. There is a *gallery of portraits* in the present novel which might set up half a dozen novelists for life" (6).

V

On the first, or more painterly score, we can see that as Dickens's output extended, so too did the range of allusions that his critics used, but that many of these worked along remarkably similar lines, and with a seemingly simple common goal: to use the vocabulary of the art critical world to try to establish what Dickens's artistic *product* looked like, or how we could tell "A Dickens." In the art world, as we have witnessed, it was becoming obvious that English works, works showing scenes from common life, and works of great vivacity were generally well-liked and certainly much seen; this knowledge beckoned evidently when readers sought to describe and to account for, or sometimes even to condemn, the reasons behind Dickens's own success. When a critic wanted to underscore the significance of Dickens's engagement of the national imagination, the novelist could easily become a "painter of English manners" ("Dombey and Son," Collins 214)—or someone, as Hippolyte Taine wrote, who had the "passion and the patience of the painters of his nation" to "recko[n] details one by one" and to "not[e] the various hues of old tree trunks." Less felicitously, for Taine, Dickens also had a tendency to "be lost, like the painters of his country, in the minute and impassioned observation of small things," and to lack "love of beautiful forms and fine colours" (Hollington 1: 373). When someone wanted to flag the importance of Dickens's investment in low and quotidian subjects, he was said to have a gift for "some happy bits of Dutch painting" (Trotter 686). He was noted by George Henry Lewes, to have "painted the life he knew, the life everyone knew . . . all the resources of the bourgeois epic were in his grasp" (Hollington 1: 459–60) and he was accounted by another critic to have done "with the pen what some of the old Dutch Painters—Oustade and Teniers and Jan Steen—had done with the pencil, revealing not only the picturesque effects but the interesting moral characteristics, that lie in the commonest and even basest forms of plebian life" ("The Late Charles Dickens," Collins 517).

Dickens's flaws sometimes seemed especially to act as magnets for critics influenced or inspired by terms of art, and James Augustine Stothert railed against Dickens for "lay[ing] on colours with violent elaboration"—for, we could say, working much as a modern painter eager to catch and corner the eye might (Stothert, Collins 296). Then both Stothert—who also complained that Dickens worked with "true Pre-Raphaelite toil," adumbrating "everything that can be seen or discovered till . . . weariness takes the place of vivid perception" (296), and a reviewer for the *North British Review*, identified a detail overload in decidedly art-inflected terms. Pronounced the *Review*:

> The frequent recurrence of . . . ludicrous minuteness in the trivial descriptive details induces us to compare Mr. Dickens's style of delineation to a photographic landscape. There, everything is copied with unfailing but mechanical fidelity. . . . He lavishes as much attention on what is trivial or useless as on the more important part of the picture, as if he could not help painting everything with equal exactness . . . the very hat, and neckcloth, and coat buttons of each [character]. (Cleghorn 78)

Dickens, having lampooned the Pre-Raphaelites for making "every brick in the house . . . a portrait; . . . [and] the texture of his hands (including four chilblains, a whitlow, and ten dirty nails . . . a triumph of the painter's art" ("Old Lamps" 524), could hardly have been pleased to be faulted for painting with too much "exactness" "the very hat, the neckcloth and coat buttons of each, or to be charged with leaving "no atom . . . in natural indistinctness." Nor might he have been happy the a comparison between himself and Scott that appeared in the *Irish Quarterly Review*: "A sketcher can never be enrolled amongst the great masters; a Rembrandt outline is never put in competition with a picture of Titian's, and therefore for all these reasons, we cannot consider Charles Dickens a GREAT NOVELIST" ("Novels and Novelists" 102). But, in both positive and negative assessments, the hallmark of Dickensian style appears as a technique whose own most significant features and novelties may be best described through recourse to those of another sphere. And in the negative evaluations, as in the more favorable ones, we can see that when critics are trying to identify something very particular about Dickens, they do so by relating Dickens to the particulars of his art historical moment.

His reviewers assume there is a common audience for verbal and visual art forms, and Taine's comment on Dickens's Englishness relies for its success and sense on the reader's having seen enough English paintings so that he or she can agree with him that these are all works that tend to be too crammed with details, and at their best when working on a small scale. Lewes's comment assumes a common "everyone" who is responding to art—and then clarifies that he assumes this everyone as "bourgeois." And

Stothert's ire takes force and fire from adding Dickens to the burning heap of complaints people are already supposed to have against the Pre-Raphaelites. These comparisons all implicitly suggest first, that art was popular, and articulate then, what features marked the most popular artistic works. Ultimately they identify the same audience and tastes for art as circulating in and around the work of Dickens. There is about all of this an implicit presence—of a presumed audience—and there is also about it a theoretical *absence*; missing is any hierarchical claim of the kind that many critics—and most recently Alison Byerly—have asserted as normative between visual and verbal realist forms (*Realism* 7). In neither praising nor disparaging kinds of assessment do we find the terms of visual invocation about rank. Instead, critics work to identify *which* art style—whether old (Dutch and Italian) or new ("photographic" and Pre-Raphaelite)—Dickens's style most resembles. And to recognize the lack (or breakdown) of hierarchy that is suggested in the analogies above is to encounter the second and more important of the two points I would like to make about the visual invocations of Dickens's critics: namely, that at the same time these purport a lack of hierarchy up and down, we get in replacement a *spatialized* push on and out. This is a push into the space of the gallery, and a move to talk about *reading* and seeing, not just writing and the seen.

VI

For, even more prominent by the end of his career than allusions and analogies which cast Dickens as working in the same register as contemporary painters (or of painters who had gotten a new valuation in contemporary times), there were allusions and analogies which cast him in a kind of curatorial role, as the architect and governor of a viewing space, and though the painterly metaphors persisted, more and more the visual borrowings of Dickens's critics began to engage a vocabulary of appraisal and dimension that involved more than one frame.[16] There seemed to be an increasing recognition that Dickens's career was one of multifarious colors, of flexible shape, and, as he seemed to do more and more different kinds of things, and ever to be doing something new, the metaphor of the single canvas appears to have finally stretched just too wide to accommodate this.

Critics emphasizing the novelty of what Dickens was creating and the unique aspects of the sensations his work thus produced, critics wanting to comment not just on his subject and style, but also on the phenomenological responses these could engender (responses that were sometimes unsettling), and critics wanting to describe the challenges his experimentation (or even his success) could seem to pose to the reader's experience of the novel form itself—these critics all brought the *space* of Dickens's work and the *space* of encounter with that work to the fore. As they did, they suggested that the experience of reading Dickens came to seem like the experience of entering a gallery, since there was so much on display. There were diverse ends to which such a perceived analogy could be put, and in closing I'll adumbrate what seem to have been the three chief categories of these, now.

First, for those who found it challenging to track and relate everything in Dickens's works across hundreds of pages and multiple parts, and for those who wanted to explore the complex dynamics attendant to such difficulty, a gallery vocabulary could seem useful for this purpose, and could be a language applied to the reading of a single book. In an 1862 review of a *Collected Works* set, a reviewer for the *British Quarterly Review* started her praise of *Nicholas Nickleby* by celebrating the "so pleasant, so truthful" "picture" provided by Dickens, but as soon as she began to enumerate the characters, her vocabulary expanded: "what a pleasant gallery of veritable portraits are these" (Lawrance 138). More often it was the case that a critic started with the gallery and made explicit why. From the time of *Pickwick* forward, Dickens was sometimes cited for a tendency to fail to provide "that concentration of interest which forms the grand merit of narrative" (Hayward 494). He was seen as being better at character than plot, for critics often set these two main narrative elements in competition. And the nature of the gallery, as a space of competing views, and a place where different images pulled each, if not equally on the eye, had an obvious utility for limning this tendency. Decrying criticism of *Bleak House*, for instance, John Forster tried to claim a value for the novel as a whole by pointing to some of its parts. He sounds, however, rather like an art critic defending a bad show, on the grounds that it has at least some good works included: "Taking the story piecemeal as a mere *gallery* of pictures and persons, we are disposed to think there are particular groups in *Bleak House* finer than anything Mr. Dickens has yet produced" (Collins 291). George Brimley echoed Forster's language, now minus the latter's supportive feeling: "the whole Dedlock set might be eliminated from the book without damage. . . . This would give an exact notion of the contents of a *collection of portraits* embracing suitors, solicitors, law-writers, law stationers. . . . Even then, a comprehensive *etcetera* would be needed for supernumeraries" (Collins 284). And Henry Chorley, in the *Athenaeum*, again on *Bleak House*, had a similar worry. He suggested that Dickens was bent on "exhibiting" so many figures, such an "improbabl[e] . . . assemblage" that they "stand in one another's way" (Collins 277). In this complaint, in particular, we can hear an echo of the frustration that the *Art-Union* expressed over the "plague of blots" in the Royal Academy show, and its concern that amidst such an "assemblage" a viewer could not manage to "care" about anyone depicted ("The Royal Academy" 179). It might really be a problem, wrote a critic for the *Westminster Review*, that in the average Dickens novel, we find "a gallery of photographs, but no landscape" ("Modern Novelists" 426).

But whether with good or bad import, in all of these comments, the novel, rather than being a single "picture" painted by Dickens, becomes a whole "gallery" of images, an "assemblage" of things variously worth "exhibiting." And the spatialized vocabulary of art could be seen to resonate well with the way many of Dickens's wrapper covers were designed to look—in the plate for *Our Mutual Friend*, indeed, we find a landscape at the top, some portraits on each side, and then a genre melee below.[17] The gallery language can resonate well with such images, as it should seem to, to be historically resonant. The artistic language captures the feeling that in any work like *Bleak House* that is characterized by many different sub plots, filled with over fifty characters, and published, in its original serial run, in nineteen different parts, (the last installment being a double number), elements may interfere with one another, and compete for attention as surely as the "pictures" in the showplaces of critical allusion would do. A single work could indeed be complicated.

Then, of course, since we are talking about Dickens, it would be rare that someone would read just a particular work, or that a reviewer could resist the impulse of drawing on all that he had read. Even more than the "gallery" language of the kind we have been examining got deployed to describe single books, it seems to have become vitally present to many critics, too, as they sought to describe the experience of dealing with one of the first authors beyond Shakespeare or Scott who was perhaps as much associated in the popular imagination with a *collection* of works as with any given one. If it was confusing that not everything in a novel necessarily seemed to add up into a single whole, it was certainly at least as startling to find that the books, the pages in them, and the characters depicted, jostled for attention in your mind's eye.

When readers ranged across their mental shelf of Dickens, a second utility that a gallery vocabulary had could be to define the object of what was a discovery of delight. By the time the author of the *Collected Works* review had come to consideration of *Oliver Twist*, the "gallery" of Dickens was now oeuvre-spanning, and she noted that "The convict . . . will rank high in Mr. Dickens's gallery of portraits." (Lawrance 154). Similarly, in a review of *Our Mutual Friend*, a critic for *The Reader* praised both the canon of Dickens and his new work: "In spite of the extravagance of his plots, the men and women of his pages are living beings. When once seen they have come home with us, as persons we have known in life. Mr Pickwick and Sam Weller, Mark Tapley and Jonas Chuzzlewitt. . . . To this great Dickens portrait gallery 'Our Mutual Friend' will add not a few pictures." ("Charles Dickens"

647). In a review of *The Mystery of Edwin Drood*, a writer for *The Academy* noted how "in addition to a whole gallery of hypocrites, Dickens has favoured us with numerous personifications of cast-iron unamiability" (Lawrenny 3).

Even a mixed review could praise such characters: in its *Bleak House* review, the *Illustrated London News* faulted the novel for a shoddy plot, but lauded Dickens's creation of figures who could be extracted from that dubious book and repatriated to his "dreaded gallery . . . of the denounced"; "may the salutary terror of it increase!" (Collins 282). Moreover, in many, many obituary tributes, we find Dickens's career-spanning "gallery" of portraits invoked. The *Glasgow Herald* celebrates Dickens's creation of a "gallery of portraits . . . a greater number of living . . . characters, than any author of our own or other times, with the exception of Shakespeare and Scott" ("Mr. Charles Dickens" 3). *The Manchester Times* admires the "long gallery of . . . portraits of the men and women of his time . . . [and] of all degrees" that Dickens created ("Recollections of Dickens" 244). Then, in a review of a recent biography of Dickens, George Barnett Smith sounds an elegiac note: "His gallery of portraits may not be full of perfect portraits, but there are many whose truth and naturalness will be attested for all time" (316). Reading over these notices, we can see how often more or less these same phrases get repeated in different sources, all sounded in tones of high appreciation.

But readers who tried to think about Dickens entire could also turn up frustration, and this is the third and final reading experience I'll suggest the gallery vocabulary often got pointed towards. In 1851, David Masson summarized Dickens's career to date, and he offers perhaps the most hyperbolic encapsulation of what ultimately became a common critical tendency; he underlines Dickens's stylistic heterogeneity and the diversity of what the novelist could produce as he holds Dickens superior to Thackeray in having an "artistic faculty . . . more comprehensive" and in going over "a wider range of the whole field of art"—and when Masson means "field," he means *field*:

> Take Dickens, for example in the landscape . . . department. Here he is capable of great variety. He can give you a landscape proper—a piece of the rural English earth . . . he can give you what painters seldom attempt, a great patch of flat country by night. . . . he can even succeed in a sea piece. . . . Take him again in the figure department. Here he can be an animal painter with Landseer when he likes . . . he can be a historical painter . . . he can be a portrait painter or a caricaturist like Leech; he can give you a bit of country life like Wilkie; he can painter a haggard or squalid scene of low city-life, so as to remind one of some Dutch painters . . . or a pleasant family-scene, gay or sentimental, reminding one of Maclise or Frank Stone; he can body forth romantic conceptions of terror or beauty, that have risen in his own imagination . . . he can even succeed in a powerful dream or allegory.   (70–71)

Here, Dickens with his different "department[s]" sounds like nothing so much as a gallery, and one with some rare views on offer ("he can give you what painters seldom attempt") at that. He, like the gallery, possibly promotes multiple styles in one space—Pre-Raphaelite mimesis and Dutch care of "external effect," "landscape proper," "pleasant family-scene," and "romantic conceptions of terror or beauty," the works of Landseer, Leech, Wilkie, Maclise, and Frank Stone, all ranged side by side (hardly insignificant, indeed, that these were all painters whose canvases would have been familiar from the walls of the commercial gallery). And, as for his fellow institutions, the display of such fecund offerings can be taken by someone like Masson to promote a sense of delight in variety.

But where Masson was delighted by such a rich stock of doings, and takes much pleasure in their variety, there were many who were decidedly less pleased. To enter a space not knowing what was going to be seen exactly, or what was meant to be of most value, could be disconcerting, and George Henry Lewes noted this as he evinced unease in the face of Dickens's diversity. Lewes wrote, "Michael Angelo is intelligible, and Giotto is intelligible, but a critic is non-plussed at finding the invention of Angelo with the drawing of Giotto [together] in the work of one author" (Hollington 1: 461). To look at someone whose arrayed art always consisted in the "limn[ing]" of a Dutchman, or in obsessively "photographic" works, might be restful in a certain kind of way; if readers knew what they liked, they could either celebrate getting it, or be irritated at not finding it. Lacking such luxury, readers might appreciate Dickens's "pictures," but be put off, as a reviewer for the *Eclectic Review* wrote, summarizing a certain belief in the critical field, by "too great . . . a variety of work" (Hood 460, 459).

In considering Dickens, as in considering the commercial gallery, the act of comparison might mean that something was lost, that something seemed inferior, and it could be frustrating for readers to accommodate changes in perception and in what had seemed to be a predetermined value judgment. At the same time, embarking on the act of comparison seemed to be irresistible to Victorian consumers, and the question Henry Morley posed about the Royal Academy exhibition—"Did anybody ever go to a private view at the Academy without being asked, whether he thought this exhibition better or worse than the last?"—was a question that clearly had a readerly dimension (694). Some shared a view of Dickens like the one with which William George Clark approached painting: "The general impression which the exhibition of the present year leaves upon one's mind is, that it is neither better nor worse than those of other years" (709). For others, there was the same teleology novelistically that Titmarsh brought to the Royal Academy show: "I think every succeeding year shows a progress in the English school of painters"

(214). A *Fraser's* review comparing Dickens's earlier novels with *David Copperfield* concluded with approval. The books that had preceded that novel stood side by side with it, but were also surpassed by *Copperfield:* "The principal groups are delineated as carefully as ever; but instead of the elaborate Dutch painting to which we had been accustomed in his backgrounds . . . we have now a single vigorous touch here and there" (Collins 245–46) Conversely, a note by Ruskin on *The Old Curiosity Shop* was far less satisfied. Following his own act of comparison, holding that book against the ones that had come before it, the sage fretted: "Can it be possible that this man is so soon run dry? . . . there is a want of the former clear truth . . . there is a vivid effective touch, truthful and accurate, but on the surface only; he is in literature very much what Prout is in Art" (36: 25–26).

For the kinds of readers who would complain at seeing everything up to *Great Expectations*, "Give us back the old *Pickwick* style," the experience of Dickens's "gallery" of works could be distinctly unpleasant (Dallas 6). And Ruskin had his echo in the assessments of others, including a critic for the *Saturday Review*, who considered each Dickens work itself a finished picture—but who was not necessarily pleased when putting these pictures side by side: "There is no possibility of pretending that *Bleak House*, *Little Dorrit* and *The Two Cities* were not surprisingly bad—melodramatic and pretentious, and above all, deadly dull. It seemed scarcely conceivable that a writer who had *drawn* Sam Weller and Mrs Nickleby should really compose the dreary narrative of *Little Dorrit* and her wooden lover" ("Uncommercial Traveller" 195). What seemed often most irksome about Dickens was how bad "draw[ings]" and good ones hung side by side; successful portraits were surrounded by lame or sketchy ones; effects by Michelangelo sat near ones by Giotto; details of Dutch delineation and modern photographic style clashed; landscapes intermingled with genre pictures; and somehow you had to find a way to evaluate it all together.

P. G. Hamerton, trying to define what the skill and the purview of art critics should be, had written in 1863, "The one distinguishing quality of all valuable art criticism is *largeness*—largeness of acquired information, to grasp the knowledge of so many thousands of artists, and largeness of natural sympathy, to enter into the individual feelings and affections of so great a multitude of minds" (343). Clearly, Dickens's critics had to wrestle with something of the same scale of problems, with the issue of "largeness," when they dealt with the novelist's work, and they too sought to "grasp . . . knowledge"—now of myriad plot strands in many books. They too sought to make sense of "a great multitude of minds" as they confronted the inner lives of characters who had all sprung from one head.

NOTES

1. As examples of the kinds of biographical information such authors are interested in, Richard Lettis details Dickens's involvement with the Artists' Benevolent Fund and summarizes his visits to the Royal Academy Banquets. He also records that Dickens "seems . . . to have provided financial assistance to painters" (95). Leonée Ormond traces Dickens's connections with the Dulwich Gallery and also with the pictures at Hampton Court Palace and Warwick Castle (132–33).

2. I am thinking of works by Jonah Siegel, Alison Byerly, and Kate Flint, which center on the Victorians and the visual arts and some important questions about imagination and realism, but which bring Dickens into their considerations only by a casual reference, or along a more broad pathway, as part of a generalized, non-art-specific set of inquiries. For Flint, for instance, there is interest in the fact that "Dickens is especially fascinated with the act of seeing" (Introduction, xiii), but Dickens does not make it into her specifically art-concerned chapters in *The Victorians and the Visual Imagination*. Similarly, in *Realism Representation and the Arts*, Byerly has chapters on Thackeray and Charlotte Brontë, on Eliot, and on Hardy—on the novel's major practitioners and theorizers of mid- to late-Victorian realism, but Dickens barely rates. Barbara Black's *On Exhibit: Victorians and Their Museums* is a notable exception to this trend. For some commentary on Dickens and the "sketch" see Garcha and Byerly, "Effortless Art."

3. Examples of studies of Dickens's connection to these other modes of entertainment are many and well known though Schlicke and Altick (*Shows*) are obvious places to start.

4. The Royal Academy handled the question of popular access with perhaps even more timidity than did other spaces of display, and it was exempt from some of the force of popular pressure or parliamentary attention that made the British Museum and the National Gallery swing open their doors more widely. When it first began having shows in 1769 it charged an entrance fee to keep numbers manageable (and crowds genteel) and it persisted in this policy for years (Altick, *Shows* 101–03). The Royal Academy was, however, some twenty years ahead of the National Gallery in keeping its doors open at night for the benefit of the working classes, and where the National Gallery waited until 1885 to do this, the Royal Academy started in 1862 (Borzello 42).

5. Richard Altick articulates the triple possibility of exposure to the Academy as he discusses developments in the engraving trade (*Pictures* 83).

6. As Altick observes: "The conventional triple-decker novel cost 31s. 6d., or a guinea and a half" (*Paintings* 77).

7. The ratio that characterizes *Bleak House* is obviously not consistent, and it may have more illustrations featuring framed images than does the average text, but what is consistent is that even in works like *Barnaby Rudge* that do not spend much time depicting domestic scenes, their illustrations reveal pictures placed in the most unlikely of locations.

8. George Landow offers a useful treatment of the problems and utility of a comparison like this: "One may doubt to what extent the situation in Victorian art can

resemble that in literature, because the nature of painting makes it so difficult for a work to reach a large number of people. In particular, since oil painting is a medium which produces a single work at a time, a work in an edition of one, it cannot ever be quite as popular as a novel which can be printed in an edition of thousands or even tens of thousands. Nonetheless, despite these essential differences, similar changes in the relation of artist to audience did take place'' (125).

9. What Dickens is talking about here is the repetition that he finds *internal* to works by the Italian masters, but he evinced on multiple occasions a clear feeling that such a problem of redundancy could arise easily in contemporary works that took classical inspiration. In writing to Miss Burdett-Coutts in 1845, he even replicated the phrase ''Perfect nightmare'' to express this difficulty (*Letters* 4: 280–81).

10. A. H. Layard wrote that in Manchester's show, an ''attempt [was] made for the first time in this country to place before the public pictures arranged upon the [chronological] system'' (Cited in Siegel 158).

11. In this speech, Dickens praises the Dulwich Gallery, which to him is notable for how its ''pictures are seen with an unusual absence of glare and bustle.'' The Gallery at Dulwich is, as Leonée Ormond points out, ''one of the delights of Mr. Pickwick's retirement'' (132).

12. It bears emphasizing that this is not, of course, to say that the walls of the British Museum or the National Gallery (or for that matter, of earlier spaces like the Dulwich Gallery and later ones like the South Kensington Museum) were not very crowded: as Flint reminds us, it was not until the 1877 opening of the Grosvenor Gallery that ''this mid-Victorian habit of crowding walls'' was finally ''deliberately broken'' (*Victorians* 191–92).

13. This line from the preface is noted by Butt and Tillotson (37), who also remind us that the subtitle of *Sketches* included the ''challenge'' that they were to be ''*Illustrative* of Every-Day Life and Everyday People.''

14. Dickens, of course, could only have been delighted by the latter trend; for, as an 1871 *Atlantic Monthly* piece recorded, ''Dickens's admiration of Hogarth was unbounded, and he had hung the staircase . . . of his house with fine old impressions of the great master's best works.'' (''Our Whispering Gallery'' 624).

15. Other representative comparisons of Dickens and Hogarth can be found in Taine, 1: 375.

16. Brimley's review is replete with artifactual vocabulary. For him, Dickens offers a ''collection of portraits,'' and ''selects in his portraiture exactly what a farce writer of equal ability and invention would select—that which is coarsely marked and apprehended at first sight; that which is purely outward. . . .'' It then follows that ''Dickens belongs in literature to the same class as his illustrator, Hablot Browne in design, though he far surpasses the illustrator in range and power'' (Collins 284–86).

17. Dickens sometimes even had the same reaction to his own covers that he did to the gallery's ''glare and bustle'' ; referring to the cover of *Dombey and Son*, he worries in a letter to Forster, that while it is ''very good generally,'' there might be ''perhaps . . . a little too much in it.'' Charles Dickens (*Letters* 4: 620).

WORKS CITED

Altick, Richard. *Paintings from Books: Art and Literature in Britain 1760–1900.*
Columbus: Ohio UP, 1985.

———. *The Shows of London.* Cambridge: Harvard UP, 1978.

"Armadale." *Westminster Review* (Oct. 1866): 269–71. Rpt. in *Wilkie Collins: The Critical Heritage.* Ed. Norman Page. London: Routledge & Kegan Paul, 1974. 157–59.

Atkinson, J. B. "The Decline of Art: Royal Academy and Grosvenor." *Blackwood's Edinburgh Magazine* (July 1885): 1–25.

———. "The London Art Season." *Blackwood's Magazine* (Aug. 1865): 234–53.

———. "Pictures British and Foreign: International Exhibition." *Blackwood's* (Sept. 1862): 353–71.

Bagehot, Walter. "Charles Dickens." *National Review* (Oct. 1858): 458–86.

Black, Barbara. *On Exhibit: The Victorians and Their Museums.* Charlottesville: UP of Virginia, 2000.

"Bleak House." *Illustrated London News* (24 Sept. 1853): 247. Rpt. in *Charles Dickens: The Critical Heritage.* Ed. Philip Collins. London: Routledge & Kegan Paul, 1971. 280–82.

Borzello, Frances. *Civilizing Caliban: The Misuse of Art 1875–1980.* London: Routledge & Kegan Paul, 1987.

Brimley, George. "Bleak House." *The Spectator* (24 Sept. 1853): 458–86. Rpt. in *Charles Dickens: The Critical Heritage.* Ed. Philip Collins. London: Routledge & Kegan Paul, 1971. 283–86.

Buller, Charles. "The Works of Dickens." *London and Westminster Review* (July 1837): 194–215. Rpt. in *Charles Dickens: The Critical Heritage.* Ed. Philip Collins. London: Routledge & Kegan Paul, 1971. 52–55.

Butt, John, and Katherine Tillotson. *Dickens at Work.* London: Methuen, 1957.

Byerly, Alison. "Effortless Art: The Sketch in Nineteenth-Century Painting and Literature." *Criticism* (Summer 1999): 349–64.

———. *Realism, Representation and the Arts in Nineteenth-Century Literature.* Cambridge: Cambridge UP, 1997.

"Charles Dickens." *The Reader* (Dec. 1865): 647.

"Charles Dickens and David Copperfield." *Fraser's Magazine* (Dec. 1850): 698–710. Rpt. in *Charles Dickens: The Critical Heritage.* Ed. Philip Collins. London: Routledge & Kegan Paul, 1971. 243–48.

Chorley, Henry Fothergill. "Bleak House." *The Athenaeum* (Sept. 1853). Rpt. in *Charles Dickens: The Critical Heritage.* Ed. Philip Collins. London: Routledge & Kegan Paul, 1971. 276–79.

Clark, William George. "On Some Pictures in the Royal Academy Exhibition of 1855." *Fraser's Magazine* (June 1855). 707–15

Cleghorn, Thomas. "The Life and Adventures of Martin Chuzzlewit." *North British Review* (May 1845): 65–87.

Collins, Philip. Ed. *Charles Dickens: The Critical Heritage.* London: Routledge & Kegan Paul, 1971.

Crook, J. Mourdant. *The British Museum* New York: Praeger, 1972.

Dallas, E. S. "Great Expectations." *The Times* (17 Oct. 1861): 6.

———. "Our Mutual Friend." *The Times* (29 Nov. 1865): 6.

Dickens, Charles. "Artists' Benevolent Fund" (8 May 1858). *The Speeches of Charles Dickens.* Ed. K. J. Fielding. Atlantic Highlands, NJ: Humanities International, 1988. 265–69.

———. *Bleak House.* Paperback ed. New York: Modern Library, 2002.

———. *David Copperfield.* Paperback ed. New York: Modern Library, 2000.

———. "An Idea of Mine." *Household Words* (13 Mar. 1858). Rpt. in *The Works of Charles Dickens.* 36 vols. London: Chapman and Hall, 1911. 161–65.

———. *The Letters of Charles Dickens.* 12 vols. Ed. Madeline House, Graham Storey and Katherine Tillotson. Oxford: Clarendon, 1981.

———. *Little Dorrit.* Paperback ed. New York: Modern Library, 2002.

———. "Meeting of the Dramatic Profession on Dulwich College" (13 Mar. 1856). *The Speeches of Charles Dickens.* Ed. K. J. Fielding. Atlantic Highlands, NJ: Humanities International, 1988. 215–19.

———. *Nicholas Nickleby.* 2nd ed. London: Wordsworth Edition, 1998.

———. "Old Lamps for New Ones." *Household Words* (15 June 1850): 265–67. Rpt. in *Selected Journalism 1850–1870.* Ed. David Pascoe. New York: Penguin, 1997. 521–26.

———. *Our Mutual Friend.* Paperback ed. New York: Modern Library, 2002.

———. "Royal Academy Banquet." (1 May 1858). *The Speeches of Charles Dickens.* Ed. K. J. Fielding. Atlantic Highlands, NJ: Humanities International, 1988. 215–19.

————. "The Toady Tree." *Household Words* (26 May 1855): 385–87. Rpt. in *The Dent Uniform Edition of Dickens' Journalism: 'Gone Astray' and Other Papers from Household Words 1851–1859*. Ed. Michael Slater. 4 vols. London: J. M. Dent, 1994–2000.

"Dombey and Son." *The Economist*. (10 Oct. 1846): 1324–25. Rpt. in *Charles Dickens: The Critical Heritage*. Ed. Phillip Collins. London: Routledge & Kegan Paul, 1971. 214–15

"The Ensuing Exhibition." *Punch* (8 May 1847).

Flint, Kate. Introduction. *Pictures from Italy*. By Charles Dickens. New York: Penguin, 1998.

————. "Moral Judgment and the Language of English Art Criticism 1870–1910." *Oxford Art Journal*. (1983): 59–66.

————. *The Victorians and the Visual Imagination*. Cambridge: Cambridge UP, 2000.

Forster, John. "Bleak House." *Examiner* (8 Oct. 1853): 643–45. Rpt. in *Charles Dickens: The Critical Heritage*. Ed. Philip Collins. London: Routledge & Kegan Paul, 1971. 290–93.

————. "Henry Esmond." *Examiner* (13 Nov. 1852): 723–26. Rpt. in *Thackeray: The Critical Heritage*. Ed. Geoffrey Tillotson and Donald Hawes. London: Routledge & Kegan Paul, 1968. 144–50.

Garcha, Amanpal. "Styles of Stillness and Motion: Market Culture and Narrative Form in *Sketches by Boz*." *Dickens Studies Annual* (2001): 1–22.

Hall, S. C. *Retrospect of a Long Life from 1815–1883*. New York: Appleton, 1883.

Hamerton, P. G. "Art Criticism." *Cornhill Magazine* (Sept. 1863): 334–43.

Hamley, E. B. "Remonstrance with Dickens." *Blackwood's Edinburgh Magazine* (Apr. 1857): 490–503.

Hayward, Abraham. "The Posthumous Papers of the Pickwick Club &c." *Quarterly Review* (Oct. 1837): 484–515.

Hollington, Michael. Ed. *Charles Dickens: Critical Assessments*. 3 vols. Mountfield: Helm Information, 1995.

Hood, Edwin Paxton. "Charles Dickens's *Great Expectations*." *Eclectic Review* (Oct. 1861): 458–77.

Landow, George. "There Began to be a Great Talking About the Arts." *The Mind and Art of Victorian England*. Ed. Josef Altholz. Minneapolis: U of Minnesota P, 1976. 124–45.

"The Late Charles Dickens." *Illustrated London News* (18 June 1870): 639. Rpt. in *Charles Dickens: The Critical Heritage*. Ed. Philip Collins. London: Routledge & Kegan Paul, 1971. 515–18.

Lawrance, Hannah. "The Collected Works of Charles Dickens." *British Quarterly Review* (Jan. 1862): 135–59.

Lawrenny, H. "The Mystery of Edwin Drood." *The Academy* (Oct. 1870): 1–3.

Lettis, Richard. "Dickens and Art." *Dickens Studies Annual* 14 (1985): 93–146.

Lewes, George Henry. "Dickens in Relation to Criticism." *Fortnightly Review* (Feb. 1872): 141–54. Rpt. in *Charles Dickens: Critical Assessments*. Ed. Michael Hollington. 3 vols. Mountfield: Helm Information, 1995.

Lister, Thomas Henry. "Sketches by Boz &c." *Edinburgh Review* (Oct. 1838): 75–97. Rpt. in *Charles Dickens: The Critical Heritage*. Ed. Philip Collins. London: Routledge & Kegan Paul, 1971: 71–77.

"London Exhibitions and London Critics." *Blackwood's Magazine* (June–Dec. 1858): 181–200.

"Manchester Exhibition of Art Treasures." *Blackwood's Magazine* (June 1857): 758–76

Masson, David. "Pendennis and Copperfield: Thackeray and Dickens." *North British Review* (May 1851): 57–89.

Minihan, Janet. *The Nationalization of Culture: The Development of State Subsidies to the Arts in Great Britain*. New York: New York UP, 1977.

"Modern Novelists: Charles Dickens." *Westminster Review* (Oct. 1864): 414–41.

Morley, Henry. "Pictures at the Royal Academy." *Fortnightly Review* (1872). 692–704.

"Mr. Charles Dickens." *The Glasgow Herald* (11 June 1870): 3.

"A New Result of the Great Exhibition." *Illustrated London News* (28 June 1851): 607.

"Novels and Novelists." *Irish Quarterly Review* (Mar. 1856): 94–109.

Ormond, Leonée. "Dickens and Painting: The Old Masters." *The Dickensian* 79.3 (Autumn 1983): 131–51.

Orwell, George. "Charles Dickens." *Dickens, Dali & Others*. New York: Harcourt, 1973: 1–75.

Page, Norman. Ed. *Wilkie Collins: The Critical Heritage*. London: Routledge & Kegan Paul, 1974.

Prettejohn, Elizabeth. "Aesthetic Value and the Professionalization of Art Criticism." *Journal of Victorian Culture* (Spring 1997): 71–94.

"Recollections of Dickens." *Manchester Times* (6 Aug. 1870). 244.

"The Return of the Native." *Athenaeum* (23 Nov. 1878): 654. Rpt. in *The Critical Companion to Thomas Hardy.* Ed. R. G. Cox. London: Routledge, 1996. 57–58.

Roberts, Helene. "Art-Reviewing in Early Nineteenth-Century Art Periodicals." *Victorian Periodicals Newsletter* (Mar. 1973): 9–20.

"The Royal Academy." *Art-Union* (June 1845): 179–96.

"The Royal Academy: The Eightieth Exhibition of 1848." *Art-Union* (June 1848): 165–80.

"The Royal Academy Exhibition." *Saturday Review* (23 May 1857): 475–76.

Ruskin, John. "To W. H. Harrison." 6 June 1841. *Works of John Ruskin.* 39 vols. Ed. E. T. Cook and Alexander Wedderburn. 1903.

Schlicke, Paul. *Dickens and Popular Entertainment.* London: Allen and Unwin, 1985.

Sha, Richard. *The Visual and Verbal Sketch in British Romanticism.* Philadelphia: U of Pennsylvania P, 1998.

Siegel, Jonah. *Desire and Excess: The Nineteenth-Century Culture of Art.* Princeton: Princeton UP, 2000.

"Sketches by Boz." *London* (July 1837): 194–215.

Smith, George Barnett. "Charles Dickens." *Gentleman's Magazine* (March 1874): 301–16.

Stothert, James Augustine. "Living Novelists." *The Rambler* (Jan. 1854): 41–51. Rpt. in *Charles Dickens: The Critical Heritage.* Ed. Philip Collins. London: Routledge & Kegan Paul, 1971. 294–97.

Taine, Hippolyte. "Charles Dickens: Son talent et ses ouevres." *Revue des Deux Mondes* (1 Feb. 1856): 618–47. Rpt. in *Charles Dickens: Critical Assessments.* 3 Vols. Ed. Michael Hollington. Mountfield: Helm Information, 1995.

Thackeray, William Makepeace. "Letters on the Fine Arts: No. 3: The Royal Academy." *The Pictorial Times* (13 May 1843). Rpt. in *Stray Papers by William Makepeace Thackeray: Being Stories, Reviews, Verses, and Sketches (1821–1847).* Ed. Lewis Melville. London: Hutchinson, 1901.

Trotter, L. J. "Mr. Dickens's Last Novel." *Dublin University Magazine* (Dec. 1861): 685–93.

"The Uncommercial Traveller and the Pickwick Papers." *Saturday Review* (23 Feb. 1861): 194–96.

Yeazell, Ruth Bernard. *Art of the Everyday: Dutch Painting and the Realist Novel.* Princeton: Princeton UP, 2007.

Making Music with the Pickwickians: Form and Function in Musical Adaptations of *The Pickwick Papers*

Marc Napolitano

The stage musical Pickwick *(1963), which was produced in the wake of the Dickensian musical fad initiated by Lionel Bart's* Oliver! *(1960), is the descendant of numerous musical treatments of Dickens's very first novel, including W. T. Moncrieff's infamous adaptation,* Sam Weller *(1837). The haphazard use of music in this Victorian stage show stands in sharp contrast to the meticulously organized musical score of* Pickwick. *Like virtually all of the Dickensian "musicals" produced in the nineteenth-century,* Sam Weller *is written in the British tradition of the eighteenth-century ballad opera, while* Pickwick *is written in the American tradition of the twentieth-century integrated musical. Though the later adaptation is clearly more organized and coherent from a musical point of view, the freewheeling and incoherent use of songs in the earlier adaptation is arguably more reminiscent of the overall tone and form of* The Pickwick Papers *as written by Dickens. In a way, the randomness of the songs compliments the randomness of Mr. Pickwick's adventures, and likewise, fills a gap left by the omission of the interpolated tales. Furthermore, the traditional Englishness of the Dickensian source is more pronounced in the Moncrieff adaptation due to his use of canonical English songs and the ballad-opera format.*

The popularity of Lionel Bart's *Oliver!* (1960) paved the way for many other musical adaptations of Charles Dickens's works, and almost all of the creative

Dickens Studies Annual, Volume 42, Copyright © 2011 by AMS Press, Inc. All rights reserved.

minds behind these subsequent adaptations tried to duplicate the success of *Oliver!* by approaching the source material with the same methodology used by Bart. Whereas the emotional extremes in *Oliver Twist* seem conducive to musical adaptation given the fact that songs in integrated "book" musicals are built around emotional highpoints, the uproarious humor of *The Pickwick Papers* makes the original text quite suitable for the genre of musical comedy, especially when one considers the boisterous and grand qualities of the leading characters. In light of the excesses and peculiarities of Mr. Pickwick and his companions, it is little wonder that, even in Dickens's day, characters from the novel were adapted for the stage and given songs to sing.

Although musical theater as we understand it today did not exist in Dickens's age, many of the unlicensed adaptations of Dickens's works produced throughout the nineteenth century featured characters who sing. Stage adaptations of *The Pickwick Papers* that employed music began appearing as early as 1837. One of the most infamous of these early adaptations of Dickens's novel was *Sam Weller, or, The Pickwickians* (1837) by William T. Moncrieff. This particular adaptation features a good deal of singing, yet it hardly meets the standards of what we now consider a "musical." Though there are a wide variety of subgenres within the realm of the modern musical (from the book musicals of the golden age of Broadway, to the more abstract musicals of the 1970s, to the "mega-musicals" of the 1980s, and the recent string of "jukebox musicals") all of these types share an overarching premise: that music can be used to tell a story as opposed to simply embellishing that story. Conversely, *Sam Weller* highlights the conventions of the musical stage in the nineteenth-century, several of which stem from the initial production of *The Beggar's Opera* (1728): Moncrieff adopts popular melodies, modifies the lyrics slightly, and incorporates them somewhat haphazardly into the play. The songs rarely contain any explicit references to Dickens's characters or the situations in which they have been placed; in short, the ballads are used simply to entertain the audience as opposed to helping tell the story. At the opposite end of the historical/musical spectrum is Leslie Bricusse and Cyril Ornadel's *Pickwick* (1963). Written over a century later, this adaptation epitomizes the modern book musical: songs are placed strategically throughout the piece, and each character who sings has a reason for singing in the context of the scene. The musical numbers in this version are more than simple interludes or diversions. Instead, every single song serves a purpose.

The function of music in these stage adaptations reinforces the contrasts between the two eras, and likewise between the two cultures that influenced their production: Moncrieff's employment of songs in *Sam Weller* is random and sporadic, and the musical narrative of his piece is never truly coherent. His adaptation is clearly written in the British tradition of the ballad opera. Conversely, *Pickwick*'s librettist, Wolf Mankowitz, attempts to provide a more solid underlying structure to the overall story, with Bricusse and Ornadel applying specific songs to specific episodes taken from the novel; consequently, there is less of a sense of interchangeability between Mr. Pickwick's adventures. This tight, integrated musical structure is evocative of the golden age of the American book musical. The historical discrepancies between these two different forms of musical theater reveal distinct trends in the approaches used by adaptors of Dickens for the musical stage. Though it is tempting to label the later adaptation as superior given that it conforms more readily to our modern sense of what a musical should be, the more random use of music in the Moncrieff version is curiously "Pickwickian" in that its very incoherence matches the chaotic structure of Mr. Pickwick's adventures as conveyed by the narrator in the original novel. Indeed, Dickens's episodic approach to the text, along with his inclusion of the various "interpolated tales," leaves one with the distinct impression that the very idea of creating an "integrated" musical adaptation of *The Pickwick Papers* is somehow counterintuitive. Ultimately, an approach which combined the sophisticated music and lyrics of *Pickwick* with the loose musical narrative of *Sam Weller* would produce a musical adaptation that outclasses both of these earlier efforts.

W. T. Moncrieff's *Sam Weller, or The Pickwickians* is a noteworthy adaptation of Boz's first novel because of the date it was first produced and also because of the intensely personal feud that would develop between Moncrieff and Dickens over the pirating of the author's text. Though the play admirably served its purpose of attracting an audience, it was immediately reviled by many of Dickens's friends and contacts in the press. John Forster wrote a scathing review of the adaptation soon after it was produced, and in one of the earliest critical studies of Dickens and the theater, S. J. Adair Fitz-Gerald labels the adaptation "a most villainous concoction, and not to be endured" (80). Throughout his career, Dickens maintained an ambivalent view of the unlicensed adaptations of his works produced within his lifetime. Alexander Woolcott notes that Dickens "witnessed or heard of all such stage versions with mingled emotions, an enormous curiosity as to how it had been managed, an intense anguish when the impersonation departed absurdly from the portraits he had painted, and a genuine undying exasperation because, under the loose laws of the day, he could never deflect any of the royalties or profits into his own coffers" (229). Moncrieff's adaptation was particularly grating for the young author, and the play irked Dickens enough to inaugurate an ongoing dispute between the two men which would be carried out in the public sphere. Dickens's disdain for Moncrieff would continue throughout his early career and culminate in a scornful satire of the playwright in *Nicholas Nickleby*. Unwilling to endure such censure without a fight, Moncrieff stood up for his adaptation of *The Pickwick Papers*, insisting that he had worked long and hard on his piece: "I have triumphed over all the difficulties I had to encounter in my undertaking. Every wretched mongrel can, I am aware, dramatize the 'Pickwick Papers' now that I have shown them how, by closely copying all I have done" (qtd. in Woollcott 230). Moncrieff's frustration at the thought of other playwrights writing adaptations of *The Pickwick Papers* based on his specific rendering of Dickens's text seems strangely ironic given his own dubious approaches to playwriting.

In spite of its limitations, Moncrieff's adaptation can serve as a time capsule of sorts for the modern reader. Moncrieff's use of music throughout the piece is particularly interesting from a historical point of view, as it brings to light the predominant function of songs in Victorian-era plays. Simultaneously, the adaptation presents a suitable context for analyzing the history of the stage musical, for although *Sam Weller* hardly qualifies as a musical, it is still a play with music and songs. The placement and use of these songs throughout the adaptation reveals how the conventions of the early musical stage diverge significantly from the conventions of the modern integrated musical.

The musical breakdown of *Sam Weller* is incredibly simple. In almost every case, a lighthearted air of some kind is incorporated into a random scene in the adaptation, often exerting absolutely no influence on the story or the characters. Though the sheet music to these songs is not included in the surviving script, it is clear that all of these airs were simply popular melodies from the era in which the play was written—no original music was composed for the piece. The songs are placed indiscriminately throughout the adaptation, as there is never any buildup toward the numbers. Rather, the characters randomly begin singing at arbitrary moments in the play. In most cases, the lyrics are modified so as to make at least some sort of thematic reference to the stage play, but there are very few explicit allusions to Mr. Pickwick, his friends, or their adventures. The purpose of the songs is simply to entertain the audience by allowing the actors to showcase their vocal abilities while singing a modified version of a well-known song which the audience would undoubtedly have recognized and appreciated.

The first number begins just after Mr. Pickwick hires Sam as his manservant and invites the conniving Jingle to accompany the Pickwickians to Rochester. The song is sung to the melody of "Vive le Roi" and the lyrics are modified to describe the Pickwickians' journey. This modification gives the song a decidedly more particularized feel than most of the other numbers in the play, but the fact remains that its basic placement is random. The moment in the play where the song appears does not seem to warrant any sort of interlude from a narrative point of view; instead, the Pickwickians begin singing simply for the sake of singing. This convention epitomizes the use of music throughout the adaptation.

Scene 2 commences with a song sung by Isabella, Emily, and Rachael Wardle entitled "Nice Young Maidens." The song has no real influence on the plot, nor does it help to define the specific characters of the girls and their aunt; as with the first song sung by the Pickwickians, it is simply a lighthearted air sung to entertain an audience. Perhaps there is no better illustration of this random use of music throughout the play than in the final song of the third scene, as Sam Weller sings the infamous minstrel song "Jim Crow." Though the lyrics are altered slightly, the main chorus is retained: "Wheel about and turn about/And jump jist so/Laughing at their silly rout/He jumps Jim Crow!" (8). The idea of Dickens's Sam Weller, who epitomizes Cockney wit, singing a "Jim Crow" song is ludicrous, but simultaneously, Sam's character here is a negligible factor; Moncrieff simply wanted to incorporate the song into the play and he decided to use Sam as the singer—he might just as easily have chosen Jingle, as the personality of the singer has absolutely no connection to the song being sung.

The rest of the score plays out very similarly, as popular songs are incorporated into the show and sung simply to entertain the audience. Several Christmas carols are sung during the holiday scenes at Dingley Dell, while popular political ballads (such as "Hurrah! for the bonnets of blue!") are sung during the scene in which Mr. Pickwick visits Eatanswill to witness the Slumkey vs. Fizkin election. Scene 3, which focuses on the armed forces drills in Rochester, contains two brief military airs entitled "Follow the Drum," and "Oh they march'd through the Town," which, though thematically appropriate, bear no relevance to the plot or the characters. So superfluous are all of these airs to the overall narrative of the play that the scenes would play out in entirely the same way even if the songs were excised from the libretto.

It is somewhat fitting that Moncrieff would utilize popular music in this fashion given the fact that he was employing Dickens's text in virtually the same way: borrowing elements from something ingrained in the popular culture of the day and modifying those elements to serve his own purposes. Moncrieff was hardly the first playwright to approach stage music in this fashion, however. Rather, the playwright's use of music in *Sam Weller* is traceable back to the eighteenth-century tradition of the British ballad opera.

Edmond Gagey describes the ballad opera as an irreverent newcomer that took the London stage by storm. To write ballad operas, composers "ransacked the plays and themes of the past as well as the song collections in order to satisfy the prevailing taste" (3). The constant re-use of these popular tunes is probably what contributed to the early demise of the genre, as melodies were recycled so often that the novelty quickly wore off. Nevertheless, the popularity of certain ballad operas, most notably *The Beggar's Opera*, was unquestionable. *The Beggar's Opera*, written by John Gay and arranged by Johann Pepusch, is a curious mixture of the conventions of the Newgate novel, Swiftian satire, and, of course, popular music of the seventeenth and eighteenth centuries. Though ballad operas frequently adopted melodies from Italian operas, they simultaneously lampooned the perceived effeminacy of this art form. In a review of *The Beggar's Opera* written by Jonathan Swift, the famed satirist praises the piece for its parody of Continental opera: "This comedy likewise exposes, with great justice, that taste for Italian music among us, which is wholly unsuitable to a Northern climate and the genius of the people, whereby we are overrun with Italian effeminacy and Italian manners" (qtd. in Fiske 97). Thus, there was something patriotic about *The Beggar's Opera* despite the low subject matter. Much as the modern musical would prove an inherently American art form, the ballad opera was inherently British.

The debate over whether or not the integrated book musical evolved from the ballad opera is a contentious one due to the cultural issues that arise when discussing the evolution of musical theater; given the fact that the integrated musical is viewed as an American art form, various musical theater scholars are hesitant to emphasize such precursors as the ballad opera or the operettas of Gilbert and Sullivan, for to do so would imply that one of the few indigenous American art forms is actually rooted in the artistic traditions of Britain and Europe. Scott Miller dismisses the links between the early forms of musical theater—including the ballad opera—and the modern musical in his text, *Strike Up the Band*, as he insists that the musical is quintessentially American: "Musical theatre as we define it today . . . was invented in America, it was largely developed in America. . . . There are British authors who declare categorically that the Brits invented musical theatre, but they're talking about operetta, ballad opera, and other such things" (6). Conversely, other texts on the history of the musical genre emphasize the aforementioned links, and thus cite *The Beggar's Opera* as an important precursor to the modern stage musical. In *Musical! A Grand Tour*, Denny Martin Flinn states that *The Beggar's Opera* "begins the history of the musical-comedy" (56), and the author stresses that Gay was one of the most important figures in the development of what we now know as the American musical.

Kurt Ganzl reconciles these two contrary viewpoints in his text on the history of the musical, as he implies that the trends started by the ballad opera allowed for the gradual development of original music being written for the stage, which was, of course, essential to the eventual emergence of what we would today define as "musical theater":

> During the second half of the eighteenth century and the first years of the nineteenth century, much of what was produced as musical theatre entertainment followed the lines that had been established in these early years. Little by little, however, the popular pieces began to undergo important changes. Most importantly, they began regularly rather than exceptionally to take in original

rather than recomposed music: music that was of a "popular" bent, in the same
style as the favorite songs and tunes previously used as musical-theater song-
fodder, but freshly baked in a virtual imitation of the pasticcio songs.   (12)

Despite the new innovations inspired by the popularity of the ballad opera,
however, music remained a tangential element as opposed to a fully incorporated component. As in *Sam Weller*, the music written for most of the plays
of this period was meant to add to the overall entertainment value of the
piece—it did not contribute significantly to the plot or characters.

The movement toward a more consistent and structured musical emerged
in America in the early twentieth century, as the musical form itself evolved.
With the arrival of shows such as *Show Boat* and *Oklahoma!*, the concept of
the book musical was finally crystallized through the efforts of Jerome Kern,
Richard Rodgers, and Oscar Hammerstein II. Unlike the musicals of the past,
there was no longer a sense of numbers being pasted in solely to divert and
entertain. Simultaneously, in contrast to pieces like *The Beggar's Opera* that
could be staged successfully while leaving out the songs, the narrative of an
integrated musical is incomplete without the music to support the story.

If *Sam Weller* epitomizes the conventions of a Dickensian musical before
the advent of the integrated format, *Pickwick* (1963), like *Oliver!*, exemplifies
the standards of the modern, integrated Dickensian musical. The use of music
throughout the adaptation is logical and coherent, and the libretto, musical
score, and lyrics all work together to contribute to the presentation of the
narrative and the characters. Whereas the songs in *Sam Weller* are interpolated
arbitrarily and could easily be excised from the piece without hindering the
narrative, the songs in *Pickwick* are meticulously laid out so that each number
serves some function in tandem with the libretto.

Several of the songs in *Pickwick* are used either to move the plot forward
or to introduce scenes. As in the Moncrieff adaptation, the Christmas episodes
and Eatanswill scenes from Dickens's novel are retained. Furthermore, both
versions of the story employ music in these scenes. While Moncrieff employs
traditional Christmas carols and political ballads, Bricusse and Ornadel write
entirely new songs. What is more significant, however, is the function of these
songs in their respective contexts. In *Sam Weller*, the songs are thematically
relevant, but they exert no influence on the drama itself. The plot seems to
stand still while the characters take a moment to shift from speech to song.
In *Pickwick*, the shift is much more organic, and the songs are not used as
decorations. Furthermore, time is not standing still during these numbers.
Rather, the songs are used to move the story forward. "That's What I'd Like
for Christmas" is employed to transition from the Fleet Prison scenes to the
flashback scenes that dominate the adaptation. Simultaneously, the number
helps to create a smooth movement from one setting to another. The Eatanswill

number, "A Hell of an Election," provides a boisterous opening to the play's
second act while simultaneously establishing a new conflict. The organic and
operational function of music in *Pickwick* is far removed from the haphazard
and static function of music in *Sam Weller*.

The disparate use of music in relation to the characters in these two adaptations is also an important contrast. A great many of the songs in *Pickwick*
serve characterization purposes, since several characters are introduced and
defined through music. Dickens's method of revealing the basic personalities
of his characters instantaneously is well-suited for musical adaptation, given
the importance of introducing characters quickly in this particular genre.
When Mr. Pickwick and Sam first appear in *Pickwick*, Sam sets about trying
to cheer his master by singing a song entitled "Talk," where he stresses the
importance of learning how to talk one's way out of awkward situations. The
animated melody, comic tone, and witty lyrics are all befitting of Dickens's
character, and the song serves the same function as Sam's "wellerisms"—to
present the Cockney wit and street smarts of the young manservant:

> If you're stepping out in St. James's Park
> With some sweet young widder ready for a lark!
> She asks you to home to tea—
> Then a knock comes at the door—
> Her husband's very much alive and six foot
> three or four!
>
> You'll have to
> Talk your way out of it!—
> Talk your way out of it!—
> Talk around about a bit,
> But talk!
>
> Or he'll make mincemeat of you!
>
> (7)

This comic air is clearly a more appropriate anthem for Sam than a "Jim
Crow" song, and it is simultaneously far more relevant to the plot. Furthermore, this song accomplishes many different goals: it introduces Sam's comical personality, it characterizes Sam's relationship with Mr. Pickwick, and it
expresses hope that Sam will be able to get his employer out of trouble.

As in all successful integrated musicals, the character-driven songs in *Pickwick* are specific to the individual doing the singing and pertinent to the action
taking place onstage. When Mr. Jingle is introduced and sings "A Bit of a
Character," the odd syncopation to the song mirrors the character's staccato
method of speaking, while the lyrics convey his roguish personality. Later,
when Mr. Pickwick sings the most famous song from this particular show,

"If I Ruled the World," his reasons for doing so are clear: the Slumkey supporters in Eatanswill have mistaken him for their candidate and wish him to make a speech. Thus, he sings a song that epitomizes his naïve yet hopeful worldview: "If I ruled the world/Every day would be the first day of Spring—/Every heart would have a new song to sing—/And we'd sing/Of the joy every morning would bring" (52). While the songs in *Sam Weller* are virtually interchangeable, a song in *Pickwick* which is sung by Sam would lose all of its meaning if it were sung by Mr. Pickwick or Jingle. This fact is another key facet of the integrated musical. As Lehman Engel asserts in *Words with Music*, "each song must say what only this specific character *can* say, not just loosely what *any* character (for example) in love might say. It is the duty of the lyricist to find material in this particular character in this particular play in this particular scene which has not been said again and again by every character in every previous play. This requires genuine creativity, thought, patience, and invention" (Engel's emphases, 156). It is clear that Moncrieff was lacking in these qualities when he wrote *Sam Weller*; the recycled music, trite lyrics, and lack of specificity exemplify the absence of such things as creativity, thought, patience, and invention.

On the contrary, in an autobiography, the lyricist Leslie Bricusse conveys the meticulous efforts that went into the writing of the score for *Pickwick*. His struggle to come up with a big, character-defining number for Mr. Pickwick to sing at some point in the play is particularly noteworthy: "I was acutely aware that there was as yet no sign of the big song for Pickwick and Harry Secombe's glorious tenor voice, nor any likely place for it" (127). After discussing the matter with director Peter Coe, who had his own suggestions about a possible number for Pickwick, Bricusse reflected on the idea, along with the traditional conventions of the integrated musical:

> I went back to the basics. Rule one, exemplified a thousand times in the great theatre songs, was to use the verse of the lyric to link the specific context of the story to the expression of a bigger idea with universal application, viz, the chorus of the song. I decided to try to apply this theory to Peter Coe's 'If I Were Your Parliamentary Candidate' at the moment in the show where Pickwick is unexpectedly asked to make a speech. I put the essence of Peter's title into a verse, to see where it would lead me. And it led me naturally to the bigger idea I had been seeking in a dozen discarded lyrics. The idea was 'If I Ruled the World.' I knew the moment I had the title that I had the big song too. The lyric wrote itself after that, and the melody arrived with the lyric. (135)

Whereas Moncrieff's versions of Dickens's characters sing songs that are simply used to divert the audience at random moments in the play, Bricusse and Ornadel's incarnations consistently perform songs that are highly specialized and contextualized based on their personalities and the positions in which they find themselves. Music and lyrics combine with storyline, character, and dialogue to present a unified whole.

Clearly, the contrasts between *Sam Weller* and *Pickwick* highlight the dissimilar functions of stage music in the nineteenth and twentieth centuries. Combined with these historical issues are the cultural concerns raised in the two adaptations. Both plays are the result of British writers adapting a canonical British author for the British stage. Of the two works, *Sam Weller* retains a more overtly British identity in terms of the function of its musical score. Written in the tradition of the ballad opera and featuring melodies from popular British ballads, carols, and folksongs, *Sam Weller* is certainly representative of early nineteenth-century British culture; furthermore, even those songs that are not based on British melodies, such as "Jim Crow" or the numbers set to the classical works of various European composers, can help to paint a historical portrait of the Victorian musical stage, as Moncrieff's incorporation of these numbers exemplifies the techniques employed by the playwrights of the Victorian period. In comparison to *Sam Weller*, *Pickwick* marks a transition from the disjointed works of eighteenth—and nineteenth-century Britain to the unified shows of the golden age of the American musical. But, maintaining the British elements of the Dickensian source material while translating it into an American entertainment form presents certain difficulties, as will be discussed shortly.

In spite of the numerous divergences between these two adaptations, there are likewise some interesting similarities between the two plays, particularly regarding the basic structure of the script. Both Moncrieff and Mankowitz are judicious in their selection of what specific episodes from Dickens's original novel to incorporate into their adaptation; they also shuffle the order of these episodes so as to tighten up the sequence of the narrative. Chart 1 presents a brief comparison of what specific episodes are selected and omitted from the two adaptations and the new sequencing of these episodes in each musical.

Moncrieff uses a greater number of episodes from the novel, but rather than dramatize all of these scenes, he sometimes allows the action to take place offstage. *Pickwick* uses fewer episodes from the original novel and is structured around a flashback, as the play opens with Mr. Pickwick entering the Fleet. This technique immediately endows this particular adaptation with a solid sense of chronology, as the viewer knows that the play is building towards a concrete occurrence: Mr. Pickwick's and Sam's imprisonment for debt. The tighter chronological structure is well-served by the integrated musical score, which helps to reinforce the overall coherence of the adaptation's narrative. Nevertheless, the episodic quality to the plot of *The Pickwick Papers* immediately raises several questions about any attempt to adapt the novel for linear, dramatic presentation.

Chart 1

	Novel	Moncrieff	Bricusse/ Ornadel
Meeting of the Pickwick Club	1	*	*
Fight with the Cabman	2	2	*
Meeting Mr. Jingle	3	3	4
Tupman and Jingle at the Ball	4	7 (OS)	5
Winkle Challenged by Dr. Slammer	5	*	11
The Duel	6	*	12
Interpolated Tale 1: "Stroller's Tale"	7	*	*
Military Drills	8	5	*
Journey to Manor Farm	9	*	*
Interpolated Tale 2: "Convict's Return"	10	*	*
Rook-shooting Accident	11	8 (OS)	*
Jingle at the Cricket Game	12	9	*
Tupman Flirts with Rachael	13	6	6
Jingle Cons Tupman and Rachael	14	10	7
Jingle and Rachael Elope	15	13	14
Introduction of Sam Weller	16	1	*
Wardle Bribes Jingle	17	14 (OS)	17
Interpolated Tale 3: "Madman's Manuscript"	18	*	*
Expulsion of Blotton	19	*	*
Mr. Pickwick "Proposes" to Mrs. Bardell	20	15	10
Sam Becomes Mr. Pickwick's Servant	21	4	9
The Eatanswill Election	22	16	16
Interpolated Tale 4: "Bagman's Story"	23	*	*
Masquerade Party at Mrs. Leo Hunter's	24	20	*
Sam Meets Job Trotter	25	17	*
Mr. Pickwick at the Boarding School	26	18	*
Interpolated Tale 5: "The Parish Clerk"	27	*	*
Mr. Pickwick is Served with a Lawsuit	28	*	15

Chart 1 (continued)

	Novel	Moncrieff	Bricusse/ Ornadel
Mr. Pickwick is Locked in the Pound	29	*	*
Mr. Pickwick Confronts Dodson & Fogg	30	*	19
Sam Reunites with Tony	31	19	18
Interpolated Tale 6: "The Queer Client"	32	*	*
Sam and Tony Plot Against Rev. Stiggins	33	*	*
Mr. Pickwick Meets Peter Magnus	34	*	*
Mr. Pickwick Enters the Wrong Bedroom	35	24	*
The Pickwickians Before Magistrate Nupkins	36	25	*
Sam Meets Mary	37	12	8
Jingle is Exposed at Last	38	26	*
Sam Snoops on Mrs. Barde	11	39	*
Sam Visits Tony, Mrs. Weller, and Rev. Stiggins	40	*	*
Christmas at Dingley Dell	41	11	3
Interpolated Tale 7: "Goblins and the Sexton"	42	*	*
Ice-Skating at Dingley Dell	43	*	13
Mr. Pickwick Confers with Sgt. Snubbins	44	*	*
Sawyer's Bachelor Party	45	*	*
Sam Buys Mary a Valentine	46	23	*
The Trial of Bardell vs. Pickwick	47	27 (OS)	20
The Pickwickians go to Bath	48	*	*
Interpolated Tale 8: "Prince Bladud"	49	*	*
Winkle 'Elopes' with Mrs. Dowler	50	*	*
Winkle Secretly Courts Arabella	51	*	*
Mr. Pickwick and Sam Assist in the Courtship	52	*	*
Mr. Pickwick Enters the Fleet	53	28	1
Mr. Pickwick Reunites with Jingle and Trotter	54	30	21
Sam Gets Himself Arrested for Debt	55	29	2
Tony, Mrs. Weller, and Stiggins Visit the Fleet	56	*	*

Chart 1 (continued)

	Novel	Moncrieff	Bricusse/ Ornadel
Mrs. Bardell is Arrested for Debt	57	*	22
Mr. Pickwick is Persuaded to Leave the Fleet	58	*	24
Winkle Reveals his Marriage	59	22	*
Mr. Pickwick Persuades Allen and Sawyer	60	*	*
Interpolated Tale 9: "The Bagman's Uncle"	61	*	*
Mr. Pickwick Meets Mr. Winkle, Sr.	62	*	*
Tony Expels Rev. Stiggins	63	*	*
Reformation of Jingle and Trotter	64	31	23
Snodgrass Proposes to Emily	65	21	*
Tony Makes His Fortune	66	*	*
Mr. Winkle Accepts Arabella	67	*	*
Mr. Pickwick Enters His Retirement	68	*	25

Note that the numbers here, in reference to the novel, do not correlate to chapter numbers or installment numbers, but rather, to all of the significant incidents that take place in the story, and the order in which they occur. The same is true of the numbers referencing the events in the two plays (the first occurrence in the Moncrieff adaptation is the introduction of Sam, the first occurrence in the Bricusse musical is Mr. Pickwick's entry into the Fleet, and so forth).

* denotes an incident omitted from the adaptations.
"OS" denotes an occurrence which is included in the story but which takes place offstage.

The structure of the plot to *The Pickwick Papers* has been a source of contention since the era in which the text was published. In his preface to the original edition (1837) of the novel, Dickens explained his approach to the composition of *The Pickwick Papers*, highlighting how the serialized publication method that he employed necessitated an episodic plot:

> The publication of the book in monthly numbers . . . rendered it an object of paramount importance that, while the different incidents were linked together by a chain of interest strong enough to prevent their appearing unconnected or impossible, the general design should be so simple as to sustain no injury from this detached and desultory form of publication. . . . It is obvious that in a work published with a view to such considerations, no artfully interwoven or ingeniously complicated plot can with reason be expected. (6)

Critics have since debated the issue of how exactly one should read the plot of *The Pickwick Papers*. Curiously, many prominent Dickensians have made attempts to delineate an underlying structure to the novel in spite of its episodic format. Robert Patten and William Axton have addressed the issue in terms of subtle thematic links between Mr. Pickwick's adventures, with Patten focusing on the hidden relevance of the interpolated stories to the protagonist's travels, and Axton outlining the plot of the novel according to the interplay between the Wellers' cynicism and the Pickwickians' naiveté. Other scholars have expressed their reservations about these attempts to "justify" the work based on the ideals of configuration and organization. In "Fragmentation in *The Pickwick Papers*," Anny Sadrin astutely questions the logic of the various critics who have attempted to validate the novel by arguing in favor of its underlying coherence: "The trouble with these well-intentioned defenders of Dickensian unity is that they moralize art: unity is good, fragmentation is bad, they seem to say" (22). Sadrin asserts that the true spirit of *The Pickwick Papers* defies any attempts to organize the text into a solid chronological structure. Rather, the text seems to celebrate the joys of the passing moment and the pleasures of mutability. Even when the "plot" is intensifying with the filing of Mrs. Bardell's lawsuit, Mr. Pickwick is more focused on what places the Pickwickians will visit on the next leg of their excursion. Like the text itself, Mr. Pickwick seems to take life from moment to moment without worrying about any sort of overarching significance.

To a certain extent, fragmentation contributes to the fun of the novel, for, as Sadrin asserts, the narrator himself is humorously frustrated with the disjointed structure of the novel: "Fragmentation is constantly presented by the narrator as a necessary evil, unsuited to his own taste for stylistic decorum and high flown rhetoric" (27). The narrator's task as the editor of the "Posthumous Papers of the Pickwick Society" can prove difficult, especially when he discovers various holes in his records, but his drawing attention to these omissions, fragments, and inconsistencies adds to the levity of the text. When Jingle pokes fun at the corpulent Tupman by comparing him to Bacchus, the narrator humorously states that there is no record of whether Tupman took exception to this comment: "Whether Mr. Tupman was somewhat indignant at the peremptory tone in which he was desired to pass the wine which the stranger passed so quickly away, or whether he felt very properly scandalised at an influential member of the Pickwick Club being ignominiously compared to a dismounted Bacchus, is a fact not yet completely ascertained" (32). Later in chapter 7, which, according to the narrator, is lifted directly from the notes that Augustus Snodgrass took while accompanying Mr. Pickwick on his journey, the editor drops hints that Snodgrass's carousing with Mr. Pickwick, Wardle, Winkle, and Jingle made his last few notes difficult to incorporate into the novel:

> Mr Snodgrass, as usual, took a great mass of notes, which would no doubt have
> afforded most useful and valuable information, had not the burning eloquence

of the words or the feverish influence of the wine made that gentleman's hand so extremely unsteady, as to render his writing nearly unintelligible, and his style wholly so. By dint of patient investigation, we have been enabled to trace some characters bearing a faint resemblance to the names of the speakers; and we can only discern an entry of a song (supposed to have been sung by Mr Jingle), in which the words 'bowl' 'sparkling' 'ruby' 'bright' and 'wine' are frequently repeated at short intervals.   (106)

A tighter narrative would lose some of the subtle pleasures of the episodic storytelling technique that Dickens employs and make such jokes by the narrator/editor irrelevant.

Sam Weller and *Pickwick* both create a less episodic and more unified narrative as is necessitated by the medium of the stage, but whereas *Pickwick* also creates a unified musical score, the songs in *Sam Weller* are utilized much more freely. Ganzl describes the major effects of the advent of the integrated musical on the genre as a whole, stating: "There was as little place for the irrelevant numbers of the 'interpolated' kind that had flourished in the early part of the century in the score of a modern musical as there was for the irrelevant performer" (284). His use of the word "interpolated" here is particularly worthy of note given the fact that it is a word which has been applied to Dickens's novel many times: the melodramatic stories inserted throughout the text are often referred to as "interpolated" tales, and, indeed, the fragmented structure of the novel makes many episodes in the Pickwickians's travels seem as if they have been "interpolated" into the story. Consequently, although the musical score to *Pickwick* is infinitely more organized and technically coherent than the score to *Sam Weller*, the very randomness of the songs incorporated into the earlier musical seems somehow more evocative of the basic tenor of Dickens's first novel. In a sense, the songs take the place of the interpolated tales, which would be very difficult if not impossible to incorporate into a coherent stage adaptation of *The Pickwick Papers* given their irrelevance to Mr. Pickwick and his friends. However, Moncrieff's songs, by their very irrelevance to the rest of the adaptation, serve a similar function: to entertain briefly the audience merely for the sake of diversion itself. Just as the interpolated tales could easily be cut from the novel without damaging the overall story, so could the songs be struck from *Sam Weller*. *Pickwick*, as an integrated musical, does not possess the same level of freedom, for cutting the songs would render the narrative incoherent. Though Mankowitz, Ornadel, and Bricusse succeeded in creating a successful and wholly integrated musical adaptation of Dickens, the very process of integration seems at odds with the free-wheeling format of the original novel. This dissimilarity reinforces the historical and cultural contrasts between these two adaptations, as the unrestrictive musical structure of *Sam Weller* seems to emphasize the Englishness of both the adaptation and its source. The tighter and more linear narrative structure of *Pickwick* is reflective of the era in which the American style book show was the dominant form of musical theater.

Much of the traditional Englishness of the Dickensian source is thus automatically lost in musical translation, though Bricusse and Ornadel manage to preserve some of this Englishness (along with some of the source's spontaneity) through the character of Sam Weller. Though most of Sam's numbers, including the aforementioned "Talk," are integrated directly into the narrative and thus serve either story or characterization purposes, there is simultaneously a sense throughout the musical that Sam is singing songs as a way of entertaining the other characters, not to mention the audience members themselves. Almost all of Sam's numbers are sung as duets, and whereas most characters in musicals make the transition from speaking to singing without acknowledging any sort of change in their method of communication, Sam seems somehow conscious of the shift as he interacts with Mr. Pickwick, Mary, and his father through music. This sense of knowingness on the part of the character, along with the style of music that he utilizes, places him squarely in the tradition of the British music-hall performer, and it is the trademark Cockney Englishness of music-hall entertainment, along with its random, revue-style tenor, that allows Bricusse and Ornadel to preserve certain elements of their British source even while operating in the genre of the American musical.

Music-hall songs are the natural means of musical communication for an individual like Sam Weller, given that music-hall culture was distinguished in part by the same Cockney spirit that defined the character as written by Dickens. In *Best Music Hall and Variety Songs*, an archival text edited by Peter Gammond, there are numerous examples of songs that are written in the same Cockney vernacular and cynical tone as the songs sung by Sam throughout *Pickwick*. Indeed, a short section of the book is devoted entirely to Cockney songs, and the sardonic introduction to this section emphasizes the importance of Cockney culture to the music hall as a form of entertainment: "The Cockney, the creature born, by definition, within the sound of Bow Bells and irretrievably of the working-class (there is no such thing as a middle or upper class Cockney), is, without dispute, from him at any rate, the salt of the earth. . . . Some may consider that music-hall opinion on this subject may be somewhat loaded in their favour as so many of the stars of music-hall were Cockneys themselves" (203). Featuring such titles as "Wot's The Good of Hanyfink? Why! Nuffink!", and " 'Alibut, 'Addick Or 'Ake," these songs epitomize the comicality and rebelliousness of London street life—the same qualities that Dickens had presented through Sam's character in *Pickwick Papers*.

The conventions of various music-hall songs are immediately detectable in Sam's main numbers, from his cynical description of marriage in "The

Trouble with Women'' to his use of comic patter in "Learn a Little Some-thing.'' The former presents the satirical music-hall disparagement of middle-class domesticity that was so common in many music-hall comic ballads, while the latter revolves around the same sort of Cockney wit demonstrated in the songs that Gammond includes in his text. A side-by-side analysis of "Learn a Little Something" and Percy Morris and Malcolm Ives's Cockney music-hall ballad "The Council Schools Are Good Enough For Me" reveals the links between music-hall entertainment and Sam's songs in *Pickwick*, not only in terms of style and content, but likewise, in terms of the palpable celebration of Cockney culture and the distinct brand of London Englishness. This same celebration is essential to preserving the British qualities of Dick-ens's text while incorporating it into the genre of the American book musical:

When I was only four years old.
Me pore ole father
Upped and told me
'Sammy' he said
Wiv a claht rahnd the 'ead,
He said, 'Ere you are
Laying about,
When you should be out there
Earning a living
Giving instead er taking the bread
From the pore old marth er yer
Dear old muvver 'n me.'
(29)

Oh! They'll never make an 'Ighbrow Cockney aht
    o'me,
I'd rather be a Lowbrow Townie;
You won't find me in bags,
along with 'Blues' and 'Fags,'
A-knockin' cops abaht in them there Student Rags.
I ain't a one for Rolls Royce phrases.
I leaves that to the Aristocracy
And as long as I'm a-blowin',
And 'Old Father Thames' keeps flowin',
Oh! The Council Schools are good enough for me!
(206)

The lyrics to these songs underscore the connection between music-hall enter-tainment and Sam's character, and simultaneously put forth the impression of a music-hall revue show even though the adaptation is clearly written in the American tradition of the book musical. Similarly, the spontaneity of Sam's music-hall numbers, along with his sense of knowingness regarding the ability of a music-hall performer to connect with his audience, allows for the writers to incorporate some elements of the freewheeling spontaneity that defined Dickens's text.

Peter Bailey describes the chaotic yet congenial dynamic of the Victorian music hall as revolving around the close bond between the music-hall perfor-mer and his or her audience, a bond which emerged as a result of the singer's ability to engage the audience on a direct, intimate level. Just as the so-called "fourth-wall" was virtually nonexistent in the Victorian music hall, Sam repeatedly seems to break the fourth wall in *Pickwick*, and his doing so creates a sense of both naturalness and playfulness akin to the unstructured tenor of the original text. As Bailey writes, this technique of breaking the fourth wall, as utilized by many prominent music-hall performers, "secured a distinctive relationship with the audience by initiating them in the mysteries of the performer's craft and giving them a consequent sense of select inclusion'' (132). Though every audience was different, Bailey claims that a music-hall performer, by letting the crowd in on the act, effectively helped mold the audience even while allowing it to shape his or her performance.

There are important links between this technique and the technique utilized by Dickens in *Pickwick Papers* given that Boz likewise breaks the fourth wall in his presentation of the story. Through the persona of the Pickwickian editor, who frequently alludes to the amorphous tenor of the narrative, Dickens likewise invites the audience into the secret world of his craft—the craft of novel-writing. Though the 1837 preface hints that Dickens felt the need to explain the unstructured format of the novel to his public, it is that same lack of structure that contributes to the joys of Mr. Pickwick's adventures, as the lack of a ''fourth wall'' allows for the reader to share these adventures directly with the characters. Though *Pickwick* presents a far more linear and coherent story than its source, it is only through the use of Sam's music-hall style songs that Bricusse and Ornadel come close to capturing the engaging spontaneity of the original narrative. Had the writers taken this idea further, and created an even more unrestrictive music-hall style score for the entire piece, this same spontaneity might have set the tone of the entire project.

The ideal musical version of this particular novel would combine the sophistication of the musical score to *Pickwick* with the freedom and improvisational use of songs in *Sam Weller*. The concept-musical approach, which is noteworthy for its loose narrative structure and thematic use of music and song, immediately seems appropriate. Rupert Holmes utilized this same format in his musical adaptation *Drood* (1985), and Holmes's adaptation of Dickens's final novel remains one of the most frequently produced musical versions of the author's work, second perhaps only to *Oliver!* However, if *Oliver!* epitomizes the traditional, integrated approach of the golden age of the musical to a Dickensian source, then *Drood* epitomizes the experimental approach of the 70s and 80s, yet another important historical chapter in the evolution of the musical.

Most musical theater scholars designate the 1970s as the birth period of the concept musical, and Stephen Sondheim's *Company* is oftentimes described as one of the first examples of the genre. Joanne Gordon stresses the correlation between Sondheim's innovative approach to musical theater and the advent of the concept musical:

> Concept, the word coined to describe the form of the Sondheim musical, suggests that all elements of the musical, thematic and presentational, are integrated to suggest a central idea or image. . . . Prior to Sondheim, the musical was built around the plot. . . . The book structure for Sondheim, on the other hand, means the idea. Music, lyric, dance, dialogue, design, and direction fuse to support a

focal thought. A central conceit controls and shapes an entire production, for every aspect of the production is blended and subordinated to a single vision. . . . Form and content cannot really be separated, for one dictates and is dependent on the other. (7–8)

As Gordon indicates, the concept musical is built around an idea as opposed to a plot. Rather than simply integrating music into a narrative as the writers of the golden age of the American musical did, the writers of concept musicals integrate songs, narrative, dance, and staging into an overarching theme. While Gordon emphasizes the importance of total integration to the structure of the concept musical, other musical theater scholars stress the influence of the disjointed format of the musical revue on the presentation of songs in a concept musical. Stephen Citron describes the concept musical as "an off-shoot of the topical revue, often done with more seriousness of purpose. It need not have a plot or it may have a slight thread of one" (39). Sondheim's *Company*, perhaps the foremost example of this particular type of show, is built around a series of loosely connected episodes in the life of the protagonist. The unifying factor in this musical is the theme of marriage, as the show examines the tumultuous relationships of five different couples. There is no real sense of chronological order, and many of the songs—such as "You Could Drive a Person Crazy" and "What Would We Do without You?"— are presented in the same fashion as songs from a musical revue, with the characters knowingly breaking the fourth wall.

The loose narrative structure of *Company* is immediately evocative of *The Pickwick Papers*, and the idea of a conceptual or revue-style musical based on the novel is intriguing: episodes from the novel could be selected based on their entertainment value and conceptual relevance (as opposed to any narrative function they serve in the text), and lively songs that fit the scene could be incorporated accordingly. The driving concept to any such musical adaptation of *The Pickwick Papers* would have to relate to fellowship and escapade, as the novel itself is structured around the miscellaneous adventures of Mr. Pickwick and his friends. Given the centrality of drink to many of Mr. Pickwick's adventures (and misadventures), the various songs in the musical score might be written to replicate traditional English drinking songs. Just as Rupert Holmes sought to recreate music-hall culture in his conceptual adaptation of *The Mystery of Edwin Drood*, a musical team might try to replicate the saloon-singing culture that preceded the music hall in a revue-style adaptation of *The Pickwick Papers*. Such an approach could ultimately underscore the Englishness of the source material, as Holmes's own technique of utilizing music-hall songs in his adaptation helped to reinforce the British roots of both the source and its creator.

As for a conceptual framework around which to build a new Pickwickian musical, many different approaches might be taken to the source material.

The show might be structured as a meeting of various archivists compiling the posthumous papers of the Pickwick Club, and miscellaneous papers detailing specific episodes in the Pickwickians's travels could be presented as individual scenes featuring Mr. Pickwick and the other characters. The rather haphazard structuring of the musical would not undercut the liveliness and humor of the episodes, nor detract from the music and songs incorporated into each sequence; in fact, the loose structuring would resemble Dickens's approach to the original text. Another conceptual frame might revolve around the most famous scene in the novel, the trial of Bardell vs. Pickwick; the various witnesses called to the stand could present ''evidence'' in the form of flashbacks to memorable episodes in Mr. Pickwick's travels. Once again, though the narrative structure would be disjointed, the incorporation of songs in the style of a musical revue would allow for an entertaining musical variety show based on episodes from the novel, all of which would contribute to the overarching theme of companionship. The looser story arc would allow for an amount of flexibility that is lacking in the Bricusse adaptation; however, the emphasis on thematic integration would necessitate more relevant and effective songs than the random and inappropriate ballads inserted into Moncrieff's adaptation.

Simply utilizing elements of Dickens's novel as the catalyst for a series of songs may seem an ineffective use of the author's text, but this technique worked particularly well for Holmes in his adaptation of *Edwin Drood*. Furthermore, a revue-style format would correlate incredibly well to the chaotic yet comical structure of Dickens's original novel. It is ironic to imagine a musical version of *The Pickwick Papers* written in the style of a concept musical given the fact that *The Mystery of Edwin Drood* is the foremost example of a Dickensian musical written in this genre: *Edwin Drood* was Dickens's very last novel while *Pickwick Papers* was his first. Nevertheless, the flexible narrative pattern of the concept musical, along with its less rigidly structured musical score, seems to correlate perfectly with the episodic nature of *The Pickwick Papers*. Furthermore, a conceptual approach, such as the one taken by Holmes in his adaptation of *Edwin Drood*, would allow for an easier reconciliation of the divergent British and American qualities of any musical adaptation of *The Pickwick Papers*. Indeed, a concept musical interpretation of *The Pickwick Papers* might very well prove to be the most ''harmonious'' musical adaptation of this novel to date given its potential to bring the divergent cultural, thematic, and musical elements of the previous versions together.

WORKS CITED

Axton, William F. ''Unity and Coherence in *The Pickwick Papers.*'' *Studies in English Literature, 1500–1900* 5.4 (1965): 663–76.

Bailey, Peter. *Popular Culture and Performance in the Victorian City.* Cambridge: Cambridge UP, 1998.

Bricusse, Leslie. *The Music Man.* London: Metro, 2006.

———, and Cyril Ornadel. *Pickwick.* London: Samuel French, 1963.

Chesterton, G. K. *Charles Dickens: The Last of the Great Men.* New York: Press of the Readers Club, 1942.

Citron, Stephen. *The Musical from the Inside Out.* Chicago: Ivan R. Dee, 1991.

Dickens, Charles. *The Posthumous Papers of the Pickwick Club.* Ed. Mark Wormald. London: Penguin, 1999.

Engel, Lehman, and Howard Kissel. *Words with Music: Creating the Broadway Musical Libretto.* New York: Applause Theatre & Cinema Books, 2006.

Fiske, Roger. *English Theatre Music in the Eighteenth Century,* 2nd ed. Oxford: Oxford UP, 1986.

Fitz-Gerald, S. J. Adair. *Dickens and the Drama.* London: Chapman and Hall, 1910.

Flinn, Denny Martin. *Musical!: A Grand Tour.* New York: Schirmer, 1997.

Gagey, Edmond McAdoo. *Ballad Opera.* New York: Columbia UP, 1937.

Gammond, Peter, ed. *Best Music Hall and Variety Songs.* London: Wolfe, 1972.

Ganzl, Kurt. *The Musical: A Concise History.* Boston: Northeastern UP, 1997.

Gordon, Joanne. *Art Isn't Easy: The Achievement of Stephen Sondheim.* Carbondale: Southern Illinois UP, 1990.

Miller, Scott. *Strike Up the Band: A New History of Musical Theatre.* Portsmouth: Heineman, 2007.

Moncrieff, W. T. *Sam Weller, or, The Pickwickians.* London: J. Dicks, 1884.

Patten, Robert L. "The Art of *Pickwick's* Interpolated Tales." *ELH* 34 (1967): 349–66.

Sadrin, Anny. "Fragmentation in *The Pickwick Papers.*" *Dickens Studies Annual* 22 (1993): 21–34.

Woollcott, Alexander. *Mr. Dickens Goes to the Play.* New York: G. P. Putnam's, 1922.

Boz versus Bos in *Sweeney Todd*: Dickens, Sondheim, and Victorianness

Sharon Aronofsky Weltman

The 1979 Stephen Sondheim/Hugh Wheeler musical Sweeney Todd *derives (through Christopher Bond's 1973 melodrama) from the anonymously authored* The String of Pearls *(1846–47). The novel is often attributed to Thomas Peckett Prest, who so blatantly copied Dickens that he frequently wrote under the name "Bos." Certainly* The String of Pearls *imitates some identifiable characteristics of Dickens's writing—outrageous characters, Pickwickian humor, and a sensational Newgate plot, like* Oliver Twist*'s. Yet Prest crucially leaves out Dickens's powerful social critique. In contrast, Sondheim's adaptation reinserts the kind of social criticism viewers associate with Dickens. It is from Dickens—and later adaptations of Dickens—rather than from the Victorian novel from which* Sweeney Todd *descends that Sondheim receives and assembles the traits that we interpret as Victorian. Sondheim intensifies the Victorianness of his play* not *by closely following the nineteenth-century source but by inserting details chiefly inherited from Dickens's* Oliver Twist *and, perhaps more surprisingly, from the 1960 musical adaptation* Oliver!. *Examining Sondheim's* Sweeney Todd *(on stage and in the 2007 Tim Burton film) in relation to* The String of Pearls *and* Oliver! *provides a potent vehicle for considering how we have come to understand Victorianness through what we read as Dickensian.*

Dickens Studies Annual, Volume 42, Copyright © 2011 by AMS Press, Inc. All rights reserved.

Stephen Sondheim's award-winning musical *Sweeney Todd: The Demon Barber of Fleet Street* (1979) evolved through a long genealogy of adaptations—most importantly Christopher Bond's 1973 melodrama of the same name—from the now virtually forgotten serial tale of terror *The String of Pearls* (1846–47), often attributed to Thomas Peckett Prest. Ever popular, Sondheim's *Sweeney Todd* has seen major new stage productions in both London (2004) and New York (2005), continuing on tour at least through 2009. The recent Tim Burton film (2007), starring Johnny Depp and Helena Bonham-Carter, has captured critical acclaim and brought new audiences to the musical through the cinema and on DVD (2008). But, despite the musical *Sweeney Todd*'s decades of success, *The String of Pearls* remains largely unknown. A Newgate novel with characters and plot elements directly imitating Charles Dickens, *The String of Pearls* (unlike Dickens's novels) employs neither its comedy nor its depictions of villainy to offer significant social criticism. Yet Sondheim's masterpiece does. Partly by way of the musical's book by Hugh Wheeler and its hefty debt to Bond's play, Sondheim's adaptation reinserts the kind of critique viewers associate with Dickens. It also reinstates those aspects of the original novel that derive from Dickens and adds others that directly come from Dickens's novels or from later adaptations of Dickens's work. In bringing the Victorian tale to the current stage and screen, Sondheim and Wheeler make it seem more Victorian for us by making it seem more Dickensian.

Theater critics reviewing *Sweeney Todd* typically refer to it as "Dickensian" without going beyond that adjective. Examples from reviews of recent British and American productions include *Sweeney Todd*'s "Dickensian-laden revolving stage," as Roderic Dunnett in *The Independent* (May 24, 2004) describes the Derby Playhouse production in England's Midlands, and the "perverse Dickensian cartoons," as Charles McNulty in *The Village Voice* (March 9, 2004) describes the New York City Opera's production of that year. Newspapers identified Dickensian qualities even more vehemently with the original Broadway opening: *The New York Times* remembers the "Dickensian social framework" from Harold Prince's 1979 production that it does not detect in John Doyle's 2005 production. Similarly, in *Newsday* Linda Winer refers to Prince's 1979 production as a "vast Dickensian epic."[1] John Bush Jones offers a bit more when he suggests that *Sweeney Todd* reveals "that the United States today is as over-industrialized and depersonalized as Charles Dickens's London" (291). Reviews of the new Tim Burton film also recognize Dickens. According to the *Minneapolis Star-Tribune*, Timothy Spall, who plays Beadle Bamford, comes "straight out of a Dickens illustration."[2] In *The New York Times*, A. O. Scott likens Burton's London to the set in Carol Reed's movie musical *Oliver!*.[3]

While all these reviews agree that there is something Dickensian about *Sweeney Todd*, none explains precisely what characteristics they mean to invoke by that term. I say "Dickensian" because I argue that it is from Dickens—and adaptations of Dickens—that Sondheim inherits the set of characteristics that audiences read as Victorian rather than from *The Three-penny Opera* (to which Sondheim clearly owes a debt) or even from the Victorian pulp novel from which *Sweeney Todd* sprang.[4] In fact, Sondheim magnifies the Victorianness of his show based on a Victorian work *not* by faithfully following the original (which was set in eighteenth-century London) but by inserting details, characters, themes, and a setting drawn largely from Dickens's novel *Oliver Twist* (1837–39) or, perhaps more significantly, from the musical adaptation *Oliver!* (London, 1960; New York, 1963).

Although no one knows for sure who wrote the blood-and-thunder story of *The String of Pearls*, historians often identify the author (or co-author) as Thomas Peckett Prest. A prolific hack writer working for the penny press, Prest spent much of his career copying Dickens, whom he imitated so bla-tantly that he published under the name of "Bos." While Sondheim's musical play derives from Prest's novel, Prest himself continually imitated Dickens. Novels attributed to Prest include *The Penny Pickwick* (1839), *Nickelas Nick-lebery, Martin Guzzlewit,* and, most tellingly, *Oliver Twiss* (1841). Although *The String of Pearls* does not directly pirate Dickens, it imitates some identi-fiable characteristics of Dickens's writing—such as outrageous characters, Pickwickian humor, and, most obviously, a sensational Newgate plot, like *Oliver Twist*'s (1837–39). Prest deftly regurgitated Dickensian characters, plots, and titles, but crucially left out Dickens's powerful social critique. In contrast, Sondheim's adaptation emphasizes Dickensian concern for reform. Sharp class and cultural criticism in Sondheim's musical rendering of Prest's story results in a kind of re-Dickensing of it. In other words, Sondheim provides a version of Sweeney Todd that is more Boz than Bos.

What I trace through the rest of this essay are three parallel sets of relation-ships between the works of Sondheim, Prest, and Dickens. First, I discuss the relationship of *The String of Pearls* to Dickens's novels; second, what use *Sweeney Todd* makes of *The String of Pearls*; and, third, what *Sweeney Todd* owes to Dickens directly or through adaptations, such as *Oliver!,* even though *The String of Pearls* (already an imitation of Dickens), leaves them out. Examining Sondheim's *Sweeney Todd* in relation to *The String of Pearls* and *Oliver!* provides a potent vehicle for considering how we have come to understand Victorianness through what we read as Dickensian.

A Touch of Bos/z[5]

While Sondheim's *Sweeney Todd* boasts many fervent fans and many studies by musical theater scholars,[6] few in either group have read or even know of the novel that is the musical's ultimate literary source. This is because Sondheim identifies Christopher Bond's 1973 melodrama (also called *Sweeney Todd: The Demon Barber of Fleet Street*) as inspiring him. Hugh Wheeler's book for the musical follows Bond's play very closely, and it is Bond who first contributes many of the Dickensian elements I discuss here.[7] Nevertheless, the tale originated long before either Bond or Wheeler got involved. The author of the novel *The String of Pearls* is often misidentified as George Dibdin Pitt,[8] who did in fact first adapt it for the melodrama stage in 1847 at the Britannia Theatre, just before the concluding installment of the novel appeared in print; however, the novel itself was perhaps—though by no means certainly—written by Prest. The alcoholic Prest often wrote for Edward Lloyd, a successful publishing entrepreneur who created inexpensive Salisbury Square periodicals for the working class, such as *The Penny Sunday Times and People's Police Gazette* and *Lloyd's Weekly Newspaper.*[9] Additional contenders for the novel's debated authorship are other Lloyd authors: James Malcolm Rymer, George Macfarren, Lloyd himself, or a combination, with one of them beginning it and others continuing or expanding or alternating chapters.[10] Because Prest has been traditionally identified as author and because no critical consensus yet exists, I have for convenience attributed *The String of Pearls* to Prest throughout this essay.

What is certain is that *The String of Pearls* came out anonymously on Sundays from 1846 to 1847 in a Lloyd penny weekly, *The People's Periodical and Family Library*. The story filled narrow columns alongside light anecdotes, thrilling travel sketches, and recipes for rat poison. No matter what its provenance or literary merit, the novel spawned over a century and a half of wildly popular adaptation and, even for this reason alone, merits investigation.[11] It has been made into at least four films, two TV movies, radio plays, and a ballet. British actor Tod Slaughter (a serendipitous name) was able to perform the role of Todd in a version of Pitt's stage melodrama over 4,000 times by the time he died in 1956.[12] Also in 1956, comedian Stanley Holloway (perhaps best known for the role of Eliza Doolittle's father in *My Fair Lady*, both on Broadway and in film) recorded the comic music-hall favorite "Sweeney Todd: The Barber."[13] The myth of Sweeney Todd is so powerful that many people claim in print that the story was based on an actual case of murder and cannibalism, despite the fact that there is no evidence of this—at least, not on Fleet Street, not in London.[14] While Dibdin Pitt touts his stage melodrama as based in truth, Prest's earlier piece is subtitled "A Romance," underscoring its status as fiction. Sondheim renews the tradition of fictionality by subtitling his show "A Musical Thriller."[15]

The main character is so famous that Sweeney Todd hair salons flourish in cities across America.[16] However, *The String of Pearls* is so little known as to warrant a full paragraph of summary.

In the novel's opening chapter, the barber Sweeney Todd murders a customer, the sailor Mr. Thornhill, for a valuable string of pearls. Thornhill had stopped for a shave on his way to deliver the necklace to the beautiful Johanna Oakley. They were a gift from her beloved, Mark Ingestrie, presumed drowned at sea. Thornhill's friend, Colonel Jeffrey, decides to visit Johanna instead, to break the bad news about Mark's death and to mention Thornhill's worrisome disappearance with her gift. Also noticing that Mr. Thornhill is suddenly missing (and last seen at the barber shop) is Todd's apprentice, Tobias (or "Toby") Ragg, who suspects foul play. Meanwhile, a handsome and desperately poor young man takes a job baking meat pies for the buxom and attractive widow Mrs. Lovett, whose delicious pastries are famous throughout London and whose shop is around the corner from Todd's. The peculiar job requires the young baker to stay locked in the cellars below the bakeshop and never to ask where the meat comes from. Back at the barber's, Todd recognizes that his apprentice has become suspicious and claps him into Dr. Fogg's cruel insane asylum. Colonel Jeffrey goes to the magistrate and tells him of his friend Mr. Thornhill's having vanished, last seen at Todd's barber shop. A terrible stench wafts up from the cellars of St. Dunstan's church, which stands near Todd's and Mrs. Lovett's shops, causing an official inquiry, including a visit from the magistrate whom Colonel Jeffrey had consulted earlier. In the meantime, the distraught but resourceful Johanna disguises herself as a boy and fills the now vacant position of Todd's apprentice, in order to spy on the barber. Mrs. Lovett's recently hired bake-house chef grows restive in his incarceration, and so Mrs. Lovett tells Todd that it's time to kill the young man. Unknown to Mrs. Lovett, the inquisitive young cook discovers an unspeakable secret about her meat locker. Back at Sweeney Todd's shop, the magistrate impersonates a customer; because Sweeney Todd tries to kill him instead of shave him, the magistrate knows the truth. His hidden officers seize Todd, relieving readers who are at this point worrying about Johanna's safety while she is dressed as an apprentice under Todd's control. At the same time, the brave young baker puts himself on the dumbwaiter used to carry pies from the basement bake house to the pie shop. When the next load of pies is supposed to come up, he jumps out of the dumbwaiter, crying to the hungry pie-lovers, "Mrs. Lovett's pies are made of *human flesh!*"[17] In the middle of being arrested by the magistrate, Mrs. Lovett dies of the poison Todd has secretly put in her brandy so that he won't have to split the proceeds from selling the string of pearls. Johanna has come to the pie shop, too, brought there by the magistrate, the Colonel, and Toby—who had previously escaped from the madhouse and told his story to the law—so that she might be reunited with her long-lost love; indeed, the good-looking pastry cook is none other than Mark Ingestrie, thought drowned at sea. They embrace. Todd is executed at Newgate Prison.

While this summary smoothes over the novel's interpolated stories, dropped plot lines, and rushed ending, it preserves the book's solidly entertaining melodramatic narrative. But it does not point out the ways in which *The String of Pearls* imitates Dickens. The parallels between Prest's Todd and Dickens's Fagin, who both hang at Newgate, are among the most significant examples of Bos copying Boz in *The String of Pearls*. One scene in which Prest seems clearly to attempt imitating the inimitable is the scene in which Todd imagines that his apprentice, Tobias, has seen him kill a victim. The passage shows a remarkable similarity to Fagin's discovering that Oliver has observed Fagin's treasure box. In *Oliver Twist*, Fagin,

> . . . laying his hand on a bread knife which was on the table, started furiously up. He trembled very much though; for, even in his terror, Oliver could see that the knife quivered in the air.
>
> "What's that?" said the Jew. "What do you watch me for? Why are you awake? What have you seen? Speak out, boy! Quick—quick! for your life!"
>
> "I wasn't able to sleep any longer, sir," replied Oliver, meekly. "I am very sorry if I have disturbed you, sir."
>
> "You were not awake an hour ago?" said the Jew, scowling fiercely on the boy.
>
> "No! No, indeed!" replied Oliver.
>
> "Are you sure?" cried the Jew: with a still fiercer look than before: and a threatening attitude.
>
> "Upon my word I was not, sir," replied Oliver, earnestly. "I was not, indeed, sir."
>
> "Tush, tush, my dear!" said the Jew, abruptly resuming his old manner, and playing with the knife a little, before he laid it down; as if to induce the belief that he had caught it up, in mere sport. "Of course I know that, my dear. I only tried to frighten you. You're a brave boy. Ha! ha! you're a brave boy, Oliver!" The Jew rubbed his hands with a chuckle, but glanced uneasily at the box, notwithstanding.   (69)

Prest borrows several elements from Dickens, intensifying the violence with physical contact between Todd and Toby:

> In two strides Todd reached him, and clutching him by the arm he dragged him into the farthest corner of the shop, and then he stood opposite to him glaring in his face with such a demoniac expression that the boy was frightfully terrified.
>
> "Speak!" cried Todd, "speak! And speak the truth, or your last hour is come! How long were you peeping through the door before you came in?"
>
> "Peeping, sir?"
>
> "Yes, peeping; don't repeat my words, but answer me at once, you will find it better for you in the end."
>
> "I wasn't peeping, sir, at all."
>
> Sweeney Todd drew a long breath as he then said, is a strange, shrieking sort of manner, which he intended, no doubt, should be jocose,—

"Well, well, very well; if you did peep, what then? It's no matter; I only wanted to know, that's all; it was quite a joke, wasn't it—quite funny, though rather odd, eh? Why don't you laugh, you dog? Come, now, there is no harm done. Tell me what you thought about it at once, and we will be merry over it—very merry." (7)

Prest imitates Dickens's characters and their relationships, dramatic situations, and dialogue. Todd's "demoniac expressions" recall the abundant devil imagery associated with Fagin, who is at once the "merry old gentleman" and a gliding, creeping, crawling "loathsome reptile" (66, 132). In both cases the criminal/protectors worry that the boys have observed evidence that could convict them. Both enjoin the boys to say what they have seen or risk losing their lives. Both then joke to control the damage of having revealed the intensity of their concern. Neither adult finally is sure he is safe from the boy's prying.

The fun in Prest's Todd springs not only from his being an excessively bad guy, but also from the quirkiness that we associate with Dickens's creations. Fagin's "villainous-looking and repulsive face is obscured by a quantity of matted red hair" (65), but Todd sports an even more outlandish coiffure. The narrator first describes the barber's "Terrific head of hair" in one of the most memorable images from the novel: it had "the appearance of a thick-set hedge, in which a quantity of small wire had got entangled. . . . Sweeney kept all his combs in it—some people said his scissors likewise—" (2). The irony of a barber with hair so wild, thick, and unkempt that he can store all his combs and scissors in it is funny enough, but the mad villain effect is heightened by Todd's evil laugh. In the first scene in which a customer is about to be—in what becomes Todd's favorite expression—"polished off,"[18] the unfortunate says,

"What the devil noise was that?"
"It was only me," said Sweeney Todd: "I laughed."
"Laughed! Do you call that a laugh? I suppose you caught it off somebody who died of it." (5)

In addition to Todd's fearsome headdress and his hideous laugh, he has huge hands, mouth, feet, and a squint. His physical grotesqueness may remind some readers of Quilp, the villain from *The Old Curiosity Shop* (1840–41), whose disproportionate physique and alarming merriment magnifies the effect of his villainy.

The novel includes some gentle social satire in imitation of Dickens, without his reformist agenda. Prest takes aim against feminine mawkishness when the heroine Johanna Oakley's friend, Arabella Wilmot (whose name recalls Arabella Allen in *Pickwick*), bases all her actions and advice on silly novels.

Johanna herself is almost equally absurd in her romantic diction; for example when she realizes that she will soon hear news of her lover, Mark, she says,

> "Joy, joy! He lives, he lives! Mark Ingestrie lives! Perchance, too, successful in his object, he returns to tell me that he can make me his, and that no obstacle can now interfere to frustrate our union. Time, time, float onwards on your fleetest pinions!"   (34)

Johanna's dialogue sounds ripe for the melodrama stage, begging for appropriate gestures. One may hear echoes of the actress Mrs. Crummles from *Nicholas Nickleby*, whose theatrical manner of speech in everyday discourse ("What mean you? . . . Whence comes this altered tone?") already spoofs the diction of melodrama as her "tragic recoil" spoofs the gesture (596).

Like Dickens, Prest here pokes fun at women taken in by hypocritical evangelical ministers. These characters might well remind readers of other early Dickens. For example, Robert Mack argues that the Oakleys are based on the Varden family in the 1841 novel *Barnaby Rudge* (Introduction xvii). Both are (to some extent) historical novels, set around 1775. Certainly, there are parallels, including a sneaky apprentice, named Sim in Dickens and Sam in Prest. But Prest also reaches farther back in Dickens's oeuvre, as he had already done—if the authors are the same—in *The Penny Pickwick* (1839). The mooching preacher and his comic comeuppance in *The String of Pearls* seem blatantly borrowed from Sam Weller's father's revenge against the pineapple rum-and-water swilling "shepherd" in *Pickwick Papers* (1836–37).[19] In *The String of Pearls*, Big Ben (Mr. Oakley's bulky Beefeater cousin) physically chastises the Reverend Mr. Lupin (and lassoes Mrs. Oakley, dangling her unharmed but furious from a hook on the wall), just as Sam Weller's father tackles the punch-loving preacher who had long been poaching off Sam's wife and her friends (*Pickwick* 444; ch. 32). Yet such imitation seems less to interrogate evangelical hypocrisy than comically to condone a misogynist rule by the paterfamilias.

Even the cannibal pie-maker has antecedents in Dickens, as Mack points out (Introduction xvii). Dickens writes of food made of human flesh, both in *The Pickwick Papers* and *Martin Chuzzlewit* (1843–44). In Dickens, the problem simultaneously plays on the readers' anxiety about the dangers of industrial society (where impersonal machines beyond our control grind one's meat), and on the readers' sense of superiority to the foolishness of country rubes who believe that they will be either poisoned or eaten in the city. In *Pickwick Papers*, Sam Weller describes the sausage-maker who is ground up by his own "patent-never-leavin'-off sassage steam-ingin" and discovered to have been eaten by his customers only by the bits of brass button "seasonin' " (407–08; ch. 30). In *Martin Chuzzlewit*, Tom Pinch expresses his concern that John Westlock will worry he's "been made meat pies of, or some such horrible thing" because he has taken so long; the novel subsequently reassures the reader that Tom does not fall "into the dens of any of those preparers of cannibalistic pastry, who are represented in many standard country legends as doing a lively retail business in the Metropolis" (544; ch. 36). Prest's novella comes hard on the heels of both these novels, but, other than a general sense that Mrs. Lovett's pies are just too delicious to be true, her pastries provide neither a warning against the brutality of the industrial revolution nor a ridiculing of a rural population for imagining cannibals in the metropolis.[20]

No matter how many of Dickens's characters or plot elements *The String of Pearls* imitates, the social satire has no institutional or systemic object: no workhouse, no Chancery, no Debtor's Prison. Although we associate social criticism more strongly with Dickens's later novels, these critiques already appear in *Pickwick Papers*, *Nicholas Nickleby*, and *Oliver Twist*. In *The String of Pearls*, the only serious indictment of social evil is in the depiction of Dr. Fogg (from whose madhouse the apprentice Toby escapes), who incarcerates and kills patients for a fee from their families; nevertheless, his gothic asylum seems less a protest than a plot device.

Meet the Beadles

The most serious way in which Sondheim's *Sweeney Todd* derives more from Dickens than Prest is in its class commentary. A prime example is "A Little Priest," in which Mrs. Lovett and Sweeney Todd sing gleefully as they decide to eliminate the corporeal evidence of his murders by using his victims' corpses to provide meat for her pies, which an unsuspecting clientele will happily eliminate to their mutual profit. This song makes the musical's most explicit statement that Sweeney Todd turns the tables on the musical's villainous judge and beadle so that, although "The history of the world . . . Is those below serving those up above," now "those above will serve those down below" (108).[21] In this respect, Sondheim's show recalls Dickens more than Prest, who makes no attempt to depict Todd's murders or Mrs. Lovett's pie-making as a symbolic reversal of social inequities. There is some irony, however, in the fact that the expensive middle-class, middle-brow amusement of this particular Broadway musical criticizes class hierarchy and the mistreatment of the working man, while the original working-class entertainment of this particular "penny dreadful" novel does not. While Sally Ledger points out that Dickens's use of the aesthetics of melodrama serves the aesthetics of class protest in *Pickwick Papers* and *Oliver Twist* (101), that process does not extend to *The String of Pearls*. In the novel, most of Todd's victims, like himself, are small tradesmen, shop-keepers, farmers, and service providers, instead of the musical's corrupt judge and deceitful beadle. Prest restricts his criticism to schoolgirl sentimentality, evangelical hypocrisy, and foolish fashion, rather than abuse of power or exploitation of poverty. In Prest's world, law and justice coincide: the criminal barber is caught by the brave and clever magistrate Sir Richard and his officers, who serve the public faithfully and at personal risk. The heroine Johanna, her sailor boyfriend Mark, Toby the apprentice, and their friend the Colonel help. Public health is insured by Mrs. Lovett's exposure; order is restored by Todd's arrest. This is not a radical aesthetic. In Sondheim's musical, Prest's mercenary brute has become a law-abiding family man who first seeks justice and then retribution solely against the people who directly and horribly wronged him.[22] Only when Todd realizes how utterly he and his family have been mangled and mistreated by the law, which should have protected them, does he take revenge against everyone. This addition of Sweeney's motivation inserts a large measure of social protest into a story that had none.

Sondheim's embittered Sweeney Todd gains the audience's sympathy immediately. He sings in the gripping melody of ''No Place Like London'' his heart-felt grief for his lost life and love, and of his hatred of the corrupt judge who transported the honest barber on a trumped up charge in order to rape his unprotected wife, Lucy. This Todd yearns for his daughter Johanna, trapped in the judge's house as his ward and subjected to her supposed benefactor's unseemly advances. The result of these motivations is Todd's appeal and our identification with him. We pity him and want him to succeed in bringing the vile judge to justice. Because of this sympathy, Sweeney Todd's rise and fall—even after he has become a serial murderer—take on the grandeur of tragedy, allowing Sondheim's extraordinary music to enter opera repertoire, with performances by the Houston Grand Opera (1984), the New York City Opera (1984, 2004), the Chicago Lyric Opera (2002), and the Royal Opera House at Covent Garden (2002) (Grout 750).

None of this depth comes from *The String of Pearls*. The character that Prest creates in the novel is pure melodrama villainy: motiveless, malevolent, and over the top.[23] Prest tells us nothing of Todd's origin. The barber has no reason to kill people in general and none to kill anyone in particular, other than innate, overweening malignancy and greed; he steals from almost all his victims, mostly hats, canes, wallets, and jewelry, in preparation for an early retirement. The young Johanna, who has become Todd's daughter in Sondheim, is in Prest an unrelated ingenue, the daughter of a spectacle-maker, whose plot intersects with Todd's when he steals the eponymous string of pearls. Prest's Todd has no wife, no child, no sentimental attachment of any kind. In the very first installment, he murders several customers with great relish, one for the pearls, another for a cane. He beats his young apprentice

Toby and extorts his silence by threatening the destruction of the lad's hard-working mother. Before long, he even tries to poison a dog.

Sondheim's Todd, on the other hand, is never a ridiculous figure. All the humor associated with him comes from witty dialogue and song lyrics, usually with the lusty Mrs. Lovett. The plot gives him ample motivation to change from a loving husband and father to a murderer dissociated from the horror of his crimes. The rage of Sondheim's Sweeney so overtakes him and his killing so hardens him that he is able to kill his mad wife, Lucy (without recognizing her), in his rush to get at the judge. Indeed, he nearly kills his disguised daughter, Johanna.[24] While he begins killing out of a justifiable desire for revenge, he ends up reveling in the bloodbath. The contrast between the coldly executed reiterated murders and the beautiful song ''Johanna'' that he sings while slitting his victims' throats further affects our reaction to Sweeney's crimes, which develop a kind of tragically ritual inevitability. Besides the addition of his just motive for retribution, music elevates Sondheim's Sweeney beyond the bogeyman of Prest's.

''Times is hard. Times is hard,'' sings Mrs. Lovett to Todd, in a direct echo of the title *Hard Times*, suggesting that, while Mrs. Lovett arrives in some respects unchanged from novel to musical, in others, she seems more Dickensian than Prestian (37).[25] Her name and occupation as cannibal pie-maker remain intact. But the comical character that Angela Lansbury originated on Broadway is a cheery, maternal, fast-talking, opportunistic, and lusty woman in her forties or fifties.[26] She convinces us that using the free meat from Todd's tonsorial parlor is merely practical business sense: ''Waste not, want not,'' she says. The novel's Mrs. Lovett is nubile, beautiful, aloof, and diabolic. Prest's character imprisons and enslaves handsome young work-men, planning to have them murdered as soon as they figure out the business. Rather than seizing a fortuitous opportunity, she operates with icy premedita-tion. The novel describes her as ''Buxom, young, and good-looking,'' traits she uses to ensnare her hapless helpers (26). Still, if the unfortunate young men were more alert or less hungry (she entices them as much with the promise of all the pies they can eat as with her personal charms), the unlucky cooks would have noticed that ''her smile was cold and uncomfortable . . . the set smile of a ballet-dancer'' (27).[27]

While Prest's chilly femme fatale serves primarily as a monstrous vehicle for the story's cannibal horror, Sondheim's more complicated Mrs. Lovett pushes the murderous plot along through bourgeois aspirations for lace and a slightly singed harmonium. In her down-to-earth motherly manner, Mrs. Lovett even takes the orphaned Toby under her wing; she pities, feeds, and puts him to work serving her customers in the pie-shop, taking care that he continue without knowledge or access to the nefarious nature of the business. He is not Todd's apprentice. Todd, Mrs. Lovett, and Toby live together, parodying the bourgeois family and cut-throat aspirations of upward mobility. Through their unorthodox entrepreneurship, Todd and Lovett provide new clothes and a comfortable living for all three. The used harmonium that appears in their parlor in Act II stands as a particularly prominent reward for their successful entry to a state of financial security through a seemingly respectable business.[28] Mrs. Lovett as a middle-aged, middle-class anti-mother recalls Mrs. Bumble from both *Oliver Twist* and *Oliver!* more than Prest's cold dominatrix. The musical's Mrs. Lovett shares with her Dickensian predecessor a coy courtship, a habit of spousal manipulation, and a relationship based on a combination of lust and avarice; both women either misuse or do not fulfill their maternal roles vis-à-vis the boys Tobias Ragg and Oliver Twist—surely the ur-orphan here. But I stress the debt of Sondheim's musical to Lionel Bart's musical *Oliver!* over the debt to Dickens's novel because, for the 1979 Broadway audience, Mrs. Bumble already exists as a stage type—middle-aged, hypocritically maternal, very materialistic, somewhat plump, and vocalizing—so that her appearance in *Sweeney Todd* seems more Victorian to a theater-going audience than would the fiendish, tantalizing ice queen of Prest's story.

But the mock-happy bourgeois family that Todd, Lovett, and Toby compose goes sour by the end of the Sondheim play in a way that is neither Prestian nor Dickensian. Toby wants to protect his ''mother'' from his ''father,'' whom he perceives as a violent danger to the complacent Mrs. Lovett, whom he wants for himself. All this is managed in the song ''Not While I'm Around,'' at first a tender sort of declaration by Toby that he will always protect his adoptive mother. Once it becomes clear that he means to protect her from Todd, the tender way in which the simple-minded adolescent has been resting his head on Mrs. Lovett's bosom seems inflected not only with the reasonable suspicions that the plot provides, but also with some obvious Oedipal desires to replace the father, whose relations with the mother, according to Freud, appear to a witnessing child as violence. In this case, of course, Todd will actually kill Mrs. Lovett, once he realizes that she has deceived him about the fate of his wife, Lucy. Mrs. Lovett's silence about Lucy's identity inadvertently helps to cause the madwoman's death, since Todd kills the anonymous mad beggar woman—who turns out to be his wife—just to rid himself of a nuisance. And Toby will fulfill the Oedipal fantasy by killing Todd in a deranged but belated effort to keep his beloved ''mother'' safe.

A possible antecedent hovering in cultural memory here is Bill Sikes's horrific murder of Nancy in both *Oliver Twist* and in the musical *Oliver!*. The adaptation eliminates *Oliver Twist*'s Rose Maylie from the plot altogether, making Nancy the closest thing Oliver gets to a viable mother.[29] Magnifying this view of a maternal Nancy in *Oliver!* is the boy's singing ''Where is Love?'' The context of this song (a lonely orphaned child forced to sleep among coffins) makes clear that Oliver really asks, "Where is my mother?'' In "I'd do Anything,'' Oliver expresses his devotion to Nancy. She genially teases Oliver and the Artful Dodger by singing a list of questions that test the limits of what they are willing to do for her, culminating with, "Even fight my Bill?'' While the Artful Dodger artfully dodges the question with one of his own, "What, fisticuffs?'' Oliver implies his readiness to defend her with childlike alacrity by singing that he'd do anything just for her smile.[30] However, unlike the adolescent Toby (generally played on stage by an adult), Oliver is only a nine-year-old. He can't do anything at all to protect Nancy, and—properly repressing any Oedipal urge—certainly can't kill Sikes.[31]

Another strong example of how the show *Sweeney Todd* inserts or alters familiar characters from Dickens to establish itself as a Victorian tale of class struggle in Dickensian terms is Beadle Bamford, who is imported straight out of *Oliver Twist* or perhaps just *Oliver!*. The beadle barely exists in *The String of Pearls*. A very minor unnamed character, he is a self-important functionary attached to St. Dunstan's church who enters the story during the investigation into the stink wafting up from the ecclesiastical cellars, which happen to be adjacent to Mrs. Lovett's basement. *Oliver Twist*'s beadle, Mr. Bumble, is a much more important character. Recurring through most of the novel, he reports Oliver to the parish board for requesting "more'' and then dispatches the lad to Mr. Sowerby, the undertaker. He marries the Widow Corney for her "six teaspoons, a pair of sugar-tongs, and a milk-pot'' (240). Later, when his misdeeds and those of Mrs. Bumble are discovered, before he is sent to his own poorhouse, he utters the novel's famous assessment of the British legal system, "The law is a ass'' (357). His presence emphasizes a vision of a Victorian world in which petty officials keep other people in their places and puff their own minimal importance. He carries out the edicts of an unjust system, and he does so while cherishing his perks and his author-ity over the powerless. Likewise, Sondheim's sycophantic beadle enjoys lord-ing it over the poor. But the evil of Sondheim's beadle far exceeds that of Dickens's or Lionel Bart's. Sondheim's beadle salaciously enjoys advising and abetting the corrupt and perverse Judge Turpin. He physically threatens Johanna's beau and wrings her pet bird's neck. He directly assists the judge in raping Lucy. From *Oliver!* to *Sweeney Todd*, the Beadle's shift from bum-bling to brutal intensifies Sondheim's bitter indictment of law, no longer merely the "ass'' we have seen in Dickens but the catalyst for unspeakable carnage. While the show *Oliver!* gives the Beadle a solo and a duet, making it a proportionally larger role than *Sweeney Todd*'s Beadle (who has a duet and a trio), the fact that *Sweeney Todd* includes a Beadle as a prominent character, when the original story had none of significance, is remarkable. Again our sense of Victorian culture is so influenced by Dickens—and by adaptations of Dickens—that a musical version of a Victorian novel requires a large singing beadle.

Depp and Debasement

Although Sondheim's *Sweeney Todd*'s successful crossover from musical theater to opera might have seemed surprising,[32] the crossover to a pop culture horror movie might seem even less likely. Do slasher-film fans generally overlap much with musical theater buffs? Previous musical horror films are often campy send-ups, such as *Rocky Horror Picture Show* (1975) and *Little Shop of Horrors* (1986), which rely on ridiculing horror movie conventions.[33] Tim Burton's *Sweeney Todd* takes both its horror and its music very seriously. While Sondheim's musical has appealed both to middle-brow musical theater audiences and to high-brow opera audiences, for the first time it is also attracting much larger popular culture audiences. Because of Johnny Depp, fans of the *Pirates of the Carribean* series and his many other films flock to it, in a sense returning the movie musical to the story's original function as working-class entertainment, whether for the readership of Lloyd's *People's Periodical and Family Library* or for the audiences at the transpontine Britannia Theatre, Hoxton, where Dibdin Pitt's dramatization first played in 1847 (Richards 147). In addition, a Tim Burton film starring Johnny Depp raises expectations about a certain kind of gothic effect, macabre humor, and sex appeal, as well as excellent film-making. These expectations attract a considerably younger audiences than would ever attend an opera, a concert at Lincoln Center, or a Broadway show, appealing to the same age demographics that read comic books and see Johnny Depp in *From Hell*.[34]

Like the stage musical, the film also borrows Dickensian features in order to intensify its Victorianness. For example, Toby is presented as a child, like nine-year-old Oliver, rather than as an adolescent.[35] Dialogue added to the film indicates that Toby is from the workhouse, an innovation for filmgoers who apparently expect that all Victorian orphans come from workhouses—like Oliver. In this respect, Burton's film recalls King's 1936 film *Sweeney Todd*, which goes so far as to interpolate a scene directly from *Oliver Twist*: in both King's and Burton's films, it is the beadle who first brings parish boy Tobias as apprentice to Todd's shop.[36] One effect of Burton's Toby being a little boy is that, when the angelic-looking boy soprano and the fetching Mrs. Lovett sing "Not While I'm Around," the Oedipal significance of the stage play is largely muted; perhaps an older teenage apprentice's singing with his head on Bonham-Carter's breast instead of Angela Lansbury's might look less like Freudian family dynamics and more like a potential ménage-à-trois. So while Bonham-Carter's Mrs. Lovett at times seems less like Mrs. Bumble and more like Prest's attractive original, the film's Tobias Ragg resembles Oliver Twist more than ever.

The 2007 film concludes even more bleakly than the 1979 play. Focusing on the grisly demise of Todd as his blood streams over his dead wife, the ending offers no glimpse of the fate of Johanna and her lover.[37] Although, like the stage play, the musical film punishes evil and hypocrisy in high places (and, like the novel, it punishes Todd's and Mrs. Lovett's mass murder), the film goes even further than the stage play in moving outside melodrama's generic feature of restoring order. Although evil is punished, in no way does good appear to triumph. In the stage musical, the adolescent Toby's surprise murder of Todd seems tragically appropriate—not only is justice served, and not only does he save his own life, but he avenges Mrs. Lovett (in whom he still believes), and becomes a man, albeit a demented one. But in the movie, depressingly and disturbing, we see the child Toby/Oliver fill this role, as though the incorruptible Oliver had finally yielded to the depraved influence of Fagin and Sikes. We have gone from *The String of Pearls*, in which the law properly upholds justice; to the stage musical, in which Todd wreaks his own terrible vengeance on the law, with the ultimate result that the new generation will inherit a world rid of both the corrupt institutions and the vitiated avenger; to the film, in which, as a result of too-extravagant retribution, the young lovers become irrelevant, and even the child is debased.

In film and on stage, Sondheim uses his music and lyrics to show us the horrors of Dickensian drama without the sentimentality, the humor turned cynical instead of sweet. The stock characters of Victorian melodrama join with a plot that indicts social institutions guilty of wantonly victimizing a helpless population. None of this critique comes from Prest, but much is familiar from Dickens. It is from Dickens—and later rewritings of Dickens—rather than from the Victorian novel from which *Sweeney Todd* descends that Sondheim assembles the traits that we interpret as Victorian. Sondheim and his collaborators intensify the Victorianness of his play derived from a Victorian novel *not* by closely following the source but by inserting details chiefly inherited from Dickens's *Oliver Twist* and, perhaps more surprisingly, from Bart's musical adaptation. Sondheim's reworking of Bos's imitation of Boz yields a powerful locus for representations of Victorianness and the Dickensian, which audiences now read as the same thing.[38] Ultimately, Sondheim makes Prest's tale current by making it seem more Victorian; he rewards our expectations that a Victorian story will be socially significant, based on our experience of Dickens as the quintessential Victorian novelist and *Oliver!* as the quintessential neo-Victorian musical.

NOTES

1. See Linda Winer. The reason for this shift in critical opinion from the original
1979 Broadway production to the recent Doyle-directed productions on the West
End and Broadway has largely to do with Doyle's remarkable innovation of
having the actors also provide the instrumentals while on stage. Since this significant break from the melodramatic tradition explored in the original production
reduces its Dickensian qualities, my analysis will apply more obviously to the
1979 production, which—despite the striking inventiveness of the most recent
staging—will remain definitive.
2. See Covert.
3. See Scott.
4. Early critics of Sondheim's *Sweeney Todd* recognized its debt to the Brecht-
Weill musical *The Threepenny Opera* (Berlin 1928), which debuted in an English
adaptation by Mark Blitzstein on Broadway in 1954. Certainly the connection is
there: not only the murderous anti-hero, the murky staging, the Victorian back-
drop, the low-life cast, the dark humor, but also and more importantly the class
struggle, the cultural critique, and the alienating effect of horror mixed with
pathos, beautiful music, and humor. See Richard Eder in the *New York Times*
(March 2, 1979). Among other scholars who explore *Sweeney Todd*'s Brechtian
qualities are John Bush Jones (290–93), Scott McMillin (29–30), Joanne Gordon
(184–88), and Thomas Adler (40–42).
5. Dickens first became famous for his *Sketches by Boz* (1836). As any reader of
Roland Barthes might be tempted to say, what a difference there is between "s"
and "z"! My thanks go to Elsie Michie for helping me make this connection.
However, an analysis informed by *S/Z* of how Bos refashions/castrates the mas-
terpieces of Boz and how that might be interesting in terms of gender and semiotics is far beyond the scope of this essay.
6. Useful criticism on Sondheim includes studies by Stephen Banfield; Geoffrey
Block; Sandor Goodhart; and Joanne Gordon, *Art Isn't Easy* and *Stephen Sondheim: A Casebook*.
7. See Gordon, *Art Isn't Easy* for a close analysis comparing these texts (221–23,
227–28).
8. See, for example, Bond's introduction to Sondheim's published libretto (2). See,
also, Louis James (162).
9. See Graham Law for a very helpful historical study (21).
10. Helen Smith argues against Prest and for James Malcolm Rymer as author of *The
String of Pearls* (21–28). Dick Collins rejects that idea in his Introduction to
the 2005 Wordsworth Press edition of *Sweeney Todd; or, The String of Pearls*,
suggesting instead that Prest and Rymer each contributed revisions to a text
started by an as yet unidentified writer (vii–viii); in his revised 2010 introduction,
he argues more firmly for co-authorship with Rymer. Robert Mack also points
to George Macfarren and Lloyd himself as possible writers (*Sweeney Todd* xxxi).
11. Despite the two-dimensional characters, the disjointed plot, the episodes that lead
nowhere, the characters left dangling, and the very abrupt ending, the novel

creates a phenomenally popular bogeyman whose longevity exceeds Dracula's and comes within 30 years of Frankenstein's.

12. There have been many versions of this play. See Malcolm Morley for casting in the initial performances at the Britannia and a substantial list of later plays based on Pitt's. Morely reports on wholesale passages of *Pickwick* (specifically "The Madman's Manuscript") interpolated into Pitt's play as printed and performed at various times (92–93).

13. My thanks go to Professor Dick Stein for alerting me to the wonders of Stanley Holloway and sending me this song on tape.

14. The closest "true story" of a Parisian barber-murderer in cahoots with a pastry chef neighbor was republished in 1824 as "A Terrific Story of the Rue de la Harpe, Paris" in *The Tell Tale Fireside Companion and Amusing Instructor*, a London magazine. The Newgate Calendar's Scottish cannibal clan leader Sawney Beane, who lived in a cave and dined for decades off unwary travelers, is also cited as a model. Other possible antecedents include the myth of Procne and Shakespeare's *Titus Andronicus*. See Mack (*Wonderful* 159–65).

15. See Gerould for more on why Sondheim calls it "A Musical Thriller" (7–8).

16. A Google search for "Sweeney Todd hair salon" on April 24, 2008, revealed stores in Minnesota, Connecticut, New York, New Jersey, Wisconsin, and Virginia—on just the first page.

17. One can't help but wonder if Stanley Greenberg, the screenwriter of *Soylent Green* (1973), heard echoes of Mark's cry when he adapted Harry Harrison's short story and added the cannibal plot in the film's famous last line, "Soylent Green is people!"

18. In his introduction to the novel, Mack points out that the phrase "I'll polish him off!"—the exclamation most associated with Sweeney Todd—originates in Dibdin Pitt's 1847 stage melodrama adaptation (xxxi). However, the wording comes from the novel, when Todd tells Colonel Jeffrey that when Thornhill had come for a shave, he had "polished him off" (24). The joke is already there in that the Colonel responds with the question "What do you mean by polishing him off?" (24).

19. Valentine Cunningham points out that such scenes are common in the period (190–99).

20. In *Little Dorrit*, Dickens again refers to cannibal pie-making, when Mrs. F's aunt becomes the center of rumors among "credulous infants" that she had sold herself to a pie-maker to be "made up" into pies (853; bk. 2, ch. 34). Although the Penguin edition's endnote suggests that the popularity of F. Hazleton's stage adaptation *Sweeney Todd, The Barber of Fleet Street; or, The String of Pearls* might be behind this comment (984), Hazelton's version was first performed later, about 1865 at the Old Bower Saloon, Stangate Street, Lambeth (Mack, Introduction xxxii).

21. John Bush Jones points correctly to *Sweeney Todd*'s turning *The Threepenny Opera*'s "metaphorical cannibalism to actual cannibalism" (293).

22. This plot change comes from Bond's 1973 play.

23. For Victorian melodrama, see Michael Booth; Bratton et al.; Elaine Hadley; and Peter Brooks. To a theater historian, Victorian melodrama is a genre of plays

including songs or musical underscoring that allowed performance outside the patent houses of Drury Lane and Covent Garden (where Shakespeare and other "legitimate" or non-musical plays could be performed). Melodramas were characterized by sensational story lines, stock characters, a lack of moral ambiguity, good conquering evil, and emotion over intellect; in fact, the music that defines the genre helps to manipulate the audience's emotional response. However, Sondheim does not seem to have that specific genre of melodrama in mind, nor does he use the term as it appears in common parlance, suggesting the overly dramatic. He defines it "simply as being high theater," "larger than life—in emotion, in subject, and in complication of plot''; he sees little difference between melodrama and tragedy (Gerould 3).

24. Likewise, Ralph Nickleby causes his son Smike's death in ignorance of his true identity. Such mistaken identity tragedy is the stuff melodrama is made of, just as in its comic form it is a staple of farce.

25. Joanne Gordon also makes this observation (*Art Isn't Easy* 220).

26. For a feminist reading of Mrs. Lovett and Johanna, see Mary Jo Lodge 90–94. For a Brechtian reading, comparing her to Mother Courage, see Adler 42.

27. Helena Bonham Carter's interpretation of Sondheim's Mrs. Lovett harks back to Prest's in that she is younger in the film and, in spite of the pale makeup, pretty.

28. The Tim Burton film places the harmonium in her parlor from the beginning, so that—while just as funny—it loses its value as a symbol of their upward mobility.

29. In the novel, because Fagin and Sikes are—in Juliet John's terms—hot and cold sides of the same villain (9), it is as much Fagin as Sikes who kills Nancy in the bedroom, a murder directly resulting from Nancy's motherly protection of Oliver. The musical mitigates Fagin's guilt, but the parallels remain.

30. In some productions Oliver sings this line to Nancy, in some to Bet, in some to both; but, as Bet is a junior version of Nancy, the audience understands through these lines how Oliver feels about the older girl.

31. Toby in the Tim Burton film seems almost as young as Oliver in the musical play and movie, suggesting an intensification of *Oliver!*'s influence. See below for more analysis of this point.

32. Sondheim also says that his initial instinct was to write it as an opera (Gerould 8).

33. *Sweeney Todd* doesn't fit most horror film formulas. See Clover 231–40.

34. In December 2007, I heard another member of the audience whispering to her companion, "It's a musical! Did you know it's a musical? It's a *musical!*" For more about the Doyle productions and the Burton film, see Weltman. See also Calderazzo on Dolye.

35. In *New York*, David Edelstein writes that the sweet-voiced young actor Ed Sanders "splits the difference between Oliver Twist and the Artful Dodger."

36. See Richards 139–59, for a very helpful analysis of King's film.

37. In the film, our last view of a possibly traumatized Johanna is when Todd unaccountably lets her live, still alone in his tonsorial parlor. We never see the young lovers reunite. In the play, Todd was still intent on killing Johanna (whom he thinks is a boy) before he rushes away in response to screams from the basement. Johanna and her lover show up below stairs together, clinging to each other, to see what has happened.

38. This is the topic of my current book project about Victorian materials adapted to Broadway musical theater, to be called "Victorians on Broadway: The Afterlife of Victorian Literature on the American Musical Stage, 1951–2000."

WORKS CITED

Adler, Thomas P. "The Sung and the Said: Literary Value in the Musical Dramas of Stephen Sondheim." *Reading Stephen Sondheim: A Collection of Critical Essays.* Ed. Sandor Goodhart. New York: Garland, 2000. 37–60.

Anglo, Michael. *Penny Dreadfuls and Other Victorian Horrors.* London: Jupiter Books, 1977.

Banfield, Stephen. *Sondheim's Broadway Musicals.* Ann Arbor: U of Michigan P, 1993.

Barthes, Roland. *S/Z.* Tr. Richard Miller. New York: Hill and Wang, 1974.

Block, Geoffrey. *Enchanted Evenings: The Broadway Musical From Showboat to Sondheim.* Oxford: Oxford UP, 1997.

Bond, Christopher. Introduction. *Sweeney Todd: The Demon Barber of Fleet Street.* Stephen Sondheim and Hugh Wheeler. New York: Applause Theatre, 1991.

Booth, Michael. *English Melodrama.* London: H. Jenkins, 1965.

Bratton, Jacqueline, Jim Cook, and Christine Gledhill. *Melodrama: Stage Picture Screen.* London: British Film Institute, 1994.

Brooks, Peter. *The Melodramatic Imagination: Balzac, Henry James, and the Mode of Excess.* New Haven: Yale UP, 1976.

Calderazzo, Diana. "Theory of the Murderous Mind: Understanding the Emotional Intensity of John Doyle's Interpretation of Sondheim's *Sweeney Todd.*" *Theory of Mind and Literature.* Ed. Paula Leverage, Howard Mancing, Richard Schweickert, and Jennifer Marston William. Purdue UP, 2011. 93–103.

Clover, Carol. *Men, Women and Chain Saws: Gender in the Modern Horror Film.* Princeton: Princeton UP, 1992.

Collins, Dick. Introduction. *Sweeney Todd; or, The String of Pearls.* Ware, Hertfordshire: Wordsworth Editions, 2005.

———. Introduction. *Sweeney Todd; or, The String of Pearls.* Ware, Hertfordshire: Wordsworth Editions, 2010.

Covert, Colin. "Bloody Valentine with 'Sweeney Todd.' " *Star Tribune*. 20 Dec. 2007: Entertainment. <http://www.startribune.com/entertainment/movies/12672012.html>.

Cunningham, Valentine. *Everywhere Spoken Against: Dissent in the Victorian Novel.* Oxford: Clarendon, 1975.

Dickens, Charles. *Barnaby Rudge*. Ed. Gordon W. Spence. New York: Penguin, 2003.

———. *Little Dorrit*. Ed. Helen Small & Stephen Wall. New York: Penguin, 2003.

———. *Martin Chuzzlewit*. Ed. Patricia Ingham. New York: Penguin, 2000.

———. *Nicholas Nickleby*. Ed. Mark Ford. New York: Penguin, 1999.

———. *Old Curiosity Shop*. Ed. Norman Page. New York: Penguin, 2001

———. *Oliver Twist*. Ed. Fred Kaplan. New York: W. W. Norton, 1993.

———. *Pickwick Papers*. Ed. Mark Wormald. New York: Penguin, 2000.

———. *Sketches by Boz*. Ed. Dennis Walder. New York: Penguin, 1996.

Dunnett, Roderic. *"Insignificance*, Royal Theatre, Northampton." *Independent.* Theatre and Dance. 24 May 2004. <http://www.independent.co.uk/arts-entertainment/theatre-dance/reviews/insignificance-royal-theatre-northampton-564527.html>. Accessed 8 Feb. 8, 2009.

Edelstein, David. "It's a Gusher!" *New York* online edition. 24 Dec. 2007. <http://nymag.com/movies/reviews/42087/index1.html>.

Eder, Richard. *New York Times*. 2 Mar. 1979. <http://theater.nytimes.com/mem/theater/treview.html?html_title=&tols_title=SWEENEY%20TODD%20%28PLAY%29&pdate=19790302&byline=By%20RICHARD%20EDER&id=1077011431620>. Accessed 5 Mar. 2011.

Gerould, Daniel. "Larger than Life: Reflections on Melodrama and Sweeney Todd." *New York Literary Forum* 7 (1980): 3–14.

Goodhart, Sandor. "Introduction: Reading Sondheim, The End of Ever After." *Reading Stephen Sondheim: A Collection of Critical Essays*. Ed. Sandor Goodhart. New York: Garland, 2000. 3–36.

Gordon, Joanne. *Art Isn't Easy: The Achievement of Stephen Sondheim*. Carbondale: Southern Illinois UP, 1990.

———. *Stephen Sondheim: A Casebook*. New York: Garland, 1997.

Grout, Donald Jay, and Hermine Weigel Williams. *A Short History of Opera*. Columbia UP, 2003.

James, Louis. *Fiction for the Working Man, 1830–1850*. London: Oxford UP, 1963.

John, Juliet. *Dickens's Villains: Melodrama, Character, and Popular Culture.* Oxford: Oxford UP, 2003.

Jones, John Bush. *Our Musicals, Ourselves: A Social History of the American Musical Theatre.* London: Brandeis UP, 2003.

Hadley, Elaine. *Melodramatic Tactics: Theatricalized Dissent in the English Marketplace, 1800–1885.* Palo Alto: Stanford UP, 1995.

Haining, Peter. *Sweeney Todd: The Real Story of the Demon Barber of Fleet Street.* New York: Barnes & Noble, 1993.

Law, Graham. *Serializing Fiction in the Victorian Press.* London: Palgrave, 2000.

Ledger, Sally. *Dickens and Popular Radical Imagination.* Cambridge: Cambridge UP, 2007.

Lodge, Mary Jo. "From Madness to Melodramas to Musicals: The Women of *Lady Audley's Secret* and *Sweeney Todd.*" *Theatre Annual: A Journal of Performance Studies* 56 (Fall 2003): 78–96.

Mack, Robert. Introduction. *Sweeney Todd: The Demon Barber of Fleet Street.* Ed. Robert Mack. Oxford: Oxford UP, 2007.

———. *The Wonderful and Surprising History of Sweeney Todd: The Life and Times of an Urban Legend.* London: Continuum International, 2007.

McNulty, Charles. "Fleet Street Blues." Theater. *The Village Voice.* 9 Mar. 2004. <http://www.villagevoice.com/2004-03-09/theater/fleet-street-blues/1>. Accessed 8 Feb. 2009.

McMillan, Scott. *The Musical as Drama.* Princeton, NJ: Princeton UP, 2006.

Morley, Malcolm. "Dickens' Contributions to Sweeney Todd." *The Dickensian* 58.337 (Spring 1962): 92–95.

Oliver! Book, music, and lyrics by Lionel Bart. Directed by Peter Coe. Designed by Sean Kinney. Starring Ron Moody and Georgia Brown. New Theatre London. Opened 30 June 1960. 2,618 performances.

[Prest, Thomas Peckett and James Malcolm Rymer.] *The String of Pearls: A Romance. The People's Periodical and Family Library.* Ed. Edward Lloyd. 21 Nov. 1846–20 Mar. 1847, in 18 numbers.

Richards, Jeffrey. "Tod Slaughter and the Cinema of Excess." *The Unknown 1930s: An Alternative History of the British Cinema, 1929–39.* Ed. Jeffrey Richards. New York: IB Tauris, 1998. 139–60.

Scott, A. O. "Murder Most Musical." *New York Times.* 21 Dec. 2007: Movie Review. <http://movies.nytimes.com/2007/12/21/movies/21swee.html?ref=movies>. Accessed 5 Mar. 2011.

Smith, Helen. *New Light on Sweeney Todd, Thomas Peckett Prest, James Malcolm Rymer and Elizabeth Caroline Grey.* London: Jarndyce Books, 2002.

Sweeney Todd; or, The String of Pearls. Ed. Dick Collins. Ware, Hertfordshire: Wordsworth Editions, 2005; 2010.

Sweeney Todd: The Demon Barber of Fleet Street. Directed by Tim Burton. Starring Johnny Depp, Helena Bonham Carter, Alan Rickman, Sacha Baron Cohen, and Laura Michelle Kelly. Paramount Pictures. Dec. 2007. (DVD Apr. 2008.)

Sweeney Todd: The Demon Barber of Fleet Street. Music and Lyrics by Stephen Sondheim. Book by Hugh Wheeler. Directed and Designed by John Doyle. Starring Michael Cerveris and Patti Lupone. Eugene O'Neill Theatre, New York City. Opened 3 Nov. 2005. 384 performances.

Sweeney Todd: The Demon Barber of Fleet Street. Music and Lyrics by Stephen Sondheim. Book by Hugh Wheeler. Directed by Harold Prince. Starring Angela Lansbury and Len Cariou. Uris Theater, New York City. Opened 1 Mar. 1979. 557 Performances.

Weltman, Sharon Aronofsky. "Sondeheim's *Sweeney Todd* on Stage and Screen." *Victorian Literature and Culture* 37.1 (2009): 301–10.

Winer, Linda. "A Touch of the Original." *Newsday.* 4 Nov. 2005: Entertainment. n.p. <http://www.newsday.com/entertainment/stage/am-sweeneytodd,0,7817573.story>. Accessed 8 Feb. 2009.

Dickens's Immaterial Culture of Hats and *The Pickwick Papers*

Mark M. Hennelly, Jr.

Typified by Pickwick's altercation over his nightcap in the Fleet, The Pickwick Papers *provides a "diffusion of hats [and] bonnets" that perform proverbial, idiomatic and slang, class, gender, moral, psychological, and popular-culture roles. Dickens's immersion in the worlds of melodrama and the carnivalesque gives some clarifying context to his many hat performances, as do examples from his other works, relevant articles from* Household Words *and* All the Year Round, *and Carlyle's influence in* Sartor Resartus. *The result is not so much an exposé of Dickens's response to Victorian material culture as his exposure of the* immaterial *culture of hats. In fact, Dickens teaches readers how to do things with hats and even how hats themselves do things as his characters meaningfully obey, test, and violate Victorian hat codes and their cultural messages. Three sustained examples—Sam's lost hat adventure and consequent kissing game with Mary, Pickwick's exposing his nightcap to Miss Witherfield in the Great White Horse Inn, and, most prominently, Pickwick's chasing his hat in a field near Chatham barracks—significantly demonstrate these issues.*

> There are very few moments in a man's existence when he experiences so much ludicrous distress, or meets with so little charitable commiseration, as when he is in pursuit of his own hat.—Charles Dickens, *The Pickwick Papers*

Dickens Studies Annual, Volume 42, Copyright © 2011 by AMS Press, Inc. All rights reserved.

To refashion the old adage, in Charles Dickens's fiction a man's hat is his castle, his inside displaying itself habitually outside his outside, often as his crowning glory. Dickens's representation of Pickwick as an "angel in tights and gaiters" (734; ch. 45) has surely become iconic, but it also seems iconoclastic because it neglects the angel's haloing hat.[1] As Robert Patten notes, the Victorians themselves adopted "Pickwick hats" in homage to their original owner (Introduction 19), and John Bowen even cites "the cult of the Pickwick hat" (*Other Dickens* 47). Moreover, Dickens's typical head-to-toe descriptions of Pickwick, "from the crown of his hat to the lowest button of his gaiters" (385; ch. 22), prominently feature it.

Nevertheless, Dickens's focus on a "diffusion of hats [and] bonnets" (161; ch. 7), whether Pickwick's or those of others, may seem counterintuitive given those famous gaiters and the text's emphasis on Sam Weller's profession of bootblack, "in whose mind the inmates [of the White Hart Inn] were always represented by that particular article of their costume, which came under his immediate superintendence": whether "a wooden leg in number six"; "a pair of Hessians in thirteen"; or "painted tops in the snuggery inside the bar" (205; ch. 10). Perhaps Dickens's traumatic childhood labor at Warren's boot-blacking warehouse drove his literary predilections from heels to hats, though only after a parting shot at his old nemesis: Sam's gleaming "polish . . . would have struck envy to the soul of the amiable Mr Warren (for they used Day and Martin [blacking] at the White Hart)" (199; ch. 10). Still, Dickens does dramatize suggestive links between bonnets and boots in *Pickwick*, comically reversing and democratizing the occult theory of correspondences, as above so below, into the carnivalesque metaphysic of the *mundus inversus*, in heaven as it is on earth.[2]

But while Sam, the White Hart's resident "boots," may sometimes ground Pickwick and his blessed bonnet, hats more often transcend the grounds of realism. And hats are memorably associated with young Dickens's week-long-awaited "way home" Saturday evenings from Warren's to his family at the Marshalsea prison. As the older Dickens waxes nostalgic in his autobiographical fragment, "[t]here were two or three hat-manufactories" on Blackfriars road; "and among the things which, encountered anywhere, or under any circumstances, will instantly recall [my home-coming], is the smell of hat-making." Dickens also recalls his "poor white hat" (Forster 32–34), a relic of his abandoned schooling, which Michael Slater finds "a poignant reminder" of Dickens's "lost middle-class status" (10). In "Arcadian London" Dickens's narrative persona even posits that his "lodgings are at a hatter's—my own hatter's," and so he "live[s] surrounded by human hats" in this "hatter hermitage," including "seaside wide-awakes, shooting caps, and a choice of rough water-proof head-gear for the moors and mountains" (*The Uncommercial Traveller* 159, 168). On the other hand, "Fashions," an anonymous 1860 article in *All the Year Round*, balances Dickens's personal nostalgia for hats with a paradoxical, public celebration of them: "hair and head-dresses . . . are the most wild and wonderful of all the wild and wonderful things man has from time to time fashioned for his disfigurement" (127). In short, hats are perhaps the most idiosyncratic objects in Dickens's wildly over-populated and over-determined kingdom of thingdom. What is more, hats are objects that paradoxically construct and deconstruct the subject (position) in Dickens, both in terms of its subjectivity and its agency.

I

This essay is about the often conflicting, performative roles of Dickensian hats, with particular attention to *The Pickwick Papers* (1836–37). In their proverbial, idiomatic and slang, class, gender, moral, psychological, and popular-culture performances, hats function much more importantly than as mere costume accessories, part of the blur of background details that most reading experiences overlook. If J. Hillis Miller is correct, and *Pickwick* presents its readers with "a restless flitting to and fro of objects . . . [that] can no longer be distinguished from one another" (*Charles Dickens* 15), our task is to slow down Dickens's blitz of things and focus attention on headgear, just as Thomas Carlyle focuses on fashion in *Sartor Resartus* (1833–34), a major influence on Dickens.[3] Admittedly, this task may appear as ridiculous or "ludicrous" as Pickwick chasing his own hat; and Catherine Robson courts just such a critical caveat when she parodies crafting an essay on Carker's teeth in *Dombey and Son*:

> The textual insistence on those brilliant white teeth obviously demands investigation: a concise summary of the history of false teeth, with particular attention to the nineteenth century, would be provided, and a number of illustrations supplied (pictures from advertisements run in periodicals around the time of the novel's publication in serial parts would clearly be preferable, but others would serve at a pinch). And if our scholar could find Dickens saying something about false teeth in a letter, or somewhere in his journalism, all the better—failing that, any anecdote about a Victorian and his dentures would do. (245–46)

Robson continues for several more funny (and accurate) sentences, playfully exposing boilerplated academic strategies. She concludes, however, by emphasizing that "it is perhaps the prospect of the unending potential for enjoyable and revealing inquiry which justifiably continues to attract new scholars to the historical study of Dickens" (248). The irony is that Dickens also exposes artificial or naively scholarly misreadings of texts in uproarious episodes like "the Pickwick controversy" over Pickwick's "erudite speculations on the meaning of the inscription" (229, 227; ch. 11) on the rum rune he discovers and Serjeant Buzfuz's forensic analysis, during the breach-of-promise trial, of "Chops and Tomata sauce" (562; ch. 34) in Pickwick's letter to Mrs. Bardell. Perhaps this is why Mr. Blotton judges "the gigantic brain of Pickwick" to be "a humbug in a Pickwickian point of view" after Pickwick calls him a "haberdasher" (68, 72, 71; ch. 1) and why illustrator H. K. Browne crowns that "gigantic brain" with such a ridiculously small, nondescript, and unassuming hat.[4] As an 1845 article in *Blackwood's Magazine* suggests, "[t]he hat is, beyond all doubt, one of the strangest vestigial anomalies in the nineteenth century" (qtd. in Briggs 260).

While the present study doesn't claim to be particularly new historicist, Robson's near self-satire is well-taken, and any critic of Victorian material culture needs to be wary of slavishly cloning such totalizing strategies, but must still remain aware of the desired goal—"enjoyable and revealing inquiry." Put differently, the role of hats in Dickens's fiction does, indeed, waver between the philosophically ridiculous and profound ridicule, between serious sentiment and sartorial satire—in the words of *All the Year Round*, "[t]here is much philosophy, as everybody knows, or should know, in the wearing of hats" (qtd. in Briggs 260). Or, as Dickens's tell-tale phrase "ludicrous distress" above suggests, hats imply something ludic or performatively playful at the same time that their signifying practices may produce intense narrative emphasis, stressful drama, and the consequent hope for rescue and redemption from such pressures. In Peter Brooks's sense of the term, there's something inherently *melodramatic* about Dickens's Mad-Hatter routines: "the term *melodrama* most readily suggests an exciting and spectacular drama of persecuted innocence and virtue triumphant" (26). In fact, Brooks's leading example in *The Melodramatic Imagination* involves Balzac's Raphaël surrendering his hat to a mysterious stranger just before betting his final franc on roulette's revolving wheel of fortune in *Le Peau de chagrin* (1830). In Brooks's translation,

> Is this some scriptural and providential parable? Isn't it rather a way of concluding a diabolical contract by exacting from you a sort of security? Or may it be to oblige you to maintain a respectful demeanour toward those who are about to win your money? Is it the police, lurking in the sewers of society, trying to find out your hatter's name, or your own, if you've inscribed it on the headband? Or is it, finally, to measure your skull in order to compile an instructive statistic on the cranial capacity of gamblers?

Brooks's analysis of this passage is as generally true of Dickens as it is particularly true of Balzac, whose "narrator applies pressure to the gesture, pressure through interrogation, through the evocation of more and more fantastic possibilities, to make it yield meaning, to make it give up to consciousness its full potential as 'parable' " (1). Thus, Balzac anticipates Sherlock

Holmes's forensic inferences from the size, shape, age, quality, accessories, re-coloring, residual hair, odor, and dusty condition of "a very ordinary black hat" in "The Blue Carbuncle" (1892): namely, that the missing owner "was highly intellectual . . . and also that he was fairly well-to-do within the last three years, although he has now fallen upon evil days. He had foresight, but has less now than formerly, pointing to a moral retrogression, which . . . seems to indicate some evil influence, probably drink, at work upon him. This may account also for the obvious fact that his wife has ceased to love him" (Doyle 377–78). In Dickens's fiction, however, meaning derives not so often from the appearance of hats as from their performative activities as the Inimitable teaches his readers how to do things with hats, or even how hats themselves do things.[5] In this context, Catherine Waters relevantly empha- sizes contributors' repeated "device" of "the animation of commodities" (16) in *Household Words* articles. But Waters curiously neglects Mary Boyle and Dickens's co-authored (Lohrli 74) "My Mahogany Friend" (1851), the title of which refers to a talking "Hat-stand" that sports all sorts of personi- fied and performing "hats and caps," including "an Oxford boating hat, and a velvet hunting cap, and a steeple-chase cap, and a German travelling cap," not to mention an extremely rambunctious, "dark blue foraging cap" (558, 560). In *American Notes* (1842), Dickens even scripts, in dramatic form, a lengthy talking-hats, comic stichomythia between Mr. "STRAW HAT" and Mr. "BROWN HAT," illustrating Americans' compulsive repetition of "Yes, sir" (232–34; ch. 14) and thus the undistinguished sameness which he finds symptomatic of leveling, populist democracy.

The following example from Pickwick's first night in the Fleet suggests, then, that hats provide much more than "just" hyperbolic melodrama when Smangle, a clownish wag wearing "one of the common eighteenpenny French skull-caps, with a gawdy tassel dangling therefrom," addresses the night- capped Pickwick, who has been dozing in "the warden's room" (see fig. 1):

"Allow me to have the felicity of hanging up your nightcap, sir."
   With this, the speaker snatched that article of dress from Mr Pickwick's head, and fixed it in a twinkling on that of the drunken [Zephyr], who, firmly impressed with the belief that he was delighting a numerous assembly, contin- ued to hammer away at [a] comic song in the most melancholy strains imag- inable.
   Taking a man's nightcap from his brow by violent means, and adjusting it on the head of an unknown gentleman of dirty exterior, however ingenious a witticism in itself, is unquestionably one of those which come under the denomination of practical jokes. Viewing the matter precisely in this light, Mr Pickwick, without the slightest intimation of his purpose, sprang vigorously out of bed, struck the Zephyr so smart a blow in the chest as to deprive him of a considerable portion of the commodity which sometimes bears his name, and then, recapturing his nightcap, boldly placed himself in an attitude of defence.

Fig. 1. Hablot Browne's "The Warden's Room"

This entire overcharged episode (670–75; ch. 41) provides an intersection of several popular traditions, genres, modes, and motifs. With references to Shakespeare, "the Opera House," "costume," Mivins's "performing the most popular steps of a hornpipe, with a slang and burlesque caricature of grace and lightness," and Pickwick's histrionic "attitude," the surreal "scene" performatively develops into a comic theater of cruelty, or what Michael André Bernstein calls a "bitter carnival," one which both supports and subverts its melodramatic motifs.[6] Put somewhat differently, its game of pass-the-hat shuttles generically between a kind of *pantomime dialoguée* with Dickens's narrative "intertitles" providing only a "skeletal structure of verbal meanings" (Brooks x)—which Browne's illustration and the reader's imagination flesh out—and, conversely, a pompously mocking kind of self-conscious street "patter," defined by Deborah Vlock as "a *manipulation* of language which results in increased trade. . . . it represents deviance from the 'proper' methods of speech and commerce, and locates itself among working-class transients who violate capitalist industry, engaging in illegitimate forms of work" (119). Here Dickens's patter, like so many cagey narratives in *Sketches by Boz* (1835) and like the cheapjack narrator of *Dr. Marigold's Prescriptions* (1865), markets its literary "commodity" to the reader, just as Smangle's cadging sells the codger's need for sherry and cigars to Pickwick. Further, this bedroom farce focusing on Pickwick's nightcap partially restages his hilarious "horrors of a night-cap" (408; ch. 24) interlude with Miss Witherfield, which, as we will see, comically rehearses this episode. And the hornpipe prefigures Dickens's frequent use of the *danse macabre* motif from the *Vanitas* tradition in which a group of motley mummers promenade witlessly toward the grave, here located in the Fleet's underground. Smangle and Pickwick, graphically paired in Browne's illustration with fool's cap tassels, are doubled as fools, as is the Zephyr when he dons Pickwick's nightcap.[7]

This dramatic interchange illustrates just how overdetermined hats can become in *Pickwick*, since the nightcap, suspended between costume and prop, worn at the body's upper boundary, and often functioning as a fifth limb or somatic threshold, seems invested with gnostic revelations regarding the body as template for the universe, especially its upper and lower hemispheres. Indeed melodrama, like carnival, vacillates in "a continual vertical movement between extremes" as it stages its own "manichaeistic struggle of good and evil, light and darkness" (Brooks 134, 167), like Pickwick with his "solar drama" enacting "a creation myth, the birth of light and order out of chaotic darkness" (Miller, *Illustration* 97). We will see that hats also function as conjurers' caps or even pantomimic wands—transitional objects (in D. W. Winnicott's sense of the expression) or fort-da passports to the semiotic imaginary, which Brooks generally locates in melodrama: "this realm of signs that organize and decipher the world" (45).[8]

In *Gargantua and Pantagruel,* Rabelais lists more than two hundred types of fools (340–42; bk. 3, ch. 38); but here the con man Smangle, dandified by his "French" headdress, personifies the "artificial fool," while the dunce-capped and duped Pickwick, who later "innocently" buys rounds of sherry for all in a Pickwickian gesture of clubby male-bonding, becomes the "natural fool." Thus both personify the two primary carnivalesque types.[9] The dialogic between "comic song" and "melancholy strains" further suggests dual-bodied carnivalesque ambivalence, as does Dickens's repeated focus on "laughter," drunkenness, Pickwick's "pantaloons," mock-billingsgate banter like "Curse me!" and the "carnivalesque game of names" and spirited "theme of 'wind' " vested in the inflated, then deflated Zephyr (Bakhtin, *Rabelais* 461; *Dialogic Imagination* 188–89). At the same time, Pickwick ambiguously plays an unlaughing "agelast"—the somber and sober senior who must be cyclically disgraced and replaced (Bakhtin, *Rabelais* 267–68)—plus "the *veillard généreux* of melodrama [or] representative of an earlier and nobler generation" (Brooks 165) and a clownish rustic or rube.[10]

The nightcap exchanges dramatize both carnival's characteristic, class-conscious act of uncrowning and crowning and melodrama's democratic origins in the French Revolution (the synecdochic relationship linking crown and hat and metonymic relationships between crown and head and crown and currency—hat crown and half-crown—seem critical here). These origins are semiotically recalled to life by the republican blue and later red "indispensable cap[s]," the Liberty or Phrygian bonnets, of "ubiquitous Jacques" (197, 203; bk. 2, ch. 15) in *A Tale of Two Cities* (1859), which trace the Revolution's exchange of airy idealism for a terrifying reign of bloody uncrownings that Brooks would see as "representative of the struggle of the sign of innocence toward liberty" (51).[11] In the same way, Pickwick's retaliation against Smangle's attempt at scapegoating his "innocence" seems a class-coded comeuppance to this ironically "admirable specimen of a class of gentry." In fact, Jonathan Arac writes of the crowning "and uncrowning of the king of carnival" in a way that clarifies Pickwick's ultimate release from the Fleet: "In this cyclical process the pathos within the jollity becomes evident, the sadness of vicissitude and death as well as the promise of change and renewal" (487).[12] And thus Dickens's crowning glory of hats also often functions as his *crowning story* of hats. For example, Dickens enjoys some obvious fun with crowning and uncrowning in the inset tale "The True Legend of Prince Bladud" when "King Lud flew into a frightful rage, tossed his crown up to the ceiling, and caught it again—for in those days kings kept their crown on their heads, and not in the Tower" (599; ch. 36). The Zephyr's "comic song" with its "most melancholy strains" may itself recall the Cockney ballad "All Round my Hat" that Dickens features in "The Last Cab Driver" (*Sketches by Boz*), "which was then just beginning to form a recognized portion of our national music" (175). The singer of this ditty, a street patterer, wears a "greenie willow" around his hat to commemorate his lover, who has been deported for theft, and to signify that his affection will remain evergreen until her desired return ("All Round My Hat" Web). Readers can imagine the imprisoned debtors in this scene both identifying with and burlesquing such musical sentiments—and, indeed, "music is inherent to [melodrama's] representations" (Brooks 48).[13] Such issues remain to be developed; the goal here has been to provide a brief summary of the diverse motifs riddling this suggestive example.

II

Earlier I discussed the material culture of hats in Victorian England; but perhaps a more accurate phrase would be the immaterial culture of hats, which might be expected from an uncommercial traveller like Dickens and which, with help from his other novels and Thomas Carlyle, can suggest the relevant, if often ephemeral, cultural precedents and practices of hats in *The Pickwick Papers*.[14] That is, though hats in Dickens's works may appear immaterial or irrelevant, their real relevance actually transcends their materiality and becomes "immaterial." Dickens seems less interested in the specific styles of hats he invokes than, again, in their frenzied kinetics and free-floating and fleeting semiotics, which translate into a gestural hat language in his fiction, one that includes proverbial sayings, idioms, and slang, class- and gender-conscious social etiquette, and popular entertainment representations. The result is more than a hat-bound comedy of manners or even Brooks's "melodrama of manners" (131), but rather a kind of historically thick, heteroglossic riff on head coverings, one which challenges cultural codes (as much as conforming to them).

And so, like the "multitude of plans and speculations, . . . hovering in all their heterogeneous confusion and disorder, round the puckered cap of the [sleeping] little Paul" (148; ch. 7) in *Dombey and Son* (1846–48), hats play a number of contradictory roles in Dickens. For example, in *A Tale of Two Cities*, the significance of hats is sometimes manifestly clear. During the French Revolution, the "raggedest nightcap, awry on the wretchedest head, had this crooked significance in it: 'I know how hard it has grown for me, the wearer of this, to support life in myself; but do you know how easy it has grown for me, the wearer of this, to destroy life in you [the nobility and its minions]?' " (250; bk. 2, ch. 22). Some hat melodramas may seem inconsequential until we later learn their secret significance, such as when Madame Defarge "pin[s] her rose in her head-dress" (209–10; bk. 2, ch. 16) to identify Barsad as a spy to the Jacquerie, which also prefigures "the prevailing Republican colour" of the revolutionary red caps or "Redheads"

(315; bk. 3, ch. 6; 318; bk. 3, ch. 7), if not the French "people rising from [the] abyss" (404; bk. 3, ch. 15). Some other idiosyncratic head coverings may appear gratuitous or meaningful merely as expressions of Dickens's delight in grotesquerie, such as Jerry Cruncher's "old cocked-hat like a three-cornered spittoon," Miss Pross's "most wonderful bonnet like a Grenadier wooden measure . . . or a great Stilton cheese," and Sydney Carton's "eccentricities of damp head-gear [which] no words can describe" when he attempts to sober himself by "fold[ing wet towels] on his head in a manner hideous to behold" (45; bk. 1, ch. 3; 58; bk. 1, ch. 4; 119, 118; bk. 2, ch. 5). Nevertheless, Cruncher does habitually enjoy eating and spitting "out straw," which serves as a parodic counterpart to Foulon's being forced to eat "bunches of grass and straw" by the revolutionaries after infamously telling "the famished people that they might eat grass." Miss Pross's bonnet prefigures her character's epic battle defending Lucie against Madame Defarge ("Grenadier") and her championing all things English ("Stilton cheese"), while Carton's comic ablutions with his "turban" both recall him to life and prepare for his ultimate self-sacrifice: "For the first time in many years, he had no strong drink" (88; bk. 2, ch. 1; 254, 251; bk. 2, ch. 22; 395; bk. 3, ch. 14; 168; bk. 2, ch. 11; 368; bk. 3, ch. 12). More to the present point, Pickwick may often stand "hat in hand, bowing with the utmost politeness and respect" (422; ch. 25), and Sam may "always" introduce his "conversation with his master" by "a touch of the hat" (383; ch. 22); but Pickwick also indecently exposes his nightcap to a lady, and Sam deploys his hat in sexual foreplay with Mary, besides sometimes touching his hat in mock, or at least deferred, deference to Pickwick when his "master" needs to be taught a lesson.

Some of the (Victorian) proverbs and idioms involving hats are still voiced today; some have been silent for scores of years (such as forgotten slang like "tile" and "castor"). For example, in *Pickwick* when a Fleet prisoner, who "look[s] like a drunken chaplain" wearing "a "seal-skin cap," pontificates, "if I knew as little of life as [Pickwick], I'd eat my hat and swallow the buckle whole" (682–83; ch. 41), his cliché suggests a humbling loss of selfhood at the same time that it exposes his own self-righteousness. In *The Old Curiosity Shop* (1840–41), "the gayest feather in Miss Monflathers's cap" is that her boarding school boasts of attracting "a baronet's daughter" (312; ch. 31); and this fashionable idiom ironically reflects her old-fashioned (according to Dickens) class values in humiliating little Nell. In *Hard Times* (1854), Tom taunts his sister Louisa with being "mercenary" when she refuses to charm her husband Bounderby, whom she married mainly for her brother's sake, into further advancing Tom's schemes: " 'You know whether the cap fits you, Loo,' returned her brother sulkily. 'If it does, you can wear it' " (203; bk 2, ch. 7). And this self-incriminating version of "if the shoe fits, wear it," identifies Tom's own, not Louisa's, cupiditas. Similarly, Tom's commonplace evaluation of Mrs. Sparsit's jealousy of Louisa and her feigned compassion for Bounderby, "Mother Sparsit never set her cap at Bounderby when he was a bachelor" (169; bk. 2, ch. 3), remains transparent while implying the often erotic, and even fetishistic, nature of hats.[15] On the other hand, Bitzer's bromide, "While my hat covers my family, [I will feed them]," is no longer in usage; but his revision of its inclusivity to "I have only one [family member] to feed, and that's the person I most like to feed" (152; bk. 2, ch. 1) clearly identifies and indicts Bitzer's self-centered, utilitarian philosophy of Number One. In *Little Dorrit* (1855–57), Tip illogically charges his father William Dorrit with "trying on other people's hats" (428; bk. 1, ch. 31) for attempting to impose his patriarchal values on his rebellious son; but most common readers understand his somewhat tortured meaning. When Dora in *David Copperfield* (1849–50) melodramatically sends her engagement ring back to David, "enclosed in a despairing cocked-hat note, wherein she used the terrible expression that 'our love had begun in folly, and ended in madness!' " (551; ch. 33), modern readers may guess that the phrase "cocked-hat note" describes a message folded like a cocked hat. They may not realize, however, that "cocked hats" in Dickens often suggest a cocky, role-playing wearer like beadle Bumble in *Oliver Twist* (1837–38), as opposed to belittled Oliver wearing a "little brown-cloth parish cap" and so bowing as much to Bumble's "cocked hat" as he does to the bumptious, bumbling beadle (53, 52; ch. 2), just as Dora's cocked-hat epistle is characteristically histrionic and disingenuous at this early stage of her life.[16]

The contemporary phrase "thinking cap" appears literally or figuratively as "conjuror's cap" or "considering cap" in Dickens. For instance, when Wemmick tells Pip in *Great Expectations* (1860–61), "I'll put on my considering-cap, and I think all you want to do, may be done by degrees" (314; ch. 37) to provide professional opportunities for Herbert Pocket, the text implies more than that Wemmick will simply put his mind to the matter. "Considering cap" further bears the pantomimic connotation of a "wishing hat" or even Good Fairy's magic wand, which suggests that Pip is finally emulating his unselfish benefactor Magwitch in transforming Herbert into a gentleman of means, one, like now reformed Pip, who already happened to be a genial, generous, and gentle man. In *Little Dorrit*, the inventor Daniel Doyce has a "peculiar way of tilting up his hat at the back every now and then, as if he were contemplating some half-finished work of his hand and thinking about it" (163; bk. 1, ch. 10) through the figurative agency of his thinking cap. The poet Mr. Slum in *The Old Curiosity Shop* keeps his conjuring "hat . . . full of scraps of paper," one of which allows him to transform the acrostic for "Warren" into "a positive inspiration for Jarley" (282; ch. 28), the managing madam of the traveling waxworks Nell encounters, as a hat again magically transcends boots and Dickens's traumatic past at Warren's blacking warehouse. Like his maker, Slum seems capable of pulling virtually anything out of his hat. As Carlyle told Dickens, "Charley, you carry a whole company of actors under your own hat" (qtd. in Andrews, *Charles Dickens and His Performing Selves* 28).

Finally, the forgotten slang term "bonneting," which word and which practice Dickens also invokes frequently, means to humiliate, or at least tease, someone by "knock[ing]" his (usually a male's) hat "over his eyes" as Sam does to his unrecognized father when Tony Weller, in a comedy of errors, unintentionally steps on his son's toes: "You're a dutiful and affectionate little boy, you are, ain't you? . . . to come a bonnetin' your father in his old age?" Sam replies, "How should I know who you wos?" (698; ch. 43). The context here suggests that "bonneting" can mask or disguise identity—the hooded self—though ordinarily hats help reveal or even create selfhood. As Catherine Waters suggests of *Household Words* contributor George Sala, his "consciousness [in fashion articles] of the role of clothing in the performance of social identity leads to an understanding of the ways in which dress is not so much an expression, as an embodiment, of the selfhood of the wearer" (153). Further, though hats usually shelter their owner, they can also be employed in (ironic) self-defense and as weapons in scapegoating rituals, which abound in Dickens's novels. As the candle-lit Ghost of Christmas Past dramatizes in *A Christmas Carol* (1843), Ebenezer Scrooge has self-defensively " 'bonneted' " (44; stave 2) himself against the humanizing memories of missed opportunities to exchange his love of gold for the gold of love: "from the crown of its head there sprung a bright clear jet of light, . . . which was doubtless the occasion of its using, in its duller moments, a great extinguisher for a cap, which it now held under its arm" (42; stave 2). Terrified of being literally recalled to enlightened life, if not acknowledging its brief candle, Scrooge "seized the extinguisher-cap, and by a sudden action pressed it down upon [the Ghost's] head." Prefiguring Redlaw's recovered memory in *The Haunted Man* (1848) and the mantra DNF (Do Not Forget) in *Little Dorrit*, however, Scrooge could no longer "hide the light: which streamed from under [the cap], in an unbroken flood upon the ground" (65; stave 2). As indicated earlier, scapegoating usually involves uncrowning rather than bonneting. In *Little Dorrit*, though, when Pancks scapegoats Casby, the miserly landlord of Bleeding Heart Yard, after paying mock homage to "The Casby's Head," he both uncrowns and bonnets "The Last of the Patriarchs" in one decapitating and castrating, melodramatic flourish: Pancks "whipped out a pair of shears, swooped upon the Patriarch behind, and snipped off short the sacred locks that flowed upon his shoulders. In a paroxysm of animosity and rapidity, Mr Pancks then caught the broad-brimmed hat out of the astounded Patriarch's hand, and cut it down into a mere stewpan, and fixed it on the Patriarch's head" (871–72; bk. 2, ch. 32).

Breezy, tongue-in-cheek articles on hats in *Household Words*, like Henry Fothergill Chorley's "The Brown Hat" (1850) and Henry Morley's "A Hint to Hatters" (1851), use head coverings as figures with economic, historical, national, and even international significance. They habitually employ word play like "those whose thoughts are 'wide-awake' " (Chorley 133), punning on "wideawake" hats—named "according to *Punch* because they had no nap" (Briggs 268)—and metaphors such as hats "are an absurd roofing for the capital of the human column" (Morley 419), to fashion literary values. In this context, and besides referencing idiomatic proverbs and slang in Dickens, hats also reflect Victorian class, gender, and social (if not moral) standards and thus again serve as one of Brooks's melodramatic "signs that organize and decipher the world" (45). In *Hats*, Fiona Clark emphasizes both the immaterial culture of hats and their practical performances: "It is important to note that men's hats have tended to make a symbolic statement, rather than a purely visual one," suggesting "bourgeois authority, . . . democracy and revolution." On the other hand, the female "hat remained a symbol of emancipation during the eighteenth and nineteenth centuries. . . . The etiquette of hat wearing for men hinges largely on the removal of the hat, for women on its retention." In Victorian times "one gentleman would doff his hat to another if of higher status or greater age, and always to a lady, and her escort" (6–7, 85–86). Alison Gernsheim, in *Victorian and Edwardian Fashion*, significantly adds that "in outdoor costume, women were shut in and protected" (26) by prophylactic kinds of bonnets, which seem emblematic of cultural repression—the need to hood or veil a female's sexuality vested in her hair.[17]

In a remark that seems particularly relevant to the anxieties of certain male characters in Dickens, Clark suggests that Victorian men carried their hats indoors during social calls for a "subtle" reason "based on the supposition that the masculine caller feels himself privileged in being permitted to pay his respects, and, feeling himself on sufferance is ready to leave at a moment, hat in hand, should he not find his presence agreeable and acceptable" (86). However, when an American "constantly walked in and out of the room with his hat on," Dickens notes it "as characteristic of the country: not at all as being matter of complaint" (*American Notes* 240; ch. 14), indicating his tolerance for diverse cultural practices. Thomas Hill's conduct manual, *The Essential Handbook of Victorian Etiquette*, makes the point that one of the shibboleths associated with keeping one's headgear handy indoors is "Do not fidget with your . . . hat" (31), which becomes the exception rather than the rule in Dickens. A single example of the social subtlety of such hat gestures, which most readers take for granted, must suffice here. When middle-class Arthur Clennam simply removes his hat before working-class Mrs. Plornish in *Little Dorrit*, she responds, "It ain't many that comes into a poor place [like Bleeding Heart Yard], that deems it worth their while to move their hats. . . . But [poor] people think more of it than [other] people think'' (178; bk. 1, ch. 12).

Dickens's characters meaningfully obey, test, and violate these cultural dress codes as his hat language becomes a gestural idiolect with its own transgressive, "complete code of telegraphic nods and gestures" (*Pickwick* 700; ch. 43) that peculiarly defines (and distinguishes among) personalities, while at the same time both labeling and leveling social differences. Thus, hats not only transfer the inside to outside the outside, but also trope the trajectory of external influences upon subjectivity. Daniel Doyce "had an old workmanlike habit of carrying his pocket-handkerchief in his hat" (*Little Dorrit* 354; bk. 1, ch. 26), which ironically suggests how his working-class origins uphold his creative, if not artistic genius, while Kit Nubbles can be framed for carrying a "bank-note" in "his hat" (*The Old Curiosity Shop* 550; ch. 60) because the working class typically used hats as containers and were just as typically typecast as thieves by legal authorities.[18] A wide range of such possible behavior appears in *David Copperfield*. For example, during his foundation-school days, Uriah Heep was conditioned "to be umble to this person, and umble to that; and to pull off our caps here, and to make our bows there; and always to know our place, and abase ourselves before our betters" (639; ch. 39). And Uriah's characteristic acts of mock humility are practiced even by Sam Weller when he encounters Mrs. Bardell in the Fleet and "took his hat off with mock reverence, while his master turned indignantly on his heel" (747; ch. 46). On the other hand, "Mr Dick would pull off his hat at intervals to show his [genuine] respect for [Dr. Strong's] wisdom and knowledge" (310; ch. 17) whenever they walked together; and Mr. Peggotty "bared his head, as it was always his custom to do when he saw [Aunt Betsey], for whom he had a high respect" (791; ch. 51).

Conversely, in *Oliver Twist* the Artful Dodger, an outlaw, breaks the bare-headed indoor rule for males when he "wore his hat, as, indeed, was often his custom within doors" (229; ch. 25). And David's (partially) emancipated Aunt Betsey flouts female hat mores "by wearing her bonnet in any manner that happened to be comfortable to her head, without at all deferring to the prejudices of civilization on that subject" (668; ch. 41). Dickens's Words-worthian point here seems to be that one's nature confers grace and should receive priority over cultural artifice—unless it comes "naturally" as it does to Mr. Dick and Mr. Peggotty. In Bath, Sam combines nature and grace by donning "his hat in a very easy and graceful manner" (586; ch. 35); but the posturing footman Mr. John Smauker elevates "his hat gracefully with one hand, while he gently waved the other in a condescending manner" (608; ch. 37). In one of the relatively few examples of Dickens's emphasizing a particular style of hat (other than nightcaps), "Never were [there] such distortions

as Mr Tupman's frame underwent in his efforts to appear easy and graceful''
wearing a "sugar-loaf hat, decorated with ribbons of all colours" at Mrs.
Leo Hunter's "[f]ancy dress déjeuné.'' With its "band of music in pasteboard
caps" reflecting its artificiality, this event even features a farcical uncrowning
when Tupman must remove his hat in the stylish carriage because "no known
conveyance with a top to it, would admit of any man's carrying [a high-
crowned hat] between his head and the roof" (*Pickwick* 280–83; ch. 15).[19]

Dickens also repeatedly dramatizes anxiety and aggression over these social graces and disgraces. For instance, Sam and his father's attempts to give
Tony's savings to "master" Pickwick result in Sam "plucking nervously at
the brim of his hat" (882; ch. 56); and rather than carrying his hat upon
entering a residence, Mr. Tibbs, in "The Boarding House," "put[s] his hat
on the floor (as all timid men do)" (*Sketches by Boz* 334). But Dickens seems
particularly fascinated by the social incongruity and fluidity of "Shabby-
genteel People," typified by the Micawbers but also explored in his article
by that name. Here a distinguishing characteristic is predictable: "nobody
could mistake the shape of that hat, with its high crown gradually increasing
in circumference towards the top," though "[l]ong service" had discolored
it so that the hat is hidden "under the table" while its shabby-genteel "owner
crept into his seat as quietly as ever" (*Sketches by Boz* 306–07). When
Pickwick spies some "men of shabby-genteel appearance, who touched their
hats to many of the attorneys who passed" the courthouse, he finds their
status and business to be as mysterious as their appearance and deferential
gestures, but later discovers they are bailsmen who tip their crown for a
crown or at least "half-a-crown a crime" (656–57; ch. 40).

And hat crowns and half-crowns can equally confer the capital principles
of power, privilege, and general sign-value in Dickens. When class status is
more clearly at stake, however, Dickens's characters threaten, or even resort
to the (mis)use-value of violence toward and with hats and bonnets. In *Dombey and Son*, for example, proud but previously impoverished Edith Dombey,
whom her husband purchased at the marriage market, grows "disdainful and
defiant of [all upper-class house guests] as if the bridal wreath upon her head
had been a [bonneting] garland of steel spikes put on to force concession
from her which she would die sooner than yield" (594; ch. 36). In fact,
such hostility is often triggered by so-called "home invasions." Aunt Betsey
threatens the parvenu Jane Murdstone: "Let me see you ride a donkey over
my green again, and as sure as you have a head upon your shoulders, I'll
knock your bonnet off, and tread upon it!' (*David Copperfield* 271; ch. 14).
Bounderby is so angry at Mrs. Sparsit for bringing Mrs. Pegler, his shamefully
disowned mother, into his house that he screams at Mrs. Pegler, "Couldn't
you knock her cap off, or her tooth out, or scratch her, or do something or

other to her?'' (*Hard Times* 279; bk. 3, ch. 5). And Eugene Wrayburn expresses antipathy towards reciprocating Bradley Headstone, his social-climbing rival for Lizzie Hexam in *Our Mutual Friend* (1864–65), when he prepares to drop dirt ''pellets'' from his *upper* window ''on the hat'' of the ''schoolmaster,'' who is about to enter Eugene's rooms from the street *below*. Headstone's class-sensitive response echoes the dangerous doubling between these two different kinds of headhunters: ''You think me of no more value than the dirt under your feet'' (284, 289; bk. 2, ch. 6).

Reversing this violence against hats trend, working-class criminal Bill Sikes uses ''a little bit of a old hat for waddin' '' in his ''pocket-pistol'' bullets (200; ch. 20) in *Oliver Twist* when he attempts to invade Mrs. Maylie's leisure-class home in Chertsey and steal her precious plate. In a fitting, if ironic, act of retributive justice, ''the dark stain upon [Sikes's] hat'' from his bludgeoning Nancy in their London rooms—initially with this same pistol—self-incriminates the housebreaker in a *Hatfield* tavern when he snatches ''the hat'' from a stain-removing patterer (426–27; ch. 48). And before the judge sentences Fagin, mastermind of all the home invasions in *Oliver Twist*'s class warfare, he dramatically ''assumed the black cap'' (468; ch. 52), the juridical signifier of capital punishment. On the other hand, the ghoulish and even self-consuming Mr. Vholes, who typifies all-consuming Chancery's home invasions in *Bleak House* (1852–53), ''lifts off his tight hat as if he were scalping himself'' (605; ch. 39). More in the metaphoric manner of ''melo-dramas,'' Mr. Richard Swiveller pins ''a small parcel of black crepe'' on ''his hat'' as an ''emblem of woman's perfidy.'' Later, he ''made a show of tearing his hair,'' but prudently ''wrenched the tassel from his nightcap instead'' (*The Old Curiosity Shop* 513–14; ch. 36; 533; ch. 58), both hat histrionics betokening his loss of Sophy Wackles to the putative homewrecker and market-gardener Cheggs.

Class anxiety and aggression significantly merge in *Great Expectations* when Joe visits nouveau riche Pip's rooms in London. Here Dickens provides a four-page (241–44; ch. 27) examination of Joe's inability to control his hat and Pip's inability to refrain from patronizing Joe's fidgety social discomfort. Safe-guarding his own humble identity, Joe refuses to hand his hat over to Pip for safekeeping, but places it ''on the floor'' and ''persist[s] in standing talking over it in a most uncomfortable way.'' In an effort to be funny, Pip compares Joe's hat to ''a bird's-nest with eggs in it,'' a sustained trope that becomes a kind of ironic parable for Joe's nurturing of Pip, the seed. At one point, Joe unsuccessfully places his hat on Pip's mantle, from which ''it ever afterwards fell off at intervals,'' as both Joe and Pip seem ''fallen'' in different ways in this scene—Joe socially (but fortunately), Pip morally (and most unfortunately). The hat continues falling, in Pip's affected social satire, ''[a]s if it were an absolute point of good breeding that it should tumble off again,'' while, "providentially attracted by his hat," Joe makes "extraordinary play with it," employing graceful "eye and hand" coordination "very like that exacted by wicket-keeping." Joe's role as a kind of "extraordinary" ludimagister here outplays Pip's narrative pretense in attempting to uncrown the lovable "dunder-headed king of the noodles," as Mrs. Joe calls him (141; ch. 15), and to deny their prior kinship.

All of these cultural categories overlap, but none more so than gender and moral codes. Miming both the gender-bending carnivalesque and pantomimic traditions (melodrama evolved from pantomime [Brooks 62], which itself grew out of the medieval carnival [Eigner 10]), hats can even cue transvestite exchanges in Dickens. This occurs particularly in *Sketches by Boz* when travesty acts as the norm at the "Greenwich Fair" where "unbonneted young ladies," practicing carnival's "ideology of unbuttoning" (Hyman 10), patter "all the blandishments of 'Do dear,' " " 'There's a love,' " and other tricks of their trade to sell "real spice nuts," if not more intimate commodities. Here, even Dickens's chiastic rhetoric reflects promiscuous cross-dressing as revelers grow "somewhat noisy, and in the highest spirits possible: the ladies, in the height of their innocent animation, dancing in gentleman's hats, and the gentlemen promenading 'the gay and festive scene' in the ladies' bonnets" (140, 144). In "The First of May" (un)crowning rites, clowns even join the debasement of dress codes and reversals of hat-over-heels, or heaven-over-earth, standards: "a young gentleman in girl's clothes and a widow's cap" cavorts, accompanied by "two clowns who walked upon their hands in the mud, to the immeasurable delight of all the spectators" (208). As Bakhtin explains this cheeky topography, the somersaulting cartwheel represents "the primeval phenomenon of popular humor, . . . which by the continual rotation of the upper and lower parts suggests the rotation of earth and sky. This is manifested in other movements of the clown: the buttocks persistently trying to take the place of the head and the head that of the buttocks" (*Rabelais* 353). Such carnivalesque license in *Sketches by Boz* anticipates the more fully developed "gay madness of the [Roman] Carnival" in *Pictures from Italy* (1846) where women don "tiny Greek caps, all awry, and clinging to the dark hair" and cross-dressing carriage "drivers were attired as women, wearing long ringlets and no bonnets" (375, 372–73; ch. 10).

More melodramatically in *David Copperfield*, Dora's chaperone and moral guide, Miss Lavinia, "gives a little scream because [David] tumble[s] Dora's wedding] bonnet" the day *before* the ceremony at the same time that his too ardent professions of love are "fraught with . . . danger to the bonnet" (696; ch. 43). More farcically, Sam's intended Mary "pushed [him] against the wall, declaring that he had tumbled her cap, and put her hair quite out of curl" (825; ch. 52). On the other hand, Rosa Bud's mysterious chaperone Mr. Grewgious, in *The Mystery of Edwin Drood* (1870), sublimates the "entangled," erotic connotations of hats and hair in his courtly-love gestures toward her: "The respectful tenderness with which, on one knee before her, he helped [Rosa] to remove her hat, and disentangle her pretty hair from it, was quite a chivalrous sight. Yet who, knowing him only on the surface, would have expected chivalry—and of the true sort, too: not the spurious—from Mr Grewgious?" (224; ch. 20). *Chaperone* derives from the French *chaperon*, meaning "hood"; and Grewgious here partially unveils his "true" feelings toward his adopted ward, though there still seems to be something "spurious" or at least hooded about Rosa's chaperone. When predatory Mrs. Brown kidnaps six-year-old Florence, replaces her fashionable bonnet with "the crushed remains of a bonnet that had probably been picked up from some ditch or dunghill," and then cuts her hair to "disentangle" it from the substitute bonnet in *Dombey and Son*, her disturbing actions suggest not only a rape of the lock, but an uncrowning debasement, if not scapegoating, of upper-class dress codes. When shortly thereafter the "bonnet fall[s] off, [and Florence's] hair came tumbling down about her face: moving [her future husband Walter] to speechless admiration and commiseration" (130–31, 134; ch. 6), the erotic ties between hats and hair grow even more apparent, besides implying that Florence's natural grace morally transcends both upper- and lower-class distinctions. These erotic ties seem unmistakable when Mrs. Browne's daughter Alice Marwood, "the fallen angel," appears in hymenal, "disordered head-gear" with "wild hair" like "a heap of serpents": "no bonnet on her head, nothing to defend her rich black hair from the rain, but a torn handkerchief; with the fluttering ends of which, and with her hair, the wind blinded her" (572; ch. 34; 563–66; ch. 33). On the other hand, ties between bonnets and hair grow more personally obvious but idealized in "The Lazy Tour of Two Idle Apprentices" (1857), when Mr. Goodchild (Dickens) idolizes the haloed "Angel" (Nelly Ternan): "O winning little bonnet, making in conjunction with her golden hair quite a Glory in the sunlight round the pretty head, why anything in the world but you and me!" (748). And the dovetailing of moral and aesthetic values, implied here, becomes more clear in "The Boiled Beef of New England" when Dickens unfavorably contrasts plain, if not utilitarian, English bonnets with "the pretty French cap, the Spanish mantilla, or the Genoese mezzero" (*The Uncommercial Traveller* 250).

Dickens is, of course, famous for his fascination with popular culture, for his acting and directing career in amateur theatricals, and for his fictional creation of self-reflexive "strolling players" such as Jingle in *Pickwick*, Codlin and Short, the Punch showmen in *The Old Curiosity Shop*, Sleary's circus performers in *Hard Times*, and Wopsle in *Great Expectations*. But the Crummles troupe histrionics in *Nicholas Nickleby* (1838–39), who performed on and off stage "in the highest style of melodrama" (478; ch. 30) and replete with gestures "from [the] pantomime collection" (366; ch. 23), are most representative. In recent years, researchers like Malcolm Andrews, Edwin Eigner, Paul Schlicke, Juliet John, Tore Rem, and Deborah Vlock have retrieved a treasure-trove of cultural material in these areas.[20] And we have already discussed many of the carnivalesque, pantomimic, and melodramatic motifs in *Pickwick* in order to demonstrate that it is not simply "professional" thespians like Jingle who speak "in a stage whisper," gesture "melo-dramatically," or emote "with a professional (*i.e.* theatrical) air" (181–83; ch. 8). Dickens directs many critical scenes—and several of these feature hats—as melodramatic tableaux (animated with carnivalesque spirits), which Brooks repeatedly emphasizes: "In the tableau more than in any other single device of dramaturgy, we grasp melodrama's primordial concern to make its signs clear, unambiguous, and impressive" (48). For example, when the Pickwickians unmask Jingle and Job Trotter "as rogues and impostors" in the magistrate Nupkins's parlor, "[i]t was an impressive tableau. Alfred Jingle, Esquire, alias Captain Fitz-Marshall, was standing near the door with his hat in his hand, and a smile on his face, wholly unmoved by his very unpleasant situation," while Pickwick melodramatically confronts him, "inculcating some high moral lesson" (438, 437; ch. 25). Jingle's "hat in his hand"—according to the Victorian indoor dress code—signals in a "clear, unambiguous, and impressive" manner both his self-concealing artifice and his self-revealing readiness to make a stage exit at a melodramatic moment's notice. Vlock insists that Victorian audiences understood such interdependent historical and histrionic clues and cues involving common "sartorial assumptions" (23); and "Dickens frequently mixed his personal, social, and theatrical observations in this way," exploring and exploiting "the general 'confusion' in Victorian culture, of the theatrical or fictive and the 'real'" (140). Dickens reflects this insight in "The Pantomime of Life": "A pantomime is to us a mirror of life"; when Shakespeare dramatically declared that "All the world's a stage," he actually "meant a Pantomime, and we are all actors in The Pantomime of Life" (226, 234).[21]

Three other points should be made about possible theatrical influences on Dickens's hat scenes. First, characters typically use sweeping gestures with hats, most often the melodramatic convention of dashing one's hat to the floor for exclamatory emphasis, which Brooks associates with "the aesthetics of astonishment" (55), though this gestural exclamation point also suggests a leveling of upper and lower topographies and typologies. Explaining the drunken revelry at the Blue Lion Inn, for example, Pickwick celebrates the joke that the bacchanal was due to "the salmon" rather than "the wine" by exorcizing his spectatorial role and emphatically exercising his participation in the pantomime of life: "'Hurrah!' echoed Mr Pickwick, taking off his hat and dashing it on the floor, and insanely casting his spectacles into the middle of the kitchen" (176; ch. 8).[22] When Sam floors Pickwick in the Fleet by telling him that he has also been imprisoned for an unpaid debt, the dramatic intensification of Sam's typical tipping his hat to his "master" also levels the difference between man and master: "With these words, which he repeated with great emphasis and violence, Sam dashed his hat upon the ground, in a most unusual state of excitement; and then, folding his arms, looked firmly and fixedly in his master's face" (706; ch. 43). Finally, the repentant Jingle punctuates his promise to pay back "every farthing" of Pickwick's charitable gesture toward "mak[ing] a man" of him by "striking the crown of his hat with great violence" (840–41; ch. 53) as if Jingle's previous posture of kingship mastery, of lording it over Pickwick, has been replaced by fealty, if not quite kinship bonds.

Secondly, Dickens's "hat monologues" sometimes seem influenced by popular street patter. For instance, Sam describes his talismanic "old white hat" in what Dickens terms a cheap-jack "delivery": "Ta'nt a werry good 'un to look at . . . but it's an "astonishin' 'un to wear; and afore the brim went, it was a werry handsome tile. Hows'ever it's lighter without it, that's one thing, and every hole lets in some air, that's another—wentilation gossamer I calls it" (235; ch. 12). Vlock cites a very similar patter song titled "Cheap John" (comparing it to Silas Wegg's hawking in *Our Mutual Friend*): "my noble swells, here's a bran-new ventilating hat, to begin with. A tile—a castor—a skull case—a nutshell, or whatever you please to call it, my pretty dears. Look at this 'ere hat—there's a brimmer! With a bit let in at the back—it will fit everybody. Just examine this hat, while I twirl it round on a stick. Ain't it a non-such, and a bit over? Don't *I* look well in it?'' (Vlock 125–26).[23] Obviously, Cheap John is trying to sell the "bran-new ventilating hat" through the use of seductive humor and persuasive display. Since Pickwick is contemplating a job offer to Sam as his traveling valet and since Sam is perceptive enough to guess his motive, it seems reasonable that Sam's similar patter is an attempt to persuade Pickwick to hire him.

Sam's description also anticipates our third point (suggested earlier): that hats, as theatrical images of the inside outside the outside, not only reflect but also fashion selfhood in Dickens's fiction. In other words, Sam likewise promises to be "an astonishin' un," very comfortable "to wear" or attend Pickwick, no matter what his present appearance, and someone much "lighter" than the other Pickwickians since Sam won't be a burden but only a blessing during Pickwick's pilgrim's progress. Other hats serve the same self-defining purpose.[24] Tom Pinch seems to feel that the most characteristic hat in English literature is Robinson Crusoe's "goat-skin cap" (*Martin Chuzzlewit* 78; ch. 5), while the most characteristic hat in later Victorian fiction is probably Sherlock Holmes's deerstalker. The most idiosyncratic hat in Dickens is not Dolly Varden's colorful and later commodified bonnet in *Barnaby Rudge* (1841), but Barnaby's own theatrical "hat [ornamented] with a cluster of peacock's feathers, but they were limp and broken, and now trailed negligently down his back. . . . The fluttered and confused disposition of all the motley scraps that formed his dress, bespoke, in a scarcely less degree than his eager and unsettled manner, the disorder of his mind'' (74; ch. 3). In Browne's illustration, Barnaby's hat feathers appear graphically paired with those of his equally erratic familiar, Grip the raven (192; ch. 17).

Even more sustained, memorable, and pantomimic is Captain Cuttle's "glazed hat" in *Dombey and Son*, which functions more subtly than as a mere mnemonic tag phrase like "the cocked hat and mortified bonnet" (533; ch. 31) repeatedly cuing Mr. Sownds the beadle and Mrs. Miff the pew-opener at Dombey's wedding. The "glazed hat [such] as a sympathetic person's head might ache at the sight of, and which left a red rim round his own forehead as if he had been wearing a tight basin" is so characteristic of Captain Cuttle that it sometimes ironically *becomes* that "mysterious and incomprehensible character," the good Captain himself: "the glazed hat merely nodded with a mute, unutterable meaning." In fact, searching for Sol Gills, "the hard glazed hat" passed "gleaming where men were thickest, like the hero's helmet in an epic battle" (97; ch. 4; 309; ch. 17; 280; ch. 15; 435; ch. 25). At other times, it signals "a most remarkable phenomenon," becoming the Captain's familiar as it magically "skimmed into [his] room like a bird, and alighted heavily at the Captain's feet. The door then shut as violently as it had opened, and nothing ensued in explanation of the prodigy" (407; ch. 23). Captain Cuttle's weather-proof or glazed hat is cited repeatedly, its guttural alliteration echoes his own reliability and resilience, and the "glazed," if not haloing effect of the eternal "scarlet circle on his forehead swelling in his triumphant joy" (306; ch. 17) further portrays the enduring romance quality of this loveable tenant of the Wooden Midshipman (against love-starved Dombey's "realist" aura). When Cuttle "clap[s] on his glazed hat," after believing Sol has been lost at sea, "with the solitary air of Crusoe finishing his toilet with his goat-skin cap" (637; ch. 39) and when its "scarlet circle" actually becomes "a very halo of delight round his glowing forehead" (970; ch. 62), the place of the Captain's hat, proof against any of life's sea changes, seems secured in the annals of literary headgear.

More trenchant is the sole and soulless "head-dress" of the cross-dressing, legal predator Sally Brass in *The Old Curiosity Shop*: "a brown gauze scarf, like the wing of the fabled vampire" (321; ch. 33). Sairey Gamp's transformation from crass selfishness to "new-born," assertive compassion, at least toward Mercy Chuzzlewit and Mr. Chuffey, is suggested by her headgear's dramatic transformation—"her bonnet was bent into the shape of a cocked hat" (728; ch. 51; 587; ch. 40)—after contact with the wharf's lonely crowd when Sairey tries to rescue Mercy from her husband Jonas. And back in *Pickwick*, Jingle is repeatedly identified as the strolling player performing in his "pinched up hat" (78; ch. 2), which prefigures both his "pinching" or bride-theft of Rachael Wardle and his later "pinched," squalid condition in the Fleet, just as Dickens's "Cicerone" in Mantua has "so much poverty expressed in his faded suit and little pinched hat" (*Pictures From Italy* 341; ch. 8).[25]

Sometimes it is the name inside the hat which less "graphically," but no less dramatically, identifies its owner. For example, when Rachael and Sissy search for Stephen Blackpool in *Hard Times*, they discover his "hat lying in the grass" near Old Hell Shaft, down which he had mysteriously disappeared: "Stephen Blackpool was written in his own hand on the inside" (284; bk. 3, ch. 6). Similarly, in *The Mystery of Edwin Drood*, the enigmatic and presumably disguised "Dick Datchery" identifies himself by asking a waiter to read what is "written" in his hat (202; ch. 18). Shortly thereafter, Datchery walks with "an odd momentary appearance upon him of having forgotten his hat . . . ; and he clapped his hand up to his head as if with some vague expectation of finding another hat upon it" (208; ch. 18), that is, of rediscovering his real hat or former identity.

Sometimes the identification by hat is less nominal and more synecdochic (in this sense, exclamatory gestural script often proves more "expressive" than alphabetic writing). In *Oliver Twist*, the Artful Dodger's name may not be written in his headgear, but his animated hat figuratively incarnates his name's declaration of the Dodger's telltale kinetics, while also foreshadowing his precarious chances for survival: "His hat was stuck on the top of his head so lightly, that it threatened to fall off every moment—and would have done so, very often, if the wearer had not had a knack of every now and then giving his head a sudden twitch, which brought it back to its old place again" (100; ch. 8). The "devious mazes" surrounding "M. Todgers's Commercial Boarding-House," and "the mazes of bedrooms" within it, are both represented by Mrs. Todgers's head covering in *Martin Chuzzlewit*: "something made of net—you couldn't call it a cap exactly—which looked like a black cobweb," suggesting this "black" widow's strategies in keeping undesirable strangers out, while trapping desirable bachelors and widowers like Pecksniff within her "labyrinth, whereof the mystery was known but to a chosen few" (131; ch. 9; 128; ch. 8; 170; ch. 11; 129; ch. 8; 131; ch. 9). Thus, like other characters in Dickens, Mrs. Todgers's hat, habits, and habitat are all akin. In *Little Dorrit*, Old Nandy's hat personifies the recurring motif of "Nobody" by signifying his lack of social identity, "individuality," and adaptability—but also his "obdurate" resilience in sustaining life: "This old man wears a hat, a thumbed and napless and yet an obdurate hat, which has never adapted itself to the shape of his poor head. His coarse shirt and his coarse neckcloth have no more individuality than his coat and hat" (413; bk. 1, ch. 31). In the same novel, Pancks creates a hat trope to characterize Mr. Rugg's somewhat proud and parsimonious personality: "as to the crown of his hat, it's high. And as to the brim of his hat, it's narrow" (462; bk. 1, ch. 35). Dickens lavishes an entire paragraph in *David Copperfield* on Mrs. Markleham's "one unchangeable cap, ornamented with some artificial flowers, and two artificial butterflies" which "improved the shining hours at Doctor's Strong's expense, like busy bees" (296; ch. 16), but also at the ironic expense both of this idle and mischievous parasite and of Isaac Watts's parodied poem "Against Idleness and Mischief." In *Bleak House* the vagabond crossing sweeper Jo bears the burden of his "wretched fragment" of subjectivity like some regressive pilgrim as he "carried his wretched fragment of fur cap like a bundle, though he went bareheaded through the rain, which now fell fast" (488; ch. 31). In several of these examples, hats performatively prefigure some kind of fall from spiritual, psychic, or social grace at the same time that they dramatically bestow selfhood on their respective owners and, in the case of Nandy and Jo, preview postmodern anomie.[26]

As Mrs. Haweis's *The Art of Dress* (1879) posits, the importance of a Victorian hat rests not on its fashion statement "but rather . . . exclusively [on] the psychology of its individual wearer" (Briggs's paraphrase 261). Besides suggesting individual traits, however, Dickens's dramatic hat language can also articulate interpersonal and even transpersonal issues. After little Paul's death, Mr. Dombey decides to travel in company with that *miles gloriosus* Major Joey Bagstock, who has just insincerely eulogized the child and "wore [his hat] with a rakish air on one side of his head, by way of toning down his remarkable [blue] visage." At the railway station, they run into Mr. Toodle, humble husband of Paul's early nurse Polly, and altogether present a nearly psychomachic tableau. Toodle, "working man" foil to the Major, repeatedly tips "his oilskin cap" in deference to Mr. Dombey, besides nervously "turning [it] round and round." Dombey's "attention [is] arrested by something in connection with the cap"; namely, the "rough cap [features] a piece of new crape." When Toodle tells him that he and Polly lost a child three years ago but still rejoice in their remaining children, insensitive Dombey characteristically fails to commiserate with Toodle and to connect this lesson to his own remaining child Florence. Instead, he sees the mourning hatband as a public affront to his private grief, realizing Toodle "wore it" not for his own lost son, but "for *his* son" little Paul (350–53; ch. 20).

In *Martin Chuzzlewit*'s satire of America, headgear signifies the cruelly pretentious and clownishly hypocritical psychology of an entire culture. And Dickens's often histrionic rhetoric parrots American pretensions. For example, Colonel Diver wears "a rather broad-brimmed hat for the greater wisdom of his appearance," tilting it "back upon his ears—like a man who was oppressed to inconvenience by a sense of his own greatness" (250, 254; ch. 16), while Mrs. Hominy, "a philosopher and an authoress," dons "a highly aristocratic and classical cap, meeting beneath her chin: a style of head-dress so admirably adapted to her countenance, that if the late Mr Grimaldi had appeared in the lappets of Mrs Siddons, a more complete effect could not have been produced'' (353; ch. 22). The transcendental literary lady aptly named Miss Codger proves more patriotic as she extends the definition of *headgear*: "Sticking on [her] forehead . . . by invisible means, was a massive cameo, in size and shape like the raspberry tart which is ordinarily sold for a penny, representing on its front, the capitol at Washington" (512 ch. 34). Personifying America's "colonial" reign of terror over African slaves, the national goddess "Liberty" even "pulls down her cap upon her eyes, and owns Oppression in its vilest aspect, for her sister" (328; ch. 21).

In "Meditations in Monmouth-Street," the "burial-place of the fashions" where second-hand clothes—including "low crowns and broad brims"—are bought and sold, Dickens writes "[t]here was the man's whole life written as legibly on those clothes, as if we had his autobiography on parchment before us" (*Sketches by Boz* 98–99). And an anonymous 1847 review of three new fashion books, "Art of Dress" in *The Quarterly Review*, similarly emphasizes that dress, with specific attention to hats, becomes "a sort of symbolical language—a kind of personal glossary—a species of body phrenology, the study of which it would be madness to neglect" (375). Thomas Carlyle, the Victorian cultural critic to whom Dickens dedicated *Hard Times*, appears to be behind both of these sartorial assumptions ("Art of Dress" acknowledges Carlyle 390). At least his *Sartor Resartus*, published two years before *Pickwick*, provides the kind of cultural material assembled here, retailoring it to feature immaterial values which almost certainly influenced Dickens: "All visible things are Emblems; what thou seest is not there on its own account; strictly taken, is not there at all: Matter exists only spiritually, and to represent some Idea and *body* it forth. Hence Clothes, as despicable as we think them, are so unspeakably significant" (56; bk. 1, ch. 11). In fact, Carlyle also presumably influenced George Sala's article "Fashion" (*Household Words* 1853), in which he emphasizes that "Fashion is not tangible or palpable" (194) but culturally and psychologically emblematic. Carlyle notes that "We too have walked through Monmouth Street; but with little feeling of 'Devotion' " to "that foolish Street" (184; bk. 3, ch. 6). Deriding fashionable, commodified apparel as vain affectation commodifying selfhood, Carlyle stresses the incompatibility of hat and head, but reverses Pickwick's "gigantic brain" and small hat relationship: "How has our Head on the outside a polished Hat, . . . and in the inside Vacancy, or a froth of Vocables and Attorney Logic!" (90; bk. 2, ch. 3).

Carlyle particularly satirizes ostentatious "head-dress" like the "Clergyman, or man with a shovel-hat," and the "head-dress [by which the Dandiacal Sect] affect[s] a certain freedom: hats with partial brim, without crown, or with only a loose, hinged, or valved crown; in the former case, they sometimes invert the hat, and wear it brim uppermost, like a University-cap, with what view is unknown.'' He would rather "bow to every Man with any sort of hat" (like Pickwick) "or with no hat whatever. Is he not a Temple, then; the visible Manifestation and Impersonation of Divinity?" (213, 181; bk. 3, chapters 10, 6). Carlyle's insistent ridicule of "Fashion" even seems to include genial Mrs. Boffin in *Our Mutual Friend*, who with her "large black velvet hat and feathers" becomes in her husband's words "a highflyer at Fashion" until "Fashion, in the form of her black velvet hat and feathers . . . got deservedly crushed" by the good couple's mutual affection (62, 64; ch. 5). Carlyle's extended speculations on Fortunatus's "wishing Hat" or "Time-annihilating" and "Space-annihilating Hats" (197–200; bk. 3, ch. 8), however, like all of Dickens's "considering" and "conjuring caps," come closest to the sense of the immaterial, imaginative power of hats presented in this essay.

Put differently, the metaphoric potential of Dickens's hat creations proves as "astonishin' '' as Sam's famous Wellerisms and melodrama's "aesthetics of astonishment" as the following examples from *Martin Chuzzlewit*, *David Copperfield*, and *Pictures from Italy* suggest. Nurse Sairey Gamp's comic association with the transcendental "Philosophy of Vegetables" (284; ch. 17) seems rooted in her "yellow nightcap, of prodigious size, in shape resembling a cabbage" (394; ch. 25), while David's own sublimely grotesque hat metaphor captures the shabby-genteel dimensions of his pilgrimage to Dover and Aunt Betsey: "My hat (which had served me for a night-cap, too) was so crushed and bent, that no old battered handleless saucepan on a dunghill need have been ashamed to vie with it" (246; ch. 13). Finally, when Dickens gazes "down into" the "great Roman Amphitheatre" in Verona, his imagined "at the moment," but later self-consciously represented, hat conceit uncannily memorializes the ancient artifact. This time, however, Dickens reverses his usual tendency to compare a hat to something else and rather compares something else to an astonishing hat: "[I]t seemed to lie before me like the inside of a prodigious hat of plaited straw, with an enormously broad brim and a shallow crown; the plaits being represented by the four-and-forty rows of seats. The comparison is a homely and fantastic one, in sober remembrance and on paper, but it was irresistibly suggested at the moment, nevertheless" (338–39; ch. 8).

III

The remainder of this essay will explore three equally astonishing hat scenes from *Pickwick* in reverse chronological order so we can conclude where we commenced—with Pickwick chasing his hat.[27] The first scene (440–41; ch. 25) involves Sam descending "below stairs" at magistrate Nupkins to find his hat:

> Now, there was nobody in the kitchen, but the pretty house-maid [Mary] and as Sam's hat was mislaid, he had to look for it; and the pretty house-maid lighted him. They had to look all over the place for the hat. The pretty house-maid, in her anxiety to find it, went down on her knees, and turned over all the things that were heaped together in a little corner by the door. It was an awkward corner. You couldn't get at it without shutting the door first.
> "Here it is," said the pretty housemaid. "This is it, ain't it?"
> "Let me look," said Sam.
> The pretty housemaid had stood the candle on the floor; as it gave a very dim light, Sam was obliged to go down on *his* knees before he could see whether it was his own hat or not. It was a remarkably small corner, and so—it was nobody's fault but the man's who built the house—Sam and the pretty house-maid were necessarily very close together.

At this juncture, Sam unaccountably drops his hat again, whereupon Mary "put[s] it on for him," and Sam kisses her. " 'You don't mean to say you did that on purpose,' said the pretty housemaid, blushing." Sam replies, " 'No, I didn't then, . . . but I will now.' So he kissed her again." Pickwick impatiently calls Sam. " 'Coming, sir,' replied Sam," and explains, " 'There was something behind the door, sir, which perwented our getting it open, for ever so long, sir.' . . . And this was the first passage of Mr Weller's first love."

This scenic mating ritual activated by Sam's hat can be read on at least two levels. On the one hand, the understated narrative plays out like a sublimated and egalitarian, courtly-love match-making, in which a "below stairs," servant-class couple genuflects to each other and so previews "above stairs," higher-class couples (like new-generation Winkle and Arabella Allen) in finding comic pretexts for ingenious but innocent foreplay under the nose of the panoptic father (the repeated "sir"). On the other hand, the overstated narration seems to recount a bawdy, carnivalesque tryst featuring lower-body functions with lusty double-entendres like "went down on her knees" and "Coming," graphic examples of the "sustained current of sexual insinuation" (237) that James Eli Adams finds flowing throughout *Pickwick*. In the first scenario Sam's hat serves as a prophylactic prop, both directing and deflecting desire; in the second, it serves as a Rabelaisian codpiece, a metonym for the phallus.[28] At both levels, it becomes a transitional object which liminally transforms the two initiates participating in this amorous rite of passage—"the first passage of Mr Weller's first love." In a related, but more psychoanalytic sense, the hat also becomes a fort-da passport to the imaginary where the name of the father (again, the repeated "sir") cannot repress erotic (dis)play. The ambiguity of Mary's candlelight reinforces the ambiguity of

Sam's hat as it casts her as a parodic vestal virgin who sacrifices her spiritual light—she both inflames and enlightens Sam's cap—at the same time that her candle of life encourages a kind of *carpe diem* response to its brevity. In any event, this sustained hat gag returns when Sam unexpectedly runs into "the pretty housemaid from Mr Nupkins's" in Ipswich, next door to none other than the sought-after Miss Arabella Allen, Mary's higher-class double: Sam's "hat had fallen off a few minutes before [Mary's cry of surprise]—from both of which tokens we should be disposed to infer that one kiss or more, had passed between the parties" (638; ch. 39).

The second hat scene details "Mr Pickwick's [night-cap] adventure with the middle-aged lady," Miss Witherfield (389–96; chapters 22–23), which, like melodramatic *tableaux vivants* based on familiar paintings (Brooks, 65, 213, n. 5), restages the slapstick bedroom farce involving Parson Adams, Mrs. Slipslop, Beau Didapper, Lady Booby, Fanny Goodwill, Joseph Andrews, and a nightcap in *Joseph Andrews* (322–25; bk. 4, ch. 14). In Fielding's picaresque mock-epic, the usual suspects are all sleeping at Booby-hall when the innocent Parson hears Mrs. Slipslop scream "I will swear a rape against thee" as Didapper assaults her, mistaking her for Fanny. Adams, "without staying to put a rag of clothes on," rushes to aid Slipslop, who, mistaking him for her attacker, wrestles with Adams who, in turn, "seiz[es] her by the hair (for her double-clout [nocturnal head-dressing] had fallen off in the scuffle)" and "pinned her head down to the bolster," mistaking her for a him with a very hairy chin. Adams, still "naked" except for "a flannel nightcap," is then undeceived "by the two mountains which Slipslop carried before her," but decides she must be a witch whose prodigious breasts "gave suck to a legion of devils." Lady Booby rushes on the scene, but "could not refrain from laughter; nor did Slipslop persist in accusing the parson of any motions towards a rape." Still naked and nightcapped, Adams exits, loses his way, and climbs into bed with Fanny, quickly begging her "pardon [and] assuring her he did not know whether she was man or woman." Joseph erupts on the scene, but freezes "as the tragedians call it, like the statue of Surprize." Nevertheless, his "great opinion of Adams was not easily to be staggered," and he calmed down "when he heard from Fanny that no harm had happened." With references to "rape," Slipslop's mammary "mountains," and actual bed-sharing, eighteenth-century Fielding can obviously wax more graphic than Victorian Dickens can, but both just as obviously share a sense of social and class satire, a boudoir comedy of errors, an exposé of innocence, and concern with the sexual connotations of head-(un)coverings.[29]

Minus the relay-race tempo, Dickens's plotting is remarkably similar but zooms in and maintains focus on "the horrors of a night-cap," the "description" of which John Glavin finds "suggestively metonymic" (9). Adamic Pickwick loses his way in the Great White Horse Inn after "progress[ing] downward'' to find his watch. He eventually discovers what seems to be his room, undresses "behind the curtains" of his bed, "and slowly drawing on his tasselled night-cap, secured it firmly on his head" (nightcaps are cited ten times in this scene, besides being visually prominent in the accompanying illustration; see fig. 2). After "smiling" at the absurdity of "losing myself in this place," Pickwick is surprised by a "mysterious visitor"—"a middle-aged lady, in yellow curl-papers, busily engaged in brushing what ladies call their 'back-hair.' " She has carried "a rushlight . . . like a gigantic light-house" into the room and eventually dons her own "muslin night-cap with a small plaited border." "[C]old perspiration starting in drops upon his night-cap," Pickwick—ever "the most modest and delicate-minded of mortals"—grows obsessed with removing his troublesome headgear, the strings of which he had tied too tightly: "The very idea of exhibiting his night-cap to a lady overpowered him." (Perhaps at this point, Pickwick recalls Boz's words from "Omnibuses": "when you have seen a man in his nightcap, you lose all respect for him" [Sketches by Boz 166].) Pickwick vocally reveals himself to the lady, at first terrifying but then calming her until he exposes his "dancing" nightcap: "the sudden apparition of Mr Pickwick's night-cap [drove] her back into the remotest corner of the apartment." Pickwick's consequent anxiety causes him to nod "his head so energetically that the tassel of his night-cap danced again": "I am almost ready to sink, Ma'am, beneath the confusion of addressing a lady in my night-cap." Finally able to exit after reciting his "improbable story," Pickwick "hastily put[s] on his hat over his night-cap, after the manner of the old patrol" constabulary and "at the end of the [hall] passage" happens upon Sam, who suggests, "You rayther want somebody to look arter you, sir, wen your judgment goes out a wisitin'." The Wellerism leaves Sam's master "buried in the profoundest meditation."

Dickens's representation of the *Joseph Andrews* precursor text, like the dressing mirror in Browne's plate and the theatrical "curtains" drawn round Pickwick's bed, looks before and after—back to Parson Adams and Slipslop's madcap comedy of terrors, and forward, as a dress rehearsal, to Pickwick's tragicomic nightcap encounter with Smangle and the Zephyr. Its "improbable story"-within-a-story even ironically prefigures Sam's foreplay with Mary in its concern with losing time, female enlightenment, class (and here generational) courting practices, and, of course, a primary hat symbol connoting various kinds of crowning, uncrowning, and comically erotic tomfoolery replete with erupting body fluids.[30] Sam's exit line implies not only that the master can learn a great deal from the servant in these matters, but that age can learn a great deal from youth, while Fielding's precedent, if not picaresque archetype, likewise suggests that there's no fool like an old fool in a nightcap, whether innocently vain lord or his "lady love." The tight "strings" of the

Fig. 2. Hablot Browne's "The Middle-Aged Lady in the Doubled-Bedded Room"

fool's cap recall a similar bromide—it's very difficult to teach an old dog new tricks, to shed age's culpable innocence and fall consciously and responsibly into the world of experience, which Pickwick does not accomplish until after his tragicomedy with Mrs. Bardell and his descent into the Fleet. Still, this hat scene becomes another liminal rite of passage for Pickwick, one where he must "lose myself," meaning his foolishly vain self, or at least discipline it with wiser self-control and patrol as he "put[s] on his hat over his night-cap, after the manner of the old patrol." And so it is perhaps not coincidental that Frederic Coleman Nantz featured this episode as the "Scene of Night Caps" in his popular 1837–38 stage adaptation *Pickwick; or, The Sayings and Doings of Sam Weller* (Schlicke 55–56).

Our final hat scene (120–23; ch. 4; see fig. 3 for Seymour's plate) also involves losing and finding oneself as it returns to Pickwick "in pursuit of his own hat" in a field near Chatham barracks where two military troops march, in ranks, toward each other. At the same time, the somersaulting Winkle enjoys a ground-level view of "his venerated leader at some distance off, running after his own hat, which was gamboling playfully away in perspective":

> A vast deal of coolness, and a peculiar degree of judgment, are requisite in catching a hat. A man must not be precipitate, or he runs over it; he must not rush into the opposite extreme, or he loses it altogether. The best way is, to keep gently up with the object of pursuit, to be wary and cautious, to watch your opportunity well, get gradually before it, then make a rapid dive, seize it by the crown, and stick it firmly on your head: smiling pleasantly all the time, as if you thought it as good a joke as anyone else.
>
> There was a fine gentle wind, and Mr Pickwick's hat rolled sportively before it. The wind puffed, and Mr Pickwick puffed, and the hat rolled over and over as merrily as a lively porpoise in a strong tide; and on it might have rolled, far beyond Mr Pickwick's reach, had not its course been providentially stopped, just as that gentleman was on the point of resigning it to its fate.

Just when Pickwick is "completely exhausted, and about to give up the chase," the wind spirits his hat "against the wheel" of a carriage. Seizing the opportunity, Pickwick "darted briskly forward, secured his property, planted it on his head, and paused to take breath," whereupon he "heard his own name eagerly pronounced." Pickwick then beholds a large, extended "family": "a stout old gentleman," "two young ladies," a "young gentleman apparently enamoured of one of the young ladies," "a lady of doubtful age," and a "fat and red-faced boy, in a state of somnolency," guarding "a hamper of spacious dimensions" imaginatively associated with "cold fowls, tongues, and bottles of wine."

This threshold scene proves proleptic and much more significant than just "the broad farce of Mr Pickwick chasing his hat" (Schlicke 43): Pickwick's

Fig. 3. Robert Seymour's "Mr. Pickwick in Chase of His Hat"

"ludicrous distress" pursuing "his own hat" prefigures his episodic, romance pursuits, particularly his unself-conscious quest for "his own" selfhood, throughout the text. Commenting generally on the "hat in the wind"
motif, Fred Miller Robinson relevantly notes, "What makes so venerably
comic a hat's being suddenly whisked off a head is precisely the contradiction
between what is so intimate and what is so removable. A windblown hat is
an abruptly absent mind" (157). The topographical ups-and-downs Pickwick
experiences, as modeled by Winkle's cartwheeling, carnivalesque "perspective" and by his own hat's "gamboling playfully," finally come to rest
against Wardle's carriage wheel. And this targeted goal proves to be a providential (not "fate[d]") Wheel of good Fortune and revolving inclusivity for
Pickwick, who appropriately appears at Snodgrass's wedding "turning round
in a different direction at every fresh expression of gratification or curiosity,
and inspiring everybody with his looks of gladness and delight" (895; ch.
57).[31] Unlike the lonely crowd of the serried, militaristic rank-and-file, emancipated Pickwick learns to follow the "object of his pursuit," his self-defining
hat, according to the text's stated or suggested paradoxes. He learns these
paradoxes here, but he really doesn't accept and practice them until later in
the Fleet.

The best guide through this passage is, I think, D. W. Winnicott's *Playing
and Reality*, which models the role of playing with objects (like hats) in "the
search for the self": "The thing about playing is always the precariousness
of the interplay of personal psychic reality and the experience of control of
actual objects" (54, 47). Winnicott emphasizes "the difficult part of the
theory of the transitional object, which is that a paradox is involved which
needs to be accepted, tolerated, and not resolved" (53). Like Pickwick's
shuttling betwixt and between his private pursuit of his hat and his communal,
nearly beatific vision of the human family, we all "experience life in the area
of transitional phenomena, in the exciting interweave of subjectivity and
objective observation, and in an area that is intermediate between the inner
reality of the individual and the shared reality of the world that is external
to individuals" (64). Winnicott makes clear that this creative "area," which
he calls *potential space*, is critical for self-development and aesthetic enjoy-
ment. In both life and literature, revolving, if not revolutionary perceptions
and comic perspectives, like those of the somersaulting Winkle and Pickwick's "sportively" rolling hat, provide self-fulfillment: "It is creative apper-
ception more than anything else that makes the individual feel that life is
worth living" (65).[32] Previewing, if not influencing Winnicott and Dickens's
"object[s] of pursuit," the Victorian Carlyle seems, then, a pioneer object-
relations theorist and surveyor of immaterial culture: "Rightly viewed no
meanest object is insignificant; all objects are as windows, through which the
philosophic eye looks into Infinitude itself" (56; bk. 1, ch. 11).

With Winnicott's leads in mind, we can more clearly understand Pickwick's experience in this scene. The narrator proves a paradoxical mentor in advising "opposite extreme[s]" for capturing the flag, catching the golden ring, or grasping one's elusive selfhood symbolized by Pickwick's hat: one must "keep gently up with the object of pursuit . . . get gradually before it, then make a rapid dive, seize it by the crown, and stick it firmly on your head." In other words, one needs to develop a kind of double-consciousness—jointly reflective and spontaneous—but as Winnicott advises, this paradox cannot really be "resolved." It can only be experienced and "accepted." Menelaus learns this lesson with the shape-shifting Proteus in *The Odyssey*, and young Arthur learns it with the shape-shifting Merlin in the Arthurian tradition. Neither the visionary Proteus nor Merlin will help, however, unless their initiates hold onto them for dear life; and as James Kincaid emphasizes, this "motif of initiation" is "central" in *Pickwick* (*Dickens and the Rhetoric of Laughter* 22). Pickwick must learn the same life lesson from his shape-shifting, "lively porpoise" hat: he can't change a changing world; he can only change himself in trying to keep up with it, and so Pickwick "puffed" with the puffing wind, inhaling its carnivalesque jeu d'esprit. Such successful adaptation to his changing environment allows Pickwick to crown himself as Alice ultimately is crowned in *Through the Looking-Glass* after "pursuing a large bright thing, that looked sometimes like a doll and sometimes like a work-box" (201; ch. 5). At this point, Pickwick hears "his own name eagerly pronounced," signaling his new self-awareness; and then he is blessed with that Blakean vision of the "Echoing Green" which graces *David Copperfield*'s serial cover-design illustration—that is, a traditional tableau of the unified human family where generations, genders, and classes seem aligned and (here) where a carnivalesque horn of plenty provides bountifully potential, "spacious dimensions" for all. The problem with this beatific vision, of course, is that it is only momentary as the Fat Boy cautions like some Janus-faced, *Et in Arcadia Ego* figurine depicting Eros on one side and Thanatos on the other.[33] But later, after many more hat adventures, Pickwick and the reader reach a different conclusion, one that sustains melodrama's (and Winnicott's) contention that "light and darkness" cannot be resolved and that belief in the final victory of light over darkness must be earned: "There are dark shadows on the earth, but its lights are stronger in the contrast" (896; ch. 57).

Near the end of *The Pickwick Papers*, Solomon Pell, attorney for the debtor's court, proclaims and performs the ultimate compliment to the Pickwickians (including Sam): " 'Gentlemen,' said Mr Pell, touching his hat, 'my service to you all. I don't say it to flatter you, gentlemen, but there are not five other men in the world, that I'd have come out of that court for, to-day' " (868; ch. 55). And it is equally appropriate that in the final paragraph, when Pickwick retires to Dulwich, our angel in tights, gaiters—and a hat—"is known by all the poor people about, who never fail to take their hats off, as he passes, with great respect" (898; ch. 57). But perhaps the last astonishing, melodramatic flourish should be left to Tony Weller, who, after hearing Sam's desire to serve Pickwick happily ever after, "rose from his chair, and, forgetting all considerations of time, place, or propriety, waved his hat above his head, and gave three vehement cheers" (887; ch. 56). Tony may well have cheered, "Hats off to Dickens!"[34]

NOTES

1. In *Dombey and Son*, Mrs. MacStinger counters the sexism of the old adage by amending it to "an Englishwoman's house was her castle" (180; ch. 9). David Vincent notes that even in Victorian times, "the eponymous hero [of the *Pickwick Papers*] in a fixed pose and dress gained an iconic force" (190). In "Noctes Pickwickianae," a "plagiarism of 1840" cited by Louis James, Sam Weller illustrates this iconicity by exclaiming to Pickwick, "I hope you aren't arter changing that broad-brimmed tile . . . celebrated black gaiters, or . . . them yaller tights" (48).

2. In *Rabelais and His World*, Mikhail Bakhtin relevantly addresses "the essential topographical element of the bodily hierarchy turned upside down; the lower stratum replaces the upper stratum" (309) so that the *mundus inversus* leads to the *unus mundus*. The anonymous article "Fashions," an historical survey of British dress codes in *All the Year Round*, reflects Dickens's life-long habit of seeing connections between heels and hats: "But the boots—the feet covering—they and the head-dresses went beyond all else in extravagance and no-meaningness" (126) during the reign of Richard II. Finally, the chiastic, vertical gazes of "the tragedian" Mr. Lenville in *Nicholas Nickleby* suggest that "melodramatic performances" may have influenced Dickens's hat-to-heel dialectics: Lenville took "an upward look at Nicholas, beginning at his boots and ending at the crown of his head, and then a downward one, beginning at the crown of his head, and ending at his boots—which two looks, as everybody knows, express defiance on the stage" (458; ch. 29).

3. Like Miller, Julian Wolfreys focuses on "certain . . . overlooked idiosyncrasies of detail" (41) in *Pickwick*, specifically visual tropes, while in *Victorian Things* Asa Briggs more generally finds that "Dickens's novels are necessary reading for the historian of things, which are often brilliantly—and poetically—described" (19).

4. Jane R. Cohen reproduces the previous illustrators' (Robert Seymour's and Robert Buss's) evolving conceptions of Pickwick and his hat (44, 53). From these, it seems clear that Seymour created the specific hat that Dickens left up to the imagination and that Browne immortalized. After checking back-issue advertisements of London's *Hatters' Gazette* online (especially nos. 10, 14, Web) and

Alison Gernsheim's "Photographic Survey" of Victorian fashions (76, photo 133), I would say that Pickwick's hat, in shape, most resembles a "boater," which is in keeping with Seymour's original Cockney sportsmen motif. In fact, the reader's initial impression of Pickwick (and his hat) occurs on the cover illustration of the first installment where Seymour depicts him fishing from a boat. *Pickwick*'s subtitle also emphasizes *Sporting Transactions*, and Lucy Johnston relevantly notes "a range of men's sporting attire reflects the popularity of hunting, shooting, and archery, as well as the impact of new pastimes, such as cycling, on dress" (8). In *Dombey and Son*, Dickens stresses that among the "commodities . . . offered by the vendors" around Dombey's office were hunting dogs "with a view to the Stock Exchange, where a sporting taste (originating generally in bets of new hats) is much in vogue" (237; ch. 13). The Costume Store Online commodifies the "Pickwick hat" into an "Early Victorian hat with 6cm brim. Chestnut brown. Sizes 59–61 normally in stock. £46.00 + VAT" (*Costume Store Online* Web). In the accompanying illustration, this hat's crown appears (much) higher than Pickwick's in the Seymour and Browne illustrations. See Briggs's chapter 7, "Hats, Caps and Bonnets" (260–88), a grouping borrowed from London's Great Exhibition's (1851) classification of this clothing category, for a useful account of Victorian headgear. See also Fred Miller Robinson's *The Man in the Bowler Hat* for the particular social (and literary) significance of the bowler, a later "version" of the boater and, "with the familial (paternal, regional, national) pressure of its history," the preferred hat of the English Everyman because of its "ability to cross social boundaries" and represent "something timelessly British" (152, 2, 168–69) as Pickwick does.

5. Dickens's lack of reliance on certain styles of hats (though he includes many) may be a function of his theatrical model in which actors were required to provide "their own costumes" and so operated against standardized "accessories" like hats (Booth 114). Briggs notes that the stage greatly influenced Victorian fashion (277), while Edward Costigan discusses how the stage influenced *Pickwick* (101–21).

6. See Bernstein's *Bitter Carnival*. George Worth argues, in fact, that *Pickwick* develops as a "mock melodrama" rather than "pure melodrama"; and Peter Ackroyd relevantly stresses that Dickens "mocked theatrical conventions while at the same time always remaining instinctively theatrical himself" (950), especially in terms of dressing flamboyantly like a Dandy (see 173, 199, 302, 349, 474–75, 619, 926, 1001).

7. Of course, the Fool appears frequently in Thackeray's illustrations to *Vanity Fair* (1848). For a discussion of Dickens and the dance of death, see Michael Hollington, Nancy K. Hill (80–95), and my " 'Playing at Leap-Frog with the Tombstones': The *Danse Macabre* in Dickens." Dickens concludes both his 1847 and 1867 Prefaces to *Pickwick* with satiric references to the "Dance of Death" as "petty boards and bodies . . . keep their jobbing little fiddles going" (53) by heartless and endless imprisonment of the poverty-stricken. More to the point, the actor in "The Stroller's Tale" is "dressed for the pantomime, in all the absurdity of a clown's costume. The spectral figures in the Dance of Death, the most frightful shapes that the ablest painter ever portrayed on canvas, never

presented an appearance half so ghastly'' (106; ch. 3). Finally, though the theatrical, rather than pictorial, tradition of hats seems to have influenced Dickens most
significantly, Michael Steig stresses an ''almost endless'' list of ''fairly standard
emblematic objects,'' which are ''seemingly simple as well as subtle,'' that Dickens and Browne both utilized. One of Steig's examples involves the portrait of
Mephistopheles with a feathered hat behind Miss Mowcher's feathered hat in
Browne's *David Copperfield* illustration—whether the idea was originally Dickens's or Browne's is unknown (13, 18–20, illus. 6).

8. If such claims appear ''grandiose,'' Brooks similarly insists that melodrama creates a ''cosmic ethical drama,'' which ''reach[es] in grandiose reference to a
noumenal realm''—to ''grandiose and summary metaphor[s] of basic relations
and truth,'' the ''drama and the very principles of creation'' (54, 142–43). Indeed,
Brooks tends to wax melodramatic about melodrama. Briggs, on the other hand,
reports that ''the hatmaking trade'' was curiously linked with drinking customs
(286), which suggests a less sublime, but no less telltale connection between
Victorian headgear and carnivalesque spirits.

9. See Sandra Billington for this distinction.

10. In relating *Pickwick* to the pantomime tradition, Eigner relevantly notes that
the ''confusion between Clown and Pantaloon . . . made the conception of Mr.
Pickwick possible'' (72).

11. The ''blue cockade'' on the hats of Gordon rioters in *Barnaby Rudge*, the ironic
''sign of a loyal Englishman'' (443; ch. 48), anticipates the revolutionary caps
in *A Tale of Two Cities* as well as implying that the revolutionary impulse was
alive and active in late eighteenth-century England.

12. Bowen indicates that the ''great Russian critic Mikhail Bakhtin writes of the
way that in the medieval carnival certain historically specific claims to absolute
knowledge or transcendent power are 'uncrowned . . . and transformed into a
''funny monster''.' That is what Dickens does too: transform those who seek to
impose abstract and systematic reason, or their claims to a privileged knowledge
of the divine or the metaphysical, into funny monsters, from the Reverend Stiggins
in *Pickwick Papers* to Mr. Sapsea, the pompous mayor of *Edwin Drood*'' (''dickens and the force of writing'' [*sic*] 260).

13. In ''The Pawnbroker's Shop'' (*Sketches by Boz*), Dickens derisively plays with
''Round My Hat'' sentiments when a hung-over ''young man'' reports ''how
regularly round my hat he felt himself'' in consequence ''of some stolen joviality
of the preceding evening'' (224).

14. As George Levine notes, *Pickwick* is, according to Victoria's reign, rather than
the first Reform Bill, pre-Victorian (its fictional time is even earlier, 1827), but
it is still conventionally considered a ''Victorian'' novel (1, 37). The interested
reader might compare the idea of ''immaterial culture'' with Briggs's assertion
that ''[a]s a concept, [material culture] clearly needs refinement'' and focus
''more on the hidden meanings of things than on the range of things available''
(30–31). Elaine Freedgood similarly argues against ''the idea that the meaning
and value of things can be separated from their materiality. . . . Material things
offer starting places for metonymic flights of fancy'' (155, 165). On the other

hand, Lynn Voskuil uses Marx's notion of a "mystical veil" surrounding commodified materials to argue against any *real* immateriality and relates this bourgeois "ideological illusion" to the melodramatic sensation theater where
"commodities themselves play the roles of independent, autonomous agents"
(256–57) as hats do in Dickens.

15. David Mayer discusses Harlequin's "penis-equivalent, his magic bat or sword,
the potent instrument with which to make his own way, to secure Columbine, to
ward off and to frustrate his enemies" (59). In Dickens, the hat often functions
as either a "potent instrument" or an impotent instrument; for example, after
Mary Graham rebuffs Pecksniff's amorous advances in *Martin Chuzzlewit*, "his
hair looked too limp; his hat looked too little" (459; ch. 30). Tracy Davis further
suggests that "[i]n burlesque, opéra bouffe, pantomime, music hall, musical comedy, ballet, and extravaganza, conventions of costume, gesture, and theatrical
mise-en-scène insured that the most banal material was infused with sensuality—sensuality that was deliberately manipulated to arouse male spectators. . . .
sex was always apparent in gendered costume, whether through tights, breeches,
skirts, corsetted silhouettes, hairstyles, or headgear" (99–100, 106–07).

16. Lest anyone think that Oliver consequently remains at the bottom of the novel's
hierarchy of hats, however, class-conscious Noah Claypole later grows jealous
of the mourning "hat-band" that the undertaker Sowerberry bestows on Oliver
while Noah wears only his charity-school "muffin-cap" (85–86; ch. 6). Back in
Pickwick, Sam appropriately uncrowns the foppish and besotted "man with the
cocked hat" (as he is repeatedly dubbed) when he attempts to sleep off the effects
of the Bath "swarry" by lying in the street; and then Sam bonnets the posturing
and equally besotted "gentleman in blue": "As the cocked hat would have been
spoilt if left there, Sam very considerately flattened it down on the head of the
gentleman in blue, and putting the big stick in his hand, propped him up against
his own street-door, rang the bell, and walked quietly home" (617; ch. 37). In
his cups, Pickwick even wears "his hat cocked completely over his left eye"
(175; ch. 8); and as late as 1864, Dickens himself theatrically appeared to a
London solicitor "clad in spruce frockcoat, buttoned to show his good and still
youthful figure; and with brand new hat airily cocked on one side, and stick
poised in his hand" (Ackroyd 948). Dickens's fashion statement recalls the Crummles player in *Nickleby* who cultivated "an air of exaggerated gentility about
him, which bespoke the hero of swaggering comedy" (368; ch. 23) and may
suggest the Inimitable's personal progression from shabby-genteel to the sub-
limely-genteel status of Victorian England's greatest celebrity.

17. For an analysis of Victorian women's hair, see Gitter; for a book-length study of
Victorian hair codes, see Ofek. Tommy Traddles is a male who practices Dickens's (usually female) keep-it-under-your-hat motif: his "obstinate hair" transforms Tommy into "quite a fretful porcupine" who must hide his (erect) locks
under his hat: "Traddles's hair start[ed] up, now his hat was removed, like one
of those obtrusive little figures made of springs, that fly out of fictitious snuff-
boxes when the lid is taken off" (*David Copperfield* 656, 659; ch. 41).

18. The Artful Dodger does, in fact, transport stolen "hot rolls and ham . . . in the
crown of his hat" (*Oliver Twist* 109; ch. 9). Sarah Levitt provides a full range

of hat behaviors, including Daniel's and Kit's (106–14). More generally, Waters devotes her climactic chapter, "Fashion in Undress" (140–56), to *Household Words* articles on clothing and its relationship to the formation of subjectivity. One could write a similar account of anonymous clothing articles in *All the Year Round* (all under the magisterial facing-page headers of "Conducted by/Charles Dickens"). See, for example, "A Grumble" (1864), which argues that "The history of English dress is an epitome of human folly" (137) , and "Foolish Fashions" (1868), which agrees: "Fashion is a tyrant; always has been, . . . a cruel and oppressive tyrant, delighting in nothing so much as in bodily torture and general inconvenience" (65). Some pieces feature hats, like "Since This Old Cap Was New" (1859), which employs the author's cap as a repeated metonym for mutability, and "Business in the Black Forest" (1862), which details the German "trade in straw caps" (163).

19. Levitt notes that the "top hat was a nuisance particularly in crowded omnibuses and railway carriages" during the Victorian era (108); obviously this extended back to earlier carriage and coach days.

20. See Andrews's *Charles Dickens and His Performing* Selves, Eigner's *The Dickens Pantomime*, Schlicke's *Dickens and Popular Entertainment*, John's *Dickens's Villains: Melodrama, Character, Popular Culture*, Rem's *Dickens, Melodrama, and the Parodic Imagination*, and Vlock's *Dickens, Novel Reading, and the Victorian Popular Theatre*.

21. See Axton.

22. We can trace Dickens's fascination with this histrionic convention to his childhood theater-going in Chatham ("Dullborough Town"), where he watched a "funny countryman . . . crunch up his little hat and throw it on the ground" with comically violent emphasis—Dickens finds such stage business to be one of the "wondrous secrets of Nature" (*The Uncommerical Traveller* 117). Pickwick's gesture also recalls what French theater terms *faire feu*: "insanely" underscoring a point "by striking the boards with one's heels" (Brooks 47).

23. Although Vlock dates the popularity of this song to the 1860s (113–14), its remarkable similarity to Sam's routine suggests that it, or some patter song much like it, was familiar thirty years earlier. On the other hand, "Ventilating Hats," in midcentury known as "Idrotobolic Hats," were commonplace (Cunnington and Cunnington 225) and designed to relieve the problems of annoying heat, plus hair-oil and perspiration odor, from heavy, enclosed Victorian hats. Sam's joke is that his hat, perforated with wear, is naturally, not artificially, ventilated.

24. Again, this point has been generally made before. For example, Juliet McMaster states that "Dickens supplies voluminous information on his characters' apparel, and it furnishes evidence of personal style as well as of economic and social level and the passing fads of the day, to which he was always sensitive" (45). Malcolm Andrews asserts that "[i]n constructing a character by initially presenting carefully wrought details of clothing, physique, mannerisms, speech-style, Dickens is educating the reader in a kind of visual literacy" ("Performing Character" 74). Christine Huguet discusses "clothing as an index of moral essence," particularly with respect to "female disguise" (24) in Dickens, and David Parker

more specifically notes that the Pickwickians' "pretensions are signified chiefly by the clothes they wear" (301).

25. Lest I appear guilty of the intentional fallacy here, I am not necessarily arguing that Dickens, who is improvising with plot and characters at this early point, consciously foreshadows Jingle's future fate. The actor's habitual "green coat" (75; ch. 2) and "pinched hat" both imply avarice, which the text almost immediately confirms. Eventual, if not inevitable, poverty is the usual melodramatic punishment for this Deadly Sin. See H. N. Maclean for an account of the motif.

26. A further wrinkle on the psychological value of hats occurs when characters exchange hats, as Sam and Bob Sawyer riotously do during the Birmingham coach ride (796; ch. 50), thus indicating their shared madcap traits, though Sam, of course, also possesses other, more virtuous qualities.

27. The "Story of the Bagman's Uncle" is loaded with suggestive hat imagery (see especially 781–86; ch. 49, including the illustration depicting eleven hats) and features generationally-differentiated hats, violence against hats, crowning and uncrowning, wigs as artifice, and the sexual (or at least romance) implications of withdrawing a lady's hood.

28. Dickens owned an 1838 edition of Sir Thomas Urquhart's original 1653 English translation of Rabelais's *Gargantua and Pantagruel* (Stonehouse 96), and he helped P. W. Banks edit "Of Rabelais" (*Letters* 1: 455, 459), which eventually appeared in three lengthy installments in *Frazer's Magazine*.

29. Walters also notes that "Fielding, more robust [than Dickens,] places Parson Adams in a situation of less delicacy [than Pickwick's] though of equal innocence" (58). Dickens, of course, named one of his sons Henry Fielding Dickens in homage to the novelist (Ackroyd 556).

30. Cohen mentions the lady's "beribboned bonnet perch[ing] flirtatiously on the knob" in Browne's illustration (66), and her bed curtains reproduce the theater curtains framing the frontispiece illustration (which themselves preview the bed curtains' conical opening that frames Pickwick's nightcap). See Steig's account of the theatrical implications of the frontispiece (38–39) and Wolfrey's perceptive discussion of visual motifs in this nightcap scene (50). *Nickleby* asserts that going "to bed in a nightcap" is a "low comedy" convention, though the nightcap wearer, in this instance, happens to be a circus pony who also "ate apple-pie" and "fired pistols" (361; ch. 23), while Mrs. Nickleby delivers a spirited and detailed panegyric on the "great deal of comfort in a night-cap" (565; ch. 37).

31. Winkle's cartwheeling perspective here seems related to the Bildungsroman motif of being "turned upside down" as characters like Pip (in the opening churchyard scene) are "stood on their head" so as to "move beyond the limits of the past socially static ways of being" and to adopt "a new vision" (Levine 85, 91). Repeated childhood metaphors suggest that *Pickwick* develops as a kind of ironic coming-of-age fable. Pickwick's own "turning" figuratively illustrates Hugo Rayner's notion of the "forgotten virtue" of *eutrapelia* performed by the "well-turning" or holistically playful individual: "This refined mentality of eutrapelia is therefore a kind of mobility of the soul, by which a truly cultured person 'turns' to lovely, bright, and relaxing things, without losing himself in them; it is, so to speak, a spiritual elegance of movement" (67, 94–95). Wolfreys also addresses

the pivotal "double question of perception and perspective" in *Pickwick* (11) and generally discusses the "zoetrope ('wheel of life')" (69–70) without referencing Wardle's carriage wheel. Finally, see Campbell for a reading of the Wheel of Fortune motif throughout Dickens's fiction.

32. For an excellent anthology of essays employing Winnicott's object-relations theory, see Peter L. Rudnytsky's collection, *Transitional Objects and Potential Spaces: Literary Uses of D. W. Winnicott*. For a discussion of the role of play in *Pickwick*, see my "Dickens's Praise of Folly: Play in *The Pickwick Papers*."

33. Kincaid describes the Fat Boy as "that genderless image of engulfing, cannibalistic self-indulgence, the satisfaction of every desire worth having. . . . He promises to make our flesh creep, and he does, makes it creep and tingle sensuously by reaching out to caress it." In the flesh, he personifies *Pickwick* as "a great carnival luring us back to full eros" (*Annoying the Victorians* 24, 22, 26).

34. Such a climactic cheer also occurs after the pardon of Barnaby Rudge, when Garbriel Varden, "in a glow of joy and right good-humour, waved his hat [to the London crowd] until the daylight shone between its brim and crown" (711; ch. 79), figuratively linking the novel's imagery of solar renewal with both the miraculous saving of Barnaby's head from hanging and the Royalist or loyalist principles which the Gordon rioters previously repudiated but the present crowd reaffirms. In closing, I should note that Paul Schacht's "In Pursuit of Pickwick's Hat: Dickens and the Epistemology of Utilitarianism" appeared after the present essay had been accepted for publication. Schacht argues that "[h]ats often serve as a comic prop in Dickens's novels" and help cue "the moral turn in Pickwick himself toward awareness and responsibility," but, most importantly, they satirize "the epistemological failure of utilitarianism" (2, 6). The latter portions of Schacht's essay are, in fact, more concerned with Dickens's nuanced take on utilitarianism, which extends to *Oliver Twist* and *Hard Times*, than with his hat metaphors. The present essay, on the other hand, is more concerned with the effects of melodrama, the carnivalesque, and commodity culture on Dickensian hats. Taken together, the two approaches demonstrate, I think, the wide-ranging cultural context of hats in Dickens's fiction.

WORKS CITED

Ackroyd, Peter. *Dickens*. London: Sinclair-Stevenson, 1990.

Adams, James Eli. "Reading with Buzfuz." *Contemporary Dickens*. Eds. Eileen Gillooly and Deirdre David. Columbus: Ohio State UP, 2009. 231–44.

"All Round My Hat." *Contemplator*. Web. 20 Sept. 2008. <http://www.contemplator.com/england/round.html>

Andrews, Malcolm. *Charles Dickens and His Performing Selves: Dickens and the Public Readings*. Oxford: Oxford UP, 2007.

———. "Performing Character." *Palgrave Advances in Charles Dickens Studies*. Ed. John Bowen and Robert L. Patten. Houndmills, Basingstoke, Hampshire: Palgrave, 2006. 69–89.

Anonymous. "Art of Dress." *The Quarterly Review* 79 (1847): 372–99.

———. "Business in the Black Forest." *All the Year Round* 7 (26 Apr. 1862): 163–65.

———. "Fashions." *All the Year Round* 4 (17 Nov. 1860): 125–29.

———. "Foolish Fashions." *All the Year Round* 20 (27 June 1868): 65–68.

———. "A Grumble." *All the Year Round* 11 (19 Mar. 1864): 136–38.

———. "Since this Old Cap was New." *All the Year Round* 2 (19 Nov. 1859): 76–80.

Arac, Jonathan. "The Form of Carnival in *Under the Volcano*." *PMLA* 92 (1977): 481–89.

Axton, William F. "*Pickwick Papers* and the *Theatrum Mundi*." *Circle of Fire: Dickens' Vision and Style and the Popular Victorian Theater*. Lexington: U of Kentucky P, 1966. 60–83.

Bakhtin, Mikhail. *The Dialogic Imagination*. Trans. Caryl Emerson and Michael Holquist. Ed. Michael Holquist. Austin: U of Texas P, 1981.

———. *Rabelais and His World*. Trans. Hélène Iswolsky. Foreword by Krystyna Pomorska. Bloomington: Indiana UP, 1984.

Bernstein, Michael André. *Bitter Carnival: Ressentiment and the Abject Hero*. Princeton: Princeton UP, 1992.

Billington, Sandra. " 'Suffer Fools Gladly': The Fool in Medieval England and the Play *Mankind*." *The Fool and the Trickster: Studies in Honour of Enid Welsford*. Ed. Paul V. A. Williams. Ipswich, England: D. S. Brewer; Totowa, New Jersey: Rowman and Littlefield, 1979. 36–54.

Booth, Michael R. *Theatre in the Victorian Age*. Cambridge: Cambridge UP, 1995.

Bowen, John. "dickens and the force of writing" [*sic*]. *Palgrave Advances in Dickens Studies*. See Andrews. 255–72.

———. *Other Dickens:* Pickwick *to* Chuzzlewit. Oxford: Oxford UP, 2000.

[Boyle, Mary Louisa, and Charles Dickens]. "My Mahogany Friend." *Household Words* 2 (8 Mar. 1851): 558–62.

Briggs, Asa. *Victorian Things*. Chicago: U of Chicago P, 1989.

Brooks, Peter. *The Melodramatic Imagination: Balzac, Henry James, Melodrama and the Mode of Excess*. New Haven: Yale UP, 1995.

Campbell, Elizabeth. *Fortune's Wheel: Dickens and the Iconography of Time*. Athens: Ohio UP, 2003.

Carlyle, Thomas. *Sartor Resartus*. Ed. Kerry McSweeney and Peter Sabor. Oxford: Oxford UP, 1987.

Carroll, Lewis. *The Annotated Alice: The Definitive Edition*. Intro. Martin Gardener. Illus. John Tenniel. New York: Norton, 2000.

[Chorley, Henry Fothergill]. "The Brown Hat." *Household Words* 1 (4 May 1850): 133–35.

Clark, Fiona. *Hats*. The Costume Accessories Series. London: Batsford, 1982.

Cohen, Jane R. *Dickens and His Original Illustrators*. Columbus: Ohio UP, 1980.

Costigan, Edward. "Pickwick's Stage Manager." *The Dickensian* 99 (2003): 101–21.

The Costume Store Online. Web. 20 Aug. 2008. <http://www.shopcreator.com/mall/productpage.cfm/TheCostumeStoreOnline/_05–45/90146/Pickwick%20hat>

Cunnington, C. Willet, and Phillis Cunnington. *Handbook of English Costume in the Nineteenth Century*. London: Faber, 1970.

Davis, Tracy C. "The Actress in Victorian Pornography." *Victorian Scandals: Representations of Gender and Class*. Ed. Kristine Ottesen Garrigan. Athens: Ohio UP, 1992. 99–133.

Dickens, Charles. *American Notes for General Circulation*. Intro. John S. Whitley and Arnold Goldman. London: Penguin, 1972.

———. *Barnaby Rudge*. Ed. and intro. Gordon Spence. Harmondsworth: Penguin, 1971.

———. *Bleak House*. Ed. Norman Page. Intro. J. Hillis Miller. London: Penguin, 1985.

———. *A Christmas Carol*. Illus. John Leech. London: Penguin, 1984.

———. *David Copperfield*. Ed. Trevor Blount. London: Penguin, 1988.

———. *Dombey and Son*. Ed. Peter Fairclough. Intro. Raymond Williams. Harmondsworth: Penguin, 1985.

———. *Great Expectations*. Ed. Angus Calder. London: Penguin, 1985.

———. *Hard Times*. Ed. David Craig. London: Penguin, 1988.

———. "The Lazy Tour of Two Idle Apprentices." In collaboration with Wilkie Collins. *Christmas Stories*. Intro. Margaret Lane. *The Oxford Illustrated Dickens*. No vol. London: Oxford UP, 1966. 661–758.

———. *The Letters of Charles Dickens*. Pilgrim Edition. 12 vols. Ed. Madeline House, Graham Storey, Kathleen Tillotson, et al. Oxford: Clarendon, 1965–2003.

———. *Little Dorrit*. Ed. John Holloway. Harmondsworth: Penguin, 1967.

———. *Martin Chuzzlewit*. Ed. Patricia Ingham. London: Penguin, 1999.

———. *The Mystery of Edwin Drood*. Ed. David Paroissien. London: Penguin, 2002.

———. *Nicholas Nickleby*. Ed. Michael Slater. Harmondsworth: Penguin, 1978.

———. *The Old Curiosity Shop*. Ed. Angus Easson. Intro. Malcolm Andrews. Harmondsworth: Penguin, 1986.

———. *Oliver Twist*. Ed. Peter Fairclough. Intro. Angus Wilson. Harmondsworth: Penguin, 1985.

———. *Our Mutual Friend*. Ed. Adrian Poole. London: Penguin, 1997.

———. ''The Pantomime of Life.'' *Miscellaneous Tales, Sketches, Etc. The Works of Charles Dickens*. No vol. Booklovers Edition. Managing ed. John H. Clifford. New York: The University Society, 1908. 226–34.

———. *The Pickwick Papers*. Ed. Robert L. Patten. London: Penguin, 1986.

———. *Pictures from Italy*. *American Notes* and *Pictures from Italy*. Intro. Sacheverell Sitwell. *The Oxford Illustrated Dickens*. No. vol. London: Oxford UP, 1974. 255–433.

———. *Sketches by Boz*. Ed. Dennis Walder. London: Penguin, 1995.

———. *A Tale of Two Cities*. Ed. George Woodcock. London: Penguin, 1988.

———. *The Uncommercial Traveller*. *The Uncommercial Traveller* and *Reprinted Pieces*. Intro. Leslie C. Staples. *The Oxford Illustrated Dickens*. No. vol. London: Oxford UP, 1973. 1–362.

Doyle, Sir Conan. ''The Blue Carbuncle.'' *Adventures of Sherlock Holmes* in *The Strand Magazine*. Collector's Edition. Ed. Edgar Smith. Intro. Vincent Starrett. Norwalk, CT: Easton P, 1981. 375–95.

Eigner, Edwin. *The Dickens Pantomime*. Berkeley: U of California P, 1989.

Fielding, Henry. *Joseph Andrews*. New York: Washington Square P, 1963.

Forster, John. *The Life of Charles Dickens*. 2 vols. London: Chapman Hall, New York: Scribner's, n.d.

Freedgood, Elaine. ''Commodity Criticism and Victorian Thing Culture.'' *Contemporary Dickens*. See Adams. 152–68.

Gernsheim, Alison. *Victorian and Edwardian Fashion: A Photographic Survey*. New York: Dover, 1981.

Gitter, Elisabeth G. "The Power of Women's Hair in the Victorian Imagination." *PMLA* 99 (1984): 936–54.

Glavin, John. "Pickwick on the Wrong Side of the Door." *Dickens Studies Annual* 22 (1993): 1–20.

Hatters' Gazette. Web. 20 Aug. 2008. <http://www.hatshapers.com/images/ Mens_hat_Advertisement.jgp>

Hennelly, Mark M., Jr. "Dickens's Praise of Folly: Play in *The Pickwick Papers*." *Dickens Quarterly* 3 (1986): 27–45.

———. " 'Playing at Leap-Frog with the Tombstones': The *Danse Macabre* in Dickens." *Essays in Literature* 12 (1995): 227–43.

Hill, Nancy K. *A Reformer's Art: Dickens' Picturesque and Grotesque Imagery*. Athens: Ohio UP, 1981.

Hill, Thomas. *The Essential Handbook of Victorian Etiquette*. San Mateo, CA: Bluewood Books, 1994.

Hollington, Michael. "Dickens and the Dance of Death." *The Dickensian* 74 (1978): 67–75.

Huguet, Christine. " 'There's not a doubt of the dress': Changing Clothes in Dickens's Fiction." *The Dickensian* 102 (2006): 24–31.

Hyman, Timothy. "A Carnival Sense of the World." *Carnivalesque*. By Timothy Hyman and Roger Malbert. London: Hayward Gallery, 2000. 8–73.

James, Louis. *Fiction for the Working Man: A Study of the Literature Produced for the Working Classes in Early Victorian Urban England 1830–1850*. London: Oxford UP, 1963.

John, Juliet. *Dickens's Villains: Melodrama, Character, Popular Culture*. Oxford: Oxford UP, 2001.

Johnston, Lucy. *Nineteenth-Century Fashion in Detail*. London: V&A Publications, 2005.

Kincaid, James. *Annoying the Victorians*. New York: Routledge, 1995.

———. *Dickens and the Rhetoric of Laughter*. Oxford: Clarendon, 1971.

Levine, George. *How to Read the Victorian Novel*. Malden, ME: Blackwell, 2008.

Levitt, Sarah. *Victorians Unbuttoned*. London: Allen & Unwin, 1986.

Lohrli, Anne. Household Words *A Weekly Journal 1850–1859 Conducted by Charles Dickens, Table of Contents, Lists of Contributors and Their Contributions Based on The 'Household Words' Office Book*. Toronto: U of Toronto P, 1973.

Maclean, H. N. "Mr Pickwick and the Seven Deadly Sins." *Nineteenth-Century Fiction* 8 (1953): 198–212.

Mayer, David. "The Sexuality of Pantomime." *Theatre Quarterly* 4 (1974): 55–64.

McMaster, Juliet. *Dickens the Designer*. Totowa, NJ: Barnes & Noble, 1987.

Miller, J. Hillis. *Charles Dickens: The World of His Novels*. Cambridge: Harvard UP, 1965.

———. *Illustration*. Cambridge: Harvard UP, 1992.

[Morley, Henry]. "A Hint to Hatters." *Household Words* 3 (26 July 1851): 419–21.

Ofek, Galia. *Representations of Hair in Victorian Literature and Culture*. Burlington, VT: Ashgate, 2009.

Parker, David. "*The Pickwick Papers*." *A Companion to Dickens*. Ed. David Paroissien. Malden, ME: Blackwell, 2008. 287–307.

Patten, Robert. Introduction. *The Pickwick Papers*. By Charles Dickens. 11–30.

Rabelais, François. *Gargantua and Pantagruel*. Trans. Burton Raffel. New York: Norton, 1990.

Raynor, Hugo. *Man at Play*. New York: Herder and Herder, 1972.

Rem, Tore. *Dickens, Melodrama, and the Parodic Imagination*. New York: AMS, 2002.

Robinson, Fred Miller. *The Man in the Bowler Hat: His History and Iconography*. Chapel Hill: U of North Carolina P, 1993.

Robson, Catherine. "Historicizing Dickens." *Palgrave Advances in Dickens Studies*. See Andrews. 234–54.

[Sala, George A.]. "Fashion." *Household Words* 8 (29 Oct. 1853): 193–96.

Schacht, Paul. "In Pursuit of Pickwick's Hat: Dickens and the Epistemology of Utilitarianism." *Dickens Studies Annual* 40 (2009): 1–21.

Schlicke, Paul. *Dickens and Popular Entertainment*. London: Allen & Unwin, 1985.

Slater, Michael. *Charles Dickens*. New Haven: Yale UP, 2009.

Steig, Michael. *Dickens and Phiz*. Bloomington: Indiana UP, 1978.

Stonehouse, J. H. *Catalogue of the Library of Charles Dickens from Gadshill, Catalogue of His Pictures and Objects of Art, Catalogue of the Library of W. M. Thackeray, and Relics from His Library*. London: Piccadilly Fountain, 1935.

Transitional Objects and Potential Spaces: Literary Uses of D. W. Winnicott. Ed. Peter L. Rudnytsky. New York: Columbia UP, 1993.

Vincent, David. "Dickens's Reading Public." *Palgrave Advances in Charles Dickens Studies.* See Andrews. 176–97.

Vlock, Deborah. *Dickens's, Novel Reading, and the Victorian Popular Theatre.* Cambridge: Cambridge UP, 1998.

Voskuil, Lynn M. "Feeling Public: Sensation Theater, Commodity Culture, and the Victorian Public Sphere." *Victorian Studies* 44 (2002): 245–74.

Walters, J. Cuming. *Phases of Dickens: The Man, His Message, and His Mission.* 1911. New York: Haskell House, 1971.

Waters, Catherine. *Commodity Culture in Dickens's* Household Words: *The Social Life of Goods.* Hampshire, England: Ashgate, 2008.

Winnicott, D. W. *Playing and Reality.* London: Tavistock, 1971.

Wolfreys, Julian. *The Old Story, With a Difference*: Pickwick's *Vision.* Columbus: Ohio UP, 2006.

Worth, George. *Dickensian Melodrama: A Reading of the Novels.* Lawrence: U of Kansas P, 1978.

The Discipline of Tears in
The Old Curiosity Shop

Maia McAleavey

Little Nell's death has been a central example of sentimentality since the publication of The Old Curiosity Shop. *By dwelling exclusively on this moment, however, literary critics and philosophers dull the emotional distinctions on which Dickens insists. This essay argues that the novel depicts a carefully observed world of restrained and controlled emotion. It is only after developing this account of the dangers of public crying that the novel recuperates the positive power of observed tears. When Nell's mourners finally allow themselves to grieve publicly, they are rejecting a world of disciplined tears in favor of a social community created by fiction.*

Little Nell's death in *The Old Curiosity Shop* (1841) has been a touchstone of fictional response since the novel's appearance, eliciting emotional imperatives ranging from Margaret Oliphant's lament in 1855–"'Poor little Nell! who has ever been able to read the last chapter of her history with an even voice or a clear eye?'"—to Oscar Wilde's bon mot forty years later, "One must have a heart of stone to read the death of Little Nell without laughing" (Collins, ed., *Critical Heritage* 331).[1] This novel in particular has come to represent a strand of Dickens's writing that Aldous Huxley disgustedly termed "'[t]he really monstrous emotional vulgarity, of which he is guilty now and then in all his books and almost continuously in *The Old Curiosity Shop*'" (113). Philosophers of ethics, cognition, and fictionality have relied on the novel as an important example, issuing imperatives not of feeling or

Dickens Studies Annual, Volume 42, Copyright © 2011 by AMS Press, Inc. All rights reserved.

taste, but of discipline. Mark Jefferson, for instance, admonishes: "If we do allow ourselves to wallow in our sympathies for Little Nell we may cease to be alive to the genuinely pitiable. . . . We cannot afford to be emotionally spendthrift—to squander too much emotional energy on the likes of Little Nell" (525).[2] Marcia Muelder Eaton attempts to answer the question "Should one laugh or cry at the death of Little Nell?" by distinguishing between two kinds of sentimentality (275): "Unpernicious sentimentality . . . [is] more or less an involuntary reaction (and one that embarrasses us occasionally). Pernicious sentimentality, on the other hand, seems always to involve false belief or the deception of oneself or others" (282 n. 33). Eaton separates the wheat of emotional generosity from the chaff of sentimentality through interrogation: "Are his tears 'crocodile tears'? Is he trying to control himself or is he too easily giving in?" (278). For many of these critics, the physicality of crying, which is visible and judicable, immediately raises the issues of embarrassment and control.[3] Tears become symptoms of a faulty cognitive or ethical response. By isolating Nell's death from the rest of the novel's emotional landscape, however, philosophers and literary critics mute Dickens's own exploration of the issue of emotional response.[4]

Crying in *The Old Curiosity Shop* is never free from the snares of hypocrisy, publicity, and betrayal that beset sentimentality in philosophical and literary critical accounts. The novel situates its characters' nuanced visible emotion within complicated social contexts. *The Old Curiosity Shop* advocates tears not as easy escape or self-deceiving wallowing, but as a rare release from the social strictures it more frequently emphasizes. The novel, like many of its critics, generally renders crying punishably observable ("is he too easily giving in?"); in spite of its tear-jerking reputation, it contains more scenes of characters withholding tears than shedding them. The paradox of this twin emphasis on restraint and release is addressed in G. K. Chesterton's 1906 preface to the novel, in which he argues that "There is a great difference between Dickens thinking about the tears of his characters and Dickens thinking about the tears of his audience" (563). In this essay, I first consider the novel as a sketchbook of carefully observed tears, situated within fraught scenes of eavesdropping and sinister observation. I then turn to a concept I call "emotional transference," which Dickens develops over the course of the novel as its characters cry together and over one another. In *The Old Curiosity Shop*, I argue, Dickens connects the rich phenomenology of his fictional tears with his understanding of his audience's emotional response, developing a theory of fiction built around the publicity of private crying. This theory of shared and transferred emotion is not naively sentimental, but is instead conditioned by the competing pains and pleasures of observed tears.

The Old Curiosity Shop works against the clear oppositions of critics and philosophers, between laughter and tears, authentic and artificial, and sophistication and vulgarity. Dickens tests the limits of these binaries, from Sampson

Brass's fake tears to Nell's painfully real sobs, but the novel dwells between such extremes, considering the many ways in which tears appear in eyes, and giving equal weight to their near-appearance, suppression, faint evidence, and hearty release. When Nell is first encountered appealing to Master Humphrey for directions, her perplexity "brought a tear into the child's clear eye, and made her slight figure tremble" (8; ch. 1). From the first, she is between definable states, neither crying nor holding back tears. And only a few pages later, the contrast Wilde and Eaton presuppose between laughter and tears is dissolved: "when her laugh was over, the child's bright eyes were dimmed with tears" (13; ch. 1).

The Old Curiosity Shop creates a chromatic scale of emotion, control, and observation that puts pressure on the distinction between real emotion and crocodile tears. Nell in particular prevents or disguises her tears more often than not. She relinquishes her childhood home in silence, although "it was hard not to be able to glance round it once more, and to be forced to leave it without one kind look or grateful tear" (104; ch. 12), and she is frequently seen hurrying away "to hide her falling tears" from her grandfather or becoming embarrassed when a crowd observes her wet eyes (32; ch. 3). In one painful scene, "somebody happened to discover that Nell was crying, and all eyes were again turned towards her. There were indeed tears in her eyes, and drawing out her handkerchief to brush them away, she happened to let it fall" (245–46; ch. 31). Although she cannot prevent the handkerchief from falling, she does keep her tears in her eyes, where they are often described as "glistening" (100; ch. 12). And Nell is not alone in the novel: her grandfather's eyes repeatedly fill with tears, but he does not sob until the novel's close; Kit observes "a small tiny tear, yet trembling" on Barbara's eyelash, and so on (534; ch. 68).

If these liminal moments seem to be simply an extension of the novel's agonizingly proleptical tracking of a girl on her inevitable journey toward death, they are also signs of Dickens's awareness of the complex physiology of crying. Helmuth Plessner's phenomenological study of responses to emotional and cognitive stimuli, *Laughing and Crying* (1970), notes the act of crying's vexed relationship to control: "We do not simply burst out crying but feel a weakness, a yielding coming on, which we either master or can no longer master" (117). Plessner's contest between mastery and yielding plays out internally; he does not make plain the social setting of most scenes of controlled crying. Dickens, however, carefully notes the different contexts for the mediation of tears, elaborating the consequences of observed crying and near-crying across the novel's social panorama.

The Old Curiosity Shop opens with the pleasures and dangers of seeing and being seen: Master Humphrey walks at night, both because it favors my infirmity and because it affords me greater opportunity of speculating on the characters and occupations of those who fill the streets. The glare and hurry of broad noon are not adapted to idle pursuits like mine; a glimpse of passing faces caught by the light of a street lamp or a shop window is often better for my purpose than their full revelation in the daylight.

(5–6; ch. 1)

Nell is introduced as one of these glimpses and remains throughout the novel an image in a largely masculine line of sight. Kit, the schoolmaster, and "the bachelor" (Mr. Garland's brother) watch over Nell, while "the single gentleman" (Master Humphrey) looks for her, and Quilp looks her over. If at times Dickens seems to be part of this scopophilic chain, he also shows the physical danger of life as a glimpse. When Nell is reduced to begging, the narrator observes, "although some ladies smiled gently as they shook their heads, and others cried to the gentlemen beside them 'see, what a pretty face!' they let the pretty face pass on, and never thought that it looked tired or hungry" (159; ch. 19). Diminished from a whole (a hungry, injured person) to a part, Nell's face becomes a dark metonym.

The picaresque form of the novel highlights this particularly modern problem of sympathy. On the road, it is only the glimpse and not the "full revelation," as Master Humphrey puts it, that can be taken in. Hillary Schor shows how central Nell's exposed, peripatetic condition is to the novel's structure. Nell is sexually vulnerable, and she must endure the gaze and possible abuse of everyone whom she meets, but Schor argues that the novel complicates a simple voyeuristic interpretation: "The spectacle of the novel is organized around the alternate veiling and discovering of Nell's sexual vulnerability . . . [yet] the novel repeatedly forces our view away from [Quilp's] watching of Nell into Nell's anxiety about being watched" (34). She is encountered by observers, but she also encounters many strangers, and can herself only give emotional attention to some of them. Nell and the reader peek briefly into the hovels on the outskirts of the factory town where, within one page, she fleetingly observes "a gaunt miserable man" out of work, his dead child, another woman's deaf-and-dumb son, and the mother of a transported boy (351; ch. 45).

Close observation of emotion has the power for good in the novel, as when Mrs. Jarley takes Nell in after noticing that the child "could scarcely repress a tear as she glanced along the darkening road" (205; ch. 26). But emotional display is also the engine of the novel's threats, and structures every interaction, no matter how seemingly private. Nell's first emotional outlet in the novel is prepared by Quilp, who forces his kindly, downtrodden wife to draw out the girl's secrets, as he listens behind a door. Nell, mistakenly believing she and Mrs. Quilp are alone, allows herself to "burst into a passion of tears" (58; ch. 6). This outburst is emphatically justified by the narrator:

"[t]he fountains of her heart were opened; the child [was] overpowered by the weight of her sorrows and anxieties, by the first confidence she had ever shown" (58; ch. 6). Tears are another weight on Nell, overcoming her fortitude only in rare instances. They are also dangerous: this scene of release is shadowed by a grimacing predator, who uses Nell's tearful comments to discover her grandfather's misuse of his money. Dickens punctuates Nell's crying confession with the sound of Quilp creaking the door behind which he hides, reminding his wife and the reader of his presence and ulterior motives.

This scene is followed by an even darker scene of spied emotion. After Nell's painfully observed confession to Mrs. Quilp, she withdraws to her own house and cries to her grandfather, begging him to give up his mysterious nighttime pursuit of wealth. Emotional connection is again transformed to voyeuristic torture through Quilp's eavesdropping, but his presence here is only revealed *after* Nell's tears, shocking both her and the reader.

> The child's voice was lost in sobs as she dropped upon the old man's neck; nor did she weep alone.
>
> These were not words for other ears, nor was it a scene for other eyes. And yet other ears and eyes were there and greedily taking in all that passed, and moreover they were the ears and eyes of no less a person than Mr. Daniel Quilp. (81; ch. 9)

Dickens's sudden introduction of an observer, following the ambiguous phrase "nor did she weep alone" allows for a momentary suggestion that not only Nell's grandfather but also the anonymous observer weeps in sympathy with Nell. As is clear from the startling illustration, however (fig. 1), Quilp's unobserved observation is not sympathetic; he looks on "with his accustomed grin," even as other curiosities in the shop (such as the suit of armor or the subject of the half-covered painting in the left background) seem to look at him. Dickens moves us from one scene of eavesdropping to another, more gothic, scene, basing its terror on sudden surprise and the violation of a seemingly secure domestic space.

And yet this spy, too, is spotted, as we learn in the following chapter, which opens "Daniel Quilp neither entered nor left the old man's house, unobserved" (87; ch. 10). Dickens constructs concentric circles of surveillance in a scene that begins with assumed privacy: Nell crying at the decentered center, her grandfather also moved to tears, the grinning Quilp, and the loyal Kit, who has determined to watch Nell from afar. The scene suggests an infinite regression of observers of tears, which extends out to the reader and powerfully evokes the public and potentially dangerous nature of all crying.

Nearly all of Nell's few and unwonted emotional episodes are observed and contribute to Quilp's persecution of her grandfather for debt, her decision to flee London, and, therefore, her own subsequent death on the road. Oscar

Fig. 1: "Little Nell as Comforter," *The Old Curiosity Shop* 77; ch. 9.

Wilde characterizes sentimentalists as those who "always try to get their emotions on credit, or refuse to pay the bill when it comes in," but *The Old Curiosity Shop* is full of settled emotional accounts (Wilde 190). Far from being had on the cheap, Nell's tears are punished by death. And, in fact, the novel leaves open the question of what Nell would be getting away with if she did not have to pay for her tears so grievously. Rather than bringing cathartic relief, Nell's crying is consistently depicted as restrained and partial. The very intensity that contributes to the betrayal of the scene with Mrs. Quilp is later revealed to be incomplete:

> The child, in her confidence with Mrs. Quilp, had but feebly described the sadness and sorrow of her thoughts, or the heaviness of the cloud which over-hung her home, and cast dark shadows on her hearth. Besides that it was very difficult to impart to any person not intimately acquainted with the life she led, an adequate sense of its gloom and loneliness, a constant fear of in some way committing or injuring the old man to whom she was so tenderly attached, had

restrained her even in the midst of her heart's overflowing, and made her timid
of allusion to the main cause of her anxiety and distress.   (77; ch. 9)

Dickens builds *The Old Curiosity Shop* out of these withholding revelations,
matching the terror of external publicity with the discipline of internal restraint.

Nell's defining characteristic is her considerate self-control: in her struggle
to protect her grandfather she sensitively softens even her deepest griefs.
When the young scholar dies, Nell's sorrow derives in part from her sense
that she is also destined to die young. But she does not lose sight of other
possible analogies:

> In the midst of her grief and tears she was yet careful to conceal their real
> cause from the old man, for the dead boy had been a grandchild, and left but
> one aged relative to mourn his premature decay.
>   She stole away to bed as quickly as she could, and when she was alone, gave
> free vent to the sorrow with which her breast was overcharged. (201; ch. 26)

Nell's stolen solitude is only possible in contradistinction to the problem of
public mourning. The repeated phrase "in the midst of her heart's overflowing" (77; ch. 9) and "in the midst of her grief and tears" insists that at the
height of her emotion she retains self-control (201; ch. 26). Even giving "free
vent" suggests the oscillation between control and release that qualifies each
of the novel's instances of crying.

The Victorians developed much of our vocabulary for both grief and restraint. Charles Darwin offers a detailed biological hypothesis for the origins
of weeping in humans in *The Expression of the Emotions in Man and Animals*
(1872), in which he explores both the cultural necessity of resisting tears and
the complexity of that effort. His account of the physiological workings of
weeping centers significantly on a *reader*. The reader of "a pathetic story"
(let us suppose *The Old Curiosity Shop*), is tempted to cry, but his "tears are
restrained with difficulty" (153). The struggle between "trying to control
himself" and "giving in," in Eaton's terms, creates visible clues for Darwin,
revealing what the body is physiologically capable of at that moment:

> We may see . . . the muscles round the eyes of a person who reads a pathetic
> story, twitching or trembling in so slight a degree as hardly to be detected. . . .
> If the twitching of the muscles round the eyes . . . had been completely prevent-
> ed . . . the lachrymal glands would be eminently liable still to act, thus betraying,
> though there were no other outward signs, the pathetic thoughts which were
> passing through the person's mind.   (173)

Darwin's language of prevention and detection focuses on a reader fighting
against the betrayal of biology. In his account, fiction provides a potentially

dangerous source of tears that must be controlled. The danger of visibility and publicity seems to map onto the dangerous crying Dickens details in the first half of *The Old Curiosity Shop*, but in the following section I will demonstrate Dickens's redemption of crying over the real, or fictional, pain of others.

Emotional Transference

What Quilp watches when he watches Nell over the course of the novel is the working of her lachrymal glands. Like the scientist Darwin, Quilp transcribes the interiority that he witnesses into exterior effects. For him, Nell's tears are an index of her grandfather's financial weakness and her own attractively unprotected state. He exaggerates the public, symptomatic nature of tears by only responding to their outward signs, as when he sees Nell weeping over her grandfather's prostration, and gleefully comments, "What a pretty little Nell!" (96; ch. 11). Perfectly at home in the city and the provincial network through which he pursues the child and her maternal grandfather, Quilp manipulates the metonymy of the careless observer by consciously excluding the person, and keeping only the pretty face. Quilp may be emotionally impoverished, but, as we have seen, the novel places his sadism within a spectrum of observed scenes of emotional display. He is a villain because he responds inadequately to Nell's tears, not because he observes them.

The novel's account of observed and prevented tears moves from the concentric circles of observation with which it opens to concentric circles of effects. These effects are tracked with equal care, and they include not only Quilp's harmful externalizing of Nell's emotion but also the possibility of another kind of affective response. When an exhausted Nell is reunited with the schoolmaster, she "could not help weeping when they were left alone; whereat, and at the sight of her pale face and wasted figure, the simple schoolmaster shed a few tears himself, at the same time showing in very energetic language how foolish it was to do so, and how very easily it could be avoided, if one tried" (358; ch. 46). The schoolmaster, like his fellow scholars Eaton, Plessner, and Darwin, believes that crying can theoretically be prevented, but both he and the usually stoic Nell give way in this scene. Nell cannot help but weep, yet she waits until they are alone; the schoolmaster sheds tears, but only a few. Here the oscillation between control and the loss of control is predicated on the transference of emotion between two people watching each other cry.

Emotional release also underscores interpersonal closeness in the novel's comic plot, although here too that release is qualified. When Dick Swiveller awakens from his long illness to discover that the Marchioness has tended him, he observes her tears of joy and cries responsively: "Mr. Swiveller (being very weak) felt his own eyes affected likewise" (493; ch. 64). Their warm exchange of tears and conversation continues for several pages: "Mr. Swiveller took the small servant's hand in his again, and being, as we have seen, but poorly, might in struggling to express his thanks have made his eyes as red as hers, but that she quickly changed the theme by making him lie down, and urging him to keep very quiet" (496; ch. 64). The narrator explains Dick's response just as I. A. Richards would excuse his own illness-induced tears nearly a century later—"I reluctantly recall that the last time I had influenza a very stupid novel filled my eyes with tears again and again until I could not see the pages" (257). Dickens's irony, however, unlike Richards's critical stance, allows for the explanation of weakness to stand alongside the many good emotional reasons Swiveller has for crying. In this scene of mutual tears, the dangers of observation are transformed into the pleasures of recognition.

The Old Curiosity Shop often emphasizes this transformation by dwelling on its ambiguity. Nell and her grandfather leave a kind family on their journey in a brief episode that nonetheless evokes tears: "When she turned her head, she saw that the whole family, even the old grandfather, were standing in the road watching them as they went, and so, with many waves of the hand, and cheering nods, and on one side at least not without tears, they parted company" (130; ch. 15). Presented through litotes and practically unattributed, the tears in this parting float between possible agents. Just as Dick's moist eyes are overdetermined and their state underdetermined (he *might* have made them red, a subjunctive symptom), these tears exist only as an instance of the transmission of emotion that the novel explores.

When the schoolmaster later finds an increasingly weak Nell in the chapel, the figurative transference of tears from the novel's earlier scenes is physicalized: as he "stooped down to kiss her cheek, he thought he felt a tear upon his face" in spite of her smiles (414; ch. 53). This scene reprises many of the novel's key elements of crying: Nell disguising her tears, a public setting, the natural transference of sympathetic sorrow, and the uncertainty of their combined effects. Is Nell preventing or allowing her tears? Is the schoolmaster a sympathetic witness, or a symptomatic weeper, with "a tear upon *his* face"?

One of *The Old Curiosity Shop*'s central questions is how the physical transference of tears, from eyes to cheek, or from one face to another, is echoed in transferred action. When Kit gazes mournfully at the deserted curiosity shop, the narrator pauses to distinguish his sorrow from sentimentality:

> It must be specially observed in justice to poor Kit that he was by no means of a sentimental turn, and perhaps had never heard that adjective in all his life.

He was only a soft-hearted grateful fellow, and had nothing genteel or polite about him; consequently instead of going home again in his grief to kick the children and abuse his mother (for when your finely strung people are out of sorts they must have everybody else unhappy likewise), he turned his thoughts to the vulgar expedient of making them more comfortable if he could.

(116; ch. 14)

Dickens's defense of the practical, socially bonding power of sentiment here is typical of his repeated moral instructions to enact minor change in the domestic circle. But his willingness to play with the term "sentimental" also suggests his awareness of its dangers and limitations. Although Kit may not know the word, his "soft-hearted" gratitude might well be sentimental if not for its distinguishing effects.

Arguments against sentimentality repeatedly summon the death of Little Nell without considering the novel's own gloss on sentimentality, either in the passage above or in its sophisticated emotional description. Hugh Kingsmill, in *The Sentimental Journey, a Life of Charles Dickens* (1934), makes the complaint against the novel, frequently voiced by modernist critics, explicit:[5]

By embodying virtue in such unreal figures as Nell, the Victorians substituted the pleasure of contemplating virtue for the task of practicing it. The gold-diggers in California, according to Bret Harte, adored Little Nell, who was also the favourite heroine of Dickens himself. But neither Dickens nor the Californian gold-diggers had any use for Nell in business hours.   (84–85)

Mary Midgley's 1979 article, "Brutality and Sentimentality," also uses the death of Little Nell as the locus classicus of sentimentality. Midgley addresses the problem of absorption in fiction within a social critique (along the lines of eighteenth-century thinkers such as Rousseau and Wollstonecraft):[6]

Being sentimental is misrepresenting the world in order to indulge our feelings. Thus, Dickens created in Little Nell and various other female characters a figure who could not exist and was the product of wish-fulfillment—a subservient, devoted, totally understanding mixture of child and lover, with no wishes of her own. This figure was well-designed to provoke a delicious sense of pity and mastery, and to set up further fantasies where this feeling could continue. One trouble about this apparently harmless pursuit is that it distorts expectations; it can make people unable to deal with the real world, and particularly with real girls. Another is that it can so absorb them that they cannot react to what is genuinely pitiful in the world around them.   (385)

At stake in Midgley's argument are two dangers: misrepresentation that distorts the real, and absorption that shuts it out. Midgley and Kingsmill agree that the danger of sentimentality lies in its ability to distract and distance its consumer from real problems and duties. Crying over a novel is a significant physiological proof, in this school of thought, of the inappropriate absorption already endemic to fictional engagement.

Kit's model of sentiment and action within the domestic circle is the kind of justification of emotional power we expect from Dickens as a response to this longstanding criticism. *The Old Curiosity Shop* goes further, however; Dickens also argues for the usefulness of sentiment in the absence of action. Significantly, this is the kind of sentiment activated by fiction. When Little Nell cries sympathetically (in a carefully carved out private space) over the two separated sisters whose brief reunion she witnesses, Dickens's narrator offers a defense of seemingly fruitless tears:

> Why were the eyes of little Nell wet, that night, with tears like those of the two sisters? Why did she bear a grateful heart because they had met, and feel it pain to think that they would shortly part? Let us not believe that any selfish reference—unconscious though it might have been—to her own trials awoke this sympathy, but thank God that the innocent joys of others can strongly move us, and that we, even in our fallen nature, have one source of pure emotion which must be prized in Heaven!   (251; ch. 32)

Nell's relationship with the sisters is not close; indeed, the girls have never formally met. It is an anonymous friendship based on tears, sparked when one sister helped Nell retrieve her handkerchief in the earlier scene of embarrassing public crying, when "all eyes were again turned towards her" (245; ch. 31), and cemented when Nell observes the two sisters' reunion by chance: "Nell felt as if her heart would break when she saw them meet. They went a little apart from the knot of people who had congregated about the coach, and fell upon each other's neck, and sobbed, and wept with joy" (250; ch. 32). These two scenes frame both the shame and the communal power of public emotion, even when the connection among the actors is akin to the connection of reader and fictional character.

Nell's distant observation of the sisters echoes the loneliness of the voyeur, but is marked by the narrator as defensibly pleasurable. Linked to the sisters by shared public crying, and trailing after them through the town, Nell feels, "in her sympathy with them and her recognition in their trials of something akin to her own loneliness of spirit, a comfort and a consolation which made such moments a time of deep delight, though the softened pleasure they yielded was of that kind which lives and dies in tears" (322; ch. 42). Here Dickens isolates the brand of sentimentality that is most upsetting to philosophers. The kind of grief that Michael Tanner, for one, identifies as sentimental has "a general but not overpowering melancholy tone, [which] can be in a certain degree pleasant, and on that account sentimental" (133). Tanner distrusts pleasurable sorrow because it can be courted, whereas Dickens allows for "softened pleasure" against the dangerous context of emotion that *The Old Curiosity Shop* depicts so richly.

The novel's carefully calibrated balance of display, effects, pleasure, and pain allows Dickens to defend all such sympathetic tears, not only Nell's, but those that "move *us*," expanding the reach of his argument to include the reader's melancholy pleasure in reading of Nell's sorrows. Throughout the novel, benevolence is motivated by identification and transference—not the selfish motive of Nell crying for her own sorrows, but Nell crying with "tears like those of the two sisters." This is the importance of analogy and connection, of the kind that becomes emphatic in Dickens's later novels. For the appropriately sympathetic, crying must be contagious.

The transference of tears and sympathy among the novel's characters provides a model for their relationships. Many of the most central bonds of the novel are, like the feelings Nell has for the sisters, transferred from one object to another. The generational link between grandfather and granddaughter is the most obvious example of this kind of transference. The narrator explains the intensity of her grandfather's love for Nell near the novel's close by telling the story of the deaths he has already known in his life: "the love of two dead people who had been nearest and dearest to his heart, was all transferred to this slight creature" (543; ch. 69). The old man's feelings for his wife and daughter are distilled into his love for Nell, becoming dangerously precious and potent in the process. The schoolmaster's sequential love for his young scholar, Nell, and finally a third child, "Her little mourner," offers another instance of the transmission of sympathy and love that is less girded with threat (573; ch. 73). The schoolmaster describes this process to Nell when he tells her, "I have felt since that time as if my love for him who died, had been transferred to you who stood beside his bed" (359; ch. 46). The novel explores the power of the deathbed scene as a particular moment of emotional and relational transference, even before Nell's own death.

Nell's deathbed set-piece is the richest scene of public crying in the novel and also Dickens's most sustained meditation on the power of transference. Dickens orchestrates the characters' crying into a crescendo of falling tears and lost control. First, "Kit had no power to speak. His eyes were filled with tears" (553; ch. 71). His loss of one power is offset by the power of preventing those tears from falling. By the next page, however, the gathered men "looked into the faces of each other, and no man's cheek was free from tears" (554; ch. 71). The tears have migrated from eye to cheek, checking the masculine freedom of dry eyes and faces. Through their mutual gaze, Dickens revises the threat of group observation into a powerful social force. When Nell's death is confirmed, "there were sobs from among the group, and sounds of grief and mourning. For she was dead" (557; ch. 71). These audible records of grief alternate now with the emphatic refrain, "she was dead." Yet even in this public mourning, the characters demonstrate their continued control: when the schoolmaster kisses her cheek, he "gave his tears free vent," as Nell had done only in private after *his* scholar's death (558; ch. 71). This famously cathartic conclusion builds out of a carefully delineated system of physical and social contraction and exhalation.

This scene takes place on Nell's deathbed only in the sense that it is where her corpse lays. It is not, as so many imply, a scene in which she dies. Nell speaks no hushed parting like Paul Dombey, utters no prayer like Jo; she has long been dead when she is discovered. In this sense, Nell's death participates in Philip Fisher's model of the pointed belatedness of sentimentality:

> The tears that are so important a part of sentimentality are best understood in this context. Weeping is a sign of powerlessness. Tears represent the fact that only a witness who cannot effect action will experience suffering as deeply as the victim. For this reason stories of the long ago past play a central part in sentimentality: their only possible response is that of tears rather than revolt.
>
> (108)

But by framing scenes of crying within a multivalenced power structure, Dickens calls attention to the mediated quality of all expressions of emotion. Nell's terrifying vulnerability is too central a topic to render her occasional displays of emotion simple or protected. Her deathbed scene models not only belatedness but *necessary* belatedness, based on Nell's own consistent system of disguising her emotions to protect others. The release at her death is a long-awaited relaxation of the novel's tight control of its characters' tears.

The contagion of crying in the novel sets the stage for the larger-scale transference of grief for which Dickens hoped and that the novel's reception demonstrated. The novel itself moves from private to public by extending its phenomenology of tears to its reader in a series of analogies to the reading process. Nell's story appears within the novel in written form as a letter from the Bachelor to Mr. Garland. The story is described as "such a tale of their wanderings, and mutual love, that few could read it without being moved to tears" (535; ch. 68). The tears every character at the deathbed scene sheds become proof of the commonality of this emotional response.

Just like the schoolmaster and Nell's grandfather, many grieving parents loved Nell in memory of their own lost children. The death of a child carried a great deal more realistic weight in the nineteenth century than it does today; in 1839, nearly half of the funerals in London were held for children under ten (Ackroyd 183). John Ruskin suggests that the power of the frequent appearance of the theme of the death of a good child "rests, I suppose, on the fact that most persons of affectionate temper have lost their own May Queens or Little Nells in their time. For my own part of grief, I have known a little Nell die" (Collins, ed., *Critical Heritage* 101). Dickens writes of this transference of grief between the public and private worlds in his 1848 preface to the novel:

> In reference to the tale itself, I desire to say very little here. The many friends it owes me, and the many hearts it turned to me when they were full of private sorrow, invest it with an interest, in my mind, which is not a public one, and the rightful place of which appears to be 'a more removed ground'. (609)

As in many of his prefaces, the line between tale and life, private sorrow and public consumption, is blurred.

The Old Curiosity Shop does not give carte blanche to any readerly emotions, however. The novel contains significant admonitions about how to sympathize with and read about Nell's sorrows. Two of the many figures provided for the reader are Nell's grandfather and the factory worker tending the furnace fire in the northern city, who model opposite approaches to reading Nell. Her grandfather is blinded by his own tragedy to Nell's pain; her slightest attempt to conceal it from him succeeds, because "to the old man's vision, Nell was still the same. . . . And so he went on, content to read the book of her heart from the page first presented to him, little dreaming of the story that lay hidden in its other leaves" (78; ch. 9). His poor reading skills contribute to her death and offer a warning to the novel's reader.

A much better reader and man, the furnace tender who gives Nell and her grandfather shelter for their night in the manufacturing city, tells Nell of the stories he sees in his fire, which is "like a book to me . . . the only book I ever learned to read; and many an old story it tells me" (344; ch. 44). When Nell and her grandfather leave after spending the night warmed by his story-telling furnace, the furnace tender transforms Nell into a story as well, happy "to attach a fresh interest to the spot where his guests had slept; and read new histories in his furnace fire" (346; ch. 44). But he does not simply enjoy Nell for the variety she provides; he is the ideal ethical sympathetic reader because his careful attention to Nell improves her situation. Significantly, his sympathy is not free of ego; he readily tells her that his kindness stems from the sense of identification he feels with her: "when I saw you in the street to-night, you put me in mind of myself" (345; ch. 44). In an echo of eighteenth-century theorists of moral sentiment, the furnace tender feels and acts benevolently only after imagining Nell's sorrows as his own. The novel carries this concept of ethical reenactment to its extreme in the single gentleman's response to Nell's death. In a kind of Imitatio Christi he retraces the steps that she had wandered, dispensing charity along the way.

Nell herself transitions over the course of the novel from crier to comforter, and from interpreted emotion to emotional interpreter. She absorbs other characters' grief in a way Dickens explicitly connects to her own restrained emotion:

[Her grandfather] laid his head upon her shoulder and moaned piteously. The time had been, and a very few days before, when the child could not have restrained her tears and must have wept with him. But now she soothed him with gentle and tender words, smiled at his thinking they could ever part, and rallied him cheerfully upon his jest. (127; ch. 15)

The novel depicts the educative power of Nell's suffering. It models the power of grief to betray, to connect, and finally to heal. Each of these projects requires a meticulously charted social setting, in which no tear falls unobserved.

Dickens's correspondence emphasizes the extent to which his contemporaries felt that the novel's theory of transferred grief was its most important lesson.[7] Dickens may have been exaggerating when he claimed during a speech delivered at a banquet in Edinburgh that he finished the novel in spite of daily receiving "letters of remonstrance, especially from the ladies . . . combined with others from the sterner sex, and some of them were not altogether free from personal invective" (*Speeches* 10). In "Why We Wept for Little Nell," Richard Walsh defends the sophistication of these early readers who responded passionately to the novel's ending, or attempted to intercede on Nell's behalf: "These letters convey something of the extent of readers' emotional involvement with the story, as well as their strong sense, enhanced by serial publication, of the author's control of its as yet indeterminate outcome" (316). Dickens's friends also attempted to influence the novel's outcome in various directions as it unfolded, and John Forster claims that his suggestion steered Dickens towards Nell's death (*Letters* 2: 187–88). The actor William Charles Macready, whose own daughter had recently died, wrote to Dickens that reading of Nell's death has made him relive that pain:

This beautiful fiction comes too close upon what is miserably real to me to enable me to taste that portion of pleasure, which we can often extract (and you so beautifully do) from reasoning on the effect of pain, when we feel it through the suffering of others . . . I cannot banish the images you have placed before us.—Go on, my dear, excellent friend—make our hearts less selfish.
(qtd. in Lerner 176)

The beautiful fiction and the miserable reality were both present for Macready, who was responding to Dickens's own hope that the novel would have not merely a sentimental but also an ethical impact. While depicting Nell's death, Dickens illustrated his own goal by trying to resolve a quarrel between Forster and Ainsworth, giving the novel and Nell herself as his reason (Ackroyd 182).

Dickens codifies the connection between fictional death and factual friendship in the Edinburgh speech, in which he tells a large crowd of strangers:

> I feel as if the deaths of the fictitious creatures in which you have been kind
> enough to express an interest, had endeared us to each other as real afflictions
> deepen friendships in actual life; I feel as if they had been real persons, whose
> fortunes we had pursued together in inseperable connexion, and that I had never
> known them apart from you.   (*Speeches* 9)

In this account, the belief of an author in his characters is deeply caught up
in the reception of those characters by readers, and emotion travels freely
among author, reader, and character. Nonetheless, Dickens, like Nell sympa-
thizing with the sisters, does not feel that the public anonymity of this transference mitigates its individual power. One of those moved most personally by
Nell's death was Dickens's friend and biographer, John Forster. In a letter to
Dickens, Forster wrote:

> I was about to say that I had felt this death of dear little Nell as a kind of
> discipline of feeling and emotion which would do me lasting good, and which
> I would not thank you for as an ordinary enjoyment of literature. . . . Believe
> me at least, that if anything could have increased my affection for you, this
> would have done it. You and I have sometimes had hasty differences—such
> only as such intimate friends are apt to fall into—but certain am I, that if, at
> any time hereafter, a word or tone that might possibly give you pain should
> threaten to rise to my throat, I'd gulp it down in the memory of Nell.
>   (*Letters* 187–88)

For Forster, profound sympathy for the death of Nell does not need to be
controlled by his better self. Instead of embarrassment or pain, his emotion
connects him with a social network of transferred love, moving inward to the
novel's characters and outward to his friends and fellow readers. Rather than
disciplining his tears, his tears discipline him.

NOTES

1. Several studies have traced the historical development of sensibility over the
   course of the last few centuries. See Philip Collins's *From Manly Tear*, Fred
   Kaplan, Anne Vincent-Buffault, and Robyn Warhol.
2. Other philosophers who rely on the novel as an example include: I. A. Richards,
   Michael Tanner, and Richard Solomon, on sentimentality, and Kendall Walton,
   Robert Yanal, and Richard Moran on the paradox of fictional emotion. The plot
   of *The Old Curiosity Shop* even appears in philosophical debates that do not bear
   on these issues, as in Bernard Williams's brief observation that a "trustee is not
   entitled to gamble with the infants' money even if any profits will certainly go
   to the infants, and success itself will not remove, or start to remove, that objection," a claim that pertains not to the novel's pathetic ending, but rather to its

moral momentum—Nell's efforts to prevent her grandfather from gambling on her behalf (32). Williams's comment need not be a direct reference to the situation of the novel in order to demonstrate how philosophical that situation is in of itself.

3. Robyn Warhol observes the connection between embarrassment and the problem of fiction: "given the convergence of homophobia and misogyny in dominant culture even at the new century's beginning—having a good cry is also an embarrassing thing to do, especially when the weeping has been inspired not by a direct response to life experience, but by a narrative" (30).

4. James Kincaid also notes this oversimplification, suggesting that for many critics "the novel has been distilled into the climactic page and a half" in which Nell's death is recounted (77).

5. See I. A. Richards and Q. D. Leavis, among others. In an article on the 1935 film version of *The Old Curiosity Shop*, Jenny Dennett comments on the specific hostility of the modernists to Dickens's sentimentality, speculating that "[i]t suggests an attitude motivated in part by unease with the way in which Dickens pushed his readers—through, as Leavis has it, 'involuntary tears'—into contact with, and acknowledgement of, the neglected, the vulnerable, and the victimised" (61).

6. Jean-Jacques Rousseau writes that "[i]n giving our tears to these fictions, we have satisfied all the rights of humanity without having to give anything more of ourselves; whereas unfortunate people in person would require attention from us, relief, consolation, and work" (25). Mary Wollstonecraft argues that novels of sentiment draw women away from their duties (183).

7. George Ford provides an account of the novel's reception and its critical decline through the first half of the twentieth century (55–71).

WORKS CITED

Ackroyd, Peter. *Dickens*. London: Vintage, 2002.

Chesterton, G. K. "Introduction." *The Old Curiosity Shop*. London: Everyman's Library, 1995. 559–69.

Collins, Philip Arthur William. *From Manly Tear to Stiff Upper Lip: The Victorians and Pathos*. Wellington, New Zealand: Victoria UP, 1975.

Collins, Philip, ed. *Dickens: The Critical Heritage*. London: Routledge and Kegan Paul, 1971.

Darwin, Charles. *The Expression of the Emotions in Man and Animals*. Chicago: U of Chicago P, 1965.

Dennett, Jenny. "Sentimentality, Sex and Sadism: The 1935 Version of Dickens's *The Old Curiosity Shop*." *The Classic Novel: From Page to Screen*. Ed., Sheen, Erica, and Robert Giddings. Manchester: Manchester UP, 2000. 55–70.

Dickens, Charles. *The Letters of Charles Dickens*. Ed. Madeline House and Graham Storey. Pilgrim Edition. Oxford: Clarendon, 1965. Vol. 2.

———. *The Old Curiosity Shop*. The Clarendon Dickens. Ed. Elizabeth Brennan. Oxford: Clarendon, 1997.

———. *The Speeches of Charles Dickens: A Complete Edition*. Ed. K. J. Fielding. Hemel Hempstead, Hertfordshire: Harvester Wheatsheaf; Atlantic Highlands, NJ: Humanities, 1988.

Eaton, Marcia Muelder. "Laughing at the Death of Little Nell: Sentimental Art and Sentimental People." *American Philosophical Quarterly* 26.4 (1989): 269–82.

Fisher, Philip. *Hard Facts: Setting and Form in the American Novel*. New York: Oxford UP, 1985.

Ford, George Harry. *Dickens and His Readers; Aspects of Novel-Criticism since 1836*. Princeton, NJ: Published for the University of Cincinnati by Princeton UP, 1955.

Huxley, Aldous. *Collected Essays*. New York: Harper, 1959.

Jefferson, Mark. "What Is Wrong with Sentimentality?" *Mind* 92.368 (1983): 519–29.

Kaplan, Fred. *Sacred Tears: Sentimentality in Victorian Literature*. Princeton, NJ: Princeton UP, 1987.

Kincaid, James R. *Dickens and the Rhetoric of Laughter*. Oxford: Clarendon, 1971.

Kingsmill, Hugh. *The Sentimental Journey, a Life of Charles Dickens*. New York: Morrow, 1935.

Leavis, Q. D. *Fiction and the Reading Public*. London: Chatto & Windus, 1932.

Lerner, Laurence. *Angels and Absences: Child Deaths in the Nineteenth Century*. 1st ed. Nashville, TN: Vanderbilt UP, 1997.

Midgely, Mary. "Brutality and Sentimentality," *Philosophy* 54 (July 1979): 385–89.

Moran, Richard. "The Expression of Feeling in Imagination." *The Philosophical Review* 103.1 (1994): 75–106.

Plessner, Helmuth. *Laughing and Crying: A Study of the Limits of Human Behavior*. Evanston: Northwestern UP, 1970.

Richards, I. A. *Practical Criticism: A Study of Literary Judgment*. New York: Harcourt Brace, 1935.

Rousseau, Jean-Jacques. *Politics and the Arts: Letter to M. D'Alembert on the Theatre*. Ithaca, NY: Cornell UP, 1960.

Schor, Hilary Margo. *Dickens and the Daughter of the House*. Cambridge Studies in Nineteenth-Century Literature and Culture 25. Cambridge: Cambridge UP, 1999.

Solomon, Robert C. "In Defense of Sentimentality." *Emotion and the Arts.* Ed. Mette Horjt and Sue Laver. New York: Oxford UP, 1997. 225–45.

Tanner, Michael. "Sentimentality," *Proceedings of the Aristotelian Society* 77 (1976–77): 128.

Vincent-Buffault, Anne. *The History of Tears: Sensibility and Sentimentality in France.* Houndmills, Basingstoke, Hampshire: Macmillan, 1991.

Walsh, Richard. "Why We Wept for Little Nell: Character and Emotional Involvement." *Narrative* 5.3 (1997): 306–21.

Walton, Kendall L. *Mimesis as Make-Believe: On the Foundations of the Representational Arts.* Cambridge, MA: Harvard UP, 1990.

Warhol, Robyn R. *Having a Good Cry: Effeminate Feelings and Pop-Culture Forms.* The Theory and Interpretation of Narrative Series. Columbus: Ohio State UP, 2003.

Wilde, Oscar. *The Complete Works of Oscar Wilde.* Ed. Russell Jackson and Ian Small. 4 vols. Oxford: Oxford UP, 2000. 2: 190.

Williams, Bernard. *Moral Luck: Philosophical Papers 1973–1980.* Cambridge: Cambridge UP, 1981.

Wollstonecraft, Mary. *A Vindication of the Rights of Woman.* Ed. Carol H. Poston. New York: Norton, 1988.

Yanal, Robert J. *Paradoxes of Emotion and Fiction.* University Park, PA: Pennsylvania State UP, 1999.

Father Christmas and Thomas Malthus: Charity, Epistemology, and Political Economy in *A Christmas Carol*

Jessica Kilgore

This essay examines the interconnection between the epistemological issues raised by A Christmas Carol *and the text's often misunderstood charitable agenda. In the end, I conclude, Dickens uses his seemingly innocuous text to reestablish a sentimental link between his middle-class readers and the poor. When placed in a proper historical context, this gesture is shown to be not the conservative, socially normative one ascribed to Dickens by many modern critics, but a much more radical attempt to undermine the authority of political economics as the only available paradigm for charitable work. In short, Dickens rejects, and forces his readers to reject, the narrowly rational, scientific outlook that consigned the poor to workhouses and chooses instead a more emotional, and emotionally satisfying, personal relationship to charity. While this charitable message is quite simple on its surface, the techniques Dickens develops in* A Christmas Carol *provide the foundation for his subsequent, more highly regarded, works.*

According to one popular account, when Dickens died in 1870 a costermonger's shop girl asked: "Dickens dead? Then will Father Christmas die too?" (qtd. in Collins 158). Everyone, it would seem, knew and knows Dickens's Christmas stories. This kind of instant association of Dickens with Christmas, the general knowledge of *A Christmas Carol* (1843), and the vast cultural

---

Dickens Studies Annual, Volume 42, Copyright © 2011 by AMS Press, Inc. All rights reserved.

investment in Dickens's tale present serious problems to the would-be critic. Philip Collins writes in frustration that "one might as readily undertake a rhetorical analysis of the Lord's Prayer" as attempt serious literary work regarding *A Christmas Carol* (160). Perhaps as a result of such sentiments, the overall critical trend leans toward either dismissive or culturally relativist work, focusing on either the story's cheerful message or its value for modern popular culture.[1] Even though this text is more explicit about Dickens's views of social problems than many of his other novels, it has rarely received the depth of treatment given to the larger works. The very approachability and emotional intensity that has rendered this short novel critically uninteresting, however, give Dickens an opportunity to appeal in a concise and direct, but still critically compelling, way to his readers. Both the message and the form of *A Christmas Carol* are more complicated than many scholars acknowledge, and indeed this small text provides valuable insight into Dickens's complex relation to charity.

Those critics who do choose to treat *A Christmas Carol* as a text worthy of close study take great delight in pointing out the multitude of ways that it furthers a conservative, socially normative agenda, rather than treating the story on its own terms. J. Hillis Miller, who goes on to provide a broader reading, sums up these "faults" of the story:

> As opposed to, for example, *The Communist Manifesto*, put forth just a few years later, *A Christmas Carol* does not advocate major changes in the social system. No suggestion is made that the class and gender arrangements of Victorian England should be fundamentally altered. Scrooge is not supposed to give up his business, nor is he to cease to go daily on 'Change, nor is the capitalist system of getting, spending, production and exchange supposed to be altered in any basic way. . . . [T]he capitalist system itself he does not so much oppose as argue for reforming. . . . Nor are women to cease being primarily wives and mothers, even objects of male sexual covetousness.   (204)

Elliot Gilbert, in an even more cynical economic view, reads the story as "at least a partial failure" in that it serves as "a social document about a world in which human obligations may be satisfactorily discharged with some random charitable gestures" (24). Audrey Jaffe's intricate and interesting reading sees the text as "the story of a Victorian businessman's interpellation as the subject of a phantasmatic commodity culture in which laissez-faire economics is happily wedded to natural benevolence" (255). In her view, neither Scrooge nor the reader can ever escape from the fundamentals of capitalist exchange, since the story's charitable message serves only as an "attempt to link sympathy and business by incorporating a charitable impulse into its (male) readers' self-conceptions" (255–56). The text finally asserts only "Victorian culture's dominant value—youth, boyhood fellowship, heterosexual desire, and familial pleasure" (257). Jaffe essentially agrees with the perspective maintained by Troy Boone in his essay on the Salvation Army handbook *In Darkest England*: such works of "social exploration," in which middle-class viewers study the poor, "unite in the project of maintaining spectatorial and discursive control over a population thereby rendered essentially 'other' to them" (103, 109). These negative views correspond to a line of criticism, dating back to Dickens's own lifetime, arguing that *A Christmas Carol* emphasizes only the popular, secular, and commercial aspects of Christmas.

Each of these readings is valid, but each also loses sight of the relevant details of Dickens's social position. While modern readers can recognize that Dickens's vision is not one of deep social radicalism, dismissing the entire text as a kind of conservative propaganda entails a failure to engage with the story's basic terms. Dickens was writing, as J. Hillis Miller reminds us, in the years before Marx, when a celebration of capitalism (particularly in the forms it takes here) was not necessarily an evil, and at a time when questions of public and private charity were both of utmost importance and in genuine flux (204–05). Given the complexity and centrality of Dickens's relationship to charity in *A Christmas Carol* and beyond, such lapses translate into a disregard for the novel's most important message. Even for readers willing to examine it positively, though, the charitable message of *A Christmas Carol* is oddly slippery. The reader may, like Thomas Carlyle, come away feeling the need to purchase a turkey (Carlyle 219), but he or she is not likely to have gained an intellectual rationale for such charitable activity. Elliot Gilbert attributes this lack to the text's split between feeling and rationality:

> For Scrooge, prisons and workhouses, the machinery that a rational society has constructed to deal with the problem of the poor, are consonant with his own rational commitment to life. Charity, on the other hand, is entirely subversive of that commitment, destroying the crucial connection between cause and effect, suggesting that a man has a right to live even if he has not earned that right and can offer no logical proof that he deserves it. (27)

In Gilbert's view the reader will not come away with a logical reason to be charitable because charity and reason are presented as diametrically opposed to one another. Readers, like Scrooge himself, can be either reasonable or charitable, but not both. By ultimately privileging charity at the expense of logic, Dickens's text places its emphasis on correct feelings toward the poor, rather than more explicitly economic or practical reasons for charity. Gilbert's easy division between the two, however, splits the text a bit too neatly. *A Christmas Carol* may present a model of charity based almost entirely on emotion, but it is, at best, deeply anxious about doing so. Dickens depicts charity as a sentimental, rather than rational, act, but he never completely divorces reason and feeling. Instead, as I will argue, this text deliberately and carefully negotiates between the two states in order to encourage readers to see feeling as the primary, but not exclusive, motivation of social progress.

The text's attempt to negotiate the emotional space of philanthropy perhaps stems from Dickens's realization that in political economy he faces a foe difficult to vanquish with proper feeling alone. The speeches of the unconverted Scrooge voice the hard-line economic position that the text opposes. When presented with a plea on behalf of the poor, Scrooge responds with a series of questions: "Are there no prisons?... And the Union Workhouses?... Are they still in operation?... The Treadmill and the Poor Law are in full vigor, then?" (44–45). He shifts the responsibility of caring for the poor to the government and claims, "I help to support the establishments I have mentioned: they cost enough: and those who are badly off must go there" (45). Scrooge invests by compulsion in public, rather than private, charity and sees his poor rates as quite sufficient. Furthermore, he sanctions an explicitly Malthusian position toward the poor. His famous speech, "If they would rather die ... they had better do it, and decrease the surplus population," clearly allies him with Thomas Malthus, whose *Essay on the Principles of Population* claims:

> The natural inequality of the two powers of population and of production in the earth, and that great law of our nature which must constantly keep their effects equal, form the great difficulty that to me appears insurmountable in the way of the perfectibility of society. . . . I see no other way by which man can escape from the weight of this law which pervades all animated nature. No fancied equality, no agrarian regulations in their utmost extent could remove the pressure of [population growth] for even a single century. And it appears, therefore, to be decisive against the possible existence of a society, all members of which should live in ease, happiness, and comparative leisure; and feel no anxiety about providing the means of subsistence for themselves and families.
>
> (8)

Malthus believes that population will inevitably outstrip the means of agricultural production, so society will always exist in a state of scarcity that renders it inherently imperfect. Dickens, on the other hand, *does* believe in the perfectibility of humankind; otherwise he wouldn't have written a conversion narrative. He needs, therefore, to defend the progress of humanity against this kind of deterministic view. If science says that all men are doomed, then positive progress depends upon finding a space in which science can be denied. Dickens uses two such spaces. The first is fiction, where supernatural events can freely occur, and the second is Christmas, the one day of the year in which all humankind *can*, in Dickens's world, "live in ease, happiness, and comparative leisure" (Malthus 8).

The Christmas setting, far from just giving the text its much commented upon joviality, allows Dickens to deny several widely held ideologies. As Sandra Sherman aptly points out, works about poverty written between the rise of political economics with Smith and Ricardo and the advent of the "social problem" novels of Dickens and Gaskell tended to reduce the poor explicitly to consumers of bread, without other valid needs and desires. In Sherman's words, "Middle and upper-class readers were predisposed [by writers about poverty] to see the poor without unique desires and complex subjectivity, so that experts wielding new, quantifying protocols could manage the poor en masse, cheaply, without regard to traditional folkways" (4). This very denial of desire allows an increasing marginalization of the poor—they need and deserve no choice about what kind of relief they are given. Instead, they exist only to be "managed" as cheaply as possible, in institutions like workhouses. Dickens systematically undermines the position that the poor desire only bread. The setting of his tale allows him to catalogue, almost obsessively, desirable objects, from mouthwatering descriptions of edible Christmas luxuries to Tiny Tim's wish for heavenly peace and blessings for all. If popular and legal tendencies animalize the poor, then the use of Christmas becomes one of Dickens's strongest tools for rehumanizing them. We might consider that even within the workhouses of the New Poor Law, the first place that humanitarianism made itself felt was with the allowance of roast beef and plum pudding on Christmas (Roberts, *Social Conscience* 290). Dickens's motto could well be that of the charitable gentlemen who call upon Scrooge: "We choose this time, because it is a time, of all others, when Want is keenly felt, and Abundance rejoices" (45). Christmas, in short, provides a place outside of the normal bounds of literature on poverty from which to launch a formidable attack against that literature's statistical and mathematical stance.

The use of fiction further allows Dickens to replace the narrowly defined rationality of political economists like David Ricardo, who explicitly sought to "distance his model of political economy from the concerns of Christian morality and providence" by eliminating "social, political, psychological, moral, and cultural" discourses (Klaver xii). Dickens's model responds to such economic work by seeking to reevaluate the connection between feeling and rationality. As Mary Poovey demonstrates, both economists and fiction writers increasingly stressed the divide between fact and fiction after the turn of the nineteenth century as a way to police their contentious disciplinary boundaries (27). To accomplish his own divorce from economic "fact," Dickens chooses to appeal to his audience scientifically in early sections of his book, and then, through a series of textual maneuvers, to encourage them to abandon the strict position of the political economists. If he can, as Malthus does, force readers to accept his premises, despite their increasing oddity, then readers must acknowledge the truth of his argument and apply its merits to the realm outside of fiction. Dickens, in short, teaches his audience to read and understand his ghost story as it progresses, as a way of teaching them to apply an outlook based on feeling to their everyday transactions. The initial assertion of the factual, examined in more detail momentarily, eventually works to make the story both more "wondrous" and more believable, two goals essentially at odds with one another. As the story progresses, the strictly factual explanation becomes inadequate to explain the events and is gradually replaced by the fantastic. By opening his story with a strong appeal to the reader's ability to know the world, the narrator begins a process of gradually removing his audience's dependence on fact. At some point the reader, along with Scrooge, must abandon logic in favor of emotional engagement. This done, the reader is able to most soundly deny the negative ramifications of contemporary political economy.

Dickens's appeal to his readers' understanding begins with three conventional types of knowledge in the opening scene. The first is official. We know that Marley is dead because the record of his death is "signed by the clergyman, the clerk, the undertaker, and the chief mourner" (39). These particular members of society can be trusted as markers of official knowledge due to their state-given and socially-sanctioned roles. The second form of knowledge is ancestral and cultural. The narrator's metaphorical aside, "Old Marley was as dead as a doornail," leads him to question why a doornail is "particularly dead" (39). The answer is that "the wisdom of our ancestors is in the simile" (39). Indeed, the narrator explicitly denies our ability to question this form of knowledge, "or the Country's done for" (39). The third way we can be sure of Marley's death is that Scrooge was Marley's "sole executor, his sole administrator, his sole assign, his sole residuary legatee, his sole friend and sole mourner" (39). This knowledge, then, is largely financial; Marley must be dead, because Scrooge has inherited his money. The narrator's carefully balanced assertions, though, are inherently unstable. The reader needs to be convinced that Marley is dead in order for the story to progress. But, Marley *isn't* dead. Or, rather, he doesn't stay that way. The country may be "done for" if we question the authority of our ancestors or our bankers, clergymen, and lawyers, but the subsequent scenes call upon us to do exactly that.

The events leading up the appearance of Marley's ghost only continue this narrative balancing between the factual, the fantastic, and the simply odd. As Scrooge encounters Marley's face in his door knocker, the narrator insists that it is "a *fact* that there was nothing at all peculiar about the knocker on the door" and that "Scrooge had as little *fancy* about him as any man in the City of London, even including . . . the corporation, the alderman, and the livery" (48, emphasis mine). For the second time, the narrator attempts to establish an objective truth to the story by asserting that the events in it are both factual and verifiable. He further legitimizes such knowledge by once again invoking the social hierarchy, just in time to undermine it by shifting the responsibility for narrative comprehensibility directly to the reader: "Let any man explain to me, if he can, how it happened that Scrooge . . . saw in the knocker . . . not a knocker but Marley's face'' (48). The narrator has carefully established the factual nature of his narrative, but the moment that his facts are directly challenged he tosses the question to the reader. Readers must, in their first steps away from rigid rationality, provide for themselves whatever kind of ''truth'' they would like about Marley's appearance. By presenting the opening of this scene in factual terms, though, and by denying that Scrooge either has an elaborate imagination or has been dwelling on memories of his partner, the narrator implies that the reader should supply the supernatural explanation. Since Marley's death has been established, and since Scrooge is not a man to imagine things, the ghostly face must really be present in the door. The narrator's unwillingness to provide what might be seen as a lie echoes in the close of the scene: ''To say that they did not startle Scrooge,'' he continues, ''would be untrue'' (48). The narrator thus frames the presentation of the first magical moment in the story with assertions of truth, with the reader left explicitly to fill in the gap. The narrator's facts are simply inadequate.

A similar substitution occurs in Scrooge's second vision of Marley. As Scrooge looks into his fire, the surrounding tiles, with their depictions of Biblical scenes, are obscured by ''that face of Marley, seven years dead, [which] came like the ancient prophet's rod, and swallowed up the whole'' (50). The vision of Marley this time comes from what the narrator denied earlier—Scrooge's preoccupation with Marley: ''If each smooth tile had been a blank at first, with power to shape some picture on its surface from the disjointed fragments of his thoughts, there would have been a copy of Old Marley's head on every one'' (50). Phrasing the scene as strictly psychological does not, however, rule out epistemological questions for the reader. If Marley's ghostly head obscures the Biblical knowledge expressed in the tiles, then which is the privileged form of truth? Dickens's metaphor specifically equates Marley with the serpent that God produced from Aaron's rod to swallow up the Pharaoh's illusions. Is Marley, then, the truer messenger of charity, above and beyond Christian doctrine? If so, the narrator is again attempting to move the reader farther from acceptance of traditional thought. The entirety of Dickens's narration, in a Christmas book that doesn't mention the birth of Christ, performs much the same operation. This scene also points explicitly to the incompatibility of the acknowledged and unacknowledged forms of knowing in the text. The questioning of established authority, hinted at in the previous scenes, is finally enacted.

The culminating encounter with Marley's ghost exhibits the most direct conflict between the rational and the supernatural. When Marley appears, Scrooge is expected to believe what he sees simply because he sees it. The narrator mocks him for doing otherwise: ''Though he looked the phantom through and through, and saw it standing before him; though he felt the chilling influence of its death-cold eyes . . . he was still incredulous, and fought against his senses'' (51). The reader and Scrooge occupy very much the same position here, but the narrator has abandoned his attempts to ''ease'' us into acceptance. We, like Scrooge, are meant to accept the ghost because it is there—a simple adjustment for a reader who (as prompted) has already accepted that the ghost was present at the door. The ghost frames the narrative's position very aptly by asking, ''What evidence would you have of my reality, beyond that of your senses?'' (52). Scrooge can only answer that he, like the incredulous reader, doesn't know. Scrooge sums up neatly the intellectual opposition to the supernatural when he says that we cannot trust our senses because ''a little thing affects them'' (52). Dickens momentarily gives his rational creation the upper hand, a sign, perhaps, of his own sympathy with disbelief. Scrooge even uses the occasion to make a pun at the ghost's expense (''There's more of gravy than of grave about you, whatever you are!'' [52]), a moment that allows for comic sympathy with Scrooge. At this critical moment, however, the epistemological issue is elided; the gap is bypassed without being truly addressed. The ghost rattles his chains and makes faces until Scrooge ''must'' believe in him (54), just as the reader must further suspend disbelief to continue reading. The intellectual question is handily solved by a relentless assertion of the fictional.

   With the arrival of the spirits, the story's use of knowledge becomes more important in its implications, even though the narrative largely ceases to ask explicit questions. The ghostliness of the tale has made itself apparent enough so that the narrator wastes no more time establishing the factuality of each encounter as it occurs. By now, the readers should have learned their initial lesson. Scrooge, too, can accept the lessons of the spirits without question, immediately granting them transformative power. Scrooge's relation to supernatural knowledge still drives the text, however. The Ghost of Christmas Past serves as a reminder to Scrooge of knowledge that Scrooge already possesses, namely his own past. Here, for the first time, knowledge directly leads to charitable sentiment. Remembering his past and seeing it through his adult eyes allows Scrooge to re-imagine himself as an object deserving of pity and charity. He weeps ''to see his poor forgotten self as he had used to be,'' and ''softens'' into a veritable puddle of tears and sympathy (65). As soon as Scrooge has reclaimed his own childhood in this way, he learns to identify with a poor boy he earlier rebuffed. The mere memory of his difficult early life allows Scrooge to realize and sympathize with the difficulties faced by others. Memory's knowledge, though, can only transform on a one-to-one basis—it isn't until he has witnessed himself as an apprentice at Fezziwig's that he can also sympathize with Bob Cratchit as an employee. Memory can make him sympathetic, but only to those, it would seem, with whom he can directly identify. The other ghostly encounters will need to bridge the gap between experience and sympathy in order to complete Scrooge's transformation.

As we move into the more explicitly visual presentations of the final two ghosts, the text becomes more problematic. Critics tend to emphasize the oppressive nature of Scrooge's observation of and future responsibilities for the Cratchits as revealed in the scenes with the Ghost of Christmas Present. For all the relevance of this reading, however, it can be taken too far. The moral dichotomy of the text must be kept in mind. Scrooge can either see and sympathize with the poor, with whatever ethical and political baggage that entails, or he can remain a miser. He can be a second father to Tiny Tim, or Tiny Tim can die. Moreover, the visual element to Scrooge's conversion only figures as the mechanism of his conversion, not its substance—he needs to *see* only so that he can *feel* properly. After his conversion he lives on the "Total Abstinence Principle" (125) and gives his charity based on emotions rather than supernatural observation. More particularly, as David Roberts points out in a defense of Dickens,

> That Dickens, a many sided reflector of English life and a man who liked every kind of benevolence, would on occasion rejoice that property owners like the Cheerybles or Scrooge should do their duties should not be surprising, but it should not lead one to see in him the orthodox outlook of the paternalist; he was instinctively much too antagonistic to authority, particularly cruel, proud, and arbitrary authority, to preach the doctrines of deference and obedience.
> (*Paternalism* 94–95)

In other words, the balance of the text lies on the side of helping Tiny Tim, not in the social control of Bob Cratchit. The text is only paternalistic insofar as Dickens needs the apparatus of paternalism to perform genuine social good.

The presentation of the children Want and Ignorance by the Ghost of Christmas Present, often forgotten by critics, is crucial both to seeing the text's redemptive denial of authority and to transforming its voyeurism. At first the children are, unlike the Cratchits, not something to engage our pity, but something to provoke our fear: "Where angels might have sat enthroned" in their countenances, "devils lurked, and glared out menacing" (101). They need attention not because they are the product of social ills that deserve remedy, but because they will cause revolution otherwise. Ignorance, especially, carries "on his brow . . . that written which is Doom, unless the writing be erased" (101). Dickens's privileging of Ignorance as the greater evil stands directly in opposition to Malthus, whose theory rests on the overwhelming power of famine. The question of whose ignorance needs to be erased may be another sign of Dickens's split with contemporary theories about poverty. Traditional readings of Ignorance imagine the boy as a representation of the brutality caused by the extremely unequal state of British education. Education for the poor was a popular Victorian philanthropic cause, both because

Evangelicals lamented the absence of churches in the slums and because it was widely understood that better education could keep families off of the poor rates.[2] It was also hoped that education would lessen the influence of rabble-rousing demagogues on the working class. Reading the scene more widely, though, suggests that Dickens sees the real problem as the ignorance of the middle-class British population to the troubles brewing in their own midst. The larger thrust of the narrative, with its revelations both to Scrooge and to the reader, confirms that the middle class's ignorance of the poor needs to be rectified. If the miserly, yet wealthy, can be "shown" the miseries of the poor, then social miseries can be alleviated. The middle class cannot solve social ills of which they are unaware, and continued ignorance will only lead to resentment and, inevitably, to class conflict.

Furthermore, the narration softens the spectatorial distance by insisting that Scrooge inhabit as much as possible the scenes that he views. Time after time, Scrooge crosses the line between himself and what he watches, exactly the opposite activity from imagining himself as "other," and thus superior, to what he sees. At Fezziwig's "his whole heart and soul were in the scene, and with his former self" (71), just as at Fred's he forgets "that his voice made no sound in their ears" and takes a merry part in the guessing games (97). To this extent, the narration denies Scrooge's "otherness" and allows him to gain the sense of social unity that he fundamentally lacks. While, admittedly, Scrooge's blending with the Cratchits is much less explicit, they ultimately accept him as a family member. We can read this as a paternalistic gesture, or we can accept that Scrooge has learned the essential lesson of philanthropy—that he is not unlike people who are socially and economically different from him. Readers must remember the constant complaint of Victorian social reformers from Friedrich Engels to Benjamin Disraeli that the wealthy could exist in a world totally separate from the impoverished, even within the confines of the same city.

It is harder to reconcile a positive charitable message with the text's apparent sugarcoating of the living conditions of the "real" poor in the Ghost of Christmas Present's tour of England. In Scrooge's view of the miners, for instance, the narrator pities the desolate landscape, "glared upon" by a sun "like a sullen eye" (92), instead of the miners. Indeed, the brevity of the scene results in the landscape receiving the same amount of narrative attention as the miners themselves, who are introduced only by their singing and their "holiday attire" (92). Instead of giving a realistic description of the poor health or terrible working conditions of the miners, the narrator gives a snapshot of them at their holiday best. If this is, as Kathleen Tillotson suggests, the remnant of a pamphlet Dickens promised to write regarding the terrible effects of child labor in the mines, he seems to have changed his mind considerably (166). The given scene instead effectively ameliorates any immediate desire for action that such journalistic publications would have aroused. The knowledge that the miners have large, happy families and cheerful Christmas traditions, one might argue, can soothe middle-class readers, rather than shock them with revelations of child labor or sexual misconduct. Dickens may claim that we need to rid ourselves of ignorance about social conditions, but such knowledge is not found here. Instead, he appears on first glance to supply the social pabulum that he insists, in the description of Ignorance, needs to be denied.

Returning to the political economists and the didactic purpose of the story gives an explanation for this apparent gap. Just like Scrooge, the readers need to learn that at some level the miners are not different from themselves. In this instance, Dickens is being more optimistic than writers like Engels, who claims that mining work "gradually turns [children] into stupid animals" (67). John Stuart Mill, whose *Principles of Political Economy*, published only shortly after *A Christmas Carol*, gained a wide following among mid-Victorian audiences, gives the poor only a tiny rank above pigs, by saying that humans "do not . . . propagate like swine, but are capable, though in very unequal degrees, of being withheld by prudence . . . from giving existence to beings born only to misery and premature death" (115). Even though Mill intends his analogy to be an argument against Malthus, by its logic the more children one has in proportion to one's income, the more swine-like one becomes. Since Bob Cratchit's family is imprudently large, and since Tiny Tim is born "to misery and premature death" without Scrooge's intervention, this criticism hits very close to home. No! Dickens wants to say—no human is an animal, no matter what his condition. The claim might seem both excessively sentimental and ineffective, but it is the crucial difference between an adequate charitable understanding and Scrooge's original view of the poor as "surplus population." Dickens's gesture in this direction translates poorly to our modern understanding, with our assumed acceptance of the equality of all humanity, but it is of supreme importance in its own historical context. A public accustomed to hearing only of the misery and degradation of the poor might, in the end, be better served by this humanistic reminder.

In contrast to the other ghosts, the vision of Christmas Yet to Come steps away from social reform to focus on personal change. Instead of showing us, as we might expect, what does happen if Ignorance is not taken care of, we see what will happen to Scrooge if he doesn't make some friends, although the two scenarios are not as separate as they might seem. The force of suppressed knowledge permeates Scrooge's actions in this scene. As Scrooge and the Spirit view the division of the unidentified dead man's belongings, Scrooge recognizes that "the case of this unhappy man might be my own" (109), but he refuses to recognize the obvious and essential fact that the dead man is himself. The next scene continues this acknowledgment/evasion, which underscores the entirety of this ghostly vision. Scrooge stands at the corner of the dead man's bed, where "the cover was so carelessly adjusted that the slightest raising of it, the motion of a finger upon Scrooge's part, would have disclosed the face" (109), but he is unable to lift the corner. Whether he is incapacitated by intervention of the Spirit or his own emotional paralysis is not made clear, but in either case the message is substantially the same. Here we have knowledge, of a concrete and factual type, presented as within reach, but still unattainable. For Scrooge, the facts of his case remain unattainable until he can grasp them on an emotional, rather than rational, level.

All the revolutionary power of the text, however, is not lost, even though Scrooge's personal future supplants the vision of the future seemingly promised by the Ghost of Christmas Present. On closer reading, the endings of the second two ghostly episodes work together in a powerful way. The Ghost of Christmas Present warns Scrooge of the danger to be feared from Ignorance "unless the writing [that spells Doom] be erased" (101). Scrooge's vision of the future has him begging, not to erase those lines but to "sponge away the writing" on his own tombstone. The textual similarity between the two scenes, continued by the marked similarity of the illustrations facing each, is significant, as the second comes to answer the first. Scrooge's desperate cries against the determinacy of the future, figured in his own death, allow the reader access to the more sympathetic side of Dickens's project. If, as the text makes clear, Scrooge's future *can* be changed by his actions, the future of Want and Ignorance, phrased in such similar language, can be changed as well. This anti-determinist stance serves as a straightforward and whole-hearted rejection of the Malthusian model presented by Scrooge in the earlier chapters. By replacing the abstract image of Want and Ignorance with the concrete image of a penitent Scrooge, Dickens compels his readers to become emotionally invested in the belief that changing individual human behavior can change the future.

In order to complete his process of rejecting Malthus, while teaching the reader to do so as well, Dickens needs, after the denial of a determined future, to return the reader to the "real" world and show appropriate actions. Scrooge's awakening after his conversion serves to do this. The scene alternates between a giddy assertion of facts and a crazed denial of certainty not just once, but twice. First, Scrooge encounters the bed curtains that were being sold in his future, and exclaims, "they are not torn down rings and all. They are here: I am here," followed by an image of Scrooge struggling to put his clothes on and saying, "I don't know what to do!" (118). Immediately afterwards a similar pairing occurs: "It's all right, it's all true, it all happened! Ha ha ha!" and then "I don't know what day of the month it is! . . . I don't know anything. I'm quite a baby. Never mind. I don't care. I'd rather be a baby" (119). The juxtaposition of the two epistemological states—certainty and confusion—serves well to illustrate the fractured nature of the text's presentation of knowledge. Scrooge should either want to assert reality *or* deny it, not do both at once. He may claim that he'd "rather be a baby," but denying his knowledge also denies the very facts and process of his conversion, while not knowing the day of the month would undermine the very point of the entire ending. Scrooge recognizes this need for knowledge, whatever his own denials, by peppering the first person he sees with specific and commonplace questions. The dizzying shifts of the scene, however, serve Dickens's purposes in specific ways. Scrooge's giddiness is deliberately contrasted with his state before he realized his place in connection to the rest of the world. He had "rather be a baby" than be put back into his pro-Malthusian state of supposed rationality. Furthermore, the scene allows for a specific reminder that we still occupy the space, both fictional and temporal, that allows for the most thorough rejection of Malthus.

Scrooge's frantic childishness in this scene also serves as a reminder of an earlier, troubling scene with Belle's daughter. Critics have tended to view the scene, in which the narrator uses his spectatorial power to fantasize about a young woman, to prove the conservatism of Dickens's views about gender. In that scene, the narrator exclaims that he "should have liked . . . to have had the lightest licence of a child, and yet been man enough to know its value" (75). While in its context this line carries sexually explicit overtones, it also seems highly indicative of the state that Scrooge has reached at the end of the story. To the extent that an innocent love of humanity (embodied in Tiny Tim) is the domain of children, Scrooge has been returned to it. He has the "licence of a child" to be giddy on Christmas morning and to wish well to everyone that he meets. But, because of his ghostly visitors, he is well aware that his salvation hangs upon his good behavior. In other words, he is now "man enough to know the value" of charity and generosity, while seeing them with the good will of a child, rather than the surly rationality of an adult paying the poor rates. In this way the tension between logic and feeling in the story is resolved. Scrooge is aware of the real conditions of the poor and of his own social responsibility, but uses those factual grounds as a way to aid others joyfully, rather than dutifully.

Other than his charity toward the Cratchits, discussed earlier, Scrooge has another significant post-conversion moment, which serves as a final rebuttal of the representation of Dickens's text as deeply and truly conservative. On the street, Scrooge meets with one of the charitable gentlemen who prompted his original Malthusian statements. His response this time is radically changed, and couched in the completely irrational terms that the text has merrily accepted. What happens is not a reasonable, rational, carefully deduced charitable contribution, but rather a spontaneous overflow of benevolence. Significantly, the amount of money that Scrooge passes along is left unmentioned. Masking the numbers serves two purposes. In a way that might recall the scene with the door-knocker, readers are left to supply their own fantastic number. The contribution renders the charitable gentleman speechless, so readers need to imagine a sum even beyond what they expect a wealthy man might give in a fit of charitable generosity. By asking his audience, in effect, the price of true charity, Dickens makes a move toward suggesting that they should open their own pockets. Secondly, the absence of an amount forces the scene to hinge on feeling, rather than money. After all, what Dickens strongly wants to reassert in his text is the long out-of-fashion notion that giving to the poor *feels* good. The mediated nature of the transaction focuses exclusively on the good feelings of charity by emphasizing personal *giving* rather than reception. Instead of the gratitude of the poor, which might be received by giving alms directly, what Scrooge gains here is his reintegration into the business community, as the charitable gentleman answers affirmatively Scrooge's "Will you come and see me?" (121). Dickens pushes this idea of benevolence as feeling even further with Scrooge's language. We should notice that Scrooge is the one who thanks the charitable gentleman, not the other way around. Indeed, Scrooge asks him if he "will . . . have the goodness" to accept the money, then asks again "will you do me that favor?" of taking it (121). The scene ends with Scrooge thanking the person to whom he gives money, rather than the expected opposite. Giving to the poor isn't a duty, the scene claims; it's a pleasure.

By reemphasizing the proper feelings that should be associated with charity, Dickens drives home his claim that charity, and by implication humanity, cannot be reduced to the statistics and theorems of political economists. Moving his text into the fictional realm allows Dickens to move his readers past their insistence on facts and toward an acceptance of the fantastic. Once the readers have committed the necessary suspension of disbelief to accept the story, Dickens can most effectively remind them that the poor are still human, and that good works save worthy lives rather than simply leading to an increased number of the poor. Charity is not exclusively abstract good feeling, but rather a positive acknowledgment of our fundamental relationships to one another as parts of the same system. Dickens's project is not entirely innocent, of course, because it still depends upon deeply held beliefs about the nature of the class system that modern readers can no longer accept. It is also not entirely effective, as it relies almost exclusively upon the Christmas image and a predisposition for generosity to validate its claims. These choices, however, work to make Dickens's message more effective for his original audience. Using a time of year already associated with a heightened sense of goodwill gives Dickens a store of ready emotion to draw upon, as well as the capacity to show a moment in which everyone, rich or poor, is engaged in much the same activities. By doing so he can increase his readers' sense of common humanity, an emotion that can spread beyond being just a holiday phenomenon. It may be more common for literary critics today to examine Dickens's later, more cynical presentations of charity, as in *Bleak House*, but we should not forget that the earlier texts are engaged in the very same grappling with complex social problems. Indeed, the charity that Dickens is most likely to criticize in his later works is that which forgets the essential humanity of its object. The more positive tone and message of *A Christmas Carol* should not, therefore, remove the text from our critical sight.

NOTES

1. See, for example, Paul Davis, Philip Collins, and Michael Slater.
2. The most popular of these educational efforts was headed by the Ragged Schools Union. Ragged schools attempted to educate slum children too "ragged" to attend regular schools and/or too poor for school tuition. Their training, often explicitly aimed at preventing juvenile delinquency, was heavily moral. The schools were generally staffed by volunteers, often with little training, and varied widely in quality. For more information about this movement, including Dickens's involvement, see Norris Pope, chapter 4.

WORKS CITED

Boone, Troy. "Remaking 'Lawless Lads and Licentious Girls': The Salvation Army and the Regeneration of Empire." *Historicizing Christian Encounters with the Other.* Ed. John C. Hawley. London: MacMillan, 1998. 85–106.

Carlyle, Jane Welsh. *The Collected Letters of Thomas and Jane Welsh Carlyle.* 38 vols. Ed. Clyde de L. Ryals and Kenneth J. Fielding. Vol. 17. Durham: Duke UP, 1990.

Collins, Philip. "*Carol* Philosophy, Cheerful Views." *Etudes Anglaises* 23.2 (1970): 158–67.

Davis, Paul. *The Life and Times of Ebenezer Scrooge.* New Haven: Yale UP, 1990.

Dickens, Charles. *A Christmas Carol.* Ed. Richard Kelly. Peterborough: Broadview Literary Texts, 2003.

Engels, Friedrich. "Child Labor in the Mines." (1845). *The Portable Victorian Reader.* Ed. Gordon S. Haight. New York: Penguin, 1972. 67–69.

Gilbert, Elliot L. "The Ceremony of Innocence: Charles Dickens's *A Christmas Carol*." *PMLA* 90.1 (1975): 22–31.

Jaffe, Audrey. "Spectacular Sympathy: Visuality and Ideology in Dickens's *A Christmas Carol*." *PMLA* 109.2 (1994): 254–65.

Klaver, Claudia C. *A/Moral Economics: Classical Political Economy and Cultural Authority in Nineteenth-Century England.* Columbus: Ohio State UP, 2003.

Malthus, Thomas. *An Essay on the Principles of Population.* New York: MacMillan, 1895.

Mill, John Stuart. *The Principles of Political Economy.* 1848. New York: Appleton, 1887.

Miller, J. Hillis. "The Genres of *A Christmas Carol*." *The Dickensian* 89.3 (1993): 193–206.

Poovey, Mary. *Genres of the Credit Economy: Mediating Value in Eighteenth- and Nineteenth-Century Britain.* Chicago: U of Chicago P, 2008.

Pope, Norris. *Dickens and Charity.* New York: Columbia UP, 1978.

Roberts, David. *Paternalism in Early Victorian England.* New Brunswick: Rutgers UP, 1979.

———. *The Social Conscience of the Early Victorians.* Stanford: Stanford UP, 2002.

Sherman, Sandra. *Imagining Poverty: Quantification and the Decline of Paternalism.* Columbus: Ohio State UP, 2001.

Slater, Michael, "The Triumph of Humor: the *Carol* revisited" *The Dickensian* 89.3 (1993): 184–92.

Tillotson, Kathleen. "A Background for *A Christmas Carol*." *The Dickensian* 89.3 (1993): 165–69.

The Doppelganger Effect: Dickens, Heredity, and the Double in *The Battle of Life*

Goldie Morgentaler

Most critical accounts of the double in literature emphasize the psycho-
logical dimensions of the concept—that the double sets up a relationship
between the self and its projected image, or between the self and the
other, that it addresses the inherent duality of human nature. This essay
suggests that there is another way to account for Dickens's obsessive
depiction of the double in his fiction. Using the 1847 Christmas book,
The Battle of Life as prooftext, I argue that Dickens's use of the double
is analogous to his fictional use of heredity, which he understood as a
process of circularity and unending duplication from one generation to
the next. For Dickens, doubling erases death in much the same way
as the repetitions of biological heredity nullify the irreversible impact
of extinction.

The Battle of Life is arguably one of the least successful of Dickens's fictions; certainly it is the weakest of the Christmas books. Its prose is overwrought, its plot is sentimental and attenuated, and it betrays the promise of its master-ful opening paragraphs with an improbable plot. Yet Dickens is often as interesting a writer when he fails as when he succeeds, and his unsuccessful fictions often have the advantage of highlighting his favorite themes and clarifying their appeal precisely because the reader is not dazzled by the luminosity of his prose or the endless inventiveness of his imagination. This is certainly the case with *The Battle of Life*, which, as I intend to argue in this essay, may give us some insight into Dickens's obsessive use of the double in his fiction.

Doubling as a theme occurs so frequently in Dickens's fiction that it has almost become a critical commonplace to point to it. Indeed Maria Christina Paganoni has recently published an entire monograph on this subject entitled *The Magic Lantern: Representations of the Double in Dickens*. Nor is Paganoni the first literary critic to be seduced by this recurrent theme in Dickens's work. Edmund Wilson was no less intrigued by Dickensian duality when he published his influential essay on "Dickens: The Two Scrooges" in 1941. And since then there have been numerous critical studies of the double in Dickens's work.[1]

It is not surprising that so much critical energy has been expended on the theme of the double in Dickens's oeuvre, since there are instances of doubling in almost every one of his fictions, affecting both major and minor characters. To list only a very few examples: the Cheeryble brothers in *Nicholas Nickleby*, Mrs. Gamp and Mrs. Harris in *Martin Chuzzlewit*, Alice Marwood and Edith Dombey in *Dombey and Son*, Sidney Carton and Charles Darnay in *A Tale of Two Cities*. Even incidental characters are doubled, witness the fleeting appearance of the "flying waiter" and the "immoveable waiter" in chapter 11 of *The Mystery of Edwin Drood*. As Paganoni points out, Dickens is prone to doubling even in chapter divisions: "*Little Dorrit* is divided into two books titled antithetically 'Poverty' and 'Riches,' while its overall design appears to be built on a series of doubling paradigms: freedom/ imprisonment, past/ present, sunshine/shadow, truth/appearance" (26).

In "Dickens: Doubles: Twain: Twins," Susan Gillman and Robert Patten have suggested that Dickens inherited two conventions of doubleness. In the first the pairs of characters act out moral polarities. These kinds of doubles, claim Gillman and Patten, Dickens would have discovered in the Bible (from Cain and Abel to the prodigal son), through medieval and renaissance literature, to Hogarth and Fielding. The second model, which Dickens employs extensively at the beginning of his career, derives from the picaresque tradition: knight and squire, innocence and worldliness, youth and age, Don Quixote and Sancho Panza (Mr. Pickwick and Sam Weller) (Gillman and Patten 442). Paganoni too is given to categorizing the kinds of doubles that Dickens uses: "Dickensian doubles," she writes, "include three different typologies— the hypocrite, the Doppelgänger and the split self" (57).

Dickens was certainly not alone among nineteenth-century writers in his fascination with doubling. In fact, the double represented one of the century's major literary themes and preoccupations; it can be found in many of the major works of the century's most important writers—for instance, in Jane Austen's *Sense and Sensibility*—Emily Brontë's *Wuthering Heights*, Christina

Rossetti's "Goblin Market," Robert Louis Stevenson's *Dr. Jekyll and Mr. Hyde*, Oscar Wilde's *The Portrait of Dorian Gray*—and that is mentioning only the British writers. In 1846, the same year as Dickens wrote *The Battle of Life*, Fyodor Dostoevsky published a short story called "The Double." And the short stories of the American Edgar Allan Poe often feature doubles, most especially "The Fall of the House of Usher" and "William Wilson."

How then to account for the prevalence of this theme in nineteenth-century literature?[2] The usual explanation traces the nineteenth-century fascination with doubles to the Romantic movement. By turning their attention to the inner life of man—by emphasizing emotion, sensation, imagination—the Romantics suggested that human personality is multiple and various. According to Rosemary Dinnage, "From the Romantics onward the self was taking the place of the religious concept of the soul. Keats had written of the suspension of self, or negative capability. Matthew Arnold wrote of 'the Buried Self' and Hopkins of 'selving.' Doppelgangers became common currency, and turn-of-the-century psychology mulled over dissociation, multiple personality, the puzzle of moitité, or me-ness" (30).

At the same time, nineteenth-century ideology stressed the gulf between private life and public domain, thus creating for the individual a public and a private persona, a theme most famously exploited by Stevenson in *The Strange Case of Dr. Jekyll and Mr. Hyde*. As if to emphasize the duality, private and public life were gendered into female and male spheres. In *Making Sex*, Thomas Laqueur has argued that the nineteenth is the century in which men and women come to be considered as opposite sexes rather than as superior and inferior versions of the same sex, as had been the case earlier—a change in perception that was reflected by the fact that phrases such as "the opposite sex" and "the better half" come into wide circulation during this period.[3]

Most critical accounts of the double emphasize the psychological dimensions of the concept—that the double sets up a relationship between the self and its projected image, or between the self and the other, that the image of the double is a form of splitting of the individual into his or her component parts. This notion of inherent duality in the human psyche was advanced by such medical practitioners as A. L. Wigan, who in his 1844 treatise *A New View of Insanity* posited that human beings possessed two brains, which in turn gave rise to two minds, since "each cerebrum is capable of a distinct and separate volition, and . . . these are very often opposing volitions" (20). Insanity, he suggested, was the result of the two halves of the brain working against one another.

Thus was the double turned into the reflection of a perceived reality. It was a trope that seemed to address the inherent duality of human nature at the same time as it comforted with reassurances of sameness. Doubles, after all, can be opposites or complements; they can represent the personality at war with itself, or the personality in harmony, its two sides co-existing as the yin and yang of an integrated whole. However, I would suggest that there is another way of looking at the double, especially as it relates to Dickens's fiction. In what follows, I am going to argue that Dickens's use of the double is analogous to his use of heredity, which he understood as a process of unending duplication from one generation to the next. For Dickens, doubling erases death in much the same way as the repetitions of biological heredity nullify the irreversible impact of extinction.

What I mean by heredity is the biological process by which traits are passed on from parent to child. Dickens was intrigued by heredity and he often makes reference in his fictions to the inherited similarities between parents and children. "Both my girls are pictures of their dear mother," says a fond father, Mr. Wardle, in *Pickwick Papers* (712; ch. 54). "[H]umanity is indeed a happy lot, when we can repeat ourselves in others," proclaims the hypocritical John Chester in *Barnaby Rudge* (225; ch. 27). "In this daughter, the mother lived again," announces the narrator in *The Old Curiosity Shop* (525; ch. 69). And David Copperfield is described as being "as like his father as it's possible to be, if he was not so like his mother, too" (203; ch.13). Added to this are the frequent allusions to children as "the express image," "the living copy," "the speaking likeness" of their parents. Many of Dickens's plots revolve around the absolute resemblances of children to their parents. Oliver Twist is recognized by several characters who have never laid eyes on him before because he looks so remarkably like his middle-class parents, both of whom are dead. And in *Bleak House* the law clerk Guppy correctly guesses the mother of Esther Summerson because she is a living copy of the portrait of her mother, Lady Dedlock.

What seems to have fascinated Dickens in hereditary relationships is the idea of duplication, the reanimation in the new generation of the traits of the old. Dickens's thinking on this subject, his assumption that heredity is primarily a reiteration of resemblance, reflects the general thinking of his time—as well as of earlier times. Indeed, from the dawn of history, what has intrigued and puzzled thinkers has always been how heredity works to create resemblance and what such resemblances have to say about the nature of kinship. With the exception of the second part of the nineteenth century, when Darwin's theory of evolution launched researchers on an unproductive search for the mechanism behind variation before they knew how biological heredity worked to promote similarity—rather like trying to explain the exception without first ascertaining the rule—heredity has been primarily understood as a process of engendering resemblance.

One need only look to the Bible to see the extent to which resemblance was thought to be the key to creation. In the Hebrew Testament God makes man in His own image, and thereby turns the human body into a replica of the divine. (Gen. 1: 27 stipulates, in fact, that God creates both man and woman in His image.) The human relationship to the deity is thus established in Judeo-Christian tradition as being based in large measure on physical resemblance. It is not surprising, then, that God comes to be called Father, and that his chosen people are known as the Children of Israel. The Christian Gospels adapt and elaborate on this idea of a familial relationship between God and Man by personifying Christ as the Son of God, and intercessor for the "family of man."

But it was not just in Hebraic tradition that procreation was defined as synonymous with creating resemblance. Aristotle wrote in *The Generation of Animals*: "Anyone who does not take after his parents is a monstrosity, since in these cases Nature has in a way strayed form the generic type" (qtd. in Huet 3). Aristotle defined females as one of these deviations from the generic type, although he did concede that this deviation was "a necessity required by Nature" (qtd. in Huet 3).

Other ancient theories of heredity also emphasized resemblance. Plato believed that the relative contribution of each parent to the formation of the child depended on his or her emotional involvement at the time of conception. The degree of enthusiasm during sex would determine whether the child resembled its mother or its father. The medieval cleric Isidore put the matter this way: "Newborns resemble fathers if the semen of the father is potent, and resemble mothers if the seed of the mother is potent" (qtd. in Laqueur 56). In other words—heredity is a battle of the sexes in the most literal sense, a contest of contending seeds in which the winner is the parent whom the child most closely resembles.

Resemblance of this kind has moral implications as well, which become clear when one reads what these same theorists had to say about illegitimacy. It was taken as a matter of fact, for instance, from the Middle Ages until well into the nineteenth century, that legitimate children resembled their fathers, while illegitimate children—being primarily the mother's issue—took after their mothers. That this assumption of perfect resemblance to either the father alone or the mother alone flies in the face of observed reality was not something that theorists worried about. Since the actual genetic mechanism by which features are passed on from parent to child was unknown until the early twentieth century, earlier theories often flew in the face of what could actually be ascertained by observation.

Thus, early theories of biological reproduction emphasized absolute resemblance, despite the fact that most human beings have visibly inherited features from both parents. One of these theories, preformation, was the predominant hereditary belief of the mid-seventeenth to late-eighteenth centuries. Preformation posited that all generations that ever were or ever would be, were created by God at the dawn of time, one encapsulated within the other, like Russian dolls, so that the first mother of each species carried within herself all future generations of the race. Preformation gave a scientific legitimacy to the biblical assertion that Eve was the mother of the human race.[4]

Since the idea that growth entails the subdivision and multiplication of cells was not a concept available to the scientific mind of the seventeenth and eighteenth centuries, it was assumed that, since the structure could not disappear, the living organism had to exist as a minute version of its eventual adult self; and that this minute version was housed within a capsule that was located either in the female egg or in the male sperm. (There was much argument about which sex had the honor of harboring the capsule.) According to preformation theory, the origin of life did not occur at the moment of sexual contact, but much further back in time. The contact of egg and sperm during sex merely triggered the growth of the capsule, nothing more. It did not create the new organism. This meant that preformation regarded parents as little more than the activating agents of the capsules that they carried (Jacob 26).

Surprisingly, there seems to be a restatement of the preformationist view in Dickens's *The Old Curiosity Shop*, even though this theory had been largely discounted by the dawn of the nineteenth century. In this passage Dickens speaks of little Nell's descent from an unbroken line of virtuous women:

> If you have seen the picture-gallery of any one old family, you will remember how the same face and figure—often the fairest and slightest of them all—come upon you in different generations; and how you trace the same sweet girl though a long line of portraits—never growing old or changing—the Good Angel of the race.   (637; ch. 69)

It is doubtful that Dickens is here knowingly echoing preformationist theory, although the assumption of the repetitiveness and regularity of descent was one of the hallmarks of that theory, each generation being seen as a reenactment and reanimation of the generation that went before. Still, this notion of the regularity of descent is a seductive idea for a novelist addicted to happy endings, and Dickens makes full use of it, especially in his habit of repetitive naming. By ascribing to children the names that have been held by adults, Dickens suggests that the adult is in all essentials reincarnated and repeated in the child. There is an example of this in *The Battle of Life*, in which Grace and Alfred name their daughter Marion, as a way of reviving and memorializing Grace's run-away sister. We are told that "the spirit of the lost girl looked out of [the child's] eyes" (219), as if the name alone were sufficient to infuse Marion's essence into the newly born child.

More contemporary understandings of heredity can also be found in Dickens's novels. One of these was the use of the term "reproduction," which had replaced the older word "generation" by the middle of the eighteenth century. Reproduction represented a new way of thinking about the origins of life. "Generation" had always implied a supernatural presence. "Reproduction" conferred a past on living things by implicitly linking them to their forebears, to their producers. It also defined parents as the originators of their children, and sex as the act of creating life.

As its name suggests, reproduction, too, defined heredity as a process of duplication, of the reproducing of resemblance. In this theory, however, the physical, mental, and emotional make-up of the individual was seen to have a direct relationship to the same characteristics in the parents. How precisely this relationship came about was still a mystery at the dawn of the nineteenth century, as indeed it would be at the dawn of the twentieth. But reproduction disentangled the physiological lines of heredity to the extent of recognizing a physical, and not merely a legal, customary, mystical or even a biblical link between the generations.

Reproduction also has another, older meaning—that of the recreation or copying of an original by artificial means. In this sense, it is related to art, to the aesthetic impulse of recapturing a living reality through reproducing it in another medium such as painting or literature. Dickens fully exploited the link between art and heredity implied by the term "reproduction." His favorite means of illustrating hidden identity is through portraiture. Thus Oliver Twist, the orphan who never knew his mother, finds himself strangely drawn to her portrait even though he has no idea that the woman in the painting is his mother. And it is his resemblance to his mother's portrait that first alerts Mr. Brownlow to Oliver's true identity. Esther Summerson's identity is similarly made manifest through her remarkable resemblance to her mother's portrait. In the passage I just quoted from *The Old Curiosity Shop*, the relationship of several generations of virtuous women is filtered through the metaphor of a portrait gallery. In *Dombey and Son*, the astonishing similarity between the first cousins Edith Dombey and Alice Marwood is demonstrated through the portrait of Alice that hangs in Carker's apartments. Dickens consistently allows portraits to reveal hereditary relationships, even when the knowledge of his or her lineage has been denied the protagonist.

The most contemporary manifestation of hereditary beliefs in Dickens's novels is that of blended heredity. This idea was current throughout the nineteenth century, and was eventually adapted by Darwin in *The Variations of Animals and Plants under Domestication* (1868). Blended heredity suggests that children are formed out of the merged blood of their progenitors, that they are amalgams or alloys of the characteristics of their parents, and thus resemble both parents equally. Oliver Twist, for instance, is the "living copy" of both his mother and his father; David Copperfield is as like his father as it is possible to be if he were not so like his mother too.[5]

But what has all of this to do with the double? The answer is that doubles—at least in Dickens's work—are manifestations of the hereditary phenomenon of resemblance translated into horizontal terms—that is, if heredity is a vertical relationship in which resemblance is handed down in a straight line from parent to child, doubling is the same relationship translated into the side-by-side terms of peers and contemporaries, or of the inner self divided in two. The usual form which doubling takes in Dickens's fiction is that of siblings, witness the disreputable brother-sister pair of Sally and Sampson Brass in *The Old Curiosity Shop*, or the equally nefarious Murdstones in *David Copperfield*, or the mysterious Landless twins in *The Mystery of Edwin Drood*.

Even when the doubles are not actually related, they are defined in terms of such a strong mutual identification as to suggest kinship. In *A Tale of Two Cities*, Sydney Carton and Charles Darnay so closely resemble one another that each is constantly mistaken for the other, thus making possible the climactic substitution and sacrifice. When, as in this last example, the doubles are not blood-kin, then the assumption of consanguinity becomes generalized into a universal statement about the brotherhood of Man.

Dickens is an anomaly among writers in his depiction of doubles because he presents his doppelgangers with the kind of animation and inventiveness that other writers lavish on individuality. I would go so far as to say that he loved sameness, that it spoke to his imaginative powers, and that he found comfort in it. Sameness implies not only similarity, but also rebirth and renewal. This theme of the circularity of life, of its reanimation in identical terms, is the Dickensian equivalent of resurrection; it represents reassurance in resemblance. The kind of doubling that allows one individual to substitute for another inevitably leads—in the Dickensian universe—to altruism and self-abnegation, as when Sydney Carton goes to the guillotine in place of Charles Darnay in *A Tale of Two Cities*. In a doubling relationship, each partner of the pair can stand for the other and so be reanimated by the survival by his or her alter ego, in much the same way as the battle described in the opening paragraphs of *The Battle of Life* has resulted in the enhanced fertility of the ground, and in the continuation of the life that feeds on death. Doubling, for Dickens, confers the same reassurance of sameness as does hereditary resemblance. Since each generation is a duplication of the generation that preceded it, there need be no fear of the instabilities of change or the permanence of death.

In an early sketch called ''The Four Sisters,'' Dickens executes a number of ingenious fantasies on this theme of resemblance. The four sisters of the title have no separate existence; they are clones of one another. When one of them gets married, all four go to church together, all four take the vows, and then continue living together, so that the neighbors have no idea which one is the married sister until one of them has a baby. Dickens describes the four sisters as follows: "Three long graces in drapery, with the addition, like a school-dinner, of another long grace afterwards—the three fates with another sister—the Siamese twins multiplied by two" (30).

In *The Battle of Life*, the Christmas book with barely a trace of Christmas in it, the doubles are also sisters, sisters who are so completely identified with one another as to be virtually interchangeable. What is more, this short novel not only doubles its doubles; it triples and quadruples them. The male protagonist, Alfred Heathfield, also has a double in Michael Warden, and these two central sets of doubles are doubled by the lawyerly team of Snitchey and Craggs—or, "Craggs and Self" as Mr. Snitchey puts it—who are in turn doubled by having identical wives, who are identically suspicious of each other's husbands.

Why this compulsive duplication, which exceeds even Dickens's usual standards? The answer may lie in Dickens's own biography. Dickens had great difficulty writing *The Battle of Life*, which he began in Lausanne, Switzerland, in September 1846, shortly after starting work on his large novel *Dombey and Son*. The strain of trying to begin two different fictions at the same time brought him to the brink of a nervous collapse; he complained of nightmares and other symptoms of psychosomatic distress. Overwork was Dickens's own explanation for his problems. His biographers, however, have been nearly unanimous in seeing in this story of two sisters who love the same man a close—perhaps a too close—representation of Dickens's own domestic arrangements.

From the beginning of his married life, Dickens shared his household with his wife's younger sisters, first Mary Hogarth, and, after she died, with the still younger Georgina. Dickens was emotionally attached to both of these sisters-in-law. He had suffered a great shock when the seventeen-year old Mary died in his arms, and he was sentimentally inclined to see the dead girl reincarnated and resurrected in her younger sister. More than one commentator has suggested that some of Dickens's difficulties in writing this Christmas book stemmed from the fact that the situation it describes is in fact his own.[6] Even the names of the two younger Hogarth sisters—Mary and Georgina—are half-echoed in the names of the fictional sisters in *The Battle of Life*—Marion and Grace, although their ages are reversed in the Christmas book, so that Grace is the older of the two, whereas in life, Georgina was the younger.[7] It is as if Dickens thought that such a minor change would help transform the originals from living beings into fictional creations. Of course, both of the fictional names he confers on the sisters have religious connotations in keeping with his idealization of his two sisters-in-law and of sisterhood in general.

Whatever the reason for his difficulties, there is no doubt that the resulting book remains a puzzle, a kind of fictional miscarriage, in which the promise of the opening paragraphs, depicting an ancient battlefield restored by time and fertilized by the decomposing bodies beneath it, is dissipated by the saccharine story of sisterly self-sacrifice that follows them.

In this story, Marion runs away from home so that her elder sister Grace can marry Alfred Heathfield, the man whom Grace loves but who wants to marry Marion.[8] After a number of years, the departed Marion, who had been thought dead—or worse, dishonored—returns home, life and virginity intact. Unlike Dickens's dead sister-in-law Mary Hogarth, on whom she seems to have been modeled—Mary-Marion—Marion has, in effect, been resurrected, and not just resurrected but reestablished in her former place as her sister Grace's double, as if nothing of consequence had happened to disrupt the pattern of the sisters' parallel lives. It is not long before Marion marries Michael Warden, the double of Alfred Heathfield, and everybody lives happily ever after.

It is a pleasant vision, and it belongs in a fairy tale, which is what *The Battle of Life* aspires to be, but is not. Unlike the other Christmas books this one lacks the supernatural trappings usually associated with fairy tales. And it lacks a villain. Everyone in this Christmas book acts out of the very best motives. The two lawyers appear sinister, but are not. Michael Warden appears as a potential seducer and scoundrel, but is not. Still, if the book lacks the required fairy tale elements of magic and evil antagonists, it does not lack the happily-ever-after ending, which suggests that all things wrong can eventually be put right through marriage.

This is not where the opening paragraphs of *The Battle of Life* suggest we will go. These paragraphs, with their descriptions of the glories of nature everywhere stained and spotted by blood, with their evocation of the dead upturned faces of those same soldiers, "who had once at mothers' breasts sought mothers' eyes" (136) are as good as anything Dickens ever wrote. We are told that as time passes, Nature, far above the evil passions of men, recovers her serenity. Before long, larks are singing and swallows are flitting to and fro, while the ground, once bloody, turns green. Crops are grown, watered by the once-crimsoned stream, and the former battlefield becomes a pasture where sheep and oxen graze, and old people live and die. All living things grow and wither "in their destined terms upon the fierce and bloody battle-ground, where thousands upon thousands had been killed in the great fight" (140).

Dickens's love of the macabre causes him to underline that the greenest patches in the growing corn, which reappear year after year and are indicative of the most fertile spots, are also the graveyards where heaps of men and horses lie buried, "indiscriminately, enriching the ground." In these fertile patches, the great worms abound; everywhere life lives upon death. Or, as Dr. Jeddlar rather cannibalistically points out: "The fruit has been gathered for our eating from these trees, the roots of which are struck in Men, not earth'' (151). This notion of the dead turning into food for the living, who in turn die and are planted in the earth—that is, the notion of human life living off human death, of biological processes being circular and cyclical—occurs frequently in Dickens's work. It becomes especially insistent in the later novels where fertility is implicitly linked to decomposition and disintegration. This is the motif lurking behind the dust heaps in *Our Mutual Friend*, and it informs as well the descriptions of the cathedral town in *The Mystery of Edwin Drood*, where ''children grow small salad in the dust of abbots and abbesses, and make dirt-pies'' out of the disintegrated remains of nuns and friars (23; ch. 3).

But even in an early work like *The Battle of Life*, one can discern Dickens's insistent belief in the circularity of biological processes, as well as his understanding of heredity as a force that is endlessly repetitive—and one that is governed by resemblance and reiteration. That is, the notion of doubling, governed as it is by duplication, is for Dickens linked to heredity just as heredity is linked to the process of unending reanimation and resurrection.

Peter Ackroyd has suggested that the phrase ''the battle of life,'' which Dickens used as the title of his story, would have resonated particularly for mid-century Victorians because it was a truism of the time that struggle and domination were the twin commandments of nature. Malthus and later Darwin both described ''the struggle for survival.'' Tennyson described nature as red in tooth and claw. Gladstone talked of life as one ''perpetual conflict'' and Robert Browning, in his poem ''Prospice,'' wrote of himself, ''I was ever a fighter.'' Later in the century, Robert Louis Stevenson worked a variation on the phrase when he described marriage as a battle, writing that ''marriage is like life in this—that it is a field of battle and not a bed of roses'' (qtd. in Ackroyd 515). Even the nineteenth-century ballroom was considered a battleground, although one in which women ruled.[9]

Ackroyd goes on to suggest that Dickens reverses the significance of the title by turning his story into a moral fable of cheerfulness, goodness, and self-abnegation. But it is also possible to see the relationship between the sisters as another manifestation of a battle played out bloodlessly within the positive sphere of doubling. Sibling rivalry is, in fact, at the heart of this story, which is about two women in love with the same man, but the negatives associated with such a rivalry are transmuted and nullified by the effects of doubling.

They are also redirected into the symbolism of the battlefield turned pasture that provides Dickens with the setting on which the story of the self-sacrificing sisters is played out. In fact, the battlefield motif functions as a running metaphor throughout the book. For instance, the lawyers Snitchey and Craggs have a snug little office on the old Battle Ground, where they fight ''a great many small pitched battles for a great many contending parties'' (164). At the same time, the hostility implied by the battlefield and by the sisters' dual desire for the same man is channeled and transmuted into depictions of the ongoing processes of life that exist literally under the sisters' feet—a point that is brought home in the opening scenes when we are first introduced to the sisters Grace and Marion dancing in an orchard that has been fertilized by the decaying bodies buried beneath. The reproductive joyful profusion of nature is everywhere stressed: the onlookers watching the girls dance are a half-dozen peasant women gathering apples from the trees. The first snippet of conversation comes when Marion, the younger sister, declares that she dances because "it's somebody's birthday," to which her jaded father replies, "it's always somebody's birthday" (141).

All the doubles seem to mirror and substitute for one another. When Marion disappears, so too does the lawyer Craggs, but his is a more permanent kind of vanishing. In the words of his partner, the bereaved Snitchey, "Mr. Craggs . . . did not find life . . . as easy to have and to hold as his theory made it out" (217). The phrase "to have and to hold" derives from the marriage ceremony, and in true widower fashion, Mr. Snitchey describes the death of his partner as quite literally the loss of his "better half": "He was my right arm, my right leg, my right ear, my right eye, was Mr. Craggs. I am paralytic without him" (217).

The metaphor here says it all. It suggests that Craggs and Snitchey together made up one body. But if the right side of that body has ceased to function, the left side lives on. It is not merely the humor of Snitchey's formulation that robs Craggs's death of its sting; it is the fact that Craggs was a double, one half of a whole, with no identity of his own aside from his relationship to Snitchey. Doubling undermines the finality of death, and this is surely one reason why it so appealed to Dickens as a fictional motif. When one character can substitute for another without any vital difference between them, then no event—not even one as absolute and irrevocable as death—can be defined as unique or unequivocal.

This certainly applies to the two sisters in *The Battle of Life*. While there are superficial differences between Grace and Marion—Grace is four years older, Marion is prettier—Dickens presents them as essentially the same being, for instance in this passage: "They were very beautiful to look upon. Two better faces for a fireside never made a fireside bright and sacred. . . . Enthroned upon the clear brow of the younger sister [was] . . . the same earnest nature that her own motherless youth had ripened in the elder sister long ago" (176).

Each sister loves the other with a devotion that far exceeds her love for any man; each is capable of self-sacrifice, of the renunciation of a likely husband in favor of a sister's happiness. Apropos of this point, Craggs and

Snitchey also appear more devoted to each other than they do to their respective spouses, a situation which suggests that we tend to love our other selves far better than we do the objects of our desire.

The similarity between the sisters means that it hardly matters which sister marries which man. Grief, the usual emotional response to loss, plays virtually no role in this story. Certainly, Alfred, the abandoned bridegroom, hardly seems affected by the flight of his betrothed on the very day when he returns to marry her after a three-year absence. After a suitable period, he ends up marrying Marion's sister, and being "very happy" (213), as if the substitution made not the least difference in the world.

If one follows the logic of Dickens's symbolism, the substitution, in fact, makes no difference whatsoever. Dickens stipulates that Alfred and Grace get married on Marion's birthday, which also happens to be Alfred's birthday, which also happens to be the anniversary of the ancient battle, which also happens to be the date of Marion's return. Thus, all major events in the story occur on the same significant date, except for Marion's disappearance, which, in a belated nod to the season, takes place at Christmas—the birthday of Jesus. The simultaneous birthdays and anniversaries indicate the extent to which all elements in the story melt into each other without meaningful distinction or difference.

What is more, everyone ends by being related to everyone else. Alfred, who began by calling Grace "sister," now calls her "wife" and calls Marion "sister." Whereas Marion, who should have been calling Alfred "husband," will henceforth address him as her brother. Brother, husband, sister, wife—the terms are interchangeable, because the characters whom they describe are interchangeable—all part of the square dance of life: change partners, and do-si-do.

Thus, in *The Battle of Life*, battles of any kind, both the bloody and the bloodless, have no determining effect on the course of the action. They are merely spokes in the wheel of renewal. They do not matter in any kind of historical sense. The ancient battle that opens the story is important only to the extent that its detritus of bodies, human and animal, will enrich the ground for future generations. Dickens suggests that death—no matter how violent, cataclysmic, premature, and irrational it may be—is eventually, through the beneficent agency of time, absorbed into the regular cycle of nature, a cycle of renewal and rebirth that foreshadows the climax of the story of the sisters, when the apparently dead and/or dishonored Marion is resurrected and restored to the bosom of her family, her virginity and her life intact. Out of death comes life, out of destruction comes fertility, out of self-denial comes reward, out of sisterly love comes conjugal bliss. Everybody changes partners, everybody marries, life goes on as it has before, and we are all consoled with a happy ending.

Which is exactly the problem with doubling as a fictional motif, at least as Dickens uses it here: it deprives both people and events of their significance, because it deprives them of their uniqueness, hence of their consequence. All narrative elements in *The Battle of Life* are shorn of cause and effect through Dickens's thematic insistence on repetition, renewal, resurrection. This is certainly true of the battle with which the story begins. The very first sentence tells us how little impact this so-called "fierce battle" had on the course of history, since we are told at the outset that it does not matter where the battle was fought, nor when it was fought. This central symbol of the narrative has no historical existence.

What interests Dickens about the battle is that, in being fought, it supplied a multitude of slain men and horses, whose decomposing bodies, over the course of time, enriched the ground and fertilized the crops. Life returned to its normal course after the slaughter—and this is precisely the point. Even the depredations and destruction traditionally associated with war must eventually give way before the natural processes of regeneration and renewal that erase the traces of destruction and turn the bodies of the dead into fodder to feed the living. Dickens's insistence on the comforting aspects of repetition, whether it be in the domain of heredity, where the reanimation of generation after generation deprives death of its significance, or in the domain of natural physical processes that define the disintegrating bodies of the dead as contributing to the sustenance of the living, or whether it be in the domain of doubling, where the substitution of one double for another makes no significant difference to the overall course of events—deprives extinction of its finality.

Yet actions and events can only have consequences when there is no way back. Historical time walks hand-in-hand with irrevocability, with the idea of casting the die, or crossing the Rubicon, with the notion of never being able to stand in the same river twice. As Emily Heady writes: "History—in Christmas Books and in real life—stubbornly and persistently insists that it is anything but dead" (108). To the extent that fiction mirrors reality, then narrative time must mimic the inevitability and uniqueness of events; otherwise plots cannot advance. Dickens, of course, knew this. He knew that A gives rise to B, so that C can follow. He knew that events have significance, he knew that—with the exception of twins—most human beings do not come in duplicate—and even twins are never exactly the same. He knew that happy endings exist primarily in fairy tales. But sometimes he could not resist seeking comfort and reassurance in imagining the infinite cycles of repetition through the generations, and deducing from them the doctrine of immortality through biology.

NOTES

1. There have also been numerous studies of the double that deal specifically with Dickens and his work. In addition to the Gillman and Patten essay mentioned below, these include critical studies by Natalie Schroeder; Wendell V. Harris; Richard Currie; Athena Vretos; and Goldie Morgentaler ("Mrs. Gamp, Mrs. Harris"). More studies of the double in Victorian literature are available—see, for instance, Anna Budziaks, Robert Rogers and Otto Rank. But by the 1980s there appears to have been a reaction against a purely psychological interpretation of the double, as can be seen in such studies as the ones by Karl Miller and Paul Coates.
2. There are examples of doubling in twentieth-century literature, as well. Saul Bellow's early novel *The Victim* and Romain Gary's *The Dance of Ghengis Kahn* come to mind—both, interestingly enough, studies of anti-Semitism from the 1940s and 1950s. But it is clear that the thematic focus in twentieth- and twenty-first-century literature has shifted away from the double.
3. Laqueur is particularly good at describing the way in which beliefs about gender are incorporated into language (see esp. pages 4–5, and 96–97).
4. One of the seminal guides to the various theories of heredity throughout history is François Jacob's *The Logic of Life*. This book, published in English translation in 1973, remains, to my mind, one of the best and most thorough historical studies of hereditary theories. Much of the historical material in my discussion draws on Jacob, as well as on John Farley's *Gametes and Spores*. See, also, Marie-Hélène Huet's *Monstrous Imagination* for a study of how maternal impressions during pregnancy were supposed to affect the looks of the unborn child. And for a detailed study of the theory of preformation, see Clara Pinto-Correia.
5. Much of the material for this section on nineteenth-century theories of heredity and how they apply to Dickens's work comes from chapter 1 of my *Dickens and Heredity*.
6. See, for instance, Marcus 289–92; and Slater 96–99. Emily Walker Heady (106) identifies the self-sacrificing sister with Dickens's wish-fulfillment that Catherine, his wife, would step aside in favor of her younger sister Mary, so that he could trade "the wrong sister for the right one."
7. Steven Marcus calls this "the alphabet game" and suggests that *The Battle of Life* is the first of his works in which Dickens gives fictional characters the same initials as their real-life counterparts, the most famous example of this tendency being the name David Copperfield as a reversal of Charles Dickens's own initials. See Marcus 292.
8. For an interesting discussion of the connection between Dickens's Alfred Heathfield and Alfred the Great, see Heady 92–111.
9. An anonymous Scottish author wrote: a "A party—a ball room—is woman's battlefield. There she sways her charming scepter, and although a bold man may disregard and disobey the most sacred laws and customs, he cannot—he dare not, disregard her influence, and the amiable woman rules the haughty man" (qtd. in Aldrich 5).

WORKS CITED

Ackroyd, Peter. *Dickens*. New York: HarperCollins, 1990.

Aldrich, Elizabeth. *From the Ballroom to Hell: Grace and Folly in Nineteenth-Century Dance*. Evanston, Ill.: Northwestern UP, 1991.

Budziaks, Anna. *Text, Body and Indeterminacy: The Doppelganger Selves in Pater and Wilde*. Newcastle: Cambridge Scholars, 2008.

Coates, Paul. *The Double and the Other: Identity and Ideology in Post-Romantic Fiction*. New York: St. Martin's, 1988.

Currie, Richard. "Doubles, Self-Attack and Murderous Rage in Florence Dombey." *Dickens Studies Annual* 21 (1992): 113–29.

Dickens, Charles. *Barnaby Rudge*. Ed. John Bowen. Harmondsworth: Penguin, 2003.

———. *The Battle of Life*. *The Christmas Books*. Ed. Michael Slater. Vol. 2. Harmondsworth: Penguin, 1971. 135–235.

———. *Bleak House*. Ed. Nicola Bradbury. London: Penguin, 2003.

———. *David Copperfield*. Ed. Jeremy Tambling. London: Penguin, 2004.

———. *Dombey and Son*. Ed. Andrew Sanders. London: Penguin, 2006.

———. "The Four Sisters." *Sketches by Boz*. Ed. Dennis Walder. London: Penguin, 1995. 29–34.

———. *The Mystery of Edwin Drood*. Ed. David Pariossien. Harmondsworth: Penguin, 2002.

———. *The Old Curiosity Shop*. Ed. Norman Page. Harmondsworth: Penguin, 2000.

———. *The Pickwick Papers*. Ed. Mark Wormald. Harmondsworth: Penguin, 1999.

Dinnage, Rosemary. "The Rise and Fall of a Half-Genius." *New York Review of Books* 43.18 (Nov. 14, 1996): 30–34.

Farley, John. *Gametes and Spores: Ideas about Sexual Reproduction 1750–1914*. Baltimore: Johns Hopkins UP, 1982.

Gillman, Susan K., and Robert L. Patten. "Dickens: Doubles: Twain: Twins." *Nineteenth-Century Fiction* 39.4 (1985): 441–58.

Harris, Wendell V. "Bakhtinian Double Voicing in Dickens and Eliot," *ELH* 57.2 (Summer 1990): 445–58.

Heady, Emily Walker. "'A Steam-Whistle Modernist?': Representations of King Alfred in Dickens's *A Child's History of England* and *The Battle of Life*." *Defining Medievalism(s)*. Ed. Karl Fugelso. Cambridge: Brewer, 2009. 92–111.

Huet, Marie-Hélène. *Monstrous Imagination.* Cambridge: Harvard UP, 1993.

Jacob, François. *The Logic of Life: A History of Heredity.* Trans. Betty E. Spillman. New York: Pantheon, 1973.

Laqueur, Thomas. *Making Sex: Body and Gender from the Greeks to Freud.* Cambridge: Harvard UP, 1990.

Marcus, Steven. *Dickens, From Pickwick to Dombey.* New York: Norton, 1985.

Miller, Karl. *Doubles: Studies in Literary History.* Oxford: Oxford UP, 1985.

Morgentaler, Goldie. "Mrs. Gamp, Mrs. Harris and Mr. Dickens: Creativity and the Self Split in Two." *Dickens Quarterly* 26.1 (Mar. 2009): 3–13.

———. *Dickens and Heredity: When Like Begets Like.* London: Palgrave, 2000.

Paganoni, Maria Christina. *The Magic Lantern: Representations of the Double in Dickens.* New York: Routledge, 2008.

Pinto-Correia, Clara. *The Ovary of Eve: Egg and Sperm and Preformation.* Chicago: U of Chicago P, 1997.

Rank, Otto. *The Double.* Trans. Harry Tucker Jr. Chapel Hill: U of North Carolina P, 1971.

Rogers, Robert. *A Psychoanalytic Study of the Double in Literature.* Detroit: Wayne State UP, 1970.

Schroeder, Natalie E. "Betsey Trotwood and Jane Murdstone: Dickensian Doubles." *Studies in the Novel* 3 (Fall 1989): 268–78.

Slater, Michael. *Dickens and Women.* Stanford: Stanford UP, 1985.

Vretos, Athena. "Defining Habits: Dickens and the Psychology of Repetition" *Victorian Studies* 42.3 (Spring 1999/2000): 399–426.

Wigan, A. L. *A New View of Insanity: The Duality of the Mind.* London: Longman. Brown, Green and Longman. Rpt. Joseph Simon, 1985.

Wilson, Edmund. "Dickens: The Two Scrooges." *The Wound and the Bow: Seven Studies in Literature.* Athens: Ohio UP, 1947. 3–85.

Copperfield's Geographies

Rosemarie Bodenheimer

Although David Copperfield *is the novel most closely associated with Dickens's childhood work at Warren's Blacking, it contains very little of the London writing so central to Dickens's vision. Other landscapes—Suffolk, Great Yarmouth, Canterbury, Highgate—are more prominent and persistently memorable in David's narration. Each of them serves as a screen for the projection of certain aspects of David's obscure psychic life, while Dickens makes implicit connections among traveling, remembering, and writing. The frightening childhood scenes in London seem to be forgotten when David returns to live in the city. But we may track Dickens as he surreptitiously draws David closer to the memorable sites of his* own *London childhood, and as he buries David's memories in London writing typically associated with the disgrace of fallen women.*

David Copperfield is probably the last novel you'd choose if you wanted to concentrate on Dickensian London. Sandwiched between two consummate city novels, *Dombey and Son* and *Bleak House, Copperfield* offers very little of the London we associate with Dickens: animated descriptions of streets, houses, slums and suburban saharas, carefully mapped walking routes through named streets, or labyrinthine passages in which characters may be lost, misled, or cunningly at home.[1] This is odd: we have been repeatedly told by biographers from John Forster on that Dickens's childhood stint at Warren's Blacking Factory was the seedbed of his urban vision. Here we have Murdstone and Grinby's, and pieces of Dickens's autobiographical fragment interpolated in the text—and yet, it would seem, no urban vision. If we remember

Dickens Studies Annual, Volume 42, Copyright © 2011 by AMS Press, Inc. All rights reserved.

places in this novel, they are likely to be images of Great Yarmouth, or
Canterbury, or the village of Highgate. These, at least, are the places repeatedly revisited and re-remembered by our narrator.

Memory, we could venture, attaches just about everywhere *but* London.
From there we could easily make a leap, aided by David himself. As a child
of ten, safely out of London and its various humiliating associations, he
wishes only to forget. He begins his new life as a pupil of Dr. Strong's fearing
the exposure of his past. "How would it affect them," he asks of his invisible
schoolmates, "who were so innocent of London life, and London streets, to
discover how knowing I was (and was ashamed to be) in some of the meanest
phases of both?" (238; ch.16). Perhaps his narrative acts out this very shame
in its strange evacuation of central London?

That question is the starting point of my journey through *David Copperfield's* geography. David is always on the move in this novel, and Dickens
makes sure that writing, retrospective memory, and travel are metaphorically
intertwined. So, for instance, we get a pronounced narrative hesitation on the
brink of the bad news that Emily has eloped with Steerforth. David places
himself in the Blunderstone churchyard where his father lies, and where Mr.
Barkis has just been buried. He writes:

> A dread falls on me here. A cloud is lowering on the distant town [Yarmouth,
> about five miles away], towards which I retraced my solitary steps. I fear to
> approach it. I cannot bear to think of what did come, upon that memorable
> night; of what must come again, if I go on.
> It is no worse, because I write of it. It would be no better, if I stopped my
> most unwilling hand. It is done. Nothing can undo it; nothing can make it
> otherwise than it was.   (454; ch. 31)

As if this weren't enough, Dickens writes a geographical avoidance into
David's next movements. Instead of going north to Yarmouth, he turns south
and walks "a little distance on the road to Lowestoft. Then I turned, and
walked back towards Yarmouth" (454; ch. 31). The simultaneous hesitations
in walking, remembering, and writing tell us how clearly Dickens understood
this novel's journeys as images of the memory process, with its returns, its
blockages, its forward motion into the past. When Aunt Betsey asks David
what he would like to be, he doesn't know, but he muses: "If I could have
been inspired with a knowledge of the science of navigation, taken the command of a fast-sailing expedition, and gone round the world on a triumphant
voyage of discovery, I think I might have considered myself completely
suited." Instead, his fairy godmother sends him on a journey into his past,
"into the old part of the country again" (282–83; ch. 19). The wise woman
knows that David will never go forward until he has picked up the pieces of
his childhood idealizations and worked them through.

Similarly, the wise critic is advised to think further about Dickens's avoidance of London in this autobiographical novel. Of course, it's not that simple. To suggest the ways it isn't, I would like to approach London as David does, by way of East Anglia and Kent. "Suffolk's my county," seventeen-year-old David announces to the coach driver who takes him into London, but the ensuing dialogue makes it clear that he is no adept in Suffolk lore (292; ch. 19). Nor was Dickens. The landscapes of David's early childhood were based on a three-day holiday that Dickens took early in January 1849 with his friends John Leech and Mark Lemon, as *David Copperfield* was beginning to simmer in his mind. Their destination was Stanfield Hall near Norwich, infamous for the recent Rush murders of November 1848. Dickens, usually good for a murder, found the scene a disappointment, and so on January 9 the three friends took what Dickens described to Kate as a "two or three and twenty mile walk—to Lowestoft in Suffolk . . . and back" to the Royal Hotel in Yarmouth (*Letters* 5: 471). On the eight- or nine-mile stretch of road linking Lowestoft to Great Yarmouth in Norfolk, Dickens saw a direction post to the village of Blundeston, just to the west of the coast road. The name was enough; transformed into Blunderstone, it became the stone on which David's perceptual blunders were to be founded.

Back in London, Dickens summarized his trip for John Forster, noting that Norwich had little to offer except

> its place of execution, which we found fit for a gigantic scoundrel's exit. But the success of the trip, for me, was to come. Yarmouth, sir, where we went afterwards, is the strangest place in the wide world: one hundred and forty-six miles of hill-less marsh between it and London. More when we meet. I shall certainly try my hand at it. (*Letters* 5: 474)

In his letter Dickens was focusing on the long ride home through the network of rivers, lakes, and marshlands that make up the Norfolk Broads. In the novel, however, his fascination with the empty flatness of land moving seamlessly into water places us on the Yarmouth sands near the coastline, where Mr. Peggotty's boat-house is raked and ultimately destroyed by North Sea winds. Flatness, waste, and exposure are keynotes in David's observations: "as I carried my eye over the great dull waste that lay across the river . . . I could not help wondering, if the world were really as round as my geography-book said, how any part of it came to be so flat." Despite its personal charms, the place remains "a dull waste" or "a dim old flat" where David and Emily play as young children (40–41, 49; ch. 3). When a Norfolk reader objected to the use of the term "flats" rather than "sands," Dickens responded:

> The term "flats", is not used, I think, as any part of the local vernacular, but to explain to those who do not belong to that part of England, a general aspect

of country which would hardly be understood if described by any other term. What we call "sands", here, for example, or in Kent, or Sussex, is something very unlike the great wild level at Yarmouth.   (*Letters* 5: 59)

The "great wide level" proves to be a child's field of dreams, delusions, and portents: here a dreaming David misplaces Uriah Heep as the villain who "had launched Mr Peggotty's house on a piratical expedition . . . carrying me and Little Em'ly to the Spanish Main, to be drowned"; here David and the yet unrecognized villain Steerforth see the fallen Martha suddenly appear, fluttering on the "dark distant level" of sands and disappearing like a specter (246; ch. 16; 333; ch. 22). Death, that great leveler, plies its trade in this place, and will bring Steerforth down from the heights of his mast to join Ham below.[2]

David's childish neediness makes him dangerously oblivious to class level at Yarmouth, apparently deaf to the ways every character around him assumes and speaks class differences. Yet his own ambition later rejects such leveling; in Yarmouth with Steerforth at the age of seventeen, he "saw no suitable profession in the whole prospect; which was perhaps to be attributed to its flatness" (351; ch. 23). As the novel proceeds Dickens is more likely to locate David's own story on heights or hills with a view from above: Betsy's cottage on the Dover heights, the Buckingham Street lodging with its view of the Thames, and Highgate, then a separate village on a hill overlooking London. Such perspectives allow him safely to look down and back, at troubled moments of his past inscribed, or more likely blurred, in the scenes below. It's amusing, in this light, to consider David's first journey, made on Murdstone's horse, from Blunderstone to Lowestoft. He is too young and disoriented in this chapter to know the name Lowestoft, but he names it retrospectively in chapter 10. Here he is puzzled by the name Brooks of Sheffield; he also walks about on a cliff and looks through a telescope, through which he can make out nothing, though he pretends he can (35; ch. 2; 162; ch. 10).

David begins the second version of his childhood in Kent, a county Dickens *could* claim as his own. His own formative years from five to ten were passed in Chatham, on the River Medway. His house at Gad's Hill, acquired in 1856, sits on the small peninsula between the Thames and the Medway. For years the Dickens family vacationed from August until early October at Broadstairs, just up the coast from Ramsgate at the easternmost point of Kent. Canterbury, a crossroads town, lies thirteen miles inland from Dover, a few miles further from Broadstairs; Dickens often promised his friends day trips to Canterbury if they would come to visit him at the seaside. In the early autumn of 1849, with *David Copperfield* in train, his loyalty to the coast of Kent was deepened after an unsuccessful attempt at a holiday with John Leech at Bonchurch, off the south coast on the Isle of Wight. Dickens took his family and fled back to Broadstairs, even though the season was coming to an end. As he crowed to Leech on October 5:

> But to day is one of the most wonderful and charming days I ever saw—the air so brisk and bracing as it is nowhere but at Broadstairs—the Channel so busy and alive with shipping as it is nowhere but off Broadstairs—the hotel so cosey (*sic*) and like a private house as it is nowhere but in Broadstairs—everything as nothing is out of Broadstairs. Veeve la Broadstairs!   (*Letters* 5: 620)

Ten-year-old David Copperfield walks from London into the consolations of Kent via the Dover Road, covering about seventy-five miles in six days. He picks up the road near his old school at Blackheath, just south of Greenwich Park on the southeast edge of London, where he spends his first night as an outcast sleeping uneasily under a haystack on the familiar grounds of Salem House. The next day he toils through twenty-three miles to land in Chatham, where he takes shelter in a place Dickens probably recalled from childhood, "a sort of grass-grown battery overhanging a lane, where a sentry was walking to and fro" (193; ch. 13). Perhaps Dickens's recollections of the sleazier parts of maritime Chatham created the nightmare figure of the drunken Goroo man, who keeps the child waiting all day until he finally gives up his jacket for fourpence. Or perhaps the terror of David's walk was a re-run of Oliver Twist's walk into London. In any case, David's starvation, homelessness, and terror of tramps dissipate when he arrives in Canterbury, the novel's holy site. He muses:

> I seemed to be sustained and led on by my fanciful picture of my mother in her youth, before I came into the world . . . I have associated it, ever since, with the sunny street of Canterbury, dozing as it were in the hot light; and with the sight of its old houses and gateways, and the stately, grey Cathedral, with the rooks sailing round the towers.   (198; ch. 13)

Although he has some thirteen miles of walking before he reaches Betsey at Dover, he has come home, so to speak, to the womb.

Canterbury, the ancient religious capital of England, plays an unusual role in this novel. It's as if Dickens were seeking a geographical bedrock of memory in a place that long precedes David's existence. Many images from Blunderstone are transported to Canterbury, where the peaches ripen on the sunny south wall of the Doctor's garden, where the marriage of the Strongs may remind us of David's parents, and where the weak single parenthood of Mr. Wickfield echoes that of Clara Copperfield. The rooks that had abandoned their nests at Blunderstone thrive in Canterbury. As this town comes into view, Blunderstone becomes a deserted site, overgrown and inhabited by a lunatic inmate who sits at David's old window and figures David's own delusions. Canterbury takes its place as David's home site; thus the relocation from Suffolk to Kent underlies the wish expressed in the title of chapter 16: "I am a New Boy in More Senses than One." It suggests a pattern we will see again, one in which David is brought gradually closer to Dickens's own important places.

Canterbury, David insists, does not change; in fact its stability seems oddly to derive from the centuries of history inscribed in its ruins. Returning there after the change in Betsey's financial fortunes, David writes:

> The venerable cathedral towers, and the old jackdaws and rooks whose airy voices made them more retired than perfect silence would have done; the battered gateway, once stuck full of statues, long thrown down, and crumbled away, like the reverential pilgrims who had gazed upon them; the still nooks, where the ivied growth of centuries crept over gabled ends and ruined walls . . . everywhere—on everything—I felt the same serener air, the same calm, thoughtful, softening spirit."   (570; ch. 39)

After Dora dies, too, Canterbury looks the same, "as if there were no such thing as change on earth," even though the cathedral bells, speaking from their grand historical perspective "told me sorrowfully of change in everything" (747; ch. 52).

Yes, this is all about Agnes, her wise perspective, her quietness of spirit, the way Dickens wants her to be the stable ground beneath David's feet that has been there all along. But not only Agnes. Canterbury, like the other sites in the novel, is threatened, both by Uriah Heep and by the suspicion that Annie Strong has been unfaithful to the Doctor. When David suspects Annie, he imposes on Canterbury a fantasy brought from his Blunderstone childhood: "The impending shadow of a great affliction, and a great disgrace that had no distinct form in it yet, fell like a stain upon the quiet place where I had worked and played as a boy, and did it a cruel wrong . . . It was as if the tranquil sanctuary of my boyhood had been sacked before my face" (290–91; ch. 19). Uriah Heep invades and "sacks" the Wickfield home more directly, even to the extent of sleeping in David's old bedroom; when he takes over the business he disfigures the house by building on an addition that serves as his "new, plaster-smelling office" (576; ch. 39). It seems that Canterbury may suffer the fate of the other dissolving households: Blunderstone, the boathouse at Yarmouth, the Spenlow house at Norwood, the Steerforth house at Highgate, even Julia Mill's house in London, abandoned in a way that strikes David as "another earthquake of which I became the sport" (597; ch. 41). Unlike all these, Canterbury recovers: the Strongs' marriage is faithful, Uriah is ousted, Agnes restores the Wickfield house to its original shape. Dover recovers as well; after the exposure of Uriah Heep, Betsey's rented cottage is reinhabited by its rightful owners.

The Kent places stand fast, but they retain memories of homelessness. In a novel so often considered a central purveyor of Victorian domestic ideology, homelessness is everywhere. On the night he lands on Betsy's clean white sheets, David prays "that I might never be houseless any more, and never might forget the houseless" (210; ch. 13). When, at novel's end, David returns to the Wickfield house after three years of wandering abroad, he stands at a window and recalls memories we have never heard before: how during his schooldays he used to stand at that window on rainy evenings and watch the tramps, who remind him of his old fear, his own "toilsome journey" (843–44; ch. 60). Mr. Peggotty becomes a wandering pilgrim on the face of the earth; so do Emily and Steerforth. Micawber is always a wanderer; even Mr. Murdstone has no apparent hometown and no commitment to place, wandering as he does to become the cuckoo in other people's nests. The only rest from wandering is to be found in death, Australia—and Agnes.

The silence and changelessness that pervade descriptions of Canterbury ought to give us pause; this kind of peace is generally suspect in Dickens. When he returned to a cathedral town setting in *The Mystery of Edwin Drood*—this time choosing the nearly town of Rochester—Dickens satirized his own Canterbury writing:

> A drowsy city, Cloisterham, whose inhabitants seem to suppose, with an inconsistency more strange than rare, that all its changes lie behind it, and that there are no more to come. A queer moral to derive from antiquity, yet older than any traceable antiquity. So silent are the streets of Cloisterham . . . that of a summer day the sunblinds of its shops scarce dare to flap in the south wind; while the sun-browned tramps who pass along and stare, quicken their limp a little, that they may the sooner get beyond the confines of its oppressive respectability. (19; ch. 3)

Cloisterham, as we know, is quite literally undermined by murderousness and death. But it didn't really take Dickens twenty years to cast a dubious light on his images of Canterbury: even within *David Copperfield* he managed some undermining in the shape of Doctors' Commons, which David initially embraces as if it were an extension of the tranquility he associates with the cathedral town. This ancient and motley assortment of courts included an ecclesiastical court with advocates appointed by the archbishop of Canterbury. David associates the place with "languid stillness," a "staid air of gravity and antiquity," but it turns out to be a dusty, faded practice that's dubiously run and out of touch with reality (353, 358, 361; ch. 23). Doctors' Commons acts as Canterbury's double, a place to put Dickens's more usual skepticism about aging bureaucracies stuck in some earlier period of time.

Doctors' Commons brings us out of the provinces and into London, although its offices occupy a timeless enclave protected from the activity of the city. By mid-novel, most of the action, and most of the characters, are centered in London, where David lives continuously after the age of seventeen. What kind of London is this? What, if anything, does it have to do with David's childhood sojourns in the city?

Between the ages of eight and ten, David takes five solitary seventeen-hour coach trips between Yarmouth and London: two journeys to school and back, and one to Murdstone and Grinby's, from which he does not return. This, of course, is the period he tries to forget, saturated as it is in punishment, humiliation, parental abandonment, isolation, and shame. In chapter 11 Dickens revised and inserted a number of paragraphs about his own childhood labor from the autobiographical fragment, but much of its emotional intensity is lessened by interpolated scenes with the Micawbers; indeed David will later refer to this period as "the old Micawber times" (410; ch. 27), emphasizing that family's troubles rather than the nature of his own. Meanwhile, *David Copperfield* the novel makes its effects in the usual Dickens way: through displacement and substitution. David's first entrance into London and the scenes at Salem House school in Blackheath allow Dickens to explore complexities of feeling that were largely unavailable to him in the more naked genre of personal memoir. So, for example, the long wait to be picked up at the coaching office in Whitechapel, and the placard he's required to wear on his back, provide concrete metaphors for the child's helpless anxiety and outrage when he is abandoned in public, or when he feels wrongly identified as a working-class child by lower-class observers. When Mr. Mell is publicly humiliated and fired because his mother is an inmate in an institution for the destitute, Dickens can get at many sides of the need to conceal his own shame about John Dickens's imprisonment for debt. But I will emphasize here the more geographical games of displacement that Dickens plays in the London portions of the novel.

When twelve-year-old Charles Dickens was first sent to work at Warren's Blacking in 1824, his family was living at North Gower Street just north of the Euston Road. The blacking warehouse was located at Hungerford Stairs, Strand, so the child's walk to work would have been a pretty straight shot through the West End from Gower Street to the Thames. For *David Copperfield,* Dickens makes an eastward displacement, situating Murdstone and Grinby's in the vicinity of Blackfriars Bridge at the City of London. The Micawber lodging in Winchester Terrace just north of the City Road makes a mirror image of the relation between Gower Street and Hungerford Stairs. Dickens uses Micawber's speech about David's walking route to parody the notion that London streets are dangerously labyrinthine: "Under the impression . . . that your peregrinations in this metropolis have not as yet been extensive, and that you might have some difficulty in penetrating the arcana of the Modern Babylon in the direction of the City Road—in short . . . that you might lose yourself—I shall be happy to call this evening, and install you in the knowledge of the nearest way" (167; ch. 11). David is never to be lost in London, and the novel will later go on to make gentle fun of Aunt Betsey's provincial terror of fires, pickpockets, and city food. Of all Dickens's Londons, this is the one in which there is least to fear. Quite often it figures as a tourist town, where Steerforth's Oxford friends come to enjoy the attractions, or David takes Betsey and Peggotty to see the famous landmarks.

While Yarmouth and Canterbury are always memory-haunted, David's London at first glance seems relatively ghost-free. In the autobiographical fragment, Dickens insisted that he had long avoided the sites of his childhood labor: "Until old Hungerford Market was pulled down, until old Hungerford Stairs were destroyed, and the very nature of the ground changed, I never had the courage to go back to the place where my servitude began. I never saw it. I could not endure to go near it" (Forster 35). As if he were following Dickens's policy, David says little about earlier sites of woe when he returns to live in London at seventeen. Both as autobiographer and as novelist, Dickens was distorting a bit. In 1831, Dickens lived for a time at 15 Buckingham Street, sharing lodgings with James E. Roney, a law student and, like Dickens, a Parliamentary reporter. Buckingham Street, Adelphi, runs between the Strand and the river, a stone's throw from what is now Charing Cross Station (built in the 1860s on the site of Hungerford Market). It overlooks the Thames at just about exactly the site of the old Warren's Blacking at Hungerford Stairs. At the time Dickens lived there, six or seven years past his stint at Warren's, he was essentially next door to the destruction of the seventeenth-century Hungerford Market and the building of its elaborate Victorian successor. He would have encountered daily those spots where "his servitude began," places he later claimed to have avoided like the plague.[3]

Dickens seems to have developed fond memories of Buckingham Street: in 1856 he wrote to Roney, who had become Chief Justice in British Guinea:

> Lord! To think of a Colonial Chief Justice! And it was but the day before yesterday that we gave our first dinner at the Mansion of Mrs. Rogers in Buckingham Street, Adelphi. I bought the soup myself (it was hard, and looked like a bit of a mantel-piece), and you provided some inheritance of family teaspoons for the decoration of the festival. (*Letters* 8: 191)

This, of course, is the setting for David's first dinner parties under the thumb of Mrs. Crupp, as well as a series of other memorable scenes. In those two small rooms Uriah Heep makes his nightmare visit, Aunt Betsey announces her bankruptcy and moves in, Mr. Dick sets up two tables to do his law copying, and the assembled company holds mock Parliamentary debates to test David in shorthand.

When Dickens places David there, he plays the game of mentioning sites that are autobiographically significant to *him*, in ways that his fictional character does not comprehend. David gives little initial description of the building except to say that "sure, enough, the river was outside the windows" (362; ch. 23). Yet he too is made conscious of the past as place: after he moves into Buckingham Street, he writes, "I turned my face to the Adelphi, pondering on the old days when I used to roam about its subterranean arches, and on the happy changes which had brought me to the surface" (364; ch. 23). David, who seems especially ashamed of having "prowled," "lounged," and "roamed" about the streets at mealtimes during the Murdstone and Grinby episode (178, 180; ch. 11), is now thrilled to "walk about town with the key of my house in my pocket." Buckingham Street is a "lofty castle," the "fortification" that raises him far above those subterranean arches and the homelessness they recall (364; ch. 33).

When David visits Tommy Traddles and his downstairs neighbors the Micawbers in Camden Town, we are returned to the neighborhood where the Dickens family lived just prior to the debt crisis. Dickens launches briefly into his city-writing mode, noticing how the inhabitants "appeared to have a propensity to throw any little trifles they were not in want of, into the road," and making fun of the half-finished suburban development: "they were all built on one monotonous pattern, and looked like early copies of a blundering boy who was learning to make houses, and had not yet got out of his cramped brick and mortar pothooks." Traddles's room, rather like Dickens's head, displays blacking-brushes and blacking "among his books—on the top shelf, behind a dictionary." As if Dickens's associations were momentarily unstoppable, David continues "I looked at nothing, that I know of, but I saw everything, even to the prospect of a church upon his china inkstand, as I sat down—and this, too, was a faculty confirmed in me in the old Micawber times" (408–10; ch. 27).

Of course, the Micawbers are about to make one of their many surprise appearances, reminding David that he cannot forget. More to our point, we are watching Dickens move gradually toward his personal memory sites as the novel proceeds. David's Yarmouth friends—Mr. Peggoty, Clara Peggotty, and later Emily—are intermittently lodged in London over a chandler's shop in Hungerford Market (505; ch. 35). When the Micawbers are about to embark for Australia, David and Traddles find them "assembled on the wooden steps, at that time known as Hungerford Stairs, watching the departure of a boat with some of their property on board." The Micawbers sleep that night in "a little, dirty, tumble-down public-house, which in those days was close to the stairs"; it seems to occupy virtually the same space, overhanging the river, as Warren's Blacking (809; ch. 57). At their moment of departure, we seem to have arrived at the novel's starting point. While David's story moves him upwards and away from painful memories, Dickens's narrative is a road that travels rather deviously toward the past.

If David tracks Dickens's memory spots without knowing it, he is also allowed to create some of his own. One of these is the Golden Cross coaching inn on the Strand, just around the corner from Buckingham Street. After his second childhood in Kent, David arrives at this London landmark on the Dover coach, from which he recalls every stage of his walking marathon seven years earlier. His attempt to feel superior to that childish self fails; he's once again humiliated by coachmen and waiters, and placed in the inn's worst room. At the inn's coffee-room late that night, Steerforth reappears in David's life as if conjured by David's dazed memories and dreams, beginning the second phase of David's long infatuation with his classy anti-hero. A similarly dreamlike mood encompasses the second scene at the Golden Cross, where Mr. Peggotty unexpectedly reappears after the first phase of his quest for Emily. Walking home from Highgate in a snowstorm, David makes his way through the old St. Martin's Lane. Passing the portico of St. Martin's Church, he sees two blurred figures in the snow—first the fleeting face of Martha, then the stooping figure of Mr. Peggotty. He takes Mr. Peggotty to a public-room off the stable yard at the Golden Cross, "so memorable to me in connexion with his misfortune"; here they confer while Martha's "haggard, listening face" eavesdrops from the doorway. After Mr. Peggotty departs, the scene seems to erase itself: "I returned to the inn yard and, impressed by my remembrance of the face, looked awfully around for it. It was not there. The snow had covered our late footprints; my new track was the only one to be seen; and even that began to die away (it snowed so fast) as I looked back over my shoulder" (587–95; ch. 40). Dickens writes this hauntingly allegorical passage as a moment of memory so ephemeral that it might not have occurred.

That ghost of a face becomes the prostrate body of a fallen woman in the most sustained piece of London writing Dickens does in *David Copperfield*. After David informs Mr. Peggotty that Emily may have returned to London, they become city stalkers as they track Martha to the riverbank. Apparently it's only necessary to be near a bridge if you want to find any particular prostitute on the streets of London. Spotting Martha without much difficulty near Blackfriars Bridge, the two conspirators turn to follow her at some length as she walks upriver beyond Westminster, and down Millbank, where she comes to rest in the shadow of the Vauxhall Bridge. (David calls it the iron bridge; Vauxhall was the first iron bridge over the London Thames, built from 1809 to 1816, upriver from the present Tate Britain, then a prison site.) The detailed description of this wrecked and desolate neighborhood, with its rank, polluted marshiness, its unfinished and rotting houses, its abandoned iron shipping refuse, is unlike anything else in the novel (685–87; ch. 47).

Here, then, Dickens goes about the familiar business of creating London as a mood piece, where the quality of the description blends seamlessly—and melodramatically—with the characters' disturbed states of mind. I am not primarily interested in the way this scene displays quintessential Victorian fallen woman iconography, though it certainly does do that. Instead, I wonder why it is that Dickens's London mode is largely reserved for scenes related to Steerforth's seduction of Emily and its consequences. Similarly detailed urban description recurs in connection with that story when Martha takes David to Golden Square where Emily is hiding. Its single-family dwellings had "long degenerated into poor lodgings let off in rooms"; its "tokens of past grandeur were miserably decayed and dirty; rot, damp, and age, had weakened the flooring, which in many places was unsound and even unsafe." Among such tokens of degeneration David, now a concealed eavesdropper like Martha, will witness Rosa Dartle's humiliation of Emily (721–22; ch. 50). In this compromised position, his own psychic grounding is certainly unsound and even unsafe.

Peter Stallybrass and Allon White have suggested that nineteenth-century writing makes the city "a locus of fear, disgust and fascination" in which "the hierarchy of the body" is "transcoded through the hierarchy of the city." They identify city heights with the head and the spirit, city topography with the bourgeois body, the sewer and the slum with the lower body (125, 137, 145). This strikes me as overly schematic, but it might be a starting point for speculation about why Dickens maps a story of sexual seduction, which takes place entirely offstage, onto markedly dreamlike or nightmarish London scenes. Emily's absence from her own plot only emphasizes the truth of the matter: her story is all about David. It's about his unconfessed guilt at having brought Steerforth into her life, about his need to compensate by taking the highly unlikely role of confidante to Mr. Peggotty and Ham, and about his need to hide behind a door to see her punished for stealing Steerforth away from him. In the end, it's about the shame of unspeakable class and sexual conflict, which gets its dream-expression in figures that emerge like specters of unfinished business from London streetscapes.

Central London remains a place of unresolved distress, a hiding place for the fallen women Martha and Emily as well as for David's projections of early shame and humiliation. By contrast, the village of Highgate might be imagined as the ground of aspiration. During the *Copperfield* period, Dickens had connections with two pieces of land in this hill village: the Highgate Cemetery and the Holly Lodge Estate recently inherited by Angela Burdett Coutts. The cemetery had been consecrated in 1839 to relieve pressure on central city burial sites. When Dickens's sister Fanny Burnett died in September 1848, he had her buried there; in January 1849 her fragile young son died and was buried with her. In 1851, after the novel was complete, Dickens would bury both his father and his infant daughter Dora at Highgate. He had staked out a Dickens enclave packed with feeling and memory in this newly fashionable burial ground. Miss Coutts, perhaps the richest lady philanthropist in England, took possession of nearby Holly Lodge and its extensive grounds in May 1849. By this time she and Dickens were well-established partners in efforts of social reform, most notably the home for fallen women called Urania Cottage. They conferred frequently, and so Dickens, like David, would have become quite familiar with the Highgate Road and a wealthy mansion at the top of the hill. House-hunting in 1851, Dickens tried to buy a villa for his own family near Holly Lodge, though this plan to follow in David Copperfield's footsteps did not work out (*Letters* 6: 269).

Highgate has its own trajectory in *David Copperfield*. The proud, moneyed Steerforth household gradually disintegrates while, on the other side of the village, David's circle expands and thrives on the virtues of hard work and generous intentions. David's descriptions of the changing views from the Steerforth home measure the family crisis. His first impression places the house well above the foggy city below: "It was a genteel old-fashioned house, very quiet and orderly. From the windows of my room I saw all London lying in the distance like a great vapour, with here and there some lights twinkling through it." Later, after hearing Littimer's account of Steerforth and Emily, David watches Mrs. Steerforth and Rosa on the terrace: "I could not help observing how steadily they both sat gazing on the prospect, and how it thickened and closed around them ... from the greater part of the great valley interposed, a mist was rising like a sea, which, mingling with the darkness, made it seem as if the gathering waters would encompass them" (300; ch. 20; 680; ch. 46).

Stuck in their angry memories, Rosa and Mrs. Steerforth gradually drown in that inner urban sea, while the Copperfield circle works its way to high ground. When the Doctor retires, the Strongs move to Highgate, where Uriah attempts to work his evil and Annie extracts herself from suspicion. Employed as the Doctor's secretary, David takes "the familiar Highgate road" in pursuit of work rather than pleasure, walking so fast toward his dream of Dora that he arrives an hour too early (526–27; ch. 36). On that road he picks out a cottage for Dora and himself, very near the one they will actually take when David comes of age and marries. With Aunt Betsey placed in a tiny nearby cottage, Highgate becomes the center from which characters come and go on their various journeys. Here David becomes a successful writer and steels himself in marital patience, Agnes hovers like an angel over Dora's death, Betsey comes clean that the man who follows her is her husband, and makes her peace with the unfortunately named Peggotty.

This little community disperses in the final chapters of the novel, but it has done the work that village communities do in Dickens's early and middle novels. Mixing ambition with pathos, the Highgate scenes establish striving Victorian goodness in work and marriage as the groundwork for the novel's conclusion. After graduating from Highgate, the central couple is ready to thrive in the city; we are left with a picture of David, Agnes, and their children living, much like the Dickenses, in a London household.

In the course of this essay, I have tried to suggest that the novel makes only partial, often surreptitious moves toward coming to terms with both David's and Dickens's childhood deprivations and class humiliations. Written from the perspective of achieved ambition, it chooses finally to embrace the general idea of a forgiven past embodied in the figure of Agnes and illuminated by the holy light of historic Canterbury. But Dickens is never one to leave a novel without a counter-image embedded somewhere in the text. My favorite in this novel stars Mr. Micawber. Unhinged by his collaboration in Uriah Heep's financial frauds, he comes to London to meet with David and Traddles. His letter of announcement reads as follows:

> Among other havens of domestic tranquility and peace of mind, my feet will naturally tend towards the King's Bench Prison. In stating that I shall be (D.V.) on the outside of the south wall of that place of incarceration on civil process, the day after tomorrow, at seven in the evening, precisely, my object in this epistolary communication is accomplished. (708; ch. 49)

When the two friends meet Micawber at the appointed time, "He was standing with his arms folded, over against the wall, looking at the spikes on the top, with a sentimental expression, as if they were the interlacing boughs of trees that had shaded him in his youth." This is the "serene spot," Micawber muses, "where some of the happiest hours of my existence fleeted by"; here his children played on the intricate brick pattern of the inner court, and here he was "familiar with every stone in the place" (711–12; ch. 49). We are, of course, meant to see that Micawber feels more besmirched by his association with Uriah Heep than he ever did by his imprisonment for debt. In a wider context, however, this unabashed public embrace of a former scene of shame is precisely what David cannot do—what Dickens cannot do, as yet, except through the comic genius of Mr. Micawber.

NOTES

This essay was originally written as a lecture for the 2009 Dickens Universe at UC Santa Cruz. I thank many friends associated with the Dickens Project who helped it come into being.

1. F. S. Schwartzbach's thorough survey of London in a sequence of Dickens's novels has no chapter on *David Copperfield*. David A. Craig comments on the disappearing London landscape in this novel.
2. For the deathscape at Yarmouth, see James Davies 191–92.
3. Here Alexander Welsh's skepticism about Warren's as trauma becomes relevant. As he writes, "We do not know when Dickens discovered or decided that his experience in the blacking warehouse was traumatic" (156).

WORKS CITED

Craig, David A. "The Interplay of City and Self in *Oliver Twist, David Copperfield* and *Great Expectations.*" *Dickens Studies Annual* 16 (1982): 17–38.

Davies, James A. "Dickens and the Region in *David Copperfield.*" *Writing, Region and Nation*. Ed. James A. Davies and Glyn Purseglove. Swansea: U of Wales, 1994. 187–96.

Dickens, Charles. *David Copperfield*. Ed. Jeremy Tambling. London: Penguin, 2004.

———. *The Letters of Charles Dickens*. Ed. Madeline House, Graham Storey, and Kathleen Tillotson. 12 vols. Oxford: Clarendon, 1965–2002.

———. *The Mystery of Edwin Drood*. Ed. Peter Ackroyd. New York: Knopf, 2004.

Forster, John. *The Life of Charles Dickens*. Ed J. W. T. Ley. London: Cecil Palmer, 1928.

Schwartzbach, F. S. *Dickens and the City*. London: Athlone, 1979.

Stallybrass, Peter, and Allon White. *The Politics and Poetics of Transgression*. Ithaca, NY: Cornell UP, 1986.

Welsh, Alexander. *From Copyright to Copperfield: The Identity of Charles Dickens*. Cambridge: Harvard UP, 1987.

Adapting the Seduction Plot: *David Copperfield*'s Magdalens on the Victorian Stage

Karen E. Laird

This essay examines the very first dramatizations of David Copperfield *and investigates their page-to-stage adaptation strategies. George Almar's* Born with a Caul *(1850), J. Courtney's* David Copperfield the Younger of Blunderstone Rookery *(1850), and John Brougham's* David Copperfield *(1850) all struggle to adapt faithfully Dickens's bildungsroman plot, even as they amplify its melodramatic content. A dramatic shift occurs in the1860s, however, when playwrights abandon David's story altogether to prioritize the novel's sensational fallen woman plot. I illustrate how Francis Cowlery Burnand's* The Deal Boatman *(1863) and Andrew Halliday's* Little Em'ly *(1869) move beyond fidelity to Dickens's source text and instead prioritize correction, originality, experimentation, and sensation as the guiding criteria for adaptation. My conclusion argues that the significant tension between the bildungsroman plot and the seduction plot is finally reconciled after Dickens's death, when adapters begin a new cycle of corrective adaptation to commemorate the novelist's life through dramatizations of his most beloved novel.*

Charles Dickens's unwavering devotion to the theater is remarkable considering how plagued he was by pirated performances of his novels. As H. Philip Bolton explains, ''To the novelist's delight and irritation, such plays often

Dickens Studies Annual, Volume 42, Copyright © 2011 by AMS Press, Inc. All rights reserved.

appeared long before the novels were complete, thereby promoting his popularity but also anticipating his plots and vulgarizing his characters" (*Oxford* 196). In *The Life of Charles Dickens*, John Forster humorously recalls how, during a performance of *Oliver Twist* at the Surrey in the fall of 1838, Dickens was so disturbed by the bastardization of his work-in-progress that "in the middle of the first scene he laid himself down upon the floor in a corner of the box and never rose from it until the drop-scene fell" (76). Although Dickens averted his gaze from this rendition of his yet unwritten ending, he no doubt heard the final lines and may have even penned his conclusion in response.

While several critics have discussed Dickens's reactions to staged versions of *Oliver Twist* and *Nicholas Nickleby*, only a handful of articles and book chapters focus on Victorian stage adaptations of *David Copperfield*.[1] This is a surprising critical oversight, considering its status as "the second most dramatized of Dickens's novels" (Fulkerson 29).[2] Perhaps our gaze has long been diverted by Dickens's own subtle stage directions. Although he reworked much of his own personal history in the pages of *David Copperfield*, Dickens simultaneously distanced himself from this history through what amounts to nothing short of a reinvention of style. Unlike the earlier novels with explicitly theatrical settings (*Nicholas Nickleby*, *The Old Curiosity Shop*) or overtly melodramatic structures (*Oliver Twist*, *A Christmas Carol*), *David Copperfield* adopts an introspective, literary tone that not only lays claim to the author's growing sense of himself as a serious artist rather than an entertainer, but also seems intended to discourage adaptations penned by less serious-minded writers of the stage. Indeed, by 1849, Dickens had come to expect with certainty that pirated versions of his work would be staged without his authorization and despite his protestations.[3]

At this mid-point in his career, with seven novels behind him and seven more to follow, *David Copperfield* might well be considered a tipping point, when Dickens abandons his overtly melodramatic style of writing in favor of a less theatrical style of fiction.[4] Yet *David Copperfield* retained one crucial element of the nineteenth-century stage melodrama that proved endlessly popular with adapters: the fallen woman. The story of little Emily, the orphaned fisherman's daughter who becomes so dazzled by the prospect of becoming a lady that she leaves her loving home, constitutes one of the most memorable plotlines of Dickens's novels, despite being one of the least original. Since the cautionary tale of a poor girl's seduction at the hands of a rakish gentleman was a staple of nineteenth-century theater, Dickens's novelistic version of the familiar narrative invited dramatization. As Sos Eltis argues, "the seduced maiden, the wicked seductress, and the repentant magdalen" evolved throughout the century from a ubiquitous plot device into a complex figure demanding intense character analysis (223, 227). The

Victorian adapters of *David Copperfield* participated in this evolution by increasingly complicating Emily's psychology, even at the expense of diminishing David's.

This essay resurrects the first stage adaptations of *David Copperfield* in order to investigate how adapters negotiated the formidable tension between the introspective, difficult to adapt bildungsroman plot with the sensational, highly adaptable fallen woman plot. I'll chart a surprising evolution from the 1850s, when the inaugural playwrights struggled to translate David's memories of childhood to the stage, through the 1860s, when dramatists abandoned David's story altogether to give greater voice to the novel's fallen women. I'll conclude that this tension is only resolved after Dickens's death, when commemorative performances fuse both narratives in tribute to the celebrity author whose death was mourned on the international stage.

I. Adapting the Bildungsroman: The First Three Dramatizations

In the weeks surrounding the November 1, 1850, publication of the final double installment of *David Copperfield*, four different theaters in London and two theaters in America simultaneously staged adaptations of the novel (Bolton 321).[5] Although George Almar, John Courtney, and John Brougham are all but forgotten today, these playwrights were well-known in the mid-nineteenth century for their ambitious attempts to translate current popular fiction to the stage. In adapting Dickens in 1850, these dramatists took a risk in adapting an author who was no longer a stage novelty. H. Philip Bolton calculates that at least 240 Dickensian productions had been staged by this midpoint in the novelist's career; as a consequence, the "market for 'Dickens-dramas' was saturated" and "[t]he first generation of playwrights, actors, and actresses to profit from Dickens began, after fifteen years, to turn their attention elsewhere" (*Oxford* 196). Thus it was unlikely that these seasoned adapters presupposed critical acclaim as they grappled with *David Copperfield*'s formidable challenges, including its sheer length, its proliferation of characters, the importance of grand settings, and the first-person narrator's periodic movement between past and future events. To get a handle on this unwieldy novel, dramatists had to make decisive moves of elimination. Almar, Courtney, and Brougham proved pioneers of compression, that decidedly unglamorous task which, in the words of Thomas Leitch, involves the "hard work of whittling the material down to the right size for an evening's entertainment" (99).

Debuting at the Strand Theatre before Dickens penned his final installment to *David Copperfield*, George Almar's *Born with a Caul* presumed to capitalize on the timeliness of Dickens's current serialization without even so much as acknowledging the novelist's name in its promotional playbill. George Almar had established himself as a Dickens adapter over a decade earlier, when his dramatization of *Oliver Twist* ran for eighty nights at the Surrey Theatre during the 1838–39 season (Fulkerson 29). Almar's *David Copperfield* met with a comparatively lackluster reception, running only slightly over one week at the Strand (October 21–29, 1850) before being revived for one night only at both the Standard and the Queen's (Bolton 323–24). Despite the titular allusion to the unusual remnant of David's birth, Almar's play omits David's childhood and begins instead with David as a young man concisely recounting his family's history to James Steerforth and Miss Mowcher. The awkward opening lines illustrate the difficulty which Almar faced as he translated the first-person narrator's memories of childhood into stage dialogue. David confides: "I was born upon a Friday with a Caul . . . I was a posthumous child—my mother married again to a Mr. Murdstone. . . . She died shortly afterwards" (1). As David becomes (according to the stage directions) "Affected" and muses on his lost mother "in the land of dreams and shadows," Steerforth derails his confession by reminding him of the terrible "suet pudding" at Mr. Creakle's school and steering his attention to the present. Thus, David's retrospectives of childhood constitute only two pages of Almar's 124–page manuscript. Nearly every subsequent Victorian adapter would imitate Almar's elision of the scenes of David's childhood and education (chapters 1–18 in Dickens's novel), parts of which were based on Dickens's own autobiographical fragment.[6] Considering that most Victorian stage adaptations of *Jane Eyre* begin after Jane's education is completed (Stoneman 4), it seems that adapters of the bildungsroman form doubted whether the appeal of childhood scenes was worth the logistical headaches of casting child actors or young women in the requisite youthful parts.

With only such fleeting references to David's past to guide them, Almar's audience members have little opportunity to understand this character's motives and desires. As the play progresses, David's story is derailed by aggressively masculine characters who steal the limelight away from him. Two detectives, Bullock and Tipkins, investigate Emily's disappearance and follow hotly on the trail of the odious Uriah Heep. David's former stepfather, the villainous "Mandrake" Murdstone, doubles as Martha's seducer, and his accomplice, Hurricane Flash, turns out to be Aunt Betsy's n'er-do-well husband. This energetically named sidekick was played by none other than George Almar, whose presence on stage as the melodramatic villain reminds us of the multiple hats that a playwright could wear throughout the adaptation process. Such innovative character additions heighten the novel's interest in crime and anticipate the detective genre. The play's multiple chase and rescue scenes, which culminate in a shoot-out between Murdstone and Flash, create a frenetic pace that feels more akin to the sensation novel than the contemplative bildungsroman.

Although Almar set the standard for all subsequent adaptations by focusing much of his play on the search for the missing Emily, he missed an opportunity to present her as a sympathetic character. In an attempt to diffuse the sexual politics of the fallen woman plot which provided so much action and suspense, Almar transforms Emily's seduction into a happy domestic triumph by the play's end. To exonerate Steerforth, Almar presents Emily as a common jilt, devoid of any understandable motive. In her final line, Emily asks Ham: "Can you forgive my fickleness?" (122). Ham, who does not die as in Dickens's novel, philosophically answers: "Love has no meaning when the heart believes its idol is perfection" (122). James Steerforth's final role is glorious in comparison, as he emerges in the flesh after being presumed dead, shocks the entire cast with the news that he and Emily are actually married, and vows to emigrate to Australia with the Peggotty clan. This relentlessly happy ending proves as unconvincing as Steerforth's final lines of the play, which assert his possession over the vapid Emily: "Here my wife—my friend—my Emily" (124). In this tripartite list of signifiers, Emily's very name bears the final syntactical force of all the descriptors beyond "wife" and "friend" that the entire play worked to establish. Although the charge of her pollution is thus swept under the nominal rug, Emily's very name connotes her fallen state by this late stage of the drama.

The second British dramatization, *David Copperfield the Younger of Blunderstone Rookery*, was performed from 13 to 20 November 1850, at the Surrey Theatre (Bolton, *Dickens* 323), then considered to be "the leading minor theatre in London" (Davis and Emeljanow 5).[7] Submitted anonymously to the Lord Chamberlain's office, the British Library manuscript now credits the manuscript to J. Courtney, who penned at least sixty plays throughout his prolific career, including the very first *Jane Eyre* adaptation in 1848 (Stoneman 20).[8] Courtney's *David Copperfield* stands out as one of the few Victorian dramatizations to include a scene from David's childhood. The opening prologue depicts the novel's chapter 14, in which Miss Betsy Trotwood hosts a meeting with the Murdstones to determine the future of her runaway nephew. The young David (played by Miss Mandlebert[9]) proves remarkably articulate throughout the scene, even describing the abuse he endured at his stepfather's hands, while Murdstone listens. David begs his aunt to intervene on his behalf in a frank speech that probably elicited sympathy from its audience:

> Oh no aunt—do not let me go—they never liked me Aunt—were never kind to me & their cold looks always brought a [?] chill on me, & my dear mother when living dared not speak her mind in my behalf. Oh aunt, I cannot speak what I have suffered from them, oh, [?] day, too, because his eyes struck me with fear, and I forgot the task I had well learnt before he stood before me, he sent me to my room & with a heavy weapon beat me till I was mad with grief and pain.[10] (643–44)

The emotional honesty of this plea is particularly remarkable when we consider its striking absence from the novel. In a scene rich with heated dialogue between the adult characters, David paraphrases his own plea for help and admits to a failure of memory when he explains: "I forget in what terms now, but I remember that they affected me very much then" (185). By fleshing out David's speech on stage, Courtney gives voice to a memory that was perhaps too traumatic to be precisely recalled by the adult narrator of the novel.

In the subsequent scene that jumps ahead to David's young adulthood, Courtney continues to suggest the protagonist's childhood memories through short soliloquies. When David is momentarily alone on stage, he muses aloud: "Lo here I stand in the old spot fraught with so many [?] who in my boyish fancy seemed to me the only star that could guide me through a life of love, or hope" (648). His most poignant soliloquies convey the significant nostalgia of Dickens's first-person adult narrator. In one brief moment in act 1, scene 2, for example, David ruminates, "Let me think a moment of past times for my visit to Blunderstone, and my mother's grave, has thrown me back to boyhood" (649). Although we have no way of knowing how an individual actor performed these lines—whether he began to cry, whether he punctuated the sentence with long caesuras—the words seem to invite the audience to accompany David mentally "back to boyhood," if only momentarily, in a soliloquy that functions as the theatrical equivalent of the bildungsroman's intense interest in childhood.

Despite such initial spotlights on David's emotional life, his centrality to the play fades as the seduction plot gains momentum. One of the first reviewers of Dickens's novel lamented that "from the time that David Copperfield emerges from boyhood, the interest in *his* adventures ceases, beyond that sort of feeling which many readers entertain to know 'how it ends' " (*International* 1 Jan 1851). Courtney's play suggests that he shared this contemporary critic's opinion, as he abandons his interest in David after scene 2 to devote more energy to the adventures of Emily and company. As Richard Fulkerson astutely observes, Courtney's attempt to incorporate faithfully so much of the novel's plot resulted in mere summary of the most compelling scenes, specifically Emily's seduction scene, and rendered David "simplified to the point of being uninteresting" (32).

Emily, too, is oversimplified, especially in several scenes' final tableaux, a popular Victorian stage convention that foregrounds the actors' visual presence by freezing their movements and speech. The reviewer for the *Illustrated London News* attributed the play's failure in the overuse of such visual moments and likened the entire production to "a series of tableaux by which the novel is symbolized, rather than represented" (qtd. in Fulkerson 31). This critique could certainly be extended to Courtney's characterization of Emily, who ultimately exists as the play's figurine rather than a rounded character. In her last appearance on stage, Emily is literally muffled by Steerforth's servant, Littimer. Repelling his untoward advances, Emily declares, "I have a friend at hand, & my voice will raise" (689). Littimer menacingly replies, "Let me stifle it," and stage directions specify that he "quickly throws [a] handkerchief over her head" while Emily "utters faint cry" (689). Although Littimer is promptly arrested by two police officers, Emily never speaks again in the play—an omission that illuminates her weak role in this second London dramatization.

The first *David Copperfield* dramatization to enjoy popular and critical success was penned by John Brougham, an Irish-born actor, theater-owner, and playwright who had relocated to New York after managing London's Lyceum Theatre for a decade (Stoneman 67–69). Curiously, Brougham's adaptation of *David Copperfield* did not debut at his own theater (Brougham's Lyceum on Broadway, which opened in 1850), but rather at Barnum's Museum in Philadelphia, November 6–9, 1850 (Bolton, *Dickens* 323). Malcolm Morley posits that American museums secured audiences otherwise morally opposed to theaters: "Puritans of those days, and there were many, wishing to see a play, raised to objection no visiting a Museum for that purpose, whereas a theatre would be anathema to them" (78). Brougham must have appeased even the Puritanical strain of his American audience, for his play became the definitive version to be staged in America for the next two decades.[11] Even Charles Dickens's eldest son commended Brougham's version, assigning it the high rank of being one among "only two of any importance" (qtd. in Fitz-Gerald 233).

Although he faithfully adapted both the novel's Peggotty/Emily plot and its Micawber/Wickfield plot, Brougham made no attempt to depict David's youth through scenes of his childhood or sentimental soliloquies. He does, however, retain the bildungsroman's interest in David's growth and development by granting David more involvement with the fallen woman plot. In scenes that pit David against the masculine strength of Mr. Peggotty, the plot of Emily's fall becomes a platform to test David's heroic potential. As a consequence, Emily serves only as a vehicle for David's maturation.

Brougham's play almost immediately thrusts us into the story of Emily and Steerforth, since act 1, scene 1 establishes Steerforth as a womanizer who is piqued by Mr. Peggotty's description of his beloved "little Emily." By act 1, scene 3, Steerforth has traveled with David to Peggotty's Ark and brazenly confides to the audience his intentions to thwart Emily and Ham's marriage in melodramatic asides. Upon this first introduction to Steerforth, Emily proves shaken and regrets her engagement to Ham. As the men discuss her impending marriage, Emily confesses to the audience: "Ah! I have been rash and hasty—too hasty. What is to become of me I know not!" (12). Emily's aside creates dramatic irony by revealing her to be more uncertain of her imminent fall than the audience is; in this last declaration, Emily voices her sense of being a spectator rather than a force of action in her own unfolding life's drama. This powerful direct address, uttered right before her fall, invites the audience to imagine Emily's unhappiness in the scenes to come and grants Emily a voice, albeit only momentarily.

Emily's voice will never again be so clearly heard, as is subsequently revealed through Brougham's staging of one of the most theatrical scenes from the novel. In act 2, scene 3, Ham thrusts Emily's letter into the hands of David, who reads the opening line aloud to Mr. Peggotty: "When you, who love me better than I ever have deserved—even when my mind was innocent—see this, I shall be far away." As Peggotty repeats aloud the last phrase, David continues reading the remainder of Emily's letter: "When I leave my dear home—oh! so dear—it will be never to come back—unless he brings me back a lady. God bless all. I'll pray for all, often, on my knees—and I don't pray for my own self. My parting love to uncle—my last tears for uncle" (17). This moment of David's reciting Emily's written words constitutes nothing short of a narrative emergence. Until this point in Brougham's play, David has appeared lackluster at best. Lacking the verbal finesse of Micawber, the grotesque body of Uriah Heep, or even the creative madness of Mr. Dick, David exists only as the undeveloped character who links together more interesting ones. Powerless until this point to guide anyone's perspective, David reclaims his novelistic role of first-person narrator only by reading Emily's words aloud to his spellbound friends. As David concludes reading, he pauses for effect, and then lets loose an uncharacteristically brash order to Peggotty: "I entreat you, sir, to have command over yourself!" (17). David distances himself from the emotional letter, and falls back on a masculine code of honor. As Peggotty screams, "Who's the man! I want to know his name!", David fills in the blank by announcing "Steerforth!" (17).

While Peggotty's selfless resolve to seek his niece meets with reward in Dickens's novel, this play refuses to grant the sentimental father-figure any power of action. Peggotty simply waits for the news that David eventually brings. David's masculinity is further reinforced by announcing Emily's imminent return, and he condescendingly advises the much older Mr. Peggotty, "Bear it like a man, Daniel" (22). The stage directions even specify that David is allotted the role of physically ushering Emily back into her home: "David goes to door, L. H., and brings on Emily" (22). Emily, in turn, is granted only one short speech: "I dare not lift my sinful eye, suncle [sic]. I don't deserve a thought word of kindness now" (22). Containing typographical or grammatical errors, Emily's last words, perhaps reflecting a printer's haste, cede narrative victory to David.

II. The Sensational Seduction Plot: *The Deal Boatman* (1863) and *Little Em'ly* (1869)

In the thirteen-year period following Dickens's initial publication of *David Copperfield*, at least twenty-five versions of these early adaptations appeared internationally. Most were imitations of Brougham's play; although none garnered widespread critical acclaim or set a new precedent, popular demand for these familiar *David Copperfield* productions increased steadily. By 1860, *The Times* lamented that the public appetite for stage adaptations of novels was uncontrollable, announcing, "'once a tale becomes generally popular, a desire to see it as a dramatic form immediately spreads like an epidemic . . . people only want to see the personages they have read about clothed in a visible form and turn from the book to the stage as a child turns from letter-press to pictures" (qtd. in Law and Maunder 119). This notion of adaptation as an immature and inevitable form took root so firmly that a prejudice against adaptation is still discernible today, despite great popularity with audiences.

When Francis Cowlery Burnand (better known as F. C. Burnand) set out to create a dramatically new version of Dickens's frequently adapted novel in 1863, the time had arrived for an innovative, fresh approach to adaptation.[12] Burnand was a graduate of Cambridge, an unfulfilled barrister, a new convert to Catholicism, and a disinherited son before he found his career as an adapter of fiction to the stage ("'Burnand'" 891). Although his first substantial financial success would come from adapting Douglas Jerrold's 1829 play *Black-Eyed Susan* in 1866, *The Deal Boatman* earned him critical recognition (Stephens 60). Although this play was Burnand's "first attempt at serious dramatic composition,'' it was declared to be "the most successful of all'' the *David Copperfield* adaptations in 1870 by Dickens biographer Theodore Taylor (qtd. in Fitz-Gerald 238, 239). Significantly, it debuted at Drury Lane, marking "one of the first times—if not *the* first time—that a drama from Dickens played at one of the 'Patent' playhouses of the metropolis'' (Bolton, *Dickens* 321). Fitz-Gerald hails it as "one of the best versions, of certain portions, that has been done . . . a good two-act drama'' that was "decidedly popular'' enough to have been revived at many other theaters after its month-long run at Drury Lane (237–38). What's so surprising about this unanimous praise is that it is lavished on an adaptation that nowhere mentions either Charles Dickens or *David Copperfield*.

In *The Deal Boatman*, Burnand distilled Dickens's extremely lengthy novel into eight characters and two major plot-lines. Taking his cues from the previous adapters, Burnand realized that the most dramatic event of the novel was Emily's disappearance and Peggotty's resolve to find her. Unlike previous *David Copperfield* adaptations, however, Burnand's play takes the Yarmouth characters and freely reinvents their identities. Peggotty becomes Jacob

Vance, a boatman who has raised a young girl as his daughter after saving her from a shipwreck. This adopted daughter, Mary, is engaged to marry a simple but respectable pilot's apprentice, Matt Bramber. Unfortunately for Matt, Mary's affections have been lately captured by a dashing gentleman named Edward Leslie, whose dalliances in Kent include sailing and seduction. Act 1 opens with Mary repelling the kiss of her intended husband, and, soon after, promising Edward to run away with him before her impending wedding, which is slated for the very next day—her eighteenth birthday.

By keeping the novel's Emily-Ham-Steerforth love triangle perfectly intact—but by reimagining the characters as Mary-Matt-Edward—Burnand asserts his authority as a playwright qualified to rewrite significantly Dickens's celebrated novel. The *Dictionary of National Biography* suggests that Burnand's reputation was founded on such bold adaptation strategies when it notes with a hint of judgment that he "[e]gotistically . . . asserted that he merely imitated Shakespeare in appropriating sources" (891). He also makes a radical change in setting the play in 1748, nearly a century before the serialization of Dickens's novel begins. Burnand understood the nostalgic appeal of historical distance, and thus directs any would-be actor to "Halstead's History of Kent" on page 1 of his playscript as a way of ensuring that all efforts are made at historical accuracy. "Jacob Vance's cottage, on the shore of Deal" (where act 1 in its entirety is set) must have seemed a littoral escape for the London theatergoer of 1863 (3).

The idyllic glow of this historical distance does not lend its rosy hue to Mary's prosaic life. Although the young woman enjoys the comfortable protection of a kindly father figure and the outstretched hand of an honorable man, her complaints are clearly articulated through confessional asides, physical acting, and a soliloquy. These various modes work together to reveal her complex personality as alternatively regretful, ungrateful, and cantankerous. For instance, the curtain rises on Mary "sitting before the fire, R., on a stool, mending a coarse looking pair of stockings" while devoted Matt looks on "fondly and sadly" (3). The stage directions throughout their opening conversation emphasize Mary's activeness. She is alternatively directed to act "annoyed," to look "defiantly," and to move "impatiently, and busying herself with tea things" (3–4). In stark contrast, Matt's stage directions present him as acting alternatively "timidly," "reproachfully," "pointedly," "bashfully," and "coaxing" (3–4). As Mary repulses Matt's efforts at physical intimacy, she even burns his hand with a scalding tea kettle. Instead of apologizing, she merely explains, "You would get in my way" (4). These brash actions signify this heroine's dramatic break from the Dickensian "angel in the house" tradition, so effectively illuminated in the quiet grace and beauty of Agnes Wickfield, the contented heroine who silently reminds readers of the Victorian ideal of womanhood to which Emily might have aspired.

Because these terse interactions with her would-be husband stretch the Little Em'ly/Mary Vance character from its former template, the playwright works overtime to garner the audience's sympathy for the unhappy young woman. A conventional soliloquy displays her sensitive awareness of how her inability to return her fiancé's love will render him—and her adoptive father—heartbroken: "Poor fellow! I can't bear to think of the change that's come over me for his sake—let alone Jacob" (4). Voicing her love for Edward "*with painful intensity*," Mary even momentarily contemplates death: "Oh! that I could die before to-morrow morning! No, no—(*clasping her hands*) Heaven forgive me for the thought" (5). Finally, Burnand ensures empathy for Mary by reminding audiences of the fact that she had no mother to stand as a role model. As stage directions specify that Mary "*slowly takes out a gold miniature, suspended round her neck by a gold chain, and regards it fondly,*" she exclaims: "Oh mother, mother! whom I never knew in life—would you were here now to guide and help me in my sore distress" (5).

As Mary "*presses the portrait in an agony to her breast, and bends her head over it, as if in silent prayer,*" Burnand seems to be evoking the all-important locket in *Oliver Twist*, which eventually reveals the orphan Oliver to be the son of Agnes Fleming (5). In a parallel plot-line that deliberately merges this inheritance plot of *Oliver Twist* into *David Copperfield*, Mary's origins are revealed via her locket in act 2, when her long lost father (Sir John Houghton) recognizes the woman in the miniature portrait to be the wife whom he deserted to advance his political career. In the wildest of coincidences, Sir John Houghton is not only Mary's father, but also Edward Leslie's uncle and financial benefactor. This unlikely connection is a clear example of melodrama's "nonclassical narrative structure," which Ben Singer defines as: "a preference for outrageous coincidences, implausibility, convoluted plotting, deus ex machina resolutions, and episodic strings of action that stuff too many events together to be able to be kept in line by a cause-and-effect chain of narrative progression" (46). Because Sir John Houghton had forbidden his nephew to form a romantic attachment to a poor girl under penalty of being disinherited, audiences familiar with melodrama's formula could only trust that the said girl will be none other than Sir John's own flesh and blood.

Although Mary's newfound status unites her to Sir John's wealth and title, Burnand exaggerates the unconventionality of her parents' union. Sir John confides to his nephew Edward the sensational secret of his youth: "When about your age, I held a small appointment under the Governor of Jamaica. In this station I loved and married a young native girl, whose veins were slightly tinged with Quadroon blood, though she was as fair as one of our own countrywomen. Of this kind of union the harsh law takes no cognizance" (23). Reasoning that an interracial marriage would not be recognized by

English law, Sir John explains that he separated from his wife and child "until the possession of wealth and rank should render [them] independent of the world's opinion" (23). As if in punishment for her presumptuous union with an English politician, the young Jamaican mother drowns at sea while attempting to bring her daughter Mary to English soil under an assumed name.

In contrast, Mary's inheritance of "Quadroon blood" is not presented in the play as any sort of taint, since her newly inherited fortune thrusts her immediately back into her rightful sphere of the aristocracy. Mary's nurse-maid declares to have always known that Mary "was born to be a lady," and her adoptive father, Jacob, echoes, "A real lady she's—a real lady, as we allus said ye wor" (33). This insistence of the heroine's inherent nobility is a familiar pattern in Victorian stage melodrama, as Peter Brooks observes when he describes the plight of the innocent protagonist in terms of a quest narrative: "Expulsed from its natural terrain, its identity put into question through deceiving signs, it must wander afflicted until it can find and establish the true sign in proof of its nature" (30). Thus, Mary's "true sign in proof" of her identity confirms her high status despite her lower-class positioning in society. As Elaine Hadley explains: "This traditional romance element in melodrama, in which the 'pauper' becomes a 'prince,' should not be read in terms of class betrayal. . . . Paupers become princes only if they always have been" (127).

Mary's noble status qualifies her for an equally noble partner, and Burnand does his best to insist that Edward Leslie is a far worthier mate than the humble apprentice, Matt. As in Almar's inaugural adaptation of *David Copperfield*, the ending of *The Deal Boatman* insists upon redeeming the Steerforth/Leslie character through his marriage to the Emily/Mary character. To some extent, Dickens himself betrayed his own desire to soften Steerforth's fate when he paints his death scene as a return to his boyhood pose of sleeping innocence, "lying with his head upon his arm" (669). Both Almar's and Burnand's final revisions suggest that Dickens's capital punishment of Steerforth and his heroic attempted rescuer, Ham, was too tragically final for the melodrama's shimmering, happy resolutions. This urge to forgive the seducer should be viewed as a group of adapters' rewriting of an element of the source text that they thought would perhaps be not wholly acceptable to an audience. Burnand's gentle ending is the theatrical equivalent of film adaptations that "correct what they take to be the flaws of their originals" (Leitch 100).

This comforting final closure is also a defining trait of the Victorian sensation drama—a highly suspenseful type of five-act play in which something incredibly astonishing occurs in act 4, such as a tenement erupting into flames, an explosion on a steamboat, or a heroine being thrown in front of an oncoming London underground train. Act 5 works to restore order and, as in all melodramas, allow good to triumph unfailingly over evil. This heightened style of melodrama was pioneered in London by Dion Boucicault, whose 1860 play *The Colleen Bawn* "was to the sensation drama what *The Woman in White* was to the sensation novel" (Diamond 218).[13] Nicholas Daly has shown how integral technological spectacles were to this breathtaking subgenre, which he vividly describes as an "intoxicating cocktail of the contemporary and the spectacular" (19). The sensation drama came to define the decade dubbed the "sensational sixties," an era which Lyn Pykett characterizes as "pre-eminently, the age of the sensational theatre, most notably stylized dramatic tableaux, heightened emotions and extraordinary incidents of melodrama" (1–2). Only on such a sensational Victorian stage could the cast-off child of a multiracial union be rewarded with a wealthy father, requited love, and marriage to a gentleman in two short acts.

Among the most sensational plays of 1869 were two fallen women dramas: Dion Boucicault's *Formosa, or the Rail Road to Ruin*, a tale of working girl in London who moonlights as a prostitute to support her parents (Eltis 223), and Andrew Halliday's *Little Em'ly*, a phenomenally successful dramatization of *David Copperfield* that unapologetically repositioned Emily as the lead over the novel's eponymous character. *Little Em'ly*'s initial run at the Olympic in London constituted over 200 performances (*Letters* 12:265), which was more than three times the length of the average play's lifecycle at this time.[14] The new manager of the Olympic, Mr. Liston, deliberately began his tenure with a literary adaptation to announce the focus of his managerial career, which would eventually be remembered primarily for "some marked success with adaptations of Dickens's and Wilkie Collins's novels, chief of which were *Little Em'ly* and *The Woman in White*" (Baker 272).

Little Em'ly earned glowing reviews from critics who stressed the play's good taste and respectable venue. *The London Journal*'s review praised Halliday's play as "a rich treat" and described it as a decidedly highbrow production: "There was nothing commonplace or vulgar about the performance, and the house itself was so richly-decorated that it appeared to our dazzled vision almost like one of those fairy palaces of which poets give us such rapturous descriptions." *The Illustrated London News*'s review featured a half-page illustration and proclaimed it the event of the season: "Of all the novelties of the season perhaps the present drama of 'Little Em'ly' is the most successful." Even Dickens applauded Halliday's adaptation, making this the only staged version of *David Copperfield* to enjoy the novelist's official seal of approval. Dickens's eldest son recalled of *Little Em'ly*, "The performance was thoroughly satisfactory to Charles Dickens, whose cordial and cheery congratulations to Andrew Halliday I well remember hearing." The younger Charles Dickens attributed part of the play's success to the "unusually competent cast." His father complimented the actress playing

Martha, Miss Mattie Reinhardt, according to Fitz-Gerald, who emphasizes her centrality to the play as a whole: "I find more than one reference to Dickens's admiration for her conception of the part and his general appreciation of the whole production" (Fitz-Gerald 232–35).

Dickens's recognition of Martha's performance was partially self-congratulatory, as he had provided the playwright with explicit instructions regarding her role. As a writer for *All the Year Round*, Andrew Halliday (1830–77) had an advantage over his rival playwrights in working with Dickens for seven years before adapting his novel (Stephens 237). Halliday consulted Dickens on his script at least nine months before the play opened. In a letter addressed to "My Dear Halliday," Dickens offers constructive criticism to the hired hand who dared to adapt his employer's masterpiece:

> I have gone over your notes for a dramatized Copperfield, and although I notice the usual difficulties in the way of endeavour to put so long a story into so short a space, I have no other fault to find:—-except that I do not think you can "change" after the Storm, without an anti-climax. I would assuredly end upon the Beach, and get in what you want of Miss Dartle and Emily, before that scene. It is very important to Mr. Peggotty's character—this is another point—that he should be merciful with, and sorry for, Martha; and that he should never bully her.   (*Letters* 12: 266)

In addition to revealing his attachment to this particular fallen woman, Dickens's insistence that Peggotty show mercy and compassion to Martha suggests that Halliday's first draft characterized Peggotty in a less beneficent manner. Notably absent are any specifications for fleshing out the intentions or motivations of David, the more obvious vessel of Dickens's own early life experiences.

Halliday took his editor's advice to heart by spotlighting Peggotty's compassion towards Martha, a magdalen entrenched in the cycle of prostitution. Despite the play's title, *Little Em'ly* is just as concerned with Martha's redemption as it is with Emily's recovery. The two young women are established as dopplegängers in the play's opening scene. As Emily and Ham exit the stage to "a few bars of a solemn cast," Martha is directed to appear suddenly, with her eyes intently focused on Emily. Steerforth calls the audience's attention to Martha by asking David, "What's that? that black shadow following the girl?" Although David callously dismisses her as "some beggar," Steerforth appears visibly troubled by the sight of her and enigmatically asks David always to remember him at his best.

While Steerforth experiences qualms of conscience when observing Martha, Emily reads her own inevitable fate in Martha's body. Ham denounces Martha when he expresses shock that Emily would befriend such a woman: "You can't want to know no more that poor worem (*sic*), trod under foot by all the town. Why, the mould o'churchyard don't hold any the folk shrink away from more'' (14). As in Dickens's source text, the spectacle of the prostitute causes Emily to lament tearfully her own sins: "I'm not as good a girl as I ought to be, not near, not near" (15). As Emily's involvement with Steerforth unfolds, Halliday keeps reminding his audience that Emily is repeating Martha's missteps. While Emily is missing throughout act 2, Mr. Peggotty and David bestow their attention on Martha as Emily's surrogate. After preventing the suicidal Martha from drowning in the river, the two men restore her will to live by assigning her the task of recovering Emily. Furthermore, Martha understands her mission in life to be saving her double from further disgrace: "If I am not true to it—may the object I now have in life, pass away from me, and leave me more forlorn and more despairing than this night, and then may all help, human and divine, renounce me ever more!'' (31). By collapsing Emily and Martha into one victimized character, Halliday attempts to elicit pathos for both fallen women, regardless of the circumstances that precipitated their ruin.

One scene that achieves such sympathy occurs when Martha describes finding Emily at a house of ill-repute. Although her account is taken almost exactly from Peggotty's speeches in the novel, the details of Emily's escape from a London brothel acquire a more intimate, confessional tone when voiced by Martha:

> I came, white and hurried, upon her, in her sleep, and I says to her: 'Rise up from worse than death, and come with me!' The people of the house would have stopped me, (*waves her hand angrily, and smiles scornfully*) but they might as soon have stopped the sea! 'Stand away from me,' cried I, 'I am a ghost that calls to her from beside her open grave!' I wrapped her hastily in her clothes, and took her out, faint and trembling on my arm, heeding no more what *they* said, than if I had had no ears. I walked through them with your child, minding only her—and brought her, safe out of the dead of night, from that black pit of ruin! (33)

This pivotal speech qualifies as a sensation scene due to its "intense emotional upheaval,'' the quality which survived as the sensation drama's definitive trait and legacy throughout the century (Diamond 219). As David and Peggotty recede to the sidelines to allow Martha this uninterrupted narrative, her professed courage and resolution mark her as Emily's true rescuer.

As in Dickens's novel, another woman must fall for Martha and Emily to be able to successfully escape the audience's censure. Following Dickens's template, Halliday uses Rosa Dartle to absorb all of the play's sexualized anger. This dramatized version features Rosa and Emily alone on stage, without the novel's awkward positioning of David as a silent and frozen interloper. Rosa insults Emily in every possible degree with unambiguous exclamations: she degrades her working class origins ("You were a part of the trade of your home, and were bought and sold like any other vendible thing your people dealt in!''); she strips her of all personal dignity ("A piece of pollution, picked up from the water-side, to be *made* much of, for an hour, and then tossed back to its original place!''); she assures her that her best remaining option in life is death ("Die! There are doorways and dust-heaps for such deaths and such despair—find one, and take your flight to heaven!'') (34–35). By characterizing Rosa as the most unlikeable member of this doomed love triangle, Halliday exonerates Emily and even, to some extent, Steerforth. The ferocity of Rosa's class snobbery ultimately marks her as the most symbolically fallen of women, with a heart frozen beyond redemption and a mind steeled against compassion.

III. Dickens and the Seduction Plot

Dickens himself puzzled over how to reconcile the disparate plotlines of David's rise and Emily's fall as he transformed his beloved novel into a spoken format for his public reading series. In fact, it took him six years of deliberation before he finished his *David Copperfield* reading to his satisfaction. In an 1855 letter to Arthur Ryland, Dickens agonized over the formidable challenge of condensing his magnum opus into a manageable reading version:

> I have been pouring over Copperfield (which is my favourite), with the idea of getting a reading out of it, to be called by some such name as 'Young Housekeeping and Little Emily.' But there is still the huge difficulty that I constructed the whole with immense pains, and have so woven it up and blended it together, that I cannot yet so separate the parts as to tell the story of David's married life with Dora, and the story of Mr. Peggotty's search for his niece, within the time. This is my object. If I could possibly bring it to bear, it would make a very attractive reading, with a strong interest in it, and a certain completeness. *(Letters* 7: 515)

This letter makes clear that Dickens confronted many of the same struggles that his own adapters faced, especially the challenge to replicate the novel's sense of "completeness" within a highly compressed form. Unlike his collaborator Wilkie Collins, who radically rewrote his own fiction for the stage, Dickens prioritized fidelity to his source text. He confided to his correspondent his serious anxiety over altering the novel in any way: "I no sooner try to get it into this form, than I begin to read it all and to feel that I can't disturb it" (*Letters* 7: 515). Despite this resistance to change, Dickens's plan to begin his reading with David as a young man reminiscing on his childhood imitates the opening of that unfaithful first dramatization, George Almar's *Born with a Caul.* Furthermore, Dickens's focus on the seduction plot suggests that he may have been influenced by the playwrights who had already established that this melodramatic plotline of the novel easily translated to the stage.

Dickens's most original adaptation approach to *David Copperfield* is found in his plan to structurally juxtapose the "child-wife" Dora (a character whom almost all of the Victorian playwrights omit) with Emily, the perpetually-reproduced fallen woman. His completed reading, first performed on October 28, 1861 (Collins xxviii), consists of six chapters that cross-cut between the Emily/Peggotty plot and the Dora/David plot. As Philip Collins has observed, those chapters on Dora and David's courtship and early marriage, "though delightful, are irrelevant to the Emily-Steerforth-Peggotty story, which provides the main plot of the Reading" (216). Although four of these six chapters dramatize the seduction plot, Emily never once speaks. From chapter 1, which narrates Steerforth's initial visit to Mr. Peggotty's ark on the fateful night of Emily and Ham's engagement, to the final chapter's happy revelation of Emily's recovery, male characters recount Emily's thoughts and actions. Surprisingly, Dickens chose not to narrate the pivotal scene of Emily being found at long last. Chapter 6 opens only with Mr. Peggotty proclaiming, "Mas'r Davy, I've found her!" (244). The credit for Emily's restoration is Mr. Peggotty's alone, and Dickens played the part to perfection. The audience reactions, as preserved in theater reviews and personal journals, all point to Mr. Peggotty as the scene-stealer. One audience member, Robert Lytton, wrote to Dickens: "I confess that I was heartily *blubbering* at the time that Mr. Peggotty was talking to us" (qtd. in Collins 218). The theater critic for the *Manchester Examiner* places Dickens's reading of Mr. Peggotty on par with *King Lear.* In short, Dickens immortalized the role of Mr. Peggotty throughout the seventy-one performances of the reading that became, like its source text, his personal "favourite" (Collins xxvii, 216).

Despite the theatrical bent of his last years, dramatically replete as they were with his American tour of 1867–68 and his "Farewell Tour" of Great Britain, Dickens eschewed the thought of theatrical displays that would inevitably accompany his own last act. In his last will, he famously directed to be "buried in an inexpensive, unostentatious, and strictly private manner . . . and that those attending my funeral wear no scarf, cloak, black bow, long hatband, or other such revolting absurdity" (qtd. in Schlicke 150). What Dickens perhaps never imagined was that his adoring fans would find even more theatrical ways to act out their grief over his passing. After his death on June 9, 1870, those dramatists long espoused to Dickens in a vexed author/adapter relationship commemorated his life on the international stage via dramatizations of his fiction. At least twenty-one different performances of *David*

Copperfield were staged before the end of the year; by the end of the decade, over seventy different productions were produced in England alone (Dunn 22). Most of these productions were spin-offs of Andrew Halliday's *Little Em'ly. Lost Em'ly, Poor Lost Em'ly; or, The Wreck of the Rosa, Little Em'ly's Trials, The Ark on the Sands*, and other imitations appeared at a frenetic pace throughout the 1870s.[15]

It is in these posthumous stage adaptations where the tension between the introspective bildungsroman and the sensation of the seduction plot is finally resolved. As Michael Slater has recently reminded us, Dickens's audience "knew virtually nothing of his life before he became a journalist in his late teens" prior to John Forster's publication of the first volume of *The Life of Charles Dickens* in November 1871 (619). Although the public eagerly discussed the marked connections between David Copperfield's childhood humiliations and the shocking new details of Dickens's migratory youth, playwrights reached beyond biography to celebrate their beloved Boz. When staging his most autobiographical novel in commemoration of his life, Dickens's adapters purposefully reallocated the role of hero to Mr. Peggotty, thereby directing attention away from both David and Emily. Completing a final cycle of correction via adaptation, the productions of *David Copperfield* staged in the wake of Dickens's death steer clear of any biographical allusions that might humble their fallen hero. If the theatrical world knew that Dickens's long relationship with a young actress verged on a real life seduction scandal, the commemorative plays never breathed the secret. Instead, the post-1870 *David Copperfield* plays turn on the audience's empathy towards a benevolent patriarch whose enduring love restores faith in an errant world.[16] Perhaps it is Daniel Peggotty's version of aged masculinity—so steadfast and decisive where the young David wavers and hesitates—that the mourning public needed to believe was Dickens's personal legacy.

NOTES

1. This article is especially indebted to the pioneering work on *David Copperfield* adaptations by Fitz-Gerald, and to the later studies by Bolton, Morley, and Fulkerson.

2. *David Copperfield* adaptations are excluded from two of the most influential recent books on Dickens and popular culture: Deborah Vlock's *Dickens, Novel Reading, and the Victorian Popular Theatre* and John Glavin's *After Dickens: Reading, Adaptation, and Performance*.

3. The time that I propose for Dickens's shift to fictional practices that were aimed to thwart dramatists predates Bolton's by ten years. Bolton identifies the 1860s as the decade when "the novelist began to inhibit dramatization of his novels

and stories by legal means, and as his narrative techniques became less obviously theatrical and harder to stage'' (*Oxford* 196). Dickens and Wilkie Collins agitated for authors' rights during this time, publishing stage synopses of their newest work (for Dickens, *Great Expectations* and a story, ''A Message from the Sea'') immediately to establish their copyright to the material; because the theater had, since the eighteenth century, considered published novels fair game for stage adaptation, their demands struck the theater community as greedy (Bolton, *Oxford* 196–97).

4. I include the unfinished final novel *The Mystery of Edwin Drood* (1870) in my tally.

5. H. Philip Bolton's compendious *Dickens Dramatized* considers all of plays produced through mid-November of 1850 as having appeared before the novel's final installment (324). I suspect that there is an error in Bolton's chronology, since J. Courtney's mid-November play quotes so exactly from Dickens's final chapter. Richard Fulkerson refers to Courtney's November 13 production as having occurred ''shortly after the novel's completion'' (30); Malcolm Morley specifies only the October play by Almar to have appeared ''before the total of twenty [numbers of the novel] had been issued'' (77). November 1 is the day cited by Gareth Cordery (369) as the date of the novel's final installment (a double number), and Hughes and Lund mention ''the excitement of 'magazine day' (the first of the month when new issues appeared in bookstalls across the country)'' (10). Butt and Tilloston observe, however, that a number was published ''nominally on the first day, [but] actually the last day of each month'' (14). October 31, therefore, was evidently the day that Dickens's final number of *David Copperfield* was published.

6. This paper does not discuss the second American adaptation, Mrs. Harriet Marion Ward Stevens's *David Copperfield,* which was performed at Howard Athenaeum in Cambridge, MA (Bolton, *Dickens* 324).

7. Almar's *Born with a Caul* was revived on November 18, 1850, at the Standard and Queen's (Bolton, *Dickens* 324). Presumably this was an attempt to rival *David Copperfield the Younger* at a peak moment of popularity for the novel, the final double number of which had just been published.

8. Morley speculated the dramatist to be H. Rivers (77); Fulkerson cites ''J. Courtney'' from the Lord Chamberlain's manuscript collection (31); Bolton refers to the author as anonymous but mentions these possibilities, including a third option put forth by Williams: W. Montague (*Dickens* 323). Following the British Library citation, I accept the playwright to be ''J. Courtney,'' especially since this play bears resemblance to the 1848 dramatization of *Jane Eyre* that was penned by John Courtney. As Stoneman explains, Frederic Boase identified ''John Courtney'' as a pen name for John Fuller, although this has not been widely accepted (20).

9. Although she is not credited on the playbill, Bolton identifies the actress by name (*Dickens* 323).

10. I have used ''[?]'' in place of indecipherable words in the manuscript.

11. Bolton identifies two popular productions of Brougham's play in 1850 (in Chicago and Philadelphia). Bolton also speculates that five more productions were staged in New York City throughout the 1860s (*Dickens* 324–28).

12. Bolton numbers *The Deal Boatman* as the 27th in his chronological list of *David Copperfield* adaptations (*Dickens* 321).

13. Other mid-century melodramas with notable sensation scenes include: *Still Waters Run Deep* (1855, by Tom Taylor); *Lady Audley's Secret* (1863, adapted from Elizabeth Braddon's novel by C. H. Hazlewood); *The Ticket-of-Leave Man* (1863, by Tom Taylor); *The Streets of London* (1864, by Dion Boucicault); *Under the Gaslight* (1867, by Augustin Daly); *After Dark* (1868, by Dion Boucicault); *East Lynne* (1866, adapted from Mrs. Ellen Wood's novel by John Oxenford).

14. An average run in a London theater was, according to Andrew Halliday, "from thirty to sixty nights" (*Every Day Papers* 210). Other very successful runs include Dion Boucicault's *The Colleen Bawn* (1860), which ran for 165 performances, and Tom Taylor's *Our American Cousin* (1862), which ran for 314 nights (Trussler 233).

15. Bolton lists 46 productions of *David Copperfield* staged internationally from June 1870–December 1879 (*Dickens* 329–33). 34 of these 46 plays contain the name "Emily" or "Em'ly" in their title. The most often-performed play was Halliday's *Little Em'ly,* of which Bolton located 20 separate productions. The second most popular play was *Lost Emily,* staged 7 times throughout this decade.

16. From this point forward, the role of Mr. Peggotty surpassed that of Mr. Micawber or David Copperfield as the play's most coveted male role. The famous Dickensian actor Bransby Williams recalled his 1905 performance of this lead role in his memoir. "I somehow became Dan'l Peggotty to such an extent that I really seemed to feel the loss of Em'ly, and the tears streamed down my cheeks" (96). According to Williams, his performance so affected a self-proclaimed "fallen woman" in the audience that she fled the theater in tears, and sent a letter to him the next day thanking him for inspiring her to return home. Surely, Dickens would have been pleased to know that, long after the Urania Cottage project was abandoned, his novel achieved his social mission via a stage production.

WORKS CITED

Almar, George. *Born with a Caul.* Vol. Manuscript No. 43030, British Library, London, England: Lord Chamberlain's Plays. Vol. CLXVI, 1850.

Baker, H. Barton. *History of the London Stage and Its Famous Players (1576–1903).* New York: Dutton, 1904.

Bolton, H. Philip. *Dickens Dramatized.* Boston: G. K. Hall, 1987.

———. "Dramatizations and Dramatizers of Dickens's Works." *Oxford Reader's Companion to Dickens.* Ed. Paul Schlicke. Oxford: Oxford UP, 1999.

Booth, Michael R. *English Melodrama.* London: H. Jenkins, 1965.

———. *Theatre in the Victorian Age.* Cambridge: Cambridge UP, 1991.

Brooks, Peter. *The Melodramatic Imagination: Balzac, Henry James, Melodrama, and the Mode of Excess.* New Haven: Yale UP, 1995.

Brougham, John. *David Copperfield: A Drama, in Two Acts.* New York: Samuel French, 1851.

Burnand, Francis Cowlery. *The Deal Boatman. A Serio-Comic Drama, in Two Acts.* London: Thomas Hailes Lacy, 1864. Microform.

"Burnand, Francis Cowlery." *Dictionary of National Biography: Founded in 1882 by George Smith; Edited by Sir Leslie Stephen and Sir Sidney Lee; From the Earliest Times to 1900.* London: Oxford UP, 1959–60. 891.

Butt, John, and Kathleen Tillotson. *Dickens at Work.* 1957. London: Methuen, 1963.

Rev. of "Charles Dickens's Reading Series Featuring *David Copperfield.*" *Manchester Examiner* 19 Oct. 1868. Microform.

Collins, Philip, ed. *Charles Dickens: The Public Readings.* Oxford: Clarendon, 1975.

Cordery, Gareth. *"David Copperfield." A Companion to Charles Dickens.* Ed. David Paroissien. Malden, MA: Blackwell, 2008.

Courtney, J. *David Copperfield the Younger of Blunderstone Rookery.* Vol. Manuscript 43030, British Library, London, England: Lord Chamberlain's Plays. Vol. 166, 1850.

Daly, Nicholas. *Literature, Technology, and Modernity, 1860–2000.* Cambridge, Cambridge UP, 2004.

Rev. of *David Copperfield. The International Monthly Magazine of Literature, Science and Art* 1 Jan. 1851: 183. *American Periodicals Series.* Web. 1 Dec. 2009.

Davis, Jim, and Victor Emeljanow. *Reflecting the Audience: London Theatregoing, 1840–1880.* Iowa City: U of Iowa P, 2001.

Diamond, Michael. *Victorian Sensation.* London: Anthem, 2003.

Dickens, Charles. *David Copperfield: Authoritative Text, Backgrounds, Criticism.* Ed. Jerome H. Buckley. New York: Norton, 1990.

———. *The Letters of Charles Dickens.* Ed. Madeline House, Graham Storey, Kathleen Tilloston, et al. The Pilgrim Edition. 12 vols. Oxford: Clarendon, 1965–2002.

Dunn, Richard J., and Ann M. Tandy. *David Copperfield: An Annotated Bibliography: Supplement 1, 1981–1998.* New York: AMS, 2000.

Eltis, Sos. "The Fallen Woman on Stage: Maidens, Magdalens, and the Emancipated Female." *The Cambridge Companion to Victorian and Edwardian Theatre.* Ed. Kerry Powell. Cambridge: Cambridge UP, 2004. 222–36.

Fitz-Gerald, S. J. Adair. *Dickens and the Drama: Being an Account of Charles Dickens's Connection with the Stage and the Stage's Connection with Him.* New York: Scribner's Sons, 1910.

———. "*David Copperfield* on the Stage." *Dickensian* 10 (1914): 228–34.

Forster, John. *The Life of Charles Dickens; in 2 Volumes.* Ed. A. J. Hoppé. London: Dent, 1969.

Fulkerson, Richard. "*David Copperfield* in the Victorian Theatre." *Victorian Institute Journal* 5 (1976): 29–36.

Glavin, John. *After Dickens: Reading, Adaptation, and Performance.* Cambridge: Cambridge UP, 1999.

Hadley, Elaine. *Melodramatic Tactics: Theatricalized Dissent in the English Marketplace, 1800–1885.* Stanford: Stanford UP, 1995.

Halliday, Andrew. *Every Day Papers; A Series of Essays from "All the Year Round."* London: Tinsley Brothers, 1869. 4th ed.

———. *Little Em'ly.* New York: De Witt, 1869.

Hughes, Linda K., and Michael Lund. *The Victorian Serial.* Charlottesville: U of Virginia P, 1991.

Law, Graham, and Andrew Maunder. *Wilkie Collins: A Literary Life.* Houndmills, Basingstoke, Hampshire: Palgrave Macmillan, 2008.

Leitch, Thomas M. *Film Adaptation and Its Discontents: From Gone with the Wind to the Passion of the Christ.* Baltimore: Johns Hopkins UP, 2007.

Rev. of *Little Em'ly* by Andrew Halliday, The Olympic, London. *The London Journal* 51.1302 (Jan. 1870): 62. *C19Index.* Web. 29 June 2009.

Rev. of *Little Em'ly* by Andrew Halliday, The Olympic, London. *The Illustrated London News* 4 Dec. 1868: 561. Print.

Morley, Malcolm. "Stage Appearances of *David Copperfield.*" *Dickensian* 49 (1953): 77–85.

Pykett, Lyn. *The Sensation Novel: From* The Moonstone *to* The Woman in White. Plymouth, U.K: Northcote House in Association with the British Council, 1994.

Schlicke, Paul. *Oxford Reader's Companion to Dickens.* Oxford: Oxford UP, 1999.

Singer, Ben. *Melodrama and Modernity: Early Sensational Cinema and Its Contexts.* New York: Columbia UP, 2001.

Slater, Michael. *Charles Dickens.* New Haven: Yale UP, 2009.

Stephens, John Russell. *The Profession of the Playwright: British Theatre 1800–1900.* Cambridge: Cambridge UP, 1992.

Stoneman, Patsy. *Jane Eyre on Stage, 1848–1898.* Hampshire, UK: Ashgate, 2007.

Trussler, Simon. *The Cambridge Illustrated History of British Theatre.* Cambridge: Cambridge UP, 2000.

Vlock, Deborah. *Dickens, Novel Reading, and the Victorian Popular Theatre.* Cambridge: Cambridge UP, 1998.

Williams, Bransby. *An Actor's Story.* London: Chapman & Hall, 1909.

Bleak House, Our Mutual Friend, and the Aesthetics of Dust

Leslie Simon

In this essay, I argue that dust functions as a central image in Dickens's work, its content illuminating Victorian concerns about the fragmentations of body and mind produced by industrial urbanization (including the problems of epidemic disease and the disposal of waste matter), even as its structure offers a novel way to think about and express modernity. Borrowing from postcolonial readings of dust, which affirm psychological shattering as a basic principle of modern identity, I interpret Bleak House *and* Our Mutual Friend *as novels that call on images of excess, miscellany, and material entropy to register epistemological fractures in narrative realism, a genre torn between its impulse, at once, to depict the chaotic energies of a world constantly subject to upheaval and change and to give that chaos order. In his fiction, I suggest, Dickens makes way for a modernist aesthetic that both acknowledges and validates narrative disjunctions between content and form as themselves representative of newly emerging perceptions of the postindustrial world.*

Though I will turn to Dickens momentarily, I wish to begin in contemporary literature and, more particularly, in the enjambed couplets of Derek Walcott's ode to his St. Lucian birthplace, "Becune Point." I will argue that in two of Dickens's novels, *Bleak House* (1852–53) and *Our Mutual Friend* (1864–65), as in Walcott's poem, dust works as a central image, figuring thematically in

---

these texts as a symbol of psychological fragmentation, even while functioning structurally to reconstruct modern selfhood, not by reassembling its various parts, but by offering novel approaches for understanding and even
narrating it. This paper will analyze the generic concerns of the Victorian
novel, as *Bleak House* and *Our Mutual Friend* individually consider the
monstrosity of narrative realism—its loose bagginess, its structural emphasis
on multiplicity, miscellany, transformation, upheaval—through the central
metaphor of particulate matter.

And so to Walcott:

> Dust rises easily.
>
> Haze of the Harmattan, Sahara dust, memory's haze
> from the dried well of Africa, the headland's desert
>
> or riders in swirling burnooses, mixed with the greys
> of hills veiled in Impressionist light. We inherit
>
> two worlds of associations, or references, drought
> that we heighten into Delacroix's North Africa,
>
> veils, daggers, lances, herds the Harmattan brought
> with a phantom inheritance, which the desperate seeker
>
> of well-spring staggers in the heat in search of—
> heroic ancestors; the other that the dry season brings
>
> is the gust of a European calendar, but it is the one love
> that thirsts for confirmations. . . .   (lines 8–20)

"We are history's afterthought," the speaker concludes; "in drought we
discover our shadows,/Our origins that range from the most disparate places"
(lines 25–27). Known as a poet and playwright who gives expression to the
everyday experiences of an emerging society—one still in the process of
discovering an authentic voice—Derek Walcott locates meaning in the ordinary stuff of life, using the raw elements he finds around him to articulate
the liminal spaces of West Indian experience. In this poem, memory takes on
the consistency of dust, the refuse of past civilizations from which modern
culture and the modern individual—and more to the point here, postcolonial
cultures and postcolonial individuals—are isolated. The enjambed lines of the
poem reflect the tensions of inheriting disparate, overlapping, and conflicting
cultures—inheriting, that is, the Harmattan wind of West Africa, as well as
its representation on European canvas, in European paint.

Indeed, though Walcott's is a good example, postcolonial literature frequently employs dust as a metaphor for historical displacement and the fragmentation of cultural authenticity. In *The God of Small Things*, Arundhati

Roy depicts the History House as a collector of dust, a keeper of muddled memories and the site of a literal, corporeal dismemberment that can only be corrected metapoetically, through the imaginative re-membrance of the narrative voice. Similarly, stories by Bessie Head of Botswana, Rosario Ferré of Puerto Rico, and Zadie Smith of London call upon dust to illustrate postcolonial identities as phenomena always in the process of disintegration and decay, though Roy and Smith in particular engage in a postmodern aesthetic that ultimately validates and reaffirms this psychological shattering.[1] As Chinua Achebe memorably writes, *Things Fall Apart*—they fall apart because they should, because they must—and it is in this shattering and the reconstruction that follows that cultures and individuals find meaning and find home.

While the title of Achebe's novel turns us most readily to W. B. Yeats and the modernist disavowal of nineteenth-century imperialism, what I would like to suggest is that we find things already falling apart in nineteenth-century literature—things falling apart in spite of themselves, and in the face of bombastic claims of cultural permanence and national security—as the age of empire itself saw a profusion of writing on and through dust.[2] It should be noted at once that dust meant more to the Victorians than ''any substance comminuted or pulverized; powder,'' which we recognize (and the *Oxford English Dictionary* reports) as the term's first and most common usage; to nineteenth-century urban-dwellers, rather, dust conveyed something altogether more general: rubbish, refuse, trash.[3] Waste did not have to be broken entirely down in order to qualify as dust to Victorians, and we find that this gives the image of the dustheap a certain level of complexity: what appears to be homogenous is actually miscellaneous, as used up and discarded things continue to bear marks of distinction, even when heaped into a seemingly undifferentiated mass. The dustheap, in nineteenth-century parlance, is not *one* body of useless matter, but an accumulation of many bodies, alike, perhaps, only in being deemed useless. In continuing to be different, furthermore, these things continue to *be*—that is, they are alive, though in new environs and potentially in new form. This is what we today would call recycling—things as waste maintaining their value, even as that value shifts—and I would like to argue that Dickens recycles or repurposes the image of dust itself in his novels: rather than simply conveying notions of waste, expenditure, or disuse, dust in Dickens suggests that modern life might be reinterpreted through structures of fragmentation, miscellany, and dynamic interrelation.

In a world where mudlarks scoured the banks of the Thames for recyclable refuse from middle-class homes, where the residue from kerosene lamps blackened parlor walls and ceilings, and where the architectural center of domestic life—the hearth—polluted interior air with smoke and ash, it is no wonder (practically speaking) that dust imagery appears so frequently in domestic novels of the time.[4] Henry Mayhew's *London Labour and the London Poor* (first published in 1851), various works by Thomas Carlyle, and a great many articles printed at midcentury in *Household Words*, *Punch*, and other news journals brought the realities of pollution to the fore; and the reality was this: that even the royal family, Anthony Wohl reports, endured "tragedies and near-tragedies, from bad sewers and filth diseases, [and were] forced to live amidst stink, and water and air pollution" (2). To find dustheaps in the novels of a renowned social crusader like Dickens, then, is noteworthy, though not all that surprising.[5] The pressing need for sanitation reform in mid-Victorian London, especially after the devastating effects of the cholera epidemic that directly and ironically preceded Britain's exhibition of technological advancement and progress, would certainly have informed the writing of such topical novels—to use Kathleen Tillotson and John Butt's term—as *Bleak House* and *Our Mutual Friend*.[6]

But is there a connection between the dust imagery found in these mid-Victorian novels, written at the noontime of imperial expansion, and what we see in the postcolonial novels and poems that will follow over a century later? Or, to put the question differently, can we learn anything from postcolonial applications of dust that might help us interpret the particulate chaos we find in Dickens's novels? Does dust relate to memory, to inheritance, to the place of home, as it does in the poetry of Walcott and the fiction of Roy? Does postcolonial subjectivity—bastardized, exiled, displaced—find a predecessor (problematic though the comparison may be) in the mid-Victorian sensibility of self—orphaned, dehumanized, alienated, repressed? And if so, what is the project of the Victorian novel that links dust and home, history and subjectivity in this way? Arundhati Roy and Zadie Smith embrace the entropy imagined through dust, locating new and authentic identities in the heterogeneity—in the unruliness—it makes visual, and they allow this creative unruliness to give structure to their patterns of narrative. Does Dickens? Does he, in a sense, endorse disorder?

The obvious answer is no. A number of critics, from W. J. Harvey to Robert Tracy, have argued that in *Bleak House* Esther Summerson and her narrative act as a corrective (orderly, precise, if a bit dull) to the maddening chaos of Chancery and the city streets that loom just beyond the comforts of her domestic sphere. Harvey writes that it is because "Esther's narrative is plain, matter-of-fact, [and] conscientiously plodding" that it offers the reader "stability, a point of rest in a flickering and bewildering world, the promise of some guidance through the labyrinth" of *Bleak House* (91, 97). Similarly, Tracy calls Esther a housekeeper-narrator, responsible for chaperoning her readership through a house of fiction she has kept in order by methodically cataloguing its contents: just as Esther "writes of herself writing an inventory of Bleak House," Tracy argues, "her completed narrative is an inventory of

Bleak House the novel, as she brings before us the various characters and locales of the story, orchestrates their appearances, and links them together'' (28). With her basket of keys constantly in tow, the young woman known to her companions as Little Mother provides consistency and stability for the world she narrates—*precisely by* narrating it in seemingly static, passive, and secure terms. In her most self-aware moments—when considering the possibility of marrying Mr. Jarndyce or the alteration of her face after illness—the jingle of her keys brings Esther around to sense and duty, out of reverie and the dangers of subjectivity, and back into the material realities of her position and her responsibility to those around her; by ringing her housekeeping keys, and on one occasion even kissing them, Esther reminds herself to keep ''busy, busy, busy—useful, amiable, serviceable, in all honest, unpretending ways'' (539; ch. 44).

And she, of course, gives *us* a ''key'' to this calm and orderly imagined life too—a legend or language as it were, by which to properly translate and transform the Victorian world; because she above all people knows how to manage keys, living up against a deadlock as she so constantly does. Christopher Herbert writes that ''Esther's characteristic domestic chores . . . symbolize in their imaginary containment and systematic regularity her narrative function as the sponsor of a world insulated from the disruptive processes of fantasy that her anonymous co-narrator gives rein to'' (102). Hers is a balancing act, giving weight and credibility to cultural principles of order and regulation—indeed, seeming to make this order come to life through the rhetoric of the tale she carefully weaves. We might here second the appraisal Harold Skimpole offers to Esther of herself: ''When I see you, my dear Miss Summerson, intent upon the perfect working of the whole little orderly system of which you are the centre, I feel inclined to say to myself—in fact I do say to myself, very often—*that*'s responsibility!'' (468; ch 37; emphasis in original).

Written a decade later, as Dickens was entering his twilight years without seeming to have witnessed any manifest alleviation of the social corruption charted in earlier novels like *Little Dorrit* and *Bleak House*, *Our Mutual Friend* uses dust to represent the defining value systems of Victorian culture. Money-lust acts as the controlling psychological economy among the novel's characters, and the Harmon empire of dust and decay ominously reflects the end-point of this widespread, almost systematized desire for vacuous profit. Even as Bella Wilfer mourns the decline of Mr. Boffin into a miserliness managed by suspicion and discontent, she cannot help but be drawn in by the awful fascination of money herself, as she freely admits to her father, ''I see this, and hate this, and dread this. . . . And yet I have money always in my thoughts and my desires; and the whole life I place before myself is money, money, money, and what money can make of life!'' (455; bk. 3, ch. 4). The empty repetition of this ruling force in *Our Mutual Friend* reflects its double life as it circulates among the novel's characters, gaining power with movement, but taking on no value or meaning of its own. J. Hillis Miller claims that the characters in *Our Mutual Friend* are so entirely the products of this social environment, fashioned as it is by the false value systems of capital and credit, that they themselves lose definition; as inauthentic participants in an inauthentic world, their only option, it seems, is to become detached and disguised like the narrator in the novel (106–09). Whereas *Bleak House* offers a solution to its madness in the figure of Esther Summerson, Miller continues, *Our Mutual Friend* provides no such closure, as the world of this (Dickens's last finished) novel spins continuously off its axis, decentered, destabilized, given over entirely (we might say) to the entropic aesthetic of the dust-pile.

But is this narrative decentering purely negative—that's the basic query of my essay. In his interpretation of *Little Dorrit*, Thomas Richards writes that there is too much knowledge being circulated by the Circumlocution Office for knowledge to have a center (74). While no one, surely, would defend the absurd machinations of the Circumlocution Office, which maintains centralized power by obfuscating or decentering public knowledge, postmodern readers *would* find value in decenteredness as a principle—of knowledge, and indeed, of human life in general. For, as the deconstructionists affirm, knowledge has neither origin nor center; its authenticity takes form—as Deleuze might say—in the process of its *becoming* (in its movement, in its development, in its being phenomenologically at play).[7] The ideology of centeredness is hegemonic in principle and illusory in form, as Michel Foucault demonstrates in his seminal work *The Order of Things*. "The fundamental codes of a culture," he writes, "—those governing its language, its schemas of perception, its exchanges, its techniques, its values, the hierarchy of its practices— establish for every man, from the very first, the empirical orders with which he will be dealing and within which he will be at home" (xxii). Home, then, is defined not as the location central to the private affairs, activities, and affections of a given person, but as the cultural epistemology to which he subscribes and in which he ideologically resides. The thing we call home, in other words, is an organizing system for ideas and objects alike, a taxonomy of "ordered surfaces" with which we attempt "to tame the wild profusion of existing things" (xvi).

What postcolonial texts attempt to demonstrate is that home, as space and ideology, is anything but stable, orderly, centered; it rather reflects the tensions, obscurities, failures, and improbabilities of a world built around coincidence and chance. The matrix of ordered surfaces each individual creates for himself, Foucault shows, will crumble, because the subjectivity of an individual, as of a community—to quote Homi Bhabha—is always "in the *process of articulation* . . . where meanings may be partial because they are *in medias res*; and history may be half-made because it is in the process of being made; and the image of cultural authority may be ambivalent because it is caught, uncertainly, in the act of 'composing' its powerful image'' (3; emphasis in original). The postmodern reader interprets loss, miscegenation, and displacement as facts of the human condition—that state of transcendental homelessness so aptly articulated by Lukács—and registers authenticity in the disruption (even *pulverization*) of hegemonic patterns of thought and centralized forms of expression.[8]

And my question is, would Dickens agree? Is there a positive value given in his novels to the heterogeneity, fragmentation, and disarray rendered by the image of dust? In *Hard Times*, Dickens represents a world so stifled by utilitarian systems of order and control that it *invites* characters to fall from its pattern, and to engage in a language of free association that privileges the artistic merit of Sissy Jupe's horse-wallpaper precisely because it does not make sense. Better to engage in moderated forms of spiritual anarchy than fall like mute objects into the machinery of industrial culture, this novel seems to say, one of its most touching images that of Louisa watching the ashes of her hearth-fire as they rise up momentarily and then fall and fall and fall endlessly back into the grate—a pattern of falling that prefigures not the act of sexual transgression Mrs. Sparsit painstakingly tries to engineer, but of Louisa's psychological release from the bluebook aesthetic of her father's oppressive Gradgrindery.[9]

And I argue that this drive toward mediated forms of artistic anarchy is exactly, and ironically, what gives structure to the novels under consideration in this paper. Much attention has been paid recently by critics to the role of objects in the Victorian novel, specifically to their characteristic excess and multiplicity in realist texts—characteristics, I would argue, that reach full-pitch in the image of dust, that *after*-image of things and people. Elaine Freedgood's work, in particular, has illuminated ways in which material objects are fugitive in realist narrative, for ''the protocols for reading the realist novel . . . have implicitly enjoined us *not* to interpret many or most of its objects'' (1). It is her project to locate the meanings of these objects and make them *un*fugitive, contextualized, meaningful. I would insist, however, that the aesthetic character of objects in realist novels makes their meanings always fugitive, always unlocatable, because always in flux; so that it is the structure of forgetting that becomes the real focus of study in these texts, as the objects themselves are meant to elude, or not to be necessary to, our understanding of broader narrative forms. Indeed, my contention is that the *play* of things in novels is structurally similar to the energy and organization of narration itself, and that this kind of play is only possible in realist texts, where material objects are released from allegory, often functioning only as setting (left forgotten in the background), and in their release are free to move, to shift, and to play at meaning. Loosened from overt networks of theme and signification, the objects of nineteenth-century narrative realism in some ways take on the character of the foregrounded Victorians they help define—becoming wanderers, orphans, narrative waifs. But what is important here is that their phenomenological rootlessness is expressly what brings these objects to life, because—as Lyotard suggests—the world of objects lives outside of order and rationality, as both cosmologies do violence to the objects they attempt to comprehend.[10] In his novels, Dickens seems to wonder whether or not order and rationality do violence to people (and to the imagination) as well.

The dustheap—matter broken down and forgotten, and therefore in a heightened state of play, according to my theory—has long been considered an ambivalent and therefore unusually charged image. Beginning with Eubulides of Miletus in the fourth century BC, mathematical logicians have worked to unravel the heap paradox (otherwise called the *sorites* paradox), which calls into question the very formulation of limits and boundaries. How many grains of dust or sand make a heap, and how many must be removed before the heap ceases to exist, the paradox asks. Because it is impossible to determine at what point a heap becomes a non-heap, logicians have long since determined that the means by which we institute limits must always seem arbitrary and must always remain fuzzy or vague. Bertrand Russell even uses this theory to lobby for the perpetual and ineradicable vagueness of language documentation. The figure of the heap appears throughout Dickens's work, most notably perhaps in *David Copperfield* with the character of Uriah, each time registering some thematic or structural tension, something indefinable, uncertain, at play.

And in the novels I study here we see very clearly how the dustheap figures as narrative paradox—a paradox twice over in fact. For while the dustheap serves as a thematic marker in *Bleak House* and *Our Mutual Friend* of psychological fragmentation, it works structurally to articulate modern selfhood according to the principles of difference and divergence that characterize the modernizing world; and, even within its structure, the dustheap offers up contradiction, because it at once suggests notions of fragmentation and disarray (what was once one becomes many) and of uniformity and absolute reduction (this many looks and feels, or at least is considered to be, all the same). What these paradoxes suggest is that the dustheap mediates tensions in Dickens's novels between the narrative drive to instill order and the impulses of the material and spiritual worlds—worlds that the realist novel is committed to capturing authentically—to resist it. We see through this image how Dickens was already imagining and grappling with the types of tensions that register soundly in the novels of our own time, the tensions involved in determining modern subjectivity and in knowing how to give it form.

Lest I seem to undervalue the way dust figures as negative narrative content in these novels, jumping over the fragmentations of self and culture in Dickens's work to find redemptive qualities in the patterns through which those fragmentations are narrated, let me offer examples of the people and things that do fall apart in these texts. For like Little Nell in Mrs. Jarley's waxworks, characters in *Bleak House* and *Our Mutual Friend* become commodified things, and things, along with the ideologies they contain, erode into the granulated matter of combustion and chaos.[11] Indeed, in *Our Mutual Friend*, we might read the interior of Mr. Venus's taxidermy shop, which deals in the ruins of human life (bones, bodily fragments, and articulated corporeal forms), as a physical microcosm of the novel itself, which similarly accumulates human commodities and remains. In his attempt to preserve living matter, from infants to animals to nail cuticles, teeth, and glass eyes, Mr. Venus ushers his miscellaneous world into a state of total decomposition; although, as critics like Nancy Metz have noted, his artistry is in piecing these human fragments back together (in usefully recycling what would otherwise be perceived as waste), the force of decomposition is always a step or two ahead of his endeavors.[12] Even his own crop of hair is described as being dusty (indeed, this description is one of the only physical traits of Mr. Venus we are given), as if he—like the dead-living things that surround him—is crumbling at a slow but steady pace (86; bk. 1, ch. 7). ''From dust to dust'' is the chorus the novel seems ominously to play on repeat, asking in the undertones of its echo whether its own efforts at preservation, to contain life in some meaningful way, will be any more successful than those of Mr. Venus.

Taking on, parodically, the structure of the factory and the conveyor belt, *Our Mutual Friend*, in effect, mass-produces metaphors of human commodification and decay: Mortimer Lightwood refers to Noddy Boffin as a ''curiosity'' of miserly greed (405; bk. 2, ch. 16); Bella Wilfer considers her own self to be marriage-marketable chattel, the ''property of strangers'' to be ''willed away, like a horse, or a dog, or a bird'' (371; bk. 2, ch. 13); and Silas Wegg's person is reduced to an apparatus, whose various parts may be lost, hoarded, and sold. One of the most absurd moments in the novel comes when Wegg stumps his way into Venus's shop and demands his rights not as a human but as consumer, entitled to the purchase of his own amputated limb (88; bk. 1, ch. 7). The delightfully ludicrous suggestiveness of this scene becomes ominous, however, when we turn to the novel's main character, John Harmon, whose split-identity reflects not a fragmentation of the body, but of consciousness, of imagination, of self. Wegg's questions to Mr. Venus ''Where am I?'' and ''what did you give for me?'' are mirrored in the meditations of John Harmon, though he broods over much more than a lost limb and its value in coin: he mourns a lost identity and an obscured sense of self (88; bk. 1, ch. 7). A mutual friend to various characters, Harmon is defined relationally rather than individually, and, as such, belongs everywhere and nowhere, to everyone and to no one: "A spirit that was once a man could hardly feel stranger or lonelier, going unrecognized among mankind than I feel," he muses (360; bk. 2, ch. 13), reckoning himself in his solitude to be little more than what Venus calls Wegg—"one of a warious lot," "a Monstrosity" (88; bk. 1, ch. 7).

In his "wariousness," our main character loses himself; in being too many—John Harmon, John Rokesmith, Julius Handford—he becomes no one. He might be described, to quote Mr. Grewgious of *Edwin Drood*, as "living at once a doubled life and a halved lived" (122; ch. 11), in that amplification with him leads to reduction: to be a double means to be only a half. The miscellaneous nature of his character is, in fact, put in relief by a slew of doubled or doubling persons in the novel, individuals who are either too much, playing at other characters, other roles (like Noddy Boffin who pretends to be a miser; Bradley Headstone who disguises himself as Rogue Riderhood, in his pursuit of Eugene Wrayburn [621; bk. 4, ch. 1]; and Mr. Fledgeby who masquerades as a Turk [419; bk. 3, ch. 1]), or are not enough, finding a single and whole identity only in their dialectical relations with others (just as Harmon is mirrored by Radfoot, Wrayburn is doubled first by his friend Mortimer Lightwood and then by his adversary Headstone; and Jenny Wren speaks through her doll Mrs. T). Psychic life, like its material other, is forever splitting in *Our Mutual Friend*, showing us how life in a world of pretense—a world invested in the illusory value of cash and credit, a world seen topsy-turvy through the Veneerings' gilt mirror—confuses what is and what is not, who one is and who one isn't.

Toward the end of the novel, John Harmon even wonders nihilistically if such a thing as "I" exists, his disjointed experiences of subjectivity calling into question the possibility of maintaining an authentic sense of self in the morally polluted environment of his contemporary world. Reading something like a postmodern nightmare (an identity stolen, an expulsion from self and home), Harmon describes his experience of being drugged and assailed by George Radfoot as a total loss of person: "I could not have said that my name was John Harmon—I could not have thought it—I did not know it. . . . There was no such thing as I, within my knowledge," he explains (363; bk 2, ch. 13). Indeed, the novel suggests that even when sober and lucid, Harmon lacks a sort of tangible, definable existence, his subjecthood divided between so many different characters and storylines. A living-dead man, Dickens's main character inhabits the in-between spaces of consciousness, "going un-recognized among mankind" in a haze of crippling isolation. Just as Walcott's poetry expresses postcolonial identity as inheriting too many antecedents, too many histories, so Dickens's character John Harmon lives in a world that forces him to generate multiple personas in order to cope with life in capital-ist culture.

The predecessor of Venus's workshop, of course, is Krook's Rag and Bottle Warehouse. Krook's tenants share space with the wasted stuff of the *Bleak House* world, as if they too are the decaying ruins of past lives—Nemo foremost among them, only a fragment of his former self. When the wards of Chancery follow Miss Flite into the shop early in the novel, Krook takes a lock of Ada's hair into his hand—admiring it as a fragment of her person, and admiring her person as a relic of the infamous Jarndyce case (50; ch. 5). People, it seems, become broken-down things when they enter this muddled space—either that, or their malfunction simply becomes obvious there. What Krook trades in mostly, however, is not things or people, but documents. As Miller has observed, this novel is a document about documents, an act of writing about the act of writing.[13] Letters litter this book: Mrs. Jellyby to many correspondents regarding Africa, Mr. Jarndyce to Esther, Lady Dedlock to Captain Hawdon, Lady Dedlock to Esther, and Hortense to—everyone. In addition, Skimpole authors a book; Jo dictates a will; Mr. George draws up a testament; and Sir Leicester scratches notes on his slate. And the novel overtly recognizes the marketable nature of writing by sporting various dealers of paper, pen, and script: we have Snagsby, the law-stationer; Krook, the paper-collector; and my favorite of all, Smallweed, the dealer in bills. When Ada enters Krook's shop she is metonymically reduced to a lock of fetishized hair; even more telling, however, is the novel's reduction of Nemo to scraps of paper and drops of ink: it is only in his writing that he is a someone. In its most concentrated moments, this is the main concern of *Bleak House*— considering whether novel-writing, its forms, its language, its narrative order, reduces people to mere shreds of experience and shadows of feeling.

What *Our Mutual Friend* asks of human experience (can the modern individual maintain a sense of personal authenticity, or does the human psyche decay, as material objects do?), *Bleak House* asks of the Victorian novel: can the experiences of modern selfhood be represented in literature, and will this representation *last*, or be lost as dusty remnants in what Thomas Carlyle desolately considers the inchoate oblivion of time?[14] Andrew Stauffer argues that these two novels present "London as a writer's necropolis, a city of disintegrating paper and dead letters, a failed archival space." Dickens, he writes, "is particularly haunted by an urban vision of paper as everywhere and everywhere turning into blank, wasting forms"—in other words, threatening in its proliferation to lose words and to archive improperly the thoughts of a culture. In an oft-quoted moment in *Bleak House*, Esther wonders to herself why Lady Dedlock's face should be, "in a confused way, like a broken glass to [her], in which she saw scraps of old remembrances" (225; ch. 18). If things, people, even memories can break down into fragments and dustheaps, what then is the fate of narrative, this novel asks? Does it reach a goal or write like Mrs. Jellyby into the void?

What I want to suggest is that the structure of *Bleak House* offers a solution to its thematic concerns, for while dust is bleak in theme, it is useful, even hopeful in form. The heapiness of characters in *Our Mutual Friend*, characters who seem to have inherited the split subjectivity of David Copperfield and his Uriah, is preceded by the textual heapiness of *Bleak House*, which allows not only its characters but its most basic structural device—narration—to fall into two parts that are never fully reconciled, just as their initial division dodges explanation. But maybe just maybe the very structure of division in these works—division as inexplicable as it is real—expresses the human condition in terms unique to modernity, and in this way Dickens as artist and narrator arrives at some form of resolution for the more visceral concerns of the texts: though his novels certainly cannot cure cholera or right the wrongs of Chancery or subvert the damaging effects of capital greed, they *can* provide exposure and recognition, and, even more importantly, they *do* provide new ways for understanding humankind and individual responses to the evolving world. Dickens gives us a way of seeing and thinking and feeling that registers with twenty-first century sensibilities as it is rooted in concepts of difference and variation. In their seminal works on novel theory, E. M. Forster, Ian Watt, and Erich Auerbach all agree: the novel as a genre, born out of the cultural transformations of the eighteenth century, is structurally and ideologically predicated on the principles of individualism, multiplicity, heterogeneity, and change.[15] As an art form that came into existence in order to mediate changing attitudes, the novel, Michael McKeon claims, is unique in its ability to reflect the tensions and instabilities of social experience (20–21). And the realist novel, in particular, carries this tradition onward, portraying a world of heterogeneity and change—indeed, portraying many different worlds of heterogeneity and change, as we move from Trollope to Thackeray to Dickens, because those are the worlds its lenses capture. Today we recognize Victorian realist novels as loose and baggy (as Henry James sulkily termed them in his preface to *The Tragic Muse* [84]) precisely because they faithfully mirror a loose and baggy world. As George Levine writes, "what is unconventional and most exciting about the tradition of realism is its pleasure in abundance, in energy, and the vivid engagement, through language, with the reality just beyond the reach of language" (56).

Dust, I argue, allows Dickens to play out these tensions through a central image. For though the Victorians play at ideologies of security, Robin Gilmour tells us, they were quite aware of themselves as a generation of upstarts (2–3)—a generation, Walter Houghton has written, quoting Matthew Arnold, living "in the meantime between two worlds, one dead or dying, one struggling but powerless to be born" (10).[16] By allowing the very structure of his narrative to split in *Bleak House*, to fall into halves that come together, triumphant in their imperfections, Dickens allows the ordered surfaces of

Victorian ideology—of home and of self—to erode in his text, and discovers an authentic voice for his own emerging culture through the aesthetic of dust. Refusing, as it were, to give his readers one master key (as Esther would have him do) whereby to interpret the multiplicities, divergences, and idiosyncrasies of human life, he allows his narrative to fragment, to fall into multiple parts, and to tell the story of the Victorian experience through the heteroglossia of two variant voices. In a further move, he turns convention on its head in *Bleak House*, by writing Esther's subjective account of things in terms pointedly dry and seemingly objective and impersonal, while the omniscient reportage in the novel is anything but rational or stable, conjuring up fantastical images of dinosaurs "waddling . . . up Holburn Hill" as early as the opening page (5; ch. 1). Though the political impetus for writing certainly differed from the age of empire to the various acts of reconstruction that followed its slow but inevitable fall, we find similarities in their portrayal of modern identity as homeless, erratic, and unregulated. Indeed, it seems that the Victorians created their own mythologies of security at the expense of the people and cultures they colonized, who became to the empire blank slates upon which to write and against which to compare itself. I want to argue, however, that Dickens, that master-writer of the home-myth, reflects in his novels the unsettled nature of the nineteenth century and that he registers this unsettledness as the real stuff of life, finding in the patterns of the dust-pile a way to express the heterogeneity, bagginess, liminality, and chaos of the world around him. What we ultimately learn from Mr. Venus (himself an ironic embodiment of beauty and love) is the irony of articulation, which as an art-form relies on *particulation*, not just because things must fall apart before they can be put back together, but because in the modern world, things are best expressed in this their natural state as heapy, monstrous matter.

NOTES

1. In Head's "The Collector of Treasures," for instance, Dikeledi consistently finds "gold amidst the ash" of her life, even when taking up residence in prison after having murdered her husband. See also Jamaica Kincaid's *Annie John* and Rosario Ferré's "The Dust Garden." While these stories all make use of dust to investigate modern identity in terms of disintegration and reconstruction, the novels of Zadie Smith and Arundhati Roy, I argue, actually take on the structure of the dustheap, configuring postmodern narrative as they do postmodern identity: something always in the process of change and upheaval. Smith's novel, *White Teeth*, in particular, breaks up the unities of time and place and character to create a narrative given over entirely to—and celebrating the realities of—difference and miscellany.

2. Written in the wake of World War I and the European scramble for African territory, Yeats's poem "The Second Coming" (1919) introduces the phrase that will become the title and touchstone of Achebe's novel about the imperial division of the African continent and the history that follows: "Things fall apart; the centre cannot hold;/Mere anarchy is loosed upon the world."

3. See "dust, n.[1]" *The Oxford English Dictionary*. 2nd ed. 1989. *OED Online*. Oxford UP. 31 Aug. 2009. <http://www.oed.com/>. "1. a. Earth or other solid matter in a minute and fine state of subdivision, so that the particles are small and light enough to be easily raised and carried in a cloud by the wind; any substance comminuted or pulverized; powder."

4. In the introduction to *Filth: Dirt, Disgust, and Modern Life*, William Cohen calls filth "the other face of Victorian progress"; it is, he claims, "conceptually central in the very period in which it is supposed—thanks to new technologies of sanitary science and waste disposal—to have become materially less problematic" (xxiv). Judith Flanders shows just how central filth is to nineteenth-century culture by describing the Victorian home, that haven of order, comfort, and rest, as a dust-trap, the clutter around the hearth in particular drawing dirt and ash, much of which was produced by its own fire (192–93). Even more revealing is Dale Porter, who writes that smoke from hearth-fires and gas lamps, when "mixed with caustic exhausts from coal gas works and the miasmas emanating from polluted water-courses, caused chronic respiratory ailments among its less fortunate denizens and blocked out perhaps three-quarters of the sunshine normally enjoyed by country towns" (108); and Simon Garfield reports that even popular wallpapers contained dangerous chemicals like arsenic acid, which, "[u]nder heat or agitation from brushing or cleaning," would release "particles of dust [that] would slowly poison people in the room" where the paper was hung (105). The myth of Victorian domesticity as a model of cleanliness, health, and order, then, obscures the reality of home life in nineteenth-century London, which for most people involved a constant battle with the waste produced by their daily activities and modes of living. The famous London fog, composed of "[d]ust loaded with fecal matter, hot air, sewer gases, and smoke," apparently disregarded the Victorian boundaries between interior and exterior life, invading—and in effect coming from—the spaces of intimacy that were supposed to be free from its taint (Porter 57).

5. For legal documents on sanitation reform in the nineteenth century, see Edwin Chadwick's *Report on the Sanitary Condition of the Labouring Population of Gt. Britain* of 1842; and the reports by the Poor Law Commission of 1838 (one by Dr. Southwood Smith, the other by Drs. Neil Arnott and J. P. Kay [later Kay-Shuttleworth]), the Royal Commission report from 1845 on the "Health of Towns and Populous Places," and the Public Health Bill of 1848 (all in Parliamentary Papers). Mayhew's *London Labour and the London Poor* helped popularize these reform issues, as did Carlyle's *Chartism* (1839) and *Past and Present* (1843), and articles in *Household Words* like "Health by Act of Parliament" (August 10, 1850) and "Dust; or Ugliness Redeemed" (July 13, 1850).

6. As a matter of fact, the nineteenth century experienced six waves of cholera after its initial appearance in England in 1831–1833; Bruce Haley reports that cholera

appeared twice in the 1830s and 1840s (along with influenza, typhus, typhoid, smallpox, and scarlet fever), owing to poor sanitation conditions, as well as urban overcrowding, joblessness, and the great expense of wholesome foods (8–9, 12). In their Norton Critical edition of *Bleak House*, Sylvère Monod and George Ford explain that both the cholera plague of 1848, which killed over 14,000 people, and the smallpox epidemic that followed in 1853 "were occasioned by pollution of air and water and food" ("Pollution" 901). About these issues, they report, "Dickens himself was exceptionally well informed," reading reports on pollution, delivering a speech on sanitation in 1851, and writing four articles on the outbreak of cholera at an overcrowded orphanage in Tooting that "carried off" almost two hundred children (901). It is because Dickens's commitment to this topic extended into his works of fiction that Tillotson and Butt devoted the seventh chapter of *Dickens at Work* to "The Topicality of *Bleak House*."

7. Becoming and being are post-structuralist terms used by Gilles Deleuze in *Difference and Repetition* (1968) and *The Logic of Sense* (1969), among other of his works. Breaking from Platonism, which privileges ideas over surfaces, Deleuze argues that appearances and simulacra are all we have—that universal ideas do not and cannot exist in this world, that *being*, therefore, is an illusion, and that the process of *becoming* is what defines human experience.

8. György Lukács wrote that "the novel form is, like no other, an expression of . . . transcendental homelessness," in that the subject of art has become alienated from his or her world of references, just as the modern subject has been dislocated from the real world, its created forms, and their meanings (41).

9. Early in *Hard Times*, Tom says to Louisa, "You seem to find more to look at in [the fire] than ever I could find," which he reckons to be "[a]nother of the advantages . . . of being a girl" (44; bk. 1, ch. 9). Typical of his character, and owing to his lack of education in the finer arts of judgment and sympathy, Tom mistakes Louisa's interest in the fire as a positive one, failing to see that what she forebodes as she watches "the red sparks dropping out of the fire, whitening and dying" is her own inevitable crash-and-burn in the domestic life she's obliged to lead (45; bk. 1, ch. 9). Indeed, only a few chapters later, when she consents to marry Bounderby for the sake of Tom, she perspicaciously turns from looking at her own hearth-fire to catch a glimpse of the fires of Coketown out her door, and to read in them her future with the town magnate; in this moment, Dickens's narrator tells us, "[i]t seemed as if, first in her own fire within the house, and then in the fiery haze without, she tried to discover what kind of woof Old Time, that greatest and longest-established Spinner of all, would weave from the threads he had already spun into a woman" (75; bk. 1, ch. 14). After she arrives at Bounderby's country estate, we find her, as does James Harthouse, sitting in "an opening in a dark wood, where some felled trees lay, and where she [sits] watching the fallen leaves of last year, as she had watched the falling ashes at home" (129; bk. 2, ch. 7); and though Louisa ultimately does not fall from her marriage into sexual deviancies with Harthouse—much to the dismay of Mrs. Sparsit, who imagines Louisa toppling down a great metaphorical Staircase with the interloper and into a "a dark pit of shame and ruin at the bottom" (153; bk. 2, ch. 10)—his presence does help precipitate Louisa's awareness of her own subjectivity, which

in turns precipitates her ideological descent from the utilitarianism of her childhood to an imaginative life of the Jupe-variety—a sort of life, that is, in which
horse-wallpaper and flower-carpets are welcomed simply because they are fancied
(8–9; bk. 1, ch. 2).

10. Lyotard argues that just as contemporary culture no longer finds metanarratives
    sufficient for expressing human experience (which can only be understood
    through an infinite variety of micronarratives), French structuralism is also an
    insufficient critical apparatus, as it reduces the complexity of narrative objects to
    representational simplicity: ''Thus the society of the future falls less within the
    province of a Newtonian anthropology (such as structuralism or systems theory)
    than a pragmatics of language particles. There are many different language
    games—a heterogeneity of elements. They only give rise to institutions in
    patches—local determinism'' (xxiv).

11. While Little Nell's responsibility as an agent for Mrs. Jarley's waxworks is simply
    to advertise and help display the figures in the show, it quickly becomes apparent
    to the proprietress that the child and her beauty draw more crowds than the
    characters she is meant to put in relief. Nell, as such, becomes just another (albeit
    the most popular) character in Mrs. Jarley's dumb-show—inanimate, on display,
    a spectacle for sale (221–23; ch. 29).

12. Metz argues that the novel is preoccupied with method and process, encouraging
    the use of imagination to reconstruct the chaos we encounter in the outside
    world; Mr. Venus's work offers a good example, she claims, of the imaginative
    rebuilding necessary for tolerating the change and uncertainty in the world, as
    his goal with every project is to put the pieces of fragmented matter back to-
    gether (60–65).

13. See *Victorian Subjects*, in which Miller claims that ''*Bleak House* is a document
    about the interpretation of documents. Like many great works of literature it
    raises questions about its own status as a text'' (179). Norman Page agrees that
    references to various forms of text throughout the novel ''signal the lure and
    fallibility of communication'' (Introduction xxix).

14. As Rosenberg writes, Carlyle's *Cromwell* fully explores ''the sheer inchoateness
    of the unreconstructed past'' through its exploration of ''the stagnant backwaters
    of archival research'' in the disorderly underground storehouses of the British
    Museum: ''In this Carlylean underworld of Anti-History, presided over by the
    plutonic Dryasdust, the human past has been all but eradicated under mounds of
    successive errors and mindless commentary'' (15).

15. Watt stresses the importance of individualism in the formation of the novel as a
    genre separate—in form and content—from other literary genres; he writes that
    the realist novel is predicated on the belief that truth can be discovered ''by the
    individual through his senses'' and that universal ideas and forms must be, as a
    result, rejected (12). Auerbach emphasizes the importance not only of represent-
    ing the experiences of individuals in the modern novel, but of representing the
    experiences of *random* individuals—and taking that randomness seriously (554);

and E. M. Forster explains further that in addition to the randomness and multiplicity of things that we find "bundled" in the modern novel, we should also note that the structure of this genre, its rhythm in particular, is driven by change and the narrative resolve to form relations between the movements of people, things, and time (105, 164).

16. In the fifteenth stanza of "Stanzas from the Grande Chartreuse," Arnold writes,

> Wandering between two worlds, one dead,
> The other powerless to be born,
> With nowhere yet to rest my head,
> Like these, on earth I wait forlorn.

WORKS CITED

Achebe, Chinua. *Things Fall Apart*. New York: McDowell, Obolensky, 1959.

Arnold, Matthew. "Stanzas from the Grande Chartreuse." *Poems*. New York: MacMillan, 1878. 211–12.

Auerbach, Erich. *Mimesis: The Representation of Reality in Western Literature*. Trans. Willard R. Trask. Princeton: Princeton UP, 1968.

Bhabha, Homi. *Nation and Narration*. London: Routledge, 1990.

Butt, John, and Katheleen Tillotson. *Dickens at Work*. 2nd ed. London: Methuen, 1982.

Carlyle, Thomas. *Chartism/Past and Present*. London: Elibron, 2005.

Chadwick. Edwin. *Report on the Sanitary Condition of the Labouring Population of Gt. Britain*. Clowes: London, 1843. 18 July 2009. <http://www.archive.org/details/reportonsanitary00chaduoft>.

Cohen, William A., and Ryan Johnson, eds. *Filth: Dirt, Disgust, and Modern Life*. Minneapolis; London: U of Minnesota P, 2005.

Deleuze, Gilles. *Difference and Repetition*. Trans. Paul Patton. New York: Columbia UP, 1994.

———. *The Logic of Sense*. Trans. Mark Lester and Charles Stivale. New York: Columbia UP, 1990.

Dickens, Charles. *Bleak House*. Eds. George Ford and Sylvère Monod. New York: Norton, 1977.

———. *Hard Times*. Eds. Fred Kaplan and Sylvère Monod. 3rd ed. New York: Norton, 2001.

————. *Little Dorrit*. Eds. Stephen Wall and Helen Small. London: Penguin Books, 2003.

————. *The Mystery of Edwin Drood*. Ed. S. C. Roberts. London: Oxford UP, 1968.

————. *The Old Curiosity Shop*. Ed. Norman Page. London: Penguin, 2000.

————. *Our Mutual Friend*. Ed. Adrian Poole. New York: Penguin, 1997.

"Dust; or Ugliness Redeemed." *Household Words: A Weekly Journal*. Ed. Charles Dickens. Vol. 1. Bradbury and Evans: London, 1850. 379–84.

Ferré, Rosario. "The Dust Garden." *The Youngest Doll*. Lincoln: U of Nebraska P, 1991.

Flanders, Judith. *Inside the Victorian Home: A Portrait of Domestic Life in Victorian England*. New York: Norton, 2004.

Forster, E. M. *Aspects of the Novel*. New York: Harcourt, 1955.

Foucault, Michel. *The Order of Things: An Archeology of the Human Sciences*. London: Routledge, 2001.

Freedgood, Elaine. *The Ideas in Things: Fugitive Meaning in the Victorian Novel*. Chicago: U of Chicago P, 2006.

Garfield, Simon. *Mauve: How One Man Invented a Color That Changed the World*. London: Faber, 2001; New York: Norton, 2001.

Gilmour, Robin. *The Victorian Period: The Intellectual and Cultural Context of English Literatures, 1830–1890*. London: Longman, 1993.

Haley, Bruce. *The Healthy Body and Victorian Culture*. Cambridge: Harvard UP, 1978.

Harvey, W. J. *Character and the Novel*. Ithaca, NY: Cornell UP, 1965.

Head, Bessie. "The Collector of Treasures." *Concert of Voices: An Anthology of World Writing in English*. Ed. Victor J. Ramraj. Peterborough, ON: Broadview, 1994. 152–69.

"Health by Act of Parliament." *Household Words: A Weekly Journal*. Ed. Charles Dickens. Vol. 1. Bradbury and Evans: London, 1850. 460–63.

Herbert, Christopher. "The Occult in *Bleak House*." *Novel: A Forum on Fiction* 17.2 (Winter, 1984): 101–15.

Houghton, Walter. *The Victorian Frame of Mind, 1830–1870*. New Haven: Yale UP, 1957.

James, Henry. *The Art of the Novel*. New York: Scribner's, 1934.

Kincaid, Jamaica. *Annie John*. New York: Farrar, Straus and Giroux, 1985.

Levine, George. *The Realistic Imagination: English Fiction from Frankenstein to Lady Chatterley*. Chicago: U of Chicago P, 1981.

Lukács, György. *The Theory of the Novel: A Historico-Philosophical Essay on the Forms of Great Epic Literature*. Trans. Anna Bostock. Cambridge: MIT Press, 1971.

Lyotard, Jean-François. *The Postmodern Condition: A Report on Knowledge*. Trans. Geoff Bennington and Brian Massumi. Minneapolis: U of Minnesota P, 1984.

Mayhew, Henry. *London Labour and the London Poor*. Ed. John L. Bradley. London: Oxford UP, 1965.

McKeon, Michael. *The Origins of the English Novel, 1600–1740*. Baltimore, MD: Johns Hopkins UP, 2002.

Metz, Nancy. "The Artistic Reclamation of Waste in *Our Mutual Friend*." *Nineteenth-Century Fiction* 34.1 (June 1979): 59–72.

Miller, J. Hillis. *The Forms of Victorian Fiction: Thackeray, Dickens, Trollope, George Eliot, Meredith, and Hardy*. Notre Dame, IN: U of Notre Dame P, 1968.

———. *Victorian Subjects*. Durham, NC: Duke UP, 1991.

Page, Norman. Introduction. *Bleak House*. By Charles Dickens. Harmondsworth: Penguin, 1971.

Parliamentary Papers. *Fourth Annual Report of the Poor Law Commissioners*. 1837–39, vol. 28. App. A, Suppl. No. 1: "Report on the prevalence of certain physical causes of fever in the metropolis, which might be removed by proper sanatory measures" by N. Arnott and J. P. Kay (67–83 [215–31]; App. A, No. 2: "Report on some of the physical causes of sickness and mortality to which the poor are particularly exposed; and which are capable of removal by sanitary regulations" by T. Southwood Smith (84–94 [231–42]).

———. *Nuisances Removal and Diseases Prevention Act (Amended)*. 1847–48, vol. 4. 511.

———. *Second Report of Commissioners for Enquiring into the State of Large Towns and Populous Districts*. 1845, vol. 18. "Report on the sanatory state of Bristol" by H. de la Beche and L. Playfair (61–75 [195–211]).

Porter, Dale H. *The Thames Embankment: Environment, Technology, and Society in Victorian London*. Akron, Ohio: U of Akron P, 1998.

Richards, Thomas. *The Imperial Archive: Knowledge and the Fantasy of Empire*. London: Verso, 1993.

Rosenberg, John D. *Elegy for an Age: The Presence of the Past in Victorian Literature*. London: Anthem Press, 2005.

Roy, Arundhati. *The God of Small Things*. New York: Harper Perennial, 1998.

Smith, Zadie. *White Teeth*. New York: Vintage, 2001.

Stauffer, Andrew M. ''Ruins of Paper: Dickens and the Necropolitan Library.'' *Romanticism and Victorianism on the Net* 47 (August 2007). 11 July 2009. <http://www.erudit.org/revue/ravon/2007/v/n47/016700ar.html>.

Tracy, Robert. ''Lighthousekeeping: *Bleak House* and the Crystal Palace.'' *Dickens Studies Annual* 33 (2003): 25–53.

Walcott, Derek. ''Becune Point.'' *Poetry* 173.2 (Dec. 1998): 145.

Watt, Ian. *The Rise of the Novel: Studies in Defoe, Richardson, and Fielding*. Berkeley: U of California P, 1957.

Wohl, Anthony S. *Endangered Lives: Public Health in Victorian Britain*. Cambridge: Harvard UP, 1983.

Season of Light and Darkness:
A *Tale of Two Cities* and
the Daguerrean Imagination

Susan Cook

Charles Dickens's A Tale of Two Cities *reveals a Daguerrean imagination, a photographic subtext like that of* Bleak House *or* Little Dorrit, *but one that facilitates a reconsideration of the relationship between photography and history, as well as experimentation in realism more generally. At its very inception, photographic technology destabilized categories of light and dark, past and present, and realism and representation. The image we see in a daguerreotype is, more explicitly than in any other photograph, an image created in both the past of its capture and the present of its viewing. The daguerreotype shares this dialectical negotiation between past and present with the nineteenth-century historical novel. In particular, the high-contrast illustrations and recurrent use and critique of Enlightenment imagery in* A Tale of Two Cities *reveal a simultaneous reworking of Enlightenment "truth" and Victorian realism. In its persistent focus on light, darkness, and the troubling and subjective distinction between the two, the novel sustains an explicit critique of Enlightenment discourse as well as an implicit engagement with a more experimental, more Daguerrean photographic technology.*

On June 11, 1859, the essay "Photographic Print" was published along with an installment of *A Tale of Two Cities* in Charles Dickens's magazine *All the Year Round*. "Photographic Print" both contributes to and comments on the

---

Dickens Studies Annual, Volume 42, Copyright © 2011 by AMS Press, Inc. All rights reserved.

Fig. 1. John Edwin Mayall, "Charles Dickens." Daguerreotype (c. 1855).
Used by permission of The Charles Dickens Museum, London.

proliferation of photographic discourse: "Photography has become a science, with a literature of her own. She maintains several journals, and a photographic almanac" (162). The article goes on to describe the introduction, in 1851, of Archer's collodion process, and notes that the one drawback of all this innovation is the persistent "want of stability in photography": photographs remain ephemeral (162). The author of "Photographic Print" argues that only Fox Talbot has come close to creating permanent and inexpensive photographs, and does so by returning to a "Daguerrean" process of fixing the image to polished metal. Unlike subsequent photographic developments that use negatives and affix the image to chemically treated paper, daguerreotypes have no negatives and are thus permanent, singular, and irreproducible. Imprinted on polished metal, daguerreotypes also possess a dynamic and reflective quality of light and dark particular to them alone. The future of photography, implies this article published alongside *A Tale of Two Cities*, requires its return to an older and unique "Daguerrean" technology.

By the time Charles Dickens wrote *A Tale of Two Cities* in 1859, the daguerreotype had been replaced by a new technology, the wet-plate collodion process. Yet I am going to suggest that *A Tale of Two Cities*—a novel set in a period long before the invention of either collodion or daguerreotype photography—is formally invested in the photographic imagination of the daguerreotype.[1] Dickens's critique of the past in the service of the present, his fixation on and disruption of dark and light imagery, and his concluding meditation on Sydney Carton's individual "I see" registers a dialogue with a mode of representation similarly "about" the relationship between past and present, the complex relation between dark and light, and the role of individual perception. Several Dickens texts set more or less after the advent of photography—*Bleak House*, the Christmas books, and *Little Dorrit*, for instance—have been read as abstractly "photographic," while *Oliver Twist*, *Great Expectations*, and *Our Mutual Friend* explicitly cite photography. The arguments for the literal and figurative photographic trace in Dickens's canon pervade a branch of Victorian studies committed to integrating the literary and the visual.[2] Central to this debate stands Nancy Armstrong's thesis about the constitutive relation between the realist novel and the rise of photographic technology. My own contribution to this conversation asks us to rethink the limits of the implicit photographic subtext: by reading daguerreotype photography and *A Tale of Two Cities* together, I seek to expand our perception of nineteenth-century photography and its connection to "realism" and the historical novel.

There is in *A Tale of Two Cites*, I argue, an implicit Daguerrean imagination: a photographic subtext like that of *Bleak House* or *Little Dorrit*, but one that facilitates a reconsideration of the relationship between photography and history, *A Tale of Two Cites* and its moment of composition, and the experimentation in realism more generally. The image we see in a daguerreo-type is, more explicitly than in any other photograph, an image created in both the past of its capture and the present of its viewing. The daguerreotype—as I will show, building off of Georg Lukács—shares this dialectical negotiation between past and present with the nineteenth-century historical novel. More specifically, however, the daguerreotype shares with this *particular* historical novel a persistent focus on the unstable relation between categories of light and dark. The high-contrast illustrations and recurrent use and critique of Enlightenment imagery in *A Tale of Two Cities* reveals a simultaneous re-working of Enlightenment "truth" and Victorian realism. In its persistent focus on light, darkness, and the troubling and subjective distinction between the two, the novel sustains an explicit critique of Enlightenment discourse as well as an implicit engagement with a more experimental,[3] more Daguerrean photographic technology. Reading *A Tale of Two Cities* alongside the da-guerreotype prefaces the dialectical aspect of this novel's treatment of history, giving us a richly layered context for its pervasive treatment of light and dark. Yet this essay also participates in a larger movement to complicate the nineteenth-century photorealism—and by extension the literary realism—thesis, by showing that at its very inception photographic technology destabi-lized categories of light and dark, past and present, and realism and represen-tation. Beginning with the daguerreotype, then, I will analyze Daguerrean instability in general as well as in the context of the Dickensian photographic, before tracing its implications for the historical novel and *A Tale of Two Cities* in particular.

The Daguerreotype's History

Although it is a translation of the word photography, the expression "light writing" is a curious way to describe the photographic process. The term "photography" was first used in 1839 and became the popular shorthand for describing daguerreotypes, calotypes, collodion process prints, and more throughout the century. Photographic images are, of course, dependent upon light for their very existence. They are created by the controlled harnessing of directed light through a box and onto a piece of chemically-treated metal, glass, paper, or plastic. In this way, the true subject of every photograph is light itself, more so than any other visual representation.[4] The expression "light writing" is curious, however, because it suggests but never states its reliance upon darkness, that opposite quality which is so necessary to the success of the light writing itself. The portions of a photograph that appear the lightest are those parts that have received the least, rather than the most, light: the photographic representation of light relies on the obstruction of light in the development process. Incorporated implicitly into the description "light writing," darkness is the unacknowledged coauthor of photography. Daguerreotypes highlight this paradox intrinsically.

Daguerreotypes were the first photographic experiments to become commercially successful, and yet they were unique and markedly distinct from the photographs we encounter today. Daguerreotypes are direct-positive images for which there are no negatives, and as such they are each originals, images fixed onto silver-coated copper plates. While a negative process—the calotype or talbotype—was patented in 1841, only a few years after the daguerreotype, the unique daguerreotype remained the most popular photographic process until 1851, when the introduction of collodion-coated glass negatives made reproduction cheaper and faster (Novak 9). Discussing the role of photography in *Bleak House* and Nathaniel Hawthorne's *House of the Seven Gables*, Ronald R. Thomas suggests that the daguerreotype's "quality of uniqueness" made it the preferable photographic process in America for more than a decade following the development of collodion negative photography in England (92). Thomas's argument is that American individualism made collodion reproducibility particularly distasteful, whereas in England, "the energies of radical individualism were perceived as a threat equally dangerous to the emerging order as was the oppression of an old aristocratic regime" (92). In other words, nineteenth-century America fetishistically covets the aura of the original artwork for some ten years after Victorian England has embraced reproducibility and the implicit denial of individualism that process entails. Thomas distinguishes between American and English attitudes towards the new negative photographic process. However, while radical individualism may have been a predominant threat in Victorian England, the shift from daguerreotype to collodion negative was by no means a solution to this anxiety. In fact, rather than directly analogous to radical individualism, unique images such as daguerreotypes and accidentally or deliberately experimental prints can also visually represent a process of individual incorporation into a larger social body. This occurs in two ways: first, in that they photographically represent a scene, these unique images are already mimetic, doubled by their reference to the object they represent; second, accidental or experimental images frequently acquire their uniqueness from their disruption of the typical photographic uses of light and dark. Thus, while they are themselves original, these images gesture towards the instability of light and dark inherent in all photography.

This instability is reiterated in the temporal flux constitutive of every daguerreotype. "The highlights of a daguerreotype were captured in the nineteenth century, but the shadows are from the present day," writes photographic process historian Mark Osterman in his article on "How to *See* a Daguerreotype" (14). This is because the dark spots on a daguerreotype are not part of the recorded image, but the absence of image—they are the places where the polished silver of the daguerreotype plate shows through, ready to reflect the darkness of the viewing room. In order to see any contrast in a daguerreotype, there must be enough darkness present in the viewing room for the image to reflect. Placed in direct light, daguerreotypes vanish; they are paradoxically seen mostly clearly when surrounded by darkness. "Without something dark for the daguerreotype to reflect," writes Osterman, "most people simply see themselves reflected in the plate or, even more puzzling, a negative image" (14–15). Light may have been responsible for creating the daguerreotype in the past, but darkness is crucial to its viewing in the present.

The omission of darkness in the word "photography" can be interpreted historically and culturally. The emphasis on "light" is descriptive, but not merely so: epitomized by its name, photography became a part of a nineteenth-century European discourse that borrowed Enlightenment rhetoric and reflected a Victorian critique of religious faith in favor of a more scientific epistemology.[5] At the same time, however, photography contains its opposite: the darkness constitutive of photography remains as a kind of latent quality, threatening in its connotations of obscurity, ignorance, and regression. In photography, darkness is incorporated into light, becoming obscured through the process of purported scientific and artistic "development" carried out in the name of light. Yet this darkness remains: in contrast to more "realist" uses such as crime photography, portraiture, and documentary land and cityscape panoramas, technical experimentation—both accidental and intentional—calls the stability of light and realism into question simultaneously and overtly. Photographic experimentation can and did assume many forms,[6] but these forms were predominantly light-related. When the light and dark qualities of a photograph are disrupted as they are routinely when viewing daguerreotypes, we are suddenly confronted with the mediation constitutive of all photography—as well as the problem of judging objective realism more generally.[7]

The daguerreotype remains one of the clearest illustrations of the permeability between darkness and light—the incorporation of darkness *within* light—that is implicitly employed in all photography. Explicitly calling the very fixity of light and darkness into question, the daguerreotype subtly undermines metaphoric associations of light with truth.[8] Unique objects without negatives that can thus never be duplicated, daguerreotypes are both fixed and highly subjective, contingent images. Daguerreotypes are photographic products that—like all photographs—point to their own subjective construction,[9] and resonate historically and formally with the historical novel, a form of representation that is similarly attentive to its own mediation.

Because the degree of darkness seen in a daguerreotype has to do with the darkness surrounding the viewer, a daguerreotype becomes a highly volatile, intensely individual image: "Subtle changes of point of view, room lighting, or a slight tilt of the plate create a completely different tonality that is impossible to repeat or recall. Like the fabled blind men describing an elephant, each individual experiences the daguerreotype from their own unique point of view and from a place to which they can never return" (Osterman 15). The darkness we see in a daguerreotype is *ours*, a reminder that the daguerreotype is itself an image caught between the time of its capture and the moment of its viewing.

Unique photographic images such as the original daguerreotypes are not so distinct from reproducible images, but rather exist on a continuum with them. All photographs—whether they are experimental innovations with darkness and light or reproducible attempts to capture reality— ultimately betray the attempt at mimesis and the persistence of mediation. As Jonathan Crary notes, while the earlier camera obscura was a technology designed to capture objective "Truth," nineteenth-century visual technologies such as photography implicitly destabilize this truth model. The instability of such an apparently objective form of representation was cause for mid-Victorian debate and—as in Dickens's case—an ambivalence about the technology.

The Dickensian Photographic Imagination

Dickens was recalcitrant about being photographed. Although William Glyde Wilkins attests, based on his own photographic collection, that Dickens was photographed at least one hundred and twenty times, these sittings were not always welcome.[10] Dickens sat for Richard Beard, the first English daguerreotypist, in 1841, and claims, to Miss Burdett-Coutts, to have "suffered dreadfully" (*Letters* 2:284). In a later letter to the London photographer John Edwin Mayall dated 4 October 1856, Dickens declines an offer to be photographed, writing, "I have so much to do and such a disinclination to multiply my 'counterfeit presentiments' " (*Letters* 8:199). While Dickens's reference to *Hamlet* is an archaic way of describing representation, it emphasizes an unease with duplication—a sense that however faithful, representation is nevertheless a lie, a "counterfeit" of the original. Dickens had been photographed by Mayall previously (see fig. 1 above) and would sit for photographers again. Certainly aware of, exposed to, and ambivalent about photography, Dickens records the technology's presence in his life and culture literarily, from *Oliver Twist* (1837) to *Our Mutual Friend* (1865).[11]

Numerous critics have analyzed the role photography played in Dickens's biography and literary work. For instance, Jennifer Green-Lewis, Nancy Armstrong, Ronald R. Thomas, Regina B. Oost, and Helen Groth have helped to pioneer a tradition of reading nineteenth-century literary realism—and in

particular, Dickensian realism—alongside and through photographic innovation. While photography is conventionally associated with the nineteenth-
century realist novel—and more particularly, the detective novel—scholars
have also been troubled by the category of realism from the perspective of
image as well as text. Armstrong subtly nuances the claims of realism by
writing that rather than produce a factual representation of the world, the
realist novel produced textual representations of images—not "truths."[12]
Oost argues that Dickens aligns painted portraits and photographs in his 1853
Bleak House in order to challenge the veracity of both (155). These two
critics read in Dickens a critique of "factual" photographic and literary
representation. More recently, Emily Walker Heady and Daniel A. Novak
have proposed their own distinct reassessments of photographic realism. For
Heady, the Victorian photograph "was fraught with deep contradictions: it
could tell half-truths—or lie altogether—and yet, paradoxically, still be real"
(3). According to Heady, Dickens collapses "the realms of the ghostly phan-
tasmagoria and the reliable photograph" in two of his Christmas books,
teaching us "to think beyond binaristic questions of images' reliability" (10,
4). Novak's sustained critique of photographic realism goes one step further
and "redefines what 'photographic realism' meant for the Victorians and
changes our definition of and expectations for literary realism" (6). Proposing
that photographic and literary realisms share an aesthetics of fiction or abstraction, Novak challenges the critical perception that the Victorians
"trusted" photographic objectivity (4).

   Dickens complicates the alignment of truth and light in *A Tale of Two
Cities*, depicting rational Enlightenment and dark ignorance as at times indistinguishable. Set during the years of the Revolution and Terror in France, the
novel predates the invention of daguerreotype photography by some fifty
years and does not incorporate photography into the plot. Yet as Armstrong,
Thomas, and Oost have shown us through their analyses of *Bleak House*,
Dickens was interested in and encodes photography metaphorically into his
fiction.[13] These critical readings, while different in scope and focus, make the
connection between *Bleak House* and photography through the figure of the
detective. For instance, Thomas writes that the development of photography
and the detective story are not simply "analogous or continuous occurrences
but . . . dynamically interrelated events" (91). Armstrong makes the larger
claim that realism and photography were "partners in the same cultural
project. Writing that aims to be taken as realistic is 'photographic' in that it
promised to give readers access to a world on the other side of mediation
and sought to do so by offering certain kinds of visual information. . . . In
referring to images, realism was therefore referring to something very real"
(26–27). Rather than exploring the interrelated reality effects of photography
and the nineteenth-century novel, I am interested in using these connections

between the visual and the discursive to trace a more experimental and dialectical trajectory in both photography and Dickens's fiction.

Such an implicit and experimental treatment of photography appears throughout Dickens's work. In his analysis of the photographic imagination in *Little Dorrit* (a novel that, like *A Tale of Two Cities*, does not directly address photography), Novak argues for a more embedded connection between Dickens and photography: according to Novak, *Little Dorrit* "internalizes and dramatizes" photographic and novelistic forms alike without explicitly discussing photographic technology (66). Joss Marsh similarly detects a photographic element to *Little Dorrit*, writing that "Much of the visual imagery" identified by commentators on the novel "seems to me to demand a specifically photographic frame of reference if we are to appreciate it in the full" ("Inimitable Double Vision" 267). For instance, the play between sun and shade in the novel resonates with "the dual negative-positive quality of the daguerreotype" (267). This imagery pervades *A Tale of Two Cities*, which couples it with an attention to the historical past. Not simply anachronistic, novel and daguerreotype are in fact thematically linked through their shared dialectical relation to the past.

Given Dickens's own references to photography in several of his novels and his engagement with debates surrounding the technology, it is not far-fetched to interpret a photographic subtext in these meditations on detection and light and dark: photographic discourse surrounded Dickens, whether he was working on a novel set in the 1830s or the 1780s. Dickens published an article by Henry Morley and William Henry Wills entitled "Photography" in the 19 March 1853 issue of his *Household Words*, and (as we have seen) published an essay on "Photographic Print" alongside an installment of *A Tale of Two Cities* in 1859. Much like *Bleak House* or *Little Dorrit*, *A Tale of Two Cities* shares with nineteenth-century photographic discourse a concern with the truthfulness of light and dark, of representation, and of realism and historical authenticity. Dickens's persistent use and misuse of the light/dark metaphor above all other dualisms draws our attention, as readers of this historical novel, not only to the Enlightenment and the Revolutionary reformulation of religious light imagery, but to newer technologies of light and dark.

Re-viewing Enlightenment

Light and darkness, past and present: these are *A Tale of Two Cities*'s predominant metaphors for duality, and they also mark the disintegration of such binary oppositions. The novel's opening suggests an extension of Lukács's argument about temporal slippage in the historical novel to a consideration of the flux between light and dark. We read that this was the "season of Light" as well as the "season of Darkness" (5). At once light and darkness, this particular season challenges straightforward visual perception. Explicitly, this "season" is the era of the French Revolution. Yet in this historical novel, light and darkness mark the coming together of two related but temporally distinct discourses: Enlightenment philosophy and photography. Rolf Reichardt traces the way the light/dark metaphor shifted from religious iconography to Enlightenment rationality and then to Revolutionary textual and imagistic propaganda in the late eighteenth and early nineteenth centuries. In charting this movement from religious to fervently anti-religious uses, Reichardt effectively undermines the consistency of the metaphor. Working with this metaphoricity from a different angle, art critic Melissa Miles describes the way nineteenth-century photographic theorists treated light as both excessively metaphysical as well as a controlled representation of reality: light was considered to be evocative of both stable reality and the loss of control (330). The dark/light metaphor is thus at different times used to evoke religious belief, Enlightenment rationality, and technological development. Yet this very multiplicity of uses, some of which are contradictory, destabilizes the metaphor.

Instability is written into the Bible's own first treatment of light and dark: "And God said, Let there be light: and there was light. And God saw the light, that it was good: and God divided the light from the darkness. And God called the light Day, and the darkness he called Night. And the evening and the morning were the first day" (Genesis 1:3–5). In this passage, evening and morning represent a full *day*. Conflating dusk with dawn into one day, the Bible itself describes the condensation of darkness or partial darkness into light within one temporality—even as it describes the separation of these qualities. In the post-Genesis Victorian age of photography and religious doubt, however, light and dark are no longer so distinctly separated. Drawing on this biblical passage in his interpretation of Walter Benjamin, photography, and history, Eduardo Cadava writes that "There has never been a time without the photograph, without the residue and writing of light" (5). There is, writes Cadava, a "secret rapport between photography and philosophy. Both take their life from light, from a light that coincides with the conditions of possibility for clarity, reflection, speculation, and lucidity—that is, for knowledge in general" (5). For Benjamin, this light is mercurial, providing, as Cadava writes, "simultaneous illumination and blindness" (5). Through Benjamin, Cadava links photography to history, Enlightenment philosophy, and the dialectical complication of that philosophy. It is to a similar nexus of illumination, time, and dialectics that we now turn in Dickens's novel.

Both temporally specific and expressively abridged, *A Tale of Two Cities* seems consciously to deploy—rather than unconsciously succumb to—duality.

Time, being both "best" and "worst" at once, is after all this novel's first contradiction in terms. The novel famously begins with a series of apparent binaries: best of times, worst of times, age of wisdom, age of foolishness, season of Light, season of Darkness, and so on. But 1775, this year of dualities, is, as Dickens writes, "so far like the present period, that some of its noisiest authorities insisted on its being received, for good or for evil, in the superlative degree of comparison only" (5). This introduction facilitates Dickens's subsequent meditation on France, a nation mired in the irony of a "Revolution that was running so fearfully wild" (252). This economy of contradiction is central to Dickens's engagement with the historical novel form: this is, after all, a tale of *two* cities as well as two times, and in that respect, it is a commentary on 1850s London as much as it is about 1790s Paris. This is not, in other words, a novel about merely two locations, but about two temporalities as well.

Several critics have noted the connection between historical past and compositional present both in *A Tale of Two Cities* as well as the historical novel genre at large. For instance, David Richter writes that, as a genre,

> Historical novels are set in the past but they always in some sense express the needs of the present. The popular entertainments of an age can tell us about the dreams and frustrations of its readers, its response to social and economic change, its ideology both in the Marxist sense of "false consciousness" and in the larger and more neutral sense of the way it orders and attempts to understand the experience of life and time. (265)

Lukács also writes about this connection between past and present, noting that in both the novel and drama, "there is a very complex interaction between [the writer's] relation to the present and his relation to history" (250).[14] But although the historical novel brings the present with it into its description of the past, this connection of past and present is not, for Lukács, an intentional or successful association: "quite contrary to what so many moderns think, the historical novel does not become an independent genre as a result of its special faithfulness to the past. It becomes such when the objective or subjective conditions for historical faithfulness in the large sense are either not yet or no longer present" (251). In a sense, then, the historical novel is defined by its break from—rather than its continuity with—the past.

This break in turn creates a "dreamlike 'timelessness' " in the historical novel (262). *A Tale of Two Cities*, for example, universalizes "purely moral aspects of causes and effects, weakens the connection between the problems of the characters' lives and the events of the French Revolution" (262). The historical novel is thus ironic, for it is more "subjective" and less historical than the social novels of the time. Lukács grounds his critique of Dickens's historical novel in the history of its production itself: after 1848, he argues, the historical novel genre becomes ever less directly historical and ever more abstract, mediated, and subjective. Yet this subjective abstraction is itself historically tied to the period of the novel's composition: "in the historical novel this tendency of Dickens must necessarily take on the character of modern privateness in regard to history" (263). Lukács responds negatively to the post-1848 historical novel's ironic failure to sustain direct historical specificity, and attributes its abstract quality to the way that post-1848 writers used a more mediated relationship to history. This leads these more modern writers to " 'introject' " their own "subjective problems into the 'amorphousness' of history" (263). The historical novel's temporal slippage is, for Lukács, a sign of its potential failure to understand the present.

Yet instead of an aesthetic or historical mistake on Dickens's part, I read this slippage—between the more modern, subjective present of composition and the history that forms its subject—as a manifestation of the broader duality theme foregrounded by the novel. As Richard Maxwell points out, the destabilization of time forms a larger motif in the novel, exceeding its generic uses of past and present. While the novel keeps careful track of the passage of time, emphasizing, for example, the year "one thousand seven hundred and seventy-five" three times in as many pages in the first short chapter, it also contains several "temporal ellipses," which amounts to a "drastic reduction" of the events surrounding the Revolution (Maxwell xi). What Maxwell terms the "condensations of historical time"[15] are paired with a hyper-attention to the passage of time back and forth from 1757 to 1794 (xix). For example, setting the scene in Mr. Cruncher's office at the start of chapter 1 of Book the Second (a chapter helpfully entitled "Five Years Later"), Dickens documents the time as "half-past seven of the clock on a windy March morning, Anno Domini seventeen hundred and eighty" (57). Descriptions such as this make it possible to trace, in several instances, the events contained within the novel down to specific hours as well as days within months and years.

A Tale of Two Cities does not simply use the past to comment on the present or emphasize the distinction between precisely documented and expressively fluid time; the novel also positions this historical movement spatially, featuring not one but two cities, London and Paris. The choice of these two cities—the one more properly representative of the French Revolution and the other of Dickens's own Victorian reading public—emphasizes, through place, the slippage of time from past into present. The two cities thematized in this novel belong to different epochs—London to a less historically marked, privatized, and peaceful era, and Paris to a more temporally particular, revolutionary time frame. Both depicted more impressionistically rather than realistically, the cities are, in their descriptions, more connotative than denotative. While one of our earliest glimpses of London is as a "great city by night," full of "darkly clustered houses," each of which encloses "its own secret," pre-Revolutionary Paris is introduced through the district of Saint Antoine, a place that can be best illustrated by personified "hunger": "Hunger stared down from the smokeless chimneys, and started up from the filthy street that had no offal, among its refuse, of anything to eat" (32; bk. 1, ch. 5). Compared with the more detailed account of London that introduces *Bleak House*, the introduction of London and Paris is, in *A Tale of Two Cities*, more affective and less descriptive. Individual secrecy and collective hunger characterize both of these cities. While this privatized London is more general—it could be Dickens's own London in its disengagement with historical particularity—Paris's hunger contextualizes this place, rendering it more precisely revolutionary. Thus, in terms of time and place, this historical novel incorporates past into present, specific time into a "half-imaginary cultural moment," and the more ahistorical London with the revolutionary Paris (Maxwell xix).

Rather than an opposition between two diametrically opposed qualities, the treatment of historical time in *A Tale of Two Cities* is more about the conflation of past into present—or factually historical into expressively impressionistic—not the contradiction between two uses of time. In fact, writes Grahame Smith in a different context, Dickens has a way of "reading the world in terms of dualities which, although contrasting, are not necessarily oppositional in the binary sense" (5). Smith's example here, relevantly enough, is the treatment of light and darkness in relation to London and Paris. According to Smith, the two cities—and the two qualities of light and dark—are equally privileged and are always potentially collapsing into one another. Smith's point here is to bring these apparent binaries together and to show the way they were linked for Dickens. Hence, Dickensian opposites do not conflict so much as they illuminate: they reveal something to us dialectically. In the case of *A Tale of Two Cities,* this revelation is the relation between history and contingency, a relation most clearly articulated through visual motifs. More impressionistic than realistic, neither city in this novel is described in a way that seems particularly descriptive in a photo-realistic sense of the term. Yet a notion of photography expanded to include the Daguerrean imagination allows us to read the instability between past and present in *A Tale of Two Cities*—described by Lukács as a failure of the post-1848 historical novel—both contextually as well as thematically.

"a light, or a shade"

Describing eighteenth- and nineteenth-century panoramas and dioramas—the forerunners of daguerreotypes[16]—Richard Altick notes that the first panoramists sought to bring "instant-history painting to a somewhat broader public," or to commemorate important historic events as they occurred (138).

This documentary impulse persists in photography, yet in photography, writes Roland Barthes, "I can never deny that *the thing has been there*. There is a superimposition here: of reality and of the past" (76). The past is captured or commemorated by photography, but the past is no longer "reality" as it is recognized in the present of the observation of the image. Like Dickens's treatment of history, photography captures a reality, but the passage of time transforms that reality: "truth and reality in a unique emotion" (Barthes 77). Rather than being directly involved with photography in the way that the detective elements of *Bleak House* are said to speak to the documentary uses of early photography, *A Tale of Two Cities* engages with this technology on a more implicit level through its illustrations and written descriptions of the relation between darkness and light.

As Richard L. Stein notes, visual art was crucial to the writer's understanding of himself and his fiction.[17] In the illustration "In the Bastille," featured on the title page of the first bound edition of the novel, Phiz (Hablot Knight Browne) depicts Doctor Manette sitting in the Bastille, sewing a shoe (fig. 2). He sits with his back to the light, which is coming into the cell from what appears to be a high window beyond the upper right side of the image. This illustration calls to mind Manette's description, analyzed below, of the torturous light of a freedom he is denied. Yet this picture does not depict an individual turning, in agony, away from the moonlight that represents a liberty withheld from him—it shows the doctor at work sewing a shoe. The position the doctor assumes is, in its spatial orientation, noteworthy. Manette is turned away from the light. The front of his body is in shadow, confirming that the probable light-source is the upper-right corner of the image. Yet the shoe he works on is well lit, implying that he is neither facing the light nor facing away from it, but instead positioned diagonally. He is in between the light and the darkness, his body position emphasizing this ambivalence.

A Tale of Two Cities was the last of Dickens's novels to be illustrated by Phiz. Whereas in the earlier *Little Dorrit* and *Bleak House* Phiz had used "dark plates"—a technique that allowed the illustrator to draw on more gradations between dark and light tones and "convey graphically what is for the Dickens novels a new intensity of darkness"—he returned to simple line drawings in this later work (Steig 131). Compared with the illustration from *A Tale of Two Cities*, the illustration "A new meaning in the Roman" in *Bleak House* is more tonally complex (fig. 3). While both depict a single source of light illuminating a darkened room, the *Bleak House* illustration utilizes darker grays along with blacks to give a heightened depth to this dark room. Although the reasons for this shift back away from the "dark plate" method in the later novel have to do with the practical issue of economics and turn-around time,[18] the line drawing's greater emphasis on the binary of darkness and light is, despite the critical disappointment it incited, more

Fig. 2. Hablot Knight Browne (Phiz), "In the Bastille." Illustration for *A Tale of Two Cities* (1859).

Fig. 3. Hablot Knight Browne (Phiz), "A new meaning in the Roman."
Illustration for *Bleak House* (1853).

resonant with the novel's economy of duality.[19] Read together, *A Tale of Two Cities* and its illustrations form part of a Victorian culture in which visual technologies were increasingly important. Less realistic, perhaps, than the more intricate *Bleak House* illustrations, the images in Phiz's last collaboration with Dickens nevertheless speak *more* to photography. Their stylized, high degree of contrast emphasizes those two qualities—light and dark—so important to photographic visual representation.

Dickens shows that it is futile to sustain a division between qualities such as darkness and light. In the London of *A Tale of Two Cities*, for example, Doctor and Lucie Manette live on a street where "summer light struck into the corner brilliantly in the earlier part of the day; but, when the streets grew hot, the corner was in shadow, though not in shadow so remote that you could see beyond it into a glare of brightness" (96; bk. 2, ch. 6). The light does not last all day, in other words, but in spite of the shadow that overtakes the bright corner where the Manettes live, it is possible to see beyond the darkness and back to the light. This shadow with the promise of light just out of reach is "a cool spot, staid but cheerful" (96; bk. 2, ch. 6). It remains unclear whether the cheer of this "cool spot" is in its being out of the sunlight and in the shadow, or in its proximity to the brightness from which it is nevertheless removed.

Taking a closer look at this brief description of the Manettes' street, we see that it could be describing a photographic process: what is light becomes dark, as a light space on a negative will become dark once it is printed. This imaginary image is more akin to a daguerreotype than a collodion print, however: like a daguerreotype held in the light, the darkness is eclipsed by "a glare of brightness" (96; bk. 2, ch. 6). There is a partial reversal of darkness and light—or of the introduction of light *into* something still dark. Read in conjunction with daguerreotype technology, the light in the Manettes' street that becomes shadow revealing light introduces us to a spatial and temporal indeterminacy that is both particular to the Manettes and part of the novel's larger historical frame.

In another instance, Doctor Manette complicates light/dark enlightenment rhetoric in order to explain the paradoxical torment of freedom. Using the metaphor of light-as-freedom, the doctor gestures towards the moon: " 'I have looked at her from my prison-window, when I could not bear her light. I have looked at her when it has been such torture to me to think of her shining upon what I had lost' " (196; bk. 2, ch. 17). Yet here, the light of freedom is mediated: this symbol representing light-as-freedom is the moon, not the sun. This illustrates the doctor's own ironic distance from that very freedom. The moon refracts sunlight (ostensibly the light source that most directly connotes light-as-freedom), and thus the source of this light of "freedom" lies elsewhere—on the other side of the globe, in fact. Moonlight here represents a shadowy light—the existence of darkness (as night) in light (as moon). The moon subverts metaphoric expectation by casting a light, the very benevolent freedom of which tortures rather than soothes the doctor. Inaccessible, this freedom becomes a terrible light.

The novel does, in its frequent deployment of metaphors of light and darkness, sustain traditional valuations of these qualities: for instance, the remains of the Bastille contain the expected Gothic "gloomy vaults where the light of day had never shone," with "hideous doors of dark dens and cages" and "cavernous flights of steps" (227; bk. 2, ch. 21). Yet recourses such as this to traditional light/dark categories are just as frequently challenged: in an apparent use of this traditional rhetoric, Dickens notes that in 1775 London, "The highwayman in the dark was a City tradesman in the light" (6; bk. 1, ch. 1). This sentence at once sustains a contrast between the unlawful night and the legitimate day, and dismantles the distinction between the two. The same man occupies both positions. The duplicity implied here indicates that while daylight may be a more honest sphere than the treacherous nighttime, in fact the distinction between these two times—and the difference between honesty and treachery—is merely superficial.

In the trial scene at the start of Book the Second, Dickens unsurprisingly critiques juridical honesty, exemplifying the ironic *dis*honesty of the court system through a metaphor of light and mirrors. Charles Darnay is standing trial, and in the courtroom a mirror is positioned over his head "to throw the light down upon him" (66; bk. 2, ch. 2). Yet rather than the pure light of justice or truth, "Crowds of the wicked and the wretched had been reflected in it, and had passed from its surface and this earth's together. Haunted in a most ghastly manner that abominable place would have been, if the glass could ever have rendered back its reflections, as the ocean is one day to give up its dead" (66; bk. 2, ch. 2). Instead of reflecting the true light of justice, the mirror reflects the ghostly images of past criminals—there is no justice reflected back to him in this court.

The indeterminacy of light and dark is transferred from Darnay to his doppelgänger Sydney Carton as well. Looking at Carton's face near the end of the novel, Mr. Lorry notices "A light, or a shade (the old gentleman could not have said which)" (321; bk. 3, ch. 9). It is significant that Carton here represents the impossibility of telling light from dark, for Dickens's system of duality is disrupted, perhaps most strikingly, in the conflation of Darnay and Carton. Because they look so much alike—though they initially represent far different moral motivations—the roguish Carton can conclude the novel cathartically by saving Darnay from an unjust fate. Their similar appearance is thus on one level a mere plot device: in order to change places with Darnay, it is necessary that Carton look like him. The resolution of the entire novel thus appears accidental—all contingency and no purpose. At the same time, the novel has foreshadowed this conflation of the two men from their introduction in the court scene. The story of these characters' lives may thus, like a subjective daguerreotype viewing, represent contingency in spite of an over-determined sense of purposeful, knowable historical progress. Carton takes Darnay's place in an act that disrupts the complete incorporation of the individual (here represented by Darnay) into the Terror. Though a device, this similarity between the two characters is worked into the text figuratively, by way of the novel's larger economy of darkness and light. Mr. Lorry's inability to tell whether light or shade passes over Carton's face registers, on a metaphoric level, Carton's change—and the fact that he can no longer represent the moral opposite of Darnay. Carton adopts some of Darnay's morality, though the indeterminacy of the light or shade on his face registers (perhaps his or perhaps the novel's own) ambivalence towards this morality itself.

Daguerreotype photography itself models a Lukácsian approach to Dickens's novel, a way to read in Dickens both Enlightenment past as well as Victorian present. The novel weaves together history and individual perception of that history: it demands our negotiation of the two together; it represents both in a vision of Carton's end. The novel, after all, ends with speculation about what Carton thinks he *sees*: "I see Barsad, and Cly, Defarge, The Vengeance . . . I see a beautiful city and a brilliant people rising from this abyss . . . I see the evil of this time and of the previous time of which this is the natural birth . . . " (389; bk. 3, ch. 15). This emphasis on Carton's vision is repeated fourteen times in the novel's last two pages, and drives us visually towards his final "It is a far, far better thing that I do, than I have ever done; it is a far, far better rest that I go to, than I have ever known" (390; bk. 3, ch. 15). Carton's present tense "I do" and "I go to" reflects upon and modifies the present perfect "I have ever done" and "I have ever known"; it attains its power as a hopeful finale in the turn away from an old process and towards a new future. There is, of course, another way of reading the concluding repetition of "I see," which is to emphasize the "I" of the sentence. Carton, who has throughout the novel been potentially or actually confused with Darnay, here emphasizes the individuality of his vision. Like an individual looking at a daguerreotype, Carton here sees something no one else can see: the newness, the unexpected turn, the contingent process that forms the image with which the novel concludes.

Understood alongside contemporaneous developments in photographic technology, the play of light and dark in *A Tale of Two Cities* reveals the novel's negotiation with the photographic present of its composition as well as the revolutionary past comprising its subject. The daguerreotype does not create the criticism of historical truth and representation, but rather lends this discourse a particular vocabulary. I have suggested that the daguerreotype affords us a new way of accounting for Dickens's symbolic economy of light and darkness, the Enlightenment past he evokes with this symbolism, and the present through which he understands that past. The daguerreotype—by the late 1850s an outmoded, historic form of photographic technology—complicates nineteenth-century literary and photographic realism more generally, and can be read as part of a recent critical tradition that questions the way we read those realisms. The technique's particular challenge, however, is in its explicit unsettling of the categories of light and dark, past and present. Rather than simply challenging realistic representation, the daguerreotype simultaneously calls into question the fixity, the very truthfulness of light, and thereby destabilizes the metaphoric systems of Enlightenment rationality and religious morality simultaneously. Learning to interpret this and other Victorian novels as not simply photographic but as Daguerrean, we have the chance to develop new techniques for reading the past in the present, the darkness in light, and the experimentation in realistic representation.

NOTES

I would like to thank Nancy Armstrong, Maurizia Boscagli, Mike Frangos, and Rachel Mann for their helpful comments on earlier versions of this essay. I am also indebted to Mark Osterman and Joe Struble for their help at the George Eastman House Gannett Foundation Photographic Study Center.

1. In referring to the "photographic imagination" or "Daguerrean imagination" throughout this essay, I aim to highlight the extent to which photography, for all its apparent claims to objective realism, is a cultural product, a mode of representation that intersects in creative ways with the imaginations of its viewers. The rise of photography in the nineteenth century amounted to a cultural phenomenon, and it altered the way we picture images in our minds. Yet photography is not immune to creative reimaginings, and here I want to signal both the way photography arrested the interest of an entire culture, as well as the destabilization of photography's objectivity through that imaginative process. For more on the photographic imagination, see Martha Langford. For the visual imagination more broadly, see Kate Flint and Carol T. Christ and John O. Jordan's collection.

2. See Jennifer Green-Lewis, Nancy Armstrong, Ronald R. Thomas, Regina B. Oost, and Helen Groth. See also Melissa Sue Kort's unpublished dissertation. For related theorizations of the intersections between image and text in the nineteenth century, see, for example, Vanessa R. Schwartz and Dennis Denisoff.

3. Because of its position at the origins of modern photography, the daguerreotype is inherently experimental.

4. While this concept is ubiquitous to most photographic theory, for my own understanding of it I am indebted to my first photography professor, Roy W. Traver.

5. According to Rolf Reichardt, light imagery shifts in connotation from religious truth to rational truth and finally to punitive truth. I would add photographic representation to this catalogue of shifting light/dark metaphors. A technological development, photography uses light in its attempt to convey a kind of empirical truth. As Flint notes, metaphors of vision were used not least of all by scientists themselves (33)—i.e., nineteenth-century scientists frequently used visual metaphors in order to communicate their discoveries.

6. Examples of more novel experimentations include solarization, blue-toned prints, the Vandyke process, burnt-in photography, fuming, heliography, the Kromscop, the magic lantern, the Opalotype, spirit photography, the whey process, and the Woodburytype (Peres, ed. *The Focal Encyclopedia*).

7. M. H. Abrams's distinction between the mirror and the lamp as metaphors for the mind and poetry is useful to consider and complicate in this context. Abrams argues that, beginning with Romanticism, the older metaphor of mind-as-mirror is replaced with the image of mind-as-lamp. The figure of the lamp implies a greater degree of participation on the part of the poet, for rather than merely reflecting the world, the poet actually projects a new element outwards—illuminating and thus creating. As a technology designed to reflect *and* illuminate, photography stands at the crux of these two metaphors.

8. See, for instance, Reichardt's description of the way the light/dark metaphor, in which light equals truth and darkness ignorance, shifts over time from religious imagery to Enlightenment iconography and then post-Enlightenment political figurations.

9. See Jonathan Crary's distinction between the camera obscura and nineteenth-century photographic development. Whereas the camera obscura served as a "model, in both rationalist and empiricist thought, of how observation leads to truthful inferences about the world," later photography instead inaugurated a new model, "fundamentally independent of the spectator, yet which masqueraded as a transparent and incorporeal intermediary between observer and world" (29, 139).

10. Claude Baillargeon hypothesizes that this discomfort had perhaps as much to do with Dickens's own uneasy awareness of the fiction behind photographic representation—his critique of "the very ability of the new art to convey truthful representation at all"—as it did the physical experience of sitting for a portrait (10).

11. Critics such as Grahame Smith and Joss Marsh work with Dickens's implicit connection to photography and extend its implications in order to discuss Dickens in relation to cinema.

12. Armstrong argues that "In order to be realistic, literary realism referenced a world of objects that either had been or could be photographed" (7–8).

13. *Bleak House* is, like *A Tale of Two Cities*, similarly set back in time, in this case to the 1830s, during the early years of photographic experimentation and development.

14. For more readings of the relation between historical past and compositional present in the historical novel, see, for example, Harry E. Shaw and Elliot Gilbert.

15. These condensations have long been the subject of analyses and judgments about the novel: in a letter that does not survive, Edward Bulwer-Lytton complains

directly to Dickens that the feudalism featured in the novel was anachronistic. Dickens's reply, as quoted in Maxwell, is that abridgment is necessary to his more picturesque, expressive intention: "Surely, when the new philosophy was the talk of the salons and the slang of the hour, it is not unreasonable or unallowable to suppose a nobleman wedded to the old cruel ideas, and representing the time going out, as his nephew represents the time going in" (xix).

16. Daguerre himself was originally a panorama and diorama painter, and is cited as the father of the diorama, or "drama of light."

17. Stein points to two "early examples" of Dickens's interaction with visual representation: the full title of *Sketches by Boz and Cuts by Cruikshank*, which draws a direct parallel between author and illustrator; and the illustration of Dickens himself in *Nicholas Nickleby* (167).

18. Sarah Solberg describes the practical motivations underlying this reversion to line drawings in her "A Note on Phiz's Dark Plates."

19. For more on the *A Tale of Two Cities* illustrations, see Michael Steig's *Dickens and Phiz* (311–12).

WORKS CITED

Abrams, M. H. *The Mirror and the Lamp: Romantic Theory and the Critical Tradition.* New York: Oxford UP, 1953.

Altick, Richard D. *The Shows of London.* Cambridge: Harvard/Belknap, 1978.

Armstrong, Nancy. *Fiction in the Age of Photography: The Legacy of British Realism.* Cambridge: Harvard UP, 1999.

Baillargeon, Claude. *Dickensian London and the Photographic Imagination.* Exhibition Catalogue. Rochester, MI: Johnston Lithograph, 2003.

Barthes, Roland. *Camera Lucida: Reflections on Photography.* Trans. Richard Howard. New York: Hill and Wang, 1981.

Cadava, Eduardo. *Words of Light: Theses on the Photography of History.* Princeton: Princeton UP, 1997.

Christ, Carol T., and John O. Jordan, eds. *Victorian Literature and the Victorian Visual Imagination.* Berkeley: U of California P, 1995.

Crary, Jonathan. *Techniques of the Observer: On Vision and Modernity in the Nineteenth Century.* Cambridge: MIT P, 1990

Denisoff, Dennis. *Sexual Visuality from Literature to Film, 1850–1950.* New York: Palgrave, 2004.

Dickens, Charles. *Bleak House.* 1853. Ed. Nicola Bradbury. New York: Penguin, 2003.

———. *The Letters of Charles Dickens.* Vol. 2: 1840–1841. The Pilgrim Edition. Ed. Graham Storey and Kathleen Tillotson. Oxford: Oxford UP, 1995. 284.

———. *The Letters of Charles Dickens.* Vol. 8: 1856–1858. The Pilgrim Edition. Ed. Graham Storey and Kathleen Tillotson. Oxford: Clarendon, 1995. 199–200.

———. *A Tale of Two Cities.* 1859. Ed. Richard Maxwell. New York: Penguin, 2000.

Flint, Kate. *The Victorians and the Visual Imagination.* New York: Cambridge UP, 2000.

Gilbert, Elliot. " 'To awake from history': Carlyle, Thackeray, and *A Tale of Two Cities.*" *Dickens Studies Annual* 12 (1983): 247–65.

Green-Lewis, Jennifer. *Framing the Victorians: Photography and the Culture of Realism.* Ithaca, NY: Cornell UP, 1996.

Groth, Helen. *Victorian Photography and Literary Nostalgia.* New York: Oxford UP, 2003.

Heady, Emily Walker. "The Negative's Capability: Real Images and the Allegory of the Unseen in Dickens's Christmas Books." *Dickens Studies Annual* 31 (2002): 1–21.

The Holy Bible, King James Version. New York: American Bible Society: 1999.

Kort, Melissa Sue. "Facing the Camera: Dickens, Photography, and the Anxiety of Representation." PhD Dissertation. U of Southern California, 2001.

Langford, Martha. *Image and Imagination.* Montreal: McGill-Queen's UP, 2005.

Lukács, Georg. *The Historical Novel. Theory of the Novel: A Historical Approach.* Ed. Michael McKeon. Baltimore: Johns Hopkins UP, 2000. 219–64.

Marsh, Joss Lutz. "Dickens and Film." *The Cambridge Companion to Charles Dickens.* Ed. John O. Jordan. Cambridge, Cambridge UP, 2001.

———. "Inimitable Double Vision: Dickens, *Little Dorrit*, Photography, Film." *Dickens Studies Annual* 22 (1993): 239–82.

Maxwell, Richard. Introduction. *A Tale of Two Cities.* New York: Penguin, 2000.

Miles, Melissa. "The Burning Mirror: Photography in an Ambivalent Light." *Journal of Visual Culture* 4.3 (2005): 329–49.

Morley, Henry, and W. H. Wills. "Photography." *Household Words* 7.156 (19 Mar. 1853): 54–61.

Novak, Daniel A. *Realism, Photography, and Nineteenth-Century Fiction.* New York: Cambridge UP, 2008.

Oost, Regina B. " 'More Like Than Life': Painting, Photography, and Dickens's *Bleak House.*" *Dickens Studies Annual* 30 (2001): 141–58.

Osterman, Mark. "How to *See* a Daguerreotype." *Image* 43.2 (Autumn 2005): 12–15.

Peres, Michael R., ed. *The Focal Encyclopedia of Photography: Digital Imaging, Theory and Applications, History, and Science*. 4th ed. San Francisco: Focal P, 2007.

"Photographic Print." *All the Year Round* 1.7 (11 June 1859): 162–64.

Reichardt, Rolf. "Light against Darkness: The Visual Representation of a Central Enlightenment Concept." Trans. Deborah Louise Cohen. *Representations* 61: *Practices of Enlightenment* (Winter 1998): 95–148.

Richter, David. Rev. *The Historical Novel from Scott to Sabatini: Changing Attitudes toward a Literary Genre 1814–1920*. By Harold Orel. *YES* 27 (1996): 264–65.

Schwartz, Vanessa R. *Spectacular Realities: Early Mass Culture in* Fin-de-Siècle *Paris*. Berkeley: U of California P, 1998.

Shaw, Harry E. *The Forms of Historical Fiction: Sir Walter Scott and His Successors*. Ithaca, NY: Cornell UP, 1983.

Smith, Grahame. "Dickens and the City of Light." *Dickens Quarterly* 16.3 (Sept. 1999): 178–90.

Solberg, Sarah. "A Note on Phiz's Dark Plates." *Dickensian* 76 (1980): 40–44.

Steig, Michael. *Dickens and Phiz*. Bloomington: Indiana UP, 1978.

Stein, Richard L. "Dickens and Illustration." *The Cambridge Companion to Charles Dickens*. Ed. John O. Jordan. New York: Cambridge UP, 2001. 167–88.

Thomas, Ronald R. "Double Exposures: Arresting Images in *Bleak House* and *The House of the Seven Gables*." *Novel: A Forum on Fiction* 31.1 (Autumn 1997): 87–113.

Wilkins, William Glyde. "Charles Dickens in Art and Photography." *The Victorian Web* <http://www.victorianweb.org/authors/dickens/gallery/gallery1.html>.

Cryptic Texts: Coded Signs and Signals in *A Tale of Two Cities*

Jim Barloon

A Tale of Two Cities, a novel about the past, portrays language, and communication generally, in a very modern—at times postmodern—way. Although language is used as an unambiguous means to convey ideas and information, much of the communication that occurs in the novel is buried, encrypted, dislocated, and transmogrified; the secrecy and "secret signaling" that pervade the later Dickens extend, in A Tale of Two Cities, *even to the linguistic and semiotic realms. While one of the obvious purposes of these cryptic texts is to keep incriminating or compromising communication secret, the purposes are not limited to this. Generally the text evinces a radical skepticism towards the necessary or ineluctable connection between the signifier and signified, between word and deed. Although* A Tale of Two Cities *may not offer a new or penetrating interpretation of the French Revolution, it does interrogate the very bases—language and identity—upon which we build our representations of our world and our selves.*

A Tale of Two Cities, a novel about the past, portrays language, and communication generally, in a very modern—at times post-modern—way. Though serious readers of Dickens have long recognized that he is not the sententious caricaturist of popular fame, too few readers, still, appreciate the subtle and experimental devices of the later Dickens. In an analysis of *Great Expectations*, the novel that Dickens wrote immediately after *A Tale of Two Cities*, Peter Brooks asserts, "The text constantly warns us that texts may have no

Dickens Studies Annual, Volume 42, Copyright © 2011 by AMS Press, Inc. All rights reserved.

unambiguous referent and no transcendent signified'' (132). This is also true, a fortiori, of *A Tale of Two Cities*, a novel in which language has gone underground—texts/words are buried, encrypted, dislocated, and transmogrified. The novel may not offer a new or penetrating interpretation of the French Revolution, but it does interrogate the very bases—language and identity—upon which we build our representations of our world and our selves. The first chapters set, respectively, in England and France, chapters 2 and 5, emphasize the indeterminacy and slipperiness of language, as well as the necessity for indirection. What these chapters suggest, and what the novel shows, is that the secrecy and "secret signaling" (Stone 327) that pervade the later Dickens extend even to the linguistic and semiotic realms.

In "The Mail," chapter 2, Jerry Cruncher slogs through the muck and mire of the Dover Road on a sodden autumn night to deliver a note to Jarvis Lorry. The scene, as well as Lorry's response, is shrouded in mist and mystery. Reading the note—"Wait at Dover for Mam'selle"—by the scant light of the coach-lamp, Lorry tells Jerry to "say that [his] answer was, 'RECALLED TO LIFE' " (41; bk. 1, ch. 2). After the mail has renewed its journey, the guard and coachman discuss Lorry's enigmatic answer; neither, however, can make anything of it. Jerry himself, "left alone in the mist and darkness" (42; bk. 1, ch. 2), also ponders and puzzles over the mystifying words. Unlike the guard and coachman, Jerry does makes something of the message, though not the meaning the words are intended to convey, but a meaning "of a private and personal capacity," as Wemmick would put it, a significance that Jerry Cruncher must himself be at great pains to keep buried. Nevertheless, because of the nebulousness of his answer, Lorry's message achieves its twofold purpose: it illuminates meaning, like the coach-lamp, within a narrow, circumscribed circle, while keeping those outside its ambit in the dark.

"The Wine-Shop," chapter 5 and the first set specifically in France, opens (in more ways than one) as follows: "A large cask of wine had been dropped and broken, in the street" (59; bk. 1, ch. 5). The breaking of the cask also releases the pent-up, demonic appetites of the slowly starved Parisians. Some sop up the wine with handkerchiefs, others laugh and gambol—a desperate respite from their long death march—while one lone "tall joker" "scrawl[s] upon a wall with his fingers dipped in muddy wine-lees—BLOOD" (61; bk. 1, ch. 5). This "joker," this wild card, Gaspard, has dared to spell out the unspoken, archetypal subtext of the saturnalian scene; indeed, the episode is merely a rehearsal, an impromptu, fake-blood bacchanal, for the coming apocalypse. As the narrator comments, "The time was to come, when that wine too would be spilled on the street-stones, and when the stain of it would be red upon many there" (61; bk. 1, ch. 5).

Gaspard's scrawl is, literally and figuratively, the writing upon the wall. In this novel of echoes, this echo of The Book of Daniel offers a relevatory gloss upon the scene. In Daniel, neither Baltasar, the king, nor all the king's men, can interpret the writing on the wall of the king's palace, but Daniel, a man renowned for his "interpretations of dreams and shewing of secrets," comes and does. He tells the king that the writing means that "God hath numbered thy kingdom, and hath finished it," and that "thou are weighed in the balance and art found wanting" (5:26–27). That same night Baltasar is slain. The French aristocracy, with the exception of Charles and his mother, are as benighted as Baltasar, as blind to the writing on the wall and its portentous significance. Charles, who can read the writing upon the wall—who can recognize not only the injustice of the past but the coming, cataclysmic reckoning—warns his uncle the night before *he* is slain: " 'We have done wrong,' he declares, 'and are reaping the fruits of wrong' " (154; bk. 2, ch. 9).

As many critics have pointed out, Dickens insists upon the inevitability of the events which the novel depicts. It had to be—or, one might say, the future was embedded, implanted, within the past. The "grimly determinist vision of history which [the novel] articulates" (Rignall 166) can be attributed not only to the givenness, the historicity, of the story, but also to Dickens's investment in a lisible, empirical conception of history. The past is prologue, there for all to read—Darnay himself, awaiting execution, observes, " 'It could not be otherwise' " (364; bk. 3, ch. 11)—if only in very fine print. In this instance, Dickens does construct history, with its emphasis upon determinism and class-warfare, in proto-Marxist terms; the outcome had never been in doubt, and not because Providence was directing events, but due to inalterable human and social laws. "Sow the same seed of rapacious licence and oppression over again," the narrator proclaims, "and it will surely yield the same fruit according to its kind" (399; bk. 3, ch. 5). Dickens's insistent use of the sowing-reaping metaphor—the skeletal, structuring trope of *Hard Times* (1854), another novel about ineluctable cause-and-effect processes—foregrounds the implacable trajectory of the storm the novel tracks.

But Gaspard's articulation of the subversive subtext of the scene is premature; he must learn patience, that "ripeness is all." The "jest" pointed out to Defarge, he immediately responds: " 'What now? Are you a subject for the mad hospital?' said the wine-shop keeper, crossing the road, and obliterating the jest with a handful of mud, picked up for the purpose, and smeared over it. 'Why do you write in the public streets? Is there—tell me thou—is there no other place to write such words in?' " (63; bk. 1, ch. 5). "Blood" is the one word, the one lust, that dare not speak its name—at least openly. The word, then, is obliterated, smeared over, the wall a palimpsest still bearing the muddy/merde traces of the forbidden, the dirty, word. Note, too, that Defarge does not prohibit the use or writing of the word entirely, but only "in the public streets." Is there, as Defarge intimates, a private place to write such words in, perhaps another language to use?

His sanguinary wife, Madame Defarge, secretly knits the names of those whom she and her fellow ''citizens'' plan to obliterate, to smear over, and blot out, with blood. But how exactly—literally or in code—are these names inscribed? Talking with Defarge about the register, Jacques Two observes that '' 'no one beyond ourselves can decipher it,' '' but he then worries that they themselves might one day lose the capacity to unravel it. Defarge reassures his confrere that the register is '' 'Knitted, in her own stitches and her own symbols, [and] it will always be as plain to her as the sun . . . It would be easier for the weakest poltroon that lives, to erase himself from existence, than to erase one letter of the name or crimes from the knitted register of Madame Defarge' '' (202; bk. 2, ch. 15). Using ''her own symbols,'' Madame Defarge weaves a story—a loomed Doomsday Book—that only a close-knit coterie of readers can comprehend, a coded text that both divulges and occludes, a text, like others in the novel, that is buried and that must be resurrected before it can deliver up its meaning. An underground ''historian'' (Lewis 31), Madame Defarge spins a text that is revolutionary on many fronts—particularly if one accepts the radical argument that ''unproblematic prose and . . . clarity of . . . presentation . . . are the conceptual tools of conservatism'' (Zavarzadeh 333). In its deeply, deliberately problematic symbology, Madame Defarge's register inscribes the leveling, chthonic program—one that wants to conserve nothing—that she and her fellow conspirators are plotting.

Just as wine is linked and likened to blood, so the wineshop, in Dickens's transubstantiating imagination, serves as the heart of the bloody business of the revolution. But like Madame Defarge's register, the wineshop both advertises and conceals its business. As a web of underground revolutionary activity, the wineshop has developed an elaborate system of secret signaling and coded communication, as the paragraph introducing Madame Defarge illustrates:

> Madame Defarge said nothing when her lord came in, but coughed just one grain of cough. This, in combination with the lifting of her darkly defined eyebrows over her toothpick by the breadth of a line, suggested to her husband that he would do well to look around the shop among the customers, for any new customer who had dropped in while he stepped over the way.
>
> (64; bk. 1, ch. 5)

The signs are so slight, so marginal—''one grain of cough,'' ''the breadth of a line''—that only the initiated, those who have been taught to read such liminal cues, can understand them. The secret signaling serves both as a means of empowering the Jacquerie—allowing them to protect their interests and solidifying the bond among them—while it also mutely testifies to their powerlessness, their voicelessness. One of the privileges of the aristocracy is the freedom to speak out at little or no immediate risk to themselves or their interests—for example, Foulon's contemptuous remark that the famished people might eat grass (251; bk. 2, ch. 22)—whereas the peasants can be torn apart, literally, for not prostrating themselves with sufficient humilty before the reigning powers (36; bk. 1, ch. 1). Even a look, such as the stony look that Madame Defarge bestows upon Monseigneur, constitutes a defiant, dangerous act (143; bk. 2, ch. 7). Later, ironically, Madame Defarge plans to denounce Lucie Manette and produce a witness who will testify that he saw Lucie "making signs and signals to prisoners" (373; bk. 3, ch. 12). The revolutionaries, then, trained in the perilous semiotics of the corporeal, have developed their own language—gestural, devious, and coded—which both speaks and elides.

But this underground network of signals and signs also exists to confound the spies who try to unravel the tangled semantic skein of the wineshop. The narrator, for example, remarks upon "the spies who looked in at the wineshop, as they looked in at every place, high and low, from the king's palace to the criminal's gaol" (195; bk. 2, ch. 15), and Barsad's visit only further reinforces why the revolutionaries must not only act but communicate clandestinely. The wineshop is thus a contested site, not only politically, but linguistically—it stands at the crossroads of these two realms—a place where language and meaning have gone underground, and signification occurs in the defensive shorthand of the hunted.

But (yet another turn of the screw) the revolutionaries have spies of their own. Having been informed of Barsad's "commission" by "Jacques of the police" (206; bk. 2, ch. 16), the Defarges are lying in wait for him, the spidery Madame Defarge knitting killing "shrouds" (203; bk. 2, ch. 15). Thus Barsad is, in a sense, pre-registered. In fact, even before Barsad speaks a word, Madame Defarge pins a rose in her head-dress and the other customers cease talking and "be[gin] gradually to drop out of the wine-shop" (209; bk. 2, ch. 16). Now sub rosa, the wineshop has quietly modulated into another linguistic key. The scene and exchanges that follow further dramatize how language often functions in the novel: rather than a medium designed for and used to convey meaning transparently, language/communication in *A Tale of Two Cities* often obfuscates or tells only within a prescribed, delimited range.

Barsad's unstated, unspeakable purpose is to trigger an involuntary answer or response that will betray the group's revolutionary loyalties or associations. For example, he repeatedly addresses Defarge as "Jacques," a name Defarge earnestly, if not very artfully, dodges: " 'You mistake me for another. That is not my name. I am Ernest Defarge' " (211; bk. 2, ch. 16). Throughout the interview, or interrogation, Madame Defarge continues to knit—the chapter is entitled "Still Knitting"—itself the pattern of secret signaling, of encryption, in the novel. Madame Defarge not only knits Barsad's name, presumably in code or cipher, but also "an extra something into his name that boded him no good'' (210; bk. 2, ch. 16). Like the wineshop itself, Madame Defarge's text is ''sub rosa,'' a sub-text that represents a thorny hermeneutical challenge. It is also, for Madame Defarge, as well as for other women, a displacement, an ersatz *pis aller* with an oblique metonymic significance: ''All the women knitted. They knitted worthless things; but, the mechanical work was a mechanical substitute for eating and drinking; the hands moved for the jaws and the digestive apparatus'' (215; bk. 2, ch. 16). Thus, Madame Defarge's knitting and what she knits mean several different things—all of them displacements, coded gestures or texts, of one kind or another.

Though Barsad suspects this, he is unable to break Madame Defarge's cool, coded mien; he has more success, however, with Monsieur Defarge. After failing to elicit their sympathy for Gaspard in particular or the plight of the people in general, Barsad reveals that Charles Darnay, the nephew of Monsieur the Marquis, is going to marry Miss Manette. Madame Defarge continues to knit ''steadily, but the intelligence ha[s] a palpable effect upon her husband. . . . The spy would have been no spy if he had failed to see it, or to record it in his mind'' (214; bk. 2, ch. 16). Like his adversary, Madame Defarge, Barsad secretly records what he sees and learns, a registry of names, or perhaps simply a record of unguarded, undisguised gestures. This is a struggle, a high-stakes heuristic, that takes place on the margins of the perceptible.

Throughout *A Tale of Two Cities*, and in divers ways, referentiality itself is questioned, or at least shown to be contestable. The world of the novel is hard to read—as are the words that stand for things in that world. Even the names that appear (and those that do not) reveal a breach between signifier and signified, a radical disjuncture between word and referent. Although a historical novel, *A Tale of Two Cities* includes very few real, historical figures, and it names even fewer. In the first paragraph of the novel, for example, Dickens refers to King George III of England and King Louis XVI and Marie Antoinette of France, but does not name them. Dickens might have had various good reasons for this—perhaps it has something to do, as Murray Baumgarten suggests, with Dickens's democratic sympathies (168)—but it is suggestive that Dickens, in a novel that purports to be both history and fiction, declines this early opportunity to weight his fiction with hefty historical names. Indeed, the rogue's gallery of names Dickens does not include—for example, ''there is no Danton, no Robespierre, no Marat'' (Maxwell xiv)—acts as a kind of black hole, a dark blank that teases us to interrogate this nameless absence. Dickens, though his novel owes so much to Carlyle, set out to write a very different, in some ways more modern, history of the Revolution. As Peter Ackroyd points out, ''Dickens distrusted [Carlyle's] love of the past and his worship of power, and it is noteworthy that both these aspects of Carlyle's history are missing from the novel'' (862). William J. Palmer goes so far as to argue that Dickens wrote a kind of prototypical new historical account of the Revolution, and that by writing "From below, from outside, from the margins, he is trying to 'thicken' the historical narrative of his time by making it truer, more inclusive'' (168). But if Dickens produces a 'thick' text, in the New Historical sense of the word, he does so at the expense of solidity. Given the radical skepticism evinced regarding the necessary or ineluctable connection between signifier and signified, between word and referent, the novel might also be characterized as unstable.

Further, many of the invented, purely ''fictional'' characters are given or adopt names that blur or disguise their singular individuality, among the central purposes of a proper name, especially in a fiction.[1] The male revolutionaries adopt the name ''Jacques,'' which not only blurs their identities, but multiplies it by giving them another persona. Like so much else in the novel—the dates, Dr. Manette's cell, even the formal organization of the novel—each Jacques is numbered. Numbers in this novel have the kind of stability, of accountability, normally ascribed to names. The chapter portraying the execution of Carton/Darnay is entitled ''Fifty-Two,'' the number condemned to be executed that day. And though numbers of spectators take an interest in the fate of one particular prisoner, Charles Darnay/Evrémonde, their inability to distinguish between Darnay and Carton further testifies to the unreliability of names—and faces—to single out a specific individual. The Fifty-Two are Evrémonde, everybody, and therefore nobody in particular. The nameless ''number of women, busily knitting'' (401; bk. 3, ch. 15) who witness the executions tell/toll off the roll by counting: ''Twenty-Two. . . . Twenty-Three'' (403; bk. 3, ch. 15). Earlier, when Carton assures an anxious Barsad that he '' 'will be true to the death,' '' Barsad (or Solomon Pross) responds, '' 'You must be, Mr Carton, if the tale of fifty-two is to be right' '' (382; bk. 3, ch. 13). Here again, with his use of the word ''tale'' to mean ''count'' or ''list,'' a secondary meaning, Dickens exemplifies the variable and contextual nature of language. But to the ''Republicans,'' as to ''Madame Guillotine'' herself, numbers and not names are what matter; to them, every head tells, every head counts.[2]

Just as the Jacquerie are, on some level, indistinguishable—not only because they try to be, but also because the Jacquerie are all the same (i.e., enemies) to the crown—so, too, do the aristocrats tend to collapse upon one another to form a generic composite. Chapter 7 of Book the Second, entitled ''Monsieur the Marquis in Town,'' features two separate yet hard to distinguish aristocrats. One is referred to as ''Monseigneur'' while the other (Charles's uncle) is ''Monsieur the Marquis.'' By their titles are they known—in more ways than one. Dickens, by constantly referring to them in this way, emphasizes what is most essential and determinative about them.

Further, both aristocrats display the same decadence, arrogance, and contempt for the masses. Part of the doubling, twinning pattern so central to the novel—in fact, Charles's uncle, the Marquis, had a twin brother—this conflation not only suggests that aristocrats are all the same, but calls into question, placed in the larger context of the novel, the integrity and indivisibility of identity itself. As John Bowen asks, apropos of comments that George Henry Lewes made about the psychology underlying Dickens's characters, "What if there is no psychology in the sense that Lewes thinks there is? What if the human itself was also at stake in these novels, not a given but a question?" (17). In a novel of echoes (especially Ovidian echoes),[3] it is no wonder that identity should be portrayed as fungible, as phantasmagoric.

Many other characters in the novel have names that resist the sort of semiotic stability, the unambiguous referentiality, that we tend to take for granted in nineteenth-century novels. In Paris, Miss Pross's brother is John Barsad but, as Jerry Cruncher remarks, " 'that warn't [his] name over the water' " (326; bk. 3, ch. 8). Barsad's partner, Roger Cly, seems to be all shadow and no substance. When Cruncher and his cohorts unearth Cly's grave, they find it empty; Cly is later resurrected in France, under a new identity, and once again becomes a spy. The "wood-sawyer" was once a "mender of roads," and everyone (Evrémonde) becomes, as "prescribed by decree," "citizen" (305; bk. 3, ch. 5). To Shakespeare's familiar question, "What's in a name?", *A Tale of Two Cities* would seem to answer, a word "signifying nothing."

Just as names frequently change or lose their representational significance—becoming unmoored and free-floating—so too do documents often become detached from their origin, or are misappropriated or misapplied. Albert D. Hutter argues that "The overt and seemingly relentless subtext of this novel is to give meaning to death or to the past, to disinter the historical moment and make it come alive, to recover bodies and letters and everything that may presumably have disappeared and to resurrect them, to give them meaning" (25). Texts are resurrected, but the meaning given them is often a perversion or misprision of their intended purpose. Dr. Manette, for example, is almost certainly arrested and confined to the Bastille based on a *lettre de cachet*, a " 'letter of seal,' a warrant issued in the France of the *ancien régime* for the imprisonment of a person without trial at the pleasure of the monarch" (OED). That is what Jarvis Lorry suggests when, in breaking the news about her father to Lucie, he refers to "the privilege of filling up blank forms for the consignment of any one to the oblivion of a prison for any length of time" (56; bk. 1, ch. 4). The verb *cacher* means to hide or conceal. The *lettre de cachet* hides and conceals many things: the person put in prison, of course, but also the accuser and his grievance, whatever its nature. The *lettre de cachet*, then, is a tabula rasa, a blank slate, or blank form, upon which anyone's name can be written—a warrant without any warrant. Such a letter not only has no clear referent, but it also lacks referentiality—that is, any connection with reality or a responsible body prepared to answer for the truth of its claims. This is a real prison-house of language, a totally arbitrary and factitious fiction that consigns the person designated to "oblivion."

The letter denouncing the Evrémonde "race" that Dr. Manette wrote in prison in 1767 in the Bastille is "resurrected," but only to seal Darnay's death warrant. This is done at the trial against Manette's express wishes, and is done in the name of Justice and the Republic, though the real motivation, as Dickens makes clear, is much more personal and pernicious. The murder committed in the name of "liberty, fraternity, and equality" is mostly a pretense for barely disguised blood vengeance, a displacement, a false warrant meant to sanctify unholy deeds. It is more than an expression to say that the judge, jury, and spectators at Darnay's second trial in Paris have an ax to grind. Dr. Manette's "resurrected" letter is a cry for justice—and revenge—but it is used by its appropriators to kill "an innocent man" (391; bk. 3, ch. 14).

But, of course, Darnay is not killed. Through yet another displacement, Carton takes his place, and goes to the guillotine and his posthumous reward. Carton's reward is to be resurrected, in heaven presumably, but also, and more importantly, here on earth. Sidney Carton dies in the name of—literally and figuratively—Charles Evrémonde, alias Charles Darnay, only to be resurrected in the descendants, echoing through the ages, of Lucie and Charles Darnay. What Carton supposedly "sees" may be a prophetic vision, or it may only be wishful thinking: "I see that child who lay upon her bosom and who bore my name, a man, winning his way up in that path of life which once was mine. . . . I see him, foremost of just judges and honoured men, bringing a boy of my name, with a forehead that I know and golden hair, to this place" (404; bk. 3, ch. 15). This composite grandson, his name a concatenation of Carton and Darnay, his features recalling to life Lucie Manette, will bear Sydney's name, but not his surname (Waters 148). The son of Lucie and Charles might be named Sydney, perhaps even Sydney Carton, but his official, surname would be "Darnay": Sydney Carton Darnay. Likewise, while the novel gives the final, revelatory lines to Carton, the bright, brilliant future that Carton envisions belongs to the Darnay line.

Stryver refers to Carton as "Memory" (118; bk. 2, ch. 5), but how and whether Carton is remembered by subsequent generations depends mostly upon Darnay. Whatever earthly fame, or name, Carton will have must be authored by Darnay (though Lucie will bear the child, the child will bear Darnay's name). This authorship is prefigured in the chapter entitled "Fifty-Two," in which Carton visits Darnay in prison, renders him unconscious, and takes his place. As a means to distract his attention, Carton asks Darnay to transcribe the words that he dictates; the words that Darnay writes down constitute Carton's valedictory to Lucie: " 'If you remember,' said Carton dictating, 'the words that passed between us, long ago, you will readily comprehend this when you see it' " (380–81; bk. 3, ch. 13). This is not simply a ploy—these are Carton's final words to Lucie, and he makes sure to put the paper in the unconscious Darnay's "breast" (382; bk. 3, ch. 13). Carton's words (and legacy) are in Darnay's hand, again literally and figuratively. These words that are "passed between" them are mediated by Darnay, the medium of the message that Carton secretes out of the prison. The words—like the son and grandson with Carton's name—bear Darnay's signature. This is an example of how communication works in the novel: mediated, concealed, divergent.

The novel concludes with some very memorable—and very slippery—words. The speech, or soliloquy, or prophecy, that Carton contemplates just before he is executed raises several vexing narratological and ontological questions. Dickens introduces Carton's words, which are put in quotation marks, as follows: "If he had given an utterance to his [thoughts], and they were prophetic, they would have been these" (404). Critics have understandably registered their perplexity in attempting to parse and locate Carton's "speech." Richard Maxwell says that the speech leaves us with "a mixed impression" (xxvii), while Carol Hanbery MacKay refers to their "paradoxical effect" (203). The first problem, or question, is, Are these Carton's words, or thoughts, or simply "the narrator's fantastical projection" (John 198)? Second, if he never utters them, as the use of the subjunctive mood indicates, how did we (or somebody) come by them? Third, with what sort of authority or credibility can we invest such ghostly words?

There is no way to save, to credit, Carton's words without positing and accepting the privileges[4] accorded to an omniscient narrator. Dickens's narrator has, "under the auspices of omniscience" (Stewart 96), resurrected these words.[5] Yet even here, with the godlike powers of omniscience, and resurrection, at this command, Dickens balks and chooses rather to leave us with real doubt as to the source and authority of the words with which the novel concludes. Carton's words, like the bright future he foresees, are forever prospective, forever inconclusive. Earlier in the novel Carton confessed to Lucie, "All [his] life might have been" (180; bk. 2, ch. 13). Carton himself is written in the subjunctive, the conditional. His dying words (if they are his) are no less provisional and unplaceable. His words—like so many other words in the novel—are signs with a questionable signifier and an uncertain signified.

Dickens's emphasis in A Tale of Two Cities upon the slipperiness, the instability, of language and signs has both crafty, storytelling uses and mimetic, epistemological implications. Given the story at hand—as well as various other considerations, such as the Victorian market for fiction—a reliance upon secrets and coded communication makes for a sensational serial; such is the stuff that melodramas and revolutions are made of. But Dickens considered himself to be more than an entertainer: he sought to tell, to reveal, the truth.[6] In this novel, however, Dickens shows that the ineluctable medium for conveying truths—or events or realities—is not transparent, but contingent and mediated. Language/Communication in the novel is not exactly a prison-house—a self-referential, closed system—but neither is it open and unrestricted. Communication, rather, functions like a one-way mirror, a means of exchange that disguises or obscures what is passed from one to another. Though Dickens's characters in *A Tale of Two Cities* do communicate, do exchange meaning, they do so, often, through a glass, darkly.

NOTES

1. See Watt, 18–21.
2. Even Dr. Manette is viewed by some as merely a "sum." When debating whether or not Dr. Manette can be "spared," Jacques Three comments that " 'He could count as one head' " (389; bk. 3, ch. 14).
3. See Maxwell's note (478) on the allusions to Ovid in the novel.
4. Wayne Booth argues that "Complete privilege is what we usually call omniscience" (160).
5. See Catherine Gallagher, who argues that "Resurrection [acts] as a double for omniscient narration" (140).
6. Over and over again Dickens, particularly in his prefaces, insists upon the "Truth" of his fiction. Two examples are *Oliver Twist* and *Bleak House*. Defending his characterization of Nancy, Dickens asserts that "It is useless to discuss whether the conduct and character of the girl seems natural or unnatural, probable or improbably, right or wrong IT IS TRUE" (36). In his preface to the first edition of *Bleak House*, Dickens defends the reality of spontaneous combution and his depiction of Chancery: "everything set forth in these pages concerning the Court of Chancery is substantially true, and within the truth" (41).

WORKS CITED

Ackroyd, Peter. *Dickens.* New York: HarperCollins, 1990.

Baumgarten, Murray. "Writing the Revolution." *Dickens Studies Annual* 12 (1983): 161–76.

Booth, Wayne. *The Rhetoric of Fiction*. 2nd ed. Chicago: U of Chicago P, 1983.

Bowen, John. *Other Dickens: Pickwick to Chuzzlewit*. Oxford: Oxford UP, 2000.

Brooks, Peter. *Reading for the Plot: Design and Intention in Narrative*. New York: Knopf, 1984.

Dickens, Charles. *A Tale of Two Cities*. Ed. George Woodcock. Harmondsworth: Penguin, 1970.

———. *Bleak House*. Ed. Norman Page. New York: Penguin, 1985.

———. *Oliver Twist*. Ed. Peter Fairclough. New York: Penguin, 1985.

Gallagher, Catherine. "The Duplicity of Doubling in *A Tale of Two Cities*." *Dickens Studies Annual* 12 (1983): 125–45.

Hutter, Albert D. "The Novelist as Resurrectionist: Dickens and the Dilemma of Death." *Dickens Studies Annual* 12 (1983): 1–39.

John, Juliet. *Dickens's Villains: Melodrama, Character, Popular Culture*. Oxford: Oxford UP, 2001.

"*lettre de cachet*, n." *The Oxford English Dictionary*. 2009. *OED Online*. Oxford UP. 21 April 2008. <http//dictionary.oed.com/>

Lewis, Linda M. "Madame Defarge as Political Icon in Dickens's *A Tale of Two Cities*." *Dickens Studies Annual* 37 (2006): 31–49.

MacKay, Carol Hanbery. "The Rhetoric of Soliloquy in *The French Revolution* and *A Tale of Two Cities*." *Dickens Studies Annual* 12 (1983): 197–207.

Maxwell, Richard. Introduction. *A Tale of Two Cities*. By Charles Dickens. New York: Penguin, 2000. ix–xxxiii.

Palmer, William. *Dickens and New Historicism*. New York: St. Martin's, 1997.

Rignall, J. M. "Dickens and the Catastrophic Continuum of History in *A Tale of Two Cities*." *ELH* 51 (1984): 157–67.

Stewart, Garrett. *Death Sentences: Styles of Dying in British Fiction*. Cambridge: Harvard UP, 1984.

Stone, Harry. *The Night Side of Dickens: Cannibalism, Passion, Necessity*. Columbus: Ohio State UP, 1994.

The Jerusalem Bible. Reader's Edition. Ed. Alexander Jones. New York: Doubleday, 1966.

Waters, Catherine. *Dickens and the Politics of the Family*. Cambridge: Cambridge UP, 1997.

Watt, Ian. *The Rise of the Novel: Studies in Defoe, Richardson and Fielding.* Berkeley: U of California P, 1957.

Zavarzadeh, Mas'd. Rev. of *The Pursuit of Signs: Semiotics, Literature, Deconstruction.* By Jonathan Culler. *The Journal of Aesthetics and Art Criticism* 40 (Spring, 1982): 329–33.

Clarriker, Pocket, and Pirrip: The Original Tale of Dickens's Clerk

David Paroissien

This essay offers another look at the original ending of Great Expectations. *Rather than accept the false opposition between "unhappy" "happy" versions, I consider the evidence that exists about the novel's origin, development, and composition. From the moment of its inception to the composition of its final words, Dickens planned, designed, and executed a story told by an older narrator who looked back on his life not with regret but with understanding. So sure of his intention, with two-thirds of the work completed and with the final third waiting to be "ground off," Dickens outlined in a letter to John Forster his belief that the import of Pip's story, in its working out and winding up, would be away from "all such things as they conventionally go." These targets, I suggest, are two prevailing fictional conventions, the use of weddings to signal narrative closure, and the extended use of sensational elements to add pace to the telling. Had Dickens stuck to his original design, the novel that has come down to us would have been read in a different way. We would have paid attention to the fact that Pip is a much older narrator than readers generally concede, that he's a man who has sought and obtained understanding about the events that shaped his life, and that, in the course of telling his story, he has achieved a degree of peace. In reacting to Bulwer's "objections," however, two consequences follow: (1) Dickens undercut his original design; and (2) he introduced a narrative flaw which relies on a chronological scheme incompatible with that design and with the actual telling. A close reading of various data—the events of the main thread of Pip's*

*story, the historical setting of those events, and the dating of the actual
telling time, taken together, support the case that Dickens weakened his
book and broke the integrity of an original and flawless narrative.*

Philip Pirrip and the Ancient Mariner have little in common save their skill
with a pair of oars. One is youthful and strong for the greater part of his
narrative, the other old and skinny. Pip inhabits the realistic social world of
Victorian England, Coleridge's figure fuses elements drawn from the legend
of the Wandering Jew and versions of the Flying Dutchman. But Pip and the
Ancient Mariner share one other important trait. Both have the ability to tell
an arresting story and make people listen; and had Dickens's clerk been
allowed to stick to the one he originally narrated, subsequent critical discourse
about *Great Expectations* would have taken a different turn.

We have Dickens's first biographer to thank for this development. One
can't prove that if John Forster had acted differently debate about the merits
of the two endings would never have been ignited. Evidence of Dickens's
decision to rewrite the ending exists elsewhere, in his correspondence with
Bulwer Lytton, Wilkie Collins, and with Forster himself.[1] But the choice
Forster made to include the text of the original in the third volume of his *Life
of Charles Dickens* (1874) added fuel to a fire that continues to burn. With
both endings before us, are we not invited to make a choice? Was Dickens
wise to have taken Bulwer's advice? Did he not spoil a fine novel by accepting
it? How can one read *Great Expectations* and push aside these and related
questions?[2] To ignore them would be cowardice, as Edgar Rosenberg suggests. But I want to reorient the discussion and make the case for the original
ending based on empirical grounds by following the advice of Mr. Jaggers:
"Take nothing on its looks; take everything on evidence," he counsels Pip.
"There's no better rule" (336; ch. 40).

You might express surprise that no one has suggested this before. One explanation, I think, is the way we respond to fictional characters and the appetencies
novels awaken. Given a choice, readers typically opt for one or the other conclusion depending on how they internalize the conventions of the work. Some read
Pip's story as one that invites the possibility of a "happy" ending. Others look
for something less romantic, a tale told by an unmarried man or one whose
narrative remains skeptical about the prospect of reconciliation and marital bliss.

Polarities like these lie at the heart of disputes over the two endings, further
energized by the ambiguity of the revised version.[3] Far less rarely do critics
assess the merits of each dispassionately. Readers pay insufficient attention
to the novel's gestation and composition, for example; they also tend to ignore
the narrative discourse and the way Pip tells his story.[4] Both issues illuminate
the question of an appropriate ending, I contend, and offer a way out of

critical gridlock. Whether readers like the story's original conception and ending or prefer the second version is a matter for each person to decide. What cannot be contested, I maintain, is that the revised ending breaks the integrity of a narrative Dickens planned, stuck to, and executed flawlessly. Taking a second turn at winding up Pip's narrative in deference to Bulwer Lytton, Dickens went against the grain of his own well-laid design, despite his professed satisfaction with the result. "[P]retty" though he pronounced it (*Letters* 9: 433), the second ending remains at odds with the whole, a narrative faking inferior to the original.

Before I proceed, it might be helpful to recall briefly how the story is constructed.

Great Expectations opens with the retrospective reflections of a young boy of about six whose life has been shaped by the events of two "memorable" days. The first describes his encounter with an escaped convict on the marshes, the second with Miss Havisham of Satis House, a mysterious and eccentric lady, who lives in the market town close to the forge where Pip grows up. Precision with the chronology reinforces the parallel structure of these two meetings, which occur within the span of a single year. Taken together, they shape the novel's development and serve as its keel. At Satis House, Pip meets Estella, an unobtainable star on account of the social gulf between them. She appears well-born and rich, while he is a humble orphan brought up to earn his living as a blacksmith. Common sense tells us that the two can never be united—unless his fortunes change, which, of course, they do, when Pip, later a young man of eighteen or so, is mysteriously summoned to London, where he becomes a gentleman. No longer fated to work with his hands, he learns to spend money carelessly, dress well, and acquire poise and manners, surely the design of Miss Havisham, who, he concludes, intends him for Estella.

But Pip, we discover in the final third stage of his expectations, is famously wrong. He owes his good fortune not to Miss Havisham, but to the convict on the marshes, now rich and back from Australia, whence he has returned in defiance of the law to see the gentleman he created. Pip collapses on learning the true source of his legacy, but recovers to experience first gratitude and then love for the convict who wanted to give a poor boy like him a chance for a better life. Pip and Magwitch plan to leave England by boarding a moving steamer bound for the Continent; but they are thwarted when their boat is intercepted by a customs galley, the convict receives a fatal injury and dies, and Pip loses everything. Recovery abroad gives him a second chance, employed as a clerk in the firm of his good friend Herbert. He works hard for a modest living, returning occasionally to England. Later in life he looks back on these extraordinary events. Estella was never intended for him;

he learns how she married Pip's rival, an abusive man whose cruelty leads to his own death and subsequently to her second, happy marriage. In the original conclusion, Pip and Estella meet once in London by chance. The two exchange a few words, and the novel ends with Pip expressing his relief that Estella had at least outgrown Miss Havisham's teaching and developed a heart to understand what his heart "used to be."

Let us return to the advice of Mr. Jaggers and consider the following relevant points. First, I want to examine the gestation and composition of *Great Expectations*. Dickens wrote this novel with a degree of assurance and self-confidence uncommon even for him. Never once did he doubt how the novel would work out or hesitate about the way it would close, until Bulwer Lytton's intervention after he had completed it. The second portion of my case focuses on the consequences of this alteration. This is, I think, the more ambitious part of my argument. It hinges on a reconstruction of the novel's internal dating and on inferences about the telling time crucial to the discursive frame in which events are presented. Selective evidence will support my case.

The relevant facts of the novel's gestation and composition fall into three stages conveniently designated as follows: the novel's gestation and initial conception; the composition of the weekly numbers 6 through 36; and the intervention of Bulwer Lytton following its completion.

Gestation and Initial Conception

The first trace of *Great Expectations* occurs early in August 1860. On two separate occasions Dickens mentions how he was "meditating a new book" (*Letters* 9: 284, 285) and contemplating "a new Serial Story" in the familiar format of 20 monthly parts (294). Nearly a month later, we find him in much the same position, announcing to an old friend that he was "on the restless eve of beginning a new big book" (9: 309). Also before him was a second project, "a little piece" evidently intended as one of the sketches he wrote for *All the Year Round* under the persona of the "Uncommercial Traveller" (9: 310).

Reference to the weekly journal opens a window on another of Dickens's concerns at this time: the need for an original novel serialized in weekly installments to sustain the magazine's commercial appeal. Delighted with the part played by *A Tale of Two Cities*, which Dickens had written in order to launch his new magazine enterprise in April 1859, he was anxious to maintain momentum. Wilkie Collins's hugely successful *The Woman in White* had followed (November 1859–August 1860) and was due to be replaced by

Charles Lever's *A Day's Ride, A Life's Romance*, scheduled to start on 18 August 1860.

It is difficult to imagine a work less likely to grip the serial reading public than Lever's novel. Inevitably, readers registered their verdict in the sales, a development of immediate concern in view of the revenue *All the Year Round* produced. Initially, Dickens was inclined to give Lever the benefit of the doubt and postpone action. But, as sales continued to fall, he began to consider his options, simultaneously thinking about his own "big" novel and the smaller piece destined for *All the Year Round*.

At some point towards the end of September these three concerns fused and became a single problem that had to be faced. Never one to delay, Dickens went to London on 2 October, called "a council of war" at the office of *All the Year Round*, and made his decisions. Two letters to Forster dated 4 and 6 October enable us to reconstruct Dickens's thinking. The property of *All the Year Round*, he explained on the 6th, was "far too valuable, in every way," for him to ignore the danger posed by Lever's failing novel. The fall in sales, he conceded, was not large, but the novel had no vitality and no prospect of recuperating lost income (*Letters* 9: 320). Thus it was perfectly clear that there was only one solution—for Dickens "to strike in" and begin on the first of December (i.e., in eight weeks time) a story "of the length of *A Tale of Two Cities*" (*Letters* 9: 319).[5]

Forster's response, the editors of the Pilgrim *Letters* conclude, was cool (9: 320 n.). His vote was for the monthly serial Dickens had referred to earlier, rather than for a new, shorter one in weekly parts. Dickens, however, argued the point. He noted that if he committed himself to twenty monthly numbers, he would cut off "doing anything serial here [for *All the Year Round*] for two good years—and that would be a most perilous thing." However, if he dashed in now, then Charles Reade and Wilkie Collins could follow, thus shaping the course of the journal "handsomely" for the next two or three years (9: 320). Sound reasoning, one might conclude; and so it proved. For unknown to Forster, Dickens had a card up his sleeve he had only hinted at in a previous letter.

Writing to Forster earlier in September, Dickens had referred to a "little piece" he had been writing or was writing (9: 310). At work on it and with the end in sight, he went on to explain, "a very fine, new, and grotesque idea has opened upon me," such a good one, in fact, "that I begin to doubt whether I had not better cancel the little paper [for *All the Year Round*], and reserve the notion for a new book." In the same letter, Dickens refers to giving Forster the chance to look at the short piece and judge its suitability for development as soon as Dickens could get it printed: "But it so opens out before *me* that I can see the whole of a serial revolving on it, in a most singular and comic manner" (9: 310).

Events moved with such speed that Forster had no opportunity to offer an opinion. That emphatic *"me"* provides the key: Dickens knew exactly what he was doing. And in fact, before Forster could catch his breath or interject, Dickens wrote on 4 October to say that he would have "the first two or three weekly parts to-morrow," and that he already had a title—The name is GREAT EXPECTATIONS. I think a good name?" (9: 320). Just how quickly Dickens worked we can infer from this letter. Finding a title often proved difficult, requiring pages of trial headings, lists of characters, alternatives set out for deliberation, the invention of names, and so on. Yet in this instance Dickens already had one rich in signification within days of thinking over his options. Moreover, he had even taken the story as far as the recapture of the two convicts at the end of chapter 5, which is where the third weekly installment closes.

Consider also the evidence of a second letter. This one lacks a definitive date, but is clearly a subsequent communication, tentatively given by the Pilgrim editors as "Early October." In it, we learn about the core of the novel. It will be told in the first person throughout, Dickens informs Forster, the story of "a boy-child" like David Copperfield, who will be the hero. "Then he will be an apprentice." The novel will not lack humor, he continues. Rather "the pivot on which the story will turn," which he had already got in, will provide "the grotesque tragic-comic conception" he had begun to explore in the paper for *All the Year Round* until events compelled him to put it aside. And just to make sure that he had fallen into "no unconscious repetitions" of *David Copperfield*—the significance of this I must defer for the moment[6]—Dickens added that he had read the novel again "the other day" and seen no evidence of his repeating himself (*Letters* 9: 325).

Reference to one more letter and we can bring the question of the novel's gestation and initial development to a close. We next hear about *Great Expectations* on Thursday 24 October. Three weeks after writing to Forster, Dickens is making arrangements with Collins for a trip they both agreed to take to Cornwall to gather local material for the story they were engaged to contribute to the Christmas issue of *All the Year Round*. Dickens posted that letter to Collins dated the 24th from London. In it, he proposes that they start early for Penzance from London, leaving at nine on the following Thursday, 1 November. Meanwhile, Dickens explains, he must return to Gad's Hill tonight and get back to work. "Four weekly numbers [of *Great Expectations*] have been ground off the wheel, and at least another [number] must be turned, afore we meet. They shall be yours in the slumberous Railway carriage," he promised (9: 330).

For our part we must resist the invitation to doze and pay attention to the implications of Dickens's schedule. Having "ground off" four numbers, the last of which takes us forward and opens the way for Pip's introduction to

Miss Havisham, within seven days—including the weekend of 27–28 October—Dickens proposes to write chapter 8, and then get back to London by the first of the month to meet Collins at nine in the morning. The eighth chapter constitutes the whole fifth number and supplies the second of the novel's axial lines around which the book pivots: Miss Havisham's scheme to get her revenge for the cruel way she was jilted as a young woman. Pip's encounter with her and Estella occupies the whole number, after which he sets out on his lonely return to the forge, crushed and humiliated. That episode, as Pip looks back on it from his adult perspective, constitutes the second of two memorable days, days so memorable they made great changes in him (72; ch. 9).

Collins and Dickens set off for Cornwall exactly one month before *Great Expectations* began as a serial on 1 December in *All the Year Round*. Dickens's story pushed aside Lever's lackluster contribution, restored readers to the journal, and in the course of its thirty-six weekly numbers established itself as Dickens's most highly crafted novel. Moreover, it would deserve unqualified praise had he not listened to Bulwer Lytton. Before taking up the consequences of this intervention, however, we must consider the second portion of the novel's composition, the writing of the weekly numbers 6 through 36.

Composition of Numbers 6–36

By the end of the first week in January 1861 Dickens was more than halfway through the first part of the three stages of Pip's expectations. Comments in letters during this phase fall off. We can guess about some of the reasons. Over Christmas and throughout January, Dickens reports that he had been "unwell," disinclined to accept social engagements and perhaps even reluctant to write letters. Also ahead lay six public readings he was to give between 14 March and 18 April, commitments that required concentration no less demanding than work on his serial. "Chronically, when I have a book to write I give myself up to it," he commented to one friend, an explanation that accounts for his self-described state at this time as being "in actual bondage for weeks together" (*Letters* 9: 387).

This paucity of evidence, however, fails to undermine one crucial point: the ease with which Dickens continued his work. Once the creative impulse had descended, it stayed there. We can infer this from a letter to Forster tentatively dated "[?Mid-April 1861]." By that date, two thirds of the novel had been written—that is, up to the end of chapter 39, which closes the second stage of Pip's expectations—from which position Dickens paused to look back on what he had written and forward to the remaining third stage. This letter is crucial to the second part of my case and deserves to be cited in full:

It is a pity that the third portion cannot be read all at once, because its purpose would be much more apparent; and the pity is the greater, because the general turn and tone of the working out and winding up, will be away from all such things as they conventionally go. But what must be, must be. As to the planning out from week to week, nobody can imagine what the difficulty is, without trying it. But, as in all such cases, when it is overcome, the pleasure is proportionate. Two months more will see me through it, I trust. All the iron is in the fire; and I have 'only' to beat it out.   (*Letters* 9: 403)

Not surprisingly, the forecast proved accurate. Dickens was on top of the work despite some trouble with neuralgic face pains the following month. But by retreating to Dover on 23 May for some sea air and by working "like a Steam Engine" while comfortably located in a hotel, he maintained his pace (*Letters* 9: 421). On Tuesday, 11 June 1861, he announced triumphantly to W. C. Macready, "I have just finished my book of Great Expectations, and am the worse for wear. . . . But I hope that the book is a good book, and I have no doubt of very soon throwing off the little damage it has done me" (424).

Bulwer's Intervention

The novel's completion on 11 June 1861 defines its third and final compositional stage. During the third week of June, including three days spent as Bulwer's guest at Knebworth (15–17 June), Dickens listened to his objections to the final chapter, returned to London on the 18th for an engagement and then over the following weekend at Gad's Hill made the changes Bulwer urged.[7] Let us therefore shift our attention and assess the results of Bulwer's advice.[8] I shall confine my attention to two main points.

When Dickens expressed a preference for reading the third stage of Pip's expectations as a whole rather than in detached portions, he gave reasons we should consider. Reading it in its entirety, he argued, one would appreciate the novel's "general turn and tone." One would also understand more clearly how the narrative moved away from "all such things as they conventionally go" (9: 403). One question naturally arises: to what "things" does the novel react and which conventions does Dickens contest, as Pip brings to a close his meditation on the extraordinary events that shaped his life?

Two issues stand out, obvious enough to Victorian readers: the conventional use of a wedding to signal narrative closure, and the use of horror, thrills, and excitement to enliven the narrative pace.

Let us consider how the novel in its original form would have challenged the first by seeming to play into the convention and then contesting it, so as to emphasize Pip's single fate against the marriages that take place around him. "Halloa! Here's a church!" exclaims Wemmick. "Let's go in!" (453; ch. 55). And so, as Pip follows, wedding bells ring to unite Wemmick and Miss Skiffin in holy matrimony. They also sound for Herbert and Clara and soon after for Biddy and Joe. They even peal twice for Estella, once for her wedding to the hateful Bentley Drummle and then more happily at some indeterminate time when she remarries her doctor. Only Pip in the original version stands alone, a brave challenge to novelistic conventions, until Dickens capitulated at the urging of Bulwer, and left Estella if not Pip's intended bride, then certainly an eligible widow.

Fallout from Bulwer's advice blunts Dickens's original design in a second respect, and undercuts further his determination to steer the novel towards a less conventional conclusion. From *Oliver Twist* onwards, Dickens had mastered the art of infusing his stories with "sensational" elements, "loading" them with Newgate material just as thoroughly as Pip on one occasion loads his benefactor "with all the crimes in the [Newgate] Calendar" (338; ch. 40). So drenched in violence and sensation, the novel, remarked Margaret Oliphant writing in May 1862, stood out as the epitome of a new literary genre gone wrong. In her view, *Great Expectations* was packed with "Strange situations and fantastic predicaments," a work, she concluded, "overstrained" and devoid of "humanity," the quality in which Dickens "used to delight" (575).

Oliphant's charge merits a second look. Might she and others have written differently with the original ending before them? Would Oliphant have attacked the novel for its apparent preoccupation with exciting effects? Would she have found the voice of Pip's autobiographical narrative so bereft of "humanity" and unrelentingly "overstrained"? Would contemporary readers, as Forster noted, have complained about Estella's too hasty remarriage to Pip?[9] Hypothetical questions like these admit few useful answers; but had Dickens ignored Bulwer Lytton's objections, further considerations arise worth pursuing.

The first is that the original ending represents the logical conclusion to the story told by Dickens's elderly, unmarried hero; the second is that the revision violates the integrity of both the narrative and the autodiegetic narrator Dickens invented. For despite the change wrought by the addition of an extra chapter, Pip remains what Dickens can't alter: a contemplative and reflective elderly man. Better therefore to have left him, pensive and settled, a quiet observer disengaged from the world around him. Here is the story of a man who looks back on the crucial events that shaped him and who now successfully puts his responses to those early memorable days into a meaningful perspective. Instead, the revised version strikes a note of ambiguity and perhaps hesitancy; or for those who prefer, the distant sound of more wedding bells to signal a union that stands in contradiction to all Pip has learned and come to accept. For by reading *Great Expectations* as a novel hostage to prevailing conventions rather than as defiant and ready to engage and contest them, opening up space in the process, Oliphant and her fellow critics underestimate Dickens's achievement. Deaf to the novel's originality, they pay insufficient attention to the distinctive quality of Pip's voice and so fail to notice how his mode of telling constantly undercuts the sensational and matrimonial matter he recounts. Make the case for the superiority of the original ending, and you complete the work Dickens designed; accept the revised version and a flawed narrative remains, at odds with both the whole work and with the mood and outlook of the teller of the tale.

Attention to selective passages supports these claims, so let us take up one already cited in which Pip reflects in a typically proleptic moment about the consequences of the "two memorable days" that shaped his life. Looking back on them, he can view his encounter with the convict and then his introduction to Miss Havisham from a perspective denied him when they first happened within twelve months of each other. Only in the now of the narrating time (more about that to come) does Pip understand how events make their impact and shape one's life. In figurative language perhaps borrowed from Carlyle, iron and gold and thorns or flowers have formed a long chain that bound him, bringing past and present into an alignment he can understand.[10] The chain metaphor conveys a sense of constriction, of one's inability to break loose from the force field of events. But now, seeing those events from the past for what they were, Pip assumes a degree of control. "Pause you who read this," commands the elderly narrator, adopting the imperative voice of the Roman inscription, "*Siste Viator.*" He seems anxious to let us know that he can make sense of the past, extract wisdom from it, and take satisfaction in developing a perspective that confers a comforting sense of equipoise and achievement.

Throughout I have characterized Pip as both elderly and reflective. The second adjective is hardly controversial, but the first may raise questions. Asked to put an age to Pip at the end of the novel, most students, indeed most readers, in my experience, tentatively fix him in the vicinity of thirty-something. So when I call him "elderly" and suggest that he's at the close of his life, perhaps winding things down rather than standing on the threshold of marriage, I had better offer some proof. And if I go so far as to put the case that he is just over sixty, I need to bear in mind Mr. Jagger's maxim about the importance of taking everything on evidence.[11]

Three interlocking sets of data permit a reasonably accurate computation of Pip's age when he tells his story. From the telling of the events which constitute the main portion of Pip's narrative—from the Christmas eve on which he met his convict to the day Magwitch dies in Newgate Gaol—we can use dates and details supplied in the text to calculate how much time passes. Those events, furthermore, occur in late Hanoverian England and, in turn, are set off against the actual narration, which provides a third source for dating. By the time Pip sits down to write his memoirs, approximately three decades have passed, setting the telling in the early 1860s. Thus, if we integrate the historical setting with the chronology of the main events and take into account the amount of time that passes, we are in a position to determine Pip's age.

Several specific chronological markers chart the passage of events in Pip's life. His account begins on Christmas Eve and follows the consequences of the meeting with Magwitch as they unfold over the next twenty-hours. A break in the chronology introduces the second strand of the plot, resuming almost exactly a year later, when Pip is taken to Satis House. From that point, the narrative develops with greater fluidity, blending specific scenes temporally fixed with a more general sense of passing time. A week after the first encounter with Miss Havisham, Pip returns to Satis House, meets the toady relatives, and then fights Herbert. Seven days later, he visits again, and then so on to return at "every alternate day" at noon as he enters on "a regular occupation" of pushing Miss Havisham around the room and across the landing in her chair. Once these trips settle into a steady routine, he states: "I am now going to sum up a period of at least eight or ten months" (95; ch. 12).

At this point in the narrative the chronological markers thin out. Pip has a birthday and is then formally "bound" as an apprentice. Too big for the schoolroom run by Mr. Wopsle's great-aunt, he takes his books to the Old Battery and studies there. Birthdays pass, Pip makes occasional visits to Satis House, registering on one of them the absence of Estella, now sent "abroad," to be educated for a lady (ch. 15). His sister is attacked; the birthday guineas from Miss Havisham become "an annual custom," and then his world turns upside down. In the fourth year of his apprenticeship, he learns that he has come into a handsome property and is to be sent to London to become a gentleman.

Pip's re-tailoring follows much the same pattern in which the events of specific days alternate with more general narration. He falls into debt, his sister dies, "fine summer weather" comes again, Herbert turns 21, "eight months before me," Pip attains his majority, and still no word emerges about his benefactor (286; ch. 36). Two more years pass and then the story advances in the novel's most tightly knit sequence of events. In November, one week after Pip's twenty-third birthday, Magwitch returns. From that point and continuing beyond Magwitch's death in April the next year, days and months are registered with precision. Pip collapses after he is arrested for debt, he is nursed back to health by Joe, and, once strong enough, he returns to the forge to thank his brother-in-law for all he has done. "The June weather was delicious," Pip recalls, as he arrives back home just in time to congratulate Joe and Biddy on their marriage (477; ch. 58). Immediately afterwards, he bids them goodbye, sells his possessions and leaves England to join Herbert in Cairo. In September of the same year, he takes his position as "clerk to Clarriker and Co," and works for his living. "Many a year went round," he recalls, telling us that eventually he became a partner in the firm (480; ch. 58).

Setting out the "facts" above requires the assembly of relevant details provided in the text. The more challenging exercise calls for readers to construct a hypothetical time line charting the duration of the main action and then integrate it with events outside the story to which Pip refers in the course of his narration.[12] When does Pip sit down to write his memoirs? How old is he when he makes this decision? The answer to both questions hangs on inferences we can draw from the external events and historical developments outside the text. While most of these might be read as realistic ballast to ground Pip's extraordinary tale, they also help "fix" the late telling time of his narrative. Two important examples illustrate this point. Both feature prominently in Pip's account and suggest careful attention to detail. The first involves money; the second is a reference to the changing face of London.

Once Pip recovers from the shock of Magwitch's appearance at his London chambers, he has the presence of mind to apologize for speaking so harshly. He offers his visitor a drink and then more gently asks after the "messenger" Magwitch employed to deliver "the two one-pound notes" to the young child who had befriended him on the marshes. "I was a poor boy then," Pip explains, adding that to a poor boy "they were a little fortune." But now, having done well, he insists that he must be allowed to repay the gift. "You can put [the notes] to some other poor boy's use," Pip adds, taking out his purse.

Note how deliberately Dickens stages Pip's attempt to make amends. The absence of any words renders the action all the more dramatic. When Pip withdraws two one-pound notes, he records how each was "clean and new." He then carefully spreads them out in order to hand them over. Magwitch, with his eyes resting on Pip, lays the notes down, "one upon the other," folds them long-wise, gives them a little twist, sets fire to them at Pip's reading-lamp, and drops "the ashes into the tray" (318; ch. 39).

Educated Victorian readers with a good memory, their knowledge perhaps refreshed by a joint composition of W. H. Wills and Dickens published a decade ago in *Household Words*,[13] would have known the following: that one-pound notes measured 7 inches by 4 inches and therefore required unfolding before use; that they belonged to what Dickens termed "the small-note era," which began in 1797; and that they remained in circulation until guineas reappeared in 1817, following the resumption of payment in gold, which had been suspended by the Bank of England in response to demands caused by the war against France from 1793 to 1815. For a four-year period, one-pound notes continued to circulate, until a government Commission in 1819 recommended their withdrawal on account of the ease with which notes of small denomination were forged, a step that was finally taken in 1821. Not surprisingly, the condition of notes in circulation varied. Some quickly assumed a dirty appearance on account of their intimacy "with all the cattle markets in the country," like the two banknotes slipped to Pip at the Jolly Bargemen. Others, by contrast, remained "clean and new," like the two Pip withdrew from his purse. Perhaps their newness suggests that they were of recent issue (i.e., before 1821); but whether new or older and well preserved, the crucial point is this: if we take Pip at his word that they could be of use "to some other" poor boy, then we have a serviceable clue for the historical dating of Magwitch's reappearance.

Two topographical references with historical significance add support to the contention that Magwitch returns from Australia in November 1821 and further historicize the "great event" Pip characterizes as "the turning point" of his life (299; ch. 38). When Pip resumes the thread in the next chapter, he tells us that he was "three-and-twenty years of age," and that he and Herbert had more than a year ago left Barnard's Inn and moved to the Temple. A sign of upward mobility, yes. But we also need to note the retrospective frame through which their new residence is viewed. "Our chambers," Pip relates, "were in Garden-court, down by the river." On that particular night, they were buffeted by winds and heavy rain; and exposed to the storm, they had then a "lonely character," no longer present when he recounts the night in question. "Alterations," Pip explains, "have been made in that part of the Temple," that have entirely changed the setting and its unprotected character (312–13; ch. 39). The reference, Dickens's original readers would have understood, was to the gradual embankment of the Thames and the dramatic project initiated in 1860, which began at Waterloo Bridge and proceeded east towards the Temple and Blackfriars.

The second historical marker occurs six chapters later. By this point, Pip has come to accept his obligation to protect Magwitch. In consultation with Herbert Pocket and Mr. Wemmick, he commits himself to staging an elaborate escape, preparations for which require regular rowing practice in a boat he shares with Herbert and keeps on the Thames. Their excursions take them up or down the river, according to the tides. On several occasions, they row east beyond London Bridge. "It was Old London Bridge in those days," Pip comments, a notorious hazard to watermen and small craft on account of the rapid flow of water "at certain states of the tide" through the starlings supporting the arches of the old bridge (382; ch. 47). Work on a new bridge began in 1825 and was completed and opened in 1831. In the absence of any allusion to its replacement, one can reasonably date this reference as consistent with the year I am suggesting.

If we look to Pip's own language and conversation, we find yet another embedded clue. Though no talker equal to either Dr. Johnson or Samuel Taylor Coleridge, Pip comes across as a well-read man, one familiar with a wide range of authors. Among them we can distinguish Mary Shelley, Carlyle, Shakespeare, Milton, and other English poets. Familiar, too, are the Bible and *The Book of Common Prayer* and, most significantly, Charles Darwin. Early in life, Pip had set out to improve himself; and on the evidence of his talk, we can assume that this endeavor became a life-long practice. Just recently, for example, he had come across Darwin's *On the Origin of Species* (1859), whose language he echoes in the opening chapter when he refers to how his five little brothers, all less well suited to surviving than he, had given up "trying to get a living, exceedingly early in that universal struggle." Pip, by contrast, had the will to work "pretty hard" and ultimately, to "do well."

To be familiar with Darwin's theory of natural selection, to use Darwinian phrases and terms in circulation at the time of the novel's serial publication, and to refer to topographical changes simultaneously occurring in London lead to a single conclusion: Pip's writing time is that of the moment. Let us assume then that Dickens conceived the writing time as taking place around 1860, what implications arise for the novel as a whole?

The consequences, I suggest are obvious and reinforce the logic of the original ending, in which the elderly, reflective narrator steps back from telling his story, having come to terms with all that has happened. In that frame of mind, he can relate calmly how he had heard of Estella's unhappiness, of her separation from her husband, possible now on account of the Matrimonial Causes Act of 1857, of Drummle's death—the result of his ill-treating a horse—and of her subsequently remarrying the local doctor who had attended Drummle and witnessed his abuse of Estella. Information also came to Pip that the doctor wasn't rich and that he and Estella "lived on her personal fortune." Visiting England yet again, Pip is summoned to her carriage while walking "along Piccadilly." On one of London's great thoroughfares, the two look at each other "sadly enough." Estella extends her hand and asks permission to kiss the child that accompanies Pip, assuming it to be his. A proxy kiss, perhaps; but certainly a deeply felt gesture. From the touch of her hand and the expression on her face, Pip is given to understand that she now knows how Pip felt in his heart about her. Scant consolation, one might want to add. But from Pip's perspective, his closing words record how "very glad afterwards" he was to have had that interview.

Forster explains in his comment on the novel that the change Dickens made to the ending required the addition of a single chapter. Pip's original "eleven years" become "eight," and further slight adjustments in the wording proved necessary. Dickens weakened Pip's "I am sure and certain," in response to Biddy's question about whether or not he frets for Estella to a hesitant "O no—I think not,'' after which follows a wholly different sequence of events as Pip reveals his secret intention to visit the site of the old house "*that evening*, alone, for her sake. Yes, even so, For Estella's sake'' [my emphasis]. Accordingly, Pip sets off "with an abundance of time'' at his disposal on account of the customary "early dinner-hour at Joe's.'' He walks the four or so miles that separate the forge from the market town where Miss Havisham used to live, loitering on the way "to look at old objects and to think of old times.'' The day, he records, had quite declined by the time he reached his destination. But he had enough light to see that the old house and the brewery and its adjacent buildings had gone. And so the moon comes out, the stars start to shine, and he beholds "a solitary figure'' in the ruins of the garden.

Let us put aside discussion of the Miltonic echoes and pretty touches about rising mists that sustain readers through this totally re-visioned ending and return to one seemingly inconspicuous adverbial phrase in the new exchange with Biddy: "that evening.'' Just when was *that evening* in December? According to the time scheme I have proposed, originally eleven years lapsed since Pip left England for work abroad. Knock off three and reduce the total to "eight'' and we can conclude that the action takes place towards the close of 1829, a hypothetical dating that makes both Pip and Estella, who are roughly coevals, about 32. Fine, one might say, a fitting age for the two to meet again and resume their relationship on a firmer footing.

And so the questions inevitably follow. Do they marry? Do they remain "friends apart''? Does Pip "see'' or not see "the shadow of no parting from her''?[14] For a narrator as informative and as scrupulous an observer as he is, isn't he overlooking something rather crucial? Is he trying to convince us of his not knowing what happened after an interval of another thirty years? Such questions are as awkward as they are futile, but they originate in a common source: a revised ending grafted onto a narrative whose chronology and retrospective telling time had been decided upon right from the novel's inception and opening chapter. Committed to using the figure of an older narrator looking back from a distant present, Dickens can't undo his age, no matter how hard and how skillfully he attempts to unpick the threads he has woven so consistently and so thoroughly into the story.

It is the creation of this gap, therefore, that represents the real narrative flaw in the revised ending, rather than the ambiguity Dickens built into his revision. Had the original stood, "the drift'' and consistency with the "natural working out'' Forster detected would have prevailed, leaving in place a more subversive definition of success. Instead, the revised Pip clings resolutely to the "poor dream'' that defined his earlier life and equivocates with Biddy when she asks if he still frets for Estella, just before setting off "secretly'' to revisit "the old site . . . for her sake.'' By way of calling attention to his continued indebtedness to her, Pip repeats: "Yes even so. For Estella's

sake." Equally important and no less a casualty of the revision is the fact
that these words negate all he had earlier said about the need to renounce
false reasons for wanting to make himself "uncommon" and strive for goals
the novel thoroughly discredits.

By contrast, the teller of the original tale can be seen to have accepted
with grace the humble but reputable lot of a clerk and, later, a partner. For
with respect to what Pip accomplishes in this capacity, we should pay tribute
to his achievements by taking him at his word. We know that he has the
ability to improve and do well. We know he can apply himself to his books
and learn, a point made when he flourishes under the benign tutelage of
Herbert's father. We know that he reads widely, observes carefully and accu-
rately, has an excellent memory, a head for figures, and the capacity to extract
himself from self-made snares. One might speculate that the man with an
unerring eye for boyish delusion, so apparent in the ironical assessments of
his former self, speaks now as a mature clerk. Gone is the self-described
"young Knight of romance" destined to marry "the Princess," long since
replaced by a reliable witness, one who can be trusted with "real" books.
Clearly, Herbert Pocket and Clarriker think so and share confidence in their
new employee. He has only to work for four months before he is given his
"first undivided responsibility," assumed when Herbert returns to England
to marry Clara, leaving Pip "in sole charge of the Eastern Branch." Nothing
catastrophic happened in Herbert's absence. But years—"many" years—go
round before Pip eventually becomes "a partner in the House." As this sober,
industrious and reliable chronicler records, in the course of telling his own
story, once resident in Cairo he assumes a productive role with his fellows.
Clarriker, Pocket, and Pirrip never becomes "a great House," nor does the
House make "mints of money." Instead all three partners attain a respectable
level of success, not "grand," but as owners of a limited company they
merit "a good name," work for their profits, and eventually do "very well"
(ch. 58).

Unquestionably one of them enjoys "strange power of speech" evident in
the hold Pip exercises when he tells his tale. But the "partner" to whom this
task falls presumably takes it on in the spirit of a faithful recorder, an attitude
commensurate with his clerkly duties. Settled in life rather than driven "from
land to land" like Coleridge's Ancient Mariner, forced to repeat his "ghastly
tale" at whatever "uncertain hour" happens to dawn, Pip sits down with a
good supply of pens, plenty of paper, and in a reflective mood. True to his
clerkly calling, he will be thorough and detailed. No brief memoir "short
and handy" like Magwitch's life story, his tale will review everything of
consequence that happened and provide a full account, exciting, memorable,
sensational, and moving. But, most importantly, the narrative of his written
memory is one purged of the false fancy and hope that generated the

"wretched hankerings after money and gentility" that so nearly ruined his life. Looking back, educated, well read, clerk, partner, and sound business man, Philip Pirrip emerges as one able to " 'hold his own' with the average of young men in prosperous circumstances," the fulfillment of one of the more benign links in the chain that shaped his life (197; ch. 24)—no luminary or "Eminent Author" (like David Copperfield), destined to be famous and caressed and attentive to "the roar of many voices, not indifferent" to him as he travelled on. Without a wife to stand beside him in "beautiful serenity," ready to point "upward!" when realities melt like shadows and death summons (*David Copperfield*, ch. 64). Of course not. No such blessing are in store for the clerk. As instinct told Dickens right from the start: he had fallen into "no unconscious repetitions" of *David Copperfield* when he sat down to write the opening numbers of *Great Expectations*.[15] To be sure, Dickens told Forster how reading the former again "the other day," he was affected "to a degree you would hardly believe." No less can be said of the impact of Pip's original account of the memorable days he endured as a child and that made him what he was. Submit yourself to the spell of Dickens's initial "grotesque tragi-comic conception" and you will reach a similar conclusion.

NOTES

1. See letters to Collins, Bulwer, and Forster, in *Letters*: 9: 428–29; 432–33.
2. The best account of the extensive literature about the ending is Edgar Rosenberg's witty survey, "Putting an End to *Great Expectations*," in his Norton edition of the novel (491–527). "Blasphemous as the suggestion may sound," he comments, "just maybe those of us who have written on the subject have rather inflated its importance: had Dickens written one ending only—either one—it wouldn't have occurred to us to take issue with it. Had he stuck with the unhappy ending, we should all have bought the unhappy ending . . . and had he all along gone for the happy ending, we might have been equally happy. But now that this double monster has affronted a hundred operatives, clairvoyants after the fact, prophets of hindsight, it would be cowardice to run from it" (491).
3. In "Textual Brief[s]" for the two endings, Rosenberg argues that the textual scholar must examine six rather than two and fit his conclusions into one of three slots: support for the first ending, the second ending or "the neither nors, who argue that Dickens botched both endings about equally" (500–18).
4. One early exception is Robert B. Partlow, Jr., who raises important questions about the narrator's position in relation to the events he describes and his position as he is "now." Partlow sees Pip as "a moderately successful, middle-aged businessman, a *petit bourgois*," who now, mature, sober, industrious, and saddened, is "aware of his own limitations, and possessed of a certain calm wisdom" (123). Partlow, however, makes no attempt to define the "now," explore fissures

in the narrative opened by the changed ending, or argue for one or the other final version.

5. That is, in 31 weekly installments. In fact, *Great Expectations* overran that projected total by 5.

6. One possible concern might have been have been the point of view of each. Both first-person narrators recount the hero's life in the manner of the traditional bildungsroman novel, but *Great Expectations* differs substantially in the manner of telling. In *David Copperfield*, the "retrospects" appear as single chapters, each announced somewhat mechanically. See the sixth, fourteenth, seventeenth, and final double number. No such formulaic writing characterizes Pip's telling, which moves effortlessly throughout the entire story, oscillating back and forth between the "then" of the events described and the "now" of their telling. I take this point up in more detail later in the essay. The two novels, however, are not without parallels, a point convincingly made by E. Pearlman.

7. Letters to Bulwer, Collins, and Forster supply details and dates that make possible the reconstruction of this sequence. See *Letters* 9: 423, 428–29, and 432–33.

8. No record exists of Bulwer's objections. All we know is that, in Dickens's own words, Bulwer "supported his views with such good reasons" that Dickens resolved to make the change (*Letters* 9: 433). See, also, Rosenberg, "A Note on Bulwer's Meddling" (518–27).

9. Forster refers to such objections being raised among readers, "not unfairly to the too great speed with which the heroine, after being married [to Drummle], reclaimed and widowed, is in a page or two again made love to [by Pip], and remarried by the hero" (bk. 9, ch. 3). His apparent agreement with the justice of this observation, which is based on the assumption that Victorian mourning conventions have been breached by Estella's failure to wait for years before even contemplating marriage, seems to explain his decision to include the first ending in his biography. "This summary proceeding," Forster writes, "was not originally intended," a claim he proved by disclosing how Dickens originally ended the novel and defending him against any such impressions of a lapse in taste. Less convincing, in my view, is the speculation that Forster felt overlooked: Dickens bowed to Bulwer's objections without consulting him, and so in retaliation, he backed up his own preference for the original by disclosing its existence and publishing it.

10. Compare Carlyle's "Wondrous truly are the bonds that unite us one and all; whether by the soft binding of Love, or the iron chain of Necessity, as we like to choose it" (*Sartor Resartus*, ch. 7, "Organic Filaments").

11. I am not alone in arguing for an "older" Pip, though closer definitions of the adjective would help. A. L. French sees Pip as "fifty-four, well into a futile and celibate middle age" (360), an estimate supported by Jerome Meckier (1992: 185; 1993: 50) and by Rosenberg, who opts for a Pip "at least in his mid-fifties" (503).

12. For a detailed exposition, see my Appendix One, "The Sequence of Events in Pip's Narrative," in *The Companion* (422–34). The novel's internal chronology has also been scrutinized by Mary Edminson, (30–43), Anny Sadrin (30–43), and Jerome Meckier in a detailed study (1992).

13. For the size of notes, see Johnson (''Bank Notes English A–F'').

14. The last line of the revised ending has generated much vexed energy. In the serial version published in August 1861, Dickens wrote: ''I saw the shadow of no parting from her.'' Slightly altered to ''I saw no shadow of another parting from her'' for the 1862 Library edition, this reading was allowed to stand in the Charles Dickens Edition six years later and presumably reflected Dickens's final choice. Most modern editions, often lacking any clear or persuasive explanation by the editor, retain the earlier ''exit'' line.

15. For a contrary view, see Pearlman, who argues that ''the numerous repetitions of the one novel in the other'' represent unconscious recapitulations of specific experiences. ''Just as *David Copperfield* explores, in its most affecting chapters, the miseries of sudden descents into the working class, so *Great Expectations* explores the exact opposite: the moral perils of a miraculous rise in social status'' (191).

WORKS CITED

Carlyle, Thomas. *Sartor Resartus*. Ed. Kerry McSweeney and Peter Sabor. Oxford: Oxford University Press, 1987.

Dickens, Charles. *Great Expectations*. London: Penguin, 1996.

———. *The Letters of Charles Dickens*. Vol. 9: 1859–1861. Ed. Graham Storey. The Pilgrim Edition. Oxford: Clarendon, 1997.

Edminson, Mary. ''The Date of the Action in *Great Expectations*.'' *Nineteenth Century Fiction* 13 (1958): 22–35.

Forster, John. *The Life of Charles Dickens*. 2 vols. Ed. A. J. Hoppé. London: Dent, 1966.

French, A. L. ''Old Pip: The Ending of *Great Expectations*.'' *Essays in Criticism* 29 (1979): 357–60.

Johnson, John. ''Bank Notes English A–F.'' *John Johnson Collection: Catalogue of Printed Ephemera*. Bodleian Library, Oxford.

Meckier, Jerome. ''Charles Dickens's *Great Expectations*: A Defense of the Second Ending.'' *Studies in the Novel* 25 (1993): 28–58.

———. ''Dating the Action in *Great Expectations*: A New Chronology.'' *Dickens Studies Annual* 21 (1992): 157–94.

[Oliphant, Margaret]. ''Sensation Novels.'' *Blackwood's Edinburgh Magazine* 91 (May 1862): 564–84.

Paroissien, David. *The Companion to "Great Expectations."* Mountfield, UK: Helm Information, 2000.

Partlow, Robert B., Jr. "The Moving I: A Study of the Point of View in *Great Expectations.*" *College English* 33 (1961): 122–31.

Pearlman, E. "Inversions in *Great Expectations.*" *Dickens Studies Annual* 7 (1978): 190–202, 259–60.

Rosenberg, Edgar, ed. *Great Expectations.* New York: Norton, 1999.

Sadrin, Anny. *Great Expectations.* London: Unwin Hyman, 1988.

Wills, W. H., and Charles Dickens. "Two Chapters on Bank Note Forgeries, ii." *Household Words* (10 Aug. 1850): 615–20.

The Mudworm's Bower and Other Metropastoral Spaces: Novelization and Clashing Chronotopes in *Our Mutual Friend*

David Wilkes

Bakhtinian novelization transforms traditional pastoral space into citi-fied enclaves where moral "fastening down" occurs in the form of strategic character testing, pedagogical lessons, and literal expulsion. Shepherd-teachers and faithful servants square off with rogues and imposters who attempt to subvert the "virtues of shelter" by using various forms of theatricality. Hexam's windmill, Boffin's Bower, The Six Jolly Fellowship-Porters, Riah's rooftop garden, The Wren's Nest, and the reclaimed Harmony Bower all function as "organizing centers" where idyllic and theatrical chronotopes vie for primacy.

"But come! Let's have a look at your garden on the tiles, before I go!"
—Fascination Fledgeby, *OMF* (278; bk. 3, ch. 5)

"Pastoral, like all other literary forms, was an urban invention."
—Harold Bloom, *Bloom's Literary Guide to London* (xi)

"Why is CHARLES DICKENS like one of *Little Bopeep's* sheep?
Because he's left his 'tale' behind him."
—*Punch*, December 7, 1867 (231)

On May 28, 1859, *All the Year Round* swallowed up *Household Words* on its way to becoming "a phenomenal success" (E. Johnson 946). Dickens, of course, had engineered the takeover to the dismay of Bradbury and Evans and to the delight of Chapman and Hall, who were "bent on giving Dickens anything he wanted" in order to have the prolific author back in their literary camp after a fifteen-year hiatus (943). In the months and years that followed, Dickens composed weekly installments for both *A Tale of Two Cities* (1859) and *Great Expectations* (1860–1861) while managing to write "a series of personal essays" that would soon become the 1861 edition of *The Uncommercial Traveler* (963). Add to this his whirlwind reading tours, his scandalous separation from Catherine, his incessant letter-writing, his ongoing task of finding the next serial for *AYR*, his declining health, and his strained relationships, and it is no wonder that the thinly veiled autobiographical voice in Dickens's fictive travelogue longs for "complete solitude and uninterrupted meditation" ("Arcadian London," *The Uncommercial Traveler* 159).[1] What's remarkable, however, is where he finds his respite: "I have taken a lodging for six weeks in the most unfrequented part of England—in a word, in London." Rather than escaping to the seashore or the countryside, the narrator chooses a room in "my own hatter's" shop on Bond Street[2] in the West End (159):

> The simple character of my life and the calm nature of the scenes by which I am surrounded, occasion me to rise early. I go forth in my slippers, and promenade the pavement. It is pastoral to feel the freshness of the air in the uninhabited town, and to appreciate the shepherdess character of the few milk-women who purvey so little milk that it would be worth nobody's while to adulterate it, if anybody were left to undertake the task. On the crowded sea-shore, the great demand for milk, combined with the strong local temptation of chalk, would betray itself in the lowered quality of the article. In Arcadian London I derive it from the cow. The Arcadian simplicity of the metropolis altogether, and the primitive ways into which it has fallen in this autumnal Golden Age, make it entirely new to me. Within a few hundred yards of my retreat, is the house of a friend who maintains a most sumptuous butler. ("Arcadian London" 160)

Like the green squares and parks that surround the hatter's shop in London, pastoral markers abound in this description of nineteenth-century urban life (see fig. 1). The "freshness of the air," the "calm nature of the scene," the "shepherdess character of the few milk-women," and the pervading "tranquility" of the "happy Golden Age" (168) are mixed with metropolitan pavement, commerce, domestic service, and a few vice-ridden descriptors such as "adulterate," "temptation," "demand," and "betray." In other words, Dickens collapses Arcade and Arcadia into one ideographic space[3] that becomes "entirely new" to the weary traveler (160).

To better understand the significance of this metropastoral space, we turn briefly to Bakhtin, whose discourse theory foregrounds the novel's ability to

Fig. 1. "London Out of Town." *Punch* 11 (1846): 42.

consume and reformulate weaker genres, resulting in "parodic styliza-
tion[s]" that engender "laughter, irony, humor, elements of self-parody and
... semantic open-endedness" (7), and whose theory of the time-place chronotope allows us to trace the "bucolic-pastoral-idyllic chronotope" (103)
from its origin in the "lyric-epic" to its transvaluation in the Victorian novel.
Since all novels contain a plethora of chronotopes, and all chronotopes seek
to "replace ... oppose ... contradict ... envelope or dominate" one another
(252), it is not surprising that the "idyllic chronotope" (224) squares off
with the "chronotope of theatrical space" (163) almost immediately in *Our
Mutual Friend*. This latter chronotope can also linked to the "chronotope of
the public square" (Bakhtin 161). In her article on the "modern urban
novel," Hana Wirth-Nesher states that "most of the action in these fictional
worlds takes place in spaces that fuse public and private, that are uneasily
indeterminate: coffee houses, theatres, museums, pubs, restaurants, hotels
and shops" (58). To a degree, *Our Mutual Friend*'s metropastoralism anticipates this modern conflation of public and private space, as does Michel
Foucault's nineteenth century "heterotopia"—a real place and "counter-
site" that represents, contests, and inverts all other sites, including utopias,
while extending its interior into the public domain and being "nurtured by
the hidden presence of the sacred" past (23–24). In other words, it is grounded
in medieval emplacement as it extends itself into the postmodern "sites"
of the future. Similarly, Bakhtin's idyllic chronotope promotes "an organic
fastening down, a grafting of life and its events to a place, to a familiar
territory with all its nooks and crannies" thus affirming "life's basic realities" which include "labor, food and drink, [and individual] stages of
growth" (Bakhtin 225). All the while, the theatrical chronotope seeks to
topple such hegemonic stability. Using street-smart rogues[4] who wear masks,
practice "cheerful deceit" (162), and spy on others, the theatrical chronotope
attempts to displace the "virtues of shelter" (Bachelard 12) by using the
vices of self-gratification.

Clashing chronotopes subsequently create the "organizing centers for the
fundamental events of the novel" (Bakhtin 250). Like knots "tied and un-
tied" along the "*temporal sequence*" of the storyline (113), chronotopes
bind spatial and temporal markers into "one carefully thought-out, concrete
whole" (84), whether the knot be a complete setting or a single image.[5]
"Time, as it were, thickens, takes on flesh" (84). Idyllic time is especially
"dense and fragrant ... like honey" (103) and manifests itself in a variety
of reformulated natural rhythms (128).[6] Bucolic space is equally novelized,
with its indicators ranging from florid carpets to sheep-like patrons, hyacinth-
root lamps, and flower box gardens set in a "wilderness of dowager old
chimneys" (*OMF* 279; bk. 2, ch. 5). In fact, *Our Mutual Friend* is full of
chronotopic knots. The very first page of the novel finds Gaffer Hexam carefully studying "every little race and eddy" (i.e., every swirling knot of river

current) between the Southwark and London Bridges. There is the "knotted" interior of the Hexams' dilapidated windmill (21; bk. 1, ch. 3), the "gnarled and riven" knots of the Six Jolly Fellowship-Porters (61; bk. 1, ch. 6), the "knotty figure" (491; bk. 3, ch. 7) of Silas Wegg and his wooden leg, the homonymic Noddy Boffin with his "knotted stick" (47; bk. 1, ch. 5), the "knot of . . . amphibious human creatures" that gather around the causeway near the river's edge (75; bk. 1, ch. 6), the "slip-knot" around Gaffer's lifeless neck (174; bk. 1, ch. 14), the "ragged knot" in Pleasant Riderhood's disheveled hair (352; bk. 2, ch. 12), and the *un*knotted cascade of Jenny Wren's "golden bower" (439; bk. 3, ch. 2). All of these fastenings and unfastenings are chronotopic, as are the larger knots in Dickens's storyline, those Gordian places where the transformational bindings are even more complex; where shepherd-teachers guide their pupils from the "transitory past" into the "immediate future . . . in which real problems must be solved and in which real becoming takes place" (Morson and Emerson 420–21); where traditional game-playing re-emerges as strategic character-testing (i.e., as a *con*-test) in which the rogue's cony-catching trick is pitted against the faithful servant's "pious fraud" (*OMF* 771; bk. 4, ch. 13), both of which rely on "pastoral masking" and "bucolic impersonation" (Alpers 75, 141); and where the locus amoenus (or pleasant place) resurfaces as the locus moralis (or ethical place) in order to reconfigure the boundaries of self-definition, familial obligation, and interclass marriage.

I

Opening as it does on the Thames River, *Our Mutual Friend* posits two significant metropastoral elements: the rogue's presence in the theatrical chronotope and the traceable "echo" (Morson and Emerson 374) of the bucolic-pastoral-idyllic chronotope issuing, in this case, from Alexander Pope's "Four Pastorals" where the brackish water and "riparian habitation" of the Thames (Ackroyd, *Thames* 340) provide a traditional set of pre-novelized pastoral markers in "Spring"[7]:

> Fair Thames, flow gently from thy sacred spring,
> While on thy banks Sicilian Muses sing;
> Let vernal airs through trembling osiers play,
> And Albion's cliffs resound the rural lay.   (1; st. 1)[8]

Willow trees, like Aeolian harps, sing with rustic ballads that echo off Albion's cliffs. The Thames is even more idyllic than the Pactolus and Po Rivers, declares Strephon:

O'er golden sands let rich Pactolus flow,
And trees weep amber on the banks of Po;
Blest Thames's shores the brightest beauties yield,
Feed here, my lambs, I'll seek no distant field.   (3; st. 12)

The shepherd's reference to Pactolus also makes a semantic connection with the Greek river-god, Paktolos, whose mixed morphology includes "a bull-horned man with the body of a serpentine-fish" (Atsma, "Potamoi"). River-shepherd meets mythological fish-man (i.e., fisherman) in this profile, just as it does in Jacopo Sannazaro's *Piscatorial Eclogues* where another hybridized shepherd inhabits a "transformed body" that "beat the foaming surface [of the sea] with forked tail" (161).[9] In Nonnos's fifth-century epic *Dionysiaca*, Pactolus appears as both a river god and a personified pastoral setting:

Pactolus glad to gratify . . . murmured as he poured the goldsowing water upon the purple sands, and the gilded fish went swimming in wealthy soundings where the rich ore lay deep. Playful Satyrs lifted their heels in air, and tumbled plunging headover into the river. . . . then [Seilenos] trod his two feet firmly into the glittering sand hunting for good nuggets of ore in the river.
                                                                    (339; bk. 10)

Here the fluid edge of the pastoral's "goldsowing water" expands to include King Midas and his golden touch:

Desperate, Midas pleaded to Dionysus for help. Dionysus instructed Midas to bathe in the headwaters of the Pactolus River, and the wish would be washed away. Midas went to the river, and as soon as he touched the water, the river carried away the golden touch. The gold settled in the sands of the Pactolus River.   (Baldwin)

The shimmering river with its riparian zones and fishermen-shepherds all resurface as novelized hybrids in the opening chapter of *Our Mutual Friend*. The Thames and its urbanized shoreline provide the metropastoral context; Gaffer appears as a nocturnal shepherd of the dead whose "dirty and disreputable" little boat is piloted by his cloaked accomplice, daughter Lizzie, who turns out to be a disguised bucolic maiden with calloused hands; the gold dust that once lined the bottom of the sylvan river becomes the cold hard cash lining the wet pockets of suicides and murder victims (their bodies wandering like lost sheep beneath the murky surface of the river); violence replaces riparian tranquility; and the personal grief of pastoral elegy resurfaces as an impersonal list of names found in the lawmen's "Book of the Dead" (Ackroyd, *Thames* 381).

To use the "dead as a resource" (Baumgarten 65) is again to underscore the novel's metropastoralism. Gaffer drives this point home when he reminds Lizzie that finding bodies is "your living" as well:

As if it wasn't meat and drink to you! . . . How can you be so thankless to your best friend, Lizzie? The very fire that warmed you when you were a baby was picked out of the river alongside the coal barges. The very basket that you slept in, the tide washed ashore. The very rockers that I put it upon to make a cradle of it, I cut out of a piece of wood that drifted from some ship or another.
(3; bk. 1, ch. 1)

First asserting that the Thames is Lizzie's "best friend," Gaffer goes on to imply that the river is also her surrogate mother. Yet it holds no such value for Lizzie (or her brother, Charley):

"It's my belief you hate the sight of the very river."
"I—I don't like it, father."   (3; bk. 1, ch. 1)

In rejecting her father's transvaluation, Lizzie marks him as a theatrical rogue who fails to own up to his sordid vocation[10] and absentee parenting,[11] as if scavenged coal and washed-up baskets were acceptable substitutes for the safety and comfort of the shepherd himself. Even Hexam's nickname blows the etymological whistle on his true identity[12]: "gaffer" is initially defined as an "elderly rustic" thus connecting Hexam with Theocritus's aged fisherman, Virgil's Menalcas, and Shakespeare's Corin; the verb "to gaff" means "to seize or strike (a fish)" with a barbed spear or "to draw out [a body?]" with an iron hook," thus referencing the violence of his grim occupation; as a bit of nineteenth-century slang, "a gaff" denotes "the low class of [the] theatre or music-hall," thus associating Gaffer with the theatrical chronotope[13]; and, more recently, the verb has come to mean "deceive or trick; to make (a game or device) crooked or dishonest"—a gloss that foregrounds Gaffer's situational ethics. By redefining theft as a recovery operation, the bird of prey rationalizes his "unassailable position" as a shepherd of the dead:

"Has a dead man any use for money? Is it possible for a dead man to have money? What world does a dead man belong to? T'other world. What world does money belong to? This world. How can money be a corpse's? Can a corpse own it, want it, spend it, claim it, miss it? Don't try to go confounding the rights and wrongs of things in that way."   (4–5; bk. 1, ch. 1)

Gaffer has indeed borrowed from maritime salvage to create his own brand of recovery ethics. By reclassifying dead bodies as lost property, he not only circumvents the "no remuneration for the salvage of dead persons" clause and sidesteps the piracy label; he also asserts his de facto "right to reward" for the time, effort, and skill needed, along with the risk incurred, to retrieve his sunken treasure ("Salvage").[14] This moral "sleight of hand" is consistent with the rogue's propensity to mask disreputable practices.

Moving from the river to its riparian habitation, we find Gaffer's "dreary old house that had once been a working windmill" (348; bk. 2, ch. 11). The dilapidated domicile is the first of several metropastoral enclosures to appear in *Our Mutual Friend*:

> There was a rotten wart of wood upon its forehead that seemed to indicate where the sails had been. . . . [Inside was] a low circular room, where a man stood before a red fire, looking down into it, and a girl sat engaged in needle-work. The fire was in a rusty brazier, not fitted to the hearth; and a common lamp, shaped like a hyacinth-root, smoked and flared in the neck of a stone bottle on the table. There was a wooden bunk or berth in a corner, and in another corner a wooden stair leading above—so clumsy and steep that it was little better than a ladder. Two or three old sculls and oars stood against the wall, and against another part of the wall was a small dresser, making a spare show of the commonest articles of crockery and cooking-vessels. The roof of the room was not plastered, but was formed of the flooring of the room above. This, being very old, knotted, seamed, and beamed, gave a lowering aspect to the chamber; and roof, and walls, and floor, alike abounding in old smears of flour, red-lead (or some such stain which it had probably acquired in warehous-ing), and damp, alike had a look of decomposition.   (21; bk. 1, ch. 3)

Gaston Bachelard reads the windmill as a transcendent enclave capable of moving the dreamer toward both the simple security of the hut (50) and the imaginative flight of the ''cosmic house''(51):

> We should find ourselves indulging in similar daydreams if we started musing under the cone-shaped roof of a windmill. We should sense its terrestrial nature, and imagine it to be a primitive hut stuck together with mud, firmly set on the ground in order to resist the wind. Then, in an immense synthesis, we should dream at the same time of a winged house that whines at the slightest breeze and refines the energies of the wind.   (64)

Yet Gaffer's windmill is stripped of its sails and left standing like a defeated giant from *Don Quixote*. The structure is further novelized into a decrepit river creature with a ''rotten wart'' on its forehead—the stump of a broken horn perhaps like that which belongs to Achelous, ''the god of the largest freshwater river in Greece [and] . . . the god of freshwater in general,'' whose horn is savagely torn from his head during a wrestling match with Heracles (Atsma, ''Akheloios''). Later on in the myth, the bony protuberance changes into a cornucopia thus converting loss into plenitude. Like Heracles, the novel overpowers myth and pastoral poetry in order to transform them both into metropastoral fiction. The windmill's ''low circular room'' with its ''lowering aspect,'' its ''knotted'' ceiling, its ''wooden bunk or berth'' (suggesting both the shoreline and the river), as well as its small fire and common cooking utensils, all reference interiors found in traditional pastoral poetry. In Theocri-tus, we find quaint farms with ''couches of fragrant reeds and fresh-cut vine leaves'' (*Idyll* 7.86), caves with ''sugary grapes'' and flowing fresh water

(11.92), and country places filled with "old wine" and savory roasted food (14.98). In Virgil, there are humble huts (*Eclogue* 2.29), caves "dappled by a woodland vine's rare-grape cluster" (5.63), caves of rest (6.14), caves situated near the river (9.99), and a wooden structure that reads like a working home: "Here's hearth and pitch-pine billets, here's a roaring fire / Ever alight, and doorposts black with ingrained soot" (7.49–50). The windmill's "clumsy and steep" wooden stairs draw attention to the house's "verticality," that is, to "the rationality of the roof [and] to the irrationality of the cellar" (Bachelard 17–18).

Gaffer's two-room tower initially appears to be both an attic and a cellar. While the former signifies the pleasure and sanctuary of "bare rafters" where "we participate in the carpenter's solid geometry" (18), the latter is "the *dark entity* of the house that partakes of the subterranean forces" (19, 20); it's where irrational fear is coupled with criminality. Sadly, Lizzie and Charley never experience the attic's safety and refuge. Sunk by "its own weight" into the Thames riverbank (*OMF* 21; bk. 1, ch. 1), the windmill has all the markings of the irrational cellar: it is dark, terrestrial, and plastered with "BODY FOUND" handbills—the visual reminders of "buried madness" and "walled-in tragedy" that exploit the "fears . . . inherent to the dual nature of both man and house" (Bachelard 20). As a chronotopic rogue, Gaffer knows the place by heart:

> "This is him as had a nasty cut over the eye. This is them two young sisters what tied themselves together with a handkecher. This is the drunken old chap, in a pair of list slippers and a nightcap, wot had offered . . . to make a hole in the water for a quartern of rum stood aforehand, and kept to his word for the first and last time in his life. They pretty well papers the room, you see; but I know 'em all. I'm scholar enough!"   (*OMF* 22; bk. 1, ch. 3)

When Eugene Wrayburn asks Gaffer if he has found all the bodies himself, the water-rat instinctively responds with a dodge: "And what might *your* name be, now?" Wrayburn persists, only to have Gaffer put on a different rhetorical disguise: "I answer you, simply, most on 'em." To the question, "Do you suppose there has been much violence and robbery, beforehand, among these cases?" Gaffer replies with feigned indifference: "I don't suppose at all about it. . . . I ain't one of the supposing sort. If you'd got your living to haul out of the river every day of your life, you mightn't be much given to supposing" (23; bk. 1, ch. 3). In reality, Hexam is more than "scholar enough" when it comes to reading dead bodies-as-texts, both in and out of the water. He knows the mindset and nomenclature of his occupation and has the insignia to prove it, for inside his windmill are several "old sculls" and a prominent "red-lead" stain. Like piratical tibias, the crossed sculls reference the Jolly Roger while the red-lead stain is reminiscent of the "rotten stain'' outlining ''a muffled human form'' in the bottom of Gaffer's boat (2; bk. 1, ch. 1).

In fact, Hexam belongs to the brotherhood of body scavengers as one of several ''cut-throat Shepherds'' of the dead (155; bk. 1, ch. 12). As with other clandestine groups, including Dickens's own 'Prentice Knights/United Bulldogs from *Barnaby Rudge*, The Order of the Sculls and Stains has its own codes and secrets: ''These meetings of the member-rats parody to absurdity the '*insignia* of terror' said by *The Annual Register, 1838* to characterize the nocturnal meetings of trade unions: 'battle-axes, drawn swords, [and] skeletons' become a 'rusty blunderbuss,' a 'very ancient saber,' and a 'chair of state, cheerfully ornamented with a couple of skulls' '' (qtd. in Pionke 38). Under the metamorphic pressure of the novel, Gaffer's underclass brotherhood chooses rigor mortis over the intellectual rigor of Phi Beta Kappa and the safeguarding of national treasures. According to one critic, Dickens cites ''individual wrong-doing'' as the source of such secret societies (Pionke 40).[15] Thus, it is stealing from the dead that binds Jesse ''Gaffer'' Hexam, Roger ''Rogue'' Riderhood, and Silas Wegg (son of ''Waterman'') together in their fraternal order (*OMF* 188; bk. 1, ch. 15).

As a scholar, Gaffer also tries to teach his children about the ways of the river. Each metropastoral space in *Our Mutual Friend* contains such a pedagogue who seeks to inculcate his or her truth. Returning once again to the Bond Street area of Arcadian West London, we find another self-appointed scholar who not only ''resembles Gaffer as a bird of prey'' (Reed 6) but has an equally weathered ''face carved out of very hard material'' (*OMF* 45; bk. 1, ch. 5). This ''street-hawker of ballads'' (Page, *Companion* 236) also has a ''wooden peg'' that testifies to the hardness (i.e., poverty) of his life (Morgentaler 93). His edible merchandise causes face-aches, stomach-aches, and tooth-aches (45; bk. 1, ch. 5). His ''halfpenny ballads''[16] are equally hard to swallow with their extra feet and parenthetical interjections, as are his services as a trustworthy ''errand-goer'' and credible ''literary man'' (49; bk. 1, ch. 5). Truth be told, Silas Wegg is nothing but a bucolic impersonator from a particular ''class of impostors'' (53; bk. 1, ch. 5) with the countenance and disposition of a shepherd's crook[17]: he is knotty, twisted, and very close-grained. While Gaffer's chronotopic lineage can be traced back to Greek shepherd-fishermen, Silas's legacy originates with the singing shepherd-turned-peddler-rogue, the fullest expression of which is found in Shakespeare's *The Winter's Tale* where Autolycus visits a ''sheep-shearing feast'' in Bohemia (4.4.203) in order to sell his ballads and ''unbraided wares'' to unsuspecting marks.

When Autolycus appears in act 3, he too is disguised as a ''literary shepherd'' (Alpers 211).[18] Like Wegg's ballads, Autolycus's songs parody traditional pastoral subjects; his verse is not about lovesick rustics or bucolic singing matches but about thieving desires and summer whores, the inspiration of which Autolycus attributes to his own tangled lineage: "My father nam'd me Autolycus, who being, as I am, litter'd under Mercury, was likewise a snapper-up of unconsider'd trifles" (4.3.24–26). In addition to being a divine messenger, the Roman god Mercury oversees both shepherding and thievery (Atsma, "Hermes"). Thus, to father Pan *and* Autolycus is to create a shepherd capable of fleecing his own flock.

Just as Autolycus "sells his trinkets and tawdry wares, and plies his customers with his broadside ballads until they are anesthetized for his purse-cutting" (Smith 1614), so Wegg peddles his popular ballads and poetasting proclivities in order to drop down on the Golden Dustman. The method by which he does so comes from Robert Greene's "Notable Discovery of Cozenage." Greene identifies three basic players in the Elizabethan extortion scenario known as the "cony-catching trick":

> The Whore, [or] the *Traffic*.
> The man that is brought in, the *Simpler*.
> The villains that take them, the *Crosbiters*.   (qtd. in Kinney 176)

Initially, Wegg plays the Traffic (i.e., the literary trull) who seduces Noddy Boffin, the Simpler. Once Mr. Venus is brought into the trick, Wegg transitions to primary Crosbiter so as to humiliate Boffin at just the right moment.

As the Traffic, Wegg sells intellectual gratification rather than carnal pleasure for "double the money!" (*OMF* 52; bk. 1, ch. 5). In no time at all, Silas becomes a 'kept literary man' in Boffin's Bower. A reference to Rosamond Clifford, King Henry II's mistress, further reinforces the trull motif: "The Bower was as difficult to find, as Fair Rosamond's without the clue" (54; bk. 1, ch. 5). According to W. H. Matthews,

> King Henry the Second (A.D. 1133 to 1189) adopted [Rosamond] as his mistress, and that, in order to conceal his illicit amours from his Queen, Eleanor of Aquitaine, he conducted them within the innermost recesses of a most complicated maze which he caused to be made in his park at Woodstock. Rumours of her spouse's defections having reached the ears of Queen Eleanor, that indignant lady contrived to penetrate the labyrinth, confronted her terrified and tearful rival, and forced her to choose between the dagger and the bowl of poison; she drained the latter and became forthwith defunct.   (164)

The traditional locus amoenus as escapist enclave is reformulated into a complicated maze of secret desire, royal subversion, and personal destruction.[19] For the maze to resurface during Wegg's search for Boffin's Bower is initially to identify Silas with the dispossessed queen who seeks to destroy her usurper. Wegg certainly does appear to poison Boffin's mind with the greed and eccentricity found in *Kirby's Wonderful Museum, Caulfield's Characters*, and *Merryweather's Lives and Anecdotes of Misers* (479, 481; bk. 3, ch. 6). Seemingly infected with acute parsimony,[20] Boffin overreacts when Wegg all but drops the volume containing the miser Daniel Dancer: " 'Don't drop that one under your arm. It's Dancer. Him and his sister made pies of a dead sheep they found when they were out a-walking' " (479; bk. 3, ch. 6). "The Story of the Mutton Pies" (481; bk. 3, ch. 6) once again illustrates the novel's ability to consume and reformulate weaker genres. In this case, irresponsible shepherding (i.e., allowing sheep to wander off and die) becomes profitable scavenging as the road-kill bakers[21] turn rural failure into urban success through clever chicanery.

Without question, Wegg's fabricated histories and outlandish biographies are a key part of his seductive Trafficking. And what better place to perform than in the novel's second major metropastoral space, in a "room below the stairs" (184; bk. 1, ch. 15) where the veracity of Wegg's claims can go unchecked. Like Gaffer's windmill, Boffin's Bower is a symbolic cellar filled with personal fears and inveigling criminality.

Initially, Wegg cannot even find The Bower until it is redefined as the "Harmony Jail." As its oxymoronic name suggests, the otium of rustic living and the tedium of incarceration are joined to produce a hybridized space with chiasmic significance: it is both the shepherd's pen(itentiary) and the thief's bower. Boffin quickly becomes a prisoner in his own home as Wegg assumes complete control of the space, subsequently forcing the Golden Dustman to move to another house near Cavendish Square. The pen/bower motif is registered further in the "dark mounds" that dwarf the pathway leading to the house (55; bk. 1, ch. 5). Wrapped with "serpentine walk[s]," the highest "Mound is crowned with a lattice-work Arbour" perfectly suited for doing surveillance and for dropping down into poetry (57; bk. 1, ch. 5).

Inside the Bower, the Crosbiting game continues in the "queerest of rooms fitted and furnished more like a luxurious amateur tap-room than anything else within the ken of Silas Wegg":

[t]here was a flowery carpet on the floor; but, instead of reaching to the fireside, its glowing vegetation stopped short at Mrs. Boffin's footstool, and gave place to a region of sand and sawdust. Mr. Wegg also noticed, with admiring eyes, that, while the flowery land displayed such hollow ornamentation as stuffed birds and waxen fruit under glass shades, there were, in the territory where vegetation ceased, compensatory shelves on which the best part of a large pie and likewise of a cold joint were plainly discernible among other solids. The room itself was large, though low, and the heavy frames of its old-fashioned windows, and the heavy beams in its crooked ceiling, seemed to indicate that it had once been a house of some mark standing alone in the country.

(55–56; bk. 1, ch. 5)

Metropastoral markers abound in this interior: it has a low, crooked ceiling and heavy wooden beams that give the room a subterranean oppressiveness consistent with cellars, dens, run-down windmills, and criminal hideouts, while the room's warm fire and cold victuals (the pie, the joint of meat, and the gin) signify the hospitality of the locus amoenus. The "amateur tap-room" description connects the space with Bacchanalian revelry via the Victorian Public House which has three distinct rooms—(1) the antechamber or "the bar-room where organ-grinders, Punch and Judy showmen, sellers of hot eels or watercress, Jewish dealers of old clothes" gather (Spiller 16); (2) the "more respectable" parlor where "lower middle class, tradesmen, clerks, actors, obscure literary men and reporters" congregate; (3) and the tap-room where "mechanics and artisans" interact in "a self-contained, male-dominated community. . . . [where] matchboard walls and ceilings, hard furniture and sanded floors are perfectly suited to the customers' mood" (16–17). Boffin's side is sparse like the tap room: the floor is covered with "sand and sawdust"; the "hospitable" larder is located there (58); Wegg the artisan and Boffin the rude mechanical meet over Edward Gibbon's eight volumes of *The History of the Decline and Fall of the Roman Empire*[22] which "were arranged flat, in a row, like a galvanic battery" (55; bk. 1, ch. 5)—a simile connecting Wegg's theatrical pedagogy with the "artful snares laid for giving galvanic shocks to the unwary" (Morus).[23]

By contrast, Mrs. Boffin's side of the room reads more like the parlor with its garish furniture and florid ornamentation. Wegg's role as "obscure literary" man is emphasized here, along with several other parodic stylizations. The "flaring gaslight pendant" shines like a phony Phoebus upon the flowery carpet with its "glowing vegetation" as the open pasture is novelized into artificial floor covering; "stuffed birds" and "waxen fruit"[24] translate bucolic warbling and Edenic provision into lifeless collectables trapped under glass shades in what amounts to a satirical commentary on the irrelevance of traditional pastoralism.

During one of his performances, the Traffick temporarily unmasks himself when he draws a distinction between "Rooshan" and "Roman" empires—an observation based on spelling rather than historical knowledge. But Wegg quickly conceals his charlatanism by turning the Simpler's question into a faux pas and using it as a rhetorical shield: " 'The difference, sir? There you place me in a difficulty, Mr. Boffin. Suffice it to observe, that the difference is best postponed to some other occasion when Mrs. Boffin does not honour us with her company. In Mrs. Boffin's presence, sir, we had better drop it' " (59; bk. 1, ch. 5). By turning the Greek historian Polybius into the titillating "Polly Beeious . . . supposed by Mr. Boffin to be a Roman virgin, and by Mrs. Boffin to be responsible for that necessity of dropping it," the Simpler is chastened into curtailing any further inquiry. By withholding Polly's illicit (and fictive) backstory, Wegg actually draws Boffin deeper into the cony-catching trick. Equally effective is the Traffic's use of the attraction of repulsion. Among the cruel tyrants cited in *The Decline and Fall of the Roman Empire* is the Emperor Commodus (Gibbon 222), whom Wegg refers to as "Commodious," thus filling Boffin's head with bloody feats and childhood chamber pots. By the end of the first evening, Noddy is so glutted with "unprovoked cruelties" that he can hardly think straight:

> "Commodious fights in that wild beast-show, seven hundred and thirty-five times, in one character only! As if that wasn't stunning enough, a hundred lions is [sic] turned into the same wild-beast-show all at once! As if that wasn't stunning enough, Commodious, in another character, kills 'em all off in a hundred goes! As if that wasn't stunning enough, Vittle-us (and well named too) eat six millions' worth, English money, in seven months![25] . . . I didn't think this morning there was [sic] half so many Scarers in Print. But I'm in for it now!"
>
> (59–60; bk. 1, ch. 5)

Commodus, like Wegg, is a rogue (albeit a sadistic one) who uses his theatricality to maintain his tyrannical authority. Moreover, both the Emperor and the literary man go on to acquire infamously lower reputations: Commodus chooses the bloody "habit and arms of the *Secutor*" in order to fight in the amphitheatre (Gibbon 232), while Wegg styles himself as the usurped heir who subsequently recruits Mr. Venus to his cony-catching trick by playing upon the taxidermist's unrequited love for Pleasant Riderhood and by appealing to his own violated "cause of right" (302; bk. 2, ch. 7).[26] Just as Gaffer's river ethics allow him to rifle through a dead man's pockets with impunity, so Wegg's bower ethics allow him to claim Boffin's inheritance with no compunction.

Having been lured to the Bower with the promise of doing business, Mr. Venus is inundated with metropastoral "quotation and hospitality" (477; bk. 3, ch. 6). The cozy fire, the hot rum, the lit pipe, and the bitter injustice of Wegg's disappointment all convince the lonely taxidermist in a moment of "reckless madness and desperation" to say "Yes" to the Traffic's proposed partnership (304; bk. 2, ch. 7). With Venus on board, Wegg exchanges his Trafficking role for that of the primary Crosbiter.

The cozening scene itself takes place inside Boffin's Bower. The Crosbiter greets the Simpler at his door with several lines from Thomas Moore's popular Victorian poem, "Will You Come to the Bower?" The original verse reads as follows:

> Will you come to the bower I have shaded for you?
> Our bed shall be roses all spangled with dew.[27]
> Will you, will you, will you, will you
> Come to the bower?   (355)

In the novelized version of the poem, Wegg's rhetorical violence displaces Moore's "gentle seduction" (Dvorak 153). The homonymic shift from *dew* to *doo* also marks the presence of the Rabelaisian chronotope with its "defecation series" (Bakhtin 170) used "to purge the spatial and temporal world of those remnants of the transcendent world" (167):

> "If you'll come to the Bower I shaded for you,
> Your bed shan't be roses all spangled with doo:
> Will you, will you, will you, will you, come to the Bower?
> Oh, won't you, won't you, won't you, won't you, come to the Bower?"
>
> (*OMF* 652; bk. 4, ch. 3)

Wegg's taunt backfires, however, when his tangled use of the double-negative comically declares that Boffin's figurative bed will not be filled with doo-spangled roses. In fact, it is Wegg who will eventually end up in the refuse pile, having first been recast as the Simpler in a cony-catching *counter*-trick orchestrated by Rokesmith, the Boffins, and Mr. Venus: " 'I tell you this, that you may know we knew enough of you to persuade Mr. Boffin to let us lead you on, deluded to the last possible moment, in order that your disappointment might be the heaviest possible disappointment' " (788; bk. 4, ch. 14). Wegg's disappointment is heavy indeed, despite the ease with which Sloppy tosses him like a sack of chronotopic waste into a nearby scavenger's cart. In the end, the perfidious "mud worm" (788; bk. 4, ch. 14) is beaten at his own game by the "worm of the hour" (307; bk. 2, ch. 8) and his metropastoral friends.

II

Tossing Silas Wegg into the public square brings us to the novel's third major metropastoral space, the Six Jolly Fellowship-Porters. Once again, idyllic and theatrical chronotopes clash inside a novelized enclave shepherded, in this case, by "a tall, upright, well-favoured woman" with the "air of a schoolmistress" (*OMF* 63; bk. 1, ch. 6). The raised public house—with its tap-room, parlor, and "wooden verandah impending over the water" (61; bk. 1, ch. 6)—seems more like an attic than a cellar since it "increases reality" by addressing the daily ethical concerns of those who frequent the pub (Bachelard 20). Like other attic spaces, the Six Jolly Fellowship-Porters values honest labor, sustenance, and "organic fastening down" (Bakhtin 225). Its interior is also studded with plenty of metropastoral indicators:

> The wood forming the chimney-pieces, beams, partitions, floors, and doors . . .
> seemed in its old age fraught with confused memories of its youth. In many

places it had become gnarled and riven, according to the manner of old trees; knots started out of it; and here and there it seemed to twist itself into some likeness of boughs. In this state of second childhood, it had an air of being in its own way garrulous about its early life. Not without reason was it often asserted by the regular frequenters of the Porters, that when the light shone full upon the grain of certain panels, and particularly upon an old corner cupboard of walnut-wood in the bar, you might trace little forests there, and tiny trees like the parent-tree, in full umbrageous leaf.   (*OMF* 61; bk. 1, ch. 6)

The Golden Age of literary pastoralism resurfaces as a gnarled old man with outstretched limbs whose interlocking "memories" provide the pub's regulars with a dual sense of shelter and rootedness: "This haven was divided from the rough world by a glass partition and a half-door with a leaden sill upon it for the convenience of resting your liquor; but, over this half-door the bar's snugness . . . gushed forth" (62; bk. 1, ch. 6). Warmth and safety are so abundant in this "Arcadian Saloon"[28] (180) that they spill over into the adjacent street. Back inside, "the bar's snugness" translates into moral snugging or fastening down for those who regularly attend The SJFP academy. "*I* am the law here, my man," Miss Abbey tells Rogue Riderhood, "and I'll soon convince you of that, if you doubt it at all" (*OMF* 63; bk. 1, ch. 6). Snugging and snuggery are further reinforced by a novelized cluster of Bacchanalian images found in the same description:

> that space was so girt in by corpulent little casks, and by cordial-bottles radiant with fictitious grapes in bunches, and by lemons in nets, and by biscuits in baskets, and by the polite beer-pulls that made low bows when customers were served with beer, and by the cheese in a snug corner, and by the landlady's own small table in a snugger corner near the fire, with the cloth everlastingly laid.   (62; bk. 1, ch. 6)

The ethical mooring and physical comfort of Miss Abbey's public school/ house are registered in the "polite" and "cordial" casks, bottles, and beer-pulls, and in the nets and baskets that signify containment, provision, and protection. Directly across from the bar is a "very little room like a three-cornered hat" called the "Cosy" (62; bk. 1, ch. 6), an enclave that serves as Bella and John Harmon's temporary little prison cell. "With extended arms," Mr. Inspector initially corrals the married couple "as if they had been two sheep" (763; bk. 4, ch. 12), only later to learn the truth of Harmon's secret identity and set the couple free.

Those who defy Miss Abbey's law are eventually expelled from The Six Jolly Fellowship Porters, as is the case with Rogue Riderhood and Gaffer Hexam. The compliant and "deferential faces of her school" (66; bk. 1, ch. 6) review their lessons in the taproom adjacent to the bar. George Jones, for example, is working on his promptness: "I told your wife you should be punctual,'' declares Miss Abbey, and so ''Jones submissively rose, gave the company good-night, and retired'' (65; bk. 1, ch. 6). William Williams, Bob Glamour, and Jonathan are dismissed with similar accountability assignments. Captain Joey is learning moderation, Tom Tootle is being prepared for marriage, and Jack Mullins is busy acquiring much needed self-discipline.

Miss Abbey then instructs her potboy to ''run round to Hexam's and tell his daughter Lizzie that I want to speak to her'' (66; bk. 1, ch. 6). Sitting at ''a snug little table by the bar fire,'' the schoolmistress invites the prospective pupil to join the SJFP academy: '' 'Lizzie, come under my direction. Don't fling yourself away, my girl, but be persuaded into being respectable and happy' '' (68–69; bk. 1, ch. 6). Try as she may, Miss Abbey cannot ''persuade her to come to me for a refuge'' (439; bk. 3, ch. 2). Rather, Lizzie chooses familial loyalty over respectability and personal happiness, risking being tarred herself with the same ''dirty brush'' that ruins her father (69; bk. 1, ch. 6). Her implied status as a ''tainted woman'' raises ''the specter of fallen female sexuality and, specifically, [that] of the prostitute'' since such an association ''would have been familiar to Dickens's readers through one of any number of literary and visual representations of the prostitute on the river'' (Allen 100). By rejecting Miss Abbey's invitation, Lizzie may seem to become a symbolic whore in the rogue's theatrical chronotope.[29] But perhaps Lizzie's refusal to join the pub-school simply highlights her need for a different kind of teacher in a more private kind of educational setting which she eventually finds in another ''weird patch of pastoral island'' (Alter 55), up in Riah's rooftop garden—the novel's fourth major metropastoral site.

The ''garden on the tiles'' (*OMF* 278; bk. 2, ch. 5) sits atop the Pubsey and Co. building and is a dreamer's refuge where ''a more tranquil solitude'' exists for those who visit there (Bachelard 26): '''We are thankful to come here for rest, sir,' said Jenny. 'You see, you don't know what the rest of this place is to us; does he, Lizzie? It's the quiet, and the air' '' (281; bk. 3, ch. 5). Like its metropastoral counterparts, this elevated locus moralis contains urban, pastoral, and pedagogical markers. Here these same elements also create a nest-like snugness for the disabled little wren and her troubled friend:

> Seated on [a carpet], against no more romantic object than a blackened chimney-stack over which some humble creeper had been trained, they both pored over one book; both with attentive faces; Jenny with the sharper; Lizzie with the more perplexed. Another little book or two were lying near, and a common basket of common fruit, and another basket full of strings of beads and tinsel scraps. A few boxes of humble flowers and evergreens completed the garden; and the encompassing wilderness of dowager old chimneys twirled their cowls and fluttered themselves, and looking on in a state of airy surprise.
>
> (279; bk. 3, ch. 5)

The open pasture is reformulated into a floor covering here (see fig. 2), just as it is in Boffin's Bower. The "blackened chimney-stack" (a sign of the urban/industrial) is covered by a "humble creeper" thus suggesting the power of metropastoralism to reclaim the world of bricks and mortar. So as to connect the rooftop garden with the surrounding "wilderness of dowager old chimneys," illustrator Marcus Stone adds a trunk-like chimney pot with severed limbs and a curved cowl. Boxes of transplanted "flowers and evergreens" further rusticate the city while a "basket of common fruit" cross-references the metropastoral sustenance found in the Six Jolly Fellowship Porters. Down on the carpet, a "little book or two" earmark the space's pedagogical function. At first glance, the illustration would have us believe that Lizzie is in charge of the garden school, given her posture, size, and placement in the frame. Yet physiognomy suggests that Jenny is the "sharper" of the two readers (Lizzie, the more "perplexed"). It is Jenny, after all, who first leads Lizzie to the urban enclave. Although a "child in years," Miss Wren is nonetheless a "woman in self-reliance and trial" (439; bk. 3, ch. 2) while Lizzie all but flees her difficult circumstances like a frightened child. In Bakhtinian terms, it is Jenny who plays the novelized shepherdess to Lizzie's wandering sheep.

Further evidence of Jenny's role as shepherd/teacher surfaces during her initial encounter with Fascination Fledgeby wherein she gives him a short lesson on the transcendent power of metropastoralism. During this exchange, Lizzie hardly says a word. To Fledgeby's general complaint that there is "not much good to be got out of that [book-learning]," Jenny snaps back with "Depends upon the person!"—immediately correcting her misinformed pupil. While Jenny's applied creativity—what Dickens calls her "doll-fancy"—puts "rather strong demands" on Fledgeby's intellect (280; bk. 2, ch. 5), her business sense speaks directly to his "bill-brokering" mentality (272; bk. 2, ch. 5). Jenny's "great calmness" also exerts a quiet authority over Lizzie when the latter becomes uneasy due to Fledgeby's inquiries: "Jenny stole her hand up to her friend's, and drew her friend down, so that she bent beside her on her knee" (280–81; bk. 2, ch. 5). With Lizzie safely under her wing, Jenny launches into Fledgeby's tutorial. She tells him that the inner "rest" and "quiet" found in the rooftop space allow her and Lizzie to transcend the "City's roar" below; that the rarified air of the tiled garden dispels the oppressive smoke; that the "golden arrows" (i.e., the sunlit spires of All Hallows by the Tower, St. Michael's Church Highgate, St. Botolph's Church Aldgate, St. Bride's Fleet Street Church, and the dome, cupola, and cross of St. Paul's Cathedral to the west, all within a mile's radius of St. Mary's Axe) point skyward with future hope; that the winds of change sweep away their temporal cares and leave a "strange good sorrowful happiness." Jenny finishes her lesson with "Come back [up] and be dead!" effectively driving Fledgeby away from their metropastoral community.

Fig. 2: "The Garden on the Roof" (*OMF* 257; bk. 2, ch. 4).

Like Jenny, Lizzie understands that being "dead" is synonymous with rest, relationship, and ongoing moral training. As the two young women talk, eat, and pore over their books "early and late" (280; bk. 2, ch. 5) in the rooftop garden, they are temporarily released from the weariness of their daily lives. Both are acquiring facts about the world around them, yet it is Jenny who "fastens down" certain moral convictions in her friend's unsettled life. A clearer sense of this emerges in another metropastoral space symbolically connected with Riah's rooftop garden, namely, the Wren's Nest on Church Street, just off of Smith Square (221; bk. 2, ch. 1), where Lizzie again finds rest "up-stairs" in "a quiet, and pleasant, and airy" little enclave (226; bk. 2, ch. 1). The Wren's Nest also plays host to a variety of teachers: Bradley Headstone volunteers his educational services there; Jenny continues to assert her mentoring influence over Lizzie while attempting to correct her derelict father, Mr. Dolls; and Eugene Wrayburn renews his offer to hire " 'some qualified person of your own sex and age, so many (or rather so few) contemptible shillings, to come here, certain nights of the week, and give you certain instruction which you wouldn't want if you hadn't been a self-denying daughter and sister' " (235; bk. 2, ch. 2). Wrayburn, however, must first dismantle Lizzie's ethical assumptions about her own self-denial before she is willing accept his offer. Lizzie's "false pride," he argues, wrongs both herself and her dead father " 'by perpetuating the consequences of his ignorant and blind obstinacy. By resolving not to set right the wrong he did you. By determining that the deprivation to which he condemned you, and which he forced upon you, shall always rest upon his head' " (237; bk. 2, ch. 2). Despite his disclaimer that "I might have got myself up, morally, as Sir Eugene Bountiful," Wrayburn does indeed take the high road as his "earnestness, complete conviction, injured resentment of suspicion, generous and unselfish interest" (236; bk. 2, ch. 2) all succeed in persuading Lizzie to drop her "vain misgiving" and receive the proffered instruction.

The pedagogical exercise that follows then focuses on Wrayburn himself. When he playfully declares that "I think of setting up a doll," Jenny replies, "You had better not."

> "Why not?"
> "You are sure to break it. All children do."
> "But that makes good for trade, you know, Miss Wren. . . . Much as people's breaking promises and contracts and bargains of all sorts, makes good for *my* trade."
> "I don't know about that . . . but you had better . . . set up a penwiper, and turn industrious and use it."

Jenny admonishes Sir Bountiful to live by the same honest self-evaluation that he advocates for Miss Hexam. Initially, Eugene deflects Jenny's challenge: "Why, if we were all as industrious as you, little Busy-Body, we should begin to work as soon as we could crawl, and there would be a bad thing!'' (238; bk. 2, ch. 2). But Jenny only hears "body . . . bad thing" and assumes that Wrayburn is ridiculing her infirmity: "Do you mean . . . bad for your backs and your legs?'' His mortification instantly derails his self-protection which suggests that he too is learning a valuable lesson in the locus moralis. Unlike the pretentious banter of the Veneerings's dinner parties, conversation among real friends in the Wren's Nest is both candid and constructive.

In addition to its ethical influence, the Wren's Nest manifests three extrasensory (rather than physical) descriptions of its own metropastoralism. Jenny's segue into flowers, birdsongs, and shining children begins with a pragmatic observation that Church Street is "not a flowery neighborhood'' at all:

> "It's anything but that. And yet, as I sit at work, I smell roses till I think I see the rose-leaves lying in heaps, bushels, on the floor. I smell fallen leaves till I put down my hand—so—and expect to make them rustle. I smell the white and pink May in the hedges, and all sorts of flowers that I never was among. For I have seen very few flowers indeed, in my life.''   (239; bk. 2, ch. 2)

The fragrance of Jenny's metropastoral roses with their aromatic virtues of love, loyalty, purity, unity, and friendship overpowers the "villainous smells" of the nearby Thames (Picard 6). Flowering hedgerows call to mind enclosed sheep pastures, while rustling leaves invoke the autumnal months of Spenser's *Shepheardes Calender*, especially the October eclogue "made in imitation" of Theocritus's Idyll 16 wherein "Poetes [have] . . . the power to make men immortal for theyr good dedes, or shameful for their naughty lyfe" (Spenser 458). To "restraine/The lust of lawlesse youth with good aduice" is the aphoristic intent of both the bucolic poet and the metropastoral shepherdess (457). Jenny then speaks of her ephemeral little warblers which (like some of Miss Flite's songbirds in *Bleak House*—"Hope, Joy, Youth, Peace, Rest, Life" [200; ch. 14]) symbolize future release, as do the shining children she encounters: " 'They were not like me: they were not chilled, anxious, ragged, or beaten; they were never in pain. They were not like the children of the neighbours; they never made me tremble all over, by setting up shrill noises, and they never mocked me' " (239; bk. 2, ch. 2). Again, metropastoral pleasaunce consumes and reformulates urban oppression as Jenny is swept up and made light by the "delicious ease and rest" of her bright visitors, who are also manifestations of what Bachelard calls the "phenomenology of nests" (93). Along with its quiet simplicity (98), the nest-as-enclave has the ability "to recapture the naïve wonder we used to feel when we found a [real] nest. This wonder is lasting, and . . . it takes us back to our childhood or, rather, to a childhood; to the childhoods we should have had" (93). But

Jenny's transportation—"the hand was raised, the late ecstatic look returned, and she became quite beautiful" (*OMF* 240; bk. 2, ch. 2)—is soon truncated by the arrival of her drunken father, whose presence triggers a change in Jenny's attitude and demeanor:

> "Go along into your corner! . . . Oh-h-h you naughty, wicked creature! . . . Oh, you disgraceful old chap! . . . Ain't you ashamed of yourself? . . . How should you like to be transported for life? . . . Put down your money this instant. . . . Turn all your pockets inside out. . . . Go to bed this moment!"
>
> (241–42; bk. 2, ch. 2)

The heavenly wren becomes a pedagogical shrew in the blink of an eye.

This ability to slide between shiny and mundane worlds suggests that Jenny is not limited to the physical proximity of her own nest. Not only does she possess a transportable "bower" of golden hair (439; bk. 3, ch. 2); she also works on a diminutive scale as a doll's dressmaker and, as such, is in the habit of "miniaturizing the world," which allows her to get back to the imaginative reality of childhood through the re-experiencing of "*interior beauty*" in "tiny things" (Bachelard 149). Upon learning of Eugene Wrayburn's brutal beating, the doll's dressmaker immediately heads upriver to establish a temporary Wren's Nest: "They provided Jenny with materials for plying her work, and she had a little table placed at the foot of his bed. Sitting there, with her rich shower of hair falling over the chair-back, they hoped she might attract his notice" (736; bk. 4, ch. 10). The metropastoral shepherdess, the medical attendant, the best friend, and the lover then fill the temporary enclave with spiritual guidance, physical sustenance, moral support, and unconditional love. That Wrayburn's first halting conversation focuses on Jenny's three extrasensory perceptions is further proof of the nest's regenerative power. Having briefly regained consciousness, Eugene asks Jenny if she "has seen the children? . . . smelt the flowers?" She asks,

> "You mean my long bright slanting rows of children, who used to bring me ease and rest? You mean the children who used to take me up, and make me light?"
>
> Eugene smiled, "Yes."
>
> "I have not seen them since I saw you. I never see them now, but I am hardly ever in pain now."
>
> "It was a pretty fancy," said Eugene.
>
> "But I have heard my birds sing," cried the little creature, "and I have smelt my flowers. Yes, indeed I have! And both were most beautiful and most Divine!"
>
> "Stay and help to nurse me," said Eugene, quietly. "I should like you to have the fancy here, before I die." (737; bk. 4, ch. 10)

Perhaps she no longer sees the shining children because she has become such a child to Wrayburn himself, lifting his damaged spirit by the "secret sympathy" and "power" of her own golden transformation:

> through this close watching (if through no secret sympathy or power) the little creature attained an understanding of him that Lightwood did not possess. Mortimer would often turn to her, as if she were an interpreter between this sentient world and the insensible man; and she would change the dressing of a wound, or ease a ligature, or turn his face, or alter the pressure of the bed-clothes on him, with an absolute certainty of doing right. The natural lightness and delicacy of touch, which had become very refined by practice in her minia-ture work, no doubt was involved in this; but her perception was at least as fine.   (739; bk. 4, ch. 10)

Empowered by birdsong and fragrance, Jenny leads Eugene's wandering spirit back to "this sentient world" with "an absolute certainty of doing right." Her physical care is matched by her moral certitude as Jenny attends to Wrayburn's body while fastening down his moral sensibilities, as is evi-denced by Eugene's adamant plea "that the perpetrator ... never [be] brought to justice" (738; bk. 4, ch. 10). His is not some deathbed sophistry meant to exact revenge from beyond the grave but a true desire, in his per-ceived last moments, to protect (i.e., to "do right" by) the woman he loves. Put in practical terms, Wrayburn understands the retaliatory wrath of the hegemony when it comes to victims who indict the system: " 'She would be punished, not he. I have wronged her enough in fact: I have wronged her still more in intentions. . . . Don't think of avenging me; think only of hushing the story and protecting her. You can confuse the case, and turn aside the circumstances. Listen to what I say to you. It was not the schoolmaster, Bradley Headstone' " (738; bk. 4, ch. 10). Nor does Headstone need any formal punishment since he acts as his own judge, jury, jailer, and execu-tioner. Condemning himself and Rogue Riderhood to death-by-drowning, Headstone throws an "iron ring" around his tormentor's waist before tum-bling headlong into the chilly lock at Plashwater Mill (802; bk. 4, ch. 15). His final cry to "Come down [and be dead]!" inverts Jenny's life-giving invitation to "Come up and be dead!" as the teacher-turned-Rogue seeks to redeem his failed life with one last counter-trick.[30]

Jenny, meanwhile, continues to exert her honest influence in the temporary Wren's Nest. When Mortimer Lightwood declares, "Oh, Jenny, if you could only give me the right word!" she replies, "I can. Stoop down" (741; bk. 4, ch. 11). His bent posture recalls Lizzie's teachable position in Riah's rooftop garden. The whispered word ("wife") transforms the space into a "warm little corner" (a makeshift Cosy) with the power to novelize Eugene out of his roguishness and into his family-man fidelity, to transform Lizzie from potential victim to nurse-wife shepherdess, and to change Mortimer Lightwood from co-dependent enabler to truly principled friend. That Wrayburn and Lightwood declare themselves "shepherds both" by the end of the novel is testimony to the shaping influence of their mutual friend, Jenny Wren (812; bk. 4, ch. 16).

That title, of course, belongs first and foremost to John Harmon, who also undergoes a novelizing transformation. With his initial misidentification as a dangerous rogue, Harmon (alias Julius Handford) is deemed an "utter stranger" (24; bk. 1, ch. 3), a "Murderer" (40; bk. 1, ch. 4), and, in Bakhtin's expression, "an alien force":

> It often happens that in the beginning the hero is homeless, without relatives, without means of support; he wanders through an alien world among alien people; random misfortunes and successes happen to him; he encounters random people who turn out to be—for unknown reasons at this early point in the novel—his enemies or his benefactors (all this is later decoded along family or kinship lines).   (232)

Harmon's alias proves to be useful since it allows him to reappear as the Boffins' trusted servant, John Rokesmith, who is able to monitor Wegg's "underhanded game" (*OMF* 776; bk. 4, ch. 13), while laying the foundation for Bella's strategic character-testing, both of which are carried out with the help of other faithful servants: "We was all of us in on it," declares Mrs. Boffin, who plays the part of the good-hearted Traffic in Boffin's and Harmon's "pious fraud" (771; bk. 4, ch. 13)—that modified version of the cony-catching trick designed to correct, rather than exploit, the Simpler's vice. While Henrietta is typecast according to her sweet-tempered nature, Noddy must assiduously study his part as the Crosbiting miser in order to cover up his affable personality: "A kind of illegibility, though a different kind, stole over Mr. Boffin's face. Its old simplicity of expression got masked by a certain craftiness that assimilated even his good-humour to itself. His very smile was cunning, as if he had been studying smiles among the portraits of his misers" (472; bk. 3, ch. 5). In fact, Kirby, Caulfield, Merryweather, and Wilson all serve as Boffin's acting teachers (479; bk. 3, ch. 6), just as Vulture Hopkins and his miserly cohort demonstrate what a skinflint's greed really looks like in action.

The pious fraud reaches its climax during the choreographed fight between the Crosbiting miser and the servant/hero/underdog in a chapter titled "The Golden Dustman at his Worst." While Mrs. Boffin (the Traffic) and Bella Wilfer (the Simpler) look on, Mr. Boffin (the primary Crosbiter) takes center stage: his "altered character had never been so grossly marked. . . . so charged with insolent distrust and arrogance" (588; bk. 3, ch. 15). In contrast, Rokesmith (the secondary Crosbiter) "was quiet and respectful, . . . [and] stood, as Bella thought (and was glad to think), on his manhood'' (589; bk. 3, ch. 15). Rokesmith is summoned and "immediately presented himself,'' right on cue. The script then calls for the miser to gather "himself together in his most suspicious attitude'' (591; bk. 3, ch. 15) in order to expose the real John Rokesmith: " 'I'm a-going to unfold your plan before this young lady; I'm a-going to show this young lady the second view of you.' '' The plan, of course, unfolds on several levels: the melodramatic haranguing of John Rokesmith is part of the contrived surface narrative meant to establish Rokesmith's victimization; Bella's reaction to the haranguing then indexes the moral strength of her character as part of the metropastoral *con*test. Time and again, the scene comically declares its own theatricality: "Let's have no pretending that you discharge yourself. I discharge you,'' Boffin announces in a blustering huff (592; bk. 3, ch. 15). "I have borne . . . with my false position here,'' Harmon replies, "that I might not be separated from Miss Wilfer. To be near her has been a recompense to me from day to day, even for the undeserved treatment I have had here, and for the degraded aspect in which she has often seen me'' (593; bk. 3, ch. 15). As Mrs. Boffin later notes, the script clearly calls for such degradation: " 'If she [Bella] was to stand up for you when you was slighted, if she was to show herself of a generous mind when you was oppressed, if she was to be truest to you when you was poorest and friendliest, and all this against her own seeming interest, how would that do?' '' (773; bk. 4, ch. 13). Mr. Boffin is equally committed to the pedagogical outcome of the pious fraud: "Look out for being slighted and oppressed, John, for it ever a man had a hard master, you shall find me from this present time to be such to you.'' At one point, the "old growler'' is so delighted with his blustering performance that he "hugged himself'' (594; bk. 3, ch. 15). Mrs. Boffin confirms the gesture's meaning later when she comments, "The way he'd say, 'I've been a regular brown bear to-day,' and take himself in his arms and hug himself at the thoughts of the brute he had pretended'' (773; bk. 4, ch. 13).

As the denunciation scene continues, it becomes increasingly painful for Bella and downright ridiculous for John Harmon, especially when Boffin suddenly departs from the script in "a burst of sarcastic eloquence'' (777; bk. 4, ch. 13): " 'Win her affections . . . and possess her heart! Mew says the cat, Quack-quack says the duck, Bow-wow-wow says the dog! Win her affections and possess her heart! Mew, Quack-quack, bow-wow!' '' (596; bk. 3, ch. 15). That Harmon suppresses his laughter while staring at Boffin "as if with some faint idea that he had gone mad'' is implied in his ensuing silence. Boffin can barely maintain his own self-control: "I was awful nigh bursting out a-laughing though, when it made John stare!'' (777; bk. 4, ch. 13). Boffin, however, quickly picks up the stalled dialogue: "What is due to this young lady . . . is Money, and this young lady right well knows it'' (596;

bk. 3, ch. 15). What Bella knows is that she has fallen in love with John Rokesmith while learning to see and reject her own debilitating avarice. In short, the benevolent cony-catching trick has worked: the Simpler has been "righted now" by the choreographed *con*test of the shepherding Crosbiters (597; bk. 3, ch. 15).

By the end of *Our Mutual Friend*, the novel's metropastoral community has almost tripled in size. All of the incorrigible rogues have been disposed of, while their teachable counterparts—the indolent barrister, the gold-digging protégée, the female water-rat, the love-sick taxidermist, and the swivel-eyed pawnbroker—have been novelized into familial shepherds and added to the relational fold. A festive gathering (albeit offstage) marks each of the happy additions: "It was a grand event, indeed, when Mr. and Mrs. Eugene Wrayburn came to stay at Mr. and Mrs. John Harmon's house: where, by the way, Mr. and Mrs. Boffin . . . were likewise staying indefinitely" (811; bk. 4, ch. 16). The Harmon mansion now brims with "the human fullness of a rural world" (Alpers 398) but with a Bakhtinian twist: it is the city-dwellers, and not the simple rustics, that incarnate the virtues of the locus moralis. It is the novelized pastoral, and not the "pastoral novel" as a mode (376), that accounts for the dramatic change. Moreover, the Harmony Bower (i.e., the Golden Dustman's novelized Mansion) is very much like the Wren's Nest when it comes to its attic elevation, its aromatic flowers, its birdsongs and shining children, and its moral fastening down. As John and Bella Harmon climb the stairs of their new home for the first time, "it was seen to be tastefully ornamented with most beautiful flowers. . . . Going on a little higher, they came to a charming aviary, in which a number of tropical birds, more gorgeous in colour than the flowers, were flying about; and among those birds were gold and silver fish, and mosses, and water-lilies, and a fountain, and all manner of wonders" (*OMF* 767; bk. 4, ch. 12). The fragrances, the aviary, and "all manner of wonders" (including the birth of their first child) correlate with Jenny's three extrasensory perceptions. The "gold and silver fish" recall the aquatic pastoral of the piscatorial eclogues, while the "moral fastening down" finds its novelized counterpart in the ethical stability of the Harmon's new home and in the displacement of the traditional "harvest supper" (Alpers 379) onto the Veneerings's dinner party in the novel's final chapter.

Among those attending the soiree are Melvin Twemlow and Mortimer Lightwood. Although labeled a "false swain" (816; bk. 4, ch. 17) by Lady Tippins—who is herself a bucolic imposter like the "china shepherdess," Mrs. Crisparkle, in *The Mystery of Edwin Drood* (50; ch. 5)—Lightwood is now a true metropastor who, along with the acolyte Twemlow, defends the virtues of the "female waterman, turned factory girl" (817; bk. 4, ch. 17) and the "gentleman's feelings of gratitude, of respect, of admiration, and affection" which "induced him" to marry Lizzie (819; bk. 4, ch. 17). By boldly placing the Wrayburns above the Podsnaps and the Veneerings, Lightwood and Twemlow invert the socio-moral hierarchy, thus declaring that the virtues of the locus moralis are greater than the "station and fortune" of Society's false bower (818; bk. 4, ch. 17). The assertion, as might be expected, falls like a "wet blanket" on the conversation (820; bk. 4, ch. 17), but Lightwood and Twemlow brighten nonetheless. Their cordial handshake and cheerful departure in the very last line suggest that the novel's metropastoralism will continue to expand, despite its hegemonic opposition.

With the novel safely "penned," Dickens guides his "readers and commentators" (821) into one last semantic fold called the "Postscript" where the writer-as-shepherd asserts that he "may perhaps be trusted to know what he is about in his vocation." Having sheared, washed, dyed, carded, and woven his narrative fleece, "the story-weaver at his loom" finishes his text(ile) by attempting to tie up three loose ends, each with a simple moral knot. The first loose end involves will cases. To dispel incredulity, Dickens asserts that real-life testators "have made, changed, contradicted, hidden, forgotten, left cancelled, and left uncancelled . . . many more wills" than the elder Harmon ever did. "Trust me," Dickens says as he ties the first knot, and we do. The second loose end pertains to Poor Law relief, which has been "infamously administered," "openly violated," and "habitually . . . ill-supervised" (822). In denouncing the Poor Law's "illegality" and "inhumanity," Dickens reminds us that he has been a faithful advocate of social reform, starting with *Oliver Twist* and running all the way to *Our Mutual Friend*. Again, the author declares his trustworthiness as he cinches down the second knot while the reader nods in approval.

The third thread, however, is badly frayed, unbeknownst to the reader. Why Dickens even mentions the Staplehurst railway accident is somewhat of a mystery. Just as none of his audience knew anything about his difficult childhood until John Forster published his autobiographical fragment in 1871 (Slater 619), so too the circle of those who had any knowledge of Dickens's relationship with Ellen Ternan was "very restricted" (536). Perhaps another unresolved "struggle" between "two powerful emotions" (622), like that which kept Dickens from publishing his autobiography during his own lifetime, also kept him from writing about his relationship with Ellen Ternan. Could it be that humiliation over the collapse of his marriage was at odds with his strong desire to be known, loved, and admired by the world? That his mentioning of the railway disaster was both a verbal disguise and a defense of his true worth? In his Postscript, Dickens talks of climbing "back into my carriage . . . to extricate the worthy couple," Mr. and Mrs. Boffin, along with several other characters, a metaphor, of course, for his manuscript (822). He then expresses his "devout thankfulness" for surviving such a traumatic event. Yet perhaps these selected details are also meant, at some level, to cover over another extrication, one that would not be well received if known by the world: "helped by a labourer, [Dickens] extricated the Ternans along with all the other injured passengers trapped in that carriage" (Slater 535). In burying the truth about his ongoing relationship with Nelly, regardless of how it is defined, Dickens desires to be remembered for his actions and not for some scandalous connection with a young, single actress.[31] In other words, he seeks to fasten down both his reputation and his personal happiness by carefully scripting the Staplehurst events for his readers, thus highlighting what he values most—humor, courage, sincerity, and gratitude.

NOTES

1. Michael Slater writes that Victorian "readers . . . would naturally have tended to identify the Traveller with Dickens himself" (515).
2. While working on the "early numbers" of *Our Mutual Friend*, Dickens rented a house at "57 Gloucester Place, Hyde Park Gardens" for "himself, Georgina and Mamie" (Slater 525).
3. According to the *Oxford English Dictionary*, "arcade" is both a "vaulted place, open at one or both sides; an arched opening or recess in a wall" and "an avenue similarly arched over by trees or shrubs." To capitalize the word as Dickens does is to combine the "ideally rural or rustic" with a shop-lined street of the city. A similar compression occurs with (G)Arden where pastoral space is translated into a controlled city environment. Smithfield Market illustrates a similar urban/pastoral mix. Other mixed references in the essay include "the pleasant open landscape of Regent-street" (161), "the innocence of the ladies' shoe-shops, the artificial flower repositories, and the head-dress depots" of the Burlington Arcade (163), and "such a deal of fleecing, and so little fleece! . . . in the Arcadian season" (165). To "chaste simplicity . . . [and the] domestic habits of Arcadia" (167) the speaker also adds "Arcadian time" (166) and "the Beadles . . . [who] turn their heavy maces into crooks and tend sheep" (i.e., the ragged boys in the marketplace).
4. Craig Dionne and Steve Mentz define rogues as sixteenth-century "vagrants who used disguises, rhetorical play, and counterfeit gestures to insinuate themselves into lawful social and political contexts" (1–2). The term later includes "rural migrants" and "urban con artists."
5. Bakhtin states that "language, as a treasure-house of images, is fundamentally chronotopic." By extension, "any and every literary image is chronotopic" (251).
6. Examples include the scheduled appointments at Boffin's Bower, the opening and closing hours at the Six Jolly Fellowship-Porters, the after-work study sessions up in Riah's rooftop garden, and the project deadlines for the dolls' dressmaker.
7. Peter Ackroyd notes that Pope "could never get away from the river; he had to live beside it, like one of those classical deities whose existence depended upon

the calm ministrations of the rivers of Greece. He declared once that there were 'no scenes of paradise, no happy bowers, equal to those on the banks of the Thames'. The river was his Arcadia, a sylvan retreat, to which he addressed his muse'' (*Thames* 341). Dickens's 1844 Inventory of Books shows that he possessed a copy of Alexander Pope's works, edited by the Reverend George Croly, LL.D., Volume 3 1835 edition. *The Works of Alexander Pope; with a Memoir of the Author, Notes, and Critical Notices on Each Poem.* This edition contains ''The Pastorals,'' ''A Discourse on Pastoral Poetry,'' and all four pastoral poems.

8. Pope again connects the Thames with the pastoral tradition in ''Summer, the Second Pastoral, or Alexis'':

> A shepherd Boy (he seeks no better name)
> Led forth his flocks along the silver Thame,
> Where dancing sunbeams on the waters play'd,
> And verdant alders form'd a quiv'ring shade. (4; st. 1)

9. Sannazaro's Lycidas wears a metamorphic disguise that is worthy of Proteus, another ''shepherd of the watery main,'' who has ''pastured . . . monsters along the salty plain'' near the volcanic island of Ischia (175). The *Piscatorial Eclogues* were published early in the sixteenth-century.

10. Dickens catalogues the ''dredgermen'' in ''Down with the Tide,'' another essay from *The Uncommercial Traveler.* Among the ''water-thieves'' are the Tier-rangers, who rob the cabins of sleeping skippers, the Lumpers, who slip stolen goods into their ''loose canvas jackets'' and sell them to ''marine store dealers,'' the Truckers, ''whose business it was to land more considerable parcels of goods than the Lumpers could manage'' using their own boats, and the Dredgermen, ''who, under the pretense of dredging up coals and such like from the bottom of the river, hung about barges and other undecked craft, and when they saw an opportunity, threw any property they could lay their hands on overboard: in order slyly to dredge it up when the vessel was gone'' (535). Henry Mayhew adds ''corpse retrieval'' to the dredgermen's job description in his *London Labour and the London Poor*:

> The dredgers . . . are the men who find almost all the bodies of persons drowned. If there be a reward offered for the recovery of a body, numbers of the dredgers will at once endeavour to obtain it, while if there be no reward, there is at least the inquest money to be had—beside other chances. What these chances are may be inferred from the well-known fact, that no body recovered by a dredgerman ever happens to have any money about it, when brought to shore. There may, indeed, be a watch in a fob or waistcoat pocket, for that article would be likely to be traced. There may, too, be a purse or pocket-book forthcoming, but somehow it is always empty. The dredgers cannot by any reasoning or argument be made to comprehend that there is anything like dishonesty in emptying the pockets of dead men.   (qtd. in Robson 130)

Peter Ackroyd's *Thames: Sacred River* also lists the ''specific Thames 'types' among the teeming humanity by the river'' (166).

11. Lizzie describes her neglected childhood while reading "the hollow down by the flare" (30; bk. 1, ch. 1): "There are you and me, Charley, when father was away at work and locked us out [of the house], for fear we should set ourselves afire or fall out the window, sitting on the door-sill, sitting on other doorsteps, sitting on the bank of the river, wandering about to get through the time. . . . sometimes we are very hungry, sometimes we are a little frightened, but what is oftenest hard upon us is the cold" (28; bk. 1, ch. 3). Out of necessity, Lizzie must rationalize neglect into compassion.

12. All definitions here are from the *Oxford English Dictionary*.

13. "Gaffer" today also denotes "an electrician in charge of lighting on a movie or television set," again reinforcing the connection with theatricality.

14. In "A Christmas Carol," one of Scrooge's serving women lives by a similar salvage ethic: "Who's the worse for the loss of a few things like these? Not a dead man, I suppose? . . . If he [Scrooge] wanted to keep 'em after he was dead, . . . why wasn't he natural in his lifetime?" (62). The pirate Pintel, in Gore Verbinski's film *Pirates of the Caribbean: Dead Man's Chest* (2006), operates by a similar standard, namely, that taking Jack Sparrow's beached ship "ain't stealin', it's salvaging," to which the one-eyed Ragetti replies, "Salvaging is saving, in a manner of speaking," thus justifying their larceny.

15. The reference here is to *Barnaby Rudge*. Pionke states that by "making the early [Haredale] murder, with its undertones of fratricide, the frame within which the Gordon Riots take place, Dickens seems to suggest that national disturbance can be traced to individual wrong-doing, thereby making the novel 'preeminently concerned with the implications of individual action' " (40).

16. See Dvorak for a full discussion of Wegg's popular ballads. As "songs of the great urban communities of the nineteenth-century," ballads nonetheless contain rustic virtues (156).

17. The *Oxford English Dictionary* glosses "crook" as (1) a hooked weapon, (2) a shepherd's tool used for grabbing the "hinder leg of a sheep," (3) "any hooked or curved appendage," (4) an "odd corner, nook" (5) a "dishonest person, swindler, sharper," (5) a "disease of sheep."

18. King Polixenes and Camillo (an exiled Sicilian lord) are also disguised as swains in order to question Old Shepherd about Prince Florizel, who has donned the mask of "an unstain'd shepherd" named Doricles (4.4.149) in order to woo Perdita. She actually wears two disguises in what Paul Alpers calls the "double pastoral: the princess who is represented as a shepherdess (knowingly in the play, though not by herself) is here recostumed as a rural goddess" (207). The reference to the Whitsun pastorals adds Bacchanalian revelry to the Satyrs' dance that follows.

19. Apparently, Fair Rosamond is "without very much foundation" when it comes to her historical veracity (Matthews 164). Yet the Rosamond story has "formed the basis of many novels," including T. Miller's *Fair Rosamond* published in 1847 (169). Closer to home perhaps is Swinburne's play *Rosamond*, published in 1860, "the most poignant and beautiful version of the tragedy" (169).

20. Pairing shepherds with infectious diseases is not as far-fetched as it sounds. Stephen Jay Gould states that " 'Syphilis,' the proper name of a fictional shepherd,

entered our language in a long poem composed in 1,300 verses of elegant Latin hexameter and published in 1530 by the greatest physician of his generation . . . Girolamo Fracastoro (1478–1553).''

21. Other examples of this type of novelized shepherd include Sweeney Todd, the Demon Barber of Fleet Street, and the ''infamous pie-maker, Mrs. Lovett'' (Mack xiv), along with Peachum and his beggars' costumes in Bertolt Brecht's *Threepenny Opera*, and Mugatu and his *Derelicte* line of haute couture clothing in Ben Stiller's *Zoolander*.

22. Dickens owned a copy of Gibbon's *History* (see Tillotson 712). Dickens-the-editor also ran Edward Fitzgerald's ''Roman'' series in *All the Year Round* from 1859 to 1861.

23. Parlor tricks, artful snares, and showmanship are all associated with galvanic cells, according to Morus, who writes that ''Eighteenth-century electrical parlour tricks like the Venus Kiss, in which male guests were challenged to kiss an electrified girl sitting on an insulated stool, remained popular well into the Victorian period. . . . Electrical displays at the Adelaide Gallery or the Royal Polytechnic Institute included 'artful snares laid for giving galvanic shocks to the unwary,' . . . . Visitors to the exhibitions were challenged to grab the poles of a galvanic battery or an induction coil and see how much of the electric fluid they could tolerate. Bodies themselves were part of the business of electrical showmanship.''

24. Francis states that modeling waxen fruit is easily accomplished with ''a little patience and a little taste'' (1), although ''it is not to be denied, that a slight knowledge of the harmony of colours and of botany will greatly assist in the perfection of the more difficult of these works of elegance'' (2). Henrietta Boffin attempted to place such believable imitations in her half of the Bower.

25. Norman Page refers briefly to Vitellius (''Vittle-us'') and Belisarius (''Bully Sawyers'') but makes no mention of Polybius. Page is primarily concerned with Dickens's implausible ''reading programme'' when it come to the amount of material covered in such short periods of time (''Silas Wegg'' 115).

26. Wegg's true motives are unintentionally revealed during his conversation with Mr. Venus: ''It ain't that I object to being passed over for a stranger, though I regard the stranger as a more than doubtful customer. It ain't for the sake of making money, though money is ever welcome. It ain't for myself, though I am not so haughty as to be above doing myself a good turn. It's for the cause of right'' (302; bk. 2, ch.7). Finding something with which to ''criminate'' that murderous Boffin is also on his list.

27. There is a similar ''dew'' phrase in Alexander Pope's ''Autumn: The Third Pastoral'':

> Thus sung the shepherd till th' approach of night,
> The skies yet blushing with departing light,
> When falling dews with spangles deck' the glade,
> And the low sun had lengthen'd ev'ry shade.   (10; st.16)

28. The phrase comes from "Arcadian Saloon," an article in *Punch* (1842): "all our readers to go to the Arcadian Saloon, where he will find a pleasant retreat for his careworn countenance" (180).

29. In conjunction with Angela Burdett-Coutts, Dickens "leased and renamed Urania Cottage" in the west end of London (Collins 99, 94). The "quaintly mid-Victorian" name gestures toward the intended "kindness and trustfulness" of the space (104, 105). "Urania" also refers to Lady Mary Wroth's foundling shepherdess, Urania, from *The Countesse of Mountgomeries Urania* (published in 1621), which connects pastoral romance with the recovered identities of disenfranchised women. By locating the establishment in Shepherd's Bush, Dickens symbolically imposes the rustic virtues of the *locus moralis* onto the Home for Homeless Women, a refuge for former prostitutes, in an attempt to inculcate honest labor, healthy living, and moral "fastening down" in the lives of the young Cottagers who, like metropastoral maidens, wore cheerful dresses rather than dull uniforms, listened to "selections from Wordsworth and Crabbe" during their needlework and straw-plaiting sessions (Collins 106, 330n39), participated in "the cultivation of little flower-beds" and the "singing of part-songs," and received "domestic training" and religious instruction (107). A century and half later, the entrance to the Red Line in Shepherd's Bush still bears witness to the area's metropastoral symbolism (see fig. 3).

30. Bradley Headstone is a schoolteacher who impersonates a rogue before attempting to murder Eugene Wrayburn. Rogue Riderhood is a water-rat who evidently murders Gaffer Hexam before impersonating a schoolteacher. Addressing Headstone's pupils as "my lambs" (793; bk. 4, ch.15), Riderhood invades Headstone's school and blackmails the teacher-shepherd. In truth, both men are rogues who use their theatricality to destroy others.

31. Slater believes that the "attention-grabbing opening" of Dickens's will—which "boldly and prominently names the woman with whom his own name *has, in knowing literary and metropolitan circles, long been scandalously linked*"— exonerates Ternan: "I believe he intended this naming of Nelly to be taken as a public assertion of the innocence of his relationship with her" (emphasis added 615). My question is not about the nature of the relationship but its length: How far back does it extend? To September 2, 1865, when the Postscript appeared? If so, then those in the "knowing literary and metropolitan circles" would have recognized Dickens's relationship with Nelly by its striking absence in the Postscript.

WORKS CITED

Ackroyd, Peter. *Dickens*. New York: Harper Collins, 1990.

——. *Thames: Sacred River*. London: Chatto & Windus, 2007.

Allen, Michelle. *Cleansing the City: Sanitary Geographies in Victorian London.* Athen, OH: Ohio State UP, 2008.

Fig. 3 "Shepherd's Bush Subway Sign." Photograph by Malcolm Edwards. Copyright © 2011 Malcolm Edwards.

Alpers, Paul. *What Is Pastoral?* Chicago: U of Chicago P, 1996.

Alter, Robert. *Imagined Cities: Urban Experience and the Language of the Novel.* New Haven: Yale UP, 2005.

"Arcade." *Oxford English Dictionary.* Web. 11 Aug. 2007.

"Arcadian Saloon." *Punch* 3 (1842): 180. Microform. Library of Congress.

Atsma, Aaron J. "Akheloios." *Theoi Greek Mythology.* Auckland, New Zealand. 2000–2008. Web. 26 Sept. 2007.

———. "Hermes." *Theoi Greek Mythology.* Auckland, New Zealand. 2000–2008. Web. 26 Sept. 2007.

———. "Potamoi." *Theoi Greek Mythology.* Auckland, New Zealand. 2000–2008. Web. 24 Sept. 2007.

Bachelard, Gaston. *The Poetics of Space: The Classic Look at How We Experience Intimate Places.* Trans. Maria Jolas. Boston: Beacon, 1969.

Bakhtin, Mikhail. *The Dialogic Imagination: Four Essays.* Trans. Caryl Emerson and Michael Holquist. Austin: U of Texas P, 1981.

Baldwin, Anna. "Midas." *Encyclopedia Mythica*. Web. 19 June 2008.

Baumgarten, Murray. "The Imperial Child: Bella, *Our Mutual Friend*, and the Victorian Picturesque." *Dickens and the Children of Empire*. Ed. Wendy S. Jacobson. New York: Palgrave, 2000. 54–66.

Bloom, Harold. *Bloom's Literary Guide to London*. London: Chelsea House, 2006.

Collins, Philip. *Dickens and Crime*. London: Macmillian, 1962.

"Crook." *Oxford English Dictionary*. Web. 15 Mar. 2008.

Dickens, Charles. "Arcadian London." *The Uncommercial Traveler*. The Oxford Illustrated Dickens. Oxford: Oxford UP, 1860; rpt. 1958.

———. *Bleak House*. The Oxford Illustrated Dickens. Oxford: Oxford UP, 1852–1853; rpt. 1948.

———. "A Christmas Carol." *Christmas Books*. The Oxford Illustrated Dickens. Oxford: Oxford UP, 1852; rpt. 1954.

———. *The Mystery of Edwin Drood*. The Oxford Illustrated Dickens. Oxford: Oxford UP, 1870; rpt. 1956.

———. *Our Mutual Friend*. The Oxford Illustrated Dickens. Oxford: Oxford UP, 1865; rpt. 1952.

Dionne, Craig, and Steve Mentz, ed. *Rogues and Early Modern English Culture*. Ann Arbor: U of Michigan P, 2007.

Dvorak, Wilfred. "Dickens and Popular Culture: Silas Wegg's Ballads in *Our Mutual Friend*." *The Dickensian* 86.3 (Autumn 1990): 142–57.

Francis, George Willam. *The Art of Modelling Waxen Flower, Fruit*. London: Simpkin, Marshall, 1849. Web. 7 July 2008.

Foucault, Michel. "Of Other Spaces." Trans. Jay Miskowiec. *Diacritics* 16 (1986): 22–27.

Gibbon, Edward. *The History of the Decline and Fall of the Roman Empire*. London: John Murray, 1872.

Gould, Stephen Jay. "Syphilis and the Shepherd of Atlantis." *Natural History* (October 2000). Web. 10 Aug. 2008.

Johnson, Derek. *Pastoral in the Work of Charles Dickens*. New York: Peter Lang, 1992.

Johnson, Edgar. *Charles Dickens: His Tragedy and Triumph*. New York: Penguin, 1979.

Kinney, Arthur F., ed. *Rogues, Vagabonds, & Sturdy Beggars: A New Gallery of Tudor and Early Stuart Rogue Literature Exposing the Lives, Times, and Cozening Tricks of the Elizabethan Underworld*. Amherst: U of Massachusetts P, 1990.

"London Out of Town," *Punch* 11 (1846): 42. Microform. Library of Congress.

Mack, Robert L. *The Wonderful and Surprising History of Sweeney Todd: The Life and Times of an Urban Legend*. New York: Continuum, 2007.

Matthews, W. H. *Mazes and Labyrinths: Their History and Development*. 1922. Rpt. New York: Dover, 1970.

Moore, Thomas. *The Poetical Works of Thomas Moore*. N.p.: Jules Didot, 1829.

Morgentaler, Goldie. "Dickens and the Scattered Identity of Silas Wegg." *Dickens Quarterly* 22.2 (June 2005): 92–100.

Morson, Gary Saul, and Caryl Emerson. *Mikhail Bakhtin: Creation of a Prosaics*. Stanford: Stanford UP, 1990.

Morus, Iwan Rhys. "Electricity on Show: Spectacular Events in London." *Fathom Consortium*. Web. 9 Sept. 2008.

Nonnos. *Dionysiaca*. Trans. W. H. D. Rouse. Cambridge: Harvard UP, 1940.

Page, Norman. *A Dickens Companion*. New York: Schocken, 1987.

———. "Silas Wegg Reads Gibbon." *The Dickensian* 68 (1972): 115.

Picard, Liza. *Victorian London*. Oxford: Oxford UP, 2005.

Pionke, Albert D. *Plots of Opportunity: Conspiracy in Victorian England*. Columbus: Ohio State UP, 2004.

Pope, Alexander. *Alexander Pope: Selected Poetry*. Ed. Douglas Grant. New York: Penguin, 1971.

Reed, John. "The Riches of Redundancy: *Our Mutual Friend*." *Studies in the Novel* 38.1 (Mar. 2006): 1–15.

Robson, John M. "Crime in *Our Mutual Friend*" in *Rough Justice: Essays on Crime in Literature*. Ed. M. L. Friedland. Toronto: U of Toronto P, 1991. 114–40.

"Salvage." *Classic Encyclopedia*. Web. 14 Jan. 2008.

Sannazaro, Jacopo. *Piscatorial Eclogues*. Trans. Ralph Nash. Detroit: Wayne State UP, 1966.

Shakespeare, William. *The Winter's Tale*. *The Riverside Shakespeare*. 2nd edition. Ed. G. Blakemore Evans. New York: Houghton Mifflin, 1997.

"Shepherd's Bush Subway Sign." Digital photograph by Malcolm Edwards. *Flickr*. Web. 14 Mar. 2011.

Slater, Michael. *Charles Dickens*. New Haven: Yale UP, 2009.

Spiller, Brian. *Victorian Public Houses*. New York: Arco, 1973.

Smith, Hallet. Introduction to *The Winter's Tale*. *The Riverside Shakespeare*. 2nd edition. Ed. G. Blakemore Evans. New York: Houghton Mifflin, 1997. 1612–1616.

Spenser, Edmund. *Spenser: Poetical Works*. Ed. J. C. Smith and E. de Selincourt. Oxford: Oxford UP, 1983.

Theocritus. *The Idylls*. Trans. Robert Wells. New York: Penguin, 1989.

Tillotson, Kathleen, and Nina Burgis, ed. *The Letters of Charles Dickens*, Vol. 4: 1844–1846. Pilgrim Edition. Oxford: Clarendon, 1978.

Virgil. *The Eclogues*. Trans. Guy Lee. New York: Penguin, 1980.

West, Gilian. "The Macabre Use of the Pastoral in *Bleak House*." *The Dickensian* 93.2 (Summer 1997): 126–32.

Wirth-Nesher, Hana. "Impartial Maps: Reading and Writing Cities." *Handbook of Urban Studies*. Ed. Ronan Paddison. London: Sage, 2001. 52–66.

Recent Dickens Studies and
Adaptations: 2009

Shari Hodges Holt

*This study summarizes the extensive body of Dickens scholarship pro-
duced in 2009, including discussion of over one hundred articles and
books. While attempting to be comprehensive, the survey calls attention
to works of special merit that may have a lasting impact on Dickens
studies. In addition, the survey addresses several recent Dickens-related
adaptations in film, fiction, and the graphic novel (represented by a
sampling of illustrations) and offers some speculations about the current
surge in pop-culture appropriations of Dickens, particularly the fascination of contemporary novelists with the final years of Dickens's life.
The materials are organized under the following headings: Intertextual
and Cross-Cultural Influences; Gender, Sexuality, Marriage, and Children; Science, Religion, and Philosophy; Law, Economics, and Politics;
Victorian Media and Spectacle; Geographical Spaces; Studies of Adaptations in Fiction and Film; Studies of Individual Works; Biographies
and Reference Works; and Recent Adaptations: Graphic Novels, Films,
and Fiction.*

Dickens has been firmly entrenched in the popular consciousness since the
publication of *The Pickwick Papers*, and the extent of both scholarly and
pop-culture products being produced under his name today demonstrates that
he remains an important vehicle for breaching the "great divide" between
high and low culture. Therefore, I am pleased that the editors of the *Dickens
Studies Annual* have allowed me to include in this survey, in addition to the

Dickens Studies Annual, Volume 42, Copyright © 2011 by AMS Press, Inc. All
rights reserved.

annual assessment of Dickens scholarship, a review of recent Dickens-related films, fiction, and graphic narratives, all remarkable evidence of the depth and breadth of the Inimitable's continuing influence in our century. The year 2009 produced a formidable body of Dickens scholarship remarkable in both its scope and quality, consisting of over one hundred articles, book chapters, and books. I admit that I experienced some considerable trepidation in approaching such a leviathan, but I was continually delighted by the accessibility as well as the erudition of the works I encountered, many of which will leave a lasting impact on Dickens studies. Victorian print culture and gender studies remained particularly prolific areas of research, with some wonderful new contributions to queer studies, while a resurgence of film studies related to Dickens produced numerous discussions of individual films as well as innovative investigations of trends in the television industry. This year witnessed the release in the United States of an unusual number of television and film versions of Dickens's novels, all discussed here, in addition to several new adaptations in the "graphic novel" format, an increasingly popular means of introducing classic literature to a visually oriented society. A fascination among fiction writers with the concluding years of Dickens's life resulted in several novels about the collapse of Dickens's marriage and the composition of the unfinished *The Mystery of Edwin Drood*, a phenomenon upon which I offer some speculations at the end of this survey. My study of this wide range of scholarly research and Dickensiana left me with lingering questions. Why do we remain mesmerized by Dickens in the twenty-first century to the extent that he continues to appear not only on our bookshelves and in our classrooms but on our television and movie screens? While we acknowledge a genius in his art that seems to give us endless things to say about his oeuvre, what is it about his life, works, and culture that has particular appeal for the postmodern world? I hope this study will prompt us to consider these especially intriguing questions as we approach the bicentennial of Dickens's birth.

I have divided my survey into the following topics: Intertextual and Cross-Cultural Influences; Gender, Sexuality, Marriage, and Children; Science, Religion, and Philosophy; Law, Economics, and Politics; Victorian Media and Spectacle; Geographical Spaces; Studies of Adaptations in Fiction and Film; Studies of Individual Works; Biographies and Reference Works; and Recent Adaptations: Graphic Novels, Films, and Fiction. I acknowledge that many of these categories overlap (which I have tried to indicate in some specific cases), and I apologize to any scholars whose works I may have missed in this endeavor.

Intertextual and Cross-Cultural Influences

The year 2009 produced a wide variety of studies related to issues of influence— Dickens's impact on Victorian literature and other authors, the influence of other writers and texts on Dickens's fiction, and the effect of cultural differences on the translation of Dickens's fiction into other languages. I turn first to James Eli Adams's *A History of Victorian Literature*, which places Dickens within the literary context of his age. Adams's thoroughly engaging "narrative history" (ix) details the development of the novel, poetry, drama, and the prose essay throughout the Victorian period. A distinctive feature of this history is Adams's reliance on contemporary reviews to help the reader envision the works of Victorian authors within their original social and historical contexts. This technique is especially illuminating in relation to Dickens (whose work, according to Adams, comprised "the single most important literary career of the Victorian era" [50]). For example, early reviews of *The Pickwick Papers* reveal the confusion readers initially experienced in classifying the work (Adams notes that one reviewer called it "a magazine consisting of only one article" [55]), forecasting the revolutionary effect that *Pickwick* would have on the development of the novel. Indeed, Adams designates *Pickwick* as "[t]he single work that more than any other shaped the Victorian novel as a literary form" (55).

Examining Dickens's rise to fame within the framework of popular literature of the 1830s, Adams deftly assesses the sources of Dickens's unique appeal. While the humorous depiction of numerous lower-class characters in *The Pickwick Papers* and Dickens's early London sketches provided "the quasi-ethnographic pleasure of contact with exotic worlds that a middle-class audience also enjoyed in both the silver-fork and the criminal novel," Dickens's work "did not provoke the hostility aroused by those other forms" because his early fiction managed to "represent social division without making it threatening" (57). Ultimately he leavened the exotic attraction of urban life with sympathy to help create "a nostalgic cultural imaginary that would echo through Victorian literature" (58).

Dickens's individual novels receive significant treatment throughout Adams's study in terms of their influence on the literature of the period, but Adams is most effective at painting the "big picture," conveying Dickens's sweeping impact on a variety of literary genres (the Newgate novel, melodrama, sensation fiction, etc.) and other prominent authors of the age. Adams's depiction of the remarkable power of Dickens's persona in the minds of the reading public is also striking, particularly in analyzing the mixed reception of Forster's biography in 1872, which failed to realize the public's inflated expectations regarding the private life of their literary idol, resulting in "Dickens's reputation being unwittingly diminished by a biographer who wrote in the spirit of adulation" (335). Finally, Adams's delightful prose makes this history eminently readable, occasionally illuminating the study with incisive statements on the significance of particular authors, as in his assessment of the contrast between Dickens and Thackeray: "If the early Dickensian narrator seemed a benevolent neighbor, Thackeray's is the acquaintance who raises awkward questions about one's bank account" (116).

Such wit combines with penetrating analysis throughout to make this a highly accessible overview of the literature of the age.

In "A Steam-Whistle Modernist?: Representations of King Alfred in Dickens's *A Child's History of England* and *The Battle of Life*," Emily Walker Heady considers the relationship of Dickens's works to the Victorian medieval revival. Heady attests that although Dickens's fiction does not show the intense interest in the Middle Ages found in the works of many of his contemporaries, his representations of medieval subjects in some of his minor works reflect attitudes towards the past that were typically Victorian. For instance, Dickens's portrayal of King Alfred in *A Child's History of England* demonstrates the didactic approach to history favored by many Victorians (particularly Carlyle), as Dickens transforms Alfred into a "pedagogical tool" for modeling "good citizenship for his young readers" (95). The highlight of Heady's essay, however, is an extended, astute reading of how Dickens handles personal, family, and national history in the critically neglected Christmas book *The Battle of Life*. Heady claims that the battlefield metaphor in this novella introduces a central Victorian debate about history—"whether it exists primarily as a collection of artifacts or as a text that teaches right living" (101). Jedder sees the artifacts of the battlefield as a muddled collection of material objects, while Alfred (who is modeled on the medieval king) sees them as "an instructive textbook" for teaching heroic ideals (103). But Dickens depicts both material and idealistic approaches as incomplete. Simply "uniting materiality with aesthetics" is also unsatisfactory, as Dickens demonstrates in his 1850 *Household Words* article "Old Lamps for New Ones," in which he critiques the medievalism of Pre-Raphaelite art as nothing more than a beautifully painted collection of details (106). Heady argues that *The Battle of Life* ultimately demonstrates that a right relationship to history is achieved only through engagement with the personal past. For Dickens, "history is autobiography, and reflecting on the struggles of the Middle Ages is a way to meditate on his own personal issues," a point reflected in the parallels between the novella's love triangle (Alfred loves the two sisters, Marion and Grace) and Dickens's own marital situation (106). Jedder and Alfred finally achieve this personal relationship to history through the loss and eventual recovery of Marion (Jedder's daughter and Alfred's fiancée). Thus, for Dickens, "we study history in order to learn to mourn; we learn to mourn in order to cultivate deeper affection for our fellow men;" and in this manner we endow each individual's history with significance within the broader scheme of the past (109).

Jerome Meckier's " 'A Wife in Two Volumes': the 'Something Wanting' in *David Copperfield* and *The Woman in White*" is a creative analysis of a significant echo between the two novels and the personal lives of their authors. Meckier examines *David Copperfield*'s famous statement of discontent after delineating his marital dissatisfaction with Dora, that "there was always something wanting" in his life (Dickens qtd. in Meckier 14), and sees the passage echoed in *The Woman in White* when Walter Hartright notices "something wanting" in his relationship with his beloved Laura Fairlie, only to discover that what was missing was a recognition of her similarity to her half-sister, the asylum fugitive Anne Catherick. Meckier attests that the "something wanting" that David and Hartright both experience is actually "the insufficiency of male-female relationships involving just one woman." "Walter's job," Meckier contends, "is to complete Laura by pairing her with the right half-sister," which he finally achieves when he establishes a household with both the beautiful, fragile Laura and her more powerful, man-like half-sister, Marian Halcombe. In pairing Laura with her opposite, "Hartright discovers the perfect combination: the idea of keeping one woman for intellectual stimulation and another who is well-off and physically attractive" (15). Meckier sees Hartright's household as a deliberate reworking of David Copperfield's domestic arrangements, which are never entirely satisfactory because "Copperfield's women come in succession instead of in pairs and as partners. Dora is never sensible; Agnes is not sexy enough" (16).

Meckier attests that Collins actually extends his parody from Dickens's fiction to his personal life, "[r]econfiguring Copperfield, Dora, and Agnes as Hartright, Laura, and Marian" in order to create "a triangular household as a parodic response to David's fumblings with Dora and Agnes, not to mention Dickens's personal difficulties with Catherine [Dickens] and Ellen [Ternan]," which strikingly contrasted Collins's "two smoothly run households presided over by [his mistresses] Caroline Graves and Martha Rudd" (16). Ultimately, Meckier traces this satirical rewrite of *Copperfield* to Collins's sense of rivalry with his more famous and accomplished colleague. There is something delightfully audacious about Meckier's reading, as he triumphantly asserts that "Collins writes the only parodic revaluation in Victorian fiction of a rival's novel and lifestyle simultaneously" (17). However, Meckier points out that Dickens "retaliated in *Great Expectations* by eclipsing both of Collins's women in white with Miss Havisham, a more unforgettable symbolic figure" who embodied the discontent of the age (18–19).

While the influence of Cervantes's *Don Quixote* on Dickens's fiction (particularly *The Pickwick Papers*) has been well explored, Pamela H. Long's "Dickens, Cervantes, and the Pick-Pocketing of an Image" traces an intriguing possible genealogy between Cervantes's novel *Rinconete and Cortadillo* and Dickens's *Oliver Twist*. Citing George Cruikshank's well-known claims of having inspired the characters of Dickens's novel through his illustrations, Long suggests that Cruikshank may indeed have had an influence, although more indirect, on the authorship of *Oliver Twist* through the "triangular relationship" of Dickens as writer and Cruikshank as illustrator to the works of Cervantes (191). Dickens first became aware of Cruikshank's work through an 1833 translation of *Don Quixote* that Cruikshank had illustrated, which possibly renewed Dickens's interest in Cervantes, prompting him to turn to a new translation of Cervantes's *Exemplary Novels* (containing *Rinconete and Cortadillo*), published in 1832 by Richard Bentley (who would, of course, publish *Oliver Twist* in *Bentley's Miscellany*). Although Long is unable to prove that Dickens was familiar with *Rinconete and Cortadillo*, the web of connections between Dickens and Cervantes's text is fascinating. Long further supports the possibility of authorial influence by expounding on several parallels between the novels, including the gang of pickpockets, the predominance of street slang, the pocket-handkerchief game, and comparable characters among the criminals, particularly the villains Fagin and Monipodio, who reflect corresponding "morphologies of the Semite bogeyman—for the Englishman, the crouching, avaricious Jew; for the Spaniard, the menacing Moor" (194). Long provocatively concludes, "Dickens may well guilelessly defend himself against the charges of pinching Cruikshank's characters because indeed he hadn't. It was Cervantes's pocket he had picked" (194).

Two articles by Rodney Stenning Edgecombe examine intertextual influences in Dickens's works. The short essay "Nonprogressive Journeys in Dickens, Twain, and Conrad" briefly discusses the trope of the "journey going nowhere" (212), examining the description of water journeys in Dickens's Christmas stories "The Wreck of the Golden Mary" (1856) and "The Perils of Certain English Prisoners" (1857) as precursors to Marlow's journey into the Congo in Joseph Conrad's *Heart of Darkness* and Huckleberry Finn's journey on the river raft in Mark Twain's novel. Edgecombe notes that in the expeditions described by all three authors, the "futile movement" of the subjects (215) would be especially problematic for Victorian readers "committed to ideas of meliorism and progress" (212). In "Dickens, Hood, and the Comedy of Language Learning," Edgecombe considers the connections between "imperialism, international travel and language-learning" (274) implicit in comic scenes of linguistic misunderstanding from Shakespeare's *The Merry Wives of Windsor*, Defoe's *Robinson Crusoe*, Thomas Hood's letters, and Dickens's *Little Dorrit* and *Our Mutual Friend*. Edgecombe's analysis of Dickens is brief but instructive. Examining Hood's epistolary account of his wife's comic attempts to teach English to their German maid, Edgecombe speculates on the likelihood that Hood's letter was a source for the scenes in *Little Dorrit* in which Mrs. Plornish and the inhabitants of Bleeding Heart Yard attempt to teach English to the Italian Cavaletto. Regardless of their possible literary genealogy, the comic language lessons in both texts replicate the "master and servant" power dynamics of imperialism, supported by an attitude of "colonial or national condescension" (274) that Edgecombe sees epitomized in Mr. Podsnap of *Our Mutual Friend*.

In "Envy and Victorian Fiction," William A. Cohen examines intertextual connections in the Victorian novel's approach to the pathology of envy. Cohen contends that envy is a powerful tool for the traditional plot's dual impetus towards both extension and closure and also serves the novel's ethical need to establish sympathetic connection between characters and audience because envy "interrupts the straight course of the marriage plot as well as the development of a capacity for sympathy" (297). Cohen investigates "psychological," "social," and "moral" envy respectively in novels by Dickens, Anthony Trollope, and George Eliot, arguing that envy "is posed against shame in *Little Dorrit*, benevolence in *The Way We Live Now*, and sympathy in *Middlemarch*" (298). According to Cohen, the major characters of *Little Dorrit* are distinguished by "different versions of shame management," whereas "[e]nvy is most obviously associated with more minor and grotesque characters," such as Mrs. Clennam, Rigaud/Blandois, and Miss Wade (298). But the envy of the minor characters is "contagious," infecting even Arthur and Little Dorrit so that they become "greedy and possessive of the love they fear they cannot secure" (299–300). Thus, Dickens "emphasizes the intrapsychic dimensions of envy, seeing its violence as a problem of individuals that needs rooting out in order to make the corrupt world a more benign and humane place" in which the shame that pervades it can be stabilized (300). In contrast, Trollope presents a "universally cynical" world in which envy is "social and systemic" and "is acutely attuned to distinctions of status and wealth" (300), while Eliot depicts a world in which sympathy "forestalls and defeats envy through its forms of identification, incorporation, and selflessness" (302).

Sarah Gates's "Intertextual Estella: *Great Expectations*, Gender, and Literary Tradition" examines how the novel's major intertexts—George Lillo's 1731 play *The London Merchant*, Shakespeare's *Hamlet*, and Mary Shelley's *Frankenstein*—help to construct an identity for Estella that combines the two most popular critical readings of her character as heartless tormentor and victim of circumstance. While other scholars have discussed the impact of these intertextual references on our interpretation of Pip's expectations, none have considered their effect on the characterization of Estella. Examining the scene in which Mr. Wopsle performs *The London Merchant* for Pip and Pumblechook, Gates points out that the evocation of Sarah Millwood, the prostitute from the play, makes a much more complex "intertextual contribution" to Estella's characterization (393) than a mere association with the destructive seductress stereotype. Gates examines Millwood's bitter speeches to her accusers in which she reveals that her wickedness resulted from her mistreatment by men and compares them to Estella's speeches to her "creator" Miss Havisham, suggesting that the play and the novel reveal that both temptresses have been shaped by forces beyond their control. Gates likewise demonstrates how parallels to *Hamlet*'s Ophelia place Estella in a more sympathetic light. Both women are schooled by their families against the dangers of affection for men, and both are deployed by their guardians as snares to entrap the young heroes. But Victorian audiences' interpretation of Ophelia as an unwilling pawn, entirely innocent of her family's machinations, reflects "the picture Estella wants Pip to see: that she has no willing part in the wicked designs on him; indeed she seems as helplessly ensnared in that plot as he is" (396). Gates also compares Ophelia's apparent suicide to Estella's marriage to Bentley Drummle, noting that each woman's only means of escaping the plots of those who use her is to sacrifice her body (397). Finally, Gates examines how references to *Frankenstein* make us consider the creation of a monstrous femininity for Estella as the result of a patchwork series of characterizations of her by other characters in the novel, especially Pip. Gates deduces in this depiction of Estella, Dickens "seems to have intuited the experience of being a woman who is shaped in accordance with the ideologies of those who would possess and explain her" and that this artificial construction of her femininity "is made visible to us by the intertextual layers that Dickens (as opposed to Pip) includes" (399).

In *Under Conrad's Eyes: The Novel as Criticism*, Michael John DiSanto explores the connections between Joseph Conrad's novels and the writings of several nineteenth–century authors, including Dickens. In particular, DiSanto examines Conrad's *The Secret Agent* as "an impressive rewriting of Dickens's *Bleak House*" (17) that highlights the epistemological uncertainties of Dickens's text. DiSanto argues that the detective narratives of both novels investigate the complicated "relationship between knowing and not knowing" (17) as the characters attempt to escape unbearable knowledge or allow knowledge of particular facts to blind them to other alternatives. Especially enlightening is DiSanto's discussion of how Conrad refashions particular characters: Lady Dedlock becomes Winnie Verloc, whose unhappy marriage results in murder and suicide; Jo parallels the mentally disabled boy Stevie; and Inspector Bucket and Tulkinghorn are transformed into Inspector Heat and the Assistant Commissioner, who ironically rely on their obsessive investigations to hide from painful knowledge.

Kirsten Wolf's "The Adventures of David Copperfield in Nova Scotia" provides an intriguing examination of the parallels between Dickens's *David Copperfield* and Icelandic-Canadian author Jóhann Magús Bjarnason's bildungsroman *Eiríkur Hansson* (1899–1903), which recounts the experiences of an Icelandic boy emigrating to Canada in the late nineteenth century. While the first half of Wolf's essay gives an exhaustive summary of Bjarnason's novel, the second half delineates its striking similarities to *Copperfield*, including resemblances in plot and characters, the unifying factor of a single first-person narrative voice, and the powerfully retrospective nature of both narratives. Most interesting are the parallels between the protagonists' love interests. Like David, Eiríkur is married twice, first to a woman distinguished by strong sexual attraction, and second to a woman who provides sisterly affection; however, in Bjarnason's novel, the sisterly love interest comes to live with Eiríkur and his first wife prior to her death, a "kind of *ménage à trois*" that "Dickens's Victorian novel does not permit" (310), but which, oddly enough, more closely parallels Dickens's own domestic arrangements with his wife and her sisters (a striking connection that Wolf fails to recognize). Wolf concludes that critics' frequent erroneous assumption that *Eiríkur Hansson* is autobiographical reveals Bjarnason's success at transforming a Victorian novel into a tale of Icelandic immigration (314).

The remaining studies surveyed in this section are concerned with cross-cultural influences in the criticism and translation of Dickens's works. Jan Lokin's "Realism and Reality in Dickens's Characters: Dickens Seen through the Eyes of Dutch Writers" surveys the critical response to Dickens's fiction by Dutch writers during the century following his death, noting that the concepts of realism and reality are central for these critics and that these concepts shift in meaning over the decades. Lokin chronologically examines the works of several critics to demonstrate how different phases in Dutch criticism were dominated by different concerns: morality in the nineteenth century, psychology in the early twentieth-century, socioeconomics in the 1950s, and the mythic imagination in the 1960s and '70s. Lokin argues that "all these 'realities' appear in Dickens, to greater or lesser degrees," making the characters of his universe "real in more than one sense" (30–31) and therefore forever fascinating to critics despite the perpetual variations in the critical lens through which they view Dickens's work.

Four outstanding studies investigate the translation of Dickens's novels into other languages. In "Charles Dickens's and Apollo Korzeniowski's *Hard Times*," Ewa Kujawska-Lis examines the first Polish translation of *Hard Times* published in 1866 by translator Apollo Korzeniowski, a Polish writer who was the father of Joseph Conrad, a particularly interesting fact in light of the Dickensian influence that scholars such as Edgecombe and DiSanto trace in Conrad (see the above discussion). Kujawska-Lis stresses the translation's contemporaneity, published just ten years after Dickens's original, as an important factor contributing to Korzeniowski's accurate representation of the original's Dickensian atmosphere and nineteenth-century language; but Kujawska-Lis likewise demonstrates that Korzeniowski succeeded in creating a text that is a work of art in its own right, carefully balancing fidelity to Dickens's original with the flexibility to alter or add occasional materials that would make Dickens's central meanings more comprehensible to a Polish audience.

Christine Raguet's "Terror Foreign or Familiar—Pleasure on the Edge: Translating *A Tale of Two Cities* into French" likewise illustrates how the translator's societal background influences the translation process. Raguet examines three significant French translations of Dickens's *A Tale of Two Cities* to demonstrate how the French cultural understanding of The Terror impacts translators' handling of Dickens's depiction, arguing that all three versions reflect "the French tendency to assuage the horror, as if all the exactions of The Terror had been (or had to be) hidden in our minds' closet" (179). Raguet insightfully attests that "the traumatic experience of The Terror is inscribed in the French collective mind and if translators cannot deny the original text they are translating, they can make choices and emendations so as to protect themselves or the group they stand for from being directly linked to the horror described" (180). This may likewise explain why, of all Dickens's works, *A Tale* is the least known in France. Raguet concludes that the treatment of *A Tale* by French translators "may prove that the qualities of a translation do not depend on the translators' practical skills but on their personal implication in the text they are reading and they are writing" (183).

Irina Gredina and Philip Allingham's essay "The Countess Vera Sergeevna Tolstaya's Russian Language Adaptation of *Great Expectations* (1895)" provides another fascinating study of Dickens's impact across cultural and linguistic boundaries. In her 1895 Russian translation of *Great Expectations*, the Countess Tolstaya "retells rather than merely translates" the original (126), suggesting an impulse on her part "to collaborate with Dickens" in addressing a new audience, the Russian working class (131). Gredina and Allingham illustrate the losses and the advantages resulting from this technique through careful comparison of Tolstaya's translated passages with Dickens's original text. The examples indicate that while Tolstaya successfully adapted "the original's atmosphere, tone, characters, and background," the complexities of Dickens's humor (particularly his irony) and Pip's "double-voiced psychology" are lost (124). Most interesting are the ramifications of Tolstaya's new title, *The Daughter of the Convict, or, from the Forge into Wealth*, which reflects Tolstaya's purpose "to demonstrate the moral superiority of ordinary people's lives" in her attempt to reach a new peasant readership (130). Gredina and Allingham finally characterize Tolstaya's adaptation as a sensitive attempt to make Dickens accessible to a new audience that ultimately expanded Dickens's Russian readership and enhanced his impact on future Russian novelists.

Paola Venturi's "*David Copperfield* Conscripted: Italian Translations of the Novel" reveals what can be lost in translation when the translator's cultural values take precedence. Venturi surveys several Italian adaptations and translations of Dickens's novel to argue that "Dickens's status as a canonized author and the Italian tendency to read (and write) for instruction" encourage "the adoption of a didactic aim and a duly elevated style for use in translations" (234–35). Venturi demonstrates a typical twofold process of adapting the original through "ethical simplification," which eliminates features that might conflict with "the sanctioned values of Italian society" (such as the elopement of Emily and Steerforth, which is omitted in children's versions), and "linguistic simplification," which "erases, elevates, and homogenizes the different linguistic varieties of the source" (such as the Yorkshire dialect of the Peggottys, which disappears into the same elevated linguistic style assigned to the middle-class characters) (236). The hyperliterary, lofty style favored in Italian translations thus unfortunately eliminates the linguistic diversity in which so much of Dickens's humor and social criticism resides.

Gender, Sexuality, Marriage, and Children

An invaluable new reference guide to Dickens scholarship in the field of gender studies is Natalie B. Cole's *Dickens and Gender: Recent Studies, 1992–2008.* Expanded from her review essay on Dickens and gender that appeared in the 2008 volume of *Dickens Studies Annual,* Cole's selection of approximately two hundred scholarly sources includes both frequently cited authors in the field and lesser known works, and her concise and illuminating summaries of the sources provide an excellent overview of a particularly rich area in recent Dickens criticism. Cole deftly organizes the sources into categories that should be useful in pointing the researcher in the right direction, with chapters on the following topics: "Families," including sections on marriage, motherhood, fatherhood, surrogate parenting, and children; "Sexualities," covering works on lesbian erotics and homoerotics, incest, theories of embodiment, and concepts of masculinity and femininity (with special sections on bachelors, "odd women," and "fallen women"); "Work," discussing studies of the domestic space as well as the relationship of masculinities and femininities to work; "Victorian and Other Cultural Contexts," including studies of imperialism, industrialism, archetype and myth; and "Gender, Genre, and Narrative," which includes special sections on gender and narrative in *Dombey and Son, David Copperfield,* and *Bleak House.* Cole's comprehensive coverage as well as her precise organization make this volume an ideal "first stop" for scholars engaged in research on this topic.

Studies by Daun Jung and Molly Clark Hillard focus on constructions of femininity in *Our Mutual Friend.* In "Gender Mobility in *Our Mutual Friend*: Spatial and Social Transformations of Three Major Female Characters— Bella, Lizzie and Jenny Wren," Jung explores the impact of urban space on female subjectivity in Dickens's novel. As a theoretical framework, Jung employs Michel de Certeau's distinction between "strategic voyeurs," the powerful who strategically envision and control the rules of space, and "tactical walkers," the underprivileged who tactically manipulate and divert the planned spaces of those in power (209). She identifies John Harmon and Eugene Wrayburn as "strategic voyeurs" who use their freedom to traverse urban spaces and alter their own identities in order to observe the women they love and shape their movements and identities to fit the men's objectives. Bella Wilfer and Lizzie Hexam are "tactical walkers" whose "spatial and social mobility is severely limited by these male practices" (211–12) and who are "forced by their male counterparts to move between different spaces" (such as Lizzie's retreat to Riah's sanctuary to escape Eugene's seduction) (212); however, Jung argues that at some points they "transcend such spatial boundaries/limitations with their own tactical moves" (211). One example is Bella's Greenwich expedition with her father in which Bella's enhanced agency is revealed through her increased mobility around the city and her transformation into "a pleasurable consumer" of London when she and her father shop and dine in an expensive restaurant (215). Bella actually becomes a strategic voyeur and temporarily "escapes the status of spectacle and becomes a spectator" when, looking down on a panoramic view of the city, she imagines a future for herself opposed to John Harmon's plans (216). Jung notes that although significant limitations remain, "[a]s tactical users of urban/social space," both Bella and Lizzie "imagine and dream about their future identities to achieve upward spatial/social mobility through marriage" (211). She concludes with a discussion of how Jenny Wren uses "tactical walking" to subvert her subjugation as a crippled female, traversing London's streets and observing real people to create her dolls, through which she critiques society (222).

In "Dickens's Little Red Riding Hood and Other Waterside Characters," Molly Clark Hillard examines the importance of the Little Red Riding Hood fable to the "narrative of fallen womanhood" that permeates Dickens's fiction (945). Hillard attests that by the nineteenth century Riding Hood "had become a cautionary lesson of fallen womanhood, her red cap shamefully emblematic" of both sexual and class transgression since her red riding cloak is a middle-class costume donned by a heroine who is apparently lower-class (952). Citing Dickens's famous remembrance of Little Red Riding Hood as his "first love" in his essay "A Christmas Tree," Hillard asserts that Riding Hood became a "lost object of desire" who appears repeatedly throughout Dickens's fiction in the form of the "lost" or "fallen" woman, particularly those working-class females whose transgressions drive them to consider suicide, usually by drowning. The association of the devouring wolf with the devouring river waters that threaten to engulf so many of Dickens's fallen females brings Hillard to *Our Mutual Friend*, Dickens's most extended linking of the Riding Hood tale with waterside imagery. The character in the novel most obviously connected to the Red Riding Hood fable is Lizzie Hexam, the endangered female whose sexual desire threatens her purity and whose refinement (evidenced in her lack of working-class accent) "clothes her in borrowed class as surely as does Red Riding Hood's cloak, and makes her equally a target for wolves" (965). But Lizzie, unlike Dickens's previous endangered females, is rescued from Red Riding Hood's fate by the displacement of class anxieties and threatening desires onto a series of carefully constructed male scapegoats, all of whom "bear elements of both wolf and Red Riding Hood" (964) and are punished for their rapacity through symbolic immersion, through which "Dickens muzzles male appetite of every kind, in every class category" (963). But Hillard concludes that it is only by immersion in the middle class through marriage that Lizzie's dangerous female desire finally "becomes sanctioned by Victorian standards for femininity" (969).

Natalie McKnight's delightful essay "The Erotics of *Barnaby Rudge*" argues that while eroticism is a quality seldom associated with Dickens's work, *Barnaby Rudge* seethes with an erotic energy that not only titillates readers, but also connects the novel's personal and historical plots and explores the dangers of sexual desire and gender stereotypes. McKnight examines how Dickens "plays with and against Victorian gender norms" to heighten sexual tensions between characters (24). Particularly striking is McKnight's analysis of the connection between Dolly and Hugh, the "two most sexually charged characters in the novel—perhaps anywhere in Dickens" (27). McKnight discusses the appeal of the potential sexual violence between them in terms of Freud's analysis of common sadomasochistic fantasies and notes that the sexual danger is heightened by the contrast between the traditional markers of femininity and masculinity associated with each character. McKnight sees this masculine/feminine "power differential" echoed in the scenes between Dolly and her father (30) and attests that the "eros of power" that Dickens associates with family dynamics becomes a conduit for uniting the romantic family plots with the orgiastic violence of the Gordon riots (33). Finally, the essay's greatest guilty pleasure lies in McKnight's playful analysis of how Hablot Browne's illustrations illuminate the erotics of the text (the illustration of Dolly dressing her father for a parade provokes an especially titillating discussion), which provides an added dimension to the novel's treatment of sexuality.

Two excellent studies by Gwen Hyman and Holly Furneaux explore constructions of masculinity in Dickens's works. Noting that gender studies of nineteenth-century culture have given ample attention to women's appetites, Gwen Hyman turns her focus instead on the gentleman "as an embodied creature" (11) in her book *Making a Man: Gentlemanly Appetites in the Nineteenth-Century Novel*. Hyman traces the embattled construction of gentlemanliness through images of eating in nineteenth-century fiction, arguing that the gentleman in "his alimental monstrousness" embodies the terrors of "the anxious, shifting middle-class" (3). Chapter 3 focuses on Dickens, providing an eloquent survey of consumption symbolism in *Little Dorrit* by narrating a "nightmare of capitalist getting and spending" (88) through contrasting the insatiable "economic gentleman" (represented in characters such as William Dorrit, Rigaud, Mr. Casby, and Mr. Merdle), whose voracious appetite for money and its attending status threatens to starve society (91), with the self-denying protagonist Arthur Clennam, whose only alternative to participation in a ravenous, grasping culture seems to be self-imposed starvation. Hyman exhibits exceptional skill in close reading of the text throughout this extensive and well-argued analysis.

A groundbreaking work that makes a unique contribution to queer studies, Holly Furneaux's *Queer Dickens: Erotics, Families, Masculinities* considers "new ways of conceptualizing queer in relation to the domestic" (14), revising conventional concepts of the "Dickensian domestic" and Victorian domesticity in general to demonstrate how Dickens's depictions of domesticity accommodate "surrogate and adoptive parenting, same-sex desire in homoaffirmative families of choice and intimate treatments of the body" (3). Furneaux argues that examination of Dickens's work "can direct us to the ways in which his culture could, and did, comfortably accommodate homoeroticism and forms of family founded on neither marriage nor blood" (3). Citing work by queer theorists such as Eve K. Sedgwick and William Cohen, Furneaux notes that queer studies of Dickens have been dominated by interpretations "that assert that Dickensian homoeroticism is most, or only, legible in acts of violence" (15). Furneaux focuses her study instead on positive "queer masculinities," particularly the "range of tender masculinities" in Dickens's fiction, examining "the ways in which Dickens's portrayals of nurturing masculinity and his concern with touch and affect between men challenge what we have been used to thinking about Victorian ideals of maleness" (7).

In an opening chapter on "bachelor dads," Furneaux examines the "adoption plot" common to much of Dickens's fiction, focusing on Dickens's celebration of the single male whose goal is not to reproduce but to nurture children. Particularly insightful is Furneaux's detailed comparison of Dickens's handling of adoption and unwanted children in his journalism and fiction with the treatment of these issues in the writings of John Brownlow, librarian of the London Foundling Hospital and possible namesake for Oliver Twist's "bachelor dad" Mr. Brownlow. Furneaux argues that by highlighting the problem of the uneven distribution of children across societal classes, the writings of both men reveal the limitations of the reproductive ideal as the basis for conceptualizing family. Another fine chapter examines "the queer possibilities of the serial form," arguing that, in contrast to the popular contemporary concept of bachelorhood as anti-domestic or unnatural, Dickens "redefines bachelor life as a positive lifestyle, rather than a state of incompleteness" (69), frequently using the serial format to disrupt the closure of the marital finale conventionally associated with the novel genre. Furneaux supports this argument with an excellent analysis of the role of bachelors throughout the serialization of *A Tale of Two Cities, The Pickwick Papers*, and *The Old Curiosity Shop*. She provides a fine reading of Sydney Carton from *Two Cities* as an example of the type of bachelor who resists incorporation within Dickens's queer conceptions of family—the bachelor of marriageable age. Even so, Carton's final speech, "positioned in the space of closure conventionally reserved for marriage in Victorian novels," is a "deeply queer statement of Dickens's total revision of the types of bonding on which family depends" (78).

In a chapter on the queer potential of marriage in Dickens's fiction, Furneaux explores how same-sex desire could be accommodated within the heterosexual marital relationship, investigating Dickens's use of the "in-lawing plot," in which close male friends marry the sisters of their comrades (111). In contrast, a chapter on "emigration plots" in Dickens's fiction considers how Dickens likewise acknowledged the limitations of domestic accommodation of same-sex desire, "recognizing the potential dissidence of homoerotics and negotiating alternative constructions of domesticity overseas" (141). A highlight of this section is a fine treatment of *Little Dorrit*'s Miss Wade, who finds her way into Furneaux's study, despite its focus on masculinities. The final two chapters concentrate on the "tender masculinities" exhibited through physical touch, analyzing same-sex nursing in the works of Dickens, Wilkie Collins, and Walt Whitman within the historical context of the feminization of professional nursing in the nineteenth century. An insightful postscript (discussed below under "Studies of Adaptations in Fiction and Film") examines queer interpretations of Dickens in recent film productions. Thus, Furneaux draws disparate materials together from film, fiction, journalism, and history to produce an impressive study that is rigorously researched and thoroughly convincing. One can only hope that a study of "queer femininities" in Dickens's works might be in Furneaux's future.

The next three studies concentrate on marriage and parenthood as methods of negotiating Victorian gender constructs. In *The January-May Marriage in Nineteenth-Century British Literature*, Esther Lui Godfrey explores gender issues through the common literary motif of marriage between an older man and a younger woman, a trope that she examines in the writings of several nineteenth-century authors, giving preeminence to Dickens as the Victorian novelist who wielded the trope with the greatest frequency and variety. Godfrey argues that the incestuous nature of the January-May marriage plot gave Victorian writers "a convenient method of integrating both subversive and normative approaches to gendered power into popular discourse under the guise of a legitimized, heterosexual union'' (57). Godfrey sees Dickens as both reinforcing and challenging gender norms through his use of this motif throughout his fiction. Through a careful and insightful examination of the failed marriage plots of Arthur Gride and Madeline Bray in *Nicholas Nickleby* and Quilp and Little Nell in *The Old Curiosity Shop*, Godfrey argues that by using intergenerational marriage to evoke horror, Dickens's early fiction ''outwardly accept[s] the incest taboo'' and ''upholds same-age heterosexuality as the ideal'' (59). In contrast, within later works, such as *David Copperfield* and *Bleak House*, Dickens uses an ''idealized incest'' (in which ''fatherly older husbands become sympathetic figures who are desired by their young brides'') to ''destabilize traditional marriage,'' ''foreground female agency'' through a new focus on female sexual desire, and ''reform 'bad' masculinity'' through evoking a new sympathy in the male characters for the sufferings of their female counterparts (58). Especially noteworthy in this study is Godfrey's exceptional analysis of intergenerational/incestuous desire in *The Cricket on the Hearth*, which provides a more complex and subtle reading of the incest motif beyond those interpretations that focus on female victimization.

''Charles Dickens and Captain Murderer,'' a chapter from Shuli Barzilai's *Tales of Bluebeard*, considers attitudes towards gender and marriage in Dickens's fiction through analysis of his frequent allusions to the Bluebeard fairy tale. Barzilai traces ''Dickens's triangulated management of the Bluebeard theme'' in various novels (35) to his personal anxieties and fantasies regarding his own domestic triangle with his wife Catherine and her sisters. While the Bluebeard fairy tale features a serial wife-murderer who is defeated by one of his brides and her sister, the Bluebeard figure repeatedly appears in Dickens's pre-1860 novels as part of a more positive ménage à trois through which the Bluebeard character is ''not merely rehabilitated . . . but rewarded in various ways'' (30). Allusions to Bluebeard in these novels accompany triangular marital relationships including an older man and a younger woman (usually a daughter) that enact ''a fantasy of ideal intrafamilial union'' (37), as in the diffusion of Gabriel Varden's marital tensions with his wife through his erotically charged relationship with his daughter Dolly in *Barnaby Rudge*, John Jarndyce's maneuverings between husband and father figure as he gives the hand of his ward Esther to his rival in *Bleak House*, and Louisa Gradgrind's reunion with her own rehabilitated father in *Hard Times* following the collapse of her marriage to the father substitute, Mr. Bounderby. Barzilai argues that in these cases, ''[i]t appears that what corrects or, at least, offsets the strains and storms of conventional marital coupling . . . is the introduction of a third'' (30), a paradigm replicated in Dickens's relations with the Hogarth sisters. However, in the tale of Captain Murderer from Dickens's 1860 essay ''Nurses Stories,'' transgressive desire is not only enacted but ultimately punished through the mutual self-destruction of the murderous husband and his brides, a version of the Bluebeard tale that expresses Dickens's guilt regarding the disintegration of his marriage and his pursuit of Ellen Ternan. Dickens's final Bluebeard allusion, made in reference not to a familial triangle but to the age-compatible, blissful marriage of Bella Wilfer and John Harmon in *Our Mutual Friend*, expresses the author's final desire "to capture the heart of the young woman who has captured his own" (42).

In *The Tragi-Comedy of Victorian Fatherhood*, Valerie Sanders examines popular nineteenth-century constructions of masculinity in marriage and parenting, setting out to dismantle the stereotype of the stern, imperious Victorian patriarch by examining fatherhood from the father's perspective through close investigation of the correspondence and diaries (in some cases unpublished) of several prominent Victorian fathers. In her introduction, Sanders demonstrates how the developing ideology of separate spheres, while placing the mother at the center of the home, left the father's domestic function (outside of his legal and financial responsibilities for his family) largely untheorized, forcing Victorian fathers to develop "their own alternative subculture" through which they could acknowledge feelings and experiences traditionally associated with the "feminine" world of childrearing and at odds with public concepts of masculinity (26).

Sanders selects case histories that cover a wide range of the Victorian intelligentsia among whom she draws illuminating parallels and contrasts. Chapter 2, "Theatrical Fatherhood: Dickens and Macready," compares Dickens and his friend Thomas Macready in terms of the manner in which each negotiated the boundaries between his private life as a father and his professional existence. While none of the material Sanders incorporates from Dickens's letters and his children's memoirs is new, her analysis of the connections between the theater and the domestic lives of both men is enlightening. Sanders demonstrates that whereas Macready saw the domestic sphere as antithetical to his theatrical career and used his family as a retreat from the rigors of a profession he abhorred, Dickens, "whenever he can, makes a drama of his children, merging them with the identities of his fictional characters, and orchestrating their performances," illustrating "his lifelong sense of the father's role as essentially performative and theatrical" (62). Most effective is Sanders's penetrating analysis of the narrative and performance history of *The Frozen Deep* (which evolved from a series of domestic to public performances). Coming at a time when Dickens's household affairs were in crisis, *The Frozen Deep* illustrated how Dickens's amateur theatrical company served as an "alternative family, composed of male friends and young adult children" (60) that offered him escape from an increasingly disappointing and oppressive household situation. Sanders notes in Dickens's fiction a similar taste for "alternative or makeshift pseudo-families" by which characters can "decide which relationships matter to them" (81) and reconstitute the domestic unit like an effective stage manager directing a play. While Sanders mentions Dickens's eventual assumption of "the female role in the household" by the end of his marriage (80), a little more attention to the overall decline of Dickens's domestic partnership with his wife might have provided additional useful evidence of Dickens's need to be the supreme "actor-manager-father" (62). But Sanders's study is still a perceptive look at the connections between Dickens's private experience as a parent and his public existence as a writer and performer, aptly set in comparison to the fathering experiences of other eminent Victorians.

In addition to Susan Zieger's "Dickens's Queer Children" (discussed below under "Studies of Adaptations in Fiction and Film"), two fine studies from 2009 offer new approaches to the trope of the child in Dickens's works. In *Conceptualizing Cruelty to Children in Nineteenth-Century England: Literature, Representation, and the NSPCC*, Monica Flegel investigates the intertextuality of Victorian literature and the writings of the National Society for the Prevention of Cruelty to Children in developing a legal concept of child abuse in England, resulting in "the emergence of 'cruelty to children' as a new type of crime" by the end of the nineteenth-century (1). While Flegel includes works from a wide variety of authors in her study, she relies heavily on examples from Dickens's novels throughout. For instance, in a discussion of the relationship between children and animals, Flegel compares Hugh from *Barnaby Rudge* and Ozias from Collins's *Armadale* as examples of the "savage child," demonstrating how the developing discourse on cruelty to animals united with the conceptualization of the endangered child to construct children and animals as "feeling subjects" (49). While she briefly refers to *Nicholas Nickleby* in a section on child performers, Flegel provides an extended, incisive analysis of Sissy Jupe in *Hard Times*, pointing out the paradoxical portrayal of Sleary's circus as both a loving alternative family and a vulgar profession from which Sissy must be rescued to enter into middle-class domesticity, a paradox that Flegel sees as indicative of Victorian audience's mixed feelings toward child performers, who seemed to evince both playful childlike innocence and rigorous adult training suggestive of hardship.

Equally effective is Flegel's analysis of Kate Nickleby and Paul and Florence Dombey (whom Flegel unaccountably designates as "Flora" despite close reading of Dickens's text throughout) as representations of the "child as victim of commerce" (111). Flegel argues that Ralph Nickleby's and Mr. Dombey's emotional neglect of the children in their care leads them to abuse the children for commercial purposes. But rather than portraying domestic and commercial spheres as antithetical, Dickens demonstrates (and even celebrates) their interdependence (particularly through the economic and emotional roles marriage plays for the female characters), suggesting that the inescapable ties between the business world and the middle-class home must be "tempered with affection, duty, generosity, and mutual benefit" (128). In her final chapter on child delinquency, Flegel expands on the role of class in the conceptualization of the endangered child, contrasting the Artful Dodger's adult criminality with Oliver's genteel innocence to suggest that Oliver, the middle-class child who is remarkably resistant to delinquency, represents what would eventually become the Victorian cultural ideal of childhood, an ideal that was distinctly bourgeois. Throughout her study, Flegel contextualizes the various literary responses to abused children within the history of the NSPCC's emerging professional discourse on child endangerment, concluding with the provocative assertion that the institutionalization of child protection by the NSPCC by the end of the century undermined the authority of popular literature in defining and reforming social problems, ultimately impoverishing the social discourse on childhood and child abuse.

Katarina Boem's article " 'A Place for More than the Healing of Bodily Sickness': Charles Dickens, the Social Mission of Nineteenth-Century Pediatrics, and the Great Ormond Street Hospital for Sick Children" examines the evolution of Victorian constructions of the homeless child as negotiated through popular narratives about the Great Ormond Street Hospital for Sick Children, the first pediatric hospital in the United Kingdom. Boem analyzes depictions of the hospital in contemporary newspaper articles, essays and stories from *Household Words* and *All the Year Round*, and Dickens's novel *Our Mutual Friend* to demonstrate how Dickens's public support of the hospital contributed to not only the advancement of pediatric knowledge, but also the "[m]oralizing [of] pediatric therapy," which transformed "the sociopolitical discourses that circulated around the children's hospital" into "mechanisms of class regulation" (159). Although there is no historical evidence that street children comprised the majority of the hospital's patients, contemporary journalistic and fictional accounts (including Dickens's) depicted the hospital primarily as "a symbolic home for the homeless children of London's streets" (159), a means to diffuse the threat of lower-class juvenile delinquency by bringing displaced children into line with the middle-class ideology of hearth and home while keeping the threatening children "at a safe remove from the parlours of the middle classes" (163). For instance, in her analysis of Johnny's death in *Our Mutual Friend*, Boem notes that although the hospital is presented as a homey and comforting alternative to the horrific workhouse which Johnny's grandmother has struggled to avoid, the hospital performs "some of the functions traditionally fulfilled by the workhouse" in that it separates Johnny from his lower-class relations and integrates him into "a 'family' of children whose father and mother are God and social philanthropy" (169). By exploring this fascinating historical

context, Boem's article thus shows how Dickens's philanthropy was motivated as much by anxieties about social containment and control as by compassion for the poor.

Science, Religion, and Philosophy

The works in this section deal with the connections between Dickens's fiction
and certain scientific, religious, and ideological controversies of his age. In
" 'Pictures in the Fire': The Dickensian Hearth and the Concept of History,"
Adelene Buckland delineates the complex interplay between the symbolic
and material significance of the fireside in Dickens's fiction, particularly
with regard to the geologic properties and commercial uses of coal. Using *A
Christmas Carol* as an example, Buckland demonstrates how Dickens associates light, fire, and warmth with characters in proportion to their spiritual
vitality and benevolence; however, Buckland notes that in assigning greater
warmth to the Cratchit fireside, Dickens ignores the actual cost of coal, which
would have been prohibitive for the poor family. The fireside's symbolic
significance outweighs its material importance. In such cases, Buckland attests, Dickens "effaces the materiality of coal—and particularly its status as
a commodity with an economic value—in order to preserve a politics of the
text that is domestic, static, and confirms essential truths." In other cases,
however, "the transformative history of coal . . . provides the structural basis
for fictional plots of transformation" (para. 12). As examples, Buckland
analyzes the use of coal's material properties as a catalyst and symbol of the
protagonist's moral rejuvenation in selected stories from *Household Words*,
as well as the use of Lizzie's fireside and Eugene Wrayburn's lime merchant
disguise in *Our Mutual Friend* as vehicles for Eugene's moral reformation.
Buckland effectively contextualizes these writings within the scientific and
political debates of the 1860s regarding the potential depletion of Britain's
coal supplies, pointing out that Dickens's journals unequivocally refused to
give credence to such fears, focusing instead on articles that revealed the
fascinating transformations in coal's geologic history and that celebrated
coal production as an indicator of Britain's industrial progress and national
superiority. Buckland concludes that Dickens's tendency to utilize the fireside's symbolic potential selectively as an emblem of domesticity, moral
transformation, and progress, while avoiding its more troubling material properties, establishes the hearth in Dickens's works not as a static domestic
paradise, but as a dynamic and problematic space, revealing many of the
unresolved tensions of Dickens's industrial society.

  Lawrence Frank's *Victorian Detective Fiction and the Nature of Evidence:
The Scientific Investigations of Poe, Dickens, and Doyle* depicts an ideological

dialogue between the great detective fiction of the age and several controversial contemporary scientific theories, including Pierre Simon Laplace's "nebular hypothesis" of the universe originating from the random heating and cooling of gases, Darwin's theories of evolution, and Charles Lyell's geological and archaeological investigations of the history of the earth and its inhabitants. Frank claims that, like the work of these scientists, the detective fiction of Poe, Dickens, and Doyle challenged Victorian audiences with "a *new*, emerging worldview that was secular and naturalistic in opposition to nineteenth-century scriptural literalism, Natural Theology, and the vestiges of an Enlightenment deism that were often conservative in their political perspectives" (3). By adopting language and methodology from the emerging sciences of "philology, geology and paleontology, archaeology, and evolutionary biology," these three writers "introduced a middle-class readership to a universe governed by chance and necessity" (4).

Section 2 of Frank's study examines how *Bleak House* and *The Mystery of Edwin Drood* dramatize the clash between contemporary scientific concepts and traditional values. Frank's analysis of *Bleak House* is innovative in two primary respects. First, as exemplified in a particularly brilliant reading of the novel's famous opening paragraphs, Frank delineates allusions throughout the novel's language and imagery to John Pringle Nichols's *Views of the Architecture of the Heavens* (1837) and the anonymous *Vestiges of the Natural History of Creation* (1844), works that promoted the Laplacean hypothesis of galaxies originating from a confusion of nebulous gaseous clouds, a theory that Frank effectively connects with the fog and mud symbolism of the novel's third-person narrative. Second, Frank provides a convincing new analysis of the novel's double narrative and its use of coincidence, arguing that the third-person, present-tense narrative (which Frank, unlike many scholars, attests is not omniscient) depicts a universe governed "by natural law *and* contingency" (72), in keeping with the theories of Laplacean scientists, while Esther's past-tense, retrospective narrative interprets the novel's coincidental events as the workings of providence, an approach Frank connects with Natural Theologists who continued to find evidence of a providential design in the workings of nature. The two narratives thus "dramatize competing worldviews—one secular and naturalistic, the other Christian—at a moment when it could not be predicted which might triumph among people of science and the men and women who were reading the novel" (6).

Similarly, Frank examines the influence of Charles Darwin's *Origin of Species* and Charles Lyell's *Geological Evidences of the Antiquity of Man* on Dickens's final novel to argue that "through a complex geological and archaeological perspective, *Edwin Drood* investigates the difficult process of reconstructing past events from fragmentary and inadequate evidence" (6). According to Frank, in its treatment of ancient settings such as the Nun's house or Mr. Grewgious's chambers in Staple Inn as "monuments to the past that retain an irresolvable ambiguity," the novel, in contrast to a simplistic antiquarian ethos, "begins to demonstrate a sophisticated archaeological awareness" similar to that evinced by Lyell in *Antiquity of Man*, in which the archaeologist was faced with the problem of reconstructing human history from excavations that produced "negative evidence," human tools without the presence of human remains (107). Frank points out that the would-be detectives in *Drood* are faced with a similar dilemma when the discovery of Edwin's personal effects fails to lead to the discovery of a body. In the attempts to blame Neville Landless for Edwin's presumed murder, Frank sees an instructive example of the dangers of "definitive" interpretations. Frank ultimately argues that every reader of *Drood* becomes a "would-be excavator" of the text as an "archaelogical curiosity" that continues to resist definitive interpretation (123). Frank's close readings of the novels in comparison to the scientific texts, as well as his analysis of Dickens's own familiarity with the selected texts and theories, prevent Frank's comparisons from becoming strained, making this book an eloquent demonstration of the intertextuality of scientific and literary works of the period.

An important contribution to the study of Dickens's personal religious beliefs and their impact on his fiction is Gary Colledge's *Dickens, Christianity, and* The Life of Our Lord: *Humble Veneration, Profound Conviction*. Colledge argues for the importance of this generally neglected text (composed for the private religious instruction of Dickens's children) as a "carefully composed and legitimate expression of Dickens's own faith" (vii) that "can help us to see in his novels a unity and coherence in what is often perceived as disparate fragments of a rather inconsistent Christian worldview" (15). Supported by rigorously detailed readings of *The Life*, selections from Dickens's fiction and correspondence, and numerous primary texts from leaders in the Unitarian movement and the High, Low, and Broad Church denominations, Colledge examines the theology that emerges from Dickens's writings to construct Dickens's Christian worldview in comparison to the dominant religious ideologies of his age. Although Colledge asserts that Dickens subordinated theological issues to "the moral-ethical concerns" of the gospel story (6) as he sought "to present to his children the person and example of Jesus unencumbered by what he saw as the trappings and distortions of an institutionalized Christianity" (7), Colledge's examination of *The Life* still provides a convincing outline of Dickens's Christian beliefs (which, according to Colledge, are grounded in the imitation of Jesus's active charity and sacrifice); but what is missing from his study is some analysis of cases when Dickens's fiction complicates or contradicts its own religious underpinnings. For instance, in his discussion of *Bleak House*, Colledge takes Esther's pious narrative at face value as exemplifying the true Christian ethic of service without considering (as Lawrence Frank does above) how the more skeptical third-person narrative counterpoints Esther's devout reliance on a providential universe, or even how Esther's continual attitude of self-effacement is frequently suspect. Nevertheless, Colledge's study as a whole provides ample evidence of how instrumental Dickens's faith was to his art (whether or not Dickens's fiction sometimes expressed conscious or unconscious uncertainties), and Colledge's work holds considerable merit as the first extended discussion of a text relatively ignored in Dickens scholarship.

Chris Louttit's *Dickens's Secular Gospel: Work, Gender, and Personality* explores Dickens's link to a popular topic of nineteenth-century philosophy, arguing for a more complex view of Dickens's attitude toward the Victorian "gospel of work" beyond Thomas Carlyle's quasi-religious unequivocal praise of work as a moral value. Louttit claims that Dickens's portrayal of "the human dimension of work" (4) not only confirms prevailing middle-class ideas about "the benefits of purpose and hard graft, but also sympathizes with those suffering the human costs of work" (5). Louttit's comprehensive study covers Dickens's approach to diverse types of work in his personal life as well as his fiction, journalism, and travel writing. Chapters include "Work and the Shaping of the Personality," which examines how Dickens uses work to define character through both external markers and psychological factors; "Gendering the Laboring Body," which demonstrates how Dickens depicts male manual labor through "sounds rather than through sights" (40) and further considers Dickens's attitudes toward female employment; "Dickens and the Professions," which places Dickens at "a moment of transition for the professions" from "distrust and satire" to "the gradual legitimization and defense of professional power" (63); "Dickens and Domestic Management," which examines how Dickens's attitude toward work inside the home complicates "separate spheres" ideology; and "Dickens's Idle Men," which considers Dickens's complicated reaction to idleness that extends far beyond the simple condemnation associated with the gospel of work.

Kathleen Blake and Paul Schacht present two new studies of Dickens's much-discussed relationship to utilitarian philosophy. In *Pleasures of Benthamism: Victorian Literature, Utility, Political Economy*, Kathleen Blake undertakes a revisionist investigation of the connections between utilitarian political economy and a range of Victorian essayists and novelists, including John Stuart Mill, Thomas Carlyle, Anthony Trollope, George Eliot, Elizabeth Gaskell, Rabindranath Tagore, and, of course, Dickens. Blake provocatively argues that "Victorian studies exhibits a high-cultural leaning . . . largely oppositional to Utilitarian, capitalist, liberal, bourgeois values" (26), a bias that has made literary scholars depict utilitarian philosophy as calculating, unimaginative, and unfeeling without recognizing its alignment with the egalitarian sympathies promoted by many writers of the period. Especially beneficial to Blake's attempt to rehabilitate Bentham in the eyes of current critics is her close reading of numerous published and unpublished texts by Bentham (as well as texts by prominent Benthamites and political economists) to provide a more extensive analysis of Bentham's philosophies than is common to Victorian literary studies.

Blake reassesses Dickens's relationship to Benthamism through provocative new approaches to *Bleak House* and *Hard Times* that reveal Dickens as "the abettor and not only the critic of Utilitarian causes" (4). According to Blake, critics have misapplied Foucault's oppressive, carceral reading of Bentham's Panoptican to Dickens's portrayal of Chancery in *Bleak House*, seeing the court as representing "forces of the modern, a newly bureaucratic state, industrialization, and market capitalism under attack by Dickens," when in fact Chancery as an ancient, aristocratic, and wasteful institution "is as far as possible from panoptical" and was denounced by Bethamite reformers in a manner similar to Dickens's attack in the novel (11). Through careful reading of *Bleak House* in comparison to primary documents by utilitarian philosophers, Blake further demonstrates Dickens's alignment with certain utilitarian views on education, class privilege, the saving and investing of capital, the value of labor as opposed to legacy, and even population control (Blake's discussion of Skimpole's ever-expanding, improvident family is instrumental to her argument here). She similarly couches her analysis of *Hard Times* within the framework of an extended and enlightening discussion of Bentham's pleasure principle, demonstrating the connections of Bentham's concept of utility to imagination, sympathy, and individualism, values represented in the novel by Sleary's circus, in opposition to the ascetic self-denial promoted by characters such as Gradgrind. Within this context, Gradgrind is a would-be utilitarian who has misapplied Bentham's principles, and Sleary's circus becomes the true utilitarian enterprise, exhibiting the appropriate balance of profit-seeking self-interest and pleasure-seeking fancy that is at the core of Bentham's utility concept.

In contrast, Paul Schacht's "In Pursuit of Pickwick's Hat: Dickens and the Epistemology of Utilitarianism" argues that Dickens depicts "the epistemological failure of utilitarianism" in his first novel "through a loose satire of an amateur scientific society and its leader" (2). Schacht points out that the Pickwick club is partly modeled on the utilitarian Society for the Diffusion of Useful Knowledge, and that Pickwick's abstract pursuit of knowledge, while failing to take in the material realities around him, parodies the utilitarian's lofty pursuit of facts, figures, and social practices regardless of their material consequences, a mindset that leads from "absent-minded blindness to social suffering" (12). This faulty perception is embodied throughout the novel by various metonyms for the head or the perceiving mind, particularly hats and spectacles. Pickwick's clumsiness with his hat throughout much of the novel is evidence of his "utter incompetence in worldly and practical matters" (3); he gains new perspective on life's realities, however, through his debtor's prison experience at the novel's conclusion. When Pickwick drops his hat upon witnessing Jingle's humiliation in the prison, the loss of the hat symbolizes not his incompetence, but his outrage, compassion, and "new sense of responsibility for his fellow creatures" (5). Schacht concludes by briefly examining how the social philosophy introduced in *Pickwick* is developed in *Oliver Twist* through an attack on utilitarianism's "reductive psychology" (with its focus on self-interest as the prime human motivation) and in *Hard Times* through "an assault on its impoverished moral calculus" (1).

Law, Economics, and Politics

Two significant studies deal with issues related to crime and punishment in Dickens's writings. The outstanding collection *Stones of Law, Bricks of Shame: Narrating Imprisonment in the Victorian Age*, edited by Jan Alber and Frank Lauterbach, provides "an explicitly post-Foucauldian intervention in the scholarship on Victorian imprisonment" (15), moving beyond readings of the prison as an embodiment of society's carceral nature to consider instead how Victorian writers "use the prison as a discursive emblem to negotiate their own identities in relation to cultural Otherness" (12). While treating a selection of canonical and noncanonical Victorian authors, as well as an American (Henry James) and a neo-Victorian novelist (Sarah Waters), the collection focuses on Dickens, since his oeuvre "presents us with an immense range of prison experience, and additionally deals with the intimate connections between the prison and the lives of the free and respectable" (13). The first essay in the collection, David Paroissien's "Victims or Vermin? Contradictions in Dickens's Penal Philosophy," provides an excellent overview of Dickens's conflicting attitudes to crime and punishment, tracing the evolution of Dickens's penal philosophy through three primary phases: Dickens's early interest in Newgate and criminal execution as evidenced in novels such as *Oliver Twist* and *Barnaby Rudge*, which complicate the popular Newgate Novel genre by portraying criminals with both harsh condemnation and striking empathy; the impact of Dickens's visit to American penal institutions in 1842 recounted in *American Notes*, resulting in both his praise for the humane reformation of juvenile offenders and his condemnation of the adult penitentiary's "separate" system of solitary confinement; and, finally, Dickens's increasing fascination in his later writings with the criminal mind that is uniquely selfish and capable of hiding behind a façade of respectability, as evidenced in his discussion of Dr. William Palmer's trial in "The Demeanour of Murderers" (1856) and his portrayal of John Jasper in *The Mystery of Edwin Drood*. Paroissien amply demonstrates that Dickens's writings are characterized throughout by "contradictory responses to crime" (28), exhibiting the paradoxical combination of "distaste for judicial murder and despair at finding an appropriate response for [the] 'wild beasts' " of the criminal world (30).

Jeremy Tambling's contribution, "New Prisons, New Criminals, New Masculinity: Dickens and Reade," traces the connection between the development of the new English penal system based on the American model of solitary confinement and a new construction of criminality (with particular gender connotations) in the novels of Dickens and Charles Reade. The eighteenth-century prison model dramatized in the Newgate Novel and the Newgate scenes of Dickens's early fiction "created, at least in myth, strongly masculine 'great criminals' who risked execution" (54), whereas the "newer, more disciplinary model" (58) based in the notion of prison as a place not only of punishment but of reformation suggested "a weakening of manliness . . . as a result of the forcing of the prisoner into self-inspection and self-analysis" (60). Surveying criminal characters from Bill Sikes and Uriah Heep to Bradley Headstone and John Jasper (with a brief comparison to Reade's representative prisoner, Tom Robinson, from *It Is Never Too Late to Mend*), Tambling convincingly argues that the new model of incarceration, which "is for those who lack masculinity, or who are made to lack it" (59), results in constructions of the criminal that are "no longer heroic" but "more duplicitous, more inward," as well as "more complicated in sexual terms, possibly homosexually charged" (63).

In " 'Now, now, the door was down': Dickens and Excarceration, 1841–2," Adam Hansen takes issue with deterministic Foucauldian approaches that interpret the prison as representing inescapable social discipline to argue instead that "Dickens's prisons are at once powerful and permeable" (95), vehicles not only of incarceration but of excarceration by which connections are revealed "between people and places that authorities and ideologies try to keep separate" (93). Hansen points out that Dickens objected to the "separate" system of solitary confinement exemplified by the Philadelphia Eastern Penitentiary described in *American Notes* because it "denied the very bonds of community upon which Dickens perceived moral life to be based" (90). In comparison, Dickens favored the "silent" system, which kept prisoners in common quarters but prevented them from communicating with each other, because "the crucial element of association (without communication) allowed prisoners to consider how their crimes affected others" (91). Hansen examines how Dickens depicts the creation of communal connections through "moments of excarceration" in *Barnaby Rudge, American Notes*, and "Pet Prisoners" (the 1850 *Household Words* essay advocating the "silent" prison model), but claims that "Dickens realizes these connections with such power that they threaten the integrity of the type of incarceration he did advocate," the "silent" system (91). Thus, Dickens's depiction of the prison, even in what he considered its ideal form, remains problematic.

In "The Poetics of 'Pattern Penitence': 'Pet Prisoners' and Plagiarized Selves," Anna Schur elaborates on Dickens's objections to the "separate" system expressed in "Pet Prisoners" and *David Copperfield*. The purpose of isolation from other prisoners was for the convict "to be drained of his pernicious vernacular in which he was used to boasting of his life of vice and depravity, and to become infused [through interaction with prison chaplains and morally uplifting texts] with a new language and a new set of representational conventions in which to tell his new story, a story of the reformed self" (137). For Dickens, the problem with this method of reform was that it placed an egotistical emphasis on the prisoner rather than the victim and represented the convict's supposed penitence through an "institutionalized script" (143) that allowed prisoners to author fictional versions of their reformed selves, such as the hypocritical protestations of model prisoners Uriah Heep and Littimer in the concluding scenes of *David Copperfield*. The "pattern penitence" exhibited in the convicts' confessions relied on "merely mastering the language of penitence" and thus revealed "the system's failure to distinguish between discourse and lived experience" (144–45).

The image of the solitary Victorian prisoner forced to tell the story of his transgressions is also central to the final Dickens-related essay in *Stones of Law*, Sean C. Grass's "*Great Expectations*, Self-Narration, and the Power of the Prison," which makes an illuminating comparison between Pip's first-person narration in *Great Expectations* and the reformatory confessions demanded of prisoners in the mid-Victorian model prison. Grass sees *Great Expectations* as Dickens's most mature expression of "the relation between the prison, the novel, and the private self" because "it shows the prison's power not only to shape Pip's identity but also to control and impel his construction of that identity through language" (173). Grass demonstrates how Pip's "long subjection to real and metaphorical prisons" creates a narrative "gap between the guilty self-account he writes and the fairy story of his life that he wants so desperately to tell" (173), revealing that "self-narration in a carceral world is a matter of *inventing*, not *disclosing*, the self" (176), an act of invention that is both enabled and controlled for Pip by his imprisoning experiences. As such essays demonstrate, *Stones of Law* approaches a much-discussed area of Dickens scholarship from fresh perspectives, making indispensable reading for those who are interested in this central motif of Dickens's fiction and personal life.

In *Forgery in Nineteenth-Century Literature and Culture: Fictions of Finance from Dickens to Wilde*, Sara Malton examines Victorian culture's preoccupation with a similar motif, financial forgery, arguing that the forgery plot found in numerous novels of the period not only reflects anxieties regarding an economic system in flux but also allows nineteenth-century writers "to engage with broader questions of epistemology and the constitution of authentic identity and origins—financial, racial, and sexual" (4). In her introduction, Malton briefly treats *Great Expectations* as "a touchstone for the literary treatment of forgery in the period" (15). By uniting the forgery plot with the bildungsroman and using the criminal forgers Magwitch and Compeyson to call into question the identity of the "self-swindler" Pip, the novel reveals "the simultaneous danger and allure presented by the promise of self-fashioning" (13). While a more extensive analysis of *Great Expectations* might have been warranted (perhaps in a separate chapter), Malton does effectively use her discussion of the novel to introduce her central approach, leading to more in-depth discussions of the forgery plots of *Barnaby Rudge* and *Little Dorrit* in the first two chapters of her study. In chapter 1, Malton contextualizes *Barnaby Rudge* and Collins's *The Woman in White* within the history of English criminal law, while examining how the forgery plot often unites with the trope of the criminal bastard in nineteenth-century novels to dramatize growing cultural uncertainties about the stability of genealogy, class, and history. In chapter 2, Malton examines Elizabeth Gaskell's *Cranford* and *Ruth* and Dickens's *Little Dorrit* to illustrate how the bank crises and widespread white-collar fraud of the 1850s "created a climate of mistrust" that "fostered a general culture of concealment" (51). She deftly compares the master swindler Merdle with other characters (Mr. Dorrit, Mrs. Clennam, and Amy) as weavers of "destructive social fictions" (66) whose forgeries are emblematic of a pervasive "suppression of knowledge" and "unwillingness to see" (66) in Victorian society. While this analysis exemplifies Malton's astute literary scholarship, her study is ultimately most illuminating in the historical context it provides for a popular literary trope.

Both Carolyn Vellenga Berman and Elizabeth Starr examine the connection between the political and economic contexts of *Hard Times* and the novel's approach to reading and education. In " 'Awful Unknown Quantities': Addressing the Readers in *Hard Times*," Berman responds to criticism of Dickens's portrayal of industrial conditions in *Hard Times* by arguing that the novel is less concerned with an accurate and detailed portrayal of labor conflicts than with a critique of "the curious new relationship between government reports and the working classes," particularly the power of parliamentary "blue books" in shaping public attitudes and policies toward "the People" (568). According to Berman, *Hard Times* mimics and mocks the rhetoric of the blue books to remind us "that the blue books do not contain bare historical realities, but representations of them" that the government constructed to further the agenda of the ruling classes (563). Through the

advent of the reports, education became "a key site for government intervention in the manufacturing districts and the lives of the workers," and education reform became a central means of policing the working classes (568);
hence, Dickens focuses the novel's social critique on government efforts
at education reform, especially "efforts to study and shape working-class
reading—of fairy tales and fiction, in particular" (564). However, while the
novel criticizes the representation of "the People" in parliamentary reports,
it fails itself to offer "a knowledgeable representation of the problems of the
working classes" (573). But the purpose of *Hard Times*, Berman argues, is
not to discredit altogether the government report and the novel as sources of
modern knowledge, but to teach us to read them better. In this case, Mrs.
Sparsit becomes "a key allegorical figure in the story Dickens tells about
modern knowledge" (576). In her misinterpretation of Louisa's elopement,
she represents the bad reader of public knowledge, both the "deaf, dumb,
and blind politicians who hear what they desire" and the "prurient readers
[of novels] who are eager for mere sensationalism" (576). In Mrs. Sparsit's
downfall, Dickens is calling for a more "perceptive reader of novelistic *and*
governmental texts" (578), who will approach the products of a burgeoning
print culture with a critical eye, wary of the "knowledge" conveyed by texts
and its potential uses.

In "Manufacturing Novels: Charles Dickens on the Hearth in Coketown,"
Elizabeth Starr similarly considers how *Hard Times* addresses Victorian anxieties about fiction's uses in the working world and its "influence or participation in social questions" (318). Starr echoes Berman in asserting that "*Hard
Times* holds up to scrutiny the relationship between its own purpose and the
purposes of other texts [such as the parliamentary blue books Berman dis-
cusses] that claim a use-value within urban economies" (318). Revealing the
dangerous influence of such texts in shaping the lives of the working classes,
Dickens distinguishes "his own work from the literal delineation of specific
problems or solutions," and instead tries to establish the link between fiction
and the more generally beneficial purpose of inspiring readers "to undefined
acts of compassion and feeling rather than enacting the will of the writer"
(330). According to Starr, the character in the novel who most embodies this
purpose is Louisa Gradgrind Bounderby, who, like the Coketown workers,
faces insidious attempts at influence and control (particularly through attempts to control her reading habits) by various characters who "assume that
their charges, whether they be a seemingly malleable Louisa or a seemingly
malleable working class, will simply absorb the content with which they are
supplied" (326). Mrs. Sparsit again provides an instructive example. While
Berman interprets Mrs. Sparsit as a poor reader of Louisa, Starr sees Sparsit
as a bad writer, constructing a narrative of Louisa's "fallenness" to which
she unsuccessfully attempts to force Louisa to conform. Starr concludes with

a dramatic rereading of Louisa's redemption, claiming that "Louisa's rehabilitation moves *Hard Times* toward a resolution invested in literary rather than domestic service" (333), as she "is drawn to the benevolent effects of storytelling" (331–32) through her association with Sissy Jupe. Starr attests that the novel's final picture of Louisa's future shows her bringing "fancy to the factory" in a manner similar to "both the periodical and the novel in which she appears" (334). In the concluding description of Louisa, "the narrator sums up Louisa's work in terms that sound strikingly like the image Dickens projected of himself" as the storyteller who "bridges the worlds of urban industry and the domestic hearth" (335).

Deborah Vlock's delightful "Teaching Marx, Dickens, and Yunus to Business Students" takes a unique pedagogical approach to the political and economic concerns expressed in *Hard Times*. Vlock describes her experience teaching the novel at a business college as part of an attempt to challenge her students' "assumptions about class, labor, and the acquisition of wealth" with texts that "are critical of the socioeconomic structures that have inspired them to choose their majors" (538–39). Vlock teaches *Hard Times* with Karl Marx's 1832 essay "Estranged Labour" and Bangladeshi economist Muhammad Yunus's 2006 Nobel Peace Prize lecture, a triad of texts in which Vlock hopes students will discover "models of good citizenship . . . as well as their own capacity to feel empathy" (539). Vlock describes strategies by which the class personalizes each text, focusing on the labor/management dichotomy in *Hard Times* as a means by which students can see "the relevance of Dickens's concerns to their own future professional plans" (544).

Particularly interesting for the Dickens scholar is Vlock's pairing of *Hard Times* with Yunus's lecture, for this conjunction can inspire us to reevaluate what has been deemed a critical weakness of Dickens's fiction, the failure to provide an alternative to the corruption of capitalism aside from a naïve belief in personal benevolence. Yunus's lecture describes his "social business" project, an attempt to reconcile doing business with doing social good, which is embodied in the Grameen Bank, an institution Yunus created to help alleviate poverty in Bangladesh by giving loans and income-generating housing to poor families, who are also shareholders in the bank. The success of this institution shows how the supposedly naïve goodwill promoted by Dickens could constitute a viable, transformative response to the abuses of capitalism. Yunus argues that businesses have a moral obligation to confront poverty, and if businessmen redefine the character of the entrepreneur to include two equally forceful motivations, "a) maximization of profit and b) doing good to people and the world," they can "change the character of capitalism radically" (Yunus qtd. in Vlock 546). In other words, reformed Scrooges can make a lasting global impact. Another of the article's highlights is Vlock's vivid account of actual classroom responses to the texts she teaches. She speaks with the voice of a dynamic and dedicated teacher who genuinely believes in the ability of Dickens's text to make a difference in her students' lives.

Amanpal Garcha's *From Sketch to Novel: The Development of Victorian Fiction* considers how class dynamics influenced the integration of the popular fictional sketch into the Victorian novel. The fictional sketch, with its "associations with quickness and fragmentary incompletion," captured the rapid pace and dynamic changeability of Victorian industrial society (15), even as the sketch "offered respite from this changeability" through its more static features (16), such as lengthy descriptive passages and a distinctive authorial style. In the section of the study devoted to Dickens, Garcha draws an important distinction between Thackeray's and Dickens's use of the sketch, claiming that while Thackeray's sketches assert his middle-class audience's "distance or immunity from rapid, potentially meaningless time," Dickens's sketches appeal to his readers "by asserting their *involvement* with such changefulness as a mark of class distinction" (114). Examining the pieces that were eventually collected in *Sketches by Boz*, Garcha notes a significant difference between Dickens's early suburban stories, which "use narratively progressive, plotted forms to depict middle-class individuals and others who work productively in the capitalist-oriented economy," and his later urban sketches that "use static, descriptive forms [rather than plotted narrative] to depict members of the *lumpenproletariat* whose destitution seems to be caused by their unwillingness or inability to take part in England's busy, forward-looking commerce" (115). The sketches' energetic, restless style and the narrator's flaneur-like persona help to distinguish the narrator and his middle-class audience from the static lower-classes and create "key ideological fantasies for his readers and for Dickens himself about their privileged position in England's commercial economy and, more importantly, their insulation from that economy's destructive effects on the lower classes and on themselves" (139).

Garcha sees similar uses of time, movement, and class distinction in Dickens's novels. Analyzing *Nicholas Nickleby* as an example, Garcha shows how the novel depicts lower-class characters through brutal, gritty descriptive passages (such as the Dotheboys Hall sections) that recall Dickens's urban sketches, while immersing the privileged middle-class characters in a melodramatic plot that gives a semblance of progress while actually insulating them from the morally and physically damaging effects of capitalist culture. Garcha concludes that Dickens's melodramatic plots appealed to Victorian readers' need for moral and social stability by offering "highly conceptualized narrative trajectories and highly moralized heroes and heroines," while the "mobile, unpredictable style" derived from his early sketches appealed to the readers' need to feel a part of the market economy's vitality and changefulness (167).

Victorian Media and Spectacle

A number of fine studies were produced focusing on Dickens's relationship to various Victorian media, from the postal service, to the publishing industry, to different forms of stage and performance spectacle. In the fascinating study *Posting It: The Victorian Revolution in Letter Writing*, Catherine J. Golden examines how the writings of Dickens and other Victorian authors reflect the evolution of the postal medium in nineteenth-century Britain. Golden investigates the extensive cultural impact of the introduction of the Penny Post in 1840, which, by making postage generally affordable, instigated a revolution in Victorian communication. The study draws examples from the lives and works of numerous Victorian writers, including Dickens, Wilkie Collins, the Brontë sisters, George Eliot, William Makepeace Thackeray, and Anthony Trollope. While Golden analyzes several letter-related incidents from Dickens's fiction as examples of the benefits and drawbacks of the Penny Post, her most extensive analysis concentrates on examples of postal blackmail. Golden points out that rather than bringing about the utopian vision of moral and social reform predicted by supporters of the Penny Post, the democratization of the post stimulated unsolicited and sometimes dangerous mailings and encouraged people to post a variety of odd items, as well as missives related to impropriety, fraud, and blackmail. Golden refers to Dickens's and Wills's *Household Words* article "Valentine's Day at the Post-Office" (1850) for examples of the oddities that Victorians mailed through the Penny Post, and she analyzes the article's metaphorical comparison of the Post Office to a slaughter house as exemplifying the anxieties and suspicions aroused by contemporary scandals of Post Office corruption. As examples of how the Penny Post facilitated criminal activities, Golden examines instances of slander and blackmail from Dickens's *Bleak House* (e.g., Mlle. Hortense's letter-writing campaign against Lady Dedlock), as well as Trollope's and Collins's novels, in comparison to an actual contemporary case of blackmail via anonymous letters. Golden concludes, "The centrality of letter-driven criminality in *Bleak House* secures the novel's position as a material memory of the collective social anxiety wrought by postal reform" (176).

A vital contribution to the growing body of scholarship on Dickens's journalism, Sabine Clemm's *Dickens, Journalism, and Nationhood: Mapping the World in* Household Words investigates the preoccupation of Dickens's journal with "Englishness, foreign nations, and nationhood in general" (13). Clemm begins with the contradictions inherent in "the journal's desire to transcend . . . all social boundaries—even while upholding national ones—and to form a single, in some sense homogenous community" (8), a goal that inevitably conflicted with the limitations of the journal's predominately "middle-class perspective" (12–13). Clemm then examines how these contradictions affect the vision of the world that *Household Words* constructs, which Clemm aptly describes as "a nest of concentric circles" with London at its center, moving outward through the following categories: "England/Britain, Ireland, Europe, the colonies, and 'the world beyond'—China, 'savages,' and other 'alien' cultures" (13). After a chapter discussing how the organization of the Great Exhibition set the standard for this system of international relations that *Household Words* would promote, Clemm devotes a chapter to each "circle" in the journal's worldview. In the chapter on English/British identity, she shows how the journal attempts to formulate an English national character primarily through "contrast to various Others," particularly European nations (78). To illustrate, Clemm analyzes the series of articles, "Foreigners' Portraits," in which *Household Words* writers critique depictions of the English in the writings of international visitors. Clemm attests, "Through contrast with 'Foreigners' Portraits' the English emerge, in *Household Words*, as freedom-loving, independent, and hard-working urban, metropolitan, middle-class males, even though many of the characteristics which *Household Words* asserts against foreign writers are questioned elsewhere in the journal" (78). In comparison, instead of asserting a homogenous British identity, *Household Words* depicts Wales as "a curious appendage to England" and Scotland as its own entity (72) and envisions the Welsh and the Scots as separate peoples who "can occasionally be 'English' " (50).

Clemm devotes a separate chapter to the journal's treatment of Ireland, since "the Irish always appear outside the collective national identity that *Household Words* constructs, while the Welsh and Scottish occasionally merge with it" (81). A striking distinction emerges between the journal's depictions of "Ireland" versus "the Irish." Ireland is a rich resource that Britain "is eager to claim," but the Irish people and their culture, while perceived as "visibly 'Other,' pagan, [and] savage," "were all uncomfortably close to Britain's own," unlike the indigenous populations of other colonial holdings (81). Thus, in its numerous articles addressing Irish difficulties, *Household Words* "implies that the trouble with Ireland is the Irish people themselves" (96), who are in need of "the intervention and benevolent patronage of the British" (97) to allow their country to realize its potential.

As she moves outward in the concentric circles model, Clemm's chapter on Europe compares *Household Words* articles to the news press of the 1850s to demonstrate that the journal "adopted a fairly moderate stance" regarding Britain's relations with European nations and was less interested in "official politics than in the nature of 'the people' " of the Continent (126). Clemm's final chapter on the colonies focuses on India, since it was the colony most frequently featured in the journal. She sees the 1857 Sepoy Rebellion as a turning point in the journal's depiction of India as a colonial subject. Articles prior to the Sepoy Rebellion portray India as a rich resource for British wealth populated by a largely passive race epitomized in the "mild Hindoo" stereotype. But articles following the Indian Mutiny, while taking a cautious approach to the rebellion, ultimately attempt to restore colonial order by suggesting that "the British rule of India needs to become both more efficient and more ruthless" (161). Clemm's close reading of numerous articles throughout *Household Words*'s publication history in comparison to other periodical publications of the day amply supports her construction of the journal's worldview and establishes the place of Dickens's periodical in the context of Victorian journalism.

In "Charles Dickens, George Augustus Sala and *Household Words*," Peter Blake provides a fascinating overview of the contentious relationship between Dickens and one of the most prolific contributors to *Household Words*, George Augustus Sala. Going back to their first meeting when Sala was a nine-year-old boy and his mother was an understudy in Dickens's operetta *The Village Coquettes*, Blake shows how Sala initially exploited his childhood acquaintance with Dickens to obtain employment and later chafed against Dickens's editorial control over Sala's submissions to Dickens's journals. Blake's study of "The Key of the Street," Sala's first submission, demonstrates the resemblances between the two writers (such as a fondness for street wandering and exploring lower-class life), as well as the divergences (particularly Sala's bohemianism) that would eventually end their professional and personal relationship. Blake argues that similarities of style and subject matter initially laid the foundation for a profitable relationship between the authors but finally led to Sala being eclipsed by Dickens's reputation and editorial control of his work. Sala ultimately becomes a prime example of the problems encountered by the myriad of talented writers who contributed to Dickens's journals: "If they failed to imitate his [Dickens's] style their work would be subject to revision, if they copied him then their contributions would be passed off as the editor's own" (32). The details of the troubled connection between the two authors provide striking evidence of Dickens's powerful and problematic influence in the Victorian literary world.

Several studies consider Dickens's place within the ideological conflicts and the material circumstances of Victorian print culture. Examining numerous contemporary reviews of Dickens's work from the leading periodicals of his day (such as the *Edinburgh Review* and the *Quarterly Review*), Lisa Rodensky's article "Popular Dickens" demonstrates how the construction of Dickens's popularity in the nineteenth-century was vitally connected to issues of cultural and commercial control in the dynamic publication market. Throughout the reviews of Dickens's fiction, "Dickens's reviewers are navigating in and around contradictory meanings of popular and popularity" in response to ''momentous developments'' in the Victorian publishing industry, including the expansion of literacy, the resurgence of the serial, and the increasing number of newspapers and periodicals. In this context, Dickens's reviewers are concerned not only with determining a literary hierarchy and Dickens's place within it but also with establishing ''the hierarchy's relation to a reading public'' in determining who would ultimately be the arbiters of taste (584). Examining the shifting meanings of the term ''popular'' when applied to Dickens and literature, Rodensky demonstrates that the term was a deeply contested ''site of tension among a now powerful reading public (with a point of view), critics who are struggling to hold on to the power to determine good and bad, authors with a complex set of motives often connected with the professionalization of writing, and a market that has interests of its own'' (587).

Sambudha Sen's ''Radical Satire and Respectability: Comic Imagination in Hone, Jerrold, and Dickens'' traces the development of radical satire in late-eighteenth- and early-nineteenth-century print culture, from the politically motivating texts of writers and illustrators such as Thomas Paine, William Hone, and George Cruikshank to the ''entertainment-oriented'' novels of Dickens (146). Noting a developing ''tension between radicalism and respectability'' in the early Victorian print market due to radicalism's origins in plebian political dissent (148), Sen discusses *Punch* as a particularly important ''interface between radical pamphlets and Dickens's novels'' through the magazine's ''refashioning . . . [of] radical tropes so that they would not offend the sensibilities of the increasing number of middle-class readers'' (149). According to Sen, radical tropes that passed from political pamphlets through *Punch*'s ''respectabilizing'' filter and into Dickens's fiction include the following: the use of the pronoun ''we'' to unite readers with the politically excluded; a ''counter emblematic technique'' that demystifies the consecrated emblems of those in power by replacing them with a new series of ridiculous or degrading images (154); a technique of ''satiric overwriting'' that incorporates repetition, exaggeration, and parody (155); and a technique of ''radical caricature'' derived from the satiric illustrations of radical journalism (158). Sen's study leads to a more enlightened understanding of Dickens's oft-criticized ''caricaturized figures'' not as ''failed attempts at realistic characterization or even as the products of Dickens's unique comic genius'' but rather as the offspring of ''a strand of radical satire oriented toward building around its irreverent representations of those who wielded political power, a community of the excluded'' (159).

In *Victorian Christmas in Print*, Tara Moore examines the seasonal publication market of Dickens's day, investigating the well-worn topic of the Victorian Christmas from a new angle. While discussing the seasonal output of numerous authors in a variety of genres (decorative literary annuals, Christmas books, ghost stories, children's literature, poetry, and periodicals), Moore gives primary attention to Dickens's influence, noting that he "cast an enormous shadow over the nineteenth century's literature of Christmas" (5). Although Moore denies the misconception that Dickens "invented" the Victorian Christmas, she notes that "authors and reviewers looked to him as a Christmas print trendsetter, and he made an impact on every genre available in the Christmas print market, from periodical frameworks to novel bindings, and even the element of poetry modeled in his periodicals" (5). Moore, of course, gives special attention to A Christmas Carol as inaugurating what would become the traditional size, appearance, and content of Victorian Christmas books of the 1840s and '50s, noting that the Carol's popularity moved the seasonal print market beyond the dominance of decorative literary annuals (volumes of poetry without a Christmas theme) to a new emphasis on sentimental tales that united Christmas topics with a rhetoric of social reform (25). Moore likewise investigates how the various genres of Victorian Christmas publications (including Dickens's books and periodicals) contributed to the development of English national identity and the myth of the "English Christmas." By examining some of Dickens's most popular works within the framework of the Christmas publication market, Moore thus reminds the reader of the inextricable, complex connection between the ideological and commercial impact of Dickens's writings.

An interesting speculation on how the circumstances of publication might have influenced the reception of Dickens's Sketches by Boz is the subject of Paul Schlicke's "Macrone, Cruikshank and the Proposed Part-issue of Sketches by Boz: A Note." When Dickens ended his business relationship with publisher John Macrone, the publisher retained the copyright of Sketches and planned to capitalize on Dickens's skyrocketing popularity by re-issuing Sketches as a monthly serial published in a format similar in appearance to The Pickwick Papers (complete with green wrappers), which was still in serialization. Although Pickwick publishers Chapman and Hall eventually purchased the copyright for Sketches from Macrone, Schlicke shows how incredibly close Macrone came to realizing his plans, as evidenced by two documents recently auctioned at Christie's, a letter from Macrone to illustrator George Cruikshank regarding the planned wrapper design for Sketches and a proof copy of Cruikshank's design (which is reproduced in Schlicke's article). Ironically, despite Dickens's objections to Macrone's project, Chapman and Hall eventually published Sketches serially in a poorly designed format that suffered low sales, making one wonder about the possibility of Macrone's producing a better publication (which might have enhanced the reputation of Sketches) if his plans had come to fruition.

Additional studies consider the impact of publication format and contextual materials, such as illustrations, advertisements, and editorials, on Victorian readers' reception of Dickens's serial fiction. The Lure of Illustration in the

Nineteenth Century: Picture and Press, edited by Laurel Brake and Marysa Denmoor, reprints two fine articles that were discussed in past issues of *Dickens Studies Annual*, but which deserve another brief mention here. Lorna Huett's superb essay, "Among the Unknown Public: *Household Words, All the Year Round* and the Mass-Market Weekly Periodical in the Mid-Nineteenth Century," investigates how Dickens "rehabilitate[d] the weekly serialization of fiction" (146) by combining the format of cheap weekly publications with that of the more expensive monthly and quarterly periodicals to appeal to a new middle-class audience "who desired good literature for family reading, but were reluctant to pay high prices for the same" (138). Huett supports her study of the class-based evolution of periodical publication with a painstakingly detailed description of the publication format of *Household Words* and *All the Year Round*, which makes readers feel as if they have seen and touched an original issue. Beryl Gray's "Man and Dog: Text and Illustration in Dickens's *The Old Curiosity Shop*," also reprinted in this collection, considers the significance of specific illustrations within the publication history of Dickens's novel in weekly, monthly, and complete-volume formats, providing evidence of how Dickens relied upon intertextual relationships to develop certain themes within his fiction.

In another essay in this volume, Laurie Garrison discusses a similar dialogue between an author's text and the surrounding context of its periodical publication. "Seductive Visual Studies: Scientific Focus and Editorial Control in *The Woman in White* and *All the Year Round*" claims that Wilkie Collins's detective novel and the adjacent contents of *All the Year Round*, the periodical in which the novel was serialized, "are deeply intertwined in an exchange of discourses of sexuality, . . . most prominently in terms of the relationship between sexuality and the sense of vision" (169). In this dialogue between Dickens as editor and Collins as author, Garrison sees Collins's depiction of Walter Hartwright, the novel's ostensible "editor" (182), as a critique of Dickens's editorial practices, while the periodical contents in which Dickens chose to embed the novel's serial installments conversely critique the limits of Walter's vision as a narrator. Although the essay ultimately gives more attention to the theme of visualization within the novel itself (since Garrison offers only limited analysis of examples from the surrounding contents from *All the Year Round*), this study is still an intriguing reminder of how the reading of serialized fiction was inevitably informed by other elements appearing within a periodical as determined through editorial choice, a point too often neglected by scholars of the nineteenth-century novel.

In *Advertising, Subjectivity and the Nineteenth-Century Novel: Dickens, Balzac and the Language of the Walls*, Sara Thornton considers how advertising influenced the reading of serial novels. Thornton begins by investigating how the redesign of city space in nineteenth-century London and Paris and the consequent effects on advertising (for example, the increased space for advertising display on city walls) revolutionized reading practices, with the result that "the act of reading itself becomes serialized" (9), as the increasingly ubiquitous presence of advertising evokes a reading style characterized by fragmentation, short attention span, and rapid movement of the eye and mind between tangentially related texts and images. Thornton then examines how Dickens and Balzac respectively capitalized on this new style of reading in the marketing and design of their serialized fiction. In the section on Dickens, Thornton argues for an attention to Dickens's serial installments "not simply as a novel surrounded by adverts and a few illustrations," but as organic entities in which all the parts function together to create the whole (105). She illustrates how advertisements would have interacted thematically and critically with Dickens's fiction by examining specific ads that appeared in the serial installments of *The Mystery of Edwin Drood* and *Bleak House*, looking at the position of ads with regard to particular illustrations and passages of Dickens's text. Like Huett's study, Thornton's has a richly tangible evocativeness as she meticulously describes monthly numbers she viewed at the British museum. Thornton concludes that the typical layout of a monthly number inspired a reading technique that involved "an amalgamation of attention and distraction . . . quite unlike the oriented and organized linear reading associated with the novel" (69) and that required readers to "get used to reading in parts, in a trail of interrupted pieces" (70), similar to the manner in which we "surf" television stations or Internet websites today. Thus, Thornton's study not only models the reading circumstances of Dickens's original audiences, but also provocatively suggests Dickens's contribution to the multimedia, multitasking style of perception dominant in current electronic media.

With a similar focus on visual frameworks in the publication of Dickens's fiction, Philip V. Allingham's article "The Illustrations for *Great Expectations* in *Harper's Weekly* (1860–61) and in the Illustrated Library Edition (1862)" considers Dickens's novel in the context of nineteenth-century illustrations. Allingham compares John McLenan's series of forty illustrations for the first American edition of the novel published serially in *Harper's Weekly* to Marcus Stone's series of eight woodcuts from the 1862 Chapman and Hall Library Edition, the first illustrated British edition of the novel. According to Allingham, McLenan's more comprehensive series "provides salient background details, offers symbols for lack of self-insight and illumination in various scenes, and describes every significant character . . . in a panoramic treatment" (113) that exemplifies the Gothic, mystery, and bildungsroman genres included in the novel, whereas Stone's much shorter series focuses on the novel's bildungsroman aspect, depicting Pip's growth from childhood to maturity in woodcuts that feature Pip in every image. Allingham effectively contrasts the styles of the two artists as representative of two different phases in Dickensian illustration (McLenan evinces the caricature style associated with Hablot Browne, while Marcus has the naturalism characteristic of 1860s illustrators); and for McLenan's series, in which illustrations were dropped into the text throughout the novel, Allingham likewise discusses how the placement of the illustrations would have influenced textual interpretation (for instance the placement on the same page of illustrations featuring Pip's relationships with Joe and Magwitch invites readers to connect the two men as foster fathers for Pip). Allingham amply supports his study throughout with superb analysis of numerous specific illustrations, which are reproduced in the *Dickens Studies Annual* to accompany the article. Such examples demonstrate how illustrations serve as interpretation rather than mere mimesis of the literary original.

Studies by Joss Marsh and Lillian Craton discuss the influence on Dickens's fiction of two popular types of nineteenth-century visual spectacle—the magic lantern and the freak show. Marsh's "Dickensian 'Dissolving Views': The Magic Lantern, Visual Story-Telling, and the Victorian Technological Imagination" provides a fascinating examination of the connection between Dickens's works and the most significant innovation in the history of the magic lantern, the development of the "dissolving view," in which one image slowly replaces another on the illuminated screen. Marsh begins with an intriguing history of the technique, which by the 1840s achieved unique symbolic significance in Victorian culture. The advent of limelight and front projection turned dissolving-view projectionists into "showmen-educators," bringing them from behind the screen to expound on the wonders of their imagery for the audience's enlightenment, with the result that "the dissolving-view lantern-show became a Victorian metaphor for transformation, truth-telling and spiritual regeneration" (335). The dissolving view also affected storytelling by making possible a type of story that "allowed travel through time and space" (335). Marsh shows how Dickens incorporated both the metaphorical significance and the narrative methodology of the magic lantern's dissolving view into two texts of spiritual transformation—"The Tale of a Sexton" from *The Pickwick Papers* and *A Christmas Carol*. She argues that for Dickens "the magic lantern was a Christian agent of hoped-for conversion," while for more pessimistic authors "the lantern experience actively encouraged scepticism by exposing the mechanics and potential for fakery in supernatural visions" (341).

In *The Victorian Freak Show: The Significance of Disability and Physical Differences in Nineteenth-Century Fiction*, Lillian Craton devotes two chapters to bodily spectacle in Dickens, making a significant contribution to Dickens criticism from the perspective of disability studies. "Littleness in the Novels of Charles Dickens" explores how unusually small female characters

illustrate "the interplay between two different presentations of physical difference in Dickens's fiction, one shaped by the tropes of sentimental fiction
and the other by traditions of freak spectacle and the aesthetics of the grotesque" (43). In an excellent study of odd bodies in *The Old Curiosity Shop*,
Craton examines the complex connections between Nell's precious smallness
and Quilp's freakish dwarfism to prove that "Dickens's frequent blending of
grotesque and sentimental imagery adds subtlety to his sentimental characterizations" (46). Comparing Dickens's presentation of Nell to Victorian freak
show marketing strategies, Craton argues that Nell is not just "an anti-freak,"
the "natural counterpart to Quilp's monstrosity," but an oddity in herself
(58), and Dickens as the showman/collector of curiosities exhibits Nell not
only to examine the "neglectful social order" that exploits her, but also to
exploit her himself for the sake of literary entertainment, a form of exploitation that makes us "recognize our complicity as consumers of pain" (59).
In comparison to Nell's exploitation, Craton discusses Miss Mowcher from
David Copperfield and Jenny Wren from *Our Mutual Friend* as "dwarf-girls
whose resistance to simplistic interpretation" allows them to "manipulate
sentimental and grotesque aesthetics to reshape both their own identities and
society's concepts of beauty and normalcy" (43). In their cases, the odd body
becomes empowering, giving them the ability "to reverse the direction of
the spectacular gaze" back onto the society that exploits them (68). Similarly,
in the chapter entitled "The Widest Lap: Fatness and Nurturance in Nineteenth-Century Fiction," Craton examines female obesity as an empowering
form of bodily difference, arguing that fat, nurturing females, such as Peggotty in *David Copperfield* and Mrs. Jarley in *The Old Curiosity Shop*, offer
a "necessary supplement" to the weakness or asceticism of the thin and
wasting female characters (e.g., Clara Copperfield and Little Nell) (107),
providing "an important alternative image of the nurturing ideal for Victorian
womanhood" (96) based not on self-denial but abundant self-nurturance.

Geographical Spaces

Dickens's perceptions of particular locales and the significance of geographical spaces in his travel writings and his fiction prompted some excellent
scholarship. In *Spaces of the Sacred and Profane: Dickens, Trollope, and the
Victorian Cathedral Town*, Elizabeth A. Bridgham convincingly argues "for
an expanded understanding of Dickens and Trollope as city writers" by
extending the literary analysis of geographical spaces in their fiction beyond
the traditional city/country dichotomy to include the cathedral town (3).
Bridgham's study demonstrates how Dickens and Trollope depicted cathedral
towns not as Romantic, escapist spaces grounded in traditions that offered

respite from Victorian England's social instability, but rather as deeply contested sites, caught in the religious, political, and aesthetic controversies of the nineteenth century. Chapter 1, "Monstrous Unions: Dickens, Trollope, and the Anglo-Catholic Question," treats the English cathedral town's problematic relationship to Catholicism and lends complexity to Dickens's well-known anti-Catholicism by contrasting the critical portrayal of Catholic clergy in *Pictures from Italy* and *Nicholas Nickleby* with the sympathetic portrayal of Catholic characters in *Barnaby Rudge*, a disparity that reveals Dickens's ability to distinguish between oppressive church institutions and their followers. Such oppression is embodied in *The Mystery of Edwin Drood* in the Catholic heritage that permeates the cathedral town of Cloisterham, suggesting that the Catholic past associated with cathedral communities in Dickens's works carries "fearful or Gothic implications" (43), as opposed to Trollope's cathedral towns in which religious unity "becomes a means not only to spiritual community, but also to secular community" (67).

Chapter 2, "Doctrinal Dissonance: Cathedral Music and the Issue of Vocation," provides an enlightening social and historical context for the ecclesiastical artists (particularly musicians) inhabiting Dickens's and Trollope's cathedral spaces. Especially noteworthy is Bridgham's intriguing examination of the Church's exploitative employment practices for cathedral musicians, which sheds new light on the divided psychology of *Drood* chorister John Jasper, casting him as a victim not only of personal demons but also of oppressive social and religious customs. Bridgham's discussion of contemporary suspicions about the potentially hypnotic, distracting, and sexually provocative effects of church music also adds new depth to Jasper's use of music as a mesmeric and seductive tool. Chapter 3, " 'Broken Niche and Defaced Statue': Creativity in the Cathedral," focuses on Cathedral architecture and architects, discussing Dickens's satiric and sentimental approaches to the Gothic Revival fad in the respective portrayals of Pecksniff's hypocritical architectural endeavors in *Martin Chuzzlewit* and Wemmick's whimsical "Castle" in *Great Expectations*. A section on characters who are associated with Gothic architectural structures provides outstanding readings of the analogy in *David Copperfield* between Agnes Wickfield and the stained-glass window, as well as the connections of *Copperfield*'s Uriah Heep and *Drood*'s Stony Durdles to the cathedral gargoyle, not only as a grotesque threat, but also as a watcher and protector. Bridgham gives equal attention to Trollope's works throughout the study, noting how his depictions of ecclesiastical space focus on contemporary political ambition through the lens of social realism while Dickens relies on Gothic conventions to invest his cathedral communities with psychological significance. However, both authors depict cathedral towns "as hybrid spaces, those in which the ancient and modern, the Catholic and Anglican, the religious and commercial, the homogeneous and cosmopolitan, exist in a constantly changing dialogue with one another" (152).

Geographical locations that are fraught with imperialist anxieties are the concern of essays by Julie M. Barst and John Kofron. In "Sensations Down Under: Australia's Seismic Charge in *Great Expectations* and *Lady Audley's Secret*," Barst explores the "dual literary representation" of Australia in 1860s sensation fiction as both a "dark underworld of convicts" and a more positive colonial space of "economic advancement and rehabilitation," arguing that "the mystery and danger of the colony was advanced to fulfill the expectations of the sensation market, while the opportunistic image of Australia was advanced to justify and promote Great Britain's imperialism to its citizens" (91–92). Barst develops her argument with an insightful comparison of Dickens's Magwitch to the Australian adventurer George Talboys in Mary Elizabeth Braddon's *Lady Audley's Secret*; each man makes a threatening return to England after accumulating a fortune in Australian exile, a paradox that effectively dramatizes England's conflicted "political unconscious" regarding its imperialist endeavors. Through such narratives, sensation fiction constructed Australia "as a space whereby repressed characters can hang in the balance, awaiting their opportunity for return, their chance to produce the uncanny and sensational in both those who repressed them and the readers themselves" (97). Thus, sensational representations of Australia became a means by which readers "could come to terms with the contradictions of empire-building in their imaginations" (99).

In "Dickens, Collins, and the Influence of the Arctic," John Kofron places selected texts by Dickens and Wilkie Collins within the broader fascination with Arctic exploration that permeated nineteenth-century British culture, focusing particularly on the controversy surrounding Sir John Franklin's lost 1845 expedition. Kofron examines how "The Lost Arctic Voyagers," Dickens's 1854 series of *Household Words* articles defending Franklin's expedition from charges of cannibalism, articulates an aesthetic of the Arctic developed through previous narratives of Arctic exploration. The explorers are depicted as heroic symbols of British civilization and self-sacrifice, braving encounters with savagery in both elemental and human form. Kofron sees this aesthetic reflected in Dickens's and Collins's 1857 play *The Frozen Deep*, which contains numerous similarities to the Franklin expedition, making the play "an adaptation of Dickens's 'Lost Arctic Voyager' articles into melodramatic form" (87). Kofron further traces the heroic Arctic aesthetic to Dickens's *A Tale of Two Cities* (1859), in which Sydney Carton embodies the self-sacrificing Englishman originally represented by Franklin's explorers in the "Lost Arctic" articles and Richard Wardour in *The Frozen Deep*. Kofron finally illuminates the influence of *The Frozen Deep* on Collins's novel *No Name* (1862), which contains numerous allusions to Arctic voyages as well as a questing heroine whose adventures are distinguished by lengthy waiting and watching. But while Dickens "envisions Arctic exploration as a moral triumph'' (91) indicative of ''sublime sacrifice'' (81), Collins takes a more ''sardonic tone'' toward the heroic aesthetic as resulting in ''sublime defeat'' (81). Kofron concludes that the two authors' contrasting means of adopting Arctic motifs suggest ''the complicated public perception of the Arctic endeavor'' (92).

Articles by Natalie McKnight, Karen Bourrier, and Sally Ledger address the perceptions of America and Italy expressed in Dickens's travel writings and the impact of these perceptions on Dickens's fiction and his reading audience. McKnight's ''Dickens, Niagara Falls and the Watery Sublime'' delineates Dickens's reaction to the falls within the context of other contemporary British travel narratives and considers how Dickens's Niagara experience influenced the imagery of his subsequent novels. McKnight compares Dickens's portrayal of Niagara in letters he wrote during his two visits to America in 1842 and 1868 to accounts in travel narratives by Frances Trollope, Harriet Martineau, and Captain Frederick Marryat, noting that while Dickens incorporates the Romantic rhetoric of the sublime typical to such descriptions, he differs in his tendency ''to make specific personal connections with the falls'' (72). For instance, while he describes the ghostly mists and rainbows above the falls as images of death, resurrection, and divinity, he likewise associates these features with the death of his beloved sister-in-law Mary Hogarth and his comforting sense of her ongoing spiritual presence. He also connects the falls with his affinity for his own nation (particularly enhanced by his negative experiences in America) by repeatedly emphasizing in his letters that he is staying on the English side of the falls. McKnight argues that Dickens thus ''tries to come to terms with the sublimity of the falls'' by making them ''part of himself, part of his own family story, part of his Englishness,'' eventually enabling him to incorporate his Niagara experience into his fiction (73). McKnight points out that in the novels published prior to Dickens's first Niagara visit, scenes of death, rebirth, and transformation are dominated by images of ''sunny little communities, flowers and other greenery, angels and churches,'' whereas subsequent novels symbolize moments of transcendence primarily through powerful water imagery (73), such as the sea imagery in *Dombey and Son* and *David Copperfield* and the rivers in *Our Mutual Friend* and *The Mystery of Edwin Drood*.

In ''Reading Laura Bridgman: Literacy and Disability in Dickens's *American Notes*,'' Karen Bourrier explores Dickens's account in *American Notes* of his meeting with Laura Bridgman, reputedly the first deaf and blind girl to be taught to read and write. Bourrier notes that Bridgman's literacy made her ''an emblem of America'' in the British imagination since she represented the general availability of education, even for the disabled, that was perceived as a distinctive feature of American democracy (46). But Bourrier likewise discusses how Bridgman's case reveals the actual limitations placed on education particularly by class and racial distinctions, asserting that "[w]hile Bridgman, as an able-minded and attractive white girl could be recuperated as fully human despite her multiple physical disabilities, in other cases [especially slavery] the role of literacy in securing one's humanity was much more tenuous" (53). Noting how the descriptions of Bridgman learning to read are racialized as a battle against darkness, Bourrier points out that *American Notes* reflects the tendency of nineteenth-century rhetoric to portray "both blackness and physical disabilities such as blindness or deafness" as "metaphors for ignorance" (55–56). Bourrier finally claims that "[t]he sentimental presentation of Bridgman" in Dickens's text allowed the audience to collapse such broader anxieties about literacy "into a singular portrait of an individual overcoming what were supposedly her personal challenges rather than larger social issues" (57).

In " 'GOD Be Thanked: A Ruin!': The Rejection of Nostalgia in *Pictures from Italy*," Sally Ledger places Dickens's 1846 travel narrative within the political framework of his 1840s publications, especially noting their denunciation of "the politics of nostalgia and of worn-out paternalism" that dominated English political rhetoric during that turbulent decade (80). In particular, Ledger draws a connection between *Pictures from Italy* and Dickens's 1844 Christmas Book, *The Chimes*, which was written during Dickens's stay in Genoa and was influenced by the frustrating sense of social stagnation Dickens experienced in both Italian and English societies. *The Chimes*'s attack on "the Tory reverence for the past and its feudal social arrangements" as expressed in the Young England movement of the 1840s is paralleled in Dickens's striking depiction of "the dead weight and enervating effect of the priesthood on Italian culture and society" in *Pictures from Italy* (81). Ledger demonstrates how Dickens's text turns away from a fascination with Rome's bloody imperial past (symbolized in the Coliseum, which is now "GOD be thanked: a ruin!" [Dickens qtd. in Ledger 79]), and instead celebrates the contemporary popular culture of the Italian people. Ledger concludes by comparing Dickens's attitudes to the historical past expressed in *Pictures from Italy* to the depiction of Roman ruins eleven years later in *Little Dorrit*, demonstrating how the earlier travel narrative anticipated Dickens's embrace of modernism and rejection of paternalism at the novel's conclusion.

Finally, with the recent opening of the Dickens World theme park in Chatham, I was not surprised to discover scholarship exploring the intriguing topic of Dickens's connections to tourism. Nicola J. Watson's "Rambles in Literary London," from the collection *Literary Tourism and Nineteenth-Century Culture* (which Watson edited), is a brief but fascinating discussion of Dickens's impact on London literary tourism. Watson argues that, due to its "overcrowdedness of implication and association" through its vast literary history, London, unlike most other destinations of nineteenth-century literary tourists, resisted the impulse of literary tourism to link a locale with a particular author (140). Victorian tourist writers responded to the dilemma of London literary tourism by developing ''a new tourist-model for conceiving literary London, based upon the aesthetic of the nineteenth-century novel . . . as practiced by—most especially—Dickens'' (141). This model of ''London as novel'' (145) is structured around the city ''ramble'' as an ''aimless form of exploration—episodic, even picaresque'' (141), similar to the ''Dickensian grotesque'' that ''yokes in sequence wildly disparate and apparently unconnected moods, modes, settings and clutches of characters'' (144). Watson's unique thesis made me consider the now traditional London literary walks (as well as my own London rambles) with fresh eyes.

Also from the *Literary Tourism* collection, Alison Booth's short essay, ''Time-Travel in Dickens' World,'' broaches some intriguing issues about Dickens and Heritage tourism that could be elaborated in future scholarship. Booth considers literary tourism as a form of ''time travel,'' noting that ''the movements of the readerly imagination and travel mimic each other,'' so that the tourist is immersed in a virtual world just as the reader is ''lost'' in the narrative of a favorite book (150–51). Like the reader, the tourist ''hopes to cross a temporal threshold, to transcend ordinary existence,'' so that trips to shrines and memorials become ''a controlled experiment with mortality'' (155). Booth considers this phenomenon in relation to her visits to three Dickens-related sites: the Dickens Museum in London, the Dickens Festival in Rochester, and Dickens World in Chatham. Her discussion of the actual locales is somewhat disappointing, consisting of interesting journalistic descriptions that could use more analysis for connections to the time-travel phenomenon in both tourism and Dickens's fiction. For instance, Booth provocatively notes the disjunction between the actual poverty one witnesses in Chatham and the ''voluntary trip into aestheticised history'' that one takes when visiting the ''Victorian slums'' of the Dickens World theme park (159); but Booth fails to make a connection to a Dickensian aesthetic, such as Dickens's own showman's tendency to exploit cultural suffering, child death, and poverty for commercial and entertainment purposes. However, Booth's essay points readers down some potentially fruitful avenues for further study of Dickens's place in this popular-culture phenomenon.

Presenting a marvelous conjunction between modern tourism and Dickens's travel writings, Jeremy Clarke's ''Dickens's Dark Ride: 'Traveling Abroad' to Meet the Heritage'' provides the literary context missing from Booth's study by comparing Heritage tourism rides, such as the ''*Great Expectations* Boat Ride'' at Dickens World, to the tourist aesthetic expressed in Dickens's ''Traveling Abroad,'' an essay from *The Uncommercial Traveller* that describes a journey Dickens took into France and Switzerland. Clarke contends that in the essay Dickens "uses his position as writer to construct his own Dark Ride," designing France "as an analogical space which can nourish his need for stasis, for safety and home-feeling," desires that are central to modern Heritage tourism (5). Like the journey of those theme park visitors who "are moved along at a predetermined pace" through the tourist environment by the theme park ride, Dickens's stage coach journey is largely passive, as he dives into his "travelling chariot" in "a determined withdrawal from the world, even as he goes out into the world" (6). Dickens's journey depends on the pleasures of *recognition* as much as novelty; he "knows *exactly* where he is going," and "[i]n the same way our Heritage tourism promises distinctiveness and surprises, while relying on dramas of identification to engage the visitor and sustain a coherent narrative" (7). Clarke likewise notes that the tourist's journey is primarily an affective experience of projecting oneself onto the environment that one is seeing, just as Dickens describes France less as a geographical entity than an embodiment of Dickens's personal experiences and emotions (10). Clarke summarizes the way in which Dickens's journey in "Travelling Abroad" prefigures today's tourist mentality: Dickens's

> withdrawn glance—the view from the chariot—helps us understand how the traveler/tourist . . . engages with a self-contained, closed, and determinate environment. The thrill of recognition . . . allows the viewer/reader/tourist the opportunity to establish an inclusive relationship with the environment like that promised by Heritage attractions. This is the feeling-of-being-a part-of which is promoted so strongly by living history events. (12)

Clarke's astute article, in conjunction with Watson's and Booth's essays, convinced me that Dickens's impact on modern tourism is a topic that warrants further attention in Dickens scholarship.

Studies of Adaptations in Fiction and Film

This year was marked by numerous noteworthy contributions to a growing area of Dickens scholarship—adaptation studies. Two works, Armelle Parey's "Peter Carey's *Jack Maggs*: The True History of the Convict?" and Irina Bauder-Begerow's "Echoing Dickens: Three Rewritings of *Great Expectations*," consider recent popular "rewritings" of *Great Expectations* that "challenge the authority of the primary text" (Parey 126), particularly from a postcolonial perspective. Both essays discuss Peter Carey's well-known revisionist novel, *Jack Maggs*, which retells Dickens's story from the perspective of the transported convict, while Bauder-Begerow's essay likewise addresses Lloyd Jones's *Mister Pip*, which features schoolchildren reading

Dickens's novel on the war-torn island of Bougainville in the 1990s. Both *Jack Maggs* and *Mr. Pip* "confer the narrative authority upon the 'colonial other' who thus obtains a hearing" (Bauder-Begerow 120); in *Jack Maggs*, the transported convict becomes the protagonist and a narrator of his own tale, while the marginalized voice is heard in *Mr. Pip* through the narrator Mathilda, the "doubly subaltern female protagonist" (Bauder-Begerow 133) who is a young native of Bougainville. However, Bauder-Begerow notes that unlike *Great Expectations*, which filters the narrative solely through Pip's perspective, both revisionist novels "democratise the autodiegetic narrative power by putting further narrators and focalisers alongside the protagonist's voice," creating a "multi-perspective structure" (121) that dismantles the authority of the parent text by exposing the unreliability of narrative itself. Parey points out that *Jack Maggs* initially seems to offer the "true history of the convict" omitted from Dickens's text (127); however, the multiple versions of the tale that the reader receives ultimately belie any one "true" version, revealing that "this re-vision of the convict is yet another construction" (135). According to both scholars, *Jack Maggs*'s metanarrative critique is enhanced by the addition of a novelist character, Tobias Oates, "an unflattering portrait" of Dickens (Parey 131) that "controverts the romantic concept of the ingenious author" and thus challenges the reader's view of how a great novel is written (Bauder-Begerow 125). Parey asserts that by "making the reader privy to the fictionalising process undergone by the convict, Carey generally states that writing is ideological and equals power, empowerment and possible entrapment" (132). Thus, in postmodern fashion, "*Jack Maggs* challenges indeed both a canonical England-centered tale but also its own rewriting of it," making us wary of the power of textual constructs (Parey 135).

Bauder-Begerow notes that Lloyd Jones's *Mr. Pip* achieves a similar effect in revealing "the instability of textual meaning" (131) as the protagonist Mathilda, who has identified her own life with Pip's coming of age narrative, discovers "that there are a plurality of versions of *Great Expectations*," the expurgated version told by her teacher in school, the printed copy Mathilda finally obtains and then loses in the war, and the version that the schoolchildren try to reconstruct from memory. When Mathilda ultimately turns her back on Dickens's novel to write her own narrative, she learns that to construct her own bildungsroman, she must free herself of the authority of the parent text. Bauder-Begerow's and Parey's essays thus effectively highlight the conflicted nature of contemporary authors' and readers' relationships to Dickens's powerful "pre-texts."

As a film studies scholar, I am delighted to review several particularly fine works about the relationship of Dickens's fiction to the cinema. In "Griffith, Dickens, and the Politics of Composure," Daniel Siegel provides a new reading of Soviet filmmaker Sergei Eisenstein's famous assessment of the connections between Dickens and filmmaker D. W. Griffith in Eisenstein's essay, "Dickens, Griffith, and the Film Today." Identifying montage as the narrative technique that most clearly unites Dickens and Griffith in their impact on future filmmakers, Eisenstein characterized montage as revolutionary; a series of apparently unrelated images are drawn together to create a composite image that suddenly takes on new meaning in a leap that is similar to social revolution (hence the appeal of cinematic montage to Soviet revolutionaries such as Eisenstein). But Siegel notes that Eisenstein faulted Dickens and Griffith for not going far enough in their montage sequences. Their use of montage reveals the struggles and sufferings in capitalist societies "without the culminating revolution that would give form and purpose" to these struggles (375). Siegel responds to Eisenstein's criticism by analyzing two narratives set in the French Revolution, Griffith's *Orphans of the Storm* and Dickens's *A Tale of Two Cities*, as texts that promote a "politics of composure" rather than revolutionary anarchy as the most effective means of social change. Siegel argues that Griffith's feverish and chaotic montage sequences reveal the inherent dangers of uncontrolled revolutionary action, while the melodramatic gesture of trembling performed repeatedly by the film's heroic characters at moments of supreme social upheaval suggests in contrast the attempt to balance revolutionary action with feeling and understanding; trembling represents heroic control and contemplation in the midst of chaos and visualizes "a thematic and aesthetic solution to the problem of revolutionary extremism" (379). Similarly, in Dickens's novel, which is governed by a specular economy that focuses on scrutiny, the act of bearing witness becomes the means by which characters attempt to understand, diffuse, and control the chaotic events that threaten to overwhelm them. Siegel concludes that through such melodramatic techniques, Dickens and Griffith attempt "to represent social crisis in a way that is neither palliative nor disabling" (387); rather than envisioning an idealistic end to social conflict, they show characters heroically adapting to a perpetually unstable social world.

The volume *Charles Dickens,* A Tale of Two Cities *and the French Revolution*, edited by Colin Jones, Josephine McDonagh, and Jon Mee (discussed in its entirety below in "Studies of Individual Works"), contains two of the finest essays on Dickens film adaptations that I have read in some time. Judith Buchanan and Alex Newhouse's "Sanguine Mirages, Cinematic Dreams; Things Seen and Things Imagined in the 1917 Fox Feature Film *A Tale of Two Cities*" is groundbreaking in its treatment of a previously ignored and currently unavailable silent film adaptation, which, according to Buchanan and Newhouse, visualizes the novel's "central opposition" between individual lives and public events (146). The camera "unsparingly intrudes on more private spaces [e.g., through visualizations of characters' thoughts or memories] to see how domestic, secret, and otherwise occluded realms . . . can relate to public event and mass spectacle'' (148). One highlight of this study is the perceptive analysis of the double-exposure technique that allowed the same actor to play both Darnay and Carton (this remains the only cinematic adaptation to take this approach), which demonstrates the film's use of double-casting to explore the novel's concerns with unstable identity. Buchanan and Newhouse also provide an excellent discussion of how the film's concluding tableau breaks with the heroic tradition of the stage adaptations to read greater psychological ambiguity into Carton's final vision. This impressive essay proves that the 1917 adaptation is an unearthed gem worthy of release to the general public.

In comparison, Charles Barr's essay, ''Two Cities, Two Films,'' provides an astute and innovative analysis of the two most well-known cinematic adaptations, the 1935 and 1958 versions produced by David O. Selznick and Betty Box, respectively. Barr examines how each film adapts particularly challenging features of the novel, including the double motif, the extended time frame, and Dickens's powerful narrative voice. But the most intriguing aspect of Barr's study is his analysis of each film's political/social context. While Selznick's production mirrors the social unrest of 1930s America through careful allusions to the American and Bolshevik revolutions (particularly by the incorporation of a rapid montage technique drawn from the battle scenes of Sergei Eisenstein's 1925 *The Battleship Potemkin*), Box's film, produced in the more politically stable environment of 1950s British cinema, foregoes revolutionary politics in favor of subversive sexuality, as expressed in the performances of Dirk Bogarde, who evokes a homosexual subtext for Carton, and Christopher Lee, who endows Evrémonde with the animal sexuality of his Dracula film persona.

Marc Napolitano's ''Disneyfying Dickens: *Oliver & Company* and *The Muppet Christmas Carol* as Dickensian Musicals'' is a beautifully researched article that makes a significant contribution to the study of Dickens adaptations by focusing on the seldom-discussed topic of children's adaptations. Napolitano examines two Dickens film adaptations for the effects of what he defines as ''Disneyfication,'' the ''transformation of something dark and sophisticated into something light and sentimental for marketing to a family audience'' (80). According to Napolitano, while the ''Disneyfying'' process simplifies the original literary text, it can likewise have the beneficial result of encouraging young viewers to return to the literary source. Napolitano begins with an effective summary of the evolution of film adaptation theory from stultifying fidelity criticism, which assesses an adaptation's quality based solely upon fidelity to the literary original, to the more productive, recent focus on adaptation as a form of interpretation or critique. While adaptation theory currently decries the demand for fidelity, Napolitano insightfully notes that ''in the case of children's film adaptations, the fidelity issue is important due to the criticality of reading to childhood development.'' Although we cannot demand that adaptations be absolute replicas of the source materials, ''it behooves filmmakers to somehow convey to young viewers that these films come from literary sources, and likewise, that these sources are worthy of their attention'' (81).

To demonstrate how an adaptation can preserve important aspects of the original text in such a way as to encourage young viewers to read the literary source, Napolitano compares the 1987 Disney animated feature *Oliver & Company* (an adaptation of *Oliver Twist*) to the 1992 Jim Henson Studios/ Disney production *The Muppet Christmas Carol*, focusing on how the musical score of each film relates to its Dickensian source. *Oliver & Company* features a cast of celebrity pop singers and a musical score in which the songs are used to showcase the performers' talents rather than develop the characters or plot: ''As a result, the distance between the film and its Dickensian source material is increased significantly'' (84), which ''ultimately rules out any chance of the film being used to draw young viewers to reading Dickens'' (88). In contrast, *The Muppet Christmas Carol* ''ultimately succeeds in drawing the young viewer's attention toward the original source'' because it unites the famous Dickens story with the equally beloved Jim Henson Muppet characters through a ''book score'' that carefully integrates the songs with the development of the characters, plot, and themes from Dickens's text (88). Napolitano explains the difference between the films' approaches to the adaptation process by placing each film within the immediate historical context of its production as well as within the broader framework of the history of stage musicals and Dickensian musical adaptations.

Chris Louttit and Iris Kleinecke-Bates address the historical and political contexts of television adaptations. Louttit's essay, ''*Cranford*, Popular Culture, and the Politics of Adapting the Victorian Novel for Television,'' examines twenty-first-century trends in television adaptations of the Victorian novel as exemplified in two BBC productions—Andrew Davies's *Bleak House* (2005) and Heidi Thomas's *Cranford* (2007). Placing the adaptations in the socio-political environment of the New Labour period, Louttit argues that ''much like the Blairite administration and other refashionings of British culture and heritage at this time, these adaptations seem on the surface to be quite innovative,'' while they in fact ''show continuities with earlier more traditional examples of costume drama, and are quite conservative both in their politics and in their approach to the genre'' (34). In his detailed analysis of the *Bleak House* adaptation, Louttit demonstrates how the film made ''major aesthetic changes'' to the costume drama genre by incorporating radical ''soap opera'' methods, such as the ''breathing camera'' shooting technique derived from TV crime dramas, an MTV-style of rapid and disjunctive editing, and a scheduling format of fast-paced half-hour episodes that aired immediately following the BBC's popular soap opera, *EastEnders* (36).

Screenwriter Andrew Davies's "dynamic reshaping of the emphases of the narrative" to focus on the "simple coming-of-age tale" of Esther, Ada, and Richard was also an attempt to uncover "the book's populist appeal" and "reach beyond the typically 'bourgeois' and 'elitist' audience associated with period drama" (36–37). However, Louttit reveals that the adaptation's approach is not as "unconventional and populist" as it seems. The film "lacks any real political bite" due to its focus on the "small-scale personal dramas" of the young characters (38); and the film's "soap opera" techniques, while innovative for contemporary costume drama, are actually quite faithful to Dickens's "intensely performative narrative voice," suggesting that although "it is important to take period drama in 'new' and innovative directions, . . . this is more acceptable if it more conservatively reflects aspects of the original text" (37). This fascinating study of the impact of Dickens's text on a film genre that is uneasily negotiating between populist/radical and elitist/ conservative paradigms reminds us that the role of Dickens's fiction as cultural capital remains a complicated issue today.

Like Louttit's study, Iris Kleinecke-Bates's essay, "Historicizing the Classic Novel Adaptation: *Bleak House* (2005) and British Television Contexts," examines the innovative production techniques of the 2005 *Bleak House* adaptation, but Kleinecke-Bates focuses on how these techniques were determined by the film's place within the extended history of BBC television adaptations. Kleinecke-Bates argues that the BBC's association with public service broadcasting, particularly its educational goals, has established a perception of BBC television as a transparent medium whose function in adapting a classic text is the unadulterated transmission of the author's work (115). This perception has resulted in a demand for realism and fidelity in BBC adaptations to which filmmakers have responded in varying ways, depending upon contemporary cultural and economic pressures. For instance, the impact of the Heritage movement of the 1980s, which celebrated a return to "Victorian values," resulted in adaptations marked by "nostalgia and idealization of the past," whereas the trend in the 1990s "to re-discover the period as a complex and real past" led to adaptations of Victorian texts that focused on "realism and period authenticity," even at the expense of faithfulness to the text (118). Kleinecke-Bates argues that there were fewer Dickens adaptations during the 1990s because the carnivalesque features of Dickens's fiction conflicted with the contemporary trend toward "a bleaker, more naturalistic representation of the period" (118). Kleinecke-Bates sees the inventive features of the 2005 *Bleak House* adaptation as a "shift towards a more carnivalesque and 'playful,' riotous and exaggerated Dickens" that represents both an attempt to capture a new popular audience through novelty and an attempt to meet the BBC's public service expectations of authenticity through fidelity to neglected aspects of Dickens's classic text (119).

Both Holly Furneaux and Susan Zieger consider the queer potential of Dickens's fiction, creatively magnified through the lens of film adaptations. Furneaux's *Queer Dickens: Erotics, Families, Masculinities* (discussed in its entirety above in "Gender, Sexuality, Marriage, and Children") devotes part of a chapter and a lengthy postscript to film adaptations of *Oliver Twist* and *Nicholas Nickleby*. Furneaux sees Oliver's adoption by the bachelor Brownlow in *Oliver Twist* as Dickens's acknowledgement of alternative family structures, deliberately rejecting "biological family as a fantasized panacea to the sufferings of institutionalized children in this period" (44). However, she argues that filmic tradition's attempt to normalize the relationship by portraying Brownlow as Oliver's grandfather in numerous adaptations suggests modern audiences' misgivings about nonbiological motives for parenting, suspicions that the novel itself arouses through its hints of pedophilia and the numerous parallels Dickens draws between Brownlow and Oliver's exploitative guardian, Fagin. Furneaux illuminates the negative queer potential of Dickens's text through analysis of Seth Michael Donsky's *Twisted* (1996) and Jacob Tierney's *Twist* (2004), two bleak film adaptations marketed to gay audiences that reject both the mainstream biological normalization of the Brownlow/Twist relationship and Dickens's own idyllic depiction of Oliver's queer domestic haven with Brownlow, instead adapting the narrative into queer tragedies of homosexual prostitution and domestic abuse that richly complicate issues of guardianship and parenting in Dickens's novel.

In the postscript to her study, "Doing Dickens: The Queer Politics of Adaptation," Furneaux extends her analysis of *Twist* adaptations to include brilliant discussions of director Douglas McGrath's 2002 film *Nicholas Nickleby*, which deliberately utilizes queer casting and focuses on the tender, tactile relationship of Nicholas and Smike, and screenwriter Andrew Davies's 2005 adaptation of *Bleak House*, which gives new status to the tender soldier Sergeant George as "the previously unsung gentle hero" of the novel (253). Furneaux contrasts these films with the Tierney and Donsky adaptations of *Oliver Twist* as illustrating the spectrum of queer interpretations of Dickens, from the celebration of queer family units and "tender masculinities" (7), to the depiction of queerness as tragically antithetical to domesticity. Furneaux insightfully points out that such adaptations not only reflect the ways in which we interpret Dickens's works but inevitably influence future readings "through the prism of their [the novels'] cultural afterlife" (245).

In "Dickens's Queer Children," Susan Zieger examines the figure of the fragile, threatened child in Dickens's novels and several of their film adaptations in light of queer theorist Lee Edelman's theory of "reproductive futurism," which argues that Western culture valorizes biological reproduction and heterosexuality as the basis for future social survival at the expense of the queer people of the present (141). While Edelman sees the threatened child as the icon of reproduction futurism, Zieger shows how adaptations of Dickens's novels likewise reveal latent possibilities for queerness in Dickens's child characters. Zieger focuses on "the queerly aged child" who has been "brought too soon to market" (144) as a queer signifier since such a child "accelerates the normative pace at which implicitly heterosexual workers mature and reproduce themselves" (143). Through close reading of both literary and filmic texts, Zieger shows how Dickens uses this trope not only to create the sympathies of reproductive futurism, but also to subvert them. For example, in his depictions of the children at Dotheboys Hall in *Nicholas Nickleby*, Dickens arouses compassion for the boys through their peril but likewise depicts them with a "subversive mirth" that undercuts the sympathy they evoke (147). Comparison with two recent *Nickleby* film adaptations reflects this paradox in Dickens's text. Douglas McGrath's 2002 adaptation arouses the sympathies of reproductive futurism by erasing "the [children's] ugliness and agedness" and "sanitizing" them for middle-class consumption, as many earlier classic adaptations of Dickens's novels had done with his child characters (149). Stephen Whittaker's 2000 production, in contrast, insinuates the boys' queer potential by depicting them in all their degradation sleeping in small groups of twos or threes, imagery that highlights their eroticism and evokes the threat of premature sexuality. Like Furneaux, Zieger also compares McGrath's *Nickleby* film to Jacob Tierney's *Oliver Twist* adaptation, *Twist* (which sets the tale in the contemporary urban sex industry), arguing that McGrath's *Nickleby* "suggests the possibilities for queer assimilation into the bourgeois family" (145) through its loving depiction of a "queer romance" between Nicholas and Smike (151), while *Twist* "demonstrates and refines Edelman's main point, that reproductive futurism makes queer lives expendable," through its tragic depiction of the doomed relationship between the Oliver and Dodger characters (145). Zieger significantly expands on Furneaux's analysis of *Twist* by providing a particularly powerful treatment of the Oliver/Dodger relationship in Dickens's text, Tierney's film, and previous adaptations. Thus, Zieger's study joins Furneaux's as another excellent example of how the dialogue between Dickens's texts, film adaptations, and contemporary theory can reveal dormant properties of Dickens's fiction.

Studies of Individual Works

Sketches by Boz

Citing Dickens's description of his early journalistic career from his 1865 fundraising speech for the Newspaper Press, Hisup Shin's essay, "Rapid and

Dexterous: A Study of Dickens' Journalistic Writing and *Sketches by Boz*,"
argues that the "rapidity and dexterity" (Dickens qtd. in Shin) of Dickens's
early journalism were not merely passing mechanical adjustments to the challenges of his career as a reporter but reflect a visceral connection to the
"shifting technological and social circumstances of Victorian England" that
became a central feature of the "uniquely Dickensian" imagination (122).
This rapid and dexterous style is a "necessary strategy" for writing about
urban scenes since it mimics the "lively, energetic modes of social and technological adjustments" that characterize city life (122). Shin argues that the
dominant structuralist critical approach to *Sketches* that has tried to determine
a "coherent sense of totality" underlying the essays has blinded scholars to
the "raw, vivid sense of immediacy in Dickens's writing" (109). He responds
in particular to J. Hillis Miller's reading (*Charles Dickens and George Cruikshank*, 1971) as exemplary of prevailing structuralist interpretations, arguing
that Miller's view of the Dickensian city as a prison in which characters are
trapped by social structures beyond their perception and control "is a bleak,
claustrophobic picture of the world, leaving us little chance to experience raw
reality" (110). In contrast, Shin sees the visceral energy and momentum of
Dickens's writing as capturing "ways in which the human body is able to
negotiate with its challenging, often objectionable surroundings" (113), evoking an "ambivalent, slippery dimension of human experience" at odds with
a deterministic vision of existence (110). Shin supports his arguments with
excellent analysis of Dickens's vibrant descriptions of urban people and objects in numerous passages from *Sketches* and his other journalistic writings.

The Pickwick Papers

In addition to Paul Schacht's "In Pursuit of Pickwick's Hat: Dickens and the
Epistemology of Utilitarianism" (reviewed above in "Science, Religion, and
Philosophy"), two excellent studies illuminate the contemporary social concerns prevalent in *The Pickwick Papers*. In "The Topicality of *Pickwick
Papers*," David Parker takes issue with the common contention that *The
Pickwick Papers* "is less socially engaged than Dickens's later novels" (212)
by investigating a plethora of intriguing topical issues reflected in the text,
including changes in hunting and trespassing legislation, governmental reforms in local politics, the debates surrounding Sabbatarianism, the vacillations of contemporary celebrity and fashion, and the state of the army
following the Napoleonic Wars. Parker also demonstrates how the novel,
through the debtors' prison episode and the depiction of the corrupt magistrate
Mr. Nupkins, actually participated in the public debates that led to reforms
of the local magistry and the laws surrounding imprisonment for debt. Most
importantly, Parker proves that the wealth of topical issues addressed in

Pickwick is not a mass of disconnected historical references but is unified around the "dizzying changes in middle-class projects between 1827 and 1837" (the novel's stated timeframe), a chronology that perfectly "straddles the Great Reform Act" of 1832, which serves as the "concealed fulcrum" of the novel (205–06). In other words, the novel is intimately attuned to the great social changes of the early Victorian period, dramatizing both the "middle-class ambition" and the "middle-class misgivings" aroused by the tectonic socio-economic shifts of the age (205). Parker aptly concludes by urging "a more demanding mode of reading" *Pickwick* "than is sometimes recommended" (212), making one wonder if a new annotated critical edition of the novel isn't in order.

Susan Shatto's "Mr. Pickwick's First Brush with the Law: Civil Disobedience in *The Pickwick Papers*" provides further proof of the novel's topicality by examining the threatened duel between Mr. Pickwick and Mr. Magnus from a historical perspective, placing it within the fascinating context of English legislation about dueling, rioting, and other examples of civil unrest. Shatto points out that the response of the Ipswich magistrate, Mr. Nupkins, to Pickwick's imagined duel and to an outbreak of schoolboy violence in the town is exaggerated, but the language he uses and the events he describes are based in fact and allude to the violent civil disturbances and widespread political unrest of the 1820s and 1830s (for example, Shatto notes that violent protests against the New Poor Law occurred in Ipswich just two months before Dickens began working on *Pickwick*). Shatto connects the novel to examples of legal advice for responding to civil disturbances drawn from contemporary handbooks for magistrates, as well as historical accounts of numerous early-nineteenth-century riots and duels, all excellent evidence that the world of *The Pickwick Papers* may seem "nostalgic, innocent, and childlike" (155), but it also has a "dark side" firmly based in the anxieties and social unrest of the early Victorian age (161). Thus, Shatto, like Parker, sees the novel less as a wistful evocation of an imagined pre-industrial Golden Age and more as a current barometer of the whirlwind changes wrought by the Industrial Revolution.

Part of a collection of essays on the theme of "Victorian vulgarity," James Buzard's "Wulgarity and Witality: On Making a Spectacle of Oneself in *Pickwick*" demonstrates how entrenched Dickens's comedy is in the vulgar and reminds us how effectively Dickens challenged the boundaries between high-brow artistic respectability and low-brow mass appeal. Buzard asserts that *The Pickwick Papers* owes its narrative energy to "the disreputable outsiders" who are placed in opposition to the "propriety, principle, and disinterested benevolence" of the respectable protagonist, a contrast that the narrative ultimately undermines as Mr. Pickwick and his club begin to "evince a deep-seated attachment to some of the shiftless, predatory, and

appetitive tendencies of their vulgar opposites'' (36). Buzard summarizes
the various forms of vulgarity embodied in the lower-class or disreputable
characters: ''Jingle represents vulgarity in its adversarial guise,'' Sam and
Tony Weller embody ''the power of the low as helper and instructor,'' and
Bob Sawyer ''presents us with a spectacle far more radical in its implications:
the vulgar man as secret sharer'' (45), who ''acts out, for all the world to
see, what Pickwick does covertly and hides from himself'' (49). Through
Pickwick's interaction with these characters, Buzard argues, Dickens's ''comedy drives toward the destruction of those boundaries dividing 'Pickvick and
principle' from the vulgar and mean'' (52). Buzard's reading of Jingle as
Pickwick's vulgar doppelganger, the energetic embodiment of mob mentality,
self-interest, and appetite, is particularly insightful and implies that Jingle
might function as a fictionalization of Dickens's own opportunistic nature
as well.

Oliver Twist

Most of the 2009 scholarship on *Oliver Twist* addresses film adaptations
(discussed above in ''Studies of Adaptations in Fiction and Film''). An exception is Robert D. Butterworth's ''The Significance of Fagin's Jewishness,''
which considers the anti-Semitic features of Dickens's portrayal of Fagin in
light of anti-Jewish Victorian sentiments and Dickens's own social criticism.
Providing an enlightening historical context of the social and legal advances
against anti-Semitic discrimination in England of the 1830s, Butterworth
demonstrates that Dickens was ''neither swept along by nor pandering to a
groundswell of anti-Jewish feeling'' in his negative depiction of Fagin (214);
however, while significant strides were made against discrimination, anti-
Semitic prejudice remained, resulting in ambivalent attitudes towards Jewishness in early Victorian culture that Dickens exploited in his fiction. Surveying the extensive body of scholarly analysis of Fagin's Jewishness,
Butterworth argues that Dickens was able to take advantage of his society's
anti-Semitic prejudices in his portrayal of Fagin ''in a subtler and more
sophisticated way than has been commonly assumed'' by critics (218). First,
Dickens is careful to depict Fagin ''as an unrepresentative Jew'' (218), an
apostate who breaks the precepts of his religion (particularly its food laws).
Second, although Fagin ''is clearly a villain,'' Dickens indicates that the
parish officials are not any more virtuous (221). Noting the particularly ''ap-
palling'' fact that ''when Oliver enters the world of an apostate and outlaw
Jew he receives better treatment, as a human being, than in the respectable
world'' of the parish, Butterworth attests, ''For all his evil, an apostate Jew
and common criminal does a better job'' than ''respectable Christian society''
that ''lives up to none of the standards of its religion'' (223). Thus, Dickens

exploits negative Jewish stereotypes in his depiction of Fagin "not so that he can indulge in meretricious anti-semitism," but in order "to jolt his respectable Christian readers out of their complacency" (223). Fagin's ethnicity becomes another barb in Dickens's attack on an ostensibly Christian society that was failing in Christian charity.

The Old Curiosity Shop

In "Dick Swiveller's Bed," Joel J. Brattin examines an important thematic contrast in Dickens's life and fiction through the emblem of Dick Swiveller's turn-up bedstead in *The Old Curiosity Shop*. The bed, which is disguised as a bookcase by day in a genteel attempt to cover Dick's poverty, but does double duty at night as the couch of an imaginative dreamer, embodies the contrast between reality and fantasy, and Swiveller himself stands as a conduit between the two worlds, continually tempering grim reality through "the transformative power of the imagination" (165). Beginning with Swiveller's bed, Brattin surveys a wide variety of convertible bedsteads throughout Dickens's autobiographical writings and fiction as symbols of the contrasts that dominated his career, pointing out that Dickens, like Dick Swiveller, often negotiated between two realms—poverty and gentility, journalism and fiction, social realism and fairy-tale fantasy—making the two worlds indivisible, just like the dual-purpose bedstead. Although many of the beds discussed in this essay visualize the dangers of poverty or the pathetic humiliation of trying to conceal it (e.g., the turn-up bedstead that smothers unwanted children in *Oliver Twist*, or the convertible bed that is a shabby attempt to conceal the Dorrits' destitution in the Marshalsea prison), Brattin sees the ever-optimistic Swiveller and the imaginative fiction of his bookcase/bedstead as the strongest examples of the positive, transformative powers of Dickens's fiction.

In "Narratives of Survival," Michal Peled Ginsburg examines *The Old Curiosity Shop* with novels by Oliver Goldsmith and Elizabeth Gaskell as narratives in which "the notion of closure is irrelevant" and in which the plot, although linear and straightforward, is not governed by a specific goal. These "narratives of survival" "foreground the continuous, in principle, endless, process of creation anew (production and reproduction) necessary for the maintenance of life, self, social group," and they undermine novelistic conventions through depiction of the home and family as "fundamentally dynamic" rather than characterized by the stasis and stability demanded by novelistic closure (411). For instance, the sufferings of the vicar's family in Goldsmith's *The Vicar of Wakefield* depict the home as the site of the continual intensification of affective experience. Elizabeth Gaskell's *Cranford* likewise violates novelistic conventions by divorcing housekeeping from the novel's traditional narrative goal of matrimony, which enables Gaskell to depict the endless domestic labor of women as an "autonomous activity" interesting in its own right and "essential to the survival of the material home" (412–13). In comparison, Ginsburg sees Dickens's *The Old Curiosity Shop* as "a narrative of survival recast midway into a narrative of homecoming" (414). The wanderings of Nell and her grandfather initially focus on the process of survival and imply a vision of the child as "weak and fragile, a potential victim of an adult world" whose death will be caused by poor parenting. But when the potential of reunion with lost family (in the form of Nell's great-uncle) emerges, Dickens "redefines the journey toward death (the story of life as a struggle of survival) as a journey home" in which the child's death becomes a symbol of "the victory of innocence over a corrupt world" (415). Ginsburg concludes that the three novels are united by a "view of plot as process rather than progress" (415). The historical development of the novel in conjunction with domestic ideology eventually produced the value judgment that plots marked by "progress and acquisition" are superior to plots of process and survival "through the exclusion of the labor of maintenance, the erasure of the constant need for individuals (as well as for a culture) repeatedly to reproduce their values and material base in order to survive" (415).

In "Quilp, Commerce and Domesticity: Crossing Boundaries in *The Old Curiosity Shop*," Gareth Cordery attempts to recover the historical and cultural significance of Quilp in light of the dominance of archetypal and psychological interpretations of the character. In particular, Cordery "demythologize[s] Quilp by relocating him in the commercial and domestic contexts of the 1830s" (210). Cordery argues, "Quilp's transgressiveness . . . is more than simply moral, but grounded in the material realities and doctrines of his time, a crossing of geographical and ideological boundaries within and between the spheres of commerce and domesticity" (210). To demonstrate Quilp's "refusal to be contained within traditional economic and national boundaries" (215), Cordery focuses on this character's connection with the Thames, which he interprets as a "liminal space" that dismantles "distinctions between legal and illegal trading, between Empire and Home" (215). Just as the Thames "enables the crossing of national as well as of economic boundaries" through the shipping of foreign goods into England, Quilp's movement back and forth across the river from the legal business world of the Custom House to the illegal smuggling activities of his Counting House demonstrates the permeable boundary between the official and black market economies of the 1830s (215).

Cordery likewise examines Quilp's traversing the Thames between his home at Tower Hill to his business at the Wharf as a transgression of the boundaries between the feminine world of domesticity and the masculine world of commerce, which are illuminated in the novel by the drinking practices associated with both worlds. Cordery effectively analyzes scenes of tea drinking (traditionally associated with women and the domestic sphere) and the consumption of alcoholic beverages (particularly rum, drunk primarily by men) to demonstrate how Quilp exposes the illusory nature of the distinctions between the two worlds. This is most effectively demonstrated in the "tea party" at the "summerhouse" (a dilapidated smuggler's hideaway) at which Quilp and the Brasses share tea and rum and meld the domestic and commercial worlds, mimicking the customs of polite society while confirming their illegal business partnership in the plot to destroy Kit Nubbles. Cordery concludes with a wonderfully provocative interpretation of the relationship of Quilp and Sally Brass as a final demonstration of the conflation of domestic and business worlds. Asserting, "Had sex change operations been available in 1840 Sally Brass would have been first under the knife" (224), Cordery examines evidence of Sally's maneuvering between genders, including her business and legal acumen, her cross-gendered appearance and her cross-dressing at the novel's conclusion, the implications of a past sexual relationship with Quilp that resulted in the Marchioness as their illegitimate offspring, and the possibility that Sally had used the Brasses' law office as a brothel in the past, a deduction (perhaps far-fetched, but certainly intriguing) which Cordery makes through Sally's association with the harlot's iconic color—green. Cordery concludes that Sally is Quilp's ideal mate since "[e]ach refuses to be pinned down by traditional roles assigned to males and females" (224).

Martin Chuzzlewit

In a unique reading of one of Dickens's most popular female characters, Goldie Morgentaler's essay "Mrs. Gamp, Mrs. Harris and Mr. Dickens: Creativity and the Self Split in Two" interprets Mrs. Gamp, the comic nurse-midwife in *Martin Chuzzlewit*, as an alter ego for Dickens, "an emanation of his own creative self" (3). Morgentaler argues that the Mrs. Gamp/Mrs. Harris configuration represents an unusual type of doubling in Dickens's fiction that illustrates "the uses of the creative self to alleviate loneliness and despair while at the same time establishing and anchoring identity" (5). Morgentaler examines several passages from the novel to demonstrate how Mrs. Gamp's apparently fictional friend Mrs. Harris "functions as both prop and foil for Mrs. Gamp" (7) by which she not only constructs her own identity, but also diverts the horrors of her life into more comic channels that make her difficulties more bearable. Morgentaler is critical of Dickens's apparent lack of sympathy for Mrs. Gamp, asserting that Dickens "never seems to give her credit for being, what she so manifestly is, a survivor, an independent woman whose lifeline is her imagination" (9). But, most significantly, Morgentaler sees Dickens's ambivalence towards Mrs. Gamp as an expression of "his own anxiety about the nature of creativity" (9). Morgentaler argues that both Mrs. Gamp and Dickens "live by the creation of imaginary beings who depend on them for existence, but the creators are also dependent on these same visionary creations for their sense of self" (10). Mrs. Gamp thus functions as a surrogate artist through whom Dickens examines the complexities of his own identity as a writer.

Dombey and Son

Three studies of *Dombey and Son* illuminate the relationship of domestic interiors to psychology and gender. Stella Pratt-Smith's essay "All in the Mind: The Psychological Realism of Dickensian Solitude" examines scenes of solitude in *Dombey and Son* as revealing a symbolic connection between interior spaces and individual psychology. In an unusual reading that incorporates Dickens's interest in mesmerism, Pratt-Smith interprets Paul Dombey's hallucinatory experiences with the wallpaper patterns and the ticking clock at his boarding school, as well as Florence Dombey's nocturnal wanderings throughout her father's house, as meditative attempts at self-treatment in response to the psychological trauma of solitude. Pratt-Smith likewise examines scenes depicting the respective isolation of Edith Dombey and Mr. Dombey within the Dombey home as examples of how Dickens uses interior spaces, especially domestic interiors, to reveal the interiority of his characters, belying contemporary critics' complaints about the lack of psychological depth in Dickens's creations. In particular, Edith's battle against the hostile interior of the house, which grotesquely comes to life, revealing her as a "bought woman" purchased through an economically convenient marriage, ultimately expands her personal psychological trauma into a broader picture of the individual's battle in Victorian society, "struggling not to become morally lost and submerged in the rapidly rising tide of commodities and consumption" (19). Dickens's use of domestic interiors in such instances thus demonstrates a "command of psychological realism" that extends far beyond his sentimental association with the clichés of the Victorian hearth and home (22).

In "Mobile Homes, Fallen Furniture, and the Dickens Cure," David A. Ellison considers the culturally symbolic significance of domestic interiors in *Dombey and Son*. Ellison asserts that the disconcerting mobility of Victorian society (technological, social, and economic) found its antithesis in "the dogmatic solidity of Victorian furniture." The stress on comfort in Victorian domestic interiors was a "claim for stasis amid the whirl of money and machines" (88). *Dombey and Son*, however, features "[m]obilized interiors composed of goods purchased, moved, renovated, seized, or evacuated.... Homes are repeatedly opened up by and to external forces—death, bankruptcy, matrimony, and its dissolution" (91), ultimately suggesting "an alarming instability within the domestic'' (92). This dangerous mobility encompasses, of course, the female as the guardian of the domestic space, whose job is to create the illusion of stability and stasis within the home, but who likewise embodies the threat of mobility through the prospect of her escape or fall from the domestic sphere. Ellison supports his argument through outstanding analysis of textual evidence from the novel, as well as imagery from Hablot Browne's illustrations, demonstrating how verbal and pictorial texts complement each other to visualize Victorian anxieties about domestic and social instability. Especially notable is Ellison's innovative reading of the novel's much-discussed railroad imagery, drawing a symbolic arc between the railroad, the home, and Florence as expressions of dangerous feminine mobility.

In "*Dombey and Son* and the 'Parlour on Wheels,' " Michael Klotz similarly focuses on the railway as an emblem of Victorian "anxiety about the stability of the domestic interior," since "the railway was a visible sign of the mobility of possessions and facilitated the distribution of domestic goods throughout the country" (61). But Klotz also connects the fears of domestic mobility inspired by the railroad to the developing interior decoration industry, which "imperiled the cherished ideal of the home as a fixed and unchanging refuge" (61). Two scenes in the novel feature homes that are dismantled by the forces of the railroad and interior design—the disappearance of the Toodles home in the railroad renovation of Stagg's Gardens, and the redecoration of the Dombey home prior to Dombey's second marriage. Interior design threatened to reduce domestic goods to commodities, items stripped of personal significance in order to emblemize instead the wealth and status of a family, a transformation that the objects in the Dombey home undergo when Dombey redecorates. Klotz notes that the two forces, the railway and interior design, were ultimately united in the railway carriage, which "was itself a site of aesthetic display and ornamentation" and which became a "parlour on wheels," supplied with all the comforts of the upper-middle-class home (67). In conclusion, Klotz provides a unique reading of the "take the house-tops off" passage in chapter 47 in which the narrator describes a vision of removing the house-tops of Victorian homes and exposing complacent families to the suffering of the poor around them. Klotz suggests that the passage is written from the perspective of a railroad passenger who is viewing the poor in passing, so that "[t]he passage gestures to the everyday moments in which we are offered access to a private spectacle of misery and have to make a choice: to stop, investigate, and inquire how to help, or look away and continue on our journey" (76).

David Copperfield

In "Dickens and the Wolf Man: Childhood Memory and Fantasy in *David Copperfield*," Robert E. Lougy draws on Freud's 1918 case history of the

"Wolf Man" to analyze the scene from chapter 8 in *David Copperfield* in which the sound of his mother's voice triggers within David an infantile memory of receiving comfort at his mother's breast. In Freud's case history, the Wolf Man described a childhood dream of being threatened by wolves which Freud traced back to the Wolf Man's primal memories of witnessing parental sexual intercourse. Freud claimed that whether such childhood memories are fictions or realities is unimportant since they have a very real impact in allowing the adult to access a primeval realm of human experience beyond his/her own individual understanding. Lougy applies Freud's reasoning to David's childhood memory, noting that the memory "enables David to inhabit a dream time that collapses distances, dissolves separation or loss" (413), allowing him to access a primal time of imagined wholeness with his mother that makes it possible to handle the anxiety of separation. Applying theories of the pre-subjective state before language and separation from the mother allow the construction of a sense of self, Lougy notes: "This story's indeterminate status in the novel as memory or fantasy allows Dickens to imagine those liminal sites from which subjectivity is born" (415). Lougy eloquently summarizes the significance of this memory: "[T]his scene . . . registers the mystery of the human mind, giving us access to a moment both in David's history and outside his history, one that imagines a David before David was David, before he moved, in other words, into language and into the loss and separation that our entrance into a world of symbolic structures carries with it" (416).

Daniel Lewis examines eating and drinking as bodily indicators of social class in "The Middle-Class Moderation of Food and Drink in *David Copperfield*." Lewis contends that David Copperfield's class "ascension centers not simply on his profession, marriage, and family, but also upon his dietary habits, which mark his body as middle class" (80). Lewis briefly examines two instructive scenes of eating and imbibing, David's encounter with the hungry waiter on his way to school and his "first dissipation" when he gives a party for Steerforth and his male companions. Both cases demonstrate to David how "society enforces rules about moderation of food and alcohol through various verbal abuses, such as mockery, friendly laughter, and chastisement" (79). Lewis deduces that regulation of food and drink intake was connected to class stereotypes and social aspirations: "Middle-class men did not overeat because that was a practice of lazy aristocrats, but they did not drink too much because that was a characteristic of working-class men. Moderation of food and drink situates the middle-class man between two undesirable points: the bloated, overfed aristocracy and the drunken violent working class" (79).

Clare Pettit's essay, "Peggotty's Work-Box: Victorian Souvenirs and Material Memory," provides a fascinating reading of Peggotty's sewing box in

David Copperfield from both a cultural-historical approach, considering the social and historical ramifications of the workbox as a Victorian souvenir, and a narratological approach, considering the workbox's importance in structuring the narrative of David's memory and of the novel itself. Pettit begins by surveying the history of souvenirs of St. Paul's Cathedral (the image of which adorns the cover of Peggotty's workbox), providing photographs of several memorial commodities similar to the workbox and analyzing their cultural significance as symbols of national values and ambitions. Pettit points out that while Peggotty's workbox is not actually a personal souvenir, since she does not see St. Paul's until later in the novel, it inspires her visit to the cathedral during her tour of the capital, thereby suggesting the power in shaping national consciousness that tourist souvenirs were beginning to acquire for the Victorian public in the midcentury. The essay's second half examines the workbox as an emblem of memory. Pettit argues that the workbox's recurrence throughout David's memories reveals that Dickens relied not only upon an associationist model of memory in which an object is associated with a particular idea or event, but also upon Romantic models of memory as organic and process-oriented, since the workbox's significance shifts throughout David's life and differs between characters (it is a tool by which Peggotty shapes her own subjectivity and a souvenir by which David fetishizes his servant's loyalty). Pettit concludes by calling for a more nuanced application of ''thing theory'' to the study of Victorian texts that would give more attention to the ''fluctuating values'' of objects (para. 25) as they are ''activated and deactivated over the course of a novel'' (para. 27).

Bleak House

As an instructor who has longed to teach *Bleak House* but has been repeatedly cowed by the challenge, I was delighted to review *Approaches to Teaching Dickens's Bleak House* (edited by John O. Jordan and George Bigelow), a long-overdue addition to the Modern Language Association's acclaimed ''Approaches to Teaching World Literature'' series (which last featured Dickens in a 1984 volume on *David Copperfield*). Packed with practical tactics for teaching one of Dickens's most pedagogically intimidating novels, the volume is divided into two primary sections. Part 1, ''Materials,'' discusses the broad range of resources available to teachers, based on a survey of over sixty instructors who regularly teach *Bleak House*. This section assesses editions of the novel, related bibliographies and reference works, supplemental readings for students and teachers, visual aids and paratextual materials that appeared in the novel's original serial installments (including illustrations and advertisements, several of which are reproduced within the volume), Internet resources, and film adaptations. Part 2, ''Approaches,'' contains twenty-four essays from various contributors detailing numerous pedagogical approaches to the novel. Since the scope of this survey prevents me from discussing all of the essays in detail, I will instead summarize the central topics covered. A section on "Victorian Contexts" focuses on teaching the novel within the context of nineteenth-century British culture and includes essays on the novel's connections to the 1851 Great Exhibition; the 1841 Niger expedition and its relationship to the condition-of-England debate; the development of commodity culture, advertising, and print culture; and topics in contemporary scientific discourse. This section is distinguished by both scholarly and pedagogical approaches, and there is more than enough excellent critical analysis (in addition to teaching techniques) to make it appeal to scholars as well as teachers.

A section on "Teaching Specific Scenes, Patterns, or Problems" provides classroom techniques for dealing with particularly challenging or rewarding aspects of the novel, including its double narration, its connections with the detective novel, its serial publication format, and its integration with the original illustrations. The section "Intertextual Approaches" discusses teaching the novel in conjunction with other texts, such as works by contemporary Victorian nonfiction prose writers (e.g., Thomas Carlyle, John Stuart Mill, and John Ruskin), as well as comparable nineteenth- and twenty-first-century novels, such as Hannah Craft's American slave narrative *The Bondswoman's Narrative*, Victor Hugo's *Les Miserables*, and South African writer Phaswane Mpe's novel *Welcome to Our Hillbrow* (2001), whose depiction of the AIDS epidemic in an inner-city neighborhood of Johannesburg has striking parallels to Dickens's depiction of disease-ridden London.

Finally, a section on "Specific Teaching Contexts" describes teaching the novel in different settings, from the advanced placement high school classroom, to law school, to urban community colleges. Diverse teaching environments inspire innovative pedagogical methods. Especially notable in this section are Kathleen Breen's and Joel J. Brattin's useful accounts of teaching *Bleak House* serially, which provide excellent discussions of time management in teaching such a lengthy and complex text, and Denise Fulbrook's exciting exercise of designing a class library exhibit to accompany the novel, a particularly interactive and creative means of involving students with specific features of the novel's aesthetics and cultural context.

My only disappointment with this remarkably diverse and otherwise comprehensive collection is the absence of any significant attention to film as a teaching supplement (other than a brief acknowledgment of Dickens film adaptations in the "Materials" section), which is a singular omission given the existence of two excellent BBC television adaptations of *Bleak House* (from 1985 and 2005), one of which has garnered much recent critical attention in academic circles. Using film as an avenue into Dickens's text might be a beneficial approach for teachers who are struggling to engage students with literature in a culture dominated by visual and electronic media; therefore, teaching methodologies that incorporate film might warrant more attention (at least comparable to that given to other visual aids) in a volume devoted to pedagogy. But this is a relatively small omission in an otherwise outstanding collection that details numerous techniques that I look forward to trying in my own classroom. Any instructor faced with the challenge of teaching *Bleak House* or any student looking for astute critical analysis of Dickens's novel would do well to consult this exceptional volume.

The remainder of *Bleak House* scholarship from 2009 consists of articles devoted to specific features of the novel. Caroline Levine's essay "Narrative Networks: *Bleak House* and the Affordances of Form" presents a creative analysis of the much-discussed social web in *Bleak House* through the lens of contemporary network theory. Levine argues, "*Bleak House* represents social relationships not as static structures but as constantly superimposed, conflicting, and overlapping relational webs" similar to what contemporary network theorists term "distributed networks," and each character acts as a "node," a point of connection, in one or more networks (518). Some characters function as "hubs," nodes "that are more highly linked than others" within a network (520). For example, Jo is a hub, "a node in multiple social processes," reappearing repeatedly in the text, "not because he represents poverty or childhood or social marginality but because his literal location in the city at specific times and places makes him relevant to a murder investigation, efforts at urban reform, and even the institution of marriage" (519). As the hub of multiple networks, Jo exposes "the importance of impersonal (and transpersonal) networks over personal agency" in the novel because he is both "entirely neglected by the social world and yet also unable to escape the webs of interconnection that link him to that world" (520). Thus, *Bleak House* undermines "the usual novelistic reliance on individual agency" by "replacing the centrality of persons with the agency of networks" (519–20). Because networks are ever-expanding, they defy representation and therefore challenge the tenets of realist fiction, particularly the closure expected in the realist novel. Levine contends that narrative theory's emphasis on the impulse toward closure has blinded us to the importance of the suspenseful complexity of the middle, which is the most significant feature of the networked novel's narrative structure in that "the suspense of the long middle" demonstrates "that at any moment our knowledge of social interconnections can only ever be partial" (522). Levine therefore concludes that "the vast mimetic project of *Bleak House* affords not individual agency, not the primacy of families, and not realism in any conventional sense, but a kind of narratively networked sublime" (522–23). Levine's arguments are neatly presented and provide a beautiful defense of the unique potentialities of Victorian fiction's sprawling, loose leviathans, particularly for a twenty-first century audience enmeshed in massive global networks and deeply attuned to networked experience as never before.

A lengthy, complex, but well-argued study, Rachel Teukolsky's ''Pictures in Bleak Houses: Slavery and the Aesthetics of Transatlantic Reform'' places *Bleak House* in the context of mid-Victorian debates about both aesthetics and slavery. Teukolsky explores how ''mid-century activist texts—protesting the plight of the 'slave,' whether British or African-American—wrestled with the politics of aesthetics within genres that were becoming increasingly commodified'' (492). Teukolsky envisions *Bleak House* in a complicated dialogue with other abolitionist texts, including Harriet Beecher Stowe's *Uncle Tom's Cabin*, Hannah Crafts's *The Bondswoman's Narrative* (which rewrites *Bleak House* as an African-American slave narrative), and the travel writings of former African-American slaves who toured Britain in the early 1850s. Despite Dickens's apparent dismissal of slavery as a foreign issue through *Bleak House*'s intense nationalist localism, most famously expressed in the satiric portrayal of Mrs. Jellyby's philanthropic project for the African natives of ''Boorioboola-Gha,'' Teukolsky points out that, like much mid-Victorian discourse of industrial reform, Dickens racializes the bodies of the oppressed workers in the novel, depicting working-class bodies that have been blackened and disfigured by labor, thereby evoking the trope of the African slave in support of his critique of local poverty (496). Dickens contrasts the slave bodies of the working poor with ''a parade of fine art objects'' surrounding upper-class or morally indifferent characters, acting ''as degraded signs of an opulent and immoral economy'' (492). But Dickens not only criticizes ''bankrupt fine art objects,'' but also ''popular modes of melodrama or sensation—which exploit graphic scenes of poverty or slavery'' (492). Here Teukolsky characterizes *Bleak House* as a critique of melodramatic abolitionist narratives such as Stowe's *Uncle Tom's Cabin*, which threatened to turn anti-slavery accounts into ''mere commodified spectacles'' (493). Teukolsky argues that ''[b]y making a discursive turn away from melodrama toward realism,'' most notably in *Bleak House*'s detached third-person narration that counterbalances the sympathy of Esther's first-person narrative, Dickens ''proposes a puissant social fiction that might escape the impotence of commodification,'' even as he himself participates in the commodification of the Victorian novel (493).

Teukolsky sees a similar contradictory discourse in the writings of former slaves, noting that ''African-American travel writers performed a Victorian reformist consciousness modeled by Dickens in *Bleak House* when they eschewed sensation or sentiment in accounts of their own slave histories and travel experiences,'' instead writing ''in imitation of Victorian gentlemen, describing tourist encounters with the art objects of Europe as signs of a new cultural mastery'' (493). But even as they resisted being commodified as slaves, they did so ''by producing their own commodified genre in the form of the high-art travelogue'' (511). The essay concludes with a penetrating analysis of Hannah Crafts's *The Bondswoman's Narrative*, which replicates *Bleak House*'s manner of social critique by paralleling slave bodies with the fine art objects that slave owners enjoyed as the fruits of slave labor.

In '' 'Not a Love Letter': Epistolary Proposals of Marriage and Narrative Theory in *Bleak House* and *Middlemarch*,'' Allan C. Christensen examines two cases of ''fancifully misread marriage proposals'' in Dickens's and Eliot's novels in light of the psychoanalytic theory of transference (64). In *Bleak House*, Esther Summerson reads John Jarndyce's marriage proposal in terms of her own personal history (her obligation to Jarndyce for his generosity and her sense of her unworthiness due to her illegitimacy and disfigurement). In Esther's reading, the letter seems to illuminate Jarndyce's benevolence and her own shame in such a way that she is obliged to submit to his proposal. The paradox of this misreading, according to Christensen, ''is that the illumination that she has discerned in his narrative, to which she must submit, is only the power that her own narrative has transferred to his. The binding or mastering power of his text has entered it not at the moment of his writing but at the moment of her reading of it into the context of her own narrative'' (62). Christensen argues that Jarndyce's writing ''has thus offered a genuine opportunity for free choice, which the reader's vocation for self-punishment has perversely turned into a very different sort of text'' (62). In contrast, Casaubon's letter proposing marriage to Dorothea in *Middlemarch* ''is very much a narrative that he controls'' in order to project onto Dorothea ''the role of fitting into and completing the pattern of his life story.'' Unlike the effect of Jarndyce's letter, the power of Casaubon's letter over Dorothea ''originates in the intention of the writer rather than in the interpretation of the reader'' (63). In both cases, however, the heroines must ''escape the meshes of masculine texts'' in order to find self-fulfillment (65).

In ''A Tale of Two Dandies: Gore, Dickens and the Silver-Fork Novel,'' Sarah C. Alexander examines the evolution of the dandy stereotype from the silver-fork novels of the 1820s and '30s to the social novel of the 1840s and '50s by comparing Catherine Gore's novel *Cecil* (1841) to Dickens's treatment of dandyism in *Bleak House*. Alexander sees Gore and Dickens as dramatizing a perilous societal shift from Regency to Victorian dandyism. In the wake of the reforming mindset established by the First Reform Act of 1832, the dandy's excessive consumption, instead of being merely ridiculous, ''is understood to be increasingly destructive'' because it embodies a commodity fetishism ''that seeks to undermine social consciousness'' (297). *Cecil* demonstrates this shift through the life of the eponymous hero, who straddles both eras as a Victorian dandy recounting his past life of privilege during the

Regency, whereas *Bleak House* registers the change through its depiction of Mr. Turveydrop, who embodies the Regency dandy's absurd obsession with superficial fashion and "Deportment," versus Harold Skimpole, who exhibits the Victorian dandy's more insidious tendency to "aestheticize" profound social and moral problems (292). Alexander shows that in an age in which earnestness and self-denial have become the markers of middle-class morality, the Regency dandy's solipsism is transformed into the Victorian dandy's dangerous denial of communal responsibility.

A Tale of Two Cities

Part of the esteemed series Palgrave Studies in Nineteenth-Century Writing and Culture, *Charles Dickens,* A Tale of Two Cities *and the French Revolution* (edited by Colin Jones, Josephine McDonagh, and John Mee) is an important collection of current scholarship on Dickens's novel, ranging from discussions of the novel's political and historical contexts to analyses of its history in stage and film adaptations. The introduction takes the novel beyond the "exclusively British context" in which it has traditionally been viewed (5) to consider its reception in France and its relationship to events in contemporary international politics, such as the Indian Mutiny of 1857. The first two essays, "The New Philosophy: The Substance and the Shadow in *A Tale of Two Cities*," by Mark Philip, and "The Redemptive Powers of Violence? Carlyle, Marx and Dickens," by Gareth Stedman Jones, reconsider the famous impact of Thomas Carlyle's *French Revolution* as one of Dickens's central sources, arguing for a more nuanced, expansive view of Dickens's politics. Philip demonstrates how, instead of seeing the novel through the anti-democratic, anti-French lens of Carlyle's work, *A Tale of Two Cities* "can be read as a sympathetic representation of the 'new philosophy' of the late eighteenth century and its critique of power and privilege" (24). Jones compares concepts of revolutionary violence in the works of Carlyle, Marx, and Dickens to argue that, despite Dickens's reliance on Carlyle's book for historic details, Dickens ultimately portrays the Revolution not as an indiscriminate wave of violence instigated by a societal loss of faith (as Carlyle envisioned the event), but as a justified uprising in response to the lack of government reform, the result of "a laissez-faire complacency" that Dickens saw threatening his own nation in the 1850s (57).

   The next two essays in the collection consider inspirations for particular characters or plot devices in the novel. Keith Michael Baker's "A Genealogy of Dr. Manette" traces Manette's origins to the popular Bastille narratives of the late eighteenth century, particularly the tale of Comte de Lorges, whose story and supposed likeness Dickens encountered at Madame Tussaud's waxworks. In "From the Old Bailey to Revolutionary France: The Trials of

Charles Darnay,'' Sally Ledger (to whose memory the volume is dedicated) demonstrates the astute erudition and lively prose that distinguished her career as a Dickens scholar through her revealing analysis of the novel's trial scenes, the inspiration for which she traces to Dickens's legal and theatrical experience, as well as his acquaintance with street literature (e.g., broadsides and ballads) and records of actual espionage and Chartist trials. Essays by Kamilla Elliot and John Bowen focus on the novel's symbolic imagery. Elliot's "Face Value in *A Tale of Two Cities*" considers how the motif of face and name identification functions throughout the novel to destabilize notions of identity and individualism. In a distinctly dark reading of Carton's penultimate sacrifice, Elliot argues that the doubling of Carton and Darnay reinforces middle-class patriarchal power by "ushering in a perpetual identity theft that allows the individual sins and class crimes of ruling males not only to pass unaccounted for, but also to figure as innocence and heroism" (101). In contrast, John Bowen's "Counting On: *A Tale of Two Cities*" argues that Dickens uses naming and numbering to investigate the problematic nature of democracy, expressing a deep political awareness of "the complex relations of prioritization and subordination . . . between the claims of the many and the few" (107). Bowen moves beyond the much discussed motif of doubling to consider triangular and small group relationships in relation to mass action in the novel.

One especially innovative feature of this collection is its attention to the novel's ongoing cultural impact through the process of adaptation, a topic addressed in the final three essays. In "Mimi and the Matinee Idol: Martin-Harvey, Sydney Carton and the Staging of *A Tale of Two Cities*, 1860–1939," Joss Marsh traces the history of the novel's early theatrical adaptations, focusing on actor John Martin-Harvey's remarkably successful production, *The Only Way*, which ran for 4,000 performances from 1899 to 1939. Martin-Harvey's incredible popularity in the role of Carton, which the actor privileged as the main character in an attempt to create a star vehicle for himself, helped create "the cult of Sydney Carton" as an emblem of British heroism (136). Marsh's fascinating essay does much to explain how the novel achieved iconic status as a representation of British national identity, a phenomenon that colored academic readings of the text throughout the twentieth century and promoted a view of Dickens's politics as wholly anti-revolutionary, conservative, and naïve, a perception that this volume of essays attempts to dispel. Marsh's cultural studies approach is extended in the anthology's last two selections on film adaptations, Judith Buchanan and Alex Newhouse's "Sanguine Mirages, Cinematic Dreams; Things Seen and Things Imagined in the 1917 Fox Feature Film *A Tale of Two Cities*" and Charles Barr's "Two Cities, Two Films" (both reviewed above in "Studies of Adaptations in Fiction and Film"). Such innovative studies of the cultural impact of *A*

Tale of Two Cities demonstrate the appeal of this anthology, which should leave a lasting impression on the body of scholarship related to this novel.

Three additional essays devoted to *A Tale of Two Cities* appeared in 2009. Teresa Mangum's "Dickens and the Female Terrorist: The Long Shadow of Madame Defarge" focuses on "the problem of reading *A Tale of Two Cities* post 9/11" (144), particularly in light of the questions it raises about female terrorism. Mangum argues that the threat of the domestic morphing into the political is a terror that progresses through Dickens's novel in complex ways, dramatized in the various plots that frame Madame Defarge (147). The narrative initially ties the domestic to the political through a "marriage plot" depicting Madame's powerful partnership with her husband. After Madame breaks faith with her husband to pursue her own revenge, her tale then morphs into the "sisterhood plot," which Mangum beautifully contextualizes within an extended examination of women's participation in the Revolution and the Terror, a historical framework that induces condemnation of the female *sansculottes'* terrorist methods while arousing sympathy for their cause by revealing the reasons for their violence. Mangum argues that this mixed reaction is likewise evoked in Dickens's novel by the context of Madame's personal history. Mangum sees the revelation of the rape of Madame Defarge's sister as the most significant feature of the sisterhood plot because through it the novel "illuminates another possible explanation for our horror and repulsion in the face of women terrorists. . . . [W]e know deep down they hold fast one of war's dirtiest secrets—that rape has so often been a crucial weapon of subjugation and oppression not just of the individual woman but of her community" (154). When Madame Defarge turns from her political work to her personal revenge, the novel finally submerges the sisterhood plot in "a plot of murder," featuring the conflict between Madame Defarge and Miss Pross. Mangum illuminates the numerous similarities between the two women to interpret them as powerful figures of female devotion and violence, both of whom "kill in the name of women they quite legitimately love" (157). The novel ostensibly justifies the violence of one and condemns the other, but the resemblances between the women call into question such simple distinctions.

Mangum culminates her study with provocative questions that relate the novel to the complexities of the current war on terror. Sydney Carton's heroic death eclipses Madame's at the novel's conclusion, but "can Madame Defarge also claim the status of martyr?" (157). Can the perpetrator of violence also be a victim? A stunning reminder of Dickens's continuing relevance, Mangum's essay ultimately reads as an intensely moving appeal for a more enlightened and compassionate understanding of one of Dickens's most fearsome characters, whose rage sadly lives on today in the atrocities of modern warfare and terrorism.

Jan Alber's "Darkness, Light, and Various Shades of Gray: The Prison and the Outside World in Charles Dickens's *A Tale of Two Cities*" reveals the relationship of the prison to the novel's well-discussed dichotomies, arguing that the prisons in the novel are the focal points at which "the narrative's binary oppositions are negotiated and then restructured" (96). Examining the imprisonment of Dr. Manette in the Bastille and Charles Darnay in La Force, Alber demonstrates the psychological effects of the prison in erasing the prisoner's identity but notes how a similar policing and restructuring of identity occurs in the outside world when the revolutionaries reshape Manette and Darnay for their own purposes. Alber examines such instances, as well as the existence of external prison-like environments (e.g., Tellson's Bank and Manette's room at the Defarge wineshop) and "metaphorical prisons" (e.g., revolutionary France and Sydney Carton's imprisoning loneliness) as evidence of the permeable boundaries between the prison and the "free" world, which is, in fact, "infected" by the prison agenda (101). Most innovative is Alber's treatment of the aristocratic prisoners that welcome and comfort Darnay at La Force. Alber argues, "These decent prisoners are diametrically opposed to both France, which is dominated by public violence, and the individualist Carton, who retreats into privacy and dies a noble death," since the prisoners achieve "a decent sense of community" beyond the capacities of both the revolutionaries and Carton (104). Alber sees Carton's supposedly redemptive self-sacrifice at the novel's conclusion as an extension of the metaphorical prison of his individualism that has prevented him from healthy interaction with others. In a striking rereading of Carton's triumphant final prophecy, Alber reminds us that it remains a "private vision," "a hidden potentiality that is never realized" (105) and that necessitates Carton's erasure of his own identity.

In "A Tale of Two Mimeses: Dickens's *A Tale of Two Cities* and René Girard," Kevin Rulo sets out to read Dickens's novel as "a narrative mimesis of the Gospel texts," asserting that "Biblical-narrative mimesis can be rightly seen as a persuasive textual strategy in Dickens's work as a whole" (5). Rulo applies René Girard's anthropological theories of "mimetic desire, the sacred, and victimization" to reveal how Dickens's Christian discourse imitates the way in which the Gospels "dramatize and expose the scapegoat mechanism" (6). Rulo provides a brief synopsis of Girard's theories, which focus on the interpersonal, triangular workings of "mimetic desire," between "the self, the mediator (or model), and the object" (9). Mimetic desire properly channeled results in love and self-sacrifice, or conversely leads to a destructive "mimetic rivalry" that can become contagious within the community, necessitating the transference of collective and individual animosities onto an innocent scapegoat (7). Rulo first illustrates these principles at work in Dickens's text through a complex but convincing reading of the scene of Charles Darnay's English trial. Rulo then demonstrates how the dynamic of mimetic desire between Lucie and those who desire her (Dr. Manette, Charles Darnay, and Sydney Carton) channels desire away from rivalry into love and self-sacrifice, while the violence of the French Revolutionaries dramatizes the dangerous, communal form of ''mimetic rivalry'' that must be displaced onto a series of scapegoats, culminating in Carton. This dynamic illustrates ''that the love and war of the novel are fundamentally mimetic in nature and represent two paths that humanity's mimetic nature can take,'' making the novel ''a tale of two mimeses'' (8). Rulo concludes with a fine application of these theories to Carton's mimesis of Christ's sacrifice, arguing that the self-centeredness of Carton's final vision, which has troubled some critics, is actually in keeping with ''true sacrifice,'' which is not associated with ''a gift that expects no return-gift but with the resurrection, the hope of redemption, which is very much a return-gift'' (20).

Great Expectations

Jerome Meckier's ''*Great Expectations*, 'a good name?' '' is a wonderfully illuminating examination of the complexities of one of the finest titles in literary history. Meckier aptly points out the uniqueness of the title, noting that most Dickensian titles are based on the name of the protagonist or a place name, while ''*Great Expectations* is the only Dickens novel with a multifaceted literary allusion for its title'' (249) that also takes on multiple levels of irony as the narrative progresses. Meckier traces the title's allusions to Sir Philip Sidney's sonnet sequence *Astrophel and Stella*, John Milton's *Paradise Lost*, Charles Lever's novel *A Day's Ride*, and Dickens's own novel *Martin Chuzzlewit*. While *Great Expectations* echoes the names of the writer and the two lead characters of *Astrophel and Stella*, as well as the protagonist's destructive desire for an inaccessible love, Meckier points out that Dickens ''darkens the psychological situation he borrows'' from Sidney and invests the hero's sexual obsession with greater ''sociological significance'' (250). The allusion to Milton also takes on a darker hue in Meckier's view. Although most scholars focus on the themes of sin and redemption evoked by Miltonic references in Dickens's text, Meckier reveals Dickens's ''anti-Miltonism'' by comparing the scene in which Adam welcomes mankind's ''great expectation'' of future redemption to the scene in chapter 18 of Dickens's novel in which Mr. Jaggers, ''a parodic divine messenger,'' announces Pip's ''great expectations.'' Dickens's parody transforms Milton's scene into ''the archetypal instance of . . . the snobbish self-importance that comes from being overly expectant rather than industrious, persevering, and self-reliant'' (251). It is this theme which is also apparent in the allusion to Charles Lever's novel *A Day's Ride*, in which Lever uses the phrase lightheartedly when his protagonist makes a false claim of having ''great expectations'' of an inheritance in order to escape an embarrassing situation. The phrase had similar connotations of a future inheritance when Martin Chuzzelwit used it in Dickens's earlier novel, but Meckier points out that by the time Dickens chose the title for his later novel, overexpectancy had become "a national psychosis, not just an individual malady" (252). Meckier finally surveys the various uses of the phrase throughout the novel's text, illustrating the increasing metaphorical richness that the title assumes as the narrative progresses. Meckier's efficient summary of the literary, sociological, and ironic significance of this title has convinced me to assign this essay as supplementary reading the next time I teach the novel.

Our Mutual Friend

David McAllister's "Artificial Respiration in *Our Mutual Friend*" examines the episode of Rogue Riderhood's resuscitation after drowning to determine what methods of artificial respiration would most likely have been used and how they might affect our understanding of the scene's thematics in relation to the novel as a whole. Surveying the history of various resuscitation methods, McAllister shows that, shortly before Dickens began *Our Mutual Friend*, the efficacy of artificial respiration was dramatically improved by the development of two new techniques—the Marshall Hall method, which featured repeatedly rolling the body from stomach to side, and the Henry Silvester method, which featured raising and lowering the patient's arms. McAllister's examination of Dickens's text indicates that Riderhood's rescuers deliberately reject more traditional methods of resuscitation in favor of modern techniques. Most importantly, however, the Hall and Silvester methods encourage group involvement in the resuscitation, which is in keeping with Dickens's emphasis on the community effort involved in Riderhood's revival. The two mid-Victorian techniques, like Dickens's text, place "less emphasis . . . on the individual rescuer who somehow magically revives the dead [as in mouth-to-mouth resuscitation], and a greater emphasis on teamwork" (107). Therefore, what might seem to be an insignificant detail in the text, the methodology of resuscitation, actually enhances not only the narrative's thematics but also the irony of Riderhood's revival, since he ultimately fails to recognize the lesson inherent in his resuscitation—the significance of community over self-interest.

Invoking the title of Milan Kundera's famous novel, Marie-Amelie Coste's essay "Eugene Wrayburn, or The Unbearable Lightness of Being in Dickens" demonstrates that Dickens, like Kundera, was concerned with "the light, careless character, detached from the world and from himself, indifferent to everything, including his own plight" (109). The recurring careless males of Dickens's fiction (such as Jack Maldon, Steerforth, Harold Skimpole, and Henry Gowan) represent "a new trend in Dandyism" in the Victorian age that Dickens saw as socially dangerous, a shift in focus "from a superficial attention to dress to a philosophy of life characterised by an absence of earnestness" (109). However, in Eugene Wrayburn, the epitome of the Dickensian Dandy, Dickens vividly exhibits the allure as well as the danger of the Dandy's detachment from self and society. Coste gives a particularly fine reading of Lizzie's attraction to Eugene in *Our Mutual Friend*, arguing that Lizzie gravitates toward Eugene's indifference as a relief from the excessive passions of Bradley Headstone and her brother, and she likewise experiences the "wish indifference triggers in others to breach its surface, to see it crumbling down and turned into its opposite," as she "longs to be the anchoring point of his [Eugene's] fluttering self, the only exception to his general playfulness" (111–12).

Coste contrasts Eugene with Bradley Headstone, who embodies the opposite state of overly passionate involvement, but Eugene's indifference is just as dangerous as Bradley's passion. Coste argues that Eugene's irony and his ability to play with and deconstruct language, as exhibited in his cruel verbal sparring with Bradley, reflect a level of disengagement from community that ultimately threatens to reduce self and society to absurdity. Bradley's attack on Eugene at the novel's conclusion brings a necessary balance between the extremes that the two men represent by infusing "some earnestness into the lawyer's lightness," allowing Lizzie to lead him "from selfish detachment from the community to selfless devotion to another" (120).

In "Improvising Character in *Our Mutual Friend*," Brian Cheadle sets out to counter Henry James's famous derogatory assessment of Dickensian methods of characterization published in his review of *Our Mutual Friend*. In contrast to James's assertion that a great novelist must evince a "spirit of intellectual superiority" to the characters' passions and a "philosophical" ability to analyze the complexity of their motives (James qtd. in Cheadle 216), Cheadle shows that "Dickens's métier is the spurt of improvisation" (220), which can be just as effective as a careful, analytical approach at conveying the "field of diverse energies" that comprise a character (212). And Cheadle claims that Dickens's improvisational technique is as much a *deliberate* authorial choice as a natural tendency of his genius. Cheadle cites Dickens's telling criticism to Wilkie Collins that the characters in *The Woman in White* "are too prone to self-analysis; they have a DISSECTIVE property in common, which is essentially not theirs but yours . . . my own effort would be to strike out more of what is to be got . . . out of them by collision with one another" (Dickens qtd. in Cheadle 218). Thus, Dickens consciously eschewed the analytical approach, preferring instead "to improvise characters and then to engineer collisions between them" (218) as a means of exposing and developing their natures, a method more indicative of the actual spontaneity of the human mind. Cheadle supports his analysis throughout with outstanding close reading of several characters from the novel, including Bella,

Mrs. Wilfer, Mr. Dolls, and Eugene Wrayburn, whose "fragmentation of self is a century before its time" (230). Clearly, in the case of such a conflicted character, Dickens's improvisational "spurts" resulted in a more natural, complex reflection of human character than his contemporary detractors realized.

In "Dolls and Imaginative Agency in Bradford, Pardoe, and Dickens," Victoria Ford Smith places *Our Mutual Friend* in the context of nineteenth-century doll narratives in which the doll becomes a subversive symbol. Smith sees Jenny Wren's dolls as generating an agency that allows her "to interrogate and manipulate social hierarchies" (171). In comparison, Smith examines Clara Bradford's *Ethel's Adventures in the Doll Country* (1880), a tale of a girl who delights in manipulating and abusing her dolls, to demonstrate how dolls can be used to "reconfigure power relationships" (178). Instead of being a tool of "female acculturation" preparing the girl for motherhood, the doll becomes a "site of female agency," enabled by the doll's miniaturized replication of the human being, which fuels the girl's sense of possession and control of others (175). Similarly, Julia Pardoe's *Lady Arabella, or, The Adventures of a Doll*, the story of a doll that passes from a wealthy to a poor child, uses the doll to negotiate class positions. Smith argues that in *Our Mutual Friend*, Jenny Wren "incorporates strategies of violence present in Bradford's text and strategies of class subversion present in Pardoe's" (174). Jenny imaginatively transforms "those who physically and socially overpower her into dolls that can be manipulated and mastered" (189). Smith likewise examines how Jenny's dolls facilitate "fantasies of revenge" that sometimes become more than fantasy, as when she manipulates and punishes Fledgeby's injured body in a manner similar to the imaginative control she exerts over her dolls (189). Smith finally argues that "the agency Jenny appropriates through miniaturization and magnification, however, is transient," since the social realities of her situation continually reassert themselves (190). But Smith sees the possibility of true transcendence through Jenny's implied future relationship with Sloppy, someone who finally recognizes Jenny as "a true artisan" (192).

The Mystery of Edwin Drood

Two exceptional studies of *The Mystery of Edwin Drood* situate the novel within contemporary legal and medical contexts. Stephanie Peña-Sy's "Intoxication, Provocation, and Derangement: Interrogating the Nature of Criminal Responsibility in *The Mystery of Edwin Drood*" is a study of the issue of criminal responsibility in *Edwin Drood* through the lens of Victorian case law. Assuming that Edwin Drood is murdered in Dickens's unfinished novel, Peña-Sy sets out to construct legal defenses for the two most probable suspects, Neville Landless and John Jasper, citing numerous precedents from contemporary court cases in which the accused committed murder while in an altered state of consciousness. According to such case law, Neville could claim involuntary intoxication (based on Jasper's apparent drugging of the wine that led to Neville's violent altercation with Edwin, as well as Jasper's apparent mesmeric influence over both men), or he could claim provocation (based on his passion for Rosa and Edwin's repeated and deliberately infuriating jibes). In terms of John Jasper's defense, Victorian case law drew a significant distinction between simple and habitual intoxication that could apply to Jasper's opium addiction, which seems to result in repeated delusions. But the most significant case law to impact a potential defense for Jasper is the 1843 trial of Daniel McNaughton, who assassinated the prime minister's secretary while under a delusion that he was the victim of a conspiracy. While the criteria for criminal insanity that this trial established had not yet been used in a multiple-personality case, the criteria could certainly apply to Jasper if he committed the murder under the influence of a split personality disorder, which, of course, is the most popular theory associated with the novel. Peña-Sy concludes that while many critics have characterized Dickens's approach to the law in his novels as backward looking, in his final novel Dickens engages "with a current, emerging medico-legal discourse that he foresaw would change the structure of future criminal defenses" (215). With such grounding in actual court cases, this essay is an absolutely fascinating addition to the extensive body of scholarship and speculation surrounding Dickens's unfinished novel.

In " 'Opium is the True Hero of the Tale': De Quincey, Dickens, and *The Mystery of Edwin Drood*," Robert Tracy discusses contemporary sources about opium use that Dickens most likely drew upon for his depiction of John Jasper's opium fantasies, including medical texts, such as Dr. John Elliotson's *Human Physiology* (1835) and Dr. Robert MacNish's *The Anatomy of Drunkenness* (1827) and *The Philosophy of Sleep* (1840), Wilkie Collins's experiences with laudanum (particularly the impact on his art as a writer), and, most significantly, Thomas De Quincey's *Confessions of an English Opium Eater* (1821). Tracy argues that De Quincey's dreams of dangerous heights and vast buildings described in *Confessions* and his accounts of the opium-eater's tendency to enlarge buildings into infinity in his essay "The English Mail-Coach" (1849) are paralleled in *Edwin Drood* in the perilous journey that characterizes Jasper's violent opium dreams, imagery that implies that Jasper intends to murder Edwin in the Cloisterham cathedral. Tracy likewise attests that Dickens draws upon De Quincey's aesthetic of murder established in his essay "On Murder Considered as One of the Fine Arts" (1827, 1839) to depict Jasper's repeated rehearsals of the murder as "an artist's performance" that is more aesthetically satisfying to Jasper in his opium dreams than in the real commission of the crime (211).

Tracy also connects De Quincey's analysis of the murderer's bloodlust that requires repetition of the crime to implications in Dickens's novel that Jasper will murder again, an intriguing suggestion that connects him to modern-day serial murderers.

Biographies and Reference Works

One of my great pleasures in conducting the 2009 scholarship survey was reading Michael Slater's much anticipated *Charles Dickens: A Life Defined by Writing*, a comprehensive 670-page biography that makes a superb addition to the many fine biographies of the Inimitable, including Slater's own, much shorter biographical overview published by Oxford University Press in 2007. With the completed publication of Dickens's letters, as well as his collected journalism (of which Slater was the editor), Slater is able to draw upon materials unavailable to previous biographers to provide a stunningly detailed portrait of Dickens as a writer. From Dickens's earliest known schoolboy letter to his Last Will and Testament, Slater demonstrates how Dickens relied on writing to construct a multifaceted public and private identity composed of an exhausting number of diverse roles, which he continuously negotiated through letters, journalism, and fictional writings that were complexly inter-locked. Slater's study is particularly illuminating at revealing connections between apparently "disparate pieces of writing going on at the same time" (166), an approach that is critical to investigating the works of a novelist who often had multiple publications running simultaneously.

In keeping with this scholarly focus, Slater carefully avoids excessive spec-ulation regarding aspects of Dickens's personal life (particularly his relation-ship with Ellen Ternan) about which we have little clear evidence. And while such speculation has its place and has lent power to other biographies, Slater's thrilling reconstruction of Dickens's breathtaking rise to fame and the fasci-nating history of Dickens's mercurial relationships with publishers, friends, and family as evidenced in his lively business and private correspondence provide this biography with plenty of excitement without the need for sensa-tional conjecture.

The most powerful accounts of the intersections between Dickens's per-sonal life and writing career occur in chapters 4 through 7, recounting Dick-ens's evolution from sketch writer to novelist, and chapter 19, recounting the dissolution of his marriage. The depiction of Dickens's early career in serial publication is exhilarating and reads with something of the excitement that his installment stories must have evoked in his readers. Slater follows his progress from month to month, demonstrating the amazing skill (and frequent serendipity) with which Dickens juggled his various publication commitments along with growing professional and family obligations, revealing how often chance and immediate circumstance shaped the development of his fiction. Most instructive is Slater's examination of how Dickens's perception of himself as a writer altered through the act of writing, particularly his composition of the prefaces to the volume editions of his early novels, in which he increasingly depicted the writing of his early works as more carefully planned and less haphazardly executed than the initial serial publication format had actually allowed. Slater reveals how gradual this evolution in Dickens's self-perception was, as he moved from the role of a "periodical essayist" composing a "series of papers," as he described himself in the 1839 preface to *Nicholas Nickleby* (Dickens qtd. in Slater 136–37), to the role of respected novelist. Slater reminds us that with works prior to *Barnaby Rudge*, Dickens did not intend to write novels and did not realize he was doing so until well into (or after) their publication, a fact that tends to be obscured by the single-volume tomes (containing Dickens's written-in-hindsight prefaces) that we see on our bookshelves and use in our classrooms today. This study thus augments our understanding of the original composition and publication of Dickens's works with a vibrant, moment-by-moment portrayal of the development of an accomplished novelist out of a largely improvisational format.

Similarly absorbing is Slater's depiction of Dickens's "process of gradually writing Catherine out of his life" throughout 1857 and 1858, culminating in their separation. Slater reconstructs the disintegration of their marriage through letters from Dickens and Catherine's family, demonstrating how Dickens began to rewrite Catherine's place in the narrative of his life, assigning her the roles of "failed mother" and "a 'humour' character out of Ben Jonson, dominated by the emotion of jealousy" (439). Slater likewise shows how Dickens's obsession with Ellen Ternan and resentment against Catherine are reflected in selections from *The Lazy Tour of Two Idle Apprentices* and concludes the chapter with a remarkably painful and illuminating study of "New Year's Day," the last piece Dickens wrote for *Household Words*, which appeared in the 1 January 1859 issue. Nostalgically incorporating many features of Dickens's past, the essay tellingly includes events from Dickens's family life while glossing over references to his children and omitting any indication that the narrator is married. It is a "wonderful essay for the New Year" that sadly "completes the process of [Dickens] writing off his marriage and altogether banishing Catherine from his life" (460).

Finally, I particularly enjoyed Slater's compelling account of Dickens's public readings from the perspective of his role as a writer. The theatrical analogy is typical in descriptions of Dickens's writings, and the public readings are often seen as a bridge from the world of literature to the stage, which continued to beckon Dickens throughout his career, but Slater crosses this bridge in the opposite direction, describing Dickens's theatrical endeavors, culminating in the readings, through an analogy to writing. Slater notes that during the readings Dickens "performed alone just as he wrote alone in his study. Here, however, he was working not with his mind's eye upon a host of imaginary readers but with his physical eyes upon real readers . . . responding, as he sometimes expressly encouraged them to, with audible sobs and laughter to his narrative as it came from his lips" (467). The readings thus become exhilaratingly interactive compositions. Viewed in this light, the public readings are not simply a scheme for charity or personal profit or a means to satisfy Dickens's lust for the theater and public adulation, but they represent the penultimate act of writing for Dickens in its most intense and vital form. Slater concludes, "For this audience the thrilling feeling of hearing a book being written for them there and then would have been intensified by Dickens's habit of improvising new text as he was actually reading" (467), a description that deftly pulls together Dickens's love of theatrics, his genius at writing, and his cherished intimacy with his audience.

Although the academic focus of Slater's study means that it may not be suitable for the beginner, it is indispensible for the serious student of Dickens. Erudite, but eminently readable, this splendid biography will undoubtedly be a welcome addition to the bookshelf of any Dickens scholar.

While Slater's book is the only full-length biography of 2009, two fine essays investigate specific facets of Dickens's domestic life. Margaret Flanders Darby's article "The Conservatory at Gad's Hill Place" is a fascinating biographical study of the significance of the glass conservatory Dickens built at his home at Gad's Hill Place just prior to his death. Darby interprets the conservatory as "a contradictory space" (138) that embodies many of the paradoxes of Dickens's life, such as "his passionate housekeeping in the largest sense, his fear of penury at a time of great demand on his purse, and his deeply engrained ambivalence about upper middle class extravagant display" (139). Even as Dickens ridiculed the materialism of his peers, his mansion and its conservatory, which cost over one-quarter of the purchase price of the property, emblemized his obsession with genteel status. Pointing out that Dickens began planning the conservatory at the time when his marriage was disintegrating and his troubled liaison with Ellen Ternan was beginning, Darby argues that Dickens's strict management of household affairs and improvements such as the conservatory reflected his attempt to manage household emotions and maintain an illusion of stability and control. Darby similarly connects the conservatory with Dickens's home theatricals (which many scholars have seen as evidence of his need to "stage manage" his family), noting that Dickens "loved the theatrical potential of a conservatory" and "knew it would contribute to the theatre of domesticity that was Gad's Hill Place" (139). Darby suggests that the "contradictory meanings" that the conservatory had for Dickens may explain why he delayed building it for

twelve years (139), and she concludes with the crowning irony of its completion just days before his death. Significantly, it served as the setting of his
final conversation with his daughter Katey, in which he expressed the great
regrets of his life.

John Bowen's article "John Dickens's Birth Announcements and Charles
Dickens's Sisters" is a neat little piece of biographical/literary investigation
that examines a recently identified birth announcement placed by John Dickens in the September 18, 1818, issue of *The Morning Chronicle* indicating
the birth of an unidentified daughter of whom there are no records in the
biographical sources of the Dickens family. Bowen speculates that the announcement could actually indicate the birth of Dickens's younger sister Harriet, who was christened in September of 1819 and died in childhood at an
unspecified date. If this is the case, Harriet may have lived longer than biographers have previously assumed, suggesting that she may have been "a much
more significant presence in the young Charles's life," and her death may
have had greater impact on the family, and, by extension, on Dickens's
subsequent treatment of female children and child death in his fiction (199).
Bowen notes that whether the announcement refers to Harriet or to another
hitherto unknown sister, it reminds us of "the importance of sisters to Dickens's early years," which established a "pattern of the solitary male among
a group of sisters" that would be repeated later in all Dickens's "most
important erotic attachments" (199). This article reminds us of the potential
biographical materials yet to be discovered that could significantly affect our
readings of Dickens.

Reference works published in 2009 include Natalie B. Cole's outstanding
Dickens and Gender: Recent Studies, 1992–2008 (discussed above in "Gender, Sexuality, Marriage, and Children") and Natalie McKnight's witty and
erudite survey, "Recent Dickens Studies: 2007" (which I gratefully acknowledge as a model for my own survey). Routledge Library Editions reissued
several classics of Dickens scholarship in a ten-volume set, most notably John
Butt and Kathleen Tillotson's *Dickens at Work* and John Gross and Gabriel
Pearson's collection *Dickens and the Twentieth Century*, while Angus Easson
and Margaret Brown continued their invaluable work on Dickens's correspondence, publishing three more supplements to Dickens's collected letters in
The Dickensian.

Finally, Robert C. Hanna's "Before Boz: The Juvenilia and Early Writings
of Charles Dickens, 1820–1833" provides an important resource for Dickens
scholars by collecting Dickens's earliest known writings from 1820 through
November, 1833, one month prior to the appearance of Dickens's first published sketch. The collection includes poems (such as those Dickens composed
for Maria Beadnell), plays (most notably the incomplete *O'Thello*), and nonfiction writings (the list of "Private Theatrical Regulations" is interesting in

the snapshot it provides of Dickens as a stage manager). Hanna also reproduces Dickens's first two known letters, his accounting entries in the Cash Account Book of the Ellis and Blackmore law firm, and his notes on two court cases at the Doctors' Commons. Some of the texts appear in print for the first time, including *The Stratagems of Rozanza* (often thought to be Dickens's own adaptation of an eighteenth-century Italian play for home performance) and Dickens's transcriptions of his shorthand notes for the court cases Jarman vs. Bagster and Jarman vs. Wise, which provided inspiration for the sketch "Doctors' Commons" that appeared in *Sketches by Boz*. The texts are carefully annotated throughout, and six appendices present selections from related works by Dickens and authors who influenced his juvenile writings, while a seventh appendix presents for the first time three texts by literary forger John Payne Collier that continue to be identified erroneously as the work of Dickens. The various features of the collection work together to construct a beautifully comprehensive picture of Dickens's earliest efforts as a writer, providing particular insight into his work in the legal profession as well his endeavors at home theatricals.

Recent Adaptations: Graphic Novels, Films, and Fiction

Because a remarkable number of Dickens adaptations in other media were produced in 2009, I have included a discussion of the following Dickens-related products from popular culture and the arts. I conclude the section on "Fiction" with a speculation on the significance of this surge in pop-culture appropriations of Dickens.

Graphic Novels

Dickens's fiction has had a long and vital partnership with the visual arts, from the original illustrations that accompanied the serial publication of most of the novels, to the numerous film adaptations the novels have inspired. But developments within the global publishing industry within the last decade suggest that a relatively new means of visualizing Dickens's works may be gaining popularity with readers and educators—the graphic novel. Before discussing some examples of recent comic book and graphic novel adaptations, let me explain how Dickens's novels have entered this field. Dickens had long been a staple of comic book adaptations largely due to the highly popular Classics Illustrated series (1941–1971), which over its thirty-year history produced multiple adaptations of five Dickens novels (Jones, Jr. 48). With the demise of the Classics Illustrated line in 1971, Dickens and canonical literature virtually disappeared from the comic book world, aside from a few short-lived and financially unsuccessful attempts to create "classic" lines of comic book adaptations, including two notable attempts to resurrect the Classics Illustrated series in the 1990s (Jones, Jr. 191, 199). However, two relatively recent phenomena—the rising popularity in the late twentieth century of "graphic novels" (novel-length comic books aimed at mature audiences) and the early twenty-first-century movement among librarians and educators in the United Kingdom and the United States to incorporate graphic novels as educational tools in libraries and classrooms—seem to have prompted a resurgence in comic book/graphic novel adaptations of canonical literature. Dickens returned to comics in 2003, when comic industry icon Will Eisner published the graphic novel *Fagin the Jew*, an outstanding revisionist adaptation of *Oliver Twist* that responded to anti-Semitic stereotypes in Dickens's novel by creating a sympathetic "backstory" for Fagin based on the history of Jewish immigration in eighteenth- and nineteenth-century England. In the period from 2005 to 2009, several comic book companies, as well as mainstream publishers, started new lines of "classic" adaptations, resulting in numerous graphic novels based on Dickens's works. I will discuss four of the most noteworthy titles, all of which were available for purchase at the time I composed this survey.

In 2007, Papercutz, publishers of graphic novel mysteries for teens, started two new lines of graphic novel adaptations, "Classics Illustrated," which consists of hardback reprints of the short-lived 1990s Classics Illustrated comic book series, and "Classics Illustrated Deluxe," which consists of new full-length graphic novel adaptations of literary classics illustrated by top graphic novelists from France (where comic book illustration is a highly regarded artistic tradition). While the "Deluxe" line did not yet include Dickens adaptations at the time I composed this survey, for the first issue of the "Classics Illustrated" line, Papercutz chose to reprint artist Rick Geary's wonderful 1990 version of *Great Expectations*. Although the 1990s Classics Illustrated series to which this comic book originally belonged was financially unsuccessful, the series has since become prized by collectors and comic book historians for its use of stunning artwork by famous graphic novelists whose visual styles corresponded to the verbal styles of the writers they were adapting (Versaci 197). Geary's *Great Expectations* adaptation in particular has achieved some fame in academic circles due to Jay Clayton's superb analysis of it in his 1996 article, "Is Pip Postmodern? Or, Dickens at the End of the Twentieth Century," which now appears as the representative "cultural studies" essay in the Bedford/St. Martin critical edition of *Great Expectations*. Clayton compared the bizarre imagery and focus on gender in Geary's adaptation to the heroic masculinity of the 1946 Classics Illustrated adaptation of *Great Expectations*, contrasting the two versions as postmodern and modernist readings of the original text. Geary's illustrations (see figs. 1–5) feature fragmented identities and distorted settings that examine Pip's quest for wealth and status and reveal the postmodern features nascent in Dickens's

Fig. 1. The cover of Rick Geary's Classics Illustrated adaptation of *Great Expectations* highlights artifice and the male gaze through an optical illusion; framing devices make Pip look as if he is staring at a wall tapestry depicting the females in static poses. Copyright © 1990 First Classics, Inc. The Classics Illustrated name and logo is Copyright © 2007 First Classics, Inc. All Rights Reserved. By permission of Jack Lake Productions Inc. Classics Illustrated ® is a registered trademark of the Frawley Corporation.

Fig. 2. Distorted and fragmented imagery dominates the postmodern aesthetic of Rick Geary's Classics Illustrated adaptation. Characters often appear trapped within crooked framing devices. Copyright © 1990 First Classics, Inc. The Classics Illustrated name and logo is Copyright © 2007 First Classics, Inc. All Rights Reserved. By permission of Jack Lake Productions Inc. Classics Illustrated ® is a registered trademark of the Frawley Corporation.

novel, making the adaptation especially useful for classroom discussions of Dickens's connections to postmodern culture (I have used the original 1990 paperback edition in my classes many times). Therefore, the republication of this comic in a hardback edition is particularly noteworthy for instructors teaching the novel. Those interested in incorporating graphic novel adaptations in the classroom should review the Papercutz selection of classic titles (which continues to expand). There are numerous fine adaptations of works by other authors (the Classics Illustrated versions of *Dr. Jekyll and Mr. Hyde* and *Hamlet* are among my favorites).

While Geary's 44-page adaptation is standard comic-book length, the British company Classical Comics produced a beautiful 157-page graphic novel adaptation of *Great Expectations* in 2009, following their equally admirable 2008 adaptation of *A Christmas Carol*. Publisher Clive Bryant founded Classical Comics in 2007 primarily as an educational series with the intention of creating "exciting and engaging graphical novels of classical literature" in order to "introduce new generations to the world of classic fiction" ("Classical Comics"). Beginning with an outstanding series of Shakespeare graphic novels, Classical Comics offered their adaptations in three formats: "Original Text" (in the original language), "Plain Text" (translated into contemporary

Fig. 3. The grotesque urban environment parodies Pip's distorted expectations in Rick Geary's adaptation. Copyright © 1990 First Classics, Inc. The Classics Illustrated name and logo is Copyright © 2007 First Classics, Inc. All Rights Reserved. By permission of Jack Lake Productions Inc. Classics Illustrated ® is a registered trademark of the Frawley Corporation.

English), and "Quick Text" (reduced and simplified for young readers). In adapting classic novels, Classical Comics retained the "Original Text" and "Quick Text" formats; and while the "Original Text" version of *Great Expectations* is abridged, Jen Green's adaptation is true to Dickens's prose and is incredibly thorough, including such minor characters as Mr. and Mrs. Pocket, the Aged P, and Miss Skiffins, who are usually eliminated in the adaptation process. Classical Comics's *Great Expectations* is also organized to match the original volume and chapter divisions of Dickens's three-volume publication of the novel, making it easy to use the adaptation side-by-side with a complete edition. Classical Comics has designed a wealth of supplementary teaching resources for using the adaptation in the classroom, including a study guide with printable images from the graphic novel and a broad range of

Figs. 4a and b. Characters frequently appear to drop off the frame, creating images of fragmentation that critique Pip's quest for identity. Copyright © 1990 First Classics, Inc. The Classics Illustrated name and logo is Copyright © 2007 First Classics, Inc. All Rights Reserved. By permission of Jack Lake Productions Inc. Classics Illustrated ® is a registered trademark of the Frawley Corporation.

Fig. 5. John Stokes offers a richly Gothic vision of the Hulks from the Classical Comics adaptation of *Great Expectations*. © Classical Comics Ltd.

classroom exercises related to Dickens's original text, as well as "Comic Life" computer software that allows students to create their own graphic adaptations of the novel.

The educational potential of this fine adaptation is further enhanced by artist John Stokes's gorgeous visuals. While Rick Geary's artwork in the Classics Illustrated version emphasizes the comic and grotesque features of Dickens's novel, Stokes's images, particularly in their use of light and shadow, highlight the text's elements of Gothic horror. For instance, the graphics call attention to the ominous artifice of Miss Havisham's realm through a visual association with artificial light sources, such as Estella's candle and Miss Havisham's fireside, which create a shadow world that threatens to consume Pip (Stokes's images of Estella are especially useful for classroom discussion of the symbolic candlelight and starlight imagery associated with her character in Dickens's text [fig. 6]). Artificial and natural light sources also frequently play against each other within the graphics to visualize the text's themes. One striking example is the full-page illustration of Pip's first meeting with Miss Havisham (fig. 7). While the text accompanying the image approximates the novel's description of a candlelit room and includes Miss Havisham's comment about never having seen the sun since Pip's birth, the image contains one significant interpolation by the artist. A beam of sunlight peeks through a rent in the dilapidated curtains and falls full upon Pip, who stands on one side of the room gazing upon Miss Havisham, who is seated opposite, engulfed by the candlelight reflected in the ornate mirror of her dressing table. The opposing placement of the characters and their association with competing light sources visualize Pip's developing self-division, and the image likewise utilizes the sunlight symbolism of Dickens's text to foreshadow Pip's eventual redemption even at the moment when he is being drawn into Miss Havisham's web. I have used this stunningly illustrated volume in my classes to highlight the novel's Gothic image strands (ghosts, the haunted house, starlight, moonlight, etc.), which are most effectively evoked in Stokes's drawings of the Hulks and Satis House (figs. 5–8); and the adaptation's final panels (figs. 9–10) are particularly good supplements for discussion of the novel's ambiguous concluding scene when Pip and Estella exit the grounds of Satis House.

In 2009, IDW Publishing began a line of graphic novel adaptations of classic literature that included adaptations of *Oliver Twist* and *A Christmas Carol* illustrated by noted French comic book artists. While marketed as "graphic novels" and published in hardback format, these adaptations are actually comic-book length (not more than 55 pages), making the abridgement significant. This is particularly regrettable in the case of *Oliver Twist*, in which the adaptor, Philippe Chanoinat, has eliminated most material from the novel's final chapters, including the murder of Nancy. The Monks inheritance plot is omitted, Oliver is returned to Mr. Brownlow immediately after

Fig. 6. Pip's entrance to Satis House evokes the haunted house motif and highlights Estella's association with candlelight in John Stokes's visuals. © Classical Comics Ltd.

Fig. 7. Stokes depicts Pip's introduction to Miss Havisham in terms of competing artificial and natural light sources. © Classical Comics Ltd.

Fig. 8. Competing Gothic and chivalric images call Pip's relationship with his "benefactress" into question. © Classical Comics Ltd.

the botched burglary with Bill Sikes, and both Sikes and Fagin are arrested and hanged. Despite this unforgivable truncation, David Cerquiera's harsh and uncompromising artwork, which eradicates humor and caricature to focus on the realistic hardships of the paupers and criminals, provides some striking visual approximations of Dickens's social criticism, such as the image of Bumble escorting Oliver from the baby farm to the workhouse past a tattered street poster of the young Queen Victoria, or the long-shot image of the workhouse children sleeping in perpetual rows of boxes resembling coffins. The graphic novel ends with a particularly disturbing two-page layout that encapsulates this adaptation's bleak approach to the social problems addressed in the novel. The previous pages depict Oliver's visit to Fagin in the condemned cell, concluding with Fagin's removal for execution while Oliver is still present. In the final layout, the left page is topped by a series of small

Fig. 9. Stokes's depiction of the novel's conclusion highlights the Gothic image strands of the text. Stokes visualizes how Dickens transfers the ghost imagery associated with Magwitch throughout the novel to Magwitch's daughter, the "resurrected Estella," in the final scene. © Classical Comics Ltd.

panels depicting Oliver approaching the window of the prison to look out. The entire bottom half of the page is dominated by a dramatic image of what he sees out the window—the black silhouettes of Fagin and Bill Sikes swinging from the hangman's noose—beneath which appears the final passage of the text, drawn from chapter 52 of the novel: "Everything told of life and animation, but one dark cluster of objects in the center of all—the black stage, the cross-beam, the rope, and all the hideous apparatus of death" (*Oliver Twist* graphic novel 54). The opposite page features a single concluding image of Oliver, who appears not in his newfound prosperity but in his pauper's rags, isolated, shivering, and curled in a fetal position in the center of the page. The reader knows that Oliver has been returned to Mr. Brownlow, but the artist gives no visualization of his middle-class comfort, preferring to conclude with images evoking the horror of poverty and crime that has dominated the adaptation throughout. I have not yet had the opportunity to use this adaptation in the classroom, but I suspect that these final images might be effectively contrasted with Oliver's withdrawal into a bourgeois country paradise at the conclusion of Dickens's text to provoke discussion of the weaknesses in Dickens's social criticism. Although the novel might inadvertently encourage us to forget the suffering of the lower-class characters with

Fig. 10. Melancholy Gothic imagery evokes the ambiguity of Dickens's revised conclusion in the final panels of the Classical Comics adaptation. © Classical Comics Ltd.

the protagonist's ascension into the middle classes, this adaptation will not allow readers to take comfort in the novel's "happily-ever-after" denouement.

The India-based company Campfire Graphic Novels began a classics line in 2008 which is now available in the United States through Random House publishers and includes a 2009 adaptation of *A Christmas Carol* and a version of *Oliver Twist* scheduled for 2011. While not quite as vibrant as the lavish Gothic horror adaptations of *Carol* and *Great Expectations* created by Classical Comics, Campfire's *Carol* is well-illustrated by Naresh Kumar and closely adapted from Dickens's text by Scott McCullar. The distinguishing feature of this adaptation, however, is that it was also published as a digital text to be read on computers and mobile devices such as cell phones and iPods (the digital version is available through the iTunes App Store and avecomics.com). Campfire partnered with Ave!Comics to provide their graphic novels through the AVE digital format, which allows readers either to navigate manually through the graphic novel, zooming in on images at will, or to activate a digital reader that creates an automatic animated reading path through the novel's artwork, using transitions, pans, and zooms to provide a dynamic visual experience somewhat similar to film. The digital reader is particularly effective with scenes of heightened drama and suspense in Campfire's *Carol*, such as the arrival of Marley's ghost or the revelation of Scrooge's name on the tombstone. While electronic texts of Dickens's novels have been available on computers and handheld devices for several years, new digital reading technologies, such as interactive graphic novels and software that allows readers to create their own digital illustrations for novels, intimate the innovative and provocative ways of experiencing Dickens that may be available for future readers.

Film Adaptations

Several new film adaptations of Dickens's novels were released in the United States in 2009. Three British television productions (originally broadcast in the United Kingdom in 2007 and 2008) premiered on American television's *Masterpiece Classic* and were distributed on DVD, while a major cinematic production of *A Christmas Carol* was released to theaters during the 2009 holiday season.

Distinguished by fine performances, well-paced direction, and an award-winning musical soundtrack, the most recent BBC serial production of *Oliver Twist* is superior to the ITV 1999 adaptation, which added a sensational backstory for the parents of Oliver and Monks that revolved around Monks's attempts to assassinate Oliver's mother. Sarah Phelps's adaptation for the 2007 version capitalizes on the novel's melodrama more effectively by focusing on the complex web of interrelations among characters from the criminal and middle-class worlds, and Coky Giedroyc's direction uses plot twists to maximum effect through creative use of parallel editing, cross-cutting with exhilarating speed between events in the workhouse, the criminal hideouts, and the bourgeois parlor of Brownlow's home. The whirlwind direction, fragmented plot, and raucous musical score (something between a circus and a music hall with electric guitars) give the film a carnivalesque touch of the fantastic that accentuates the grotesque aesthetic of Dickens's text. But Phelps's script never lets the narrative spin out of control, streamlining the plot by keeping Oliver with the thieves after the botched burglary and by transforming Rose Maylie into Brownlow's ward and both Monks and Oliver into Brownlow's grandsons, prompting Monks's plot to eliminate Oliver as a rival heir. Such changes are standard in film adaptations of this novel; but this production stands apart in the more drastic alterations made to several characters in an apparent attempt to emphasize the suffering of society's marginalized and dispossessed.

Young Oliver (William Miller) is not the largely passive victim from Dickens's text, carried through his trials by the protection of providence, but a tough, shrewd-minded survivor who repeatedly fights back against his abusers, most notably when he speaks up to the workhouse board in defense of a fellow pauper who has been beaten and when he takes the initiative himself to ask for more gruel. Certainly no cry-baby, Oliver similarly defies Bill Sikes (Tom Hardy in a wonderfully menacing but emotionally nuanced performance), earning the robber's grudging admiration. Continually paralleled with Sikes and Dodger, Oliver shows a resourcefulness and fearlessness that intimate how thin the line is that separates him from the criminals, a difference that will ultimately be determined solely by the chance circumstance of class. While this interpretation eliminates Oliver's allegorical significance as "the principle of Good surviving through every adverse circumstance, and triumphing at last" (Dickens, Preface 33), the changes to his character still allow him to be an effective vehicle of social protest, albeit in a more active form.

The production also emphasizes social marginalization on the basis of gender and ethnicity through the character of Nancy (portrayed with both vivacity and sweetness by Sophie Okonedo), a role that Phelps deliberately adapted for a black actress as a protest against the predominance of white performers in BBC period dramas ("A New Twist on *Oliver Twist*"). But the adaptation's most significant change in the novel's characterization is Timothy Spall's sympathetic Fagin. Past productions have attempted to humanize Fagin by eliminating his violence (as in Ben Kingsley's kindly performance in Roman Polanski's 2005 film), by portraying him as the victim of economic circumstances (as in George C. Scott's genteel rendition of Fagin as the fallen gentleman in Clive Donner's 1982 adaptation), or by emphasizing his humor and allowing him to escape criminal prosecution (as in the respective performances of Ron Moody and Richard Dreyfuss in the 1968 musical and the 1997 Disney production). The brutality and delight in evil exhibited by Fagin in the novel are similarly expunged from Spall's performance, but a greater emphasis in this case is placed on Fagin's victimization by racial and religious prejudice. Spall claims he envisioned Fagin as a German Jew who has become "an outcast, a pariah," someone who has been "kicked from pillar to post," but "has learned how to ingratiate himself" ("Timothy Spall as Fagin"). He is depicted throughout the film as observing Jewish rituals in dress and daily habits, including the refusal to partake of pork even when he cooks generous amounts for his boys. Most importantly,

Spall sees Fagin as a Jew of "very strong faith" who "completely believes that he will be delivered by providence" ("Timothy Spall as Fagin"), embodied in this instance in the form of Oliver. Rather than planning to corrupt Oliver, Fagin plots to undermine Monks's schemes and return Oliver to his wealthy family, hoping for rich compensation as "my reward for keeping the faith" (*Oliver Twist* film). With cruel irony, the authorities mistake him for Oliver's intended killer rather than his protector; and the providence that protects Oliver in the novel fails to deliver the faithful Fagin in the film, ultimately leaving him to the mercy of a deeply anti-Semitic society. With such a strong focus on Fagin's suffering, the film runs the risk of exchanging one sentimentalized victim for another, but Spall avoids this, for the most part, through the humor, common sense, and charisma that he lends the character, as exhibited in the moment that Fagin welcomes the starving Oliver to his abode with a theatrical flourish, surrounded by a blazing fire, steaming sausages, and a stunningly colorful collection of stolen pocket handkerchiefs. The focus on Fagin's ethnic marginalization becomes a bit strained, however, in the trial scene, in which the judge offers a lighter sentence for Fagin's "conspiracy to murder a Christian child" if the Jew will convert to Christianity (*Oliver Twist* film). His refusal, of course, warrants the death sentence. While rather heavy-handed, this gesture towards *The Merchant of Venice* evokes the specter of anti-Semitic stereotypes and Jewish oppression throughout drama, literature, and European history, demonstrating how this *Twist* capitalizes in intriguing ways on postcolonial sensibilities regarding ethnic and religious difference.

Whereas the *Oliver Twist* adaptation takes several largely successful liberties with Dickens's text, the BBC production of *Little Dorrit*, winner of seven Emmy Awards (including Outstanding Miniseries), and adapted by Andrew Davies (screenwriter for the 2005 *Bleak House*), reveals the benefits to be gained from a close serial adaptation. While lacking the complex exploration of the novel's gender dynamics that distinguished Christine Edzard's two-part 1988 adaptation (told from the opposing perspectives of the male and female protagonists), Davies's eight-hour production, broadcast episodically in both the United Kingdom and the United States, captures the intricacies of Dickens's massive cast of characters as well as the novel's wide-ranging critique of capitalist society, which was particularly timely for twenty-first-century audiences caught in an international financial crisis. A magnificent cast of accomplished actors, many of whom are "old hands" at portraying Dickensian characters, gives distinctiveness to even the smallest roles, resulting in an abundance of outstanding performances. Matthew Macfadyen, although too young and vigorous for Dickens's world-weary, middle-aged protagonist, still portrays Arthur Clennam with the melancholy of a genuinely good man who feels paralyzed in the face of a culture cruelly indifferent to human suffering. Claire Foy as the titular heroine gives convincing depth to Little Dorrit's self-denying devotion, portraying the repressed pain and resentment with which she struggles in the face of her family's pride and selfishness. And the supporting characters are unforgettable, even down to Mr. F's Aunt (Annette Crosbie, who provides a shockingly hilarious portrayal of senile rage) and Mr. Merdle's Chief Butler (Nicholas Jones, whose icy stare could cool raging volcanoes). While the remainder are too numerous to delineate here, I will mention three of the most nuanced performances. Russell Tovey adds a surprising layer of heart-wrenching pathos and nobility to the comical John Chivery; Tom Courtenay deftly manages William Dorrit's mixture of self-pity, shame, and denial; and Anton Lesser epitomizes Mr. Merdle, the "man of the age" swallowed whole by his surroundings, wandering myopically through the glittering soirees of "Society" with an air of heart-sick amusement at the sheer absurdity of the social and financial trap in which both he and his investors are enmeshed.

Striking performances are complemented by equally striking visuals, as elaborate camerawork and evocative set designs give a distinctly cinematic quality to this television production. One of the most creative set designs is the Circumlocution Office, satirically envisioned as an infinite spiral staircase lined on each side by carefully stacked trails of documents that explode into a mess of loose papers on the floor below, where impenetrable walls of filing cabinets tower over the chaos. The novel's prison motif likewise permeates the film's visual composition. Scenes in the Marshalsea are filmed with an unusual predominance of long shots that emphasize the characters' isolation within the cavernous, empty rooms while likewise stressing their imprisonment through the oppressive convergence of the seemingly endless floors and ceilings. Even characters outside the prison are repeatedly shot through framing devices (window panes, doorways, archways, railings, and cages) that visualize their entrapment on both private and societal levels. A fine example is a scene that dramatizes Tattycoram's servitude to the Meagles family by capitalizing on the cage motif. Tattycoram and Pet Meagles are playing a game on the lawn of the Meagles' middle-class home, as Mr. and Mrs. Meagles sit contentedly on a swing in a large white gazebo behind them, the human counterparts of the pairs of lovebirds swinging in numerous ornate white cages that surround the girls (a vivid image of the bourgeois complacency imprisoning them). The girls stand in the foreground of the shot on opposite sides of the frame, a composition that highlights their opposing social positions—a contrast accentuated by the fact that Tattycoram is played by a black actress (Freema Agyeman), casting that arouses even more disturbing misgivings about the Meagles' condescension. When a symbolically significant storm approaches and Pet orders Tattycoram to fetch her shawl, the girl rebels against her servitude, racing away through a flock of wild birds only to find her flight prevented by the arrival of Miss Wade. As the storm breaks, the camera shoots their confrontation through a series of Gothic stone arches that frame the women on opposite sides of the composition in a sinister replica of the earlier shot that had paralleled the servant girl with the pampered daughter. Tattycoram has merely run from one prison to another. Such a richly complex use of mise-en-scène is rare in television, but the series is fortunately filled with similarly evocative images which are prevented from becoming too distracting or fanciful by the deeply human quality of the performances. This detailed attention to the cinematic possibilities of Dickens's characters and themes, therefore, makes *Little Dorrit* a visual feast for the attentive viewer.

The series' only significant weakness is its conclusion, which is rushed in the final episode and which unaccountably deviates from the novel's uncompromisingly dark vision. While the novel famously concludes with Little Dorrit and Clennam going down together into the roaring city streets to achieve what limited good they can in the midst of an irretrievably fallen world, the film depicts the newlyweds exiting a lovely country church into a sunny, idyllic setting accompanied by a parade of the film's most colorful characters (a scene reminiscent of the many sentimental paintings of Dickens surrounded by his most beloved creations). The previously inescapable taint of the prison that dominated the film's mise-en-scène is completely missing. This retreat into sentimentality is a regression to the paradisiacal conclusions of Dickens's early novels that is a disservice to the more mature social criticism of his later fiction. Even so, this flaw does not diminish the achievements of the series as a whole, which deserves to be ranked among the finest Dickens adaptations.

Lacking the cinematic flair and finely nuanced performances of *Little Dorrit*, the ITV production of *The Old Curiosity Shop* is a major disappointment. Sophie Vavasseur as Little Nell does not have the winsome quality that Sally Walsh gave to the role in the 1995 Disney Channel production; and while the ITV version retains the sexual connotations of Quilp's interest in Nell (an element which was expurgated from Disney's production), Toby Jones's Quilp lacks the charisma to make him a truly convincing threat. Jones seems unwilling to depict Quilp's lecherous pursuit of a child with the wholehearted gusto evident in the text, ultimately avoiding a sexual dynamic that most film productions have been reluctant to tackle. The supporting performances are likewise lackluster, notwithstanding the presence of a noteworthy cast. Although Derek Jacobi and Zoë Wanamaker stand out as Nell's grandfather and Mrs. Jarley, the adaptation's truncation to ninety-three minutes leaves little time to devote to Dickens's brilliant collection of side characters, with the result that many seem randomly inserted and lack the delightful eccentricities that justify the characters' presence in the novel despite its haphazard structure. The camerawork is similarly uninspired, and the opportunity for outstanding visuals inherent in adapting a novel so marked by carnivalesque/ grotesque imagery is entirely lost. But the film's most glaring weakness is its altered ending, an apparent attempt by the filmmakers to avoid the excesses of Dickens's sentimentality while providing a conventionally neat dénouement, resulting in a conclusion that is just as jarring to the audience's sensibilities as Dickens's original pathos might be. While Nell and Quilp die, an odd interpolated plot twist virtually nullifies the impact of their presence in the narrative. The "single gentleman" who finally locates Nell and her grandfather is not the grandfather's younger brother (revealed to be Master Humphrey in Dickens's original manuscript), but Nell's long-lost father, who was estranged from Nell's grandfather shortly after her birth. He returns in time to beg forgiveness of the dying Nell, reconcile with his father, and whisk the old man away to the safety of the Old Curiosity Shop, where all the characters, including Nell's grandfather (who seems to have entirely forgotten both his gambling fever and his exploitation of Nell) return happily to their normal occupations as if nothing significant has happened (as, indeed, little has in this mediocre production).

The failure of this adaptation reveals certain obstacles inherent in reworking *The Old Curiosity Shop* for film. The novel's sentimentality and sexual subtext make it particularly difficult to adapt for contemporary audiences that shy away from both emotional excess and unconventional forms of sexuality; hence, the filmmakers in the ITV production rush back to normality as soon as Nell and Quilp, who most embody the narrative's maudlin and melodramatic potential, have been eliminated. Consequently, no film adaptation has yet done justice to the comic and melodramatic extravagance of Dickens's text, which hopefully will someday be recognized as rich cinematic material by stylistically flamboyant filmmakers with the courage to embrace the novel's more challenging features.

Although there have been plenty of mediocre adaptations of *A Christmas Carol*, the 2009 version is not one of them. Big-budget special effects, a lead performance by comedian Jim Carrey, and a Disney studios production stamp might seem to guarantee a shallow, sugary Christmas confection, but *Disney's A Christmas Carol*, directed by Robert Zemeckis, is an adaptation of surprising depth with a genuine respect for its literary source. The film is, indeed, a visually spectacular production that incorporates 3–D imagery and motion-capture technology (which produces digitally animated versions of live actors). But it is (happily) not the standard fare for either a Disney family feature or a special effects extravaganza. Zemeckis, who also adapted the screenplay, avoids over-sentimentalizing the story by retaining much of the novel's biting social criticism and focusing on the story's elements of Gothic horror. The sequences with the Ghost of Christmas Present best preserve

Dickens's social indignation and topical criticism, even including a moving rendition of the ghost's commentary on the Victorian Sabbath Bills. Similarly, the ghost's "death" at the midnight hour after introducing Scrooge to Ignorance and Want (who rapidly age with each stroke of the clock to become the Victorian icons of urban horror—the pickpocket and the prostitute) is a nightmarish scene not easily forgotten in its disturbing combination of Gothic terror and social critique.

The adaptation thus remains remarkably close to Dickens's text, while incorporating creative touches that visualize Dickens's themes in new ways. For instance, Dickens's brief reference to Marley's funeral in Stave 1 of the novel provides the basis for the film's unnervingly funny opening scene, in which Scrooge bargains mercilessly with the undertaker over his colleague's corpse, snatching the coins from the corpse's eyes in a parting gesture of greedy defiance. The scene effectively links Dickens's criticism of capitalism with the fear of death, setting in motion the narrative's cycle of characters profiting from the deaths of others. Throughout the film, Scrooge's miserliness takes on greater psychological depth as Zemeckis deftly employs such visual motifs as coins, candles, and clocks to imply that the moral blindness and materialistic abuses of capitalism arise from the human need to horde time and stave off death.

The production's 3–D effects are also surprisingly unobtrusive (the film should function just as effectively in 2–D), and the exaggerated animation technique ultimately does not diminish the film's humanity (despite an ill-judged, special-effects-laden chase scene inserted near the film's conclusion). Jim Carrey, who plays Scrooge and the three Christmas Ghosts, gives a complex performance that transcends the distortions of motion-capture animation to imbue the computer-generated characters with genuine emotion. One remarkable example occurs when Scrooge and the Ghost of Christmas Yet to Come visit the Cratchits after Tiny Tim's death. Bob Cratchit (Gary Oldman) is descending the stairs having visited his son's body in the bedroom above. As Scrooge watches on the stairwell, Bob comes face to face with him. From the change in Scrooge's facial expression, the audience thinks for a brief moment that Bob has seen and recognized Scrooge despite his ghostly form—until it becomes clear that the recognition is within Scrooge himself, as he witnesses and suddenly experiences the grief and compassion reflected in his fellowman's countenance. It is a stunning and unexpectedly human moment in an animated film, and it quite effectively encapsulates Scrooge's spiritual transformation. Such creative and moving moments leave us with no need to ask, "Why *another* adaptation of *A Christmas Carol*?" This version is a worthy addition to the novel's extensive history on film.

Fiction

Recent fiction produced an unusual number of novels dealing with Dickens, particularly the final years of his life and the unfinished *Mystery of Edwin Drood*. Although each novel that I reviewed approaches Dickens from a unique perspective, they all project a notable tone of emotional ambivalence toward the Inimitable, frequently combining admiration with censure, and in some cases expressing a deeply conflicted, almost obsessive sense of adoration and envy that attests to Dickens's powerful hold over the imaginations of later authors.

A novel not to be missed by Dickens enthusiasts is Richard Flanagan's lyrically mournful *Wanting*. Of the five novels I surveyed, Flanagan's perhaps provides the most complex and realistic portrait of Dickens as an exceptional genius tormented by common human desires and weaknesses. The narrative is built around the interconnected stories of Dickens, the Arctic explorer Sir John Franklin, his wife Lady Jane Franklin, and the aboriginal girl Mathinna, whom Franklin and his wife adopted during his tenure as governor of the Australian penal colony Van Diemen's Land (now Tasmania). The novel begins after Franklin's final Arctic expedition disappears. When reports emerge from the native Inuit that the explorers possibly resorted to cannibalism in an unsuccessful survival attempt, Lady Franklin asks Dickens to write a defense of her husband, resulting in the infamous *Household Words* articles "The Lost Arctic Voyagers," extolling the restraint and heroism of the civilized Englishman in contrast to the barbarism of the "savage." Flanagan places this episode within the context of Dickens's turbulent private life in the 1850s, as the collapse of his marriage and his escalating attraction to Ellen Ternan threatened to overturn his own self-control. Dickens, like his creation David Copperfield, is struggling with his "undisciplined heart": "[H]e bound and chained it, buried it deep, and only such severe disciplining of his heart allowed him his success, prevented him from falling into the abyss like his debtor father, like his wastrel brothers; from becoming, finally, the savage he feared himself to be" (Flanagan 43–44). In this context, Dickens's defense of Franklin's expedition against charges of savagery is as much a defense of himself against his own consuming passions as it is an imperialist vindication of the English national character. Indeed, Dickens attempts to restrain his desires further through the heroic portrayal of the initially selfish but ultimately self-denying Arctic explorer, Richard Wardour, in the play *The Frozen Deep*, which Flanagan depicts as ironically enmeshing Dickens even more in uncontrollable emotions as he becomes involved with actress Ellen Ternan.

The novel connects Dickens's tortured longings to those of the Franklins, depicted through flashbacks to Franklin's time as governor of Van Diemen's

Land, a post Franklin reluctantly accepts to satisfy the ambitions of his wife. Driven as much by private maternal yearning as by a wish to "improve" and "civilize" the local natives, Lady Franklin adopts the aboriginal child Mathinna and subjects her to a cruelly oppressive education in an attempt to demonstrate that the natives can be transformed into proper English citizens. Mathinna becomes the exploited object of both spouses' futile and destructive longings, and when their respective colonial projects fail, they abandon Mathinna and Van Diemen's Land, leading to Franklin's final withdrawal to the Arctic in a desperate attempt to bury his unpardonable passions within his own "frozen deep." The intersection of these tragic lives results in a broad reflection on the devastating power of desire that also has specific connotations for British colonialism. As a Tasmanian native and postcolonial novelist, Flanagan provides an intensely personal depiction of each historical character's connections to colonialism, revealing that the desires motivating British imperialism were rooted in paradoxical and profoundly human longings that were frequently as "savage" as the supposed barbarism that the imperialists were attempting to suppress.

Another moving portrait of the final years of Dickens's marriage, this time from the wife's perspective, can be found in *Girl in a Blue Dress: A Novel Inspired by the Life and Marriage of Charles Dickens*, in which first-time novelist Gaynor Arnold attempts "to give voice to the largely voiceless Catherine Dickens" (Arnold 4). Arnold re-imagines the Dickens marriage through the fictional chronicle of Dorothea Gibson, widow of Victorian England's premiere novelist Alfred Gibson (a sparkling fictional rendition of Dickens). As Dorothea reminisces on her failed marriage to the great author shortly following his death, the novel effectively constructs a sympathetic, yet unsentimentalized portrait of the possible hardships Dorothea's real-life counterpart endured as a wife and mother, inevitably defined and ultimately eclipsed by a brilliant and energetic husband who, for all his genius and sympathy for the oppressed, could not fully empathize with the restrictions that the Victorian domestic ideal imposed upon the women in his life. The novel's fictional framework allows Arnold several liberties with Catherine Dickens's biography, such as an imaginary meeting between the author's scorned wife and his mistress (here embodied in the character of young actress Wilhelmina Ricketts, who tells Dorothea her own story of her supposed affair with "The One and Only"), as well as a royal audience between Dorothea and Queen Victoria in which the women debate the nature of being wives and mothers. Although these meetings are highly contrived, allowing Dorothea to voice an implausibly sophisticated feminist awareness, they are still interesting opportunities for examining the damaging effects of contemporary gender roles not only in the Dickens marriage but in Victorian society as a whole. With the insight gained from her thirty-year career as a social worker, Arnold likewise provides a penetrating portrait of the family dynamics that revolve around a parent of genius and celebrity who is both domineering and adored, resulting in an unsettling picture of what it must have been like to be a close relative of Dickens. The profound love that the self-absorbed and charismatic Alfred arouses in Dorothea and her children convincingly intimates their pathological attraction to him, which overrides both his dismissive treatment of them and their deep resentment of him. However, Arnold's goal of recovering Catherine Dickens from her unfortunate role as footnote to a famous man is only indifferently achieved due to Arnold's own obvious fascination with Dickens, who emerges in the charming guise of Alfred Gibson as the novel's most compelling and attractive character, despite his infuriating selfishness. The novel is saturated by the admiration that both Arnold and her fictional females feel for the male protagonist, an adoration that amply withstands any critique of his myopic chauvinism. Consequently, Dorothea's decision to turn author in order to complete her husband's unfinished novel rather than to write her own memoirs, a decision that Arnold casts in the light of an unproblematic feminist triumph, suggests instead that Dorothea remains in her husband's shadow, uncomfortably reminding us that Catherine Dickens and her children aroused the interest of writers like Arnold in the first place only because they were the satellites of the adored author (after all, the novel's subtitle is *A Novel Inspired by the Life and Marriage of Charles Dickens*). Perhaps this novel's most striking quality is its proof of Dickens's continuing mesmeric power over audiences (as both an artist and an individual) even when we view his most unattractive characteristics with critical eyes.

Just as Dorothea Gibson decides to finish her husband's last incomplete work, the hypothetical completion of Dickens's final unfinished novel is likewise central to the next three novels in this survey. In *The Last Dickens*, Matthew Pearl, best-selling author of the "literary mystery" novels *The Dante Club* and *The Poe Shadow*, concocts a mystery surrounding the composition of Dickens's last novel that makes entertaining "light reading" for Dickensians. The Inimitable has done the unthinkable—proven his mortality in the most dramatic manner by dying in the midst of composing *The Mystery of Edwin Drood*, which is the bread-and-butter of Dickens's struggling American publishers Fields, Osgood & Company. When the proofs of Dickens's last completed installment go missing upon their arrival in America, and the publishing firm's delivery boy turns up dead of an opium overdose, James Osgood, the firm's junior partner, embarks on a dangerous adventure involving much more than a solution to the theft and murder, as Osgood attempts to realize the dream of any publisher—locating the concluding chapters of Dickens's ostensibly unfinished manuscript. While the mystery/adventure that Pearl fabricates is mediocre, relying on the standard plot twists and one-dimensional heroes and villains of conventional melodrama, the novel is still appealing in that it approaches Dickens's later years from the unique perspective of his publishers, enmeshing the Inimitable in the vibrant struggles of the fiercely competitive nineteenth-century publishing industry, whose tactics of creating and marketing literary celebrity contain the nascent qualities of our own celebrity-obsessed culture. The novel's historically based flashbacks of Dickens's extraordinary 1869 American tour, as well as the fictional depiction of competing publishers' mad scramble for "the last Dickens," are entertaining reminders of what a phenomenon Dickens actually was, as his life and career encapsulated the exciting vacillations of not only an industry but an entire society in flux.

French author Jeanne-Pierre Ohl's brilliant first novel, *Mr. Dick or the Tenth Book*, which was translated into English in 2008, is a fiction that Dickens scholars may find all too compellingly real. Ohl's mystery surrounding the supposed conclusion of Dickens's final novel is constructed from the perspective not of Dickens's publishers but of his academic devotees, who in this case suffer from an obsession with their literary idol that far exceeds intellectual admiration. In a postmodern parody of Dickens's bildungsroman, the central narrative recounts the biography of literature student Francois Daumal, whose passion for Dickens from childhood has inadvertently shaped every aspect of his identity. Daumal meets his doppelganger in the form of fellow Dickens scholar Michel Mangematin, a charismatic and insidiously manipulative intellectual, who becomes Daumal's adversary in the academy and beyond (through their professional and personal rancor, Ohl paints an especially dark portrait of academia). Daumal's narrative is likewise peppered throughout with excerpts from the diary of another Dickens devotee, young French author Evariste Borel, a contemporary of Dickens who claims to have received the conclusion of *Drood* from Dickens himself while visiting Gad's Hill Place on the day of Dickens's death. Borel's story sparks a literary investigation by Daumal and Mangematin that has diabolical ramifications for the rivals on academic, individual, and metaphysical levels. Ohl's novel is obsessed not only with Dickens and scholarly/literary passions, but also with how such passions problematize the nature of identity, a theme that is embodied through the novel's pattern of doubling in the narrative structure, the characterization of the fictional protagonists, and the depiction of Dickens himself, who emerges as a man who is his own doppelganger, a compulsive creator of fictional worlds who in his final years is haunted by his own creation, reputation, and past genius.

Any academic who has been both elated and intimidated by the creations of a favorite author will relate to the mania of Ohl's Dickens-besotted scholars, whose love-hate relationship with their literary icon is rendered with disturbing and convincing intensity. Consider, for instance, Daumal's description of his struggle to channel his infatuation with Dickens in the typical academic fashion, by wrangling his desires and frustrations into a book:

One day I would in any case have had to sit down at this desk, or some other, and look Dickens in the eye. For too long I had pretended to be in control of my life. But it did not belong to me: it was just a footnote to a book written by someone else. And I knew, I had always known, that the only way to get anywhere was to write my own book, and close the circle. To make use of *him*, and at the same time root him out of myself as one might remove an organ, drown him in the formaldehyde of a book. Force him out of my body, like a virus. But how? My whole being was infected. What would I say? He had already said it all. It was pointless and absurd: as absurd as drawing a full-scale map of the world.   (143–44)

As a scholar who has recently experienced my own lengthy and complete immersion in Dickens's world in order to produce this survey, I can't help but admire Ohl's strangely compelling, even terrifying homage to the power of literature in shaping human subjectivity and reality itself.

I turn at last to Dan Simmons's thriller *Drood* because it seems to summarize the recent trend in Dickens-related fiction and raises provocative questions about Dickens's afterlife in the twenty-first century. Like the two previously discussed novels, Simmons's *Drood* focuses on Dickens's composition of his final unfinished novel, imagined this time through the first-person narration of the friend and collaborator of Dickens's later years, Wilkie Collins. Addressing future generations of Dickens's readers through a "secret manuscript" that he has ordered suppressed for over a century following his death, Collins tells the "true" story of the last five years of Dickens's life. The horror of the Staplehurst Railway accident introduces Dickens to a phantasmal fellow train passenger known only as "Drood," who begins to haunt both Dickens's and Collins's lives. Drood is a criminal mastermind, an Egyptian-born serial killer from London's criminal underground, who enslaves the novelists to write his biography through a pact that exacerbates the already escalating tensions between the collaborating and competing authors and leads to the composition of Collins's *The Moonstone* and Dickens's last, incomplete manuscript. Simmons's sprawling narrative of almost 800 pages is uneven but fascinating, combining biography and historical fiction with scenes of fantastic terror typical of Simmons's horror fiction. A tauter psychological thriller could perhaps result from some significant editing of the exposition, which too often becomes awkward when Simmons inserts unnecessary (and sometimes erroneous) biographical materials, as if trying to prove that he has done his research. However, like Ohl's novel, Simmons's narrative makes effective use of doppelgangers, from Collins's laudanum-induced visions of the "Other Wilkie," his more accomplished twin who writes Collins's best fiction and is responsible for his greatest triumphs, to the mesmerically gifted and murderous Drood, the obvious embodiment of the darkest, most subversive desires of both novelists. But the most compelling doppelganger is Dickens himself, who encapsulates all that Collins desires (and sees missing in himself) in terms of human charisma and artistic genius, and who becomes an adored and despised reminder of the envious Collins's own comparative mediocrity. The story is at its best when it focuses on the relationship between the rival novelists, two flawed but fascinating artists that recognize much to admire and resent in each other. While Simmons creates an utterly engaging portrait of Dickens as a diabolically charming enigma, the kind of domineering and infuriatingly honest mentor who always makes you second guess yourself, the novel's highlight is Collins's delightfully acrimonious narrative voice that rings with humor and irrepressible rancor throughout, doing much to compensate for the novel's more cumbersome moments.

Elizabeth Bridgham, whose perceptive analysis of *Drood*'s strengths and weaknesses in her December 2009 *Dickens Quarterly* review is highly recommended for anyone interested in Simmons's novel, sees Collins's uneven narrative tone as one of the novel's most mystifying weaknesses, asking why, if Collins's narrative was intended "to shape his own legacy," he would reveal his petty jealousies and possible criminal activities, depicting himself "as a drug-addicted, untalented madman" (270). In the answer to this question lies a potential answer to the broader critical question with which Bridgham concludes her review: why have so many twenty-first-century novels focused on Dickens and the Victorian age? I would argue that Simmons's Collins is irresistibly compelled by his fascination with Dickens's genius to return to his relationship with Dickens, to reveal his adoration and hatred for his mentor even at the expense of his own reputation. And I would argue that his compulsion is in fact our own. We are fascinated with an author whose century contains the embryonic features of our own and who reflects as many of our weaknesses as our strengths, an author who acts as a kind of Victorian doppelganger for the postmodern audience. While I agree with Bridgham that Simmons's novel may be disappointing from an academic standpoint, Simmons approaches Dickens not as an academic, but as a popular novelist awed by another novelist who, despite significant flaws in his character and his art, has transcended mere popularity with sheer genius. The scathing bitterness of Collins's narrative voice (which reaches astounding levels by the novel's conclusion as Collins realizes he will be eclipsed by Dickens even after the Inimitable's death), combined with the decidedly sinister but entirely appealing depiction of Dickens, suggests to me Simmons's own paradoxical relationship with Dickens as a fellow writer, as well as our paradoxical relationship with him as readers and critics.

As I read *Drood*, I could not help thinking that Simmons had "a score to settle" with Dickens, as did all the novelists I have surveyed in this section. In turning to the controversies surrounding Dickens's final years and his unfinished novel, these writers are exploring various unresolved issues with an admired author who has cast an incredibly long shadow over fiction.

Flanagan is concerned with Dickens as an author of empire and his tangential but revealing connections with a colony that signified both imperial success and the failure of imperial ideals. Arnold is troubled by Dickens's ambivalent relationships with the women in his life, despite his iconic status as extoller of the domestic ideal. Ohl deals with Dickens's continuing hold over academic studies and reading audiences despite his detractors, while Pearl is fascinated by Dickens as a forerunner of the kind of celebrity that threatens to eclipse artistic genius. And Simmons (today's equivalent of a sensation novelist) expresses any author's inevitable envy and admiration for a novelist whose genius set painfully high standards for the fiction writers to come. The diverse concerns of these authors dramatize the wonderfully rich, ambiguous relationship that scholars, readers, and writers maintain with Dickens today.

As I conclude my study, I am grateful for being allowed to explore these less traveled regions of Dickensiana while expanding my acquaintance with Dickens scholarship. I was astonished at the breadth of the knowledge I encountered and gratified that I am part of a scholarly community capable of producing such consistently innovative and wide-ranging work. As the Dickens bicentennial approaches, the amount of Dickens-related materials still being produced in the academy and the arts is astounding and attests to the author's continuing fascination and relevance for readers of the twenty-first century. This ever-expanding body of scholarship, fiction, and pop-culture products devoted to an author born almost two-hundred years ago proves that the works of 2009 are far from "the last Dickens."

WORKS CITED

Scholarship

Adams, James Eli. *A History of Victorian Literature*. Oxford: Wiley-Blackwell, 2009.

Alber, Jan. "Darkness, Light, and Various Shades of Gray: The Prison and the Outside World in Charles Dickens's *A Tale of Two Cities*." *Dickens Studies Annual* 40 (2009): 95–112.

———, and Frank Lauterbach, ed. *Stones of Law, Bricks of Shame: Narrating Imprisonment in the Victorian Age*. Toronto: U of Toronto P, 2009.

Alexander, Sarah C. "A Tale of Two Dandies: Gore, Dickens, and the 'Social Fork' Novel." *Women's Writing* 16.2 (Aug. 2009): 283–300.

Allingham, Philip V. "The Illustrations for *Great Expectations* in *Harper's Weekly* (1860–61) and in the Illustrated Library Edition (1862)—'Reading by the Light of Illustration.' " *Dickens Studies Annual* 40 (2009): 113–70.

Barst, Julie M. "Sensations Down Under: Australia's Seismic Charge in *Great Expectations* and *Lady Audley's Secret.*" *From Wollstonecraft to Stoker: Essays on Gothic and Victorian Sensation Fiction.* Ed. Marilyn Brock. Jefferson, NC: McFarland, 2009. 91–101.

Barzilai, Shuli. *Tales of Bluebeard and His Wives from Late Antiquity to Postmodern Times.* New York: Routledge, 2009.

Bauder-Begerow, Irina. "Echoing Dickens: Three Rewritings of *Great Expectations.*" *Semiotic Encounters: Text, Image, and Trans-Nation.* Ed. Sarah Sackel, Walter Gobel, and Noha Hamdy. Amsterdam, Netherlands: Rodopi, 2009. 119–35.

Berman, Carolyn Vellenga. " 'Awful Unknown Quantities': Addressing the Readers in *Hard Times.*" *Victorian Literature and Culture* 37.2 (Sept. 2009): 561–82.

Blake, Kathleen. *Pleasures of Benthamism: Victorian Literature, Utility, Political Economy.* Oxford: Oxford UP, 2009.

Blake, Peter. "Charles Dickens, George Augustus Sala and *Household Words.*" *Dickens Quarterly* 26.1 (Mar. 2009): 24–40.

Boem, Katharina. " 'A Place for More than the Healing of Bodily Sickness': Charles Dickens, the Social Mission of Nineteenth-Century Pediatrics, and the Great Ormond Street Hospital for Sick Children." *Victorian Review* 35.1 (Spring 2009): 153–74.

Booth, Alison. "Time-Travel in Dickens' World." *Literary Tourism and Nineteenth-Century Culture.* Ed. Nicola J. Watson. New York: Palgrave Macmillan, 2009. 150–63.

Bourrier, Karen. "Reading Laura Bridgman: Literacy and Disability in Dickens's *American Notes.*" *Dickens Studies Annual* 40 (2009): 37–60.

Bowen, John. "John Dickens's Birth Announcements and Charles Dickens's Sisters." *The Dickensian* 105.3 (Winter 2009): 197–201.

Brattin, Joel J. "Dick Swiveller's Bed." *Dickens Quarterly* 26.3 (Sept. 2009): 165–74.

Bridgham, Elizabeth A. "Rev. Dan Simmons, *Drood.*" *Dickens Quarterly* 26.4 (Dec. 2009): 267–71.

———. *Spaces of the Sacred and Profane: Dickens, Trollope, and the Victorian Cathedral Town.* New York: Routledge, 2007.

Buckland, Adelene. " 'Pictures in the Fire': The Dickensian Hearth and the Concept of History." *Romanticism and Victorianism on the Net* 53 (Feb. 2009). Web. 14 May 2010. <http://www.erudite.org/revue/ravon/2009/v/n53/029902ar.html>.

Butt, John, and Kathleen Tillotson. *Dickens at Work*. 1957. London: Routledge, 2009.

Butterworth, Robert D. "The Significance of Fagin's Jewishness." *The Dickensian* 105.3 (Winter 2009): 213–24.

Buzard, James. "Wulgarity and Witality: On Making a Spectacle of Oneself in *Pickwick*." *Victorian Vulgarity: Taste in Verbal and Visual Culture*. Ed. Susan David Bernstein and Elsie B. Michie. Burlington, VT: Ashgate, 2009. 35–54.

Cheadle, Brian. "Improvising Character in *Our Mutual Friend*." *Essays in Criticism* 59.3 (July 2009): 211–33.

Christensen, Allan C. " 'Not a Love Letter': Epistolary Proposals of Marriage and Narrative Theory in *Bleak House* and *Middlemarch*." *Letter(s): Functions and Forms of Letter-Writing in Victorian Art and Literature*. Ed. Mariaconcetta Constantini, Francesco Marroni, and Anna Enrichetta Soccio. Rome: Aracne, 2009. 59–69.

Clarke, Jeremy. "Dickens's Dark Ride: 'Traveling Abroad' to Meet the Heritage." *The Dickensian* 105.1 (Spring 2009): 5–13.

Clemm, Sabine. *Dickens, Journalism, and Nationhood: Mapping the World in* Household Words. New York/London: Routledge, 2009.

Cohen, William A. "Envy and Victorian Fiction." *Novel* 42.2 (Summer 2009): 297–303.

Cole, Natalie B. *Dickens and Gender: Recent Studies 1992–2008*. New York: AMS, 2009.

Colledge, Gary. *Dickens, Christianity and* The Life of Our Lord: *Humble Veneration, Profound Conviction*. New York: Continuum Logo, 2009.

Cordery, Gareth. "Quilp, Commerce and Domesticity: Crossing Boundaries in *The Old Curiosity Shop*." *Dickens Quarterly* 26.4 (Dec. 2009): 209–33.

Coste, Marie-Amelie. "Eugene Wrayburn, or the Unbearable Lightness of Being in Dickens." *The Dickensian* 105.2 (Summer 2009): 109–21.

Craton, Lillian. *The Victorian Freak Show: The Significance of Disability and Physical Differences in Nineteenth-Century Fiction*. Amherst, NY: Cambria, 2009.

Darby, Margaret Flanders. "The Conservatory at Gad's Hill Place." *Dickens Quarterly* 26.3 (Sept. 2009): 137–50.

Dickens, Charles. Preface. *Oliver Twist*. New York: Penguin, 1985.

DiSanto, Michael John. *Under Conrad's Eyes: The Novel as Criticism*. Montreal: McGill-Queen's UP, 2009.

Easson, Angus, and Margaret Brown. "The Letters of Charles Dickens: Supplement XI." *The Dickensian* 105.1 (Spring 2009): 36–53.

―――. "The Letters of Charles Dickens: Supplement XII." *The Dickensian* 105.2 (Summer 2009): 135–53.

―――. "The Letters of Charles Dickens: Supplement XIII." *The Dickensian* 105.3 (Winter 2009): 225–39.

Edgecombe, Rodney Stenning. "Dickens, Hood, and the Comedy of Language Learning." *English Studies* 90.3 (June 2009): 274–83.

―――. "Nonprogressive Journeys in Dickens, Twain, and Conrad." *Explicator* 67.3 (Spring 2009): 212–15.

Ellison, David A. "Mobile Homes, Fallen Furniture, and the Dickens Cure." *South Atlantic Quarterly* 108.1 (Winter 2009): 87–114.

Flegel, Monica. *Conceptualizing Cruelty to Children in Nineteenth-Century England: Literature, Representation, and the NSPCC.* Burlington, VT: Ashgate, 2009.

Frank, Lawrence. *Victorian Detective Fiction and the Nature of Evidence: The Scientific Investigations of Poe, Dickens, and Doyle.* New York: Palgrave Macmillan, 2009.

Furneaux, Holly. *Queer Dickens: Erotics, Families, Masculinities.* Oxford: Oxford UP, 2009.

Garcha, Amanpal. *From Sketch to Novel: The Development of Victorian Fiction.* Cambridge: Cambridge UP, 2009.

Garrison, Laurie. "Seductive Visual Studies: Scientific Focus and Editorial Control in *The Woman in White* and *All the Year Round.*" *The Lure of Illustration in the Nineteenth Century: Picture and Press.* Ed. Laurel Brake and Marysa Denmoor. New York: Palgrave Macmillan, 2009. 168–83.

Gates, Sarah. "Intertextual Estella: *Great Expectations*, Gender, and Literary Tradition." *PMLA* 124.2 (Mar. 2009): 390–405.

Ginsburg, Michal Peled. "Narratives of Survival." *Novel* 42.3 (Fall 2009): 410–16.

Godfrey, Esther Lui. *The January-May Marriage in Nineteenth-Century British Literature.* New York: Palgrave Macmillan, 2009.

Golden, Catherine J. *Posting It: The Victorian Revolution in Letter Writing.* Gainesville: UP of Florida, 2009.

Grass, Sean C. "*Great Expectations*, Self-Narration, and the Power of the Prison." *Stones of Law, Bricks of Shame: Narrating Imprisonment in the Victorian Age.* Ed. Jan Alber and Frank Lauterbach. Toronto: U of Toronto P, 2009. 171–90.

Gray, Beryl. "Man and Dog: Text and Illustration in Dickens's *The Old Curiosity Shop.*" *The Lure of Illustration in the Nineteenth Century: Picture and Press.* Ed.

Laurel Brake and Marysa Denmoor. New York: Palgrave Macmillan, 2009. 97–118.

Gredina, Irina, and Philip V. Allingham. "The Countess Vera Sergeevna Tolstaya's Russian Language Adaptation of *Great Expectations.*" *The Dickensian* 105.2 (Summer 2009): 122–34.

Gross, John and Gabriel Pearson, ed. *Dickens and the Twentieth Century.* 1962. London: Routledge, 2009.

Hanna, Robert C. "Before Boz: The Juvenalia and Early Writings of Charles Dickens, 1820–1833." *Dickens Studies Annual* 40 (2009): 231–364.

Hansen, Adam. " 'Now, now, the door was down': Dickens and Excarceration, 1841–2." *Stones of Law, Bricks of Shame: Narrating Imprisonment in the Victorian Age.* Ed. Jan Alber and Frank Lauterbach. Toronto: U of Toronto P, 2009. 89–111.

Heady, Emily Walker. "A Steam-Whistle Modernist?: Representations of King Alfred In Dickens's *A Child's History of England* and *The Battle of Life.*" *Defining Medievalism(s).* Ed. Karl Fugelso. Cambridge, UK: D. S. Brewer, 2009. 92–111.

Hillard, Molly Clark. "Dickens's Little Red Riding Hood and Other Waterside Characters." *SEL* 49.4 (Autumn 2009): 945–73.

Huett, Lorna. "Among the Unknown Public: *Household Words, All the Year Round* and the Mass-Market Weekly Periodical in the Mid-Nineteenth Century." *The Lure of Illustration in the Nineteenth Century: Picture and Press.* Ed. Laurel Brake and Marysa Denmoor. New York: Palgrave Macmillan, 2009. 128–48.

Hyman, Gwen. *Making a Man: Gentlemanly Appetites in the Nineteenth-Century British Novel.* Athens: Ohio UP, 2009.

Jones, Colin, Josephine McDonagh, and Jon Mee, ed. *Charles Dickens, A Tale of Two Cities and the French Revolution.* New York: Palgrave Macmillan, 2009.

Jordan, John O., and George Bigelow, ed. *Approaches to Teaching Dickens's Bleak House.* New York: MLA, 2008.

Jung, Daun. "Gender and Mobility in *Our Mutual Friend*: Spatial and Social Transformations of Three Major Female Characters—Bella, Lizzie, and Jenny Wren." *British and American Fiction to 1900* 16.2 (Summer 2009): 207–26.

Kleinecke-Bates, Iris. "Historicizing the Classic Novel Adaptation: *Bleak House* (2005) and British Television Concepts." *Adaptation in Contemporary Culture: Textual Infidelities.* Ed. Rachel Carroll. London: Continuum International, 2009. 111–22.

Klotz, Michael. "*Dombey and Son* and the 'Parlour on Wheels.' " *Dickens Studies Annual* 40 (2009): 61–80.

Kofron, John. "Dickens, Collins, and the Influence of the Arctic." *Dickens Studies Annual* 40 (2009): 81–94.

Kujawska-Lis, Ewa. "Charles Dickens's and Apollo Korzeniowski's *Hard Times*." *Dickens Quarterly* 26.2 (June 2009): 86–107.

Ledger, Sally. " 'GOD be thanked: a ruin!': The Rejection of Nostalgia in *Pictures from Italy*." *Dickens Quarterly* 26.2 (June 2009): 79–85.

Levine, Caroline. "Narrative Networks: *Bleak House* and the Affordances of Form." *Novel* 42.3 (Fall 2009): 517–23.

Lewis, Daniel. "The Middle-Class Moderation of Food and Drink in *David Copperfield*." *Explicator* 67.2 (Winter 2009): 77–80.

Lokin, Jan. "Realism and Reality in Dickens's Characters: Dickens Seen Through the Eyes of Dutch Writers." *The Dickensian* 105.1 (Spring 2009): 21–32.

Long, Pamela H. "Dickens, Cervantes, and the Pick-Pocketing of an Image." *The Cervantean Heritage: Reception and Influence of Cervantes in Britain*. Ed. J. A. G. Ardila. London: Legenda, 2009. 190–95.

Lougy, Robert E. "Dickens and the Wolf Man: Childhood Memory and Fantasy in *David Copperfield*." *PMLA* 124.2 (Mar. 2009): 406–20.

Louttit, Chris. "*Cranford*, Popular Culture, and the Politics of Adapting the Victorian Novel for Television." *Adaptation* 2.1 (Mar. 2009): 34–48.

———. *Dickens's Secular Gospel: Work, Gender, and Personality*. New York: Routledge, 2009.

Malton, Sara. *Forgery in Nineteenth-Century Literature and Culture: Fictions of Finance from Dickens to Wilde*. New York: Palgrave Macmillan, 2009.

Mangum, Teresa. "Dickens and the Female Terrorist: The Long Shadow of Madame Defarge." *Nineteenth-Century Contexts* 31.2 (June 2009):143–59.

Marsh, Joss. "Dickensian 'Dissolving Views': The Magic Lantern, Visual Story-Telling, and the Victorian Technological Imagination." *Comparative Critical Studies* 6.3 (Oct. 2009): 333–46.

McAllister, David. "Artificial Respiration in *Our Mutual Friend*." *The Dickensian* 105.2 (Summer 2009): 101–08.

McKnight, Natalie. "Dickens, Niagara Falls, and the Watery Sublime." *Dickens Quarterly* 26.2 (June 2009): 68–78.

———. "The Erotics of *Barnaby Rudge*." *Dickens Studies Annual* 40 (2009): 23–36.

———. "Review of Recent Dickens Studies: 2007." *Dickens Studies Annual* 40 (2009): 365–431.

Meckier, Jerome. "*Great Expectations,* 'a good name?' " *Dickens Quarterly* 26.4 (Dec. 2009): 248–58.

———. " 'A Wife in Two Volumes': The 'Something Wanting' in *David Copperfield* and *The Woman in White.*" *The Dickensian* 105.1 (Spring 2009): 14–20.

Moore, Tara. *Victorian Christmas in Print.* New York: Palgrave Macmillan, 2009.

Morgentaler, Goldie. "Mrs. Gamp, Mrs. Harris and Mr. Dickens: Creativity and the Self Split in Two." *Dickens Quarterly* 26.1 (Mar. 2009): 3–14.

Napolitano, Marc. "Disneyfying Dickens: *Oliver & Company* and *The Muppet Christmas Carol* as Dickensian Musicals." *Studies in Popular Culture* 32.1 (Fall 2009): 79–102.

Parker, David. "The Topicality of *Pickwick Papers.*" *The Dickensian* 105.3 (Winter 2009): 201–12.

Parey, Armelle. "Peter Carey's *Jack Maggs*: The True History of the Convict?" *Rewriting/Reprising: Plural Intertextualities.* Ed. Georges Letissier. Newcastle-upon-Tyne, UK: Cambridge Scholars, 2009.

Paroissien, David. "Victims or Vermin? Contradictions in Dickens's Penal Philosophy." *Stones of Law, Bricks of Shame: Narrating Imprisonment in the Victorian Age.* Ed. Jan Alber and Frank Lauterbach. Toronto: U of Toronto P, 2009. 25–45.

Peña-Sy, Stephanie. "Intoxication, Provocation, and Derangement: Interrogating the Nature of Criminal Responsibility in *The Mystery of Edwin Drood.*" *Dickens Studies Annual* 40 (2009): 215–30.

Pettit, Clare. "Peggotty's Work-Box: Victorian Souvenirs and Material Memory." *Romanticism and Victorianism on the Net* 53 (Feb. 2009). Web. 14 May 2010. <http://www.erudite.org/revue/ravon/2009/v/n53/029896ar.html>.

Pratt-Smith, Stella. "All in the Mind: The Psychological Realism of Dickensian Solitude." *Dickens Quarterly* 26.1 (Mar. 2009): 15–23.

Raguet, Christine. "Terror Foreign or Familiar—Pleasure on the Edge: Translating *A Tale of Two Cities* into French." *Dickens Quarterly* 26.3 (Sept. 2009): 175–86.

Rodensky, Lisa. "Popular Dickens." *Victorian Literature and Culture* 37.2 (Sept. 2009): 583–607.

Rulo, Kevin. "A Tale of Two Mimeses: Dickens's *A Tale of Two Cities* and René Girard." *Christianity and Literature* 59.1 (Autumn 2009): 5–25.

Sanders, Valerie. *The Tragi-Comedy of Victorian Fatherhood.* Cambridge: Cambridge UP, 2009.

Schacht, Paul. "In Pursuit of Pickwick's Hat: Dickens and the Epistemology of Utilitarianism." *Dickens Studies Annual* 40 (2009): 1–22.

Schlicke, Paul. "Macrone, Cruikshank and the Proposed Part-Issue of *Sketches by Boz*: A Note." *The Dickensian* 105.1 (Spring 2009): 33–35.

Schur, Anna. "The Poetics of 'Pattern Penitence': 'Pet Prisoners' and Plagiarized Selves." *Stones of Law, Bricks of Shame: Narrating Imprisonment in the Victorian Age*. Ed. Jan Alber and Frank Lauterbach. Toronto: U of Toronto P, 2009. 134–53.

Sen, Sambudha. "Radical Satire and Respectability: Comic Imagination in Hone, Jerrold, and Dickens." *The Working-Class Intellectual in Eighteenth- and Nineteenth-Century Britain*. Ed. Aruna Krishnamurthy. Burlington, VT: Ashgate, 2009. 143–65.

Shatto, Susan. "Mr. Pickwick's First Brush with the Law: Civil Disobedience in *The Pickwick Papers*." *Dickens Quarterly* 26.3 (Sept. 2009): 151–64.

Shin, Hisup. "Rapid and Dextrous: A Study of Dickens's Journalistic Writing and *Sketches by Boz*." *British and American Fiction to 1900* 16.2 (Summer 2009): 99–123.

Siegel, Daniel. "Griffith, Dickens, and the Politics of Composure." *PMLA* 124.2 (Mar. 2009): 375–89.

Slater, Michael. *Charles Dickens: A Life Defined by Writing*. New Haven: Yale UP, 2009.

Smith, Victoria Ford. "Dolls and Imaginative Agency in Bradford, Pardoe, and Dickens." *Dickens Studies Annual* 40 (2009): 171–98.

Starr, Elizabeth. "Manufacturing Novels: Charles Dickens on the Hearth in Coketown." *Texas Studies in Literature and Language* 51.3 (Fall 2009): 317–40.

Tambling, Jeremy. "New Prisons, New Criminals, New Masculinity: Dickens and Reade." *Stones of Law, Bricks of Shame: Narrating Imprisonment in the Victorian Age*. Ed. Jan Alber and Frank Lauterbach. Toronto: U of Toronto P, 2009. 46–69.

Teukolsky, Rachel. "Pictures in Bleak Houses: Slavery and the Aesthetics of Transatlantic Reform." *ELH* 76.2 (Summer 2009): 491–522.

Thornton, Sara. *Advertising, Subjectivity and the Nineteenth-Century Novel: Dickens, Balzac and the Language of the Walls*. New York: Palgrave Macmillan, 2009.

Tracy, Robert. " 'Opium is the True Hero of the Tale': DeQuincey, Dickens, and *The Mystery of Edwin Drood*." *Dickens Studies Annual* 40 (2009): 199–214.

Venturi, Paola. "*David Copperfield* Conscripted: Italian Translations of the Novel." *Dickens Quarterly* 26.4 (Dec. 2009): 234–47.

Vlock, Deborah. "Teaching Marx, Dickens, and Yunus to Business Students." *Pedagogy* 9.3 (Fall 2009): 538–47.

Watson, Nicola J. "Rambles in Literary London." *Literary Tourism and Nineteenth-Century Culture*. Ed. Nicola J. Watson. New York: Palgrave Macmillan, 2009. 139–49.

Wolf, Kirsten. "The Adventures of David Copperfield in Nova Scotia." *The Nordic Storyteller: Essays in Honour of Niels Ingwerson*. Ed. Susan C. Brantly and Thomas A DuBois. Newcastle-upon-Tyne, UK: Cambridge Scholars, 2009. 297–315.

Zieger, Susan. "Dickens's Queer Children." *LIT: Literature, Interpretation, Theory* 20.1–2 (Jan.–June 2009): 141–57.

Graphic Novels and Related Works

A Christmas Carol. By Charles Dickens. Illus. Naresh Kumar. Adapt. Scott McCullar. New Delhi, India: Campfire, Kalyani Nauyug Media, 2009. Digital file.

"Classical Comics: Press Area." *Classical Comics: Bringing Classics to Life*. N.d. Web. 27 July 2009.

Clayton, Jay. "Is Pip Postmodern? Or, Dickens at the End of the Twentieth Century." *Great Expectations*. By Charles Dickens. Ed. Janice Carlisle. Boston: St. Martin's, 1996. 607–24.

Eisner, Will. *Fagin the Jew*. New York: Doubleday, 2003.

Great Expectations. By Charles Dickens. Adapt. and illus. Rick Geary. Ed. Jim Salicrup. New York: Papercutz, 2007.

Great Expectations: The Graphic Novel. By Charles Dickens. Original Text Version. Adapt. Jen Green. Illus. John Stokes. Ed. Clive Bryant. Litchborough, UK: Classical Comics, 2009.

Jones, William B., Jr. *Classics Illustrated: A Cultural History, with Illustrations*. Jefferson, NC: McFarland, 2002.

Oliver Twist. By Charles Dickens. Illus. David Cerquiera. Adapt. Philippe Chanoinat. Ed. Justin Eisinger and Kris Oprisko. San Diego: IDW Publishing, 2009.

Versaci, Rocco. *This Book Contains Graphic Language: Comics as Literature*. New York: Continuum, 2008.

Films and Related Works

Disney's A Christmas Carol. Dir. and adapt. Robert Zemeckis. Perf. Jim Carrey, Gary Oldman, and Colin Firth. Walt Disney Pictures, 2009. Film.

Little Dorrit. Dir. Dearbhla Walsh, Adam Smith, and Diarmuid Lawrence. Adapt. Andrew Davies. Perf. Claire Foy, Matthew Macfadyen, and Tom Courtenay. 2008. BBC Video, 2009. DVD.

"A New Twist on *Oliver Twist*." *Oliver Twist*. Dir. Coky Giedroyc. 2007. BBC Video, 2009. DVD.

The Old Curiosity Shop. Dir. Brian Percival. Adapt. Martyn Hesford. Perf. Sophie Vavasseur, Derek Jacobi, and Toby Jones. 2007. BBC Video, 2009. DVD.

Oliver Twist. Dir. Coky Giedroyc. Adapt. Sarah Phelps. Perf. Timothy Spall, William Miller, Tom Hardy, and Sophie Okonedo. 2007. BBC Video, 2009. DVD.

"Timothy Spall as Fagin." *Masterpiece Classic: Oliver Twist*. WGBH Educational Foundation, 2009. Web. 5 June 2009.

Fiction

Arnold, Gaynor. *Girl in a Blue Dress: A Novel Inspired by the Life and Marriage of Charles Dickens*. New York: Crown, 2009.

Flanagan, Richard. *Wanting*. New York: Atlantic Monthly, 2008.

Ohl, Jeanne-Pierre. *Mr. Dick or the Tenth Book*. Trans. Christine Donougher. Sawtry, UK: Dedalus, 2008.

Pearl, Matthew. *The Last Dickens*. New York: Random House, 2009.

Simmons, Dan. *Drood*. New York: Little, Brown, 2009.

INDEX

(Page numbers in italics represent illustrations)

447